THE GUMILEV MYSTIQUE

A volume in the series
Culture and Society after Socialism
Edited by Bruce Grant and Nancy Ries

A list of titles in this series is available at
www.cornellpress.cornell.edu.

THE GUMILEV MYSTIQUE

Biopolitics, Eurasianism,
and the Construction of
Community in Modern Russia

Mark Bassin

CORNELL UNIVERSITY PRESS   ITHACA AND LONDON

Cornell University Press gratefully acknowledges receipt of a generous grant from The Foundation for Baltic and East European Studies, Stockholm, which aided in the publication of this book.

First published 2016 by Cornell University Press
First printing, Cornell Paperbacks, 2016
Printed in the United States of America

Library of Congress Cataloging-in-Publication Data

Bassin, Mark, author.
  The Gumilev mystique : biopolitics, Eurasianism, and the construction of community in modern Russia / Mark Bassin.
     pages cm. — (Culture and society after socialism)
  Includes bibliographical references and index.
  ISBN 978-0-8014-4594-1 (cloth : alk. paper)
  ISBN 978-1-5017-0271-6 (pbk. : alk. paper)
  1. Gumilev, L. N. (Lev Nikolaevich), 1912–1992. 2. Ethnology—Soviet Union—History. 3. Soviet Union—Historiography. 4. Eurasian school. 5. Soviet Union—Intellectual life. I. Title.
    DK38.7.G86B37 2016
    305.80092—dc23   2015032013

Cloth printing   10 9 8 7 6 5 4 3 2 1
Paperback printing   10 9 8 7 6 5 4 3 2 1

Moim drogim
Ani, Dorianowi, Kalinie

Contents

Foreword by Ronald Grigor Suny   ix

Acknowledgments   xiii

Introduction   1

Part 1   **GUMILEV'S THEORY OF ETHNOS AND ETHNOGENESIS**

    1. The Nature of Ethnicity   23

    2. Ethnogenesis, *Passionarnost'*, and the Biosphere   43

    3. Varieties of Ethnic Interaction   60

    4. The Ethnogenetic Drama of Russian History   81

Part 2   **THE SOVIET RECEPTION OF GUMILEV**

    5. Soviet Visions of Society and Nature   117

    6. Ethnicity as Ideology and Politics   146

    7. Gumilev and the Russian Nationalists   177

Part 3   **GUMILEV AFTER COMMUNISM**

    8. Neo-Eurasianism and the Russian Question   209

    9. Biopolitics and the Ubiquity of Ethnicity   244

    10. "The Patron of the Turkic Peoples"   273

Conclusion: The Political Significance of Gumilev   306

Bibliography   317

Index   365

Foreword

Russian intellectuals have pondered and fretted over the differences and distance of their country from what they imagine as "the West." Those on the other side of the divide who have tried professionally or casually to comprehend Russia have likewise circled endlessly around the matter of likeness and difference. The Russian intelligentsia who might be considered "Westernizers" have always been more accessible and legible to European and American observers than the opposing powerful strain of Russian thought that circled around Slavophilism, religious Orthodoxy, Eurasianism, and the grandly synthetic speculations of Russian religious philosophers and conservative historians. The writings of the more spiritual thinkers have usually mystified those who have lightly approached them. The "Russian idea," the "Russian soul," the sense of self and others articulated by Feodor Dostoevsky, Nikolai Danilevskii, Konstantin Leontiev, or Nikolai Berdiaev defy easy explanation or reduction to a sound bite. It is in this distinctly Russian philosophical tradition that the influential and difficult figure of Lev Nikolaevich Gumilev belongs.

Gumilev had a most distinguished pedigree. He was the son of two of twentieth-century Russia's greatest poets, Nikolai Gumilev and Anna Akhmatova. His father was arrested and executed by the Bolsheviks as a counterrevolutionary. His mother was repeatedly castigated by the Soviet authorities and suffered the imprisonment and alienation of her only child. Lev Gumilev had both a successful career as an author and ethnographer and repeatedly fell from grace into the prisons and camps of the Soviet regime. His greatest fame came at the end of his life and posthumously when Russian nationalists and members of the post-Soviet ruling elite embraced his work.

In his intellectual biography of Gumilev, the geographer and historian Mark Bassin lays bare the intricacies, insights, and even absurdities of this unique, unpredictable, courageous thinker. Gumilev elaborated his own theory of the generation of ethnicities, their combination into civilizational superethnies, and the impossibility of a common human history. He wrote his own interpretations of Russia's history, revising the conventional narrative of Slav versus Tatar to one of Russian, Mongol, and nomad collaboration on the steppe. He proposed that certain civilizational elements, in his reading the Jews primarily, have disrupted certain civilizations, boring from within with their devious and deceptive practices and ideas.

Gumilev learned from and remained close to émigré Eurasianists like Georgii Vernadskii and Petr Savitskii, who wrote of a unified Russian-Asian civilization that distinguished Russia from the West. As an empire, he argued, tsarist Russia was relatively benign in its relations with its subject peoples. His two ideological enemies were the Soviet regime and the Jews, the two intimately tied together. The Soviet leaders destroyed old Russia and Jewish revolutionaries suppressed the Russian people. He also despised liberals and dissenting intellectuals, whereas he applauded the USSR's Cold War confrontation with the West and Stalin's "anticosmopolitan" campaign against Soviet Jews.

Bassin shows how many of Gumilev's ideas related to the intense reformulation of historical and scientific understanding that followed the revolution. His natu-ralization of ethnicity was consonant with the primordialization of nationality under Stalinism. Nationality flowed from parents to children, but a constructivist remnant remained. Rather than purely determined by "race," a concept that the Soviets rejected, choice was permitted in cases of parents of different ethnicities. Gumilev was among the most prominent Soviet ethnographers who promoted the essentialist idea that nationalities were distinct organic formations with a long ethnogenesis. But he went further than most of his Soviet colleagues in denouncing attempts to "bring together" (*sblizhenie*) or to "merge" (*sliianie*) one ethnicity into another or into a cosmopolitan "Soviet people" (*sovetskii narod*). He stayed closer to the Stalinist notion of "friendship of the peoples" (*druzhba narodov*), in which distinct nations lived in multicultural harmony with one another, and opposed the notion of Nikita Khrushchev that rapprochement and eventual merger of peoples into a supraethnic Soviet people was taking place. At the same time he further biologized ethnicity, not in terms of race—that would have gone too far in the Soviet Union—but in terms of energy circulation and the influence of landscape.

Gumilev's idea found a hungry audience among the growing circles of Rus-sian nationalists in the late-Soviet years. Upset with what they perceived to be privileges given to non-Russian peoples and disadvantages placed on ethnic Rus-sians by the Soviet state, the nationalists appreciated Gumilev's opposition to "hybridization" and the merging of peoples, his irreverence directed at Soviet power, and his anti-Semitism. But they were displeased by his unwillingness to see the foundational moment in Russian ethnogenesis in the struggle with the Mongols. For Gumilev, Russians were forged in a cooperative relationship with the peoples of the steppe, and he refused to grant a special superordinate role for Russians over other nationalities.

Ironically, Gumilev became most influential during the Gorbachev years of radical reform. He sided with the "empire savers," who resisted the reforms of perestroika and the opening to the West. Like other conservative opponents of the First Secretary, he feared the breakup of the USSR. His Eurasianist ideas caught fire within the Soviet establishment, even in the Ministry of Foreign Affairs. His popularity as a critic of democratization and Westernization carried his ideas through the chaotic Yeltsin years into the era of twenty-first-century Putinism. The reactionary Communist leader Gennadii Ziuganov took up his banner, and Vladimir Putin deployed language—like "unity in diversity"—that was identified with the Eurasianists. In 2011 Putin became an enthusiastic supporter of the proposal by Kazakhstan's president Nursultan Nazarbaev for the formation of a Eurasian Union of former Soviet republics.

Mark Bassin's brilliant study of Gumilev's ideas and influence reveals the complexities and subtleties of conservative and Eurasianist thought in Russia. Fair to a fault, Bassin takes Gumilev seriously and carefully parses the seeming contradictions of his sometimes bizarre, even absurd, musings. If we want to understand what often appears unfathomable in current Russian pronouncements, attitudes, and actions, it is imperative to look as deeply and carefully as Bassin has at those whom at first we might dismiss or avoid altogether.

—Ronald Grigor Suny

Acknowledgments

My interest in Lev Gumilev dates back to my graduate studies, and so I begin these acknowledgements by thanking my teachers: Jim Gibson in Toronto, and Nicholas Riasanovsky, Martin Malia, David Hooson, Clarence Glacken, and Alexander Yanov in Berkeley. In different ways, each of them stimulated and helped shape my thinking about the themes and subjects examined in this book. The book itself has taken a very long time to complete—although not, I think it is fair to say, through any undue negligence on my part. The simple fact is that the sensational growth of Gumilev's celebrity over the past decade has meant that the range and complexity of the materials I needed to digest never ceased to expand, yearly and indeed monthly, under my increasingly horror-stricken eyes. I began work on the project as a Reader in Cultural and Political Geography at University College London (UCL), continued with it after moving to the University of Birmingham as Professor of Human Geography, and have completed it in my present position as Baltic Sea Professor of the History of Ideas in the Center for Baltic and East European Studies at Södertörn University in Stockholm. I am grateful to my colleagues in all of these institutions for their interest and support throughout the many years I have been preoccupied with it.

My work would not have been possible without the support of my good friends and colleagues Konstantin Aksensov in St. Petersburg and Aleksei Postnikov in Moscow, both of whom provided expert knowledge, critical feedback, and not least of all a bed to sleep in during the many trips I made to Russia in the course of my research. At UCL I benefitted greatly from the skillful help of Alexander Titov, who served as my research assistant at an early stage of this project—and went on to write his doctoral dissertation about Gumilev! My research has also been greatly enriched by numerous individuals who knew Gumilev personally and shared their experiences and insights with me: El'za Dil'mukhamedova, Viacheslav Ermolaev, Tat'iana Frolovskaia, Aleksandr Kozyrev, Marina Kozyreva, Sergei Lavrov, Aleksandr Prokhanov, Gelian Prokhorov, and Andrei Rogachevskii. In Almaty and Astana, I learned a great deal through discussions with Meruert Abuseitova, Marat Auezov, Karl Baipakov, Zharas Ermekbaev, Mambet Koigel'diev, Sanat Kushkumbaev, Nurbulat Masanov, and Abdimanapov Sarsengali. In Kazan, Rafael Khakimov, Damir Iskhakov, and Iskander Izmailov generously shared their insights and reflections with me. I also thank Aliya Masanova, Marina Mogilner, and Ilya Gerasimov for their assistance in helping me to arrange these research trips. I am additionally grateful to Marina

Kozyreva, Director of the Gumilev Collection at St. Petersburg University, and Ilya Vikovetsky for their kind permission to use the photographs of Gumilev reproduced in this book.

Ron Suny's seminal scholarship on the Soviet and post-Soviet periods has provided a critical background and foundation for many of the themes that I engage in my own analysis. My friendship with Ron has been an unfailing source of inspiration for me over many years, and one of the greatest pleasures I have in presenting this volume is that it is graced with a foreword by him. I am also extremely grateful to my academic editor Bruce Grant. Without Bruce's unflagging encouragement and astute guidance, there is no question that this manuscript would never have left my laptop's hard drive. I would also like to thank my in-house editors at Cornell University Press: John Ackerman, for his early interest in my work and for taking on the project in the first place, and Roger Haydon for seeing it through.

Many colleagues have in different ways, direct and indirect, made a contribution to my research: David Anderson, Nick Baron, Michał Bron, Yitzhak Brudny, Martin Beisswenger, Valentin Bogorov, Gennadii Bordiugov, Denis Cosgrove, Nicholas Dejenne, Evgeny Dorbrenko, Peter Duncan, Chris Ely, Aleksandr Etkind, Orlando Figes, André Filler, Boris Gasparov, Abbott Gleason, Sergei Glebov, Steven Grosby, Michael Hagemeister, Francine Hirsch, Geoffrey Hosking, Sergei Nikitich Khrushchev, Catriona Kelly, Pål Kolstø, Irina Kotkina, Walter Laqueur, Marlène Laruelle, Athena Leoussi, Bernard Marchadier, Steve Marks, John McCannon, Holt Meyer, Andrzej Nowak, Sergei Panarin, Daria Panarina, Gonzalo Pozo-Martin, Alberto Masoero, Tetsuo Mochizuki, Harsha Ram, Anatolii Remnev, Paul Richardson, Richard Sakwa, Benjamin Schenk, Karl Schlögel, Dmitry Shlapentokh, Vasilii Shchukin, David Schimmelpenninck van der Oye, Viktor Shnirel'man, Dmitry Sidorov, Jeremy Smith, Sergey Sokolovskiy, Mark Steinberg, Richard Stites, Melissa Stockdale, Willard Sunderland, Mikhail Suslov, Galin Tihanov, Valerii Tishkov, Maria Todorova, Vera Tolz-Zilitinkevich, Igor Torbakov, Andrei Tsygankov, Vadim Tsymburskii, Sanna Turoma, Andreas Umland, Ilya Vinkovetsky, Doug Weiner, Stefan Wiederkehr, Larry Wolff, and Richard Wortman.

It is a pleasure to acknowledge the generous financial support this project has received from the Arts and Humanities Research Council and the Leverhulme Trust in the United Kingdom, and the National Council for Eurasian and East European Research in the United States. Work on the manuscript was completed as part of the research project "The Vision of Eurasia" funded by the Foundation for Baltic and East European Studies in Stockholm, which has also helped facilitate the publication of this book.

My greatest debt, as always, is to my family: to Kalina, for her strange love of lemons, to Dorian, for helping to revive the lost art of rapping, and to Ania, for her occasional reassurances *że wszystko będzie dobrze*. My book is dedicated to them, with all my love.

THE GUMILEV MYSTIQUE

INTRODUCTION

In a sense, this book was born on a chilly Leningrad morning in the spring of 1980. I was spending the year in the USSR as a doctoral exchange student at Moscow State University, conducting research on a dissertation in historical geography about Russian perceptions of Siberia and the Far East. The Soviet Union had invaded Afghanistan a few months earlier, chaotic preparations were underway in the city of Moscow to host the Olympics later that summer, and I had escaped to Leningrad for several weeks to work in the archive of the Russian Geographical Society. As part of my *komandirovka*, I had arranged consultations with a number of specialists, one of whom was a researcher in the Faculty of Geography at Leningrad State University: Lev Nikolaevich Gumilev. Although Gumilev had no direct connection to my topic, it was he who I was most excited about meeting. His name was well known to Western geographers who specialized on the Soviet Union and translations of his articles were published in our journals. For us geographers, Gumilev was in every respect a sensation. We knew about his illustrious parentage—both his father and his mother were famous poets—and that he had endured many years of banishment in the Gulag. Above all, however, we were fascinated by the unconventional and daring manner in which he challenged Stalinist doctrines about the relationship of human society to the natural world—issues that related directly to concerns in our own work in human geography. In the post-Stalinist 1960s and 1970s, new ecological perspectives about the interconnection between society and nature were being debated and Gumilev's work was at the forefront of these debates, boldly setting out original and

1

manifestly unorthodox perspectives. So when I traveled that spring to Leningrad, I simply had to meet this distinctive and interesting individual.

In the event, the meeting was not a success. Gumilev, a short stocky figure who bore a remarkable resemblance to his mother, Anna Akhmatova, was ill at ease. He did not seem very interested in my work and did not even respond to my questions about his ideas on the society-nature relationship. Nervously chainsmoking *Belomorkanal* papirosy, speaking excitedly and not always very clearly (he had a slight speech impediment), he delivered what seemed to me a thoroughly bizarre lecture, filled with outlandish notions and using terms that—despite my strong knowledge of Russian—I had never heard. He told me that ethnic groups originated as a result of radiation from outer space and that this process was driven by some strange feature he called *passionarnost'*. The relations between the groups that resulted were based either on natural friendship, which he called *komplimentarnost'*, or on a hostility that was equally natural. Sometimes a group became deformed and corrupted—a *khimera*, or chimera—and was very dangerous to other groups. I had not inquired about any of this, and none of it made much sense to me. Throughout our discussion, moreover, he seemed to have a sort of suspicious reserve toward me personally. It became clear that he was bothered that I was an American and—as he took care to establish early on in our meeting—that I was Jewish. I took my leave of Lev Nikolaevich with some relief, no more enlightened about his geographical ideas but rather less curious about them, or indeed about any other aspects of his scholarly work.

What I could not have foreseen at the time was the altogether extraordinary degree of popularity, authority, and influence that Gumilev and his ideas would achieve over the following decades. His rise to celebrity began during perestroika at the end of the 1980s, and since the collapse of the USSR has continued virtually nonstop to the present day. Two decades after his death in 1992, he has in the estimation of one authoritative observer of the Russian scene become "perhaps the most widely read and influential historian of the post-Communist era."[1] His stature and reputation today are indeed immense, not only in Russia but across the former Soviet Union as well. Gumilev is freely compared to Herodotus and Karl Marx, Oswald Spengler and Albert Einstein, and his works have sold literally millions of copies. In bookstores they fill not shelves but entire bookcases. Since the 1990s, there have been at least half a dozen competing projects to publish his collected writings, and many books and dozens of graduate dissertations have

---

1. Polonsky 2012; also see Menzel 2007, 8: Gumilev's popularity in Russia today "cannot be over-estimated." Translations of all foreign sources are my own unless otherwise indicated.

been written about his life and work.[2] One of his books has been adopted as a textbook for Russian high schools, and his ideas can be found littered throughout the curriculum. Organizations have been established dedicated exclusively to developing his legacy, the largest of which—the Lev Gumilev Center based in Moscow—has branches in St. Petersburg, Baku, and Bishkek, and continues to expand. There is a Lev Gumilev Street in the capital of the Kalmyk republic Elista, a large public monument to him in the center of Kazan, and his bust is prominently displayed in scientific institutes in Moscow, Ufa, Yakutsk, and elsewhere. In Kazakhstan, a major university in the capital Astana proudly bears his name. On the centenary of his birth in 2012 the Kazakh government reaffirmed its veneration of his memory by naming a mountain in the Altai range in the eastern part of the country "Gumilev Peak" and issuing a commemorative postage stamp in his honor. Gumilev's ideas are regularly invoked by leading politicians across the former Soviet Union, not least the Russian president Vladimir Vladimirovich Putin, who praises Gumilev's "extraordinary talents" and the "unique impact" that his ideas have had. Indeed, Putin makes very clear the Gumilevian inspiration behind a major foreign-policy initiative of his third term—the establishment of a "Eurasian Union" among the former Soviet states. Gumilev's celebrity has spilled over even into the West, where he features as a central character in an opera by Bruno Mantovani that premiered in Paris in 2011.[3]

And so I have come back to Gumilev to try to make some sense of the mystique that surrounds him. In writing this book, I have been motivated by two broad concerns. One of these is to provide a detailed examination of Gumilev's work itself—the sources, structure, and meaning of his principal hypotheses. Most fundamentally, Gumilev devoted himself to two projects: on the one hand a universal and panhistorical "ethnos theory" about the nature of nationality and ethnicity, and on the other a radically revisionist reinterpretation of Russia's historical development. In both cases, Gumilev drew on material from a wide range of scientific disciplines for ideas and inspiration. He then refracted the bits and fragments that he absorbed through the prism of his own rich imagination before reassembling them into theories that were characteristically Gumilevian. Consequently, these theories are highly, at times excruciatingly, complex, and

---

2. The fullest study of Gumilev's life and work is Beliakov 2012a; also see Lavrov 2000; Abdymanapov 2004; Karel'skaia 2005; Demin 2008; Pavochka 2011; Akhmetshin 2011. For doctoral dissertations on Gumilev at Western universities see Brownson 1988; Titov 2005; Gołąbek 2008. Dissertations from the former Soviet Union are too numerous to list.

3. The opera *Akhmatova* is based on the story of the poet's difficult relationship with her son (http://akhmatova.operadeparis.fr/, accessed 6/2/2015); "Mutter-Sohn-Konflikt" 2011.

the chapters in part 1 are devoted to unpacking and arranging them in what is hoped to be an orderly and meaningful fashion. Yet for all of his undisputed ingenuity and intelligence, Gumilev was not a credible theoretician. As will become apparent, his hypotheses are filled with inconsistencies, misunderstandings, and misapplications of the concepts he borrowed, and are often plainly contradictory in regard to basic principles. Moreover, although Gumilev believed that his work was based on entirely objective evidence and the dispassionate truth of hard science, his arguments reflected wild flights of fancy guided not by any empirical verification but rather by his own private convictions, superstitions, and biases. I do appreciate the severity of this judgement, but it is one that is shared by many, and even his most devoted followers acknowledge the large degree of fantasy in his thinking. Indeed, no less an authority on scientific and intellectual life in the Soviet Union than Loren Graham dismissed Gumilev's theoretical oeuvre out of hand as "a ridiculously speculative and scientifically baseless scheme."[4] However this may be, there is no question that, with only very minor exceptions, his scientific arguments are not very compelling. As a thinker and system-builder, Gumilev was clearly neither a Marx nor an Einstein. A book devoted to nothing more than his ideas themselves would arguably not need to be written.

What does make this book necessary is its second objective, which is to analyze Gumilev's impact and significance across a range of Soviet and post-Soviet contexts. In this regard, the scientific quality of his arguments ceases to be of central importance. From virtually the moment he began to develop his ideas, Gumilev has not ceased to exert a major influence on academic discourses, public debates, and attitudes in Russia, an influence that as of this writing extends even to the shaping of political policy. A number of factors combine to fix him so securely in this key position. The most important is that in his analyses Gumilev addressed two fundamental yet contending social, political, and ideological dynamics in Russia, what might be called alternative paradigms of belonging. On the one hand was the imperative for ethno-national individuation and autonomy on the part of the country's many nationalities; on the other was the assertion of a fundamental cohesion between these same nationalities that was somehow deeper than their ethno-national differentiation—an effective unity that was and still is perceived to be a *conditio sine qua non* for the existence of the state. Both of these contending paradigms were intrinsic parts of the chemistry of the Soviet

---

4. Graham 1987, 255. Gumilev's biographer Sergei Beliakov has great admiration for his subject, but even he stresses the mixture of positivism and mysticism in his thinking, in which "concepts from biology, geography, and physics took on a religious sense." He concludes that Gumilev was more of an artist than disinterested researcher. Beliakov 2012a, 345, 347, 517–18, 569.

system, and they have become yet more pronounced after its collapse. The collision between them created one of the major fault lines running through Soviet and post-Soviet society, and Gumilev's teachings served to position him directly on top of it. His own overriding interest was to reconcile the two principles of ethno-national *samobytnost'* and internationalism. He believed he had done so, and many of his followers appreciated him precisely for this reason. As our examination of Gumilev's reception will indicate, however, his teachings can be taken up à la carte, which means that it was and is possible to embrace his explanation of ethnic individuality while ignoring or rejecting his arguments about supranational unity, or vice versa. This fundamental ambivalence makes it possible for constituencies with differing and even conflicting interests and agendas to embrace his legacy and invoke his authority.

As indicated in the title, this book is a study of, among other things, the "biopolitics" in Gumilev's thinking. First formulated in the early twentieth century[5], the term has become popular for the post-modern sensibilities of recent decades. Perhaps the most influential example is the work of Michel Foucault, where biopolitics broadly describes the practices and technologies with which the modern state exercises political control over the bodies and biological functioning of its subject citizenry.[6] In its initial formulation, however, the term referred to something very different. Biopolitics was originally conceived as a naturalistic *Staatsbiologie* or "state biology" based on the principle that all political and social life rested on biological foundations.[7] At the center of this perspective was the belief that the institution of the state itself was a biological organism or "life form," which had an anatomy and physiology and went through lifecycles of birth, growth, maturity, and eventual decline. Indeed, the term was devised by the Swedish political scientist Rudolf Kjellén precisely to emphasize that the political state shared the very same "dependency" on the "laws of [biological] life" that was characteristic for all organic life.[8] Deployed in this sense, biopolitics flourished during the interwar period, and the belief in the direct correlation of political behavior with biological factors—if not the organismic state model as such—was revived in the 1970s, among other places in the academic field of sociobiology.[9] It is this original legacy of biopolitics as a naturalistic understanding of social and political life that I associate with Gumilev. As we will see, his entire "ethnos theory" was based on the conceptualization of the ethnic group as

---

5. For overviews of this highly contested concept see Esposito 2008; Lemke 2011.
6. Fouault 1990, 133–60; Nilsson and Wallenstein 2013.
7. Von Uexküll 1920; Lemke 2011: 9; Lemke 2008.
8. Kjellen 1920, 94 (quote); Kjellen 1924: 38, 175; Lagergren 1998.
9. Davis 2009.

a biological organism. To be sure, Gumilev did not refer to the political state as such in these terms; indeed he insisted apparently to the contrary that there was a principled distinction between *etnos* and *gosudarstvo* in this regard. The point however is that in the Russian context—Soviet no less than post-Soviet—ethnicity itself was always profoundly politicized, such that the ethnic phenomena and behavior Gumilev sought to explain using biological principles were effectively political phenomena and behavior. Gumilev's biopolitical approach was and remains utterly unique in Russia, and it is one of the most important factors conditioning the reception of his work.

A Soviet Life

Lev Nikolaevich Gumilev was born on 1 October 1912, the son of Nikolai Stepanovich Gumilev (1886–1921) and Anna Andreevna Akhmatova (1889–1966).[10] Both of his parents were major modernist poets of Russia's Silver Age, although it was the work of his mother that would leave the deeper mark on Russian culture in the twentieth century. Until well into middle age, Lev Gumilev's personal and professional life was completely overshadowed and in vital respects determined by the separate tragic fates of each of his parents. In an affectionate verse dedicated to young Lev in 1916, Akhmatov's friend Marina Ivanovna Tsvetaeva (1892–1941) inadvertently foretold the hardships that awaited him:

> Redheaded L'vyonysh
> With his green eyes,
> You are the bearer of a dreadful legacy![11]

Nikolai Gumilev's marriage to Akhmatova in 1910 had already broken down by the time their son was born, and he left the family home soon thereafter. In 1921, he was arrested by the Cheka on allegations of participation in a monarchist conspiracy and was executed in August of that year. Lev thus barely knew his father, but he would cherish his memory throughout his life. He was able to recite much of his poetry by heart and was always immensely proud of the two Georgian Crosses awarded for his military service in the First World War. There is little doubt that Nikolai Gumilev's irrepressible fascination with exotic

---

10. For biographical material on Gumilev's life, see Lavrov 2000; Demin 2008; Beliakov 2012b; Gershtein 1998. Gumilev himself left a number of fragmentary biographical accounts: Gumilev 2003a; Gumilev 2003b; Gumilev 2003d; Varustin 1990. Except where otherwise noted, the following account is based on these sources.

11. Tsvetaeva 2009, 55.

places and historical figures—he was known as the "Rudyard Kipling" of Russian literature[12]—influenced his son's own imagination and intellectual inclinations.

Gumilev's relationship with his mother was enormously complex and fraught. Throughout the turbulence of world war, revolution, civil war, and postrevolutionary reconstruction, Lev was left in the care of his paternal grandmother and spent his childhood and adolescence on the family estate at Slepneva, near Bezhetsk in Tver oblast'.[13] Akhmatova herself moved to Petrograd, where she devoted her attention to developing her oeuvre and her career. In the provinces, the Gumilevs struggled with extreme poverty and the stigma of hostile "class origins" (Nikolai Gumilev came from the minor nobility)—a difficult situation exacerbated by his father's execution of as an "enemy of the revolution." Most painful of all, however, was his separation from his mother. Akhmatova rarely wrote and almost never visited: from 1921 to 1929, she made the trip from Leningrad on only two occasions. The separation was a tribulation for Akhmatova herself, who in her heart never abandoned her son and also suffered considerably because of their separation. Her anguish was to grow yet more acute and tormented through the sufferings of later decades and would be given voice in some of her greatest poetic work. The private sorrows of his mother understandably provided no solace for young Lev, however, who grew up with a sharp resentment of having been abandoned by his charismatic parents, both of whom were "practically strangers" to him.[14] When asked as a teenager about some sums he was scribbling, he explained that he was calculating "by what percent Mama remembers me," and in his letters at the time he agonized heartbreakingly over *chto ia delal* ("what I have done") to deserve such neglect.[15] On his deathbed, he expressed his bitterness in his confession that in his entire life he felt genuinely loved by only two people: his grandmother Anna from Slepneva and his wife Natal'ia Viktorovna.

In 1929, Lev moved to join his mother in Leningrad, where he completed his final year in secondary school and set about to continue his higher education. By this time, Akhmatova was living with her third husband, the art historian and critic Nikolai Nikolaevich Punin (1888–1953). The pair shared a room in a communal apartment, where Punin's former wife and daughter also lived. The arrangements were unsatisfactory, as both space and food were in short supply,

12. Martynov 1987; Hodgson 1998.

13. Kupriianov 1995.

14. Gumilev 1990c, 3.

15. Pozdniakova and Kozyreva 2005, 12. Gumilev's teenage letters remain unpublished; for excerpts see the Russian television documentary *Ty syn i uzhas moi*, devoted to his troubled relationship with his mother (http://my.mail.ru/mail/zhans_1959/video/20703/20712.html, accessed 5/2/2015).

and Punin apparently made it clear that his wife's son was not a welcome guest. With no available space in any of the rooms, Gumilev was consigned to the humiliation of sleeping on a wooden trunk in the corridor. He had no more luck in his academic progress. As the son of a well-known counterrevolutionary, Gumilev was a *lishenets*, that is, legally deprived of certain civil rights, among them the right to a higher education. As an alternative, he took part for several years in geological and archaeological expeditions, large numbers of which were being dispatched to remote corners of the country in the frenzy of the first five-year plan. One of these, to southern Russia to study the remains of the ancient khaganate of the Khazars, was led by Mikhail Illarionovich Artamonov (1898–1972), a leading archaeologist and historian who later would become director of the Hermitage Museum. Artamonov was a founder of Khazar studies in the Soviet Union, a topic that would be one of Gumilev's most important scholarly subjects. For many years Artamonov was one of his most important mentors.

In 1934, Gumilev was finally admitted to the recently reestablished Faculty of History of Leningrad University to study ancient Russian history and the history of the steppe nomads. It took him fifteen years to complete his studies, in the course of which he developed strong personal contacts with many of the leading Soviet historians, archaeologists, and other specialists in his field. He was taught by a number of eminent authorities on Oriental studies, including Vasilii Vasilevich Struve (1889–1965), Aleksandr Iur'evich Iakubovskii (1886–1953), and Nikolai Vasilevich Kiuner (1877–1955). Gumilev's relations with these professors were extremely close, and subsequently they were to help him as they could during his long periods of prison and exile. Other important contacts from his university studies were the historians Vladimir Vasil'evich Mavrodin (1908–1987), Boris Dmitrievich Grekov (1882–1953), and Evgenii Viktorovich Tarle (1874–1955), and the archeologist and ethnographer Aleksei Pavlovich Okladnikov (1908–1981).

With his move to Leningrad, Gumilev became fully engaged in the cultural and literary life of the capital. He began to develop the poetic talents that he had inherited from his parents and he moved actively in the circles around his mother. He became friendly with the poet Osip Emilevich Mandel'stam (1891–1938), who had been closely associated with both Nikolai Gumilev and Akhmatova since before the revolution. Mandel'stam had a sense of the impending doom that awaited both mother and son, and at one point he remarked to Akhmatova: "It will be difficult for you to protect him, he carries his own demise (*gibel' nost'*) inside himself."[16] Through Mandel'stam, the young Gumilev came into contact with other important poets, including Sergei Antonovich Klychkov (1889–1937)

---

16. Demin 2008, 30; Pozdniakova and Kozyreva 2005, 46.

and Nikolai Alekseevich Kliuev (1884–1937).[17] At this time Gumilev also met the young literary scholar Emma Grigor'evna Gershtein (1903–2002), with whom he had a brief affair and maintained a close friendship and correspondence throughout his long years in the Gulag.[18] Gumilev was among the small circle of friends to whom Mandel'shtam read his short satirical caricature of Stalin "The Highlander in the Kremlin" (*Kavkazskii gorets*) in 1933. This poem, which was immediately discovered by the authorities, set in train the persecutions of Mandel'sham's final years, which ended in 1938 with his death from typhoid in a prison transit camp in the Russian Far East.[19]

Gumilev himself was arrested in 1933 and 1935, but in both cases released after a brief detention—the second time after a personal appeal from Akhmatova to Stalin himself, supported by an intervention from Boris Pasternak.[20] His third arrest, in March 1938, was not so benign. The charges against him were extravagantly implausible: he was accused of having organized a terrorist group seeking a monarchist restoration and even of planning an assassination attempt on Andrei Aleksandrovich Zhdanov (1896–1948), at that time chairman of the Supreme Soviet of the RSFSR.[21] Akhmatova's poem *Requiem*, written in the second half of the 1930s, gives epic voice to the anguish that these arrests caused her.

They took you away at dawn. I followed behind,
As if a corpse was being removed.
. . . .
For seventeen months I have been screaming,
Calling you home.
I threw myself at the hangman's feet—
You are my son and my terror.

Sentenced at first to four years of hard labor, he was dispatched to work on the Belomor Canal, but recalled to Leningrad in 1939 when prosecutors decided that this punishment was too light. After several months of deliberations at Kresti prison in Leningrad, he was resentenced to five years of hard labor and sent to the newly established prison camp complex at Noril'sk, on the Siberian peninsula

---

17. Hearing young Gumilev recite some of his own poetry, Klychkov is said to have commented that "Lyova will never make a poet, but he will make a professor." Loseff 1994, 11.

18. In the 1990s, Gershtein published her memoirs and large sections of their correspondence, which provide the fullest source of information about Gumilev's life up to the 1960s. Gershtein 1998 (English trans., Gerstein 2004).

19. On Gumilev and Mandel'stam, see Gerstein 2004, 56–58, 166–67, 341–42, 380, 383–84, 387, 399; Feinstein 2005, 143.

20. Kozyrev 2003; Golovnikova and Tarkhova 2001; "Osvobodit' iz-pod aresta i Punina" 1999.

21. For an account by a friend who was arrested along with Gumilev, see Shumovskii 2003.

of Taimyr.[22] Gumilev spent a difficult half decade in the Siberian Arctic, where conditions were brutally harsh and he suffered physical privations that would affect him for the rest of his life. Many of his fellow prisoners were academics and scholars like himself, and with some of them—the astrophysicist Nikolai Aleksandrovich Kozyrev (1908–1983) and the future science-fiction writer and philosopher Sergei Aleksandrovich Snegov (1910–1994)—he formed close relationships that influenced his thinking as he continued to develop his ideas and theories.[23] Released from captivity in March 1943, Gumilev immediately enlisted in the military and joined the westward advance of the Red Army, eventually taking part in the occupation of Berlin.[24]

In 1945, Gumilev returned to Leningrad and was reunited with his mother, who in the brief interlude of postwar euphoria was enjoying a measure of official approval and success. It was at this time that the British scholar Isaiah Berlin (1909–1998) made his famous late-night visit to Akhmatova's flat, where Gumilev was also living. Berlin later recalled how Akhmatova's son joined their conversation at one point late in the evening and quickly made a strong impression on him. Gumilev, Berlin reported, was "at least as civilized, well-read, independent, and indeed fastidious, to the point almost of intellectual eccentricity, as the most admired undergraduate intellectuals in Oxford or Cambridge."[25] The distinguished Oxford academic testified to the affection between mother and son. Gumilev completed his undergraduate exams in 1946 and in the same year enrolled as a postgraduate in the Institute for Oriental Studies. He also returned to his expeditionary work, now accompanying the ethnographer and archaeologist Sergei Ivanovich Rudenko (1885–1969) on excavations in the Altai mountains. Like Artamonov, Rudenko would become an influential mentor for Gumilev. This relative academic stability, however, did not last long. In August 1946, Andrei Zhdanov, by this time effectively the head of Soviet cultural policy, made his infamous "half nun, half harlot" denunciation of Akhmatova, and his coarse condemnation had a direct effect on her son's fate as well. He was expelled from the institute in 1947, although the rector of Leningrad State University, Aleksandr Alekseevich Voznesenskii (1898–1950), agreed to allow him to defend his candidate's thesis in his own Faculty of History in 1948.

---

22. Gumilev claimed that his prosecutor was determined to sentence him to death, and that he survived only because the latter was himself arrested and executed. Panchenko 1997.

23. For Gumilev's recollections of his time on Taimyr see Gumilev 2003d; Ryzhkov 2003.

24. Novikova 2007. The contemporary fascination and reverence for all aspects of Gumilev's persona can be seen in the fact that there is a dedicated webpage displaying his various military commendations and decorations. http://gumilevica.kulichki.net/fund/fund34.htm (accessed 6/2/2015).

25. Cited in Dalos 1998, 37; also see Ignatieff 1998, 158–59; Feinstein 2005, 217–19. Gumilev believed that Berlin's visit to his mother, which was certainly noted by the Soviet authorities, was a factor in his arrest two years later.

In November 1949 Gumilev was once again arrested and sentenced to a labor camp, this time *za chervonets*: for ten years. He served out his sentence in camps in Kazakhstan, the Kuzbass, and near Omsk. Gumilev had always tried to keep his academic interests alive even during imprisonment, and now—equipped with a handful of historical texts sent by Akhmatova and Gershtein—he was able to make progress on several manuscripts. Although Stalin's death in March 1953 was followed by a general amnesty, Gumilev's personal background once again worked against him, for he belonged to a special category of "class enemy" who did not automatically receive a state pardon.[26] Akhmatova continued to petition on his behalf, supported by an impressive array of powerful figures from the cultural and academic establishment, including the writers Ilya Grigor'evich Ehrenburg (1891–1967) and Mikhail Aleksandrovich Sholokhov (1905–1984).[27] Increasingly frustrated and desperate in his Siberian prison, however, Gumilev's correspondence at the time betrayed a growing obsession with the thought that his mother was not pressing his case energetically enough. It was only three years later, in 1956, that an official review of Gumilev's case ordered his immediate release and full rehabilitation. A single bureaucratic clarification was offered: *za otsutstviem sostava prestupleniia*—"for the absence of any criminal act."[28]

In all, Gumilev spent thirteen hard years in Stalinist prisons and labor camps. His experiences there, the people he met and the observations he made, were to provide fundamental inspiration for the ideas and theories that we will examine in the following chapters. The impact of the camp experience on his thinking has been stressed by those who knew him best; his long-standing friend and colleague from Leningrad University Sergei Borisovich Lavrov (1928–2000) observed that "there, in the camps, his ideas were born."[29] On a psychological and emotional level, however, the period of imprisonment was utterly devastating. Like the overwhelming majority of his compatriots who suffered similar fates, he was entirely innocent of any infraction or crime. Unlike them, however, his persecution by the state was not entirely wanton, for he was the son of two famous individuals against whom the authorities did indeed hold specific political and cultural grievances. Thus Gumilev did not, strictly speaking, suffer for nothing as did so many others, but rather for his parents—which might well have been worse. This was certainly his own perception of his tribulations. As he wryly put it, his first *srok* or prison term had been *za papa* ("for papa") and his

---

26. Dalos 1998, 118–20.
27. "V prokuraturu SSSR" 2003.
28. Gumilev 1990c, 6.
29. Lavrov 2003, 209. Another colleague maintained that his camp experience was "his school for working out the theory of ethnogenesis on the basis of people's behavior; in the camps he could observe the full variety of Russian (*rossiiskii*) reality." Kurkchi 1994.

second *za mama*. The knowledge that neither of his parents could bear personal responsibility for this persecution-in-proxy did not entirely alleviate the bitterness of the injustice, and the experience exacerbated the sense of abandonment and betrayal he had developed as a child.

The intensity of his chagrin was to lead eventually to the complete breakdown of his relationship with Akhmatova in the years after his return from exile in 1956. He blamed her extravagantly for not supporting him and failing to intervene actively enough during his incarceration. Gumilev made his resentment clear to Gershtein in a letter written on the eve of his release: "Mama herself knows everything about my life and that the sole reason for my difficulties is my kinship with her."[30] Gumilev's contempt extended even to his mother's attempt to immortalize her concern for her son's fate in the poem *Requiem*—a work generally considered to be one of her most moving masterpieces. He pointed out that she is focused on her own suffering and that in it Akhmatova actually trivialized the objects of her anguish—her husband and her son—by referring to them throughout as dead or corpses. "I'm still alive," Gumilev pointed out matter-of-factly: "who was the 'requiem' supposed to be for?" He dismissed the entire piece as a *pamiatnik samoliuvobaniiu*—"a monument to her narcissism."[31] Their encounters became increasingly fraught, and for the last five years of her life they did not meet at all. The coterie of young poets who were close to Akhmatova during this period—among them the future Nobel Laureate Joseph Brodsky (1940–1996)— all testify to the emotional torment that her estrangement from her son caused her, and it was something she was never able to overcome.[32] At the end, relations between mother and son had declined to the point that when Gumilev arrived at the Moscow hospital where Akhmatova lay dying in the autumn of 1965, he was turned away in the lobby by her friends with the blunt message that her weakened heart would simply not survive the sight of him. He was reunited with his mother only at her funeral.[33]

---

30. Quoted in Gerstein 2004, 456–57.
31. Vasilii 2012, 165; El'zon 2003, 208.
32. Feinstein 2005, 248–50, 256.
33. Feinstein 2005, 276; Beliakov 2012a, 305. Interest in the dynamics of the mother-son relationship, and in particular the question of Akhmatova's role during Gumilev's imprisonment, has been much stimulated by the growth of interest in Gumilev since the 1990s. His supporters have now published parts of their correspondence from his second exile attempting to demonstrate his mother's negligence, whereas Emma Gershtein—who had had close contacts with both of them throughout this period—offered a more positive evaluation of Akhmatova's role. "Perepiska A. A. Akhmatovoi i L. N. Gumileva" 1994; Gershtein 1993; Gershtein 1998. Several recently discovered letters by Gumilev to his mother, posted in the mid-1950s but apparently never delivered, give an unmistakable flavor of the chagrin Gumilev felt toward her. "L. N. Gumilev—A. A. Akhmatovoi" 2011.

Akhmatova believed that the tribulations of camp life had damaged her son's character and degraded his human goodness. After his return, she noted in her diaries, he "began to despise and hate people, and he himself ceased to be a normal person (*on sam perestal byt' chelovekom*). May God forgive him. My poor *Levushka*. . . . No! He didn't used to be like this. They [the camps] made him this way, [they ruined him] for me."[34] Indeed, at one point she described her son as *odna peredonovshchina*—an allusion to the callous provincial pedagog Peredonov in Fedor Kuz'mich Sologub's (1863–1927) 1905 novel *Melkii Bes*, who embodied the qualities of envy, ill-will, and egoism.[35] However this may be, in his subsequent professional life Gumilev certainly did develop a general reputation as an extremely difficult individual. While friends and supporters could be fierce in their protective devotion, others who knew him commented on his utter inability to countenance criticism, his paranoid inclination to see enemies lurking all around him, and his absolute belief in the correctness of his views and his alone. "He had a nasty (*skvernyi*) character, he argued with everyone," recalled Sergei Nikolaevich Semanov (1934–2011), a leading figure in the Russian nationalist movement and otherwise quite supportive of Gumilev.[36] Aleksandr Iur'evich Borodai, the son of one of Gumilev's earliest and closest collaborators, knew Gumilev personally from his childhood as a family friend. "Gumilev was not a benevolent professor, not a purely academic scholar. He possessed enormous energy and immense charm, and he attracted people to himself. But his energy was the energy of hate, nurtured over the years toward those whom he considered to be his enemies. He was a fighter: brutal (*zhestkii*) toward himself and severe toward others."[37] We will see these qualities on display at many critical points throughout this book.

Borodai goes on to point out that the greatest of Gumilev's perceived "enemies" was the Jewish people. Indeed, Gumilev's anti-Semitism was legendary.[38] In this regard, as in so many others, however, he was ambivalent, at least to some extent. On the one hand, he had Jewish friends throughout his life and had at

---

34. Cited in Pozdniakova and Kozyreva 2005, 46; Gerstein 2004, 235; Demin 2008, 30.

35. Beliakov 2012a, 299.

36. Semanov 2012. Gumilev reportedly astonished his audience at a public lecture in the mid-1980s by declaring that he held no bad feeling toward the Stalinist security apparatus responsible for his imprisonment and banishment. "They weren't the ones who put me in the camps," he explained. "So who did?" questioned a voice from the audience. "My colleagues, of course," he answered calmly. Burovskii 2012.

37. "Passionarnost'" 2012. This is the same Aleksandr Borodai who participated in the Russian incursion into Ukraine in 2014, acting as the self-styled "prime minister" of the Donetsk People's Republic in the spring and summer of that year.

38. Rogachevskii 2001; Rossman 2002a; Shnirelman 2002; Tiurin 1992; D'iakonov 1992; Chernykh 1995.

least two close personal relationships with Jewish women.[39] The archaeologist Lev Samuelovich Klein knew Gumilev professionally for many years, and emphasized that in their relationship Gumilev was always cordial and sincere. At the same time, however, Klein made it clear that Gumilev had an extremely strong antipathy against the Jews as a people.[40] His sentiments appear to have been formed by the 1930s, when despite his connections to the Mandel'shtams and others he already had something of a reputation for anti-Semitism. In the camps, Gumilev's worldly background and education, plus his speech impediment, often led his fellow inmates to assume that he was Jewish. One of his camp comrades later recollected how this infuriated Gumilev, who declared angrily after one such incident that "if that guy calls me a yid (*obzovet menia zhidom*) again, I'll tear his balls off!"[41]

Gumilev was well aware that his antipathies ran counter to his mother's philo-Semitism, and he apparently believed this played some role in their estrangement.[42] Indeed, in the 1980s his public reputation for anti-Semitism had become so formidable that Mikhail Davidovich El'zon, the editor of the first Soviet collection of Nikolai Gumilev's work, did not dare even to approach him until after the book was published. Among other things, Gumilev plainly had something of a persecution complex regarding the Jews.[43] He believed that his arrest in the 1940s had followed a denunciation from a Jewish professor,[44] and explained to El'zon: "Mikhail Davidovich, it's not my fault that the commissars responsible for my father's and my own persecution were all Jewish, and that they beat me very badly."[45] As we will see, Gumilev's antagonism toward the Jews was

---

39. The Jewish poet Matvei Mikhailovich Grubiian (1909–1972) recounted how he befriended Gumilev in the camps and, after they were released, brought him home to meet his mother—who promised to find him a nice Jewish girl to marry. Gumilev translated some of Grubiian's Yiddish poetry into Russian. "Matvei Grubian slushaet Vladimira Vysotskogo" 2009. Gumilev's good friend Gelian Mikhailovich Prokhorov denied that he was anti-Semitic in any respect (personal communication, St. Petersburg, May 2008). Also see Lavrov 2000, 332; Sorokin 2003, 20.

40. Klein 1992.

41. Savchenko 1996, 250.

42. Luk"ianov 2003, 66; Feinstein 2005, 158, 251; also see Gumilev's comments in "Etnologicheskaia karta" 1988. During perestroika, Gumilev insisted that it was Akhmatova's "non-Russian" acolytes that had turned her against him. At the time, however, he apparently had no difficulties with the young Jewish poets who had been close to his mother and then supported him in his legal battle over her estate. Joseph Brodsky, for example, met with Gumilev on several occasions and never noted any reservation or hostility. Beliakov 2012a, 306–7, 577.

43. Beliakov 2012a, 578.

44. The professor, Aleksandr Natanovich Bernshtam, is discussed below, pp. 104–5.

45. Cited in Beliakov 2012a, 581, 578; El'zon 2003, 206; Varustin 1990, 5, 27; Rogachevskii 2001, 359–60, 364; Shnirelman 2002, 47–49. Gumilev recounted how on one occasion one of his interrogators excitedly urged the other to brutalize him: "beat this goy on his head—he's clever (*bei etogo goia po golove, on umnyi!*)." Galkovskii 1995.

an underlying element present in nearly all of his work, influencing and indeed shaping his most important hypotheses about the nature of ethnicity and the meaning of Russian history.

Gumilev's return from banishment in 1956 marked the beginning of a new phase in his life in which he sought to establish an academic position and develop his scholarly interests. He was initially supported by his mentor Artamonov, who by then had become director of the Hermitage Museum in Leningrad. Artamonov took Gumilev on to work in the library of the Hermitage, where he remained until 1962, when the rector of Leningrad State University, the mathematician Aleksandr Danilovich Aleksandrov (1912–1999), approved his appointment as a research associate (*nauchnyi sotrudnik*, later *starshii nauchnyi sotrudnik*) on the Faculty of Geography.[46] Gumilev would remain in this position for the rest of his professional life, up to his retirement in the early 1980s. Compared with the awful turbulence of his early years, his life now began to approach something resembling normalcy, and he was finally able to settle down, get married, and set about developing his academic career. As we will see throughout this book, however, nothing for Gumilev would ever really be normal, for physical repression was replaced by the turmoil of an endless succession of academic controversies and disputes. Many of these were trifling, but others involved matters of high ideological and even political significance.

The research profile that he developed over this period was broad ranging and diverse, and will be examined in detail in part 1. On the one hand, he continued work on the ethnographic history of the Eurasian steppe, authoring major studies on the Xiongnu people (third to second centuries BC), the Göktürk Khaganates (sixth to eighth centuries AD), the Khazars (mid-seventh to mid-tenth centuries AD), and the Mongol empire. Along with his historical work, Gumilev now also became engaged in theoretical debates about ethnicity, ethnogenesis, and the nature of interethnic relations in the USSR. These had been vitally important issues in the Soviet Union since the revolution, and in the post-Stalinist ferment of his day were being freshly debated by ethnographers and other specialists.[47]

Gumilev always maintained that he was strongly disadvantaged and marginalized in the Soviet academic system, and moreover that the official persecution that blighted his early life continued—albeit in a more subtle form—for decades

---

46. Ironically, Gumilev had been offered an opportunity to enroll as a geography student in the 1930s. According to Gerstein, however, he was at that time "mortally offended" by the proposition, convinced that he was a historian and nothing else. Gerstein 2004, 203.

47. For full bibliographies of Gumilev's work see Diagileva 2012; Karimullin 1990. An extensive collection of materials by and about Gumilev is available on the website Gumilevica: http://gumilevica.kulichki.net/works.html.

after his release and rehabilitation.[48] On both counts there was much truth. His scholarly oeuvre was often at odds with standard Soviet perspectives and contravened many of the conventional canons and holy truths of the academic establishment. Gumilev seemed to relish this role as a sort of maverick, and unsurprisingly it won him little empathy from many quarters. Moreover, there is now documentary evidence that he did indeed remain politically suspect and was kept under various sorts of observation by the KGB until well into the 1980s, both at home and at work. Despite a publication list that would have been the envy of any Soviet academic, along with active duty teaching courses and supervising dissertations, Gumilev never received a regular academic appointment as professor. Moreover, from the late 1970s, his freedom to publish was severely curtailed by the authorities, such that his two magna opera—both of them culminations of research he had conducted during his entire career—could be published only at the end of perestroika.

At the same time, however, it is critical to note that Gumilev also enjoyed a considerable degree of support, and that much of it came from this same establishment. Although rejected by some, his research was received with great interest and enthusiasm by many of his academic colleagues, in disciplines ranging from the natural sciences to history and even philosophy. His early teachers and mentors remained doggedly faithful to him, and this support was important in later decades. His social and cultural background may have earned him the disdain of the state, but the same factors served to make him very special in the eyes of those contemporaries who viewed this legacy positively. The university rectors Voznesenskii and Aleksandrov, who came to his assistance at critical moments, were examples of this admiration, but it was true more generally for the lay intelligentsia. Everyone knew about his illustrious parentage, and the fact that he was one of the unfortunate subjects of Akhmatova's *Requiem*—still unpublished in the USSR but widely circulated in samizdat—added to the aura of interest around him. With his unorthodox approach and the simple eloquence of his writing style, gracefully unencumbered as it was by official jargon of any sort, Gumilev represented "a star in the heavens" at the end of the 1960s. "We were so overfed on Marxism," recalled the literary critic Dmitrii Borisovich Oreshkin, "that this sounded a fresh note and offered a fresh point of view."[49] Along with the portraits of Tsvetaeva, Mandel'shtam, and Pasternak that the intelligentsia liked to hang in their living rooms in the 1960s and 1970s, a picture of Lev Gumilev as a young child together with his parents was especially popular.[50]

---

48. Gumilev 1988a.
49. "Vse svobodny" 2005.
50. Loseff 1994, 13.

Gumilev received invitations to speak at leading scientific institutions, including Moscow State University and the prestigious Center of the Siberian Academy of Sciences at Akademgorodok, outside Novosibirsk. Despite restrictions on publishing, he was nonetheless able to disseminate his work broadly, and across several decades assembled a publication list that was, as noted, highly distinguished. His work appeared not only in major scholarly journals but also leading official periodicals such as *Ogonek*, *Druzhba Narodov*, and *Komsomolskaia Pravda*. Dozens of his articles and several of his books were translated into foreign languages, including one monograph published by Oxford University Press.[51] And entirely beyond the world of academics and intellectuals, Gumilev had important supporters within the political establishment, although they were not to bring their full influence to bear in his support until very near the end of his life. Indeed, at one point at least, Gumilev was in good enough standing with the authorities to be granted the nontrivial privilege of traveling abroad to attend professional meetings in Prague, Budapest, and Kraków.

Thus Gumilev was not only a scholarly and political outcast, as he liked to style himself. A good indication of the complex intertwining of suspicion and support that characterized his position in the Soviet Union can be seen in his attempts to defend a second doctoral dissertation. His first doctorate in 1961, based on his study of the Göktürk Khaganates, was in history. Thirteen year later he submitted a second dissertation, in three volumes, based on his more recent research into the nature and history of ethnicity and ethnogenesis. He sought this second degree in geography, which had been his disciplinary home since coming to the university. The defense took place at Leningrad University in May 1974. Out of a scientific counsel of twenty-two university colleagues, twenty voted in favor of awarding the degree and two were opposed—a very clear majority. All decisions about degrees, however, needed to be approved by an official oversight agency—the Vyshii Atestationnyi Komitet—and in this case VAK declined to confirm the university's decision. Although it recognized Gumilev's work as a "significant scientific achievement," VAK determined (with characteristically twisted logic) that in its broad scope and interdisciplinarity Gumilev's work was "higher than a doctoral dissertation, and therefore not a doctoral dissertation." Undaunted, Gumilev claimed his second doctoral title anyway and was never subsequently challenged. But it is the fate of the dissertation itself that indicates the remarkably widespread appeal of Gumilev's work at this early date. There was of course no question about any normal publication of the thesis. Instead, Gumilev deposited his three typewritten volumes in VINITI, a center for scientific

---

51. Gumilev 1987b.

information in Moscow, where photocopies could be ordered on an individual basis.[52] The popularity of the work proved to be extraordinary, despite the fact that all orders had to be accompanied by a payment for the copying. To service the flood of requests it received, VINITI eventually produced two thousand photocopies, and these copies were in turn copied by their recipients and further disseminated. It is estimated that eventually thirty thousand copies were in private circulation and were even available on the black market for a hefty price.[53]

Gumilev was seventy-three and well into his retirement when Mikhail Gorbachev launched the fateful program of reforms that would lead eventually to the breakup of the country. Nonetheless, it was in the course of perestroika that the now-elderly Gumilev emerged as a national celebrity and the subject of ever-greater attention and adulation. There were two elements to Gumilev's appeal, one personal and one conceptual. Personally, Gumilev had by this time become a veritable living monument, a unique personal link back to the sublime cultural heights of fin de siècle Russia's Silver Age as well as to the arbitrary brutality of decades of Soviet repression. For a society now eager to reengage with these aspects of its twentieth-century history that had long been taboo, Gumilev embodied legacies that were equally and endlessly alluring. No less important, this same society was keen to discard the tired truisms of Soviet Marxism and search out new rationales and interpretations, new ways of understanding the nation and new visions for its future development. In this regard as well, Gumilev's scholarly work offered a variety of original and unorthodox perspectives that seemed increasingly compelling. Any remaining political proscription of Gumilev was formally lifted in 1986, although it took a further three years for his two magna opera to be published.[54] Throughout this period, Gumilev's star shone ever brighter. He was the subject of innumerable interviews for the press, radio, and television. Documentary films were made about him and some of his lectures were televised nationally. Overcoming his traditional disinclination to comment on contemporary affairs, he now speculated broadly on what his scientific theories meant for his country's history, its current travails, and its future imperatives. In his final years, he was drawn ever more directly into the political tumult leading up to the collapse of the USSR, but his involvement was cut short by declining health. Gumilev died on 15 June 1992 and was buried in the

---

52. As Loren Graham points out, this was a further indication of the ambivalence of Gumilev's position: although the high academic bureaucracy refused to confirm his doctoral degree, he would not have been able to deposit his thesis at VINITI without significant support from within the establishment. Graham 1987: 251.

53. Gumilev 1994c, 258; Kurkchi 1994; "25-letie" 2004.

54. Gumilev 1989b; Gumilev 1989c.

Nikol'skii Cemetery at the Aleksandr Nevskii Monastery in St. Petersburg. His funeral was attended by over ten thousand people.[55]

The Structure of This Book

In analyzing the structure, reception, and influence of ideas or theories, it is typical to begin first by setting out the context in which they developed—where they came from and what prior influences they were responding to—before taking up a detailed analysis of the ideas themselves. Although this approach is the most intuitive and logical, it has not been strictly followed in the present work. In Gumilev's case there were always multiple contexts at work, and his place in them involved complex and highly nuanced patterns of conceptual interaction that were quite different in each case. Without a full prior appreciation of the essential contours of his theoretical models and interpretations, it is simply not possible to contextualize them meaningfully and evaluate their relationship to the dynamics of the broader environment. In this spirit, the present book is organized into three parts. In part 1, four chapters are devoted to a critical reconstruction of Gumilev's ideas and focus on his two principal concerns: the nature of ethnic being and ethnogenesis on the one hand, and his interpretations of Russia's historical experience on the other. In this discussion, the more important immediate sources of his thinking are identified, but the broader context itself is considered only in part 2. There, three chapters discuss the areas of Soviet intellectual and political life that are most important for understanding Gumilev's work: debates about the society-nature relationship; discourses around "ethnos theory" and nationality policy, and finally the emergence of a post-Stalinist movement of Russian nationalism, in which Gumilev occupied a significant if ambivalent position. Finally, part 3 discusses Gumilev's ideas and influence in the post-Soviet period, with chapters considering his relationship to neo-Eurasianism, his influence on new biopolitical preoccupations with the factor of ethnicity, and the profound interest in Gumilev's work beyond ethnic Russia, both within the Russian Federation and more broadly across the former Soviet Union.

---

55. Public concern with Gumilev's condition as he lay in hospital was such that newspapers provided regular updates. Beliakov 2012a, 694.

Part 1

GUMILEV'S THEORY OF ETHNOS AND ETHNOGENESIS

THE NATURE OF ETHNICITY

What Is an Ethnos?

All of Gumilev's theories rest on a highly essentialized understanding of the nature of ethnicity. The ethnic unit or ethnos (pl. ethnies) is conceived as one of the most fundamental and durable categories of human organization. Ethnic belonging is an existential mode of being that forms an intrinsic and immutable part of the very persona of all individuals. It is a feature of human nature, which can be neither transcended nor transformed.[1] "No human being can live outside of an ethnos," he affirmed, indeed any attempt to do so would be tantamount to "pulling oneself out of a swamp by one's own hair."[2] Although all ethnies share a similar organizational structure and go through the same evolutionary life cycle—what he called *etnogenez* or ethnogenesis—each ethnos was nonetheless unique: a self-contained and self-sustaining entity. Gumilev placed great emphasis on ethnic individuality, maintaining that real-existing differences between groups were reflected in a subjective group awareness of an "us-them" juxtaposition that provided cohesion and solidarity.[3] All ethnic groupings share "the particular quality of the species homo sapiens to group in such a way as to

---

1. Gumilev and Ivanov 1992, 51.
2. Gumilev 1989c, 145 (quote), 22, 142–45; Gumilev 1988c; Gumilev and Ermolaev 1993, 178; Gumilev 1994c, 254.
3. Gumilev 1976, 121.

oppose oneself and one's own (*svoi*) to the outside world. This [process of] distinction is characteristic for all ages and all countries."[4]

As essentialized entities, Gumilev's ethnies were primordial formations with ancient lineages. In its full scope, he reckoned that the ethnogenetic cycle of birth, blossoming, and eventual decline lasted around 1,500 years. In the course of its life cycle, the ethnos developed and evolved in certain ways, but its basic character remained constant (under normal circumstances, at least). This same cyclical pattern was characteristic across all of world history, moreover, which meant that the ethnic formations of the ancient world were structurally identical to those of the present day and shared the same institutions.[5] On this basis, he tended to use examples drawn from history—frequently ancient history—in order to illustrate present-day processes. The inherent differences between ethnies did not necessarily result in antipathy or hostile relations, but ethnic individuality did mean that they could not be combined or merged without injuring their integrity. Ethnic separation was very much a part of the natural order of what he called the ethnosphere. "It is impossible to unite (*ob'edinit'*) ethnies, for the resulting union will always involve the principle of compulsion. Ethnies cannot simply be made to love each other."[6] Even long centuries of cohabitation of adjacent spaces and mutual interaction among different groups did not necessarily lead to the loss of a sense of ethnic individuality, regardless of how much convergence there may have been between them economically and socially.

What, for Gumilev, was the essential marker of ethnicity? He rejected commonly invoked attributes such as language, religion, material culture, *genre de vie*, or simple folkways and customs. Ethnicity was rather embodied most vitally in what he called a "behavioral stereotype" (*stereotip povedeniia*), shared by all members of a given ethnic group.[7] The behavioral stereotype referred to an established pattern of interactions, a "strictly defined norm governing the relationships between the collective and the individual and between the individuals themselves."[8] All interactions among the member of an ethnos were shaped in a similar way by behavioral stereotypes, and because all ethnies possessed them, they served to establish the fundamental unity of the ethnosphere as a whole. At the same time, each stereotype was unique to the respective ethnic unit. Indeed, in the final analysis it was the very uniqueness of its behavioral stereotype that conditioned the singularity of the group noted above. The principle of ethnic

---

4. Gumilev 1970a, 47; Gumilev 1978a, 97–98; Gumilev 1989c, 41, 48, 51, 169.
5. Gumilev 1970a, 47.
6. Gumilev 1989d, 33.
7. Gumilev and Ivanov 1992, 52–53.
8. Gumilev 1970a, 49 (quote); Gumilev 1989c, 91, 131.

THE NATURE OF ETHNICITY   25

exclusivity insured that members of one group would be incapable of assimilating the behavioral norms of any other, and were frequently unable even to understand them.

For the most part, the behavioral stereotype operated on a subconscious level of personal and group psychology, where it worked to shape personal interactions, tastes, and attitudes, giving them all a distinctive ethnic stamp.[9] Gumilev illustrated how this worked with the following anecdote. Imagine four men on a Moscow tram, he proposed—a Russian, a Tatar, a German, and someone from the Caucasus. They all dressed alike, spoke Russian equally well, had a similar educational background and social values, and even enjoyed the same films. In short, you would think there was no difference between them. Yet when a drunken youth stumbles onto the tram and begins to harass a young woman, the differences in behavioral stereotype become immediately clear. "I know, and we all know, that the Russian will say to him, 'hey you, *kiriukha* [an affectionate term for a drunk], you're going to get caught. Look, get off at the next stop and take another tram.' But not the German! He will stop the tram with the emergency brake, call the police, and demand that they 'arrest this hooligan.'" The fellow from the Caucasus "will not call anyone but simply lose control and hit the offender in the face—and hit him hard. The Tatar, however, will observe the whole affair with disdain and turn away in silence."[10]

Gumilev's conceptual modeling of the ethnos was strongly influenced by systems theory and cybernetics, both of which were popular in the Soviet Union in the 1960s and 1970s.[11] The biologist and geneticist Aleksandr Aleksandrovich Malinovskii (1909–1996), an important proponent of this perspective, was a personal friend of his.[12] Each individual ethnos, Gumilev argued, represented a self-contained organism. More than a mere assemblage of ethnically similar individuals, an ethnos was a systemic entity, a "complex of elements" defined by the system of functional relationships and interconnections between them. It was these interconnections that provided the ethnos with its coherence as an

---

9. Gumilev 1994c, 248.

10. Gumilev 2003f, 58. This story was a favorite of Gumilev's and he repeated it frequently with subtle variations. For other versions see Gumilev 1989c, 86; Gumilev 2001, 22; Lavrov 2000, 328; Annenskii 2005, 141.

11. Rindzeviciute 2010.

12. Malinovskii was the son of Aleksandr Aleksandrovich Malinovskii—better known by his Bolshevik pseudonym Aleksandr Bogdanov. Bogdanov himself had pioneered an early version of systems theory in prerevolutionary Russia. Bogdanov 1989 [1913]; Malinovskii 1970; Susiluoto 1982. On Malinovskii and Gumilev, see Berg 2003, 376. Gumilev's thinking about systems theory was further influenced by the work of the Austrian biologist Ludwig von Bertalanfi and the Russian-Belgian chemist Il'ya Romanovich Prigozhin. Bertalanfi 1969.

integrated unit.[13] The "elements" involved included not only human individuals but also various animate and nonanimate parts of the external environment with which the former interacted. The ethnos operated on different levels as a sort of ecological network, which like all systems was based on certain organizational principles and dynamics.[14]

As we will see, neither Gumilev's notion of the behavioral stereotype nor his conceptualization of the ethnos as a system-organism defined by the functional interrelationships between its parts were particularly out of line with mainstream Soviet ideas about ethnicity.[15] What set him apart were his radical ideas about where ethnies fit in the fundamental juxtaposition between the natural world and human society. Whatever distinctive characteristics an ethnos might possess, it was always understood in the USSR to be a social phenomenon. This point was very important for a number of reasons, not least because it meant that in the final analysis ethnic groupings always remained in some way a part of the matrix of social relations that Marx had described, and thus they remained subject to the same laws and imperatives that drove social development universally. Ethnies might not evolve at the same tempo or in the same manner as society's material means of production, but like all other social phenomena they did evolve and did undergo transformation.

This was a perspective that Gumilev rejected, consistently and unequivocally. Throughout all of his work, he insisted that an ethnos was not a social but rather a natural formation. There were two separate categories or modes of human collective existence, he explained, which corresponded to the juxtaposition between the natural and the social. The *obshchestvennyi* or social category took the generic form of a *sotsiuum* or society. By contrast, the natural mode of collective existence took the form of ethnies and their variants: superethnies and subethnies.[16] In developing his argument he appealed directly to the authority of Marx.

> If we use the word "social" (*sotsial'nyi*) in our Marxist sense, we need to understand it as a form of collective existence connected with production, that is to say, "society" (*obshchestvo*). But are there human collectives that are not social? Collectives that are different and separate from (*krome i pomimo*) society? On this question, Marx expressed himself precisely and definitively. He referred to society using the German word

---

13. Gumilev 1989c, 100–101, 131; Gumilev 2003c, 11; Gumilev 1988b, 48; Beliakov 2012a, 433.

14. For an appraisal of systems theory as a dimension of Gumilev's work see Kuz'min 1998, 281, 284, 291–92.

15. Rybakov 2001b, 14–15. Gumilev's relation to Soviet ethnography is discussed in chapter 6.

16. Gumilev 1989c, 18, 49, 50.

Gesellschaft. [But] he distinguished society from primeval collectives, which he called *Gemeinwesen.* . . . These primeval collectives existed long before the emergence of the material production among human-kind that Marx considered to be a necessary condition for the emergence of society. The first formations, the first collectives or groups of homo sapiens, indeed had no relation to a means of production that had not yet come into existence. They lived as collective groups simply because they could not exist individually.

These *Gemeinwesen*, he concluded, did not disappear with the emergence of society, "but on the contrary, gradually developed [into] those entities that we call ethnies."[17]

Every human individual operated simultaneously in both modes of existence, as a member of society and a representative of an ethnos. He likened the distinction between them to the contrast between units of length and weight, that is to say, variables that were "parallel but incommensurable."[18] Each human being combines the "innate [natural] laws of life with specific [social] manifestations of technology and culture." Social connections and entanglements, while enriching the individual, do not remove the latter's enduring "connections (*soprichastnosti*) to the natural elements out of which he or she were born."[19] And if individuals can be natural and social at the same time, he reasoned, the same is true for human collectives. He supported the position, staked out by Soviet dialecticians since the 1930s, that the realms of the social and the natural operated in entirely different ways, each controlled by its own respective laws and patterns of regular development (*zakonomernosti*). This meant that, by their very nature, "social and ethnic processes are different."[20] As Marx had taught, the laws controlling the *sotsiuum* dictated that its development over history would be spontaneous and would move in a linear direction, progressively evolving into more developed and "advanced" forms of organization: slave-owning societies evolve into feudalism, feudalism into capitalism, and capitalism gives way to socialism.[21] These processes played out autonomously in the social sphere, however, and were "in no way connected with the group's biological structure," which remains unchanged throughout it all.[22] This biological structure was materialized in the ethnos: a "biophysical reality," a "natural phenomenon," and an organic part of the natural world.[23]

17. Gumilev 2001, 24 (quote); Gumilev 2003e, 233.
18. Gumilev 1989c, 18, 21, 51, 175; Gumilev 2004 [1967]: 38–39; Gumilev 1968c, 40.
19. Gumilev 1989c, 21.
20. Gumilev 1970a, 50; Gumilev 1971a, 80.
21. Gumilev 1968c, 36; Gumilev 1967c, 55.
22. Gumilev 1989c, 22 (quote); Gumilev 1990b.
23. Gumilev 2001, 45.

All ethnic phenomena and processes, according to Gumilev, belonged strictly to the natural realm. "Human heritability, the physiological energy of the individual cell and the entire organism are biochemical phenomena, and . . . do not depend on socioeconomic formations, productive forces and relations, economic conditions, or profitability."[24] Collective entities such as political states, by contrast, are exclusively social in nature. They can include ethnies but cannot be identified with them.[25] The particular distinction between ethnic groupings and political units was a fundamental point for Gumilev and a key element in the Soviet as well as post-Soviet reception of his ideas, as we will see. In contrast to social development that was progressive and linear, the ethnos moves "like any other living organism" through a predetermined life cycle that is cyclical in form: an ever-repeating succession of growth and decline that is organically bound to the natural rhythms of the natural world.[26] As a natural—*prirodnyi* or *estestvennyi*—phenomenon, the ethnos was more properly the subject of natural science than sociology.[27] Ethnicity was a "biophysical reality. . . . Ethnic belonging, which manifests itself in the human consciousness, is not a product of this consciousness. It obviously reflects a dimension of the nature of the person that lies much deeper; [it is] a biological dimension located beyond consciousness and psychology, on the boundaries of the physiological."[28]

Gumilev made frequent use of the metaphor of a biological organism, likening the ethnos either to an individual human being—which in a similar fashion "is born, matures (*muzhat'sia*), grows old, and dies"[29]—or to aggregate organisms found in the natural world. "Collective forms of existence can be seen in many species of terrestrial animals: ants, herds of hoofed animals, flocks of birds, and so on." For the species homo sapiens, "the corresponding form [of collective life] is the ethnos."[30] Given the high scientific and ideological stakes of such a radical position, even Gumilev—typically categorical and uncompromising in his assertions, however outlandish—equivocated to some degree in his pronouncements on this point, but the bulk of his work can leave no doubt about his position.[31] For him, ethnies represented "biological communities" in an entirely literal sense, communities that operated in terms of "biological time" (predetermined successions of organic growth, decline, and rebirth) as opposed to sociohistorical time

---

24. Gumilev 1994c, 271 (quote); Gumilev 1989c, 23.
25. Gumilev 1989c, 50, 85, 104, 134.
26. Gumilev and Balashov 1993, 159; Gumilev 1991e, 133.
27. Gumilev 1989c, 20; Gumilev 1990c, 8; Gumilev 1994c, 277.
28. Gumilev 2004 [1967], 40, 41; Gumilev 2001, 45.
29. Gumilev and Panchenko 1990, 6.
30. Gumilev 1989c, 226; Gumilev 2001, 24.
31. Filippov 2010, 202.

(progressive development in a linear fashion).[32] Ethnicity, he asserted in an early essay on the subject, was quite simply a "biological reality."[33]

But how, exactly, was an ethnos biological? It is important to appreciate that Gumilev's understanding of ethnic naturalism was two-sided in a manner that corresponded to two different dimensions of nature itself—what might be called "internal" and "external" nature. Both of these were important for the constitution of ethnicity. Internally, the naturalism of the ethnos involved physiological aspects of the individual, more specifically, its genetic properties and structure. Externally, nature was identified as the geographical environment of the ethnos, with which it formed an intimate ecological relationship. Although these two dimensions might seem to correspond to the familiar juxtaposition between "nature"—that is, inborn physiological traits—and "nurture"—the external milieu—in fact they do not, for in this case internal and external factors were equally natural and biological, and both figured fundamentally in Gumilev's conception of the naturalism of the ethnos.[34] He elaborated his naturalist perspective using ideas and theories from the respective scientific disciplines devoted to them: genetics on the one hand, and geography, ecology, and landscape science on the other. Gumilev himself was aware of this dualism in his approach, and he believed that in his ethnos theory he was successful in combining the two dimensions into a single grand perspective.[35] As we will argue in the rest of the chapter, this was not the case. Despite his obvious enthusiasm for genetic models and hypotheses and his imaginative attempts to deploy them, in the final analysis he—along with the rest of his Soviet colleagues—did not accept their implications for the nature of ethnicity. For Gumilev, therefore, the biological naturalness of the ethnos was primarily environmental, elaborated in terms of what we will call his ecology of ethnicity.

Ethnicity, Genetics, and Race

Gumilev believed that individual ethnies, as biological or quasi-biological organisms, possessed a distinctive genetic composition. Each ethno-organism

---

32. Gumilev 1974b; Gumilev 1989c, 227.

33. Gumilev 2004 [1967], 41. Certain aspects of Gumilev's naturalistic view of ethnicity were anticipated in the work of Sergei Mikhailovich Shirokogorov (1887–1939), a Russian ethnographer who emigrated to China after the revolution and in the 1920s and 1930s actively developed his own ethnos theory. Shirokogorov 1923; Shirokogoroff 1924. Although Gumilev was highly critical of Shirokogorov, there were significant resonances in their thinking, and recent studies have argued for the direct influence of the latter on Gumilev. Gumilev 1989c, 69–70; Revunenkova and Reshetov 2003, 109–10; Danchenko 1997; Elez 2001, 198; Filippov 2006, 93.

34. For a fuller discussion see Bassin 2009b.

35. Gumilev 2004 [1967], 44.

was associated with its own gene pool (*genafond*), which had to be protected from exogenic influences if the integrity of the group was to be maintained. Failure to do so could lead to *metisatsiia* or interbreeding among different ethnies—a process that, he claimed, nearly always brought negative consequences for succeeding generations. On this basis, he always underscored the importance of endogamy as an institutionalized group practice. Endogamy was critically important to sustaining individual ethnic units, for it operated in a natural fashion to restrict the penetration of foreign elements and thereby helped the group maintain its distinctive ethnic character.[36] Should this institution break down, he pointed out, it could lead to the decline of the ethnic group, a point that he illustrated through copious historical examples.[37] "Open contact and free love," he declared, "destroy nature and culture."[38] Endogamy served a specifically genetic function in "stabilizing [i.e., protecting] the composition of the gene pool" and thereby helping to consolidate the "sustainability of the ethnic collective."[39] In a conversation with a youthful acolyte in the early 1980s, Gumilev pointed out bluntly that failure to observe endogamy "creates a mixed (*smeshannyi*) gene pool, which will produce descendants that are inferior (*nepolnotsennyi*)." As an illustration, he referred to Sinclair Lewis's 1947 novel *Kingsblood Royal*—popular at the time in the Soviet Union—which described the travails of a successful banker in the American Midwest who discovers he is part black.[40]

The Soviet science of genetics was undergoing a major renaissance in the 1960s after decades of political and personal repression associated with the notorious Stalinist agronomist Trofim Denisovich Lysenko (1898–1976).[41] Gumilev followed developments in this field with great interest. He had close personal links with geneticists such as Malinovskii and Raisa L'vovna Berg (1913–2006), and throughout the 1970s was a regular participant in the so-called Seminar on Theoretical Biology organized in the Department of Biology at Leningrad

---

36. Gumilev 1989c, 90
37. Naarden 1996, 73.
38. Gumilev 1989c, 89.
39. Gumilev 1989c, 227 (quote), 85, 87–88.
40. Author's interview with Andrei Rogachevskii, March 2015; also see Rogachevskii 2001, 363. Emma Gershtein recounted how he reflected pessimistically on the future of their relationship in the late 1930s: "How stupid people in mixed marriages are to have children. When Russia is fascist in about eight years' time, children with a Jewish parent will not be allowed to do anything and, just like mulattos and half-castes, they won't be accepted by society." Cited in Gerstein 2004, 230.
41. On the history of Soviet genetics, see Zakharov 1999; Kneen 1998; Adams 1979; Adams 1990b; Gaissinovitch 1980.

University.[42] The strongest influence on his conceptualization of the internal biological dynamics of ethnicity, however, came through his contacts with two outstanding Soviet geneticists, Nikolai Vladimirovich Timofeev-Resovskii (1900–1981) and Mikhail Efimovich Lobashev (1907–1971). Both had contributed to the dramatic advances of Soviet and (in Timofeev-Resovskii's case) European genetics in the interwar period, both had suffered from the repression of the field in the USSR, and both regained prominence with the eclipse of Lysenkoism in the 1960s. Gumilev based important aspects of his own theories of ethnicity and ethnogenesis on their ideas and made constant use of their scientific terminology. Terms such as "gene pool," "genetic drift" (*dreif*), "genetic diversity," "genetic memory" (*pamiat'*), "selection," "mutagenesis" (*mutagenez*), "population," and "mutant" (*mutant*) were all standard parts of his own analytical vocabulary. He deployed them generously, not only in his technical discussions of ethnicity but in his historical writings as well.[43] Timofeev-Resovskii's influence on Gumilev related largely to the latter's ideas about the mechanics of ethnogenesis, and thus will be considered in the next chapter. Lobashev, however, provided vital concepts that allowed Gumilev to understand the essential marker of ethnicity—the behavioral stereotype—in biological terms.

From the 1940s, Lobashev worked primarily in behavioral genetics, which drew heavily on Pavlovian psychology and the principles of "conditioned reflexes."[44] The teachings of Ivan Petrovich Pavlov (1849–1936) enjoyed official endorsement in the Stalin period, especially in the twilight years from the late 1940s when the scientist was lionized as one of the great figures in world science.[45] Pavlov maintained that behavioral patterns developed as "conditioned reflexes" in response to two categories of external stimuli or "signal systems." The first signal system referred to the real-life events themselves that triggered the reflexes, whereas the second system comprised the symbolic representation of these events through the "signal of signals" (*signal signalov*), in other words,

---

42. Vakhtin 2002; Chebanov 1998. Raisa Berg was the daughter of the eminent geographer and naturalist Lev Semenovich Berg (1876–1950), whose ideas about the relationship of organic life to the geographical environment were foundational for Gumilev's own theories, as we will see. Berg described the strong personal solidarity she, Gumilev and Malinovskii felt as "three persecuted and disfigured children" of great luminaries of Russian culture. Berg 2003, 377.

43. For example, Gumilev 1989c, 217, 227, 455, 477; Gumilev 1968c, 43–44; Gumilev 2004c, 189.

44. *M. E. Lobashev i problemy sovremennoi genetiki* 1978; Birstein 2001, 46, 289, 292. Lobashev grew up as an impoverished *besprizornik* orphan in Tashkent. His childhood experiences—which included a prolonged bout of muteness—provided the inspiration for the hero Sania Grigor'ev in Veniamin Aleksandrovich Kaverin's celebrated *Two Captains* (1944). Lobashev had been a leading advocate for the introduction of eugenics in the USSR. Adams 1990c, 121; Kovach 1971; Berg 2003, 163.

45. On Pavlov and Stalin, see Pollock 2006, 136–67; Joravsky 1977; Tucker 1956.

human speech.[46] In the 1960s, Lobashev was one of the pioneers in ethology—the science of animal behavior—in the USSR. He was particularly interested in how behavioral patterns were transferred between generations and developed his own theory of "signal inheritance" (*signal'naia nasledstvennost'*) to explain this. Lobashev suggested that, although these patterns themselves were not genetically inscribed or inherited and had to be taught afresh to each new generation, a certain predisposition to learning them did indeed form a part of an organism's genetic inheritance. "Organisms of a single species but with different genotypes," he explained, "assimilate different conditioned reflexes at different rates."[47]

Although Gumilev noted the importance of Pavlov and disciples such as L.A. Orbeli for his ideas about ethnicity, it was Lobashev's ethological principles that provided the explanation for his notion of "behavioral stereotypes."[48] All ethnies, Gumilev reasoned, are distinguished from one another by the "special behavioral language" that is a behavioral stereotype. This stereotype is passed between generations "not genetically, but rather—as M. E. Lobashev has demonstrated—by means of signal inheritance."[49] The process enables children spontaneously "to assimilate a behavioral stereotype that represents adaptive skills," and in the final analysis is the key to all ethnic survival.[50] "In the animal world, individual adaptation takes place with the help of conditioned reflexes, which enable the animal to select . . . the optimal conditions for its life and self-defence. These conditioned reflexes are passed on from parents to their children . . . [and] represent the highest form of adaptation. In humans, this phenomenon is called the 'continuity of civilization,' which is made possible through the 'signal of signals,' that is, human speech." The term "civilization" here refers to the cluster of customs, modes of thought, aesthetics, perceptions, sexual norms, and so on, that taken together comprise the ethnic behavioral stereotype. This stereotype represents everything that "facilitates the best adaptation to the environment, passed on across generations by means of signal inheritance."[51] It was specifically in terms of this process of adaptation that Gumilev ultimately defined the biological quality of ethnos. "I see the biological character (*biologichnost'*) of the ethnos not in its anatomical and genetic features but in its behavioral characteristics, in the system of conditioned reflexes that since the time of I. P. Pavlov have been considered to be a branch of biology."[52]

---

46. Tucker 1956, 474–75, 478.

47. Lobashev 1967, 593, cited in Barnakov 2004; Lobashev 1961; Lobashev 1947.

48. Gumilev 1989c, 295, 309. According to Gumilev's wife, Lobashev—who like Gumilev worked at Leningrad State University—was aware of and supported Gumilev's use of his theories. Gumileva 1994, 615; Beliakov 2012a, 430, 452.

49. Gumilev 1989c, 226, 295, 309; Gumilev 1968b, 601; Gumilev 1977; Lavrov 2000, 341.

50. Gumilev and Ivanov 1984.

51. Gumilev 1989c, 226–27 (quote); Gumilev 1970a, 50, 51; Gumilev 2001, 29; Gumilev 1967c, 55.

52. Quoted in Lavrov 2000, 325.

For Soviet sensibilities in the 1960s and 1970s, Gumilev's intimation that genetic factors were significant in the constitution of ethnic life was little short of incendiary. With it, he appeared to be crossing the line that separated the legitimate scientific study of ethnicity from the notorious *Rassenkunde* or racial science of the nineteenth and twentieth centuries. Gumilev himself was by no means unaware of this, and was not entirely comfortable with the description of the "internal" biological character of ethnicity that we have just seen. This was an issue with which he wrestled throughout all of his work. Despite his own arguments for the inherent *biologichnost'* or biological character of ethnicity that we have just considered, he nonetheless rejected any suggestion of *biologizm* or "biologism" in his thinking. "[My critics] scream at me, 'This is dreadful biologism!' I beg your pardon, but it is nothing of the sort."[53] He roundly denounced reactionary "social Darwinism"—flourishing, as he claimed, not in the USSR but in "foreign countries" (i.e., the West)—which sought to apply "biological laws to social life."[54] Such "biologism" had no place in his work, he insisted, because he always separated society from ethnos in the most categorical manner. His comparison of ethnies to herds of animals, he maintained rather obscurely, did not mean that the two entities were "analogous." And in direct contradiction to his own statements cited above, on numerous occasions he denied outright that an ethnos was fully biological.[55]

Most important, and despite all he had to say about the importance of genetics, Gumilev clearly rejected the suggestion that the biological factor of race played any role in the phenomenon of ethnicity. He was indignant that he should be accused "even of racism" and earnestly tried to distance himself from such a position.[56] In no way, he maintained repeatedly, is ethnicity racially determined or conditioned. The physical-anthropological attributes commonly identified as racial features—skin pigmentation, bone structure, phrenological characteristics, and so on—"have no significance for ethnogenetic processes."[57] Although he did emphasize the need to preserve respective ethnic gene pools intact, he also affirmed precisely the opposite, namely, that ethnies are commonly made up of different races and genetic pools. Indeed, this sort of mixing was a necessary condition for the initiation of the ethnogenetic process. "At the beginning of their existence, all ethnies are the product of the mixing (*skreshchenie*) of two or

---

53. Gumilev 1994c, 255.
54. Gumilev 1989c, 225–26.
55. Gumilev 1978a, 98n; Gumilev 2001, 29; Gumilev 1989c, 24; Gumilev 2001, 348. Even in these cases, however, he always qualified the disclaimer by pointing out that "certain biological features" of human individuals do indeed still "play a definite role." Gumilev 1989c, 223.
56. Gumilev 1994c, 258.
57. Gumilev 1989c, 90.

more racial types."[58] Gumilev illustrated the point with the illustrious example of the poet Alexander Pushkin—racially mixed but ethnically of course quint-essentially Russian—which may be taken as an indication that he was entirely sincere about it.[59]

Gumilev's dismissal of the significance of race is, however, confirmed most conclusively by his behaviorist understanding of the nature of ethnicity. As we have seen, he identified the essential ethnic marker not in genetic structures but rather in the behavioral patterns—the behavioral stereotype—of the respective group.[60] And these patterns were *not* passed on biologically but rather were learned and acquired. On this one important point at least, Gumilev was unambiguous and consistent. Membership in an ethnos is determined "not by a genetic code, but by upbringing. Racial differences play no role."[61] "The child in its mother's womb does not yet belong to any ethnos. It is nonethnic. Its ethnic belonging forms out of the relations the child develops in the first four or five years after birth. Whatever is close, familiar, and pleasant for the child in the first years of its life will define its ethnic belonging."[62] Lobashev's signal inheritance may predispose an infant toward the rapid and successful assimilation of a particular behavioral stereotype, but the latter still needs to be learned. From this perspective, the significance of endogamy could be understood in an entirely nonbiological sense, as a means of regulating not a "genetic apparatus" but rather what Gumilev called the "ethnic field" (*etnicheskoe pole*) to which all infants are exposed and which works to insure that behavioral features and patterns foreign to the respective ethnos are not absorbed. "It is clear that endogamy is necessary for the preservation of ethnic tradition, because an endogamous family passes on a [single] established behavioral stereotype to the child."[63]

The Ecology of Ethnicity

With the characterization of the behavioral stereotype as the "highest form of adaptation" of the ethnos to the conditions of its external milieu, Gumilev signaled the second aspect of his naturalist understanding of ethnicity.[64] This was an

---

58. Gumilev 2001, 346 (quote); Gumilev 1989c, 132, 217, 219; Gumilev 2001, 27; Gumilev 1991e, 139. For Gumilev's ambivalence on this important point see Ivanov 1992.

59. Gumilev 2001, 347; Lariuel' 2009; Beliakov 2012a, 434.

60. Pursiainen 1998, 11; Titov 2005, 62.

61. Gumilev 1976, 121.

62. Gumilev 2003f, 58–59 (quote); Gumilev 1989c, 142; Gumilev 2003c, 10; Gumilev 1994c, 271.

63. Gumilev 1989c, 90 (quote), 295.

64. Gumilev 1970a, 50.

ecological or environmental perspective in which the focus was not on the internal genetic and physiological constitution of ethnies but rather on their complex interconnections with the external geographical environment. If Gumilev made liberal use of the terminology of genetics in his descriptions of the ethnos, his lexical borrowings from ecological science—"landscape," "ecosystem," "geobiocenosis," "symbiosis," "ecological niche," and many other terms that we will encounter throughout this book—were no less extensive or important.[65] Gumilev's environmentalism was not necessarily at odds with his ideas about the inner nature of the ethnos as a biological organism. At the same time, the two were evidently juxtaposed, and he could deploy environmentalism as an alternative to the *biologizm* that for the reasons we have just considered he found problematic. In a seemingly neat rhetorical flourish, he frequently noted that geography offered a sort of middle ground: "An ethnos is neither a biological nor a social phenomenon. . . . I suggest we think of it rather as a geographical phenomenon, always tied with its surrounding landscape"[66] But this equivocation was completely misleading, for his environmentalism was in no way less biological, natural, and nonsocial than genetics.

In developing his ecological or geographical perspective, Gumilev continued to draw heavily on theories from the natural sciences—in this case, the long and distinguished legacy of Russian research in ecology and the earth sciences. At the end of the nineteenth century, scientists such as Vasilii Vasilevich Dokuchaev (1846–1903), Georgii Fedorovich Morozov (1867–1920), and Georgii Nikolaevich Vysotskii (1865–1940) had described the dynamic networks of mutual dependency that developed between the organic and inorganic phenomena in given geographical regions. These ecosystems were conceived as discrete physical-geographical entities, the territorial extent of which was determined by the size of the ecological networks themselves. Thus, Dokuchaev divided Russia into a series of macroregions that he called "natural-historical zones" (*estestvennoistoricheskie zony*), each associated with characteristic forms of life and habitats: tundra, taiga, steppe, and so on.[67] The "natural zone" concept was extended and refined in the decades after the revolution. In order to describe different aspects of these spatially delimited ecosystems, the botanist and forest ecologist Vladimir Nikolaevich Sukachev (1880–1967) borrowed terms such as *biotope*, *biochore*, and *biocenosis* from German ecology. More important, he created his own new term "biogeocenosis" (*biogeotsenos*) to emphasize the emplacement of a network

65. Graham 1987, 253–54.
66. Gumilev 2001, 29 (quote); Gumilev 1994c, 268.
67. Dokuchaev 1899; Vucinich 1988, 154–55.

of ecological interrelationships within a specific geographical region.[68] At the same time, the geographer Lev Semenovich Berg (1876–1950) also borrowed German scientific terminology—this time from physiography and physical geography—and rechristened Dokuchaev's natural zones as *landshafty* or landscapes. Berg described these as "combinations or grouping of objects and phenomena in which the peculiarities of relief, climate, water, soil, vegetation, and fauna, and to a certain degree human activity, blend into a single harmonious whole, typically repeated over the extent of the given zone of the earth."[69]

In describing the interconnections between the organic and inorganic phenomena in a given region, there was an inclination to stress the formative influence of the latter on the former and examine how the animate flora and fauna of the system adapted to the inanimate—or "geographical"—factors of climate, relief, soils, and so on. It was precisely this adaptation to the unique conditions of a given region that gave the respective ecological system its individuality, and at the same time represented the basis for its sustainability. The emphasis on adaptation, and the associated implication that the material conditions of the geographical environment were the principal formative elements for the creation of ecosystems, was reflected in the scientific perspectives just noted. Berg, for example, suggested that all organisms were compelled to adapt to the physical conditions of their respective landscapes in order to survive, and to that extent they were fundamentally shaped by them. He emphasized the importance of physical-geographical influences for the constitution of organic life.

> The geographical landscape affects organisms in *a compulsory manner* (*prinuditel'no*), compelling all the individuals, so far as the organization of the species permits, to vary in a determined manner. There is no place here for chance: consequences follow with the same fatal constancy as chemical reactions or physical phenomena. If geographical conditions [in different regions] are identical or similar, then identical or similar results are bound to follow. . . . Tundra, forest, steppe, desert, mountains, aquatic environments, island life, life in lakes and seas: each of these natural environments stamps its mark on the organisms [that inhabit them].

"Species that are unable to adapt" to their geographical environment, he concluded, "are obliged to emigrate into other geographical landscapes or perish."[70]

---

68. Sukachev 1949; Sukachev 1947; Raney 1966. On Sukachev and early Soviet ecology see Weiner 1984, 685; Weiner 1987, 65–66.

69. Berg 1947, 5, cited in Shaw and Oldfield 2007, 112.

70. Berg 1969 [1922], 265 (emphasis in original).

This sort of holistic thinking about the intrinsic interconnection between organic life and geographical environment received new public attention in the 1960s as part of a new interest in ecology and environmental problems in the Soviet Union. Gumilev fully shared this interest, and he believed that the concept of unique ecological networks occupying delimited geographical spaces was essential to the model of ethnicity that he wanted to develop. The principle that human communities might figure as natural elements in these ecological networks had been noted by Dokuchaev, Sukachev, and Berg, but they did not elaborate on it. From Gumilev's standpoint, it remained only to provide the specifications for this final point, and he believed that with his theory of ethnos he was in a position to do so. As a biological community, he explained, an ethnos fit into a biocenosis or "landscape" as a natural and organic element, in exactly the same manner and on the same basis as indigenous plant and animal species. All ethnies not only displayed a "close interconnection with their respective geographical landscape" but also represented a "necessary component part" (*sostavnaia chast'*) of it, "interacting with its fauna and flora" to form an *etnolandshaftnaia tselostnost'* or "ethno-landscape totality."[71]

Indeed, the natural-geographical landscape acted as a sort of vital platform for ethnic development, one that "shelters and nourishes" the ethnos and defines thereby its most important life parameters.[72] "Regardless of their size, the overwhelming majority of ethnies live or lived in particular territories, where they formed a part of the biocenosis of the respective landscape, and together with it formed a sort of 'closed system.'" Ethnies may spread "beyond the limits of their biochore, but this extension eventually ends with them following the standard pattern [i.e., becoming a part of the biocenosis] in their newly tamed and stabilized regions of adaptation."[73] Although Gumilev used Sukachev's terms "biochore" and "biogeocenosis" (rearranging the latter as "geobiocenosis"), he felt that an entirely new concept was necessary in order to capture the full sense of the ecological "totality" of ethnos and geographical landscape that he had in mind.[74] Toward this end he coined the term *etnotsenos* or "ethnocenosis," which he defined as "a geobiocenosis, in which an ethnic system adapts in order to live, and by so doing becomes the highest, crowning (*zavershchaiushchii*) link."[75]

In regard to the nature of the ecological interactions between the ethnos and its respective landscape, Gumilev was clearly ambivalent. In principle, all the

71. Gumilev 1994c, 131, 258, 304.
72. Gumilev 2001, 182–83; Gumilev 1991e, 133.
73. Gumilev 1989c, 307 (quote); Gumilev 1968b, 595.
74. Gumilev 2004 [1967], 44, 52–53; Gumilev 1989c, 172.
75. Michurin 2004, 572 (quote); Gumilev 1989c, 289–91.

elements that made up the system were mutually interdependent and interacted on an equal basis, with the anthropological element both influencing and being influenced by its surrounding environment. At times, Gumilev stressed the former and described how an ethnos operates as a formative agent in affecting and shaping the geographical landscape. Elsewhere, however, he argued strongly for the existential dependency of the ethnos on the landscape and the role of the latter in shaping and determining ethnic life. "Any species of animal is modified under the influence of adaptation. The degree of modification is determined by the diversity of the geographical conditions of the region it occupies."[76] Ethnies, he judged, were particularly heavily influenced by the conditions and dynamics of their external geographical milieu.[77] Gumilev referred repeatedly to Berg's position, and he explicitly deferred to it.[78] He endorsed the latter's thesis regarding the dependency of organic life on its immediate geographical environment— "confirmed by all materials available to science"[79]—and then adopted it for his own purposes with the argument that those "individuals" Berg spoke about as subject to environmental determination included ethno-organisms as well. "The geographical landscape influences ethnic processes in a compulsory manner."[80] He referred repeatedly to the interactive process between an ethnos and its native region as a process of "adaptation" (*adaptatsiia* or *prisposoblenie*) on the part of the former to the material conditions of the latter: a fundamental conditioning by a "nourishing landscape" that created an existential dependency.[81] For Gumilev, this dependency provided further "scientific" evidence of the differences that set an ethnos apart from a *sotsiuum*. In the case of the latter, developing as it does spontaneously and in a progressive fashion, "neither geographical nor biological factors have any influence." It is, however, "entirely obvious" that geographical factors do indeed "influence the development of that special phenomenon that we call ethnos."[82]

Over much of their life histories, Gumilev maintained, ethno-organisms remained dependent on their respective geographical environments. Landscape acted to condition the ethnos in its earliest stage, in the sense that the process of ethnogenesis itself could only be initiated in regions that possessed significant

76. Gumilev 2004 [1967], 53.
77. Gumilev 1976, 120.
78. In his fullest formulation of his ethnos theory, *Ethnogenesis and the Earth's Biosphere*, Gumilev cites the passage quoted above from Berg's *Nomogenesis* at least two times (37, 180) and uses the same language throughout. He also used the passage in an earlier work, although without attribution. Gumilev 1970a, 51.
79. Gumilev 1993a, 207.
80. Gumilev 1989c, 173; Gumilev 1993a, 270.
81. Gumilev 1989c, 167; Gumilev 1987a.
82. Gumilev 1989c, 37; Gumilev 1976, 120.

landscape variability.[83] Certain geographical regions offered more favorable conditions for ethnogenesis, a point Gumilev illustrated through complex maps and tables correlating landscape zones to specific incidences of ethnogenesis in history.[84] Ethnogenesis had occurred at a rapid rate in Europe—where there was a great variety of contrasting landscape types—and much more slowly in Central Asia.[85] And from the moment of their emergence as discrete entities, ethnies were compelled to adapt to the geographical conditions they encountered. This was "above all a process of active adaptation (*adaptatsiia*) of human collectives in a milieu—ethnic and natural—in the course of which the landscape compels people to develop complex adaptive skills, that is, ethnic behavioral stereotypes. Consequently, the unique combination of landscapes in which a given ethnos originated determines (*opredeliaet*) its distinctive character—behavioral and even in many respects cultural."[86] The most important evidence for this was the behavioral stereotype itself, a bundle of reflexes shaped by external environmental influences and passed down through the generations, which enabled the ethnos to sustain itself in a similar environment over its entire life history.[87]

Ultimately, ethnic diversity itself was a product of the ecological dependency of ethnies on the landscape. The differences that set ethnies apart "reflect the deep ties between a human population and the surrounding landscape, which comprises an area for habitation, provides food, and even shapes aesthetic and moral values."[88] Precisely because geographical landscapes themselves are so different across the globe, "the biocenoses they support are unique, and thus the respective forms of adaptation in each one must be different."[89] In all of this, Gumilev saw a basic biological principle at work. Adaptation to external geographical conditions was a method deployed by all organisms in order better to meet their evolutionary tasks of survival and reproduction. Because humankind is in principle able to live in such a wide variety of environments, the adaptive challenges it faces are uniquely complex and diversified. The division of homo sapiens into ethnic groups, Gumilev suggested, was essentially a response to this challenge, that is to say, a natural species strategy for survival. As discrete ethnies, each with its own adaptive response to the unique conditions of the particular geographical landscape it occupies, the chances for sustaining its existence and enhancing its welfare are maximized, for each individual group and for the

---

83. Gumilev 1968c, 42–43, 45.
84. For example, Gumilev 1993a, 257–59; Gumilev 1970b, 1: 52–54; Gumilev 2001, 122–24.
85. Gumilev 1956.
86. Gumilev 1992b, 3.
87. Gumilev 1977.
88. Gumilev 1994c, 254.
89. Gumilev 1971a, 82.

species as a whole. The fact that this adaptation was "in the behavior and not the [genetic] structure" of the ethnic groupings in no way altered its character as a biological mechanism as far as Gumilev was concerned.[90]

Building on all of these points, Gumilev developed the notion of an "ecological niche," another concept borrowed from ecological science.[91] In scientific use, it refers to the set of environmental and ecological conditions that determine and delimit where a species is able to maintain populations.[92] Gumilev deployed it rather more loosely to refer to the geographical region of origin for a given ethnic group. His point in using the concept, once again, was to stress the natural embeddedness of an ethnic group in a particular area, which represented the most fundamental condition of its existence. It was only here in its natural home, fully integrated into the local ecological network, that an ethnos could secure its survival in a normal and healthy manner. Its behavioral stereotype, its material culture, economy, *genre de vie*, and even spiritual life were all inextricably tied to the specific natural-environmental conditions of its respective ecological niche. This natural-ecological emplacement was then psychologically and emotionally reified across the group as a whole, which recognized its respective ecological niche as its native *rodina* or homeland and displayed the corresponding affective attachments to it.[93] "All ethnies have their own regions of origin, each defined by a unique combination of landscape elements. As such, this 'homeland' represents one of the component parts of that system we call ethnos."[94] The survival of the ethnos outside of this region for any protracted period of time was unthinkable.[95] "Whoever is used to living in the mountains will not [be able to] live on the plains, and whoever is used to living on islands will be bored by the steppes of Mongolia."[96] Significantly, Gumilev argued further that under normal conditions any given landscape zone could provide a niche for only a single ethnos. Every ethnos is thus attached to a "different environing landscape" and has undergone "a different historical experience."[97]

The full power of geographical conditions over the life of the ethnos became apparent at those moments when these conditions underwent some sort of alteration. Gumilev had a special expertise on these questions, as some of his

90. Gumilev 2004 [1967], 53.

91. Chase and Leibold 2003; Schoener 1989. The term was first used by the California biologist Joseph Grinnell (1877–1939). Grinnell 1917.

92. Stigall 2012, 773.

93. Bassin 2009c.

94. Gumilev 1989c, 180.

95. Gumilev and Ivanov 1992, 54–55.

96. Gumilev 2003f, 66.

97. Gumilev 1995, 36.

early research was concerned with processes of environmental change across major historical periods. Specifically, he had examined long-cycle fluctuations of climate and sea level in the Caspian basin, and he generalized his conclusions into universal principles. When confronted with the alteration of environmental conditions in its native landscape zone, an ethnos has three alternatives. It can readapt to the new conditions, which would involve developing a new set of adaptive reflexes and thus a new ethnic character.[98] Alternatively, it can remain in the region without new adaptation, which would lead eventually to its demise. Finally, the ethnos can emigrate to a new region. In the latter option, emigrant ethnies tend naturally to seek out landscapes resembling those they have left behind, but are almost always unsuccessful.[99]

In the case of migration, three alternatives are once again possible. Commonly, the ethnos simply perishes. It is possible, however, that under the formative influence of the natural conditions of a new landscape, a process may take place that Gumilev—again adopting a natural-scientific term—called "ethnic divergence" (*divergentsiia*). The original group was transformed into an entirely new ethnos, often by means of amalgamation with other immigrant groups.[100] "Settling a new region, human beings do not alter their anatomy or the physiology of their organism, but rather change their behavioral stereotype. This means that a new ethnos is created."[101] Gumilev offered numerous examples of how, in the process of divergence, novel geographical conditions acted to reshape and transform the ethnic character of the groups who migrated into them. Medieval Norse fishermen settling in Normandy became French peasants, he asserted, whereas the same fishermen in the Tweed Valley became shepherds in the Scottish lowlands.[102] In the case of Italy, an entirely new ethnos developed out of the amalgamation of numerous newcomer groups. "All of the peoples who settled in Italy—Eutruscans, Latins, Gauls, Greeks, Syrians, Arabs, Normans, and French—lost their former character (*oblik*) gradually, over two or three generations, and combined to form an Italian mass, a distinctive and mosaic ethnos with specific character traits, behavior, and structure."[103] The process of divergence was also apparent over the centuries of Russian migration into Siberia, where it produced two different sets of results. In those cases where the pioneers managed to settle in landscapes resembling those in European Russia, they formed new "subethnies" but remained a part of

98. Gumilev 2001, 291–92.
99. Gumilev 1972a; Gumilev 1968c, 42.
100. Gumilev and Ivanov 1992, 54; Gumilev 1989c, 132, 167.
101. Gumilev 1989c, 172.
102. Gumilev 1968c, 41.
103. Gumilev 1989c, 173.

the Great Russian ethnos. Where the new landscapes were substantially different, however, the settlers eventually developed entirely new ethnic traits.[104]

Finally, a third possibility remained, namely, that the original ethnos would survive its displacement from its original ecological niche and successfully establish itself in a new landscape without divergence taking place. This could only come, however, at the cost of the fundamental deformation of its ethnic character, leading to the emergence of what Gumilev famously called an ethnic chimera. Invariably, this process had fatal consequences for the indigenous ethnic populations of the regions in question. As we will see, the operation and effects of the deformation process form a vital element in Gumilev's interpretation of world history, and more specifically Russia's historical experience.

---

104. Gumilev and Ivanov 1992, 54.

ETHNOGENESIS, *PASSIONARNOST'*, AND THE BIOSPHERE

The Circulation of Energy

In an interview given shortly before his death, Gumilev provided a dramatic account of how his theory of ethnogenesis first began to take shape. The year was 1939, the scene was a cell in the transfer prison Kresty in Leningrad, to which he had been recalled from a labor camp on the Belomor Canal for a review of his sentence. Like all the cells in the prison, this one was severely overcrowded, and those inmates who could not find space for themselves on the planks that served as bunks had to make do with the bare asphalt floor underneath them. "*Usloviia daleko ne kurortnye*," Gumilev recollected sardonically: it wasn't exactly a spa, but at least it was possible to sit peacefully and ruminate about whatever interested you. And ruminate Gumilev did, for many weeks on end. "At one point, a young man with disheveled hair crawled on all fours out from under the bunk. In some sort of joyful and ridiculous confusion, he screamed, 'Eureka!' It was none other than me. My cellmates, sitting higher above me—there were eight of them— looked at me grimly and decided that I had lost my mind. 'There goes another one! He's flipped.' This sort of thing happened frequently. But this time, they were wrong." For a long time, he explained, he had been tormented by the question about the rise and fall of ethnic groups. From ancient times down to the present day, history recorded a seemingly endless succession of different peoples who flourished and then always declined. What forces underlay this ceaseless cycle? On that day, languishing on the floor of his cell, Gumilev believed he had begun to find the answer. "I think I found the solution, having finally guessed what lies at the heart of this powerful natural process. I identified the mechanism that triggers it and gave it an excellent name: '*passionarnost'*,' from the Latin word *passio* or passion (*strast'*). I realized that the birth of each new ethnic group was preceded by the appearance of a certain number of individuals with a new passionary character."[1]

When Gumilev finally presented a full elaboration of his theory of ethnogenesis in the 1960s, *passionarnost'* emerged as the key element of the entire process, and he would come to regard it as his most important theoretical discovery. At this early point, however, he had no clear conception of it, beyond the fact that it represented some sort of force or energy driving certain people to initiate activities that led to the formation of ethnies. As we will see, his intuitions in the 1930s were influenced by elements of Stalinist culture and ideology, in particular the notion of a "new Soviet person" characterized by boundless energy and creative determination. But Gumilev, who from the outset did not doubt that his new discovery would match Marxist theory in importance, wanted to provide a genuinely natural-scientific account of this phenomenon that explained exactly what sort of energy it represented and where it came from.[2] The latter quest was to take him several decades. The first step came during his incarceration in Noril'sk, where he arrived shortly after his eureka moment in 1939. In 1942, he was joined there by Nikolai Aleksandrovich Kozyrev (1908–1983), an astronomer and astrophysicist, originally arrested as part of the so-called Pulkovo affair of 1936. Gumilev warmly described how Kozyrev's colorful bunk-bed accounts of the physics of the universe—its constant expansion and the exchange of energy among cosmic bodies—had been a sort of "intellectual bacchanalia" that mesmerized all of his fellow inmates. "It was precisely N. A. Kozyrev's account of the birth of a star out of collapse, its expansion, [and] its transformation into a luminous new entity . . ., that brought to my mind an association with the eruption of ethnogenesis"—the origins of ethnies as a burst of passionary energy.[3] Fascinated by the processes that Kozyrev described, Gumilev decided that the energy that powered *passionarnost'* was also somehow cosmic in origin.[4] After his third arrest in 1948, Gumilev found himself once again sitting in a cell—this time in Lefortovo prison in Moscow. Observing the play of the sun's rays on the floor of the cell, he recounted, "I now understood that *passionarnost'* was that surplus

---

1. Cited in Varustin 1990, 20; also see Gumilev 2003f, 62–63; Gumilev 2003c, 14.
2. Gerstein 2004, 163.
3. Gumilev 2003d, 227–28. Kozyrev's accounts were equally inspiring for Gumilev's fellow inmate in Noril'sk Sergei Aleksandrovich Snegov (1910–1994), who went on to a successful career as a science-fiction fantasist.
4. Ignatova 2008, 778.

energy that is absorbed by humans and then is impossible [for them] not to give off in the form of labor. It is not solar energy, but some other kind."[5]

Exactly what sort of energy this was Gumilev would only discover in the 1960s. And it was not astronomy, but rather the principles of energetics or energeticism (*energetika, energetizm*)—the science of the movement, transformation, and storage of energy throughout the universe—that provided the explanatory models that Gumilev eventually adopted for his own theories. Energetics grew out of the work of the chemist Wilhelm Ostwald (1853–1932), who maintained that all phenomena of nature are essentially representations of energy in its manifold transmutations and forms.[6] A Baltic German from Riga, Ostwald had numerous contacts in Russia and his ideas were highly popular there, influencing leading scientists such as the chemist and Nobel Laureate Dmitrii Ivanovich Mendeleev (1834–1907) as well as radical intellectuals.[7] Among the latter was the Ukrainian physician Sergei Andreevich Podolinskii (1850–1891), a socialist and one of Karl Marx's correspondents in the Russian empire. Podolinskii emphasized the function of human society in converting solar energy into labor. A specific link between energy cycling and social processes was similarly emphasized by Marxist "God-builders" such as the Bolshevik Anatolii Vasil'evich Lunacharskii (1875–1933) and Maksim Gorkii (1868–1936).[8] After the revolution, the discourse of energetics became yet more widespread and influential. Prominent revolutionaries such as Aleksandr Bogdanov and Nikolai Ivanovich Bukharin (1888–1938) believed that the principles of "social energetics" provided key insights into the nature of productive forces and their correlation to the dynamics of social growth.[9] At the same time, the precepts of energetics powerfully influenced the Soviet cultural ethos, both the radical avant-garde of the 1920s as well as the doctrine of socialist realism that replaced it. One particular enthusiast for the aesthetics of *energetika* was Akhmatova's partner Nikolai Punin, who might have discussed it with the young Gumilev at some point in the early 1930s.[10]

Energetics and energy circulation also figured centrally in the natural-scientific thinking of the postrevolutionary period, not least in the landscape science research noted in the last chapter. Lev Berg emphasized the role of the sun in shaping geographical landscapes, and Sukhachev treated the biogeocenosis as "a uniform system for the reception and conversion of matter and energy, and

5. Bondarenko, Ermolaev, and Ivanov 1992.

6. Ostwald 1912; Jammer 1967, 517.

7. Vucinich 1988, 254, 268, 367; Geller 2009.

8. Podolinskii 1880; Chesnokov 2010.

9. Gare 2000, 239; Martinez-Alier 1987, 125, 226; Rosenthal 2002, 72, 80; Susiluoto 1982; Stokes 1995.

10. Geller 2009.

its circulation with neighboring biogeocenoses and other natural phenomena."[11] His perspective was influenced by the ideas of Vladimir Ivanovich Vernadskii (1863–1945), a towering figure in the early decades of Soviet science and one of great thinkers of the twentieth century.[12] Vernadskii is perhaps best known for the concept of the "biosphere," a term originally coined in the 1870s by the Viennese geologist Eduard Suess but reformulated and made famous by Vernadskii himself in the 1920s. In the latter's conception, the biosphere represented the totality of worldly matter, in which inert mineral and geological material combined together with the organic life of the earth to form what he called the *zhivoe veshchestvo* or "living matter" of the universe.[13] This living matter was organized as a single organic system, into which humankind was integrated as a vital natural component.[14] Vernadskii had studied under Dokuchaev and was a colleague of Berg, and with his biosphere concept he expanded the notion of "ecological interconnections" that the latter two had identified in localized geographical landscapes into a single integrated network of global or indeed cosmic dimensions.[15]

Vernadskii stressed the principles of energy circulation in his conceptualization of the biosphere and he acknowledged the importance of Podolinskii's pioneering work. This meant, among other things, that the physical extent of the biosphere was not—as the name could be understood to suggest—limited to the earthly space of the *zhivoe veshchestvo*, but rather extended dramatically outward to include cosmic bodies as well.[16] It was from the latter, above all the sun, that the earth received its input of raw primal energy in the form of a constant influx of *izlucheniia* or cosmic radiation.[17] Although extraterrestrial in origin, Vernadskii argued that this radiation was nonetheless an integral part of the biospheric system. Indeed it was its most vital component. The transfer and conversion of this energy represented the most fundamental biospheric processes, with the effect that the biosphere "is at least as much a *creation of the sun* as it is a result of terrestrial processes." Indeed, he defined the biosphere basically in terms of energy conversion, describing it as that part of the earth's crust containing

---

11. Sukachev 1961, cited in "Sukachev Vladimir Nikolaevich (1880–1967)" 2007; Berg 2003, 432, 436; Weiner 1984, 687, 695; Weiner 1982, 49.
12. On Vernadskii see Levit 2001; Bailes 1990; Ianshina 1996; Aksenov 1994; Polienovich 2005.
13. Vernadskii 1926; Vernadsky 1998.
14. Vernadskii 1994; Aksenov 1988.
15. Berg 2003, 96; Shaw and Oldfield 2006, 147.
16. Vernadskii's inclusion of a cosmic dimension as an integral part of the biosphere contrasts with other conceptualizations such as the "biogeocenotic covering" (Sukachev) or "biogeosphere," both of which refer more exclusively to the earth's biomass by itself. See Dylis 1969.
17. Vernadsky 1998, 55; Bratel′ 1993.

the "transformers that convert cosmic radiations into active energy in electrical, chemical, mechanical, thermal, and other forms."[18] Having been transformed by these biospheric agents into usable forms of "free terrestrial energy," this cosmic force then served to power all earthly processes, organic as well as inorganic. Vernadskii referred to the aggregate of all of these different forms of converted biospheric energy with the single term "biogeochemical" energy.[19] By virtue of all this, life itself was a "cosmic phenomenon."[20]

The notion that cosmic radiation powered the organic life of the earth logically suggested that the latter was influenced and even controlled by it. This influence was explored in the work of the biophysicist Aleksandr Leonidovich Chizhevskii (1897–1964), who founded the fields of helio- and cosmic biology to study of the effects of the sun's insolation on human organisms and the historical development of human civilization.[21] Chizhevskii believed that all terrestrial life—from the macrolevel of the biosphere as a whole down to the microlevel of the individual cell—reacted in a direct fashion to the "cosmic information" that streamed down to earth from outer space.[22] All life on earth, he suggested, comes into being "through the effect of the creative dynamics of the cosmos on the inert material of the earth. All life exists through the dynamics of these forces, and each beat of the organic [terrestrial] pulse resonates with the beating of the cosmic heart—the grand totality of stars, star clouds, the planets, and the sun."[23] Chizhevskii's most important work related to the question of cosmic influences on the *longue durée* of human history. He attempted to determine the functional interdependence between humanity's behavior and the fluctuations of the sun, arguing that the periodicity, intensity, and location of major social unrest such as wars, epidemics, and revolutions could be correlated directly to cycles of solar activity.[24] "We must assume that there exists a powerful factor *outside* our globe," he summarized, "that governs the development of events in human societies and synchronizes them with the sun's activity; and thus, we must also assume that the electrical energy of the sun is the superterrestrial factor that influences historical processes."[25]

---

18. Vernadsky 1998, 44, 47 (emphasis original), 50; Vernadskii 1994, 321–32.

19. Vernadskii 1978, 311; Vernadskii 1965, 196; Gorham 1991.

20. Aksenov 1988, 65.

21. Chizhevskii and Shishina 1969, 4, 105–7; Chizhevskii 1955; Chizhevskii 1963; Chizhevskii 1973; Iagodinskii 1987; Klenskaia 1985.

22. Kon'shina 1993, 34; Bochkarev 2008, 128–36.

23. Quoted in Kon'shina 1993, 34; also see Chizhevskii and Shishina 1969, 109–10; Golovanov 1995.

24. Djordjević 1999, 106–7.

25. Tchijevsky 1971, 20 (emphasis added).

The ideas of Vernadskii and Chizhevskii were rediscovered in the 1960s as part of the reengagement with intellectual and scientific legacies that had been marginalized or suppressed under Stalin.[26] For Gumilev, who at this time was busy assembling his own theories, these perspectives were inspirational, and he was among their most enthusiastic admirers.[27] Vernadskii's unfinished *Chemical Structure of the Earth's Atmosphere*, in which the scholar had sought to summarize his most important ideas, was published in 1965, and this work had a particularly strong influence.[28] On the basis of Vernadskii's teachings about the nature of the biosphere, Gumilev deduced three vital principles that provided the foundation for his conception of ethnicity as a natural phenomenon. To begin with, he could now answer his original question as to what sort of energy *passionarnost'* consisted of. In Vernadskii's "remarkable book," this very energy "was called the biogeochemical energy of the living matter of the biosphere. It is the same energy that plants receive in the form of photosynthesis and then pass on to animals in the form of food."[29] This was the same energy, he explained elsewhere, "that raises swarms of voracious locusts into the air, directs the assaults of tropical ant armies, and in general causes all those wondrous migrations in the animal realm that are so stunning in their massive dimensions. . . . This energy exists in each natural organism, in each ethnos, and in agglomerations of ethnies called superethnies."[30] In the ethnosphere, this cosmic energy was most dramatically manifested in the form of *passionarnost'*.

Second, he argued that the ethno-organism was an integral component or "substratum" of the earth's biosphere. It shared all the qualities of the living matter of the biosphere and was subject to all of the laws and processes that Vernadskii had identified.[31] In principle, these laws, and the ecological interlinkages across the biosphere as a whole, simply replicated those of local biocenoses on a grander scale. "The laws of nature are the same for its various levels, from the macroworld of the galaxy to the microworld of the atom."[32] In practice, however, the juxtaposition between the emplacement of an ethnos in a geographically delimited

---

26. Vernadskii died in 1945, but Chizhevskii made a triumphal return after many years in the Gulag and in the early 1960s was given his own laboratory. His book *The Rhythms of the Sun*, published in 1969, had an initial print run of sixty thousand copies. Engel'gart 2000, 7, 15; Hagemeister 1997, 186, 196.

27. Hagemeister 1989, 420–21. For Gumilev's discussion of Vernadskii see, for example, Gumilev 1989c, 305–16; Gumilev 1988b, 48; Gumilev 1994c, 227. On Gumilev and Vernadskii, see Medved' 1994; Karpenko 2011.

28. Vernadskii 1965; Gumilev 2003f.

29. Gumilev 2001, 46–47 (quote); Gumilev 2003c, 14; Beliakov 2012a, 447.

30. Gumilev 1994c, 258 (quote); Gumilev 1990c, 4.

31. Varustin 1990, 21.

32. Gumilev 2003d, 227–28.

terrestrial "ecological niche" and its inclusion as a part of a biosphere of cosmic dimensions created a tension that, as we will see at various points in this study, took on a subtle but quite important significance. Finally, the most important of the biospheric processes just referred to was the circulation of energy. Indeed, Gumilev described an ethnos—in good Ostwaldian fashion—quite simply as a "manifestation of energy (*iavlenie energicheskoe*)" that was directly involved, like all other organisms, in energy circulation and transfer.[33] Ethnies were constantly exposed to irradiation from cosmic sources, and this irradiation played a key role in their constitution and development. We "live in a great galaxy, which has an effect on us, as do all the other factors determining the development of the biosphere."[34]

The Mechanics of Ethnogenesis

The identification of the energetic nature of ethnies and of biogeochemical energy as their driving force did not, however, explain the phenomenon of ethnogenesis itself. How did ethnies come into being in the first place, and what sort of developmental trajectory did they follow? In searching for answers, Gumilev continued to draw on theories and models from the natural sciences, now turning to research in radiobiology and genetics. In the 1920s, the American Herman J. Muller had demonstrated the phenomenon of radiation mutagenesis, whereby organisms exposed to X-rays developed alterations in their genetic structure that were then passed on to successive "mutant" generations. This subject attracted considerable interest in the USSR, where Muller had worked for several years.[35] The Soviets made highly significant contributions in the new field of radiation genetics before the entire discipline of genetics fell victim to Stalinist repression in the late 1930s.[36] It would fully reemerge only decades later in the 1960s.

Gumilev had heard about mutagenesis in the 1930s from his friend Nikolai Davidenkov, a biology student arrested along with him in 1938.[37] The idea fascinated him, and he became increasingly convinced that this process played a central role in the dynamics of ethnic life. As he developed these ideas in later decades, he sought the counsel of the leading geneticists noted in the preceding chapter. Gumilev's Leningrad colleague M. E. Lobashev had worked with Muller

---

33. Gumilev 1989c, 313.
34. Gumilev 2001, 38.
35. Carlson 1981. Muller won a Nobel Prize in 1946 for his work on X-ray mutation.
36. Adams 1990b, 179, 192–97.
37. Beliakov 2012a, 448.

in the 1920s and conducted research in mutagenesis in addition to behavioral genetics and ethology.[38] Gumilev's most important contact, however, was with Nikolai Vladimirovich Timofeev-Resovskii (1900–1981), a seminal figure in international genetics in the twentieth century.[39] Timofeev-Resovskii studied the mutagenetic effects of radioactive energy on individual organisms as well as the distribution and circulation of this energy throughout entire ecosystems. In his work, he drew heavily on the conceptual foundations of Vernadskii and also the ecological research of Sukachev. Timofeev-Resovskii developed his ideas within the new field of radioecology, or as he called it, radiation biogeocenology.

Timofeev-Resovskii had an extraordinary life, which is significant for our story in that it brought him into contact with Gumilev at the critical moment when the latter was working out his theory of ethnogenesis.[40] He had left the USSR as a young scholar in the mid-1920s to work at the Kaiser-Wilhelm Institute for Brain Research then being established in the Berlin suburb of Buch, eventually taking over as director of the Institute's Department of Genetics. In 1945, he was arrested in Berlin by occupying Soviet troops and repatriated back to the USSR. He was sent to a labor camp in Karaganda and later transferred to work in a *sharashka*, or secret institute for imprisoned scientists, in the Urals near present-day Ekaterinburg.[41] Released after Stalin's death but not rehabilitated, Timofeev-Resovskii was not permitted to settle in Moscow, and finally in 1965 took up a position at the Institute of Medical Radiology at Obninsk, some 100 kilometers southwest of the capital. The timing was fateful, for Gumilev, who lived in Leningrad, spent his summers in Moscow. In the summer months of 1967 and 1968 he made regular weekend trips to Obninsk to visit Timofeev-Resovskii's laboratory and discuss his ideas with him. The two developed a friendship and also something of a working relationship.[42]

---

38. Lobashev 1947.

39. Timofeev-Resovskii 1962; Weiner 1999b, 67, 285, 384, 387–88; Adams 1979; Reif, Junker, and Hossfeld 2000, 64–65; Graham 1993, 242.

40. On Timofeev-Resovskii, see Granin 1987 (English translation, Granin 1989); Berg 1990; Korogodin, Polikarpov, and Velkov 2000; Ratner 2001; Birstein 2001, 242, 247.

41. Timofeev-Resovskii's prison-camp experiences are discussed in Aleksandr Solzhenitsyn's *Arkhipelag Gulag*. Solzhenitsyn 1973, 149n, 207n, 493, 597–600.

42. For accounts of these meetings see Iarilin n.d.; Zelinskii 2012, 102–3. Timofeev-Resovskii's failure to be rehabilitated was explained in part by doubts about his scientific activities in Nazi Germany. In the late 1980s, he was posthumously accused of participating in genetic experiments on human subjects. Kuz'min 1988. In a vigorous rebuttal, Raisa Berg argued that these attacks were motivated by resistance on the part of extreme Russian nationalists to the pro-Western and liberalizing dynamics of Gorbachev's perestroika. Berg 1990. It might be noted that Timofeev-Resovskii's detractor in this particular case was the historian Apollon Grigor'evich Kuz'min, who was at that time one of Gumilev's most trenchant opponents as well, as we will see. Timofeev-Resovskii was officially rehabilitated only after the collapse of the Soviet Union, in 1992.

There were a number of reasons why these two individuals should have felt a sense of personal solidarity. They both came from the prerevolutionary aristocracy, and they of course had the common experience of the Gulag. Ideologically, they both happened to be attracted to the doctrines of Eurasianism, which for Gumilev at least were at the very center of his historical and political perspective.[43] Moreover, both were positioned on the fringes of the Soviet scientific establishment, albeit in very different ways. But there was a specifically scientific dimension to their exchanges that, for Gumilev at least, was crucial. He was convinced that the dynamics of ethnogenesis could be explained in terms of the biological processes of mutagenesis that were the subject of Timofeev-Resovskii's own research. Indeed, not only did Gumilev want to use Timofeev-Resovskii's theories for his own explanation of ethnogenesis, but he actually sought to enlist the eminent geneticist as a formal collaborator and coauthor for the first major exposition of his theory—an endorsement that he hoped would establish the natural-scientific credentials of his own work beyond question. Timofeev-Resovskii was clearly beguiled by Gumilev's ideas, and initially agreed to participate in their joint venture. He even drew another eminent geneticist, Boris L'vovich Astaurov (1904–1974), into the project as an additional coauthor.[44] When Timofeev-Resovskii finally saw Gumilev's theory in manuscript form, however, these plans quickly unraveled. He refused to accept the description of the ethnos as a biological organism and was skeptical about whether such a thing as *passionarnost'* really existed outside of Gumilev's fertile imagination. To Gumilev's ill-concealed chagrin, Timofeev-Resovskii withdrew his support, and the first presentation of his theory of ethnogenesis was published under the former's sole authorship.[45]

---

43. Beliakov 2012a, 452–56. In the 1930s, Timofeev-Resovskii met frequently in Berlin with leading figures of the Eurasianist movement, including Petr Nikolaevich Savitskii (1895–1968) and Nikolai Nikolaevich Alekseev (1879–1964). During a trip to the United States in 1932 he met with Georgii Vladimirovich Vernadskii (1887–1973), the son of Vladimir Vernadskii and an important historian in the Eurasianist movement, who at that time was teaching at Yale University. Gumilev himself would eventually establish personal contacts with Savitskii and Vernadskii. (I am grateful to Dr. Martin Beisswenger for sharing this information from the Savitskii archive in GARF.) On Timofeev-Resovskii's meetings with other Russian émigrés in Berlin, see Birstein 2001, 243–44. Gumilev's own relationship to Eurasianism is discussed below, pp. 104–7.

44. On Astaurov, see Berg 1979.

45. Gumilev 1970a; Gumilev 1970b. For revealing fragments of the correspondence between Gumilev and Timofeev-Resovskii, see Gumileva 1994, 615; Gumileva 2003b; Gumilev 1990c, 7. An extremely defensive and thin-skinned individual in any event, Gumilev took enormous offense at Timofeev-Resovskii's skepticism. Although the latter subsequently apologized—and Gumilev continued to refer to the work of "my friend" Timofeev-Resovskii in his writings—the two never reestablished their relationship. Gumilev 1989c, 56, 219; Gumilev 2004c, 12; Gumilev 1994d, 214; Gumilev 2004c, 12.

Gumilev's hypothesis about the role of cosmic radiation in the ethnogenetic process thus took shape as a sort of hybrid mélange of energeticist notions crossed with aspects of mutagenesis gleaned from the work of Timofeev-Resovskii and others. On the origins of the radiation in question, he displayed a certain ambivalence, occasionally describing it as the same energy that causes photosynthesis (i.e., solar radiation), while maintaining elsewhere that it came primarily not from the sun but rather from "scattered galaxies." He suggested that it was precisely during phases of decreased solar activity—for example, low points in the solar cycle, or at night when the sun did not shine—that optimal conditions existed for the penetration of the energy in question. At these times, the "defensive qualities of the ionosphere are reduced, allowing individual quants or bundles of energy to approach near to the earth's surface."[46] So positioned, this cosmic irradiation had the power to "cause mutations" (*vyzyvat′ mutatsii*) across the entire *zhivoe veshchestvo* of the biosphere.[47] "At night, cosmic radiation (visible or ultraviolet) penetrates through the ionosphere and continues right down to the earth's surface, where it affects minor organisms. Viruses [for example] are very sensitive to them, and they mutate under their influence."[48] This same mutagenetic process, Gumilev maintained, represented the vital source of ethnic formation. "Ethnies emerge as a result of a particular mutation, which is connected to cosmic energy."[49]

Cosmic influxes were distributed unevenly across space and time, and occasionally occurred in particularly concentrated bursts—what Gumilev called "excesses" of "intense (*zhestkii*) radiation."[50] Like all of the organic matter of the earth's biosphere, human beings were able to absorb a portion of this energy and convert it metabolically into different forms of terrestrial energy.[51] In principle, this process was constant, taking place universally and at all times. At certain places and at certain times, however, it happened that a burst of "hard radiation" produced very special results. The intense influx of energy exposed the *genafond* or genetic pool of the inhabitants of the affected area to a significant "mutagenetic influence," which could lead to a mutation—or what Gumilev, in a bid to appear more scientifically precise, usually called a "micromutation"—in the genetic makeup of a portion of the affected population.[52] "The point of departure

46. Gumilev 1990a, 30; Gumilev and Panchenko 1990, 114; Gumilev 2001, 46–47; Lavrov 2000, 342.
47. Gumilev and Balashov 1993, 144; Gumilev 1994c, 269.
48. Gumilev 2003f, 62.
49. Gumilev 2003f, 61 (quote); Gumilev 1994c, 259.
50. Gumilev 2001, 48; Gumilev 1989c, 308; Gumilev 2003f, 61.
51. Gumilev and Panchenko 1990, 95.
52. Gumilev and Panchenko 1990, 6; Gumilev and Ermolaev 1997, 241.

for all ethnogenesis is a specific *mutation* in a small number of individuals in a particular geographical region. Although this mutation does not affect (or affects insignificantly) the phenotype of the person, it does alter fundamentally their behavioral stereotype. This latter transformation occurs indirectly, of course, insofar as it is not the behavioral pattern itself that is subjected to influence but the genotype of the individuals concerned."[53] Through the mutagenetic effect of cosmic irridation, the stage was set for the emergence of a new ethnos.

The creation of a new genotype, however, did not by itself represent the creation of a new ethnos. Rather, the mutation provided those affected with an entirely new physiological feature, one that enabled their bodies to absorb and convert relatively larger quantities of irradiated energy than their nonaffected counterparts. "It is this surplus of absorbed energy that forms a new behavioral stereotype and consolidates a new systemic [ethnic] entity."[54] This surplus of absorbed energy was precisely that passionary energy or *passionarnost'* discussed earlier in the chapter—what Gumilev sometimes called the "passionary charge" (*zariad*) of a given individual or ethnic group.[55] Because all human beings were natural organisms, they were capable of absorbing energy to some degree. Gumilev's passionary individuals, however, were able to absorb and convert much greater amounts, which meant that their capacity for sustained labor output was entirely exceptional. *Passionarnost'* was thus always characterized by hyperexertion (*sverkhnapriazhenie*), accompanied by the psychological element of an "insuperable inner striving" for some sort of "purposeful activity" and an all-consuming determination to accomplish some predetermined goal.[56] As passionary actors Gumilev named the most adventurous and charismatic of history's heroes: Alexander the Great, Genghis Khan, Julius Caesar, the Prophet Muhammad, Joan of Arc, Jan Hus, Alexander Nevskii, Avvakum, Isaac Newton, Captain Cook, Napoleon Bonaparte, and many others.[57]

The "discovery" of *passionarnost'* was Gumilev's proudest achievement, and he always saw it as his most original and important scientific contribution.[58] He believed that it represented the key element of all ethnic life, which conditioned the formation of ethnic groups and then continued to influence them throughout their entire subsequent course of development. *Passionarnost'* was a physiological quality, a biological feature of the human organism that exerted a

---

53. Gumilev 2001, 75.
54. Gumilev 2001, 75 (quote); Gumilev 1978a, 99.
55. Gumilev 1970b, 50.
56. Gumilev 1970b, 46; Gumilev 1978a, 98n; Gumilev 1989c, 308; Gumilev and Ermolaev 1993, 179.
57. Gumilev 2004 [1970], 123–28.
58. Lavrov 2000, 333.

fundamental influence on its attitude and behavior. It was the product of external cosmic influences, but once created it was inscribed internally onto the genetic material of the affected organism—at one point Gumilev identified it specifically as a "recessive gene."[59] Like other genetic characteristics, *passionarnost'* was heritable, and the original passionary *mutanty* or "mutants" passed it on to successive generations.[60] It is important to note, however, that Gumilev's emphasis on the significance of this genetic and heritable element of ethnic being did not in any way indicate that he understood ethnicity itself as an inborn genetic and heritable quality. In fact, he was arguing precisely the opposite. By asserting that *passionarnost'* was a genetic feature, he was also indicating that it was a universal human feature, potentially shared by all people and all ethnic groups. The nature and effects of *passionarnost'* were identical for everyone and had always been so throughout history. *Passionarnost'* conditioned the emergence of all ethnic groups and regulated their passage through their life trajectories, but it had nothing whatsoever to do with the unique qualities that characterized them as individual entities and differentiated them from all others. The qualities representing the group's ethnic identity per se were controlled rather through the behavioral stereotype, which was conditioned through adaptation to the external environment and not subject to genetic determination.[61]

Ethnogenesis as a Life Cycle

Gumilev used the term "ethnogenesis" in two closely related but slightly different meanings. On the one hand, the term referred to the moment of ethnic formation when an assemblage of individuals first took shape as a distinct ethnic entity. Ethnogenesis also referred more generally to the entire life cycle of the newly formed ethnos. Gumilev viewed the ethnos as a biological organism, and like all organisms it developed through a fixed process of growth, maturation, and

---

59. Gumileva 1994, 624–25.

60. Gumilev 2003f, 62, 64; Gumilev and Panchenko 1990, 12; Gumilev 2001, 144; Gumilev 1978a, 99.

61. Raisa Berg inadvertently confirmed this important point. She recounted how she and Aleksandr Malinovskii had initially been intrigued by Gumilev's ideas and tried to discuss with him how his "eruptions of *passionarnost'*" might correlate to the "eruptions of genetic mutability" that they studied in their own laboratory research. She was, however, quite surprised when Gumilev showed no interest in this possibility and dismissed it out of hand, and she quickly concluded that he in fact "rejected (*otvergal*) . . . all of genetics in general." Rather than genetics, Berg noted quite presciently that Gumilev's theories were formed under the influence of "foggy Lamarckian ideas," which emphasized adaption to external environmental conditions. This was also true of her father Lev Berg, who was a Lamarckian and one of Gumilev's most important inspirers. Berg 2003, 377, 263.

decline. All aspects of ethnogenesis were ultimately controlled by natural law—indeed Gumilevian ethnogenesis was itself for all practical purposes supposed to be a natural law—and so in principle it operated in the same way at all times and for all ethnies. Thus throughout his work Gumilev discussed ethnogenetic processes in ancient China alongside those in medieval Islam, the Roman Empire, and the pre-Colombian New World as if they were generically the same thing. Deviations from the normal course of the ethnogenetic process did occasionally occur, which Gumilev called "zigzags." These were of great significance, and as we will see he devoted considerable attention to examining their origins and consequences.

Generally speaking, ethnogenesis proceeded in the following manner. At certain historical moments, certain regions of the earth's surface were exposed to heightened levels of insolation of cosmic energy. Gumilev maintained that if two natural conditions were present in these irradiated regions—a mix of different physical-geographical features or a "combination of landscapes" on the one hand and the presence of protoethnic "substrata" or groupings of individuals on the other—then the scene was set for the onset of ethnogenesis.[62] Among a small number of the region's inhabitants, the radiation would have a mutagenetic effect, as a result of which they were capable of absorbing higher amounts of energy. These "mutants" (*mutanty*) became *passionarii* or passionary individuals. The fact of their shared mutagenetic experience, together with the new qualities that it created, combined to produce a subconscious but powerful attractive draw between them. Random passionary individuals quickly came together to form small clusters, which coalesced into ever-larger agglomerations, into which the *passionarii* brought their protoethnic cohorts.

Invariably, this process involved movement and geographical dislocation for the groups involved. The demands of the new forms of communal existence with foreign peoples, together with the challenges of adapting to unfamiliar environmental conditions, led to the development of novel patterns of social and environmental interactions and laid the basis for a new behavioral stereotype. As the latter took shape, the subgroupings merged seamlessly into a single new ethnic unit. A new ethnos could only form out of the fusion (*sliianie*) of existing groups: it is "like a child with a father and a mother, which itself is an extension of both of them but also different from both. . . . For this fusion to take place, a high charge of biogeochemical energy of living matter is necessary, [which brings about] a micromutation."[63] A new ethnos was thus born, culminating the first stage of Gumilev's ethnogenesis. Gumilev characterized this as an eruption or explosion

---

62. Gumilev 1989c, 132; Gumilev 1994c, 267.
63. Gumilev (quote); Gumilev 1990a, 35; Gumilev 1991e, 139.

(*vzryv*) of *passionarnost'*, which provided a "passionary impetus" (*passionarnyi tolchek*) that set the entire ethnogenetic process in train. "Every ethnos comes into being as a result of a particular eruption of *passionarnost'*."[64]

Thus the process of ethnic formation began when the population of a given region was exposed to heightened insolation of cosmic energy. The resulting passionary charge stimulated activities that brought about the creation of a new ethnos, but it did much more. Effectively, Gumilev explained, this initial energetic surge loaded the incipient ethnos with the energy that would drive it across its entire life history, from its formation to eventual decline and collapse. An ethnos operated as a closed system, which meant that in principle there would be no opportunity for supplemental energy infusions at any later point. The fact that Gumilev himself frequently disregarded this principle should not diminish its logical importance for his ethnogenetic model. Over the life of the ethnos, the unreplenished charge of initial passionary energy behaved like all biogeochemical energy everywhere in the biosphere, that is to say, it dispersed and dissipated. Invoking the second law of thermodynamics as a fundamental ethnogenetic principle, Gumilev argued that every ethnic "system" was constantly losing its energy because of entropy.[65] "Ethnogenesis is an inertial process, in the course of which an initial charge of biochemical energy . . . dissipates as a result of resistance from its surroundings."[66] This entropic process did not lead to an eventual sustainable "steady state," however, for the energy balance was never stabilized at any level of intensity. The initial passionary impetus "imparts a limited inertia to the object it touches [i.e., a new ethnos], which is then set in motion for some time before being brought to rest by external resistance."[67] Ethnic energy thus continued always to decline until it fell below the point necessary for survival. When this happened, the ethnogenetic cycle came to an end and the respective ethnos perished.[68] At the most fundamental level, therefore, the life history of the ethnos was conditioned by the single dominating reality of constant energy loss.

Gumilev discussed the ethnic life cycle itself in considerable detail and even prepared a graphic illustration correlating the surge and dissipation of passionary

---

64. Gumilev 1991e, 132.

65. Gumilev 2004c, 425.

66. Gumilev 1989c, 324. Gumilev was by no means alone in his conviction that the physical process of entropy was an active force in human development. Friedrich Engels developed this idea in his *Dialectics of Nature*, and it was popular among Soviet scientists and philosophers, including the ecologists we have been considering. Weiner 1984, 687. For the most part, however, Gumilev's contemporaries drew very different conclusions about its significance. Hagemeister 1989, 260n.

67. Gumilev 2003f, 62.

68. Gumilev 1991e, 132.

energy to the succession of ethnogenetic stages or phases.[69] He postulated that all ethnies moved through these stages—the exact number varied but in his most complete account he identified nine.[70] The characteristics of each phase were related to the intensity and dynamics of the passionary "tension" (*napriazhenie*) present at that particular moment in the ethnogenetic cycle.[71] The stages were divided into roughly two groups, the first of which represented the "active" or "dynamic" phases of the ethnogenetic cycle when the passionary charge was high and there was a relative energy surplus. Thus, ethnogenesis commences with a *passionary impetus* (approximately 180 years), during which time the mutations caused by the initial energy infusion begin to spread and affect group behavior. After this comes the *incubation period* (20 years), when the young ethnos consolidates and gathers its forces for the following passionary *pod"em* or "phase of ascendancy" (100 years). It is a period of high *passionarnost'* and intense activity, when the ethnos makes its first dramatic impact on the world-historical scene. This activity becomes yet more accelerated in the "acmatic phase of passionary *peregrev*" or "overdrive" (300 years), when the conversion of energy and its release in the form of human activity is at its frenzied height.

The second phase of ethnogenesis is "static," reflecting the increasingly reduced levels of passionary energy. *Peregrev* is followed by the turbulent catharsis of "breakdown" (*nadlom*) (200 years) when the passionary impulse loses about half of its charge and the first signs of lassitude and decline begin to become apparent. The cohesive unity of the "ethnic field" begins to fracture at this point. This is followed by phases of *inertia* (300 years)—a slowing down and softening of the loss of energy—*obscurity* (200 years), and a final "memorial phase" of *homeostasis* (200 years). The latter is the time of maximal energy exhaustion and is thus a period of near-total quietude and inaction. Like all the others, however, it is ultimately ephemeral, for ethnic energy continues to dissipate, leading to the inevitable "degeneration" (*vyrozhdenie*) of the ethnos altogether. Overall, Gumilev reckoned that a single ethnogenetic cycle lasted approximately 1,500 years. It is important to note that Gumilev did not directly correlate the entropic exhaustion of passionary energy to declining standards of ethnic well-being or cultural production. To the contrary, the periods of highest passionary energy were precisely the times of the greatest social turmoil and suffering: wars, revolutions,

---

69. Gumilev 2000, 288–89; Gumilev 1989c, 339–436; Gumilev 1990c, 4; Gumilev 2001, 74, 335; Gumilev 1990a, 239. The graph illustrating the ebb and flow of passionary energy across the ethnogenetic life cycle was reproduced in many of his works, and as we will see was to become famous in its own right as the "*krivaia Gumileva*," or "Gumilev's Graph."

70. Gumilev 1989c, 475. For a comparison of Gumilev's different versions, see Beliakov 2012a, 439.

71. See the chart in Gumilev 1989c, 328.

and bloodshed. By contrast, it was during the declining phases of *nadlom* and especially obscurity that the ethnos could enjoy the greatest peace, harmony, and cultural flowering, before passing on to its ultimate collapse. Gumilev often referred to this period of the ethnic life cycle as its "golden autumn."[72]

Gumilev's description of the function of *passionarnost'* in his scheme of ethnogenesis involved a subtle but significant nuance in the relationship of an ethnos to the geographical landscape that it occupied. In the last chapter we saw that Gumilev stressed the dependency of the ethnos on its ecological niche very heavily—indeed he adopted Lev Berg's geo-determinist position more or less wholesale. The introduction of a vital cosmic dimension into the process, however, shifted the terms of the argument. Charged with an uncontrollable dynamism by bolts of intergalactic energy, an ethnos acquired a certain freedom from the natural-geographical conditions of its terrestrial homeland and to some extent became a landscape-shaping force in its own right. Gumilev was aware of these contrasting characterizations of ethnos—as dependent subject or as activist perpetrator—but apparently did not recognize an inherent contradiction between them. He referred casually to the "mutual interaction" (*vzaimodeistvie*) or indeed the "mutual dependency" (*obratnaia zavisimost'*) between an ethnos and its "environing landscape," in which the former "adapts a certain landscape zone to its own needs while simultaneously adapting itself to [the conditions of] this zone."[73] Eventually, he concluded opaquely, in a symbiosis of ethnos and landscape, the two would "begin to complete each other" (*dopolniat' drug druga*).[74] As we will see, Gumilev's ambivalence about these ethno-landscape dynamics resonated with broader post-Stalinist debates about the nature of the relationship between society and the natural world.

Indeed, Gumilev located this variation within the process of the ethnogenetic cycle itself. A single ethnos "impacts the landscape in different ways during different phases of its ethnogenesis."[75] In its dynamic phase, the ethnos was restless and active, full of passionary energy. Its "adaptive capabilities" in regard to the external environment were at their height. The ethnic group often undertook major migrations to new regions at this time, and its high passionary charge put it in a position of dominance, with both the power and the inclination to shape the environment at will.[76] This was the Promethean phase of the ethnos, characterized by "its active influence on its ethnocenosis: the overhunting of various

72. Gumilev 2001, 268–95; Gumilev 2004c, 335–49.
73. Gumilev 1989c, 325 (quote), 312; Gumilev 1977.
74. Gumilev and Ivanov 1992, 54.
75. Gumilev 1989c, 345.
76. Gumilev 1970a, 55; Gumilev 1970b, 50.

animal species to extinction, the clearing of forests, domestication of plants and animals, and so on." Its power declined as the passionary energy dissipated, however, and by the time the static phase was reached the ethnos had lost its "role as a transformer" of the natural world.[77] After a transitory "optimal" interlude during the *nadlom*, when the mutual influences of ethnos and the natural world were matched and balanced, the ethnos slipped ever more fully under the control of external environmental forces. The nadir came in the phase of homeostasis, at which point the ethnos had entirely exhausted its passionary charge and became a "relict" or "historical vestige, devoid of any creative forces."[78] It survived in a passive state of what Gumilev misleadingly called *ravnovesie* or equilibrium with the external environment, "entirely dependent on the historical-geographical conditions of the given territory" for its own existence.[79] This inert condition was not a genuine state of equilibrium, however, for it inexorably gave way to the eventual demise and disappearance of the ethnic unit.

---

77. Michurin 2004, 572.
78. Gumilev 1989c, 324.
79. Gumilev 1970b, 46, 48, 50.

VARIETIES OF ETHNIC INTERACTION

Modes of Ethnic Interaction

The final element of Gumilev's theories about the nature of ethnos and ethnogenesis are his ideas about what he called "ethnic contacts," in other words, the ways in which ethnies coexist and interact with one another. He described these patterns of interaction in terms of four categories: assimilation (*assimiliatsiia*), miscegenation or mixing (*metisatsiia*), fusion (*sliianie*), and symbiosis (*simbios*).[1] Assimilation involves the absorption of one ethnos by another, in which process the memory of the assimilated group's origins, heritage, and traditions is entirely lost and it becomes a component part of the assimilator ethnos. Assimilation occurs mainly in cases where one of the groups involved has a high level of *passionarnost'* and the other's passionary energy had largely dissipated. Miscegenation between ethnies takes place when two groups with similar levels of *passionarnost'* encounter and engage with each other.[2] The result is a composite group, a sort of amalgamated ethnos in which each part finds a way to keep alive its own particular ethnic memories and traditions. By their nature, such formations tend to be unstable and short-lived.[3] The third mode, *sliianie* or fusion, has been noted in the last chapter. It occurs when the merging of groups is accompanied by the wholesale dissolution of their respective past ethnic identities. In the

---

1. Gumilev 1989c, 85, 305, 479; Michurin 2004, 544–55.
2. Gumilev 1989c, 305.
3. Ibid., 87–88.

natural ethnogenetic scheme, this process results—for better in certain circumstances, for worse in others—in the creation of an entirely new ethnic unit with a novel behavioral stereotype that bears no resemblance to any of the multiple ethnic "substrata" out of which it was created.

Gumilev's final category was symbiosis between two or more ethnic groups. In this arrangement, the affected ethnies live side by side "in a single region" (*region*) but each remains naturally ensconced in its original ecological niche.[4] Relations are based on the principles of mutual respect and noninterference, which enable all ethnies involved to retain their original ethnic individuality. They do not undergo fusion, and precisely for this reason the basis is laid for a genuine interethnic fraternity. Gumilev considered symbiosis to be the "optimal variant of ethnic contact"—all ethnies live "next to one another but separately (*porozn'*), cultivating peaceful relations and not interfering in the other's affairs."[5] This symbiotic variety, what he described as a "colorful diversity" (*pestrota*) or "mosaic quality" (*mozaichnost'*), was an important biological aspect of ethnic survival, indeed "the optimal form for human existence." It helped to minimize competition for resources while enhancing opportunities for helpful cooperation.[6] The historical pattern of interrelation among the various ethnic groups in Siberia provided a good example of what he had in mind. "These ethnies occupied the different landscape regions that corresponded to their cultural-economic patterns, and they did not disturb other ethnies but rather helped them. The Yakuts settled in the broad floodplains of the Lena River, the Evenks in the watersheds of the taiga uplands, and the Russians along the river valleys. The expanses of the steppe were left to the Kazakhs and Kalmyks, and the forests to the Ugrian peoples."[7]

A symbiosis forms on the basis of a special empathy between the groups involved. Gumilev referred to this empathy with one of his most important neologisms: *komplimentarnost'* or "complementarity." In principle, complementarity could be either positive or negative. Positive complementarity was "a sensation of ethnic compatibility," an awareness of "a subconscious mutual sympathy between the members of [different] ethnic groups."[8] Its most important function was to enable mature ethnies to form solid and sustainable associations without losing their essential individuality. Gumilev emphasized the subjective character of complementarity as an intuitive, emotional, and subconscious psychological quality. Negative complementarity, by contrast, was an "irrational antipathy,

4. Gumilev 1989f, 157.

5. Gumilev 1995, 36; Gumilev 1994a, 130–31 (quote); Gumilev 1994c, 267.

6. Gumilev 1989c, 302.

7. Gumilev 1989c, 133–34. For a slightly different geographical arrangement of the same ethnic groups, see Gumilev 2001, 292.

8. Gumilev and Ermolaev 1997, 238 (quote); Michurin 2004, 526 (quote), 540.

accompanied by attempts either to restructure or to destroy the other ethnos."[9] Both qualities played a key role in his thinking, although they operated in different and even contradictory ways, as we will see.[10]

The Ethnic Hierarchy

Gumilev believed that every ethnic system consisted of taxonomical units or levels of ethnic organization arranged into a hierarchy.[11] He was not consistent on the precise number of levels, but the principles on which they were based logically indicate four. The hierarchy was strictly symmetrical, such that each level possessed an identical dualistic nature. On the one hand, each formation was an individual, self-contained entity (*tselostnost'*), while at the same time it fitted matrioshka-like as a subordinate component of the formation at the next highest level to create another, greater integral whole.[12] Across his entire system, all forms of ethnic association were at once homogeneous and heterogeneous, unitary and plural. Gumilev termed this complicated pattern *ierarcheskaia sopodchinennost'*, literally the hierarchical co-subordination of ethnic systems, in which "each ethnic system of a higher rank is comprised of several ethnic systems of the next lower rank." He likened it to the proton-electron-neutron-atom-molecule hierarchy in physics.[13] The bonding of individual ethnic units into the single entity that formed the next higher level was facilitated precisely by the quality of positive complementarity. Relations between the groups involved were not always peaceful and harmonious, but whatever conflict did occur took the form of what he called nonantagonistic competition (*neantagonisticheskaia sopernichestva*). Such conflict was not genuinely pernicious and could not ultimately damage either the competing elements or the greater whole that they formed. Each level of the hierarchy was able to sustain a vital internal diversity—the "mosaic systemic totality" just referred to—that helped to retain its ultimate unity.[14]

At the lowest level of Gumilev's hierarchy were the paired entities of consortium (*konsortiia*) and conviction (*konviksiia*).[15] These played the least important

---

9. Gumilev 1994c, 293; Gumilev 2004c, 351.

10. Gumilev explained that the notion of "complementarity" first came to him as he observed the behavior of the prison camp inmates in Noril'sk. Gumilev 2003d, 225–26; Beliakov 2012a, 483–84.

11. Bassin 2011, 54–59.

12. Gumilev and Ermolaev 1997, 238; Michurin 2004, 565; Beliakov 2012a, 431.

13. Michurin 2004, 565; Gumilev 1989c, 106.

14. Gumilev 1989c, 110; Gumilev 1994c, 256.

15. Like many of his other terms, Gumilev borrowed "consortium" from Soviet plant ecology, where it had been developed in the 1950s. Negrobov and Khmelev 2000, 118–21. The origins of the term *konviksiia* are unclear.

role in his scheme and his discussions of them were vague and unclear. A consortium was a small coterie of individuals, often from different protoethnic backgrounds, who were brought together by some combination of common interests and goals. Examples of consortia were certain types of religious sects, medieval artisan artels, and colonizer communities such as the Russian *zemleprokhodtsy* in Siberia or the Puritan immigrants to North America.[16] More significant than consortia were *konviksii*, which were of similar size and appearance but in addition shared common conditions of life (*byt*), were united by family ties, and lived together in the same area. Whereas consortia could be ephemeral phenomena, *konviksii* were generally sustained over several generations. They played a role in the earliest phases of ethnogenesis by mobilizing and catalyzing the rising passionary forces. This was the historical function of the early Christian disciples, for example, who were the harbingers of Byzantine civilization, or the groups of warrior comrades assembled around Genghis Khan—the *liudi dlinnoi voli*—which eventually coalesced to create the Mongol empire.[17]

Gumilev's primary attention was focused, however, on the trinity of remaining hierarchical levels: subethnos, ethnos, and superethnos. It was across these three categories that the micro-macro symmetry and balance of his system was the most faithful and complete. Thus, a subethnos was a subunit or microcosm of an ethnos, which had a similar structure as a self-conscious community marked by its own distinct behavioral stereotype and usually rooted in a particular geographical locality.[18] Within the corpus of the French ethnos, for example, Gumilev identified Bretons, Burgundians, Gasconians, Basques, and Alsatians as subethnics, whereas the Great Russian ethnos was made up of Pomory, Cossacks, Chaldony (Russian Siberians), Kriasheny (Orthodox Tatars), and other groups.[19] In all cases, Gumilev insisted that these subunits—held together internally by special ties of complementarity and juxtaposed to one another by "nonantagonistic competition"—were important for maintaining the vigor and resilience of the ethnos itself. The ethnos-organism was naturally aware of the beneficial effects of subethnic diversity, for which reason it spontaneously sought to enhance it under certain conditions by creating new subethnic groupings. This was the case in Russia, for example, where in the face of foreign threat in the fourteenth and fifteenth centuries the formation of subethnies—the Cossacks in the south or the Pomors in the north—was actively promoted.[20] The structural symmetry

16. Gumilev 1989c, 108–9; Gumilev 1990b.
17. Michurin 2004, 527.
18. Ibid., 548.
19. For illustrations, see the charts in Gumilev 2001, 33, 35.
20. Gumilev 1989c, 107–8.

between ethnos and subethnos was, however, limited in a number of respects, the most significant of which was the fact that not all subethnies were necessarily associated with a distinct ecological niche. The Old Believers, for example, represented one of the most enduring and significant of the Great Russian subethnies, but their remarkable resilience as a community was founded precisely on their physical mobility and ability to adapt to and thrive in very different geographical regions.[21] In the case of subethnies, moreover, Gumilev was prepared to cross the red line he himself had drawn between ethnos and society. In certain cases, he acknowledged, a *soslovie* or social class could constitute a subethnos, for which he identified the Russian aristocracy itself as one notable example.[22]

The principle of *ierarcheskaia sopodchinennost'* extended in the other direction as well, and in the same way that subethnies clustered to form ethnies, the latter themselves under certain circumstances bundled together to create yet greater entities. These were superethnies, and represented the highest stage of Gumilev's hierarchy.[23] Although there was a formal symmetrical balance between subethnos and superethnos, the latter played a far more important role in his theories. Gumilev defined a superethnos as an "ethnic system made up of several ethnies that formed at the same time in the same landscape zone, and that appears in history as a mosaic totality (*mozaichnaia tselostnost'*)."[24] Thus in many respects a superethnos simply duplicated the model of ethnos in that it possessed a discrete cohesiveness that did not abrogate or replace that of its constituent ethnies. Under normal historical circumstances, the latter coexisted symbiotically within the superethnos. Each ethnos kept more or less carefully to its own ecological niche, which as we have seen helped to preserve ethnic individuality and restrict the scale and intensity of interethnic conflict.[25] Interethnic relations within the superethnos were best characterized as a "striving for compromise" among discrete groups rather than the wholesale *sliianie* or merging of these groups into a single quasi-ethnic mass. Mixing between ethnies within a superethnos was controlled by the universal observance of the principles of endogamy.[26] This arrangement did not preclude conflict between the ethnies involved, a point Gumilev was very careful to make. "Nonantagonistic competition" was

---

21. Gumilev was not entirely consistent in his classifications, however, and on at least one occasion he identified the Old Believers as a *konsortsiia*. Gumilev 2001, 35.

22. Gumilev 1989c, 85; Michurin 2004, 549.

23. Gumilev did rank the "ethnosphere" above superethnos, but the term was used to designate the totality of ethnic life rather than an integrated structural unit organized on the model of the ethnos and superethnos. Gumilev 1989c, 131–32, 134.

24. Gumilev 1989c, 480 (quote), 116; Gumilev 1980b, 37n.

25. Gumilev and Panchenko 1990, 8.

26. Gumilev 1989c, 109, 89, 479; Laruelle 2000, 179.

an entirely natural and inevitable aspect of all interethnic contacts, which had "existed in the Paleolithic period" and always would.[27] Between ethnies with positive complementarity, however, such competition was not ultimately destructive, either to them or the superethnos itself. "Blood does flow" as a result of interethnic clashes within a superethnos, Gumilev confirmed sardonically, "but not very much, and life goes on" (*krov' l'etsia, no ne ochen', i zhit' mozhno'*).[28]

At certain points, Gumilev stressed the systemic similarities between ethnos and superethnos so strongly that it became difficult to distinguish the two. Thus, a superethnos—just like an ethnos—was formed through a complex process of ethnogenesis. The proto-superethnos required the same initial infusion of *passionarnost'* as an ethnos, which produced the same catharsis of an energetic *tolchok* setting the entire process in motion. The resulting superethnos, moreover, possessed its own distinctive behavioral stereotype, and moved through the same predetermined ethnogenetic life cycle lasting about one and a half millennia.[29] A further similarity with an ethnos was the fact that superethnies were also organically associated with a distinctive landscape zone. In the case of the superethnos, Gumilev generally referred to this zone as a "region" (*region*), apparently to distinguish it from the "landscape" (*landshaft*) or ecological niche of the ethnos, but the intended distinction remained obscure.[30] Indeed, the two fulfilled identical functions for their respective ethnic or superethnic inhabitants, beginning with the fact that in both cases the geographical environment exerted a determining effect. "A superethnos is neither a spiritual nor political entity," he explained (repeating the very point he emphasized in connection with the ethnos), but rather represents "a *geographical phenomenon*. The Russian (*rossiiskii*) superethnos, which is a genetic continuation of Orthodox Rus', is divided from Western Europe—today as in the Middle Ages—by an invisible landscape boundary: the O° C isotherm in January. To the east of this line, the qualitative shift in climatic conditions determined different forms of adaptation." On its northeastern flank, the Russian superethnos in turn abuts the Circumpolar superethnos, which in identical fashion corresponds to the characteristic and distinctive landscape features of its own respective region. The latter superethnos "is separated from 'Russia' once again by an invisible boundary: [in this case] that marking the extent of permafrost. To the north of this boundary, agriculture did not penetrate into the ... taiga and tundra landscapes. Instead, the grass cover gives way to reindeer moss, creating an ecological niche for the northern

27. Gumilev 1990b.
28. Gumilev 1989c: 302.
29. Gumilev and Ivanov 1992, 53–54; Gumilev 1989c, 133, 302, 305, 311.
30. For example, Gumilev 1989c, 302.

reindeer . . . which is closely connected to the existence of all of the groups [in this superethnos]."[31] In these characterizations, Gumilev repeated his descriptions of landscape zones of the ethnos practically verbatim.

There was, however, one significant difference between ethnos and superethnos in Gumilev's scheme. The members of an ethnos were bonded together by a shared behavioral stereotype that had been acquired in infancy and was an unconscious part of each individual's ethnic persona. Although a superethnos might also possess its own behavioral stereotype, however, this was not the primary source of the existential cohesion that united its individual ethnies into a greater whole. Superethnic cohesion derived rather from what Gumilev called ethnic *dominanty* or a set of dominant features: a "system of political, ideological, and religious values."[32] In principle, here as well Gumilev intended an ethnos-superethnos symmetry, insofar as an ethnic *dominanta* also played an important role in the formation of the ethnos by providing a core of beliefs around which protoethnic consortia and *konviksii* could consolidate and achieve the "purposeful unanimity" (*tseleustremlennoe edinoobrazie*) necessary for a new ethnic entity.[33] But the notion that subjective human values, beliefs, and ideals were part of a process that he otherwise treated quite strictly as the product of universal natural laws was awkward, and Gumilev did not stress the functions of *dominanty* in regard to ethnies. With superethnies, however, the situation was very different. Here it was precisely these subjective values, shared broadly across all of the ethnies involved, that were the most powerful source of its unanimity. These shared *dominanty* were often conditioned by a sense of "common historical destiny" among the superethnos's constituent ethnies.[34]

Although each superethnic *dominanta*, like the behavioral stereotype, was unique, they all shared two important characteristics. Effectively, they were deliberate and conscious choices that the groups made at the earliest stages of their development, and represented thereby an elemental act of superethnic self-affirmation (*zhizneutverzhdenie*). As just noted, this was a major contrast to the cohesion of an ethnos, which was "natural" and did not include any element of choice. Beyond this, *dominanty* were marked by a strict, indeed rigid uniformity in the way they were understood and embraced. For all ethnies that are part of a single superethnic system, he explained, the dominant values "possess a single uniform (*edinoobraznyi*) significance and similar conceptual dynamics." The ethnic *dominanta* provided a superethnos with a cohesive power that an ethnos—bound

---

31. Gumilev and Ivanov 1992, 55 (quote); also see Gumilev 2004c, 10.
32. Gumilev 1989c, 481; Michurin 2004, 564.
33. Gumilev 1989c, 142.
34. Gumilev and Ivanov 1992, 53.

together as it was only by a common behavioral stereotype—simply does not possess. This in turn led to the paradox that although superethnies were by definition more heterogeneous and amorphous than ethnies, they were also more tightly bonded, and therefore more resilient (*stoikii*) and more exclusive.

The behavioral implications were profound. Whereas under certain conditions ethnies could combine to form a greater whole, superethnies could not. The distinctive system of values inscribed in a particular superethnic *dominanta* was immutable, and because the identity and the unity of the superethnos derived wholly from it, the superethnos itself was very limited in the degree to which it could amalgamate or indeed even associate with others. The merging of two superethnies, Gumilev explained, would require the "rejection" of the original *dominanta* of one of the ethnies concerned, and this was simply not possible.[35] "The resulting combination (*sliianie*) of superethnies would be ephemeral, for in their soul of souls each representative of the various superethnies would remain [faithful to those original values] that seem to them to be the only natural and correct ones."[36] Because superethnies cannot combine to form larger entities, they indeed represent the highest level of Gumilev's ethnic hierarchy. He noted the hypothetical possibility of a grouping of superethnies, derisively labeling it a "hyperethnos" (*giperetnos*), but insisted that such formations would necessarily be unsustainable.[37] And there can obviously be no single panhuman entity, because there is no single universal (*obshchechelovecheskii*) *dominanta* or system of values that could form the basis for the association of all humanity.

As with ethnies, relations between superethnies were governed by the principle of positive and negative complementarity. Yet while examples of "mutual sympathy" between superethnies played an important role for Russia in particular,[38] as we will see, it was nonetheless the case that by virtue of their individualized value systems, superethnies were as a rule inclined to mutual antagonism and confrontation. Contact and mixing on the superethnic level was potentially far more dangerous and harmful than was the case with ethnies. Between the latter, conflict could take the form of "nonantagonistic competition," which was limited in its destructive effect and in a certain sense benign. Struggles, or what Gumilev preferred to call "collisions" (*kollizii*) between superethnies, on the other hand, were much more likely to be genuinely cataclysmic affairs, involving death and devastation on a grand scale.[39]

---

35. Gumilev and Ermolaev 1993, 182–83.
36. Gumilev 1989c, 142 (quote), 297; "Etnologicheskaia karta" 1988.
37. Gumilev 1989c, 116.
38. Gumilev and Ivanov 1992, 55; Gumilev 1994c, 293.
39. Gumilev 1989c, 301.

Superethnies and Civilizations

Gumilev's notion of superethnos bears an affinity with the well-known view of human history as a chronicle of the successive rise and fall of discrete "cultures" or "civilizations." These are understood as very large-scale agglomerations of various peoples and territories, which are united on the basis of some combination of shared social, cultural, or religious values. In the twentieth century this perspective was developed famously in Oswald Spengler's (1880–1936) *Der Untergang des Abendlandes* and Arnold Toynbee's (1889–1975) twelve-volume *A Study in History,* and it has been resurrected more recently in Samuel Huntington's (1927–2008) much-noted *Clash of Civilizations.*[40] At the same time, however, the civilizational approach has a long and venerable tradition in Russian nationalist discourse, beginning in the nineteenth century with the writings of Nikolai Iakovlevich Danilevskii (1822–1885), Vladimir Ivanovich Lamanskii (1833–1914), and Konstantin Nikolaevich Leont'ev (1831–1891).[41] Indeed, Danilevskii's seminal notion of "cultural-historical types," first set forth in the 1860s, anticipated Spengler's own scheme of *Weltkulturen,* and the Eurasianist Nikolai Sergeevich Trubetskoi (1890–1938) wrote his own civilizational manifesto *Europe and Humankind* in the 1920s as a sympathetic response to Spengler.[42] Gumilev became familiar with Spengler's ideas in the 1930s when the German philosopher enjoyed a certain vogue among Soviet intellectuals, and a wartime essay he wrote, "Reflections on the Decline of Europe," was obviously inspired by Spengler.[43] In his later writings, he referred frequently to the schemes of Toynbee and Spengler, noted Danilevskii's theories, and declared that Leont'ev was, of all the Russian philosophers, the closest to him.[44] Gumilev clearly felt a kinship to their project, and there is no question that he saw his own work as a part of this legacy. According to his widow, he regarded himself as a sort of "Russian Spengler,"[45] and in a lengthy introduction to a collection of Trubetskoi's writings he

40. Spengler 1918–1923; Toynbee 1934–1961; Huntington 1993; Huntington 1996. On Spengler in Russia and the Soviet Union, see Rumiantseva 2008, 41-45; Avins 1983, 35–38. The affinities between Gumilev and Huntington are further discussed below, 314–15.

41. Danilevskii 1895; Lamanskii 1916; Leont'ev 2007 [1875].

42. Trubetskoi 1921a. On Danilevskii's foreshadowing of Spengler, see Hughes 1992, 44–50.

43. Beliakov 2012a, 145. For a comparison of Spengler and Gumilev (highly unflattering for the latter), see Sapronov n.d. It is very interesting to note that Spengler anticipated Gumilev by describing the life cycle of his *Kulturen* in thermodynamic terms as a process of entropic decline. Rooney 1986, 679; Myers 1985, 35.

44. For example, Gumilev 1989c, 28, 69, 121, 131, 147, 149, 244, 358n; Gumilev 1968b, 592–95; Beliakov 2012a, 144–46ff.; Lavrov 2000, 334–43. On Gumilev and Danilevskii, see Shitikhin 2012. On Leont'ev, see Gumilev 1990b; Gumilev 1989e, 30.

45. Gumileva 2003a, 18; Gumilev 1995.

directly associated his own notion of "superethnos" with the civilizational concept, likening it both to Spengler's *Kultur*—a "distinctive entity (*tselostnost'*) of historical existence"—and to Trubetskoi's notion of "*mnogonarodnaia lichnost'*" and "historical-cultural zones."[46]

Gumilev's superethnos concept does indeed share many of the characteristics common to the different civilizational models just noted.[47] Many of the historical superethnies that Gumilev identified are commonly recognized as "civilizations" as well: India, China, Byzantium, Islam, and the Romano-Germanic civilization of Western Europe.[48] Like a civilization, moreover, superethnies are macroagglomerations of various ethnic groups, which are united by a commonality of beliefs, fundamental values, and shared historical experiences rather than ethnonational affinities. Civilizations represent the largest and most general form of human association. There is nothing above them, no higher level of association, and the notion of "universal" or "panhuman values" is explicitly dismissed. Gumilev made the same point regarding superethnies. There is no such thing as general or universal history—"to speak about a history of all humankind makes no sense."[49] And like civilizations, finally, superethnies are individualized in a manner that often makes them mutually incompatible. On some essential level, they simply do not and cannot understand one another, and their pattern of relations are therefore likely to be characterized by suspicion and hostility. "Clashes" (*stolknoveniia*) between them, Gumilev believed, were inevitable.[50]

Gumilev's terminology and perspective have an obvious resonance with Huntington's famous "clash of civilizations" (Russian: *stolknovenie tsivilizatsii*) thesis of the 1990s, which similarly stressed the reciprocal incompatibility of these macroagglomerations.[51] As a rule, Gumilev maintained, "superethnic value systems are mutually exclusive," a circumstance that confirms the functional role of the superethnic *dominanta*. "These *dominanty* block as it were the merging of superethnies among themselves. It is, for example, possible to find a great deal of commonality between Christianity, Islam, and even Buddhism. . . . However, historical practice testifies to the fact that attempts to create artificially, on the basis of these commonalities, a common value system that would be shared among even a small number of superethnies—to say nothing of a universal system of values—have always collapsed and led only to more bloodshed." In other words, he explained, "although the Muslims of Azerbaijan consider the [New

---

46. Gumilev 1995, 35, 51; Gumilev 1968a, cited in Gumilev and Ivanov 1992, 53.
47. Gumilev 1989c, 289; Matern 2007.
48. Gumilev 1989c, 135–36.
49. Gumilev 1995, 49.
50. Gumilev 2004c, 6.
51. Goudakov 2006; Iamskov 2006.

Testament] Gospels as well as the Koran to be holy books, and Jesus Christ to be a prophet, this does not and in principle cannot lead them to a reconciliation with the Christian Armenians."[52] Following Danilevskii and Trubetskoi, moreover, he applied this principle directly to Russia, characterizing relations with the country's traditional opponents—Western Europe, Islam, and China—as an opposition between rival superethnies. As such, this opposition was at once elemental and insurmountable.[53] Gumilev cited the experiences of European imperial encounters with aboriginal peoples from the sixteenth through the nineteenth centuries as examples of the horrific damage that can arise from uncontrolled superethnic contact. The grim record of the settlement of the Americas and Australia in particular, he observed, was a disquieting legacy of "extermination and enslavement."[54]

There was, however, one aspect of Gumilev's notion of "superethnies" that set it quite apart from other civilizational discourses, in particular those of his Russian predecessors. In virtually all articulations, Russia was seen as representing as a single, self-standing civilizational entity. The precise characteristics attributed to Russia qua civilization may have varied among the different accounts, but they all concurred that the totality of the historical, geocultural, and geopolitical space of the Russian imperial state represented an integral civilizational unit of world-historical significance. Gumilev, by contrast, argued strenuously *against* such an identification in most of his writings, insisting that Russia's traditional geopolitical spaces most definitely did *not* represent a single superethnic entity.

> To maintain that a single superethnos . . . has already formed on the territory of our country is to confuse both the scientific community and also those officials responsible for making decisions regarding nationalities policy. The present [1989] state boundaries of the USSR contain, as a minimum, seven different (*razlichnye*) superethnies, each of which occupies for the most part its own ecological niche or ethno-landscape zone and has its own unique historical fate, that is, an original behavioral stereotype and a particular tradition of interactions with its neighboring superethnies.[55]

These seven superethnies of the Soviet Union included the West European (Latvia, Lithuania, Estonia), Circumpolar (Samoyed, Khanty, Mansy, Tungus, Evenk, Chukchi, etc.), Steppe (Kazakh, Tatar, Buriat, Kalmyk), Byzantine (Georgian,

---

52. Gumilev and Ermolaev 1993, 182.
53. For example, Gumilev 1993b, 31; Lavrov 2000, 349, 359.
54. Gumilev 1989c, 109 (quote); Gumilev and Panchenko 1990, 33.
55. Gumilev and Ivanov 1992, 55.

Armenian), Islamic (Turkmen, Uzbek), Jewish, and Russian (*Rossiiskii*). The latter group was comprised of Great Russians, Ukrainians, Belorussians, Karels, Mordvinians, Udmurty, Komi, "Kazan Tatars," Chuvash, and others. These seven superethnic entities were further disaggregated by the fact that most of them—West European, Jewish, Islamic, etc.—were themselves part of larger superethnic bodies that existed beyond Soviet borders. Only two superethnies, the *Rossiiskii* and the Steppe, were contained wholly within the USSR, for which reason he judged them to be the country's two "foundational" (*osnovnyi*) superethnies.

The historical patterns of interaction between the Soviet superethnies were far from uniformly positive and peaceful. The Jews were perhaps the most obvious case in point, as we will see repeatedly throughout the rest of this book, but they were by no means the only one. In a fascinating observation, Gumilev described how the Chukchi peoples on the northeastern tip of Siberia, in contrast to all of the other indigenous groups of the Siberian north, had never found a "common language" with the Russians. This he explained by saying that they did not belong to the (Soviet) Circumpolar superethnos but rather were "Americanoid," a superethnic affiliation which meant that "they have no sympathy toward the Russians and have somehow always kept themselves completely separate."[56] Despite these inherent frictions, however, modern Russia nonetheless grew historically out of the positive "complementarity of interacting superethnies," more specifically the "unconscious mutual sympathy" between the two leading groups just mentioned. The synergy between them served as the "guarantor (*zalog*) for the creation of the Muscovite state, the territorial expansion of the Russian empire, and for the indestructibility of the USSR in the Second World War."[57] Gumilev did not of course intend his picture of superethnic diversity and juxtaposition to question in any way the legitimacy of the political-territorial unity of the Soviet state. He was concerned rather to indicate that this *political* unity did not rest on the solidarity within a single superethnic entity. As was the case with ethnies, so the inner cohesion of superethnies was also by its very definition nonpolitical: "a superethnos is not a . . . political community" (*obshchnost'*).[58]

The Ethnic Chimera

Although the four modes of ethnic contact discussed at the beginning of this chapter were very different, they shared one important characteristic: they were all "natural," that is, organic and normal dimensions of ethnic being. There was,

---

56. "Etnologicheskaia karta" 1988.
57. Gumilev and Ivanov 1992, 55–56; Laruelle 2000, 181.
58. Gumilev and Ivanov 1992, 55.

however, a final, fifth mode of ethnic interaction. Unlike the others, it was fundamentally unnatural and even antinatural, for which reason Gumilev usually discussed it separately.[59] This fifth mode of ethnic interaction represented one of the most important elements of Gumilev's general conceptualization of ethnicity and forms a particularly influential aspect of his legacy.

In chapter 1 we noted how the emigration of an ethnos out of its home region involved a rupture with its native landscape, which led either to the demise of the group or to its amalgamation with other groups under the influence of new natural-geographical conditions. In either case, the structure of the group is undermined, its behavioral stereotype disrupted, and the original ethnos disappears. There was, however, a third option, which allowed a migrant ethnos to survive intact despite displacement and deracination. It did so by means of a new strategy for self-preservation, namely, the calculated invasion and occupation of a landscape that served as the ecological niche of a different ethnos. Unable to establish itself naturally as an organic part of the new region and to draw sustenance from it in a normal fashion, the invader ethnos resorts to the manipulation and exploitation of indigenous ethno-ecological systems. Gumilev famously termed this particular situation, in which two ethnies occupy a single ecological niche, a chimera (*khimera*).[60] He borrowed the designation from the biological sciences, where it was used to describe a relationship that he believed to be structurally identical. "An example of a chimeric relationship in zoology is that which forms when tapeworms are present inside an animal's organs. Whereas the animal is able to exist without the parasite, the parasite will perish without its host. When the parasite lives in the body of the former, however, it takes part in its life cycle. By necessitating an increased inflow of nutrition and introducing its hormones into the blood and bile of its host organism, the parasite alters its host's biochemistry."[61] In the realm of the ethnosphere, Gumilev characterized a chimera as an "ethno-parasite" (*etnos-parazit*) or "pernicious bacteria" (*vredonosnye bakterii*) that "exploits the indigenous population of the country, along with its flora, fauna, and precious minerals."[62] And just like "a population of bacteria or infusoria [a type of single-celled organisms]" that "spreads through the internal organs of the person or animal," a chimeric invasion can be fatal for the indigenous ethnos. "The bacilli cause the latter's death, and then they themselves perish as the body grows cold."[63]

---

59. For one exception, see Gumilev 1989f, 159.
60. Gumilev 1989c, 480.
61. Gumilev 1989c, 302.
62. Ibid., 304; Gumilev 2004c, 328.
63. Gumilev 2004d, 349.

Gumilev continually stressed the comparison of ethnic chimeras to bacteria and other sorts of predatory biological organisms. All of these flourished in the same manner, by drawing on the life energies and resources of their host organisms to the necessary detriment of the latter. "The relationship between an [indigenous ethnos] and a chimera corresponds to that between a [healthy] organism and a cancerous tumor (*opukhol'*)," he noted on a number of occasions. "The latter can grow only with the organism and not beyond it, and it lives exclusively at the expense of the host organism." Just like a cancer, an ethnic chimera "sucks (*vysasyvat'*) its sustenance out of the indigenous ethnos," and just like a biological parasite, the ethno-parasite disrupts the life processes of its host and critically undermines its welfare.[64] Because the chimera stood outside of the normal ethnic life cycle, moreover, its presence had the effect of deforming the natural ethnogenetic processes of those ethnies with which it cohabited. This was what produced the "zigzags" in the natural course of ethnogenetic development mentioned in chapter 2, which could be detected throughout the course of ethnic history.[65]

Invariably, the coexistence of two groups in a single ecological niche engendered a maleficent and destructive relationship. Deprived of an organic anchor in its own primordial landscape, the character of the invader ethnos became irredeemably degraded. Degradation, however, does not necessarily mean weakness. To the contrary, deracinated ethnies survive precisely by developing traits that, however pernicious and unnatural, give them critical advantages over their more normal cohabitants. Indeed, even rootlessness itself is turned to advantage, in the sense that this independence from the natural world enables the invader ethnos—like a resilient weed—to penetrate and prosper virtually anywhere.[66] The natural energies of the indigenous ethnos are sapped and dissipated, and as long as the invader is not overcome its unfortunate host is reduced to a condition of debilitating dependency. A chimera leads inevitably to the "overloading" of the respective natural-geographical region and the transformation of a healthy ethno-ecological system into a dysfunctional morass. All of the aboriginal organic life of the geographical region—its flora and fauna no less than the ethnos itself—is seriously disrupted and threatened ultimately with destruction.[67]

The ethnogenetic dysfunctionality of a chimera is given an ideological expression in the form what Gumilev calls an antisystem (*antisistema*). Essentially, antisystems are negative world views: discrete bodies of teachings that organize and rationalize the predatory impulses that determine the behavior of an ethnic or

---

64. Gumilev 2004b, 358. Also see Gumilev 1989c, 452–69.
65. Gumilev 2004e; for a somewhat different version, see Gumilev 2004c, 108–97.
66. Shnirelman 2002, 49.
67. Gumilev 1980b, 35.

subethnic grouping. Gumilev described these as "vampire concepts (*kontseptsii-vampiry*) that embody a deep and diabolical sense of purpose."[68] In their specifics, antisystems vary greatly among different groups and across historical periods, but they share certain basic convictions and orientations. They are always characterized by a "negative view of the world" (*mirooshchushchenie*), which sees the material universe and the domains of everyday life as a realm of suffering and the source of all evil.[69] As a consequence, all antisystems advocate the rejection of the material world (*mirootritsanie* or *zhizneotritsanie*) in all its complexity and diversity in favor of oversimplified abstract principles and unyielding absolute ideals. Indeed, *zhizneotritsanie* is the principal motivational sentiment of the antisystem, commonly expressed either as a call to redesign the world or, more simply, to destroy it.[70] This general hostility to the world is linked to a more specific hostility to the ecological realities of the biosphere. In an antisystem, "man opposes himself to nature, which he sees as a realm of suffering. Despite this, he is obliged to include his own body in the biosphere, which he rejects, and from which it [therefore] becomes necessary to free his 'soul,' that is to say, his consciousness. Many ways to accomplish this have been suggested, but the underlying principle is always the same: the rejection of the [natural] world as the source of evil."[71] In the final analysis, of course, this struggle must be futile, for no chimeric antisystem is capable of extricating any ethnic group completely from its ecological emplacement in the natural world. So rather than genuine liberation from the natural environment, the antisystem summons its adherents to a struggle that can only lead to ecological desecration and destruction.

An antisystem violates all of ethnic life's positive natural qualities. The veneration of heritage and tradition, which in healthy ethnies operates within the family structure through signal inheritance and helps insure the maintenance of ethnic integrity and continuity, is shunned. To the contrary, an antisystem looks obsessively to the future rather than reverentially to the past, and is dominated by individuals "with a futuristic sense of time."[72] Antisystemic values and attitudes are codified and formalized through stylized written texts, which cannot be absorbed spontaneously but have to be explicated and taught in a formalistic manner.[73] "And the difference between 'living' traditions, absorbed by children as they are raised, and 'contrived' (*sdelannye*) traditions, in other words, those based on books, is the same as the difference between living organisms and inanimate

---

68. Gumilev 1989c, 467.
69. Michurin 2004, 518.
70. Gumilev 2004b, 360; Gumilev 2001, 180–82.
71. Gumilev 2004c, 232 (quote), 92–93.
72. Michurin 2004, 518–19.
73. Gumilev 2004c, 232–33.

objects. The former, as they perish [in a natural manner], are resurrected in the form of their posterity. The latter, by contrast, are gradually destroyed, with no hope of resurrection." Significantly, all antisystems and chimeras are characterized by a relatively high degree of passionary tension. Even this condition is abnormal, however, for the energetic infusion in question comes not directly from cosmic radiation but rather indirectly from the effluences of surplus energy (*energeticheskie perepady*) exuded by other ethnic groups.[74] Among other things, this has implications for the geographical location of chimeras, which Gumilev argues tend to form on the margins or boundaries of existing ethnic or superethnic entities. And because the chimera is removed from the normal ethnogenetic cycle and is not subject to the process of entropy, its passionary charge is not diminished over time and remains always at a high level.[75]

The Jews as the Quintessential Chimera

Throughout his voluminous writings, Gumilev described many different examples of chimeras and the antisystems they created, explaining how they blotted ethnic history across the ages and led to pernicious zigzags in the normal course of ethnic development. Practically all of the instances he identified were highly obscure and esoteric, selected from remote historical periods and geographically far removed from Russia. They included the Gnostic sects of the Classical and early Christian period, the dualist religion of Manicheism, the Zoroastrian sect of Mazdaism in Persia, Albigensianism (Catharism) in medieval France and the contemporaneous sectarian movement of Bogomilstvo in the Balkans, the Ismailist branch of Shi'a Islam, and certain forms of ancient Buddhism. In the twentieth century, Gumilev described the philosophical movement of existentialism as an example of an antisystem, particularly as developed in the writings of the German philosopher Karl Jaspers.[76] None of these would have meant a great deal to his readers, and indeed none of them really stood at the center of Gumilev's own attention. Above all else, Gumilev was preoccupied with one particular example of a chimeric relationship that was not at all obscure in nature, buried in the historical past, or geographically remote: the Jewish people. Gumilev's singular preoccupation with this particular problem runs like a red thread through the entirety of his work, indeed it can be argued that all of his theories and historical reconstructions are driven in significant measure by it.

---

74. Gumilev 2004d, 349.
75. Gumilev 2004c, 232–33.
76. Gumilev 2004b, 359–74, 338–40; Gumilev 2004d, 336–42.

In Gumilev's understanding, the Jews—not an ethnos but a superethnos, as we have seen—emerge as a prototypical chimera and antisystem whose ethnic life history provides the best evidence of the disruption and devastation that this sort of negative ethnic contact is certain to entail.[77] Their rupture with the natural environment occurred at an early moment in their ethnogenetic cycle, and they were constrained thereafter to lead the greatest part of their historical life in conditions of diaspora. This experience forced them to develop the ability to penetrate into virtually all types of natural landscapes, which gave them a unique advantage and power. Wherever they settled, they necessarily acted as a chimera in regard to indigenous populations, bringing with them the full range of problems associated with this condition. Gumilev did make one qualification of his ethno-ecological laws in regard to the Jews. He allowed that, strictly speaking, they were able to reestablish an ecological connection of sorts to a landscape, a kind of "natural" reemplacement that then became part of their ethnic character and helped shaped their ethnic identity. The ecological niche in question, however, was itself not a normal landscape but rather the "anthropogenic environment," in other words, urban settlements and trading routes created and sustained through human design rather than natural-geographical processes.[78] In this manner, Gumilev suggested, the Jews became a part of landscapes that were themselves nonorganic and unhealthy, an association that served to underscore the fundamentally antiecological and unnatural character of the Jewish superethnos overall.[79] Like all environments, these urban landscapes worked to shape the ethos of the ethnic group, fostering the detached cosmopolitanism characteristic for the Jews and their proclivity for commerce and merchantry.[80]

The Jews were a parasite chimera par excellence. Their ethnic character exemplified the sort of degradation and depravity that was the necessary result of a rupture with the natural world. They were agents of ecological destruction, either by conscious design or by the simple fact that, as foreign intruders in any given region, they did not understand local natural conditions and thus were unable to respect and manage them properly. As an example, Gumilev's refers to the demise of the ancient city of Babylon, which he attributes to the fact that the advisers of the Chaldean king were Jews who failed to take into consideration the constraints of local conditions in maintaining the vital irrigation networks.[81] Their effects on the indigenous human inhabitants of these landscapes were no less pernicious.

---

77. Gumilev and Ivanov 1992, 56–57.
78. Rogachevskii 2001, 363.
79. Gumilev and Ivanov 1992, 54, 56; Gumilev 2004ca, 123.
80. Shnirelman 2002, 56.
81. Gumilev 1989c, 414–15.

Wherever they penetrated and settled, they sought to establish themselves and gain control through devious and deceitful means.[82] Everywhere they deliberately fostered "skepticism and indifference" and "putrefaction (*razlozhenie*) and stagnation" in order to erode the spiritual and moral resistance of their hosts and more easily extend their dominance over them.[83] A particularly effective strategy toward this end, Gumilev liked to argue, was the practice of deliberate exogamy, that is, marriage outside the ethnic unit. Whereas normal ethnies naturally observed endogamy as a strategy for ethnic reproduction and survival, the Jews developed the practice of deliberately intermarrying their women into foreign indigenous elites in order to produce generations of "métis" or "bastard" offspring (Gumilev's terms) that could eventually seize power in the name of the intruder.[84] In this way, they sought to gain control over the economic life of the group and over its highest administrative offices.[85] Jewish barbarity was further demonstrated by their extensive slave-trading activities throughout history, which they pursued relentlessly and which everywhere brought them enormous profit and power at the cost of untold human misery.[86]

Finally, the Jews offered the classic example of the fetishization of the written word that Gumilev insisted was typical for antisystems. Their complete moral corruption was apparent throughout their copious holy writings, most notably those of the *Talmud* and *Kabbalah*. Here, Gumilev claimed, it was stated that the Jewish deity Jahweh, who spoke with Moses on Mount Sinai, was not a god at all but merely a "fiery demon," the "best friend" of the devil Satan.[87] In Jewish theology, he maintained, notions such as "justice," "evil," and "repentance" ceased to be absolute universal injunctions and were treated instead as relativized and opportunistic judgements. Effectively, in their laws the Jews put themselves "beyond good and evil," condoning virtually any behavior on their part as long as it helped secure the survival and prosperity of their ethnic group.[88] Jewish hostility was particularly focused on Christians, of course, but they displayed an unrelenting malevolence and hostility toward all outsiders, in pious observance of what Gumilev claimed to be a cardinal Talmudic injunction: "and kill the best of the goyim" (*i luchshego iz goev ubei*).[89]

---

82. Gumilev 2004c, 91–92.
83. Gumilev 1980b, 35; Gumilev 2004c, 260.
84. Rogachevskii 2001, 363.
85. Gumilev 2004c, 91–92.
86. Gumilev 1989c, 303–4; Gumilev 2004ca, 114–15.
87. Gumilev 2004a, 500.
88. Gumilev 2004c, 94–96.
89. Rogachevskii 2001, 364 (quote); Gumilev 2004c, 106; Rossman 2002b, 80–81.

The Ethnosphere as a Moral Domain

A final point to be made about the notions of "chimera" and "antisystem" is that through them, Gumilev introduced an explicit ethical and moral dimension into his theory of ethnogenesis.[90] The ethnosphere as a whole, he explained, was riven by an essential dualism or "bipolarity," dividing it into two separate existential realms of being.[91] One of these is the realm of *iavlenie*, or worldly natural phenomena, while the other is *deianie*, the domain of deliberate activity and deeds. The ethnogenetic cycle in all its phases belongs to the realm of *iavlenie*. As a wholly natural process, it unfolds according to laws and imperatives that inhere in the very structure of the biosphere and the universe. For this reason, it is not open to modification or rearrangement. And because of its natural immanence and immutability, Gumilev reasoned, ethnical and moral principles bear no meaningful relation to it. The realm of *iavlenie* has rather an elemental (*stikhiinyi*) character, and for this reason "stands beyond good and evil" (*vne dobra i zla*).[92] The realm of deeds or *deianie*, however, is structured through the decisions of its actors, their intentionality and their free will. Here all action is the result of "conscious strivings"—decisions taken on the basis of subjective volition, which always represent a conscious choice between multiple possibilities. Because these choices are deliberately made, they can and must be held against a moral measure, and the notion of ethical judgement becomes relevant and necessary.[93]

If we recall the emphasis Gumilev placed on the nonnatural character of chimeric formations and their associated antisystems, then their relevance for this line of argument becomes clear. At the moment that an ethnic formation becomes detached from and opposed to its natural-ecological emplacement, it crosses over from the realm of *iavlenie* to *deianie*. It is now confronted with the challenge of making moral decisions in a way that it was not previously, and by the same token it is exposed to external moral judgment. But this was not, as could be assumed, a neutral process in which the choices that the chimera as free agent had to make could be positive as well as negative. Very much to the contrary, it was precisely when it entered the realm of *deianie* that the chimera acquired its own quintessentially and unalterably evil character as an agent of disruption and despair. Evilness was apparent in the typical qualities of duplicity and deception, founded on the incorporation of what Gumilev called the "lie (*lozh'*) as a principle" into their antisystemic teachings.[94] Most of all, however, it was apparent in a special

---

90. Ivakhiv 2005, 208.
91. Beliakov 2012a, 506–18; Shishkin 1995a, 81–83.
92. Gumilev 2004d, 345 (quote), 355; Gumilev 1988b, 46.
93. Gumilev 2004d, 345, 347.
94. Gumilev 2004b, 354–57; Michurin 2004, 518–19.

proclivity for destruction or, as Gumilev called it, "annihilation" (*annigiliatsiia*). Unlike the ordinary destruction that results from the natural conflict between normal ethnies mentioned earlier in the chapter, annihilation had no rational basis or, importantly, any provision for replacing that which was destroyed. "In the [normal and] natural world of the planet," he explained, "there is no annihilation."[95] But by entering the "realm of freedom" (*polosy svobody*), Gumilev noted, the chimera necessarily develops a "behavioral syndrome, which manifests the need to annihilate both the natural world as well as human culture."[96]

Gumilev developed his point through an extended consideration of the implications of the *iavlenie-deianie* contrast for ecological issues and environmental degradation. Under normal conditions, he explained, ethnogenesis could not ultimately be harmful or threatening for the environment, for the wanton and irreversible destruction of an ecological niche obviously works against the interests of ethnic survival and thus is "not a law of nature."[97] After all, a passionary impetus "is also a phenomenon of nature, and it stimulates creative impulses, giving rise to adaptive syndromes through which an ethnos connects with its primeval landscape."[98] This is not to say that these passionary impulses are entirely without any effect on the external landscape. Nineteenth-century European migrants to the United States, for example, were driven there precisely by bursts of passionary energy, and their struggle with the primitive conditions they encountered—in the Mississippi Valley and elsewhere—involved a considerable amount of environmental transformation and destruction. But Gumilev was quick to qualify his conclusions. "Here we are dealing with a process that is determined by nature, and for which man [therefore] does not carry any moral responsibility, even if it involves the destruction of splendid virgin landscapes and magnificent foreign cultures. It's sad, of course, but what's to be done about it?" (*Grustno, konechno, no chto delat'?*) No moral reproach can be brought against a legacy of environmental destruction that is the result of natural causes, and thus the activities of the New World settlers stand comfortably beyond good and evil. If, however, destruction takes the form of annihilation, then everything is different. "But if this same immigrant should kill a Native American baby in order to claim a bounty for its scalp, or denounce his neighbor as a witch or sorceress, who is then burned by the villagers at the stake . . . all this is already *deianie*, for which the immigrant carries responsibility before his own conscience."[99] Wanton

---

95. Gumilev 2004d, 346.
96. Ibid., 352.
97. Ibid., 349.
98. Ibid., 346.
99. Ibid., 347.

annihilation begins only when an ethnic group migrates into a foreign region, confronts an indigenous group, and creates a chimera. It is not a natural process "inherent in humankind as a species, but is rather a side effect, a result of the formation and disappearance of a special [negative] view of the world"—that is, the *deianie* of the chimera.[100] Gumilev grimly concluded that in the final analysis, the principle means of preserving the natural ecology of a region was to "defend the natural environment from an antisystem."[101]

---

100. Ibid., 349.
101. Gumilev 2004b, 366.

THE ETHNOGENETIC DRAMA OF RUSSIAN HISTORY

Gumilev always thought of himself primarily as a historian, and it was in his work on ancient and medieval history that he made the fullest attempt to illustrate the operations and implications of his ethnogenetic theories. He stressed this point himself, frequently remarking that the study of more recent periods were subject to an "aberration of closeness" (*aberratsiia blizosti*) and therefore could not be objective and scientific.[1] The claim for scholarly detachment was disingenuous, in the sense that his interpretations of remote periods were heavily tendentious and always carried a clearly implied relevance for the Soviet present. Indeed, his historical studies can be read as an elaborate metaphor—a sort of "coded message" for the world that he was living in.[2] To this extent, Gumilev practiced the same ideological instrumentalization of historical interpretation that was typical for most of Soviet historiography. For the purposes of delivering his particular message, however, Gumilev presented narratives and interpretations that were radically revisionist and contravened conventional perspectives quite dramatically. His reconstructions involved a good deal of barely concealed speculation and even guesswork, which he did not deny but rather affirmed, declaring at one point that the difference between a mythic or a real event "is

---

1. Gumilev 1990c, 7.

2. Shlapentokh 2011, 113. For an appreciation of this point from a present-day admirer, see Akaev 2011a, 21. The "presentism" characteristic of Gumilev's historical writings is apparent in his frequent use of terms with a clear twentieth-century resonance—for example "total war" (*total'naia voina*), "usurper (*uzurpator*)," or "genocide (*genotsid*)"—in his discussions of the ancient past.

not important for us."[3] Although his historical research was dismissed by more orthodox academic colleagues as "fantasy" or, more generously, as "poetry," it did help lay the foundation for the yet more wanton post-Soviet manipulation of the historical past in the form of so-called alternative history. But however fanciful, his historical accounts vividly brought to life the "scientific" principles of his ethnogenetic theories, above all the juxtaposition between the contending dynamics of positive and negative complementarity—between symbioses and antisystemic chimeras. In the final analysis, his entire reconstruction of Russian history was based on this simple opposition and represented a chronicle of Manichean confrontation between *druzia i nedrugi* (friends and enemies)—the forces of good and evil.[4]

The Origins of Eurasian History

Gumilev viewed Russia's historical experience as an intrinsic part of a much older and broader pattern of historical development covering what he called the "Great Steppe"—the transcontinental expanse of low prairie grasslands that extend across Eurasia from Mongolia to Eastern Europe. Ranging over this broad geographical arena, his research focused on the historical experience of four different steppe peoples. The earliest were the Xiongnu, a nomadic group on the East Asian steppes who formed a powerful state in the third and second centuries BC. The first book Gumilev published was an historical overview of the Xiongnu, which he followed with a second focusing specifically on their relations with the Han dynasty in China.[5] Gumilev's second focus was on the Göktürk Khaganates, an empire established on the Mongolian Plateau and across Central Asia by the Ashina dynasty from the sixth through the eighth centuries AD.[6] The Khazars, his third object of study, were a semi-nomadic group settled along the northern coasts of the Black and Caspian seas. From the seventh through the tenth centuries, the Khazar state developed into a powerful trading emporium, which controlled much of the commercial traffic between China, the Middle East, and medieval Europe.[7] Finally, Gumilev studied the history of the Mongol empire, which in the twelfth and thirteenth centuries grew into the greatest land power the world had ever seen. He devoted a monograph to the legend of Prester John, a mythical patriarch of a Nestorian Christian realm located deep in the expanses

---

3. Gumilev 2004c, 318.
4. Gumilev 1994b.
5. Gumilev 1960; Gumilev 1974a.
6. Gumilev 1967a.
7. Gumilev 1966.

of Central Asia.[8] His principal interest, however, was the empire's northwestern sector—a khaganate known as the Golden Horde, which in the thirteenth century invaded and conquered the lands of ancient Russia. Although Gumilev's magnum opus on this subject was not published until 1989, shortly before his death, his research on the complex and diverse patterns of relations that developed between the Russians and the steppe nomads extended over decades and was the most significant and influential of all his historical work.[9] It forms the primary focus of this chapter.

Gumilev regarded all of these groups from the standpoint of ethnic history as he understood it, and everywhere he recognized the principles of ethnic interactions set forth in his theory of ethnogenesis. From the beginning, he believed, there had been a high degree of positive complementarity between the steppe peoples, and thus together they formed an aggregate multiethnic totality (*tselostnost'*)—a Eurasian community (*obshchnost'*) of which the Russians themselves would eventually become a natural part.[10] All these different ethnies were connected "not by a common way of life, culture, or language, but by sharing a common historical destiny. They were friends."[11] Although they did not form a superethnos *sensu stricto*, they enjoyed a sort of superethnic harmony that contrasted sharply with the hostility they encountered from the other superethnies confronting them on the open spaces of Eurasia. Chronologically, the first of these confrontations was between the Xiongnu and the Chinese. The latter viewed the former with contempt as barbaric nomad savages and were unceasingly aggressive in their relations with them. Indeed, Gumilev's account of this interaction was his first extended discussion of an ethnic chimera, created through the "collision" of these two incompatible superethnic traditions.[12] Centuries later, Islam and the West were also to intervene into the Eurasian arena, where they displayed a similar hostility and ill will toward the nomadic groups. It was, however, the relations with "people of Judaic belief" that would prove to be the most antagonistic and destructive of all for young Russia.[13]

Before considering the main lines along which Gumilev mapped out Russia's historical experience, one important and unusual aspect of his work should be noted. His naturalist understanding of ethnies and his emphasis on their close interconnection with their "environing" landscapes focused his attention on the

---

8. Gumilev 1970e; Gumilev 1987b.
9. Gumilev 1989b.
10. Gumilev 1987a.
11. Gumilev 1964a, 9.
12. Beliakov 2012a, 472.
13. Gumilev 1987a.

role of geographical factors in the historical development of these groups. This led Gumilev to an early version of what today is called "ecological" or "environmental history."[14] He explored these issues mostly in his early research before moving on to the more central questions that are the subject of this chapter. Because of the unconventionality of his environmentalist approach, however, and its unsubtle contravention of orthodox Soviet perspectives on the relations between society and the natural environment, Gumilev's work on these questions attracted a good deal of attention in the 1960s and 1970s, not only in the Soviet Union but among Western scholars as well. Specifically, Gumilev studied the impact of long-term climate and precipitation fluctuations across the Eurasian steppe. He reckoned that such fluctuations had been "strong and frequent" and had fundamentally affected the delicate ecological balance between sedentary agriculture and nomadic husbandry. These climatic fluctuations, in turn, were directly linked to the centuries of nomadic migrations crisscrossing the steppe in all directions.[15]

Gumilev's most detailed work on these questions related to the ancient Khaganate of Khazaria, which flourished on the Volga-Don steppes from the seventh to the tenth centuries. It was known that the greatest population densities of the Khazar state, focused around its capital city Itil, had been situated somewhere along the lower Volga north of the Caspian, but the precise location had never been determined. Working in collaboration with the geologist A.A. Aleksin and the ichthyologist V.N. Abrosov, Gumilev maintained that from the eighth century the Volga basin received ever-heavier inputs of moisture, causing the sea level of the Caspian to rise, a process that progressively inundated the low-lying territories of the Volga delta on its northern-western shore.[16] It was precisely here, he argued, that the capital Itil had been located, on the bountiful alluvial soils of the delta. As these agricultural lands, and eventually the city itself, became flooded, the Khazar population was pressed further to the north, to the lands of the central Volga and the Don.[17] Gumilev investigated archaeological as well as archival sources, and from 1959 through 1964 conducted a series of expeditions in the region. Through underwater excavations in the Volga delta, he uncovered what seemed to be traces of an urban settlement that, so he claimed, confirmed

---

14. On environmental history see Worster 1988; Simmons 1993; Hornborg et al. 2007.

15. Gumilev 1963; Gumilev 1967c; Gumilev 1972a. Gumilev was not the first historian of the steppe peoples to take this approach. The nineteenth-century Russian explorer Gregorii Efimovich Grumm-Grzhimailo (1860–1936) had emphasized geographical factors, as did the famous British historian and geographer Owen Lattimore (1900–1989). Lattimore 1940; Chappell 1970; Koreniako 2000. Gumilev frequently referred to Grumm-Grzhimailo's work; e.g., Gumilev 1976.

16. Aleksin and Gumilev 1962; Gumilev 1964a; Gumilev 1964c; Gumilev 1970d.

17. Gumilev 1987a.

his hypothesis. This was the "discovery" of Khazaria announced in the title of his 1966 book on the subject.[18]

The Emergence of Khazaria

What eventually emerged as Gumilev's primary interest in Khazaria, however, had nothing to do with this pathbreaking investigation into the links between climate, settlement patterns, and migration. In contrast to his iconoclastic foray into environmental history, moreover, his main interest related to concerns that were entirely mainstream in the Soviet historiography of his day. The subject of the Khazars and their relationship to ancient Russia had always been popular among Soviet historians.[19] The postrevolutionary decades pronounced a largely positive judgement on the relationship, and Gumilev's early mentor Mikhail Artamonov was one of the leading specialists on the subject. In the 1930s Artamonov claimed that Khazaria had had a progressive influence on the development of steppe culture and specifically that it had made a positive contribution to the early evolution of Russia itself. Khazaria, he maintained, had been "the most important basis for the formation of Kievan Rus."[20] This positive evaluation reflected the early Bolshevik critique of imperial Russian oppression of the steppe peoples, but it was also driven by the fact that Khazars, alone of all the steppe peoples, were known to have converted to Judaism. Although the precise details of this Jewish dimension were unclear, it meant that positive evaluations of the Khazars could also connect—albeit indirectly—with the early Soviet denunciation of tsarist oppression of the Jews. This interpretation endured until the final years of Stalin's reign when it fell victim to the anti-Semitic campaign against cosmopolitanism that would culminate in the notorious "Doctors' Plot" of 1953. In December 1951, *Pravda* published a front-page article loudly criticizing Artamonov for his "bourgeois idealization" of Khazar history. In fact, it was now asserted, Khazaria had always been a pernicious and hostile neighbor, conquering the lands of the eastern Slavs and interfering with Russia's early development.[21] This sudden interpretative inversion was quickly canonized. Artamonov and other specialists on Khazar history revised the conclusions of their earlier work to fit with the new line, and from the 1960s a new generation of specialists took up the task of elaborating the negative role that Khazaria was now deemed to have played in

18. Gumilev 1966.
19. Shnirelman 2002, 21–43; Rossman 2002b, 81–89.
20. Artamonov 1937, v–vi, cited in Shnirelman 2002, 25.
21. Ivanov 1951; Tillett 1969, 313–14.

the history of the steppe and the early Russian state.[22] From various angles, their work depicted Khazaria—always closely identified with Jews and Judaism—as an "absolute evil" whose aim had always been to "hinder the progressive development of Rus'."[23]

This generation included Gumilev. As we will see, his work on Khazar history would eventually emerge as its most influential and enduring, if not its most academically credible, product. In Gumilev's retelling, the negative view of Khazaria was pushed to its very limits. Gumilev treated Khazaria as his most fully developed historical illustration of an ethnic chimera: how it originated, what its internal deformations involved, and what sort of effect it could have on the course of other peoples and ethnic history in general. From this standpoint, Khazaria has a central place in Gumilev's scientific exposition of his ethnos theory. At the same time, the life of this particular chimera intersected with that of the eastern Slavs in a manner that shaped the latter's subsequent development and indeed continued to affect Russia to the present day. For these reasons, Gumilev's analysis of the Khazar-Russian nexus is also a major aspect of his historical interpretation of ancient Rus'.[24]

The Khazars originated as a collection of Turkic tribes occupying the Dagestani plains around the Terek River in the northern Caucasus. They were an ancient peoples, mentioned in Byzantine, Armenian, and Persian sources in the fourth and fifth centuries. At about this time, Gumilev maintained, changes in precipitation patterns across western Eurasia led to the increase of moisture in the Volga basin, which significantly transformed the arid steppe landscape.[25] As a result, the Khazars gradually shifted their activities to the newly formed oases of the Volga delta, which offered good protection against predatory steppe nomads. Here, concentrated around their major settlement of Itil, they continued with their traditional pursuits of agriculture, orchardry, and fishing.[26] At this time, Gumilev explained, the Khazars were a relict ethnos, languishing in the final phases of their ethnogenetic cycle. With their passionary charge exhausted, they

---

22. Artamonov 1962; Rybakov 1953; Shnirelman 2002, 31–34.

23. Shnirelman 2002, 42–43.

24. As noted, Gumilev developed his expertise on Khazar history under the tutelage of Artamonov himself from the mid-1930s. After the war, Gumilev participated in a series of Artamonov's archaeological digs at ancient Khazar sites, and after his final release from the camps in 1956, Artamonov gave Gumilev a position in the library at the Hermitage. As Shnirel'man points out, even after the 1951 attack in *Pravda*, Artamonov's revision of his Khazar history was halfhearted and unsatisfactory from the standpoint of the new negative perspective. Some sources claim that those parts of Artamonov's 1962 study that presented a critical view of the Khazars were not actually written by him at all but by Gumilev, who was working under him at the time. Sobolev 1997. For a dissenting view, see Shnirelman 2002, 39–40.

25. Gumilev 2004c, 27–29; also see Gumilev 1964c; Gumilev 1967c.

26. Gumilev 2004c, 32, 115–16, 129.

lived in a homeostatic state of ecological harmony and balance with the steppe landscape. The normal progression of their ethnogenetic cycle was, however, interrupted in the sixth century. In 588, the Khazars were conquered and became part of the Göktürk empire, a powerful Inner Asian confederation of nomadic tribes. Although Göktürk domination was not to last beyond the middle of the next century, it fundamentally transformed the ethnogenetic destiny of the Khazars. The nomadic Göktürk warriors used Khazar territory as a base of operations and mingled freely with the indigenous population, bringing forth entire generations of progeny with mixed parentage. Among other things, Gumilev explained, this resulted in "genetic drift" that reinfused the aging Khazar ethnos with substantial doses of fresh foreign *passionarnost'*. The effect was to turn back the Khazar ethnogenetic clock many centuries, transforming "this relict into an active and functioning ethnos."[27] For the century and a half after the end of Göktürk domination around 650, the revived Khazar ethnos developed normally, strengthening its political organization and emerging as a significant presence on the Pontic-Caspian steppe.

The Khazars developed peaceful and harmonious interactions with all of their neighboring ethnies. There was only one exception, but it would prove to be fateful. This was the Jews. Originally, Khazar contacts were with Jewish tribes in the North Caucasus. The latter were adherents of Karaite Judaism or Karaism, which did not recognize the authority of the Mishnah or Talmud. Gumilev claimed that this doctrinal independence brought them closer in spirit to Christianity and Islam than to the mainstream tradition of Rabbinic Judaism, in which the Torah and received Mosaic oral law were taken as the divine authority.[28] Significantly, the relationship between the two groups were peaceful and friendly—a good example of a symbiosis in which ethnies "live side by side, not seeking to change each other's ways and thus not interfering with each other."[29] This natural fabric of Khazar-Jewish interaction was, however, torn apart in the seventh century as a new stream of Jewish immigrants fleeing persecution in Persia and Byzantium poured into the Eurasian steppe.[30] These newcomers were Radhanite (Radaniya) Jews—medieval merchants active in the lucrative commercial networks and trade routes that connected the Christian and Islamic worlds with the Far East during the early Middle Ages. Unlike the Karaites, the Radhanites were faithful followers of the Rabbinic tradition, an orientation that, so Gumilev claimed, made them elitist and influence seeking.[31]

---

27. Gumilev 2004c, 32, 37–38.
28. Gumilev 2004c, 119; Shnirelman 2002, 49.
29. Gumilev 2004c, 108–9, 529.
30. Gumilev 2004c, 690.
31. Ibid., 110.

More problematic than their doctrinal bias, however, was the fact that the Jewish merchant caste had been irretrievably alienated from its native ecological niche and thus lost its sustaining connections with the natural environment. This situation served to distort their ethnic characteristics. Under the conditions of diaspora, the Jews "mastered not the natural but the anthropogenic landscape—cities and caravan routes. The necessary link between the landscape and ethnos became gradually deformed, and this sufficed to turn the [normal] ethnic system into a brutal (*zhestkii*) ethnos . . . automatically excluded from the course of natural development."[32] The ultimate effect was the creation of an ethnic formation that was by its very nature amoral, without scruples, and fixated exclusively on its own gain. The monopolization of the caravan trade brought the Radhanites fabulous wealth, which came in significant measure from unscrupulous usurious practices and a willingness to barter in contraband items that other traders would not touch, most notoriously slaves taken from the hapless indigenous populations of eastern Europe and Eurasia.[33] To illustrate his point, Gumilev compared Radhanite practices with the criminal activities of the Soviet underworld such as "illicit hard-currency operations and narcotics deals."[34]

Attracted by the strategic proximity of the Khazar capital Itil to a number of important caravan routes, these Jewish merchants settled there in large numbers and by the eighth century they had become a major presence. In Gumilev's account, they repeated the Göktürk practice of intermarriage with the local population, with the difference that now the Jewish spouses were women rather than men. Because the Jews were matrilineal and the Khazars, like other steppe peoples, were patrilineal, the children of these mixed marriages formed a special caste recognized as members of both groups. Accordingly, they enjoyed special rights and privileges.[35] In this manner, Gumilev explained, the Radhanite merchants came to form a sort of quasi-foreign elite that connived its way to the center of Khazar society and gained ever-increasing political influence. They drew their power from the long-distance commercial networks they operated and remained detached from the indigenous peoples, both the ethnic Khazars and the Karaite Jews. The situation came to a head in the early ninth century when the Jewish prince Obadiah seized power and made Rabbinic Judaism the official religion of state. Gumilev describes this as a "coup" (*perevorot*) and a "power grab" undertaken by Obadiah as an agent of the international "elders of

---

32. Ibid., 123.
33. Ibid., 103, 114–18, 117, 130, 200.
34. Ibid., 114.
35. Ibid., 118–19, 125.

Israel" (*mudretsy izrail'skie*), who provided the finances and organization.[36] His move was resisted by the local population, which waged a bloody civil war against it. Although the mass of ethnic Khazars were eventually constrained to submit to the authority of the Jewish elite, Gumilev was adamant that they never actually converted to Judaism, which remained exclusively a faith of the nobility and the political *verkhushka*, or high-level authorities.[37]

With this, Gumilev concluded, Khazaria was transformed into a full-fledged ethnic chimera. Internally, the indigenous Khazar population was disenfranchised and terrorized by a ruthless and despotic elite obsessed with its own enrichment and nothing else. "In their very own country," he observed, the Khazars were converted from a proud independent ethnos into "the conquered, disenfranchised, and powerless subjects of a government that was foreign to them in terms of its ethnicity, its religion, and it goals."[38] Gumilev described the tyranny of the Jewish authorities toward these subjects once again in the stark language of the twentieth century, characterizing the opposition of the two as a "total war" in which the powers that be would spare nothing and no one in order to secure their domination. Most poignantly, Gumilev indicated, this included the sale of Khazar children into enslavement. "The very saddest aspect was the fact that the children of the idol-worshipping Khazars were sold on the slave markets in Islamic countries, whereas neither the Jews nor the Christians sold their own coreligionists into slavery. It is evident that the local population of Khazaria, deprived of even a basic form of communal organization, was completely defenceless against the threats of tax collectors who were foreign to them by blood and religion."[39] The domination of the Jews was also now enhanced, ironically, by the very environmental changes that had made the Khazar occupation of the Volga delta possible in the first place. Precipitation levels had continued to increase throughout the ninth century and

---

36. Ibid., 122–23. The point was important enough for Gumilev to emphasize in his correspondence with Petr Savitskii in the 1950s. Letter to P. N. Savitskii, 19 December 1956 (personal archive of the author).

37. Gumilev 2004c, 109, 122, 125–26. Gumilev's insistence that the Khazar masses had never converted to Judaism was very important. Among other things, it meant that he rejected the thesis, advanced by Arthur Koestler, among others, that the indigenous Eurasian Khazars formed an additional "thirteenth" Judaic tribe and that they—rather than the historical Israelites—were the ancestors of the European Ashkenazi Jews. In general, Gumilev was at pains to deny any identification of the Jews as a authentically "nomadic" people, who might then have genuine affinities to other nomadic groups of the Eurasian steppes. Unlike the former, he insisted, real nomads maintained a natural and healthy connection with their particular ecological niche. Gumilev 1992b, 5; Koestler 1976; Rossman 2002b, 87–88; Beliakov 2012a, 574. The politics of this point would become significant for post-Soviet historiography on the Khazars: see below, 266–72.

38. Gumilev 2004c, 128.

39. Ibid., 131 (quote); 126, 128.

the levels of the Volga and Caspian continued to rise, with the result that some of the best agricultural land in the region became inundated and infertile. This was problematic not only for the Khazars, whose livelihood depended on their crops and who thus were driven ever further into the drier lands of the steppe, but for all of the steppe peoples. The only group not to suffer was Khazaria's Judaic merchant elite. Their commercial activities, Gumilev argued, remained largely unaffected by these ecological changes, and indeed they actually benefitted from the weakening of their subjects and neighbors. "A weak enemy," he point out, "is not dangerous."[40]

Khazars and Russians

The transformation of Khazaria into an ethnic chimera created what Gumilev called a "merchant octopus" that sought to become a powerful empire with influence extending across the Eurasian steppes and beyond.[41] To support this endeavor it formed an elaborate international network of alliances with major foreign powers, including the Tan dynasty in China, the Carolingians and their successors in Germany, the Bagdad caliphate, and the Varangians from Scandinavia. All of these powers were naturally hostile to the peoples of Eurasia and eastern Europe, for whom the "Judeo-Khazars" themselves had nothing but contempt—indeed they were determined to crush their independence and absorb them as vassal subjects into their burgeoning imperial domains. In the 830s, the fortress settlement of Sarkel on the lower Don River was established in order to facilitate the extension of Khazar power to the west and northwest.[42] The Khazars themselves were reluctant soldiers, however, preferring to hire mercenary armies and to achieve their goals by means of intrigue, deception, and betrayal.[43] One of the clearest examples was the encounter with the ancient Russians of the Rus′ Khaganate, which represented one of the principal targets of Khazar hostility.

Gumilev's explanation of Russia's interactions with the steppe peoples can only be understood in light of his complicated account of Russian ethnogenesis. Despite his own insistence on the strict universality and inviolability of the ethnogenetic process, it turned out that the Russian people, entirely exceptionally, underwent not one but two consecutive ethnogenetic cycles.[44] The first cycle occurred in the first century AD when a collection of ancient tribes. including

40. Ibid., 164–66, 194.
41. Ibid., 146
42. Ibid., 157.
43. Ibid., 128.
44. Ibid., 23; Laruelle 2000, 183.

the Skoloty, Rosomony, and Anty, merged to form a new ethnos. He referred to this entity variously as ancient Rus', Slavo-Rus', Slavo-Rossy, Rusichi, or simply Slavs. The passionary surge that brought this particular group into existence was part of an ethnogenetic wave sweeping from southern Sweden to Abyssinia.[45] Very little is known about the early life of this ethnos, and it was not until its inertia phase, from about 800 to 1100, that the historical record began to offer a more detailed picture. The principal event of this period was the emergence of the first Russo-Slavic state, initially in the form of the so-called Rus' Khaganate (late eighth to mid-ninth centuries) and then its direct successor Kievan Rus'.[46] The Rus' Khaganate was centered around the northern settlement of Holmgard (present-day Novgorod). Its population was mixed, with significant Finnic and Norse elements, and it was a major base of operations for the eastern Varangians as well. The "Slavo-Rossy" peoples, however, formed the largest and predominant ethnic group. With the decline of the Rus' Khaganate, Kievan Rus' represented the final stage of Slavo-Rus' ethnogenesis.[47]

In 859, Gumilev maintained, the Khazars made a pact with Varangian "factions" (Gumilev also called them "Normans") in Novgorod, committing them to support a Varangian attack on the Rus' Khaganate. "Two predators—the Radhanites and the Vikings—agreed on a division" of the lands of the Slavo-Rossy into their respective "spheres of conquest."[48] As a result of Khazar instigation, the Varangian prince Oleg led a successful campaign over the following years against settlements on the Dnieper, which culminated in successful attacks on Kiev and Smolensk in 882.[49] After this, the capital of the Rus' Khaganate was moved to Kiev and became Kievan Rus', with the victorious Oleg as the first grand prince of the Rurik dynasty. Gumilev described these events as a foreign Varangian "usurpation" by a "scheming politician," although it was clearly the Khazars themselves who inspired it and ultimately were to benefit most.[50] In the course of Oleg's subsequent reign, the Varangians were increasingly subject to Khazar demands for tribute and for their services as military proxies. Gumilev claimed that Kievan Rus' campaigns against neighboring steppe peoples—in particular Oleg's celebrated raid against Constantinople in 911—were all the result of Khazar instigation. The Varangians at Kiev "became vassals of the Khazar Jews, who used the Slavo-Rus' population in their wars against the Christians and the Muslims and suppressed the indigenous pagan tribes [of the steppe] with

45. Gumilev 1991e, 133.
46. Gumilev 2004c, 142–43, 261, 266; Gumilev 2000, 288–89.
47. Gumilev 2004c, 23.
48. Ibid., 154.
49. Ibid., 168.
50. Ibid., 173, 181, 183.

the arms of these mercenaries." None of this had anything to do with the natural inclinations or genuine interests of the native Slavo-Rossy population.[51]

By the end of Oleg's reign, the Khazars had significantly strengthened their position. "If in the mid-ninth century the Khazar Jews negotiated with the Normans about the division of eastern Europe," Gumilev explained, then by the beginning of the tenth century the former "had managed to seize nearly everything." They had become a true "hegemonic power" (*gegemon*) whose sphere of domination included the peoples and territories of the middle and upper Volga, the Kama, Oka, and Desna Rivers, and beyond.[52] The plight of Kievan Rus' grew progressively worse. Oleg's successor Igor' (912–945) continued to offer tribute to the Khazars, but this no longer satisfied the latter's avarice. In 941, Khazar armies led by Pesakh defeated the forces of the Kievan prince. With this, Gumilev concluded, Kievan Rus' was formally subordinated to the Khazars. The entire Slavo-Rus' population of the Dnieper was now subjected to ever more rapacious demands for tribute in the form of goods or mercenary warriors, all faithfully rendered up to the Khazars by their vassals, the Varangian princes.[53] The Khazars, for their part, used the rich resources plundered from the Russian lands to further augment their control of the "world market."[54]

Happily, young Russia did not have long to suffer the oppressive weight of Khazar domination and Varangian collusion. After Igor's death by assassination in 945, his wife Olga ascended to the throne and ruled as regent until 963. Gumilev credits her with resisting Varangian domination within Kievan Rus' and transforming the ethno-political dynamics that shaped state policies. Most important, Olga was the first Russian ruler to convert to Christianity, an act so politically incendiary that Gumilev claims she kept it a deep secret until the mid-950s. And indeed, he claimed, this conversion signaled the complete inversion of Kievan Rus' foreign relations, laying the basis for an eventual rapprochement with Byzantium at the same time that it set a collision course with their Jewish-Khazar overlords. Gumilev suggests that the implicit challenge to Khazaria was very much part of Olga's intentions, although she was herself unable to consummate it through a direct confrontation. Olga "resurrected [the genuine] Slavic-Russian tradition and set Kievan Rus' back onto the course it had been following prior to the Varangian usurpation," with consequences that proved to be "most beneficial for the Russian lands and most difficult for the Jewish elite in Khazaria."[55] Olga was succeeded by

51. Ibid., 169 (quote), 162.
52. Ibid., 166.
53. Ibid., 180, 184.
54. Ibid., 181–82.
55. Ibid., 185.

her son Sviatoslav (962–972), a warrior prince who continued her policies of promoting Slavo-Rus' welfare and opposing their natural enemies. Sviatoslav immediately undertook a series of military campaigns against Russia's steppe neighbors to the east and south, with the Khazars very much in his sights. In 965, he seized the fortress of Sarkel and pressed his offensive further, descending the Volga several years later in a campaign that devastated the Khazar capital Itil. The abrupt destruction of Khazaria had far-reaching international consequences, Gumilev argued, but most important were the implications for Kievan Rus' itself.[56] Freed at last from the interference of this chimeric menace, it could end its historical "zigzag" and return to a more normal pattern of ethnogenetic development.

Rus' and the Golden Horde

By the time of the removal of the Khazar menace in the second half of the tenth century, the Slavo-Rus' ethnos had entered its inertia phase, with the slow but steady dissipation of its remaining passionary charge. This phase was to last until around 1100, during which time ancient Russian civilization reached its zenith. The political organization of the Kievan state was highly developed, and there was an efflorescence of culture, learning, and the arts—a classic example of the "Golden Age" that Gumilev typically associated with this advanced moment in the ethnogenetic cycle. Then, in the eleventh and twelfth centuries, ethnogenetic inertia gradually gave way to the phase of obscuration and Kievan Rus' entered its final period of decline. The state structure began to fragment into hostile principalities, cultural production languished, and in general the population grew ever weaker and more languid. The stage was set for a natural culmination of the ethnogenetic cycle in a memorial phase, which—in the normal course of events according to Gumilev's scheme—should have witnessed the "complete extinction of the relict ethnies" of Kievan Rus'.[57] For a second time, however, the normal course of events was interrupted by external intervention, and ancient Rus' was diverted once again onto a historical zigzag. This second detour, however, would bring about a historical transformation with profound consequences. Effectively, it would set in train a second cycle of ethnogenetic development, the grand product of which would be the modern Russian nation.

This time, the hostile challenge came not from the steppe but from the West. A "Romano-Germanic superethnos" had begun to form in the ninth century, Gumilev explained, and by the twelfth and thirteenth centuries it reached its

56. Ibid., 193.
57. Gumilev 2000, 289.

acmatic phase.[58] Bursting with passionary energy, it was obsessively driven by a "grandiose striving . . . for world domination, which would destroy all ethnies who could not defend themselves." The ambition of this superethnos was twofold. "Politically, this was a striving to incorporate territories that had been seized from the Russians, while ideologically it represented the dissemination of [foreign] ideas, views, judgements, tastes—in short, a *mentalité*."[59] The protracted aggression of the Teutonic Order in this period against the "infidels" of the northeast—the pagan peoples of the eastern Baltic littoral and Orthodox Rus'—was the practical expression of this superethnic ambition.[60] The deep significance that the West attached to this struggle was apparent in a series of papal endorsements. In the 1230s Pope Gregory IX gave his blessing to the so-called Northern Crusades that aimed to conquer Novgorod and other important towns in the northwest of Kievan Rus', and at the Council of Lyons in 1245 Pope Innocent IV denounced the East-West schism within Christianity and called for the Eastern Church to be brought back under the authority of Rome.[61] The Teutonic knights were indeed able to score a series of important strategic advances, until they were finally stopped by the young Russian prince Aleksandr Iaroslavich Nevskii (1220–1263), who at the famous "Battle of the Ice" on Lake Peipus in 1242 heroically repulsed an attack on Novgorod, Pskov, and Izborsk. While the Teutonic Order was attacking in the northwest, moreover, the hostile forces of Catholic Lithuania were advancing against Kievan Rus' on the southwestern front in the thirteenth and fourteenth centuries, seizing significant territories and everywhere subjecting the "Russians" (*Russkie*) to "abject servitude."[62]

In his resistance to Western aggression, Gumilev maintained, Aleksandr Nevskii had important allies. Beginning with an attack in the early 1220s, Kievan Rus' had been subjected to invasion by the nomadic armies of the Jochi Ulus, the westernmost khaganate of the Chingizid Mongol empire known more commonly as the *Zolotaia Orda* or Golden Horde. Its armies were led by Genghis Khan's grandson Batu. The Slavic population was powerless to resist these mounted predators, and in a concentrated onslaught from 1237 to 1241 town after town fell under their control, culminating in the conquest of Kiev itself. Only the geographical isolation of the settlements of Pskov and Novgorod in the far northwest spared them from attack. The ancient Russian chronicles provided ample record of the ferocity of the attacks and the brutality of Batu's armies, which pitilessly ravaged the cities of Kievan Rus' and left its population

58. Gumilev 2004c, 74.
59. Ibid., 331.
60. Gumilev 2000, 121–22; Gumilev 1980a, 16; Gumilev 1989h, 34.
61. Gumilev 1995, 39; Gumilev 1991e, 135.
62. Gumilev 1991e, 136; Gumilev 2000, 139–41.

decimated and scattered. The fall of Kiev marked the beginning of two and a half centuries of domination by the Golden Horde. Although the latter did not physically occupy the lands of ancient Rus', it used the local Russian authorities as its agents to collect taxes and maintain its dominating influence.

Together with his depiction of Russian-Khazar interactions, Gumilev's interpretation of the relationship between Russia and the Golden Horde forms the basis of his entire vision of ancient Russian history. In contrast to Khazaria, however, in the case of the Mongols his views were sharply revisionist, opposed not only to official views but to mainstream historiography and even popular conceptions as well. Traditionally, the period of domination by the Tatar khans had been seen by the Russians as one of great suffering and sacrifice—a veritable Mongol or Tatar *igo* or yoke during which the hapless Russo-Slavic population languished under brutal Asiatic domination. This negative perspective was generally supported in Soviet historiography, which regarded the political, social, and moral level of the barbarian Mongols as "far inferior to that of the sedentary and civilized Russians; thus Russian borrowing of Mongol institutions was unthinkable." The only effect of the Mongols on Russian history was seen to be destructive. They razed cities, deported or massacred populations, and wrecked the economy.[63] "This yoke was a terrible force," confirmed an authoritative text from the 1960s, "which stood in the path of the development of the Russian people and the other nations of our country. It represented the greatest evil, which put a brake on all historical progress," above all the political "unification of the "Russian [*russkii*] people" within a single state structure.[64]

Gumilev rejected this popular view loudly and unceremoniously and offered his own alternative interpretation of the relations between ancient Rus' and the Golden Horde. Historical accounts of Tatar rapacity and devastation, he insisted, were not merely exaggerated but fundamentally incorrect. The thirty thousand troops that Batu commanded were simply insufficient to wreak such damage on Kievan Rus', which itself could mobilize over one hundred thousand. The famous attacks of 1237–1241 amounted to "nothing more than a big raid" (*bol'shoi nabeg*), the goal of which was not the conquest of Rus' at all but rather to extract revenge as part of a "steppe vendetta" with another nomadic people, the Polovtsy.[65] Ultimately, the Golden Horde wanted nothing more than to secure its boundaries between the Don and Volga Rivers, and any notion of conquest of the indigenous Slavic population was far from their minds. "They did not annex the Russian lands and populations to their own domains," he pointed out. They "did not attempt to subjugate the population of Kievan Rus', but rather sought

---

63. Halperin 1983, 239 (quote); Shlapentokh 2011, 108; Tillett 1969, 79, 89, 104n.
64. Smirnov 1963, 81 (quote); Nechkina and Leibengrub 1970, 74–77.
65. Gumilev 1991e, 134.

only to establish reliable boundaries that could provide security for their own country against the attacks of powerful and merciless enemies."[66] "There can be no question about a Mongol conquest of Rus'. They did not leave their garrisons behind [after they withdrew], and they had no thought about establishing permanent control. At the end of his campaign Batu withdrew to the Volga, where he built his camp at the town of Sarai. He limited himself to destroying only those towns that were on the path of his armies and that instead of making peace with the Mongols had offered armed resistance."[67]

Gumilev was prepared to acknowledge only one exception to this latter point: the destruction of the town of Kozel'sk in 1238, the exceptional brutality of which was richly documented in the Russian chronicles. Even in that case, however, Gumilev tried to justify the attackers' behavior, arguing that the Slavic population of the town had brutally murdered two envoys who the nomads, in a sincere attempt to negotiate terms of surrender, had dispatched into the town. With this, Gumilev suggested, the townspeople themselves effectively invited the retribution they received.[68] Ancient Rus' was not "conquered" at all, he concluded, but had subjugated itself "voluntarily" (dobrovol'no) to Mongol authority.[69]

If there had been no bloody conquest, then neither had the ensuing centuries witnessed the ruthless domination of ancient Rus' by the Golden Horde. The notorious Tatar yoke, Gumilev maintained, was a historical fiction, an elaborate myth concocted in later centuries by anti-Russian agents in the West. He gave his own name to the myth, calling it the *Chernaia Legenda* or "Black Legend," originally fabricated by Russia's European enemies with the intention of dividing the Turkic and Slavic peoples, setting them against each other, and thereby weakening the Russian state.[70] This false version of events was then unwittingly

---

66. Gumilev 1995, 38–39.

67. Gumilev 2000, 121.

68. Gumilev 1991e, 134. The execution of their negotiators or ambassadors was indeed considered a very serious offence by the Mongols. Weatherford 2004, 139, 142.

69. Gumilev 1991e, 136.

70. Gumilev 1994a. In fact, the expression "Black Legend" was not really Gumilev's. Although he never explained its origins, the term represents his adaptation for Russian purposes of the notorious *Leyenda Negra*, coined in the early twentieth century by the Spanish historian Julián Juderías y Loyot (1877–1919). Juderías used the term to refer to a campaign of demonization of Spain initiated in Europe in the late sixteenth century, which sought to depict the Iberian empire as a bastion of brutal repression, religious intolerance, and overall backwardness. According to Juderías, this was a profound historical distortion fabricated by Spain's European competitors for the ideological purposes of morally discrediting—and hence politically weakening—their rival. Juderías 1914; Keen 1969; Maltby 1971. In adopting this particular term, Gumilev was indicating that the notion of an oppressive *tatarskoe igo* represented the same sort of opportunistic ideological demonization, manufactured by hostile European powers determined to undermine their competitor in the east. Gumilev claimed that author of his *Chernaia Legenda* was the early-modern French historian Jacques Auguste de Thou (1553–1617), who relied on Sigismund von Herberstein's (1486–1566) highly critical work on Russia: *Rerum Moscoviticarum Commentarii*. Gumilev 1989j.

taken up in Russia itself, first by Westernizers and then eventually by most Russian historians, who based their entire understanding of early Russian history on it. In fact, however, the pattern of relations between Rus' and the Mongols displayed a strong positive complementarity, "based on national and religious toleration" that in ethnogenetic terms was entirely normal and natural.[71] An important source of this mutual appeal was the fact that many of the Mongols were Nestorians, a fifth-century Christian sect that had spread broadly across the Middle East and Central Asia. Nestorianism was particularly active in the twelfth century and for its adherents was an obvious source of affinity with Orthodox Rus'. And even when the Golden Horde eventually opted for Islam as its official religion of state, it did not attempt to impose this foreign belief on the Slavo-Rus' population, but rather allowed the latter the freedom to pursue their native beliefs.[72] Indeed, the adoption of Islam ultimately served to strengthen the interconnection of the two groups, for many of those Nestorians who were unwilling to embrace the new faith sought refuge among the Orthodox—or "emigrated," as Gumilev put it—where they became a part of early Russian society.[73]

Gumilev's insistence on the complementarity and friendship between the Slavo-Rus' and the steppe nomads led him to challenge standard interpretations of one of the most important literary monuments in Russian history: the epic poem *The Song of Igor's Campaign*. Dating from the late twelfth century, the poem is generally believed to describe an unsuccessful raid mounted in 1185 by Prince Igor Svyatoslavich against the nomadic Polovtsians, who inhabited the southern part of the Don region. Critically rejecting the scholarship of leading authorities, including the eminent historian of Russian culture Dmitrii Sergeevich Likhachev (1906–1999), Gumilev refused to accept *The Song* as evidence of hostility on the part of Kievan Rus' toward the steppe peoples. In a final chapter to his book *Searches for an Imaginary Kingdom* tellingly entitled "Overcoming Our Self-Deception," he sensationally maintained that the poem was not a genuine expression of patriotic national sentiments at all, but rather was the creation of "pro-Western" agents. Deliberately crafted to be misleading, *The Song* effectively invented an antagonism between the two groups in order better to manipulate and control them.[74]

---

71. Gumilev 2000, 132 (quote); Gumilev and Ivanov 1992, 55–56.
72. Gumilev 1989a.
73. Gumilev 1994e, 369; Gumilev 1995, 41; Gumilev 1991e, 136. On Gumilev's idiosyncratic emphasis on the importance of Nestorianism, see Laruelle 2000, 182n; Morgan 1989.
74. Gumilev 1994e, 294–95; Halperin 1982b, 318n.

This latter argument brings us back to Aleksandr Nevskii, whose own experience Gumilev offered as one of the most important examples of interethnic complementarity between the Slavs and the Tatars. After his victory in 1242, Nevskii sought the aid of Batu's forces in his ongoing struggle "against the pressure from the West—the *Drang nach Osten*—and to halt the advance of the Germans, who wanted to reduce the remnants of the ancient Russian population to serfdom."[75] In 1251 he traveled to meet Batu and befriended his son Sartaq, a Nestorian. In an elaborate Mongol ritual the two swore eternal brotherhood. With this, Gumilev explained, Nevskii became a step-son of the great khan and was able to form an alliance with him against their common foe.[76] The alliance continued after Nevskii's death in 1263. In 1268, in the wake of the inconclusive Battle of Rakovor, the Teutonic knights—driven by their inherent "Catholic aggression"—prepared to launch a fresh assault against Novgorod. In the city itself, however, "in accordance with its agreement with the Golden Horde," five hundred mounted warriors from the Mongol cavalry appeared and the Western enemy was "terrified away without even engaging in battle." For his part, Nevskii sent his own troops to help the Golden Horde in its struggles against the Alans and other nomadic groups.[77] The practical benefits of this alliance were enormous, for it brought "much-desired peace and a secure order" and enabled ancient Rus' to resist the encroachment of the forces of the West. This successful early resistance, moreover, was the key to Russia's later profile as a *velikaia derzhava* or great power. "In the final analysis, Russia (*Rossiia*) emerged as a great power in those places where the Russian princes requested help from the Tatars."[78] Ultimately, Gumilev described the close relationship between ancient Rus' and the Golden Horde "not as the subjugation (*pokorenie*) of Rus' by the Golden Horde" but rather as an "ethnic symbiosis," a union between two ethnies for their mutual benefit.[79] The Tatars "defended Rus' from attacks from the West . . . in the way that a shepherd defends his flock from the wolves."[80]

---

75. Gumilev and Balashov 1993, 145 (quote); Gumilev 1994e, 173–74, 295–96. On Gumilev and Nevskii's "anti-Occidentalism," see Schenk 2004, 452–53n.

76. Gumilev 2001, 124–25; Gumilev 1994e, 133; Gumilev 1991e, 135; Gumilev 1989c, 357.

77. Gumilev 2000, 130–31; Gumilev 1991e, 134–35; Gumilev 1980a, 16. Gumilev took care to point out, however, that Novgorod did not really appreciate Nevskii. This was because the city was governed "by supporters of the West," who deployed the "democratic" procedure of voting in the city's popular assembly (*Veche*). Gumilev 2000, 126. Gumilev made these points during perestroika, and his characterization of Novgorod's medieval democracy as traitorous had an obviously contemporary resonance. Gumilev's politics are more fully discussed in chapters 7 and 8.

78. Gumilev and Balashov 1993, 145 (quote); Gumilev 1995, 42–43; Gumilev 2000, 129–31.

79. Gumilev 1991e, 135; Gumilev 1980a, 17.

80. Gumilev 1994c, 310.

Ethnogenetic Catharsis at Kulikovo

In the fourteenth century, the symbiotic union between Rus' and the Golden Horde was profoundly destabilized and the lands of Rus' subjected once again to an existential danger. This time, the sources of the disruption came not from the West but from elements among the nomads themselves. As Gumilev explained, by the early 1300s the unity of what he called the "nomadic superethnos," made up of the various peoples of the far-flung Chingizid empire, was beginning to fracture. A period of intense internecine struggle ensued, extending geographically from the Carpathians to the Pacific.[81] The Golden Horde itself was increasingly divided between its western and eastern halves—the so-called Blue and White hordes—which competed for dominance. This conflict was exacerbated in the 1310s by the issue of religious confession. Up to that point, the Mongols had been largely pagan, with a significant number of Nestorian Christians. In 1312, Gumilev explained, the prince Uzbek seized power in Sarai and proclaimed Islam as the state religion. A harsh and brutal autocrat, he demanded that all of his subjects convert to the new faith, which as we have noted produced a stream of refugees to Orthodox Rus'. Uzbek's ascendance was not legitimate—Gumilev again uses the term *uzurpator* to describe him—and his new policies quickly disrupted the natural harmony that had characterized relations between the Golden Horde and ancient Rus'.[82] Islamic society was deeply corrupted by degenerate practices, Gumilev maintained, notably its harem culture, which undermined the endogamy necessary to maintain ethnic integrity. By the end of the eleventh century, Islam had degenerated into a chimeric antisystem.[83] More specifically, it had become a "principled opponent" of the interests of the Russo-Slavs, and so a new round of conflict became inevitable.[84]

In the 1370s, the military commander Mamai (1335–1380) seized control of the Blue Horde. He was not a scion of the Chingizid line and did not enjoy broad support within the Golden Horde. Consequently, his position was insecure, and in his ambition to extend his authority he was forced to rely on support from external allies. An "outspoken *zapadnik*" in Gumilev's description, he sought supporters primarily among wealthy Catholic merchants from Genoa, who had a major presence in Byzantium and on the Black Sea in the fourteenth century. These merchants were most interested in territorial concessions from the Rus' lands to allow them to exploit the fur trade. Mamai also concluded alliances with the

---

81. Gumilev 1980b: 34–37.
82. Gumilev 2000, 137–38.Gumilev 1991e, 135.
83. Gumilev 2004c, 332; Graham 1987, 225; Laruelle 2000, 185.
84. Gumilev and Ivanov 1992, 56.

Lithuanians, the Polovtsy, and the Crimean Jews.[85] For Gumilev, this network of alliances brought the process of ethnic degeneration begun decades earlier to its culmination. Those parts of the Golden Horde under Mamai's leadership had become a full-fledged chimera, determined "to attract their active neighbors—the Russians, Polovtsy, Mordvinians, and the Tatars themselves—into [a web of] decay and stagnation, to weaken and destroy them, having smashed their spiritual resistance."[86] The Russo-Slavs, for their part, recognized Mamai as their natural enemy and were reluctant to cooperate. In 1378, Mamai sent his warlord Murza Begich to enforce the obedience of the prince of Moscow. He was met and defeated by the forces of Dmitrii Ivanovich (1350–1389), son of Tsar Ivan II, in a battle near the river Vozha, a tributary of the Oka. Mamai then resolved to lead a second assault himself against Moscow two years later. He assembled a massive force of 150,000 soldiers and reconfirmed his alliances with the Genoan merchants and the Lithuanians, both of whom agreed to send reinforcements.[87] However, while Mamai awaited these troops at a camp near the Kulikovo field on the Don River in early September 1380, Russian forces led by Dmitrii attacked, and despite their inferior numbers were able once again to inflict a decisive defeat. Dmitrii was honored with the title "Donskoi" to reflect the location of this grand victory.

In securing this victory, Gumilev maintained that Dmitrii had a vital ally. Mamai was also opposed by the leader of the rival White Horde Tokhtamysh (d. 1406), a genuine descendant of Genghis Khan and thus a legitimate pretender to the leadership of the Golden Horde. Tokhtamysh wanted to bring the Blue and White hordes back together in order to restore the original superethnic unity of the steppe empire, in which endeavor, according to Gumilev, he enjoyed the support of the Moscow princes.[88] In 1381, as Mamai was regrouping his forces and preparing for a renewed assault on Moscow, he was attacked and routed by Tokhtamysh in a battle on the Kalka River. After this, Mamai fled to the Crimea, where he was assassinated by own Genoan allies. Tokhtamysh now turned his attention to Moscow and led an attack of his own in 1382. After an initial assault was beaten back, he laid siege to the city. When his forces finally gained access, they proceeded to slaughter the population, and tens of thousands perished. Gumilev did not deny the brutality of the nomadic armies, but once again he found a deeper justification for it. The real culprits, he explained, were the Slavic princes of Suzdal, who were hostile to Moscow and to Dmitrii in particular. They

---

85. Gumilev 2000, 158; Gumilev 1980b, 34–35; Gumilev 1991e, 137; Gumilev 1994c, 311.
86. Gumilev 1980b, 35.
87. Gumilev 2004c, 529, 535, 538–41, 579–87; Gumilev 1991e, 137.
88. Gumilev 1980b, 34; Gumilev 1991e, 137.

lied to Tokhtamysh that Dmitrii intended to betray him by forming an alliance with Lithuania, and the Mongol khan—a "good, simple, and uneducated man"—believed them. But this was not the only problem, for, as Gumilev explained, The Muscovites were themselves culpable in the city's dreadful fate. He offered the following discouraging scenario.

> Tokhtamysh's raid would not have been brutal at all if it were not for the character of the city's population. . . . Just what did the townspeople want? To drink and carouse (*vypit' i guliat'*). For this reason the population of Moscow, falling under siege, headed for the cellars of the boyars, broke open the locks, seized the barrels of honey, beer, and wine, and proceeded to get very drunk. At this point, to show how "fearless" they were, they mounted the city walls, swore at the Tatars and made vulgar gestures at them. Now the Tatars, especially those from Siberia, were easily offended, and they became extremely angry at the behavior of the Muscovites.[89]

Thus Gumilev suggested that the subsequent Tatar excesses were not at all surprising—certainly they could not be seen as evidence of any elemental hostility toward the Russo-Slavic population. Dmitrii himself was apparently of this view, Gumilev implied, for he reconfirmed the alliance with the Golden Horde, pledged loyalty to Tokhtamysh, and was duly appointed Grand Duke of Vladimir and principal tax collector for the Mongols.

These dramatic events were taking place against a broader background of ethnogenetic activity. Around 1200, an ethnogenetic *vzryv* or eruption took place in a broad band extending from Finland through Lithuania and Rus' across the Near East and south along the African coast to Ethiopia. Across these regions, a new generation of passionaries was created, of which Aleksandr Nevskii was one outstanding example.[90] It was only in the next century, however, that the incubation period of the second ethnogenetic cycle reached its final culmination in a cathartic event that would leave its stamp on subsequent Russian, and indeed world, history. This event was precisely the Battle on Kulikovo Field that we have just described. At this engagement, Gumilev argued, the disparate elements of an aging and fragmented Kievan state were freshly energized, mobilized, and amalgamated into a brand-new ethnic entity: the Russians or Great Russians. At Kulikovo, "the swelling (*nabukhanie*) of *passionarnost'* transformed ancient Rus' into Great Russia."[91] "I believe that at the Battle of Kulikovo the Russian (*russkii*)

---

89. Gumilev 2000, 161.

90. Ibid., 288; Gumilev 1991e, 133.

91. Gumilev 1994c, 286.

ethnos was born. . . . The soldiers who fought there did not [think of their home-lands primarily] as Vladimir, Moscow, Suzdal, Tver, or Smolensk. They were not representatives of disconnected principalities, all struggling against each other, but rather were Russians (*Russkie*), Great Russians (*Velikorossy*), who set out entirely consciously to defend their world: their Fatherland and their cultural-philosophical understanding of life."[92] The circumstances of Kulikovo meant that the new "Russian ethnic entity" was formed in the context of an existential and elemental struggle for its very existence. It was not, however, a struggle against the nomadic warriors of the Golden Horde but rather against the hostile super-ethnies of the Romano-German and Muslim worlds, who fought the Russians via the proxy of Mamai's forces. "This war was not between the 'forest' and 'steppe,' between 'Europe' and 'Asia,' or the 'Russians' and the 'Tatars,' but rather between a vital [new] ethnos and a chimera, which blocked the path of development for Rus' and also for the Great Steppe."[93]

It is vital to note that the active elements of this second ethnogenetic cycle involved more than the proto-Russian fragments of old Kievan Rus'. The new Great Russian ethnos, Gumilev declared, formed as a combination of three prin-cipal "components": Slavic, Finno-Ugric, and Tatar (itself a mixture of Turkic and Mongolian).[94] Of the three, the first and third were the most important. The ethnogenetic amalgamation of these two groups began in the early thirteenth century when, as we have noted, Khan Uzbek's forced conversion of the Golden Horde to Islam caused numerous Nestorian Tatars to flee to Rus'. Here, Gumilev explained, they were offered refuge by Ivan I (1288–1340), Prince of Moscow and Grand Prince of Vladimir. Ivan actively supported their integration into the local society, the most significant means of which was through intermarriage. Tatar warriors "sought out Russian princesses for wives, while young Tatar women converted to Orthodoxy in order to marry Russian boyars." This practice was sufficiently widespread to play an important role in the ethnogenetic process. Because of it, "a mixed (*smeshannyi*) ethnos" took shape, and "in the place of old Kievan Rus' emerged an entirely new Great Russian ethnos—Muscovite Rus'—with its own ethno-social system." The refugees from the Golden Horde brought with them relatively high levels of *passionarnost'*, which served to infuse the new ethnic mix with fresh dynamism and a capacity for action.[95]

---

92. Gumilev 1980b, 34.

93. Ibid., 35.

94. Gumilev 1991e, 5. Gumilev's full list of the groups that combined to become the Russians included "Eastern Slavs from Kievan Rus', Western Slavs, Viatichi, Veps, Finnish tribes (Meria, Mur-oma, Ves', the Chud' of Zavoloch'e), Ugric tribes (Balts, Goliad'), Turks (Christian Polovtsy and Tatars), and a small number of Mongols." Gumilev 1989c, 143, also see Gumilev 1988b, 47.

95. Gumilev 2000, 144–45.

Thus in Gumilev's scheme the interaction between Russo-Slavs and Tatars was not a mere symbiosis but amounted to a full ethnic fusion—a *"sliianie* of Orthodox and Nestorians" in which the two groups merged together and were transformed into something entirely different.[96] This was all in full accordance with the principles of his scheme of ethnogenesis. In the case of ethnies that were already formed, *sliianie* was unnatural and could only lead to their destruction. However, for the formation of new ethnies, the combining of disparate proto-ethnic elements was a necessary precondition. Borrowing an expression from Nikolai Trubetskoi, he maintained that the real "legacy of Ghengis Khan" was not "the threatening *bunchuki* [an ornamental horsetail that served as a sign of authority] of the Mongol [princes] but rather the Christian crosses that they wore around their necks as they wed the young beauties of Rostov, Riazan, and Moscow."[97] The legacy of Ghengis Khan was not the destruction of the civilization of Ancient Rus' but rather the creation of the modern Russian ethnos. In this way, Russia began its modern existence as a "Russian-Tatar country" (*russko-tatarskaia strana*) and has remained one ever since.[98]

Excursus: Gumilev and Classical Eurasianism

Although the historical interpretation we are considering would prove highly controversial in the 1970s and 1980s, as we will see, it was more resonant with perspectives of the 1930s when Gumilev's ideas first began to take shape. Since before the revolution, there had been a strong positive fascination on the part of Russian writers and artists with the nomadic civilizations of Eurasia. Traces of that fascination were evident in the work of both of Gumilev's parents; indeed the very surname *Akhmatova*, which his mother—née Anna Gorenko—adopted in her teenage years, was Tatar in origin. After 1917, this interest took the form of a cultural movement called Scythianism, for which the Scythians—a group of equestrian tribes roaming the plains north of the Black Sea from the ninth century BC to the fourth century AD—served as a kind of exotic metaphor-image to represent the primal and untamed energies of postrevolutionary Russia itself.[99] Alexandr Aleksandrovich Blok's (1880–1921) poetic masterpiece "The Scythians" (1918) was composed very much in this spirit, which remained

---

96. Gumilev 1994c, 307; Gumilev 1991e, 139. Gumilev traced his own ethnic identity back to this primordial fusion.

97. Gumilev 1995, 41.

98. Gumilev and Balashov 1993, 156.

99. On Scythianism, see Hoffman 1979; Brazhnikov 2011.

strong into the 1930s, inspiring among other things Evgenii Ivanovich Zamiatin's (1884–1937) play *Attila* (1925–1927) and his unfinished novel *Bich Bozhii* (*The Scourge of God*, 1937). The federalized USSR was keen in any event to emphasize the progressive historical role of its newly enfranchised Asian constituencies, and Zamiatin's positive depiction of the destruction of an aged Western imperial power at the hands of a fresh and vigorous onslaught of barbarians from the East corresponded well to the Stalinist temper of the times.[100] The scholarly study of Eurasian antiquities thrived as well in this period and Gumilev's teachers at Leningrad University included specialists such as Aleksandr Bernshtam, noted for his work on the history of the Huns and ancient Turkic tribes, and Mikhail Artamonov on the Khazars.[101]

This interest related precisely to ancient history, however, and did not specifically challenge the negative evaluation of relations between Rus' and the Golden Horde in the thirteenth and fourteenth centuries described above. Such a challenge did come from beyond the USSR, however, in the form of a political and cultural movement called Eurasianism, which developed in Russian émigré circles in the 1920s and 1930s.[102] As the name suggests, the Eurasianists saw Russia as part of a larger Eurasian civilization, one that developed autonomously over many centuries in distinction from and opposition to the European West and Asia proper. The Eurasianists elaborated their perspective in a substantial corpus of scholarly research and political polemic. One of the central elements of Eurasianism was a radical reinterpretation of the pattern of historical interaction between Russia and the nomadic peoples of the Eurasian steppes, expounded in the writings of Nikolai Sergeevich Trubetskoi (1890–1938), Georgii Vladimirovich Vernadskii (1887–1973), Petr Nikolaevich Savitskii (1895–1968), and others. They argued that Russia's relations with the steppe nomads had on the whole been positive and reflected a deeper natural unity underlying Eurasian civilization. This was particularly true in regard to the 250-year period of domination by the Golden Horde. This experience—what Trubetskoi called the "legacy of Genghis Khan"—clearly indicated the geopolitical imperative of consolidating the far-flung expanses of Eurasia into a single political and social entity, a project that Russia itself subsequently took over from the Mongols and consummated as its own *raison d'état*.[103] Although the émigré Eurasianists supported the

---

100. Shlapentokh 2011, 95; Russell 1992, 245.

101. Bernshtam 1951; Bernshtam 1946; Artamonov 1937. On the study of nomad history in this period in the Soviet Union, see Shlapentokh 2011, 108–9; 112–13; Beliakov 2012a, 216.

102. On Eurasianism, see Bassin, Laruelle, and Glebov 2015; Böss 1961; Wiederkehr 2007; Laruelle 2008b; Pursiainen 1998; Shlapentokh 2007b.

103. Trubetskoi 1925.

Russian revolution in principle, and many of them eventually sought to make their peace with the Soviet regime, within the USSR they were castigated as White Guard counterrevolutionaries and bourgeois nationalists. Their teachings were denounced and their writings suppressed.

Gumilev had encountered Eurasianist ideas in the 1930s, possibly in Punin's personal library, which might have contained their publications. He recalled how he was explicitly warned against these "most harmful teachings" by his professor Bernshtam—and how he responded that he was not only aware of them but also found them appealing.[104] He developed this interest over the following decades. One of his colleagues at the Hermitage in the late 1950s had been in a Soviet labor camp with Petr Savitskii after the war, and Gumilev began a correspondence with the latter, who was then living in Prague. This contact lasted from 1956 to Savitskii's death in 1968 and involved hundreds of letters.[105] In 1966 the two had a chance to meet when Gumilev visited Prague to attend an international conference. Through Savitskii, Gumilev also corresponded with Georgii Vernadskii, by then well established as a professor at Yale University in the United States. For their part, the Eurasianists acknowledged the importance of Gumilev's work and confirmed its relevance to their own project.[106] Gumilev himself always emphasized the significance of his connections to the Eurasianist movement. He titled his introduction to a collection of Trubetskoi's essays "The Observations of the last Eurasianist," and noted elsewhere that "In general, I am called a Eurasianist, and I do not deny it. . . . This was a powerful historical school. I studied their work carefully . . . [and] I agree with their basic historical-methodological conclusions."[107]

Studies of Gumilev differ sharply, however, in their evaluation of the relationship of his own teachings to those of the original Eurasianists.[108] In a variety of respects, the genuine affinities between them are unquestionable. These include the vision of Russia as a unique civilization on the arena of world history, a middle world between Europe and Asia but belonging to neither. Moreover, the classical Eurasianists shared Gumilev's antipathy to the West and the belief that Western hostility had been present throughout all of Russia's historical existence. Like his

---

104. Gumilev 1993b, 25; Shlapentokh 2011, 99, 106–7.

105. Gumilev 1993b, 37; Lariuel' 2001, 6. For a selection of Savitskii's letters to Gumilev, see Savitskii 1994. The entire correspondence is examined in detail in Lariuel' 2001; Beisswenger 2013.

106. In a review of Gumilev's monograph *Khunnu*, Vernadskii praised his "mastery in blending historical and archeological evidence." Vernadsky 1961, 712.

107. Gumilev 1995; Gumilev 1991e, 132.

108. For positive evaluations of Gumilev as a final representative of classical Eurasianism, see Demin 2008, 216; Lavrov 1993. More skeptical appraisals are presented by Beliakov 2012a, 659–60; Lariuel' 2001; Beisswenger 2013.

predecessors, Gumilev emphasized Russia's multiethnic character and regarded it as evidence of the solidarity of the Eurasian peoples. Where Gumilev spoke about interethnic "complementarity" as the glue for this solidarity, the classical Eurasianists had referred to the *vzaimosimpatiia* or "congeniality" between the same peoples.[109] The classical Eurasianists described a bipartite hierarchy of ethnic and national attachment that corresponded loosely but recognizably to Gumilev's ethnos-superethnos distinction: a "lower level" characterized by localized ethnic association and an "upper level" where Russia-Eurasia's multinational population was united on the basis of deep historical, cultural, and civilizational affinities.[110] Finally, the classical Eurasianists stressed along with Gumilev the special importance of the geographical environment in shaping ethnic character and historical experience. The geographer Savitskii proposed a new term *mestorazvitie*—literally "topogenesis" or "development-in-place"—to emphasize precisely the significance of local geographical conditions for historical and social development, and Gumilev used this term in his own work.[111]

At the same time, however, a number of differences set Gumilev apart from the classical Eurasianists. The latter may have identified fundamental benefits for Russia in the "legacy of Genghis Khan," but they questioned neither the historical fact of the Mongol conquest nor the great devastation that it brought. For them, the image of an *igo* was an entirely apt characterization. As Savitskii wrote to Gumilev, "the Mongol onslaught was a dreadful calamity that killed hundreds of thousands, perhaps millions of people, and destroyed a great number of priceless artifacts of ancient Russian culture."[112] The steppe nomads may have been more tolerant overall than Russia's neighbors to the west, but their effects were hardly benign.[113] The classical Eurasianists did not discuss the successful absorption of Nestorian nomads into Russian society, a fact Gumilev himself noted with some consternation.[114] In general, Savitskii gently scolded, "it seems to me that you somewhat *exaggerate* the role of the Tatars on the Russian side in the Battle of Kulikovo."[115] Moreover, while the "Eurasia" of the classical Eurasianists referred exclusively to "Russia-Eurasia" within its late-imperial boundaries, Gumilev was decidedly more expansive and included virtually all steppe civilizations from the Carpathians to the Pacific.[116]

---

109. Halperin 1982a, 487; Lariuel' 2001, 12.
110. Trubetskoi 1921b.
111. On the environmentalism of the classical Eurasianists, see Bassin 2010b; Laruelle 2015.
112. Cited in Beliakov 2012a, 649.
113. Savitskii 1994, 165.
114. Gumilev 1995, 40–41; Halperin 1982a, 479, 480, 485, 489, 493.
115. Cited in Beliakov 2012a, 647, emphasis in original.
116. Gumilev 2004c, 33n.

More important, whereas classical Eurasianism identified Russia-Eurasia as a single cultural-historical zone, Gumilev maintained that the same geographical space was divided between no less than seven different superethnies. The geographer Savitskii may have shared Gumilev's environmentalist perspective, but he showed no trace of the quirky naturalism that was so fundamental to the latter's own work—no biology or genetics, and no references to the biosphere or the cosmic irradiation that powered it. Gumilev himself drew attention to this point. "You must understand," he explained in an interview, that the classical Eurasianists "were very lacking in natural science (*im ochen' ne khvatalo estestvoznaniia*). As a historian, Georgii Vernadskii did not adequately absorb his father's ideas."[117] Finally, classical Eurasianism, unlike Gumilev, did not attempt to theorize the nature of ethnicity. Notions such as *passionarnost'*, "symbiosis," or "chimera"—so essential to Gumilev's own conceptual universe—had no place at all in any of his predecessors' deliberations.[118] The full significance of these distinctions will become apparent later, in our evaluation of Gumilev's role in the late- and post-Soviet neo-Eurasianist revival.

After the Mongols

Gumilev's primary preoccupation was with the history of ancient Rus', a chronicle that culminated in the national catharsis of Kulikovo. His discussion of Russia's subsequent historical development was far more cursory and superficial. From the late fourteenth to the sixteenth centuries, the young Russian ethnos (*russkie* or *veliko-rossy*) progressed thorough the ascendancy and acmatic phases. This period saw the final demise of the "ethnic remnants" of Kievan Rus' and the beginning of the formation of a Russian (*rossiiskii*) superethnos. The mid-sixteenth century witnessed the culmination of Russia's ethnogenetic overdrive (*peregrev*) when the initial passionary charge became uncontrollably intense and ethnogenetic development became dysfunctional. During this period, there were a series of major calamities for the Russian ethnos, beginning with Ivan the Terrible's (1530–1584) bloody *oprichnina* in the 1560s and 1570s. They were followed in the first decade of the seventeenth century by the brutal civil strife of the Time of Troubles, the *raskol* or schism of Russian Orthodoxy triggered by Patriarch Nikon's (1605–1681) reforms of church ritual in the 1650s, and Stenka Razin's (1630–1671) uprisings in the 1660s and 1670s. Throughout these upheavals, an

---

117. Gumilev 1991e, 132; Lariuel' 2001, 11–12; Shlapentokh 2011, 100. For a restatement of this position, see Vidershpan 2004, 25.

118. Shlapentokh 2012, 487.

irresistible passionary drive meant that the population at large was "drenched in spilled blood."[119] The Russian state expanded its boundaries and the Russian superethnos began to assume its full form.

Russia's *passionarnost'* finally began to decline in the eighteenth century, with the positive effect of encouraging relative harmony and peace. At the same time, however, it fostered the spread of aristocratic indolence and, yet more grievously, the "senseless admiration of everything Western"—a tendency he called "occidentalization" (*oksidentalizatsiia*), citing Arnold Toynbee.[120] Gumilev's evaluation of the most famous instigator of this process—Peter the Great—was ambivalent. He initially condemned the tsar for his Europeanizing inclinations, but eventually "amnestied" him in recognition of his services in expanding and fortifying the Russian state.[121] By the end of the century, "under the eyes of Pushkin," Russia's superethnic integration was finally completed. The momentous popular resistance to the Napoleonic invasion was a great national effort, Gumilev maintained, but it came at the very high cost of critically exhausting Russia's remaining passionary energies. By the mid-nineteenth century, he reckoned that the country had entered its breakdown phase of *nadlom*. He saw evidence for this in the growth of sectarianism, nihilism, "atheistic Gnosticism," and "intellectual vampirism"—of which Vladimir Sergeevich Solov'ev's (1853–1900) universalist vision of *vseedinstvo* or panhumanism was a particularly egregious example. It was, however, Russia's liberal and revolutionary tendencies of the nineteenth century that provided the clearest indication of the country's rapid ethnic degeneration. He had nothing but contempt for this progressive tradition, indeed "even hated the Decembrists," and saw everywhere the further entrenchment of "Westernism and Freemasonry."[122] The Bolshevik revolution was a natural culmination of this process of ethnogenetic enfeeblement.

Gumilev did, however, place special emphasis on two aspects of the historical development of modern Russia. On the one hand, he argued that the formation of the Russian imperial state, unlike its counterparts in Western Europe and North America, was an essentially harmonious and voluntary process in which non-Russians were always treated as equal members.[123] He did not deny that Russian expansion had occasionally involved forceful conquest, but this was not its principal feature. "It is clear to anyone with even the slightest superficial

---

119. Gumilev 1970b, 48; Gumilev 2000, 288.
120. Gumilev 1991e, 141.
121. The expression "amnestied" comes from Sergei Lavrov, who was mimicking his friend's ironic use of prison-camp terms. Lavrov 2000, 348. Also see Gumilev 1991e, 141.
122. Beliakov 2012a, 681; Gumilev 1989d, 30, 32.
123. Gumilev 1991e, 140.

knowledge of Russian history that the incorporation (*prisoedinenie*) of Siberia would have been unimaginable without voluntary agreement and mutual trust."

> It is true that military force was used in the Caucasus and Central Asia, but in these cases the Russians encountered a different super-ethnos, sometimes two. This was true for the Baltic as well. Georgians and Armenians were remnants of Byzantium, [whereas] the Turkmen, Uzbeks, Takzhiks, and Turks together were part of the Islamic supereth-nos [and therefore hostile]. Historically, Byzantium had had friendly relations with Russia, and the complementarity between the Christians of the Caucasus and the Russians predetermined the incorporation of the former into Russia.[124]

What made the Russian example unique were the deep natural sympathies between the Russians and the peoples they brought into their imperial structure and the toleration and respect they showed them. In contrast to the Soviet leadership, the old imperial authorities were not guided by a "universal ideology of reducing everyone to the same level," and thus the empire's subjects had been allowed to maintain their autonomy and traditional internal organization to the maximum extent possible.[125] "In [Russia's] 'prison house of peoples' it was possible [for different ethnies] to live in their own way. As we used to say in the camps: commandant, please don't do me any favors! (*nachal'nik, ne bud' ty moim blagodetelem*). From the beginning, the Russians were clever and tactful enough not do any favors, and they were answered with friendly (*druzhestvennye*), yes definitely friendly relations on the part of the conquered peoples." Even in those cases where the brutality of the Russian conquest was acknowledged, such as General Mikhail Dmitrievich Skobelev's (1843–1882) campaigns in Central Asia, the defeated Turkmen people responded positively to Russia's subsequent benevolence, and in World War I they provided battalions "to defend their conquerors."[126]

Indeed, Gumilev's determination to present a picture of harmony and symbiotic complementarity between the peoples of the empire led him to contravene one of his own cardinal principles of normal ethnic life. His account suggested that in their symbiotic enthusiasm, the various ethnies that had been part of the Russian state since medieval times did not always observe the injunction to practice the endogamy that was supposed to be a universal requirement for the

---

124. Gumilev and Ivanov 1992, 56 (quotes); Gumilev 2004c, 22; Gumilev 1992a (quote); Gumilev 1991e, 140; Lavrov 2000, 352.
125. Gumilev 1989h, 35.
126. Gumilev 2003c, 13.

maintenance of ethnic well-being. And this neglect, moreover, seemed not to have done anyone any harm. From the fifteenth through the seventeenth centuries, he explained, "our ancestors the Great Russians mixed (*smeshalis'*) easily and relatively quickly with the Tatars on the Volga, Don, and Ob' Rivers, and with the Buriats, who adopted Russian culture." The Great Russians themselves "quickly dissolved (*rastvorialis'*) among the Yakuts and were assimilated by them (*ob"iakutivalis'*), and they always had friendly contacts with the Kalmyks and Kazakhs. They easily married and lived together with the Mongols in Central Asia, just as the Mongols and Turks in the fourteenth and fifteenth centuries merged (*slivalis'*) with the Russians in central Russia."[127] Gumilev was not always talking here about the initial phases of ethnogenesis when such merging is natural and routine, but rather about relations between formed and developed ethnies, for whom such mixing should in principle have undermined their ethnic integrity.

"Sovetskaia Khazariia"

The second aspect of Russia's historical development to which Gumilev paid special attention was the role of the Jews. Sviatoslav may have succeeded in vanquishing the Khazar state in the 960s, but this did not by any means eradicate the problem of the Jewish chimera. The surviving "Judeo-Khazar" elite scattered across Eurasia and Europe, seeking everywhere to foment internal discord.[128] It remained active in Rus' lands, encouraging hostilities between the Russian princes and inciting the steppe peoples to attack the Russians. Among other things, Khazar agitation was behind the unsuccessful campaign of Mstislav of Chernigov against Kiev in 1024, and his attacking forces included Khazar troops. In Kiev itself, Gumilev maintained they sought to get power by their traditional means of intermarriage, and when Orthodox priests refused to allow mixed marriages they resorted to ideological sabotage, spreading "skepticism and indifference." This seditious activity came to a provisional end in 1113 with Vladimir Monomakh's expulsion of Jews from Kiev. The "zigzag" diverting Russia from its normal ethnogenetic course was now corrected, and Gumilev accordingly dropped the Jewish theme.[129]

The problem returned, however, in the mid-nineteenth century when the inception of Russia's *nadlom* or breakdown phase signaled the exhaustion of

---

127. Gumilev and Panchenko 1990, 90.
128. Rossman 2002b, 86
129. Gumilev 2004c, 258, 260, 344–46; Shnirelman 2002, 56.

Russia's ethnogenetic forces and offered an opportunity for the old chimeric menace to make its modern appearance. Taking full advantage of the situation, the Jews reemerged to play a central role in the various revolutionary and anarchist antisystems that plagued imperial Russia in its final decades. Gumilev attested to the growing prevalence of Jews during this period with his personal experience: "At the beginning of the twentieth century, before the revolution, I can refer to my own mother, who always said: 'We spent our entire youth in a mixed Russian-Jewish society.' This is how it was, and even later she had a huge number of Jewish acquaintances."[130] Led by opportunists such as Vladimir Lenin and Feliks Dzerzhinskii, the Jews were the driving force behind the Bolshevik maelstrom that destroyed old Russia. At this point, the old Khazar chimera emerged again, its vigor undiminished, and the Soviet Union—at least in its early decades—was completely overwhelmed by it. "According to Gumilev, the Soviet Union was created by Jewish revolutionaries. Lenin and Stalin bastardized the Russian people, turning them into Communist Untermenschen (*sovok*)."[131] His elaborate historical scenario of ancient Khazar hatred for young Russia and its determination to subjugate it was wordlessly transferred to the conditions of the early twentieth century, which represented a veritable "Soviet Khazaria" with Jewish commissars reenacting the role of the merchant Judeo-Khazar elite of old.[132] These modern tyrants ruined Russia's economy, destroyed its religion and culture, suppressed the kulaks, and deliberately organized famines that killed millions of people. In the USSR, Gumilev maintained, ethnic Russians did not suppress other nationalities, but rather themselves were suppressed as a nation along with everyone else.[133]

In the final analysis, however, things could not be quite this simple, and Gumilev did not condemn Soviet civilization in its entirety as a malign Soviet Khazaria. On the contrary, his attitude toward the USSR was highly ambivalent. On the one hand, he did indeed view the Soviet Union as a chimeric abomination dominated by iniquitous Jewish agents. Aleksandr Borodai, whose insights about Gumilev we have noted in the Introduction, testified to the intensity of his feelings.

> In essence, Gumilev had two ideological enemies: Soviet power and the Jews, whom he regarded as a parasitic ethnos. For him, these two entities were practically combined. Of course, he understood that at one point Soviet power was transformed, more or less during the period of the Second World War. [After this] it was not as ethnically colored as it had

---

130. Gumilev 1989i.
131. Yasmann 1992, 26 (quote); Gumilev and Ermolaev 1993, 187.
132. Rossman 2002a, 43; Samovarov 2013; Loseff 1994, 10.
133. Gumilev and Ermolaev 1993, 187.

been in the first decades of its existence. Nevertheless, he believed that our country was controlled by an occupying power, against which every passionary person should in principle struggle.[134]

From this standpoint, it is entirely accurate to characterize Gumilev's work as a "crusade against Bolshevism"[135] and Soviet power—*sovetskaia vlast'*, or "Sof'ia Vlasovna," as he mockingly derided it. This was a regime that after all had destroyed his parent's lives, brutally incarcerated him for many years, refused to acknowledge his scholarly achievements, and actively persecuted him virtually to the end. In indicting the Jews as the instigators of this awful project, moreover, he did not exculpate its principal executive Josef Stalin, a passionary person with "a negative, life-denying" worldview. Indeed, he ridiculed this *Korifei Vsekh Nauk* (Coryphaeus of All Sciences) as *Korifei Naukovich*, and declared that the totalitarian "meat grinder" (*miasorubka*) he created perverted the long-established principles that had historically maintained normal relations among the peoples of the Russian state.[136] "Everything Stalin did was a [harmful] oversimplification of the ethnic system," he lamented at the end of *perestroika*: "and today we are enjoying the fruits of this."[137]

This picture of Gumilev's uncompromising hostility is accurate but it is not complete. For along with his rejection of the Soviet order, he also believed there were important reasons to tolerate and even embrace it. He "was no opponent of the political order of the USSR," recalled another close acquaintance: he never openly opposed the system as such and always blamed his misfortunes on evil groups such as the Jews or malign and jealous individuals rather than the state.[138] He palpably despised the liberal and Western-oriented "dissidents" who criticized the Soviet system in the post-Stalinist 1960s and 1970s and clearly distanced himself from them. Gumilev's repeated insistence that there was nothing anti-Soviet in his work was entirely sincere, and indeed in significant respects— his fidelity to important aspects of Soviet Marxism, his materialist orientation, and his positivist approach—he adhered to standards that were typical for Soviet academic scholarship in general.[139] More important, he believed that at least some of the official policies of the USSR corresponded to his own values and priorities. Externally, the Cold War confrontation with the West indicated to him

134. "Passionarnost'" 2012.
135. Samovarov 2013.
136. Gumilev and Balashov 1993, 152; Gumilev 1994c, 267; Beliakov 2012a, 423, 520.
137. Gumilev 1994c, 267.
138. Burovskii 2012 (quote); Shlapentokh 2011, 96.
139. Beliakov 2012a, 423–24, 505, 531.

that the Soviet state appreciated the fundamental and insuperable superethnic oppositions that Russia faced. The same was true for relations with China. The nationalist writer Aleksandr Andreevich Prokhanov, who knew Gumilev from the 1960s, recalls how he was obsessed with the "yellow danger" and believed that Sino-Soviet hostilities would lead to a superethnic conflagration.[140] Gumilev denounced the liberalism of the Prague spring in 1968 as an act of Western aggression and supported the Soviet intervention.[141]

Despite his criticism of Stalin's "meat grinder," moreover, he paradoxically felt that the interethnic fraternity and solidarity of the Eurasian peoples, which underlay his scenario for the ethnogenesis of the Russian nation and its development into a grand superethnic imperial entity, had been "preserved in the Soviet period." As his widow explained, Gumilev "believed that the Soviet state in some way provided for the unity of a great power that was created over the centuries with the blood and sweat of our forefathers."[142] Finally, he was satisfied to note at least some appreciation from within the Soviet leadership of the true nature of the Jewish menace, and some preparedness to deal with it. In this regard, Borodai's reference to a "transformation" during the war period was significant, for it was precisely during this period and immediately thereafter that Stalinism demonstrated its readiness to confront the Jews.[143] "Stalin got one thing right (*bylo odno pravil'noe delo*)," Gumilev is said to have observed, namely, "the Doctors' affair." And it was no coincidence, he continued, that just two short months after its proclamation in January 1953, Stalin was dead.[144] The lethal powers of the Jewish chimera simply could not be contained.

In the Soviet Union of his day, Gumilev believed he saw precisely the same Manichean struggle between Russia's "friends and enemies"—internal and external—that he had described in his histories of the steppe and ancient Rus'. The result was the elemental ambivalence on his part to the Soviet order we have just noted. There was much that he denounced and rejected, while at the same time

---

140. Interview with the author, Moscow, September 2007. On Prokhanov and Gumilev, also see below, 220–21. Indeed, it has been suggested that Gumilev received permission to publish his books on the Xiongnu in 1960 and 1974 only because the authorities felt that his depiction of China as a historical aggressor against the steppe peoples would be useful for their own propaganda purposes. This might also explain the book's surprisingly large print run of 5,400 copies. Temirgaliev 2011; Beliakov 2012a, 551; Kurkchi 1994.

141. Beliakov 2012a, 423. However, he opposed the 1979 invasion of Afghanistan, believing that this brought Russia beyond its natural superethnic limits. Naarden 1996, 78.

142. Gumilev 1994c, 289; Gumileva 1993, 4.

143. Rossman 2002b, 145.

144. Stekliannokova 2003; Beliakov 2012a, 578. Svetlana Boym points to the similarities between the tone of Gumilev's accounts of ancient Khazaria and Stalin's campaign against "rootless cosmopolitanism." Boym 1995, 155.

there were important aspects that he wholeheartedly supported. Indeed, in certain respects, the Soviet Union even provided examples that helped to shape his own thinking. In the rest of this book, we will examine the various ways in which his contorted position formed a part of contemporary intellectual and political debates from the post-Stalinist 1960s to the present day.

Part 2
THE SOVIET RECEPTION OF GUMILEV

SOVIET VISIONS OF SOCIETY AND NATURE

Stalinist Prometheanism

The expectation that human society, given the proper forms of organization and sufficient technological capacity, could "liberate" itself from dependency on the natural world and bring it under social control has deep roots in Russian thinking. Its appeal was directly linked to the common assumption that Russia's endemic backwardness and poverty were somehow the result of the injustices of nature, which had encumbered the country with an assortment of environmental disadvantages: poor soils, harsh climatic conditions, remoteness from the civilizing influences of the sea, and the stultifying *odnoobrazie* or monotony of its endless flat expanses. This assumption was expressed, among others, by the "father" of Russian Marxism, Georgii Valentinovich Plekhanov (1856–1918), who argued that the natural-geographical conditions of the east European plain were the ultimate source of Russia's historical primitiveness and its underdevelopment.[1] But Plekhanov's bleak view of the Russian past only inspired his ultimate belief that one day socialism would enable Russia to subject the "blind, elemental forces of nature" to the "domain of human reason."[2] Plekhanov's aspiration was reaffirmed yet more ambitiously by other tendencies in the Marxist camp, notably the so-called God-building (*bogostroitel'stvo*) movement that developed in the

---

1. Bassin 1992, 11–14.
2. Quoted in Kline 1968, 143.

years after the revolution of 1905.[3] In the 1920s, Leon Trotsky (1879–1940) gave voice to this spirit with his declaration that a classless society will "command nature in its entirety, . . . change the course of the rivers, and . . . lay down rules for the oceans. . . . The effort . . . to conquer nature will be the dominant tendency for decades to come." Under socialism, people "will learn how to move rivers and mountains, how to build peoples' palaces on the peaks of Mont Blanc and at the bottom of the Atlantic."[4]

The Marxists were not alone in thinking such grand thoughts. The philosopher Nikolai Fedorovich Fedorov (1829–1903) offered an unadulterated vision of total anthropological transcendence of all terrestrial limitations and the eventual domination over the universe.[5] He believed that the powers of humankind were potentially unlimited and would be capable not merely of the "conquest" and regulation of the earth's natural world but of the colonization of outer space as well—an eschatological enterprise that Fedorov described as humanity's *obshchee delo* or "common cause." Eventually, he maintained, the power of rational science would make it possible even to resurrect dead bodies back into living beings. "The earth will be the first star in heaven to be moved not only by the blind forces of gravity but by [human] reason, which will have countered and prevented gravity and death."[6] Fedorov's ideas inspired a large variety of important thinkers, many of whom formed part of a tradition subsequently referred to as Russian cosmism.[7] In the years after the revolution, this Promethean confidence was given a scientific formulation in the notion of a "noosphere" developed by Vladimir Vernadskii.[8] As a realm of pure "noos" or human reason, Vernadsky suggested that the anthropogenic noosphere itself had become a primary geological force that exerted increasing mastery over all natural processes and was capable even of creating new resources.[9] In Soviet parlance, the "noosphere" concept was expressed in the idea of a "technosphere," indicating that industrialization and technology represented the medium through which anthropogenic control over the natural world was exerted.

These ideas were mobilized as part of the political revolution of the *Velikii Perelom* or "Great Break," through which Joseph Stalin consolidated his power in the late 1920s.[10] Because the question about the relationship of society to the natural world related directly to the projects of national development,

---

3. Kline 1968, 103–26; Kołakowski 1978, 2: 446–47.
4. Trotsky 1971 [1924], 252–54.
5. Fedorov 1906–1913. On Fedorov, see Hagemeister 1989; Young 2012.
6. Quoted in Young 2012, 81. Also see Rosenthal 1997, 403; Hagemeister 2003.
7. Semenova and Gacheva 1993; Young 2012; Shlapentokh 2001.
8. Levit 2000.
9. Vernadsky 1945; Levit 2001; Lavreonova 2007; Ianshina 1996; Shlapentokh 2001.
10. On the influence of the Fedorovian legacy on Stalinism, see Rosenthal 2002; Shlapentokh 1996a; Shlapentokh 1996b.

industrialization, and modernization that were the fundamental driving aims of the regime, it became an ideological problem of the first importance. Elaborate attempts were made to articulate an official position on the issue, based on the principles of Marxist philosophy. Friedrich Engels's notes and fragments on the philosophy of the natural world were published in Moscow in 1925 under the title *Dialectics of Nature*, and this collection provided a conceptual cornerstone for the developing Stalinist line.[11] Engels asserted that the phenomena of the natural and the social worlds were controlled by "laws of the motion of matter." He did not, however, clearly indicate either what these laws represented or—what is more important—whether those laws controlling activity in the natural world were the same as those operative for human society.[12] These were uncertainties that Stalinist dialecticians rushed to resolve. Nature on the one hand, and society on the other, were identified as ontological categories of being that were absolutely separate. Each category developed and behaved in conformity with different sets of universal laws, for which reason there could be no organic interlinkage between them.[13] "Human society is the highest link in the general chain of development of the material world. It represents a specific part of material world with its special laws of movement and development that apply to it alone. . . . The movement of society is subject to laws that are different from the laws of the natural world."[14] From this it followed logically that the evolution and organization of human society were in principle independent of the natural world.

The Stalinist conclusion was that, contra Plekhanov, the natural-geographical milieu did not and could not have any significant influence over the development of human society or the course of social evolution. To be sure, Stalin did not go so far as to deny environmental influences altogether: "The geographical milieu (*sreda*) doubtlessly is one of the constant and necessary conditions for the development of society." But whatever influence it may exert "is not a *determining influence*, and cannot be a determining influence because the changes and development of society occur incomparably faster than the changes and development of the geographical milieu. . . . From this it follows that the geographical milieu cannot serve as the principal cause for directing social development."[15] Any suggestion to the contrary, that the geographical environment could exert a controlling influence on any aspect of the course of social development, was now

---

11. Stalin 1946 [1906], 297–302.
12. Engels 1974, 243–56; Weikart 1998, 53–82.
13. Adams 1990a, 219; Weiner 1984, 689; Chappell 1975, 150.
14. Konstantinov 1950, 32, 34.
15. Stalin 1997, 266–67 (emphasis added); Konstantinov 1950, 46–68. For book-length formulations of the Stalinist perspective on the relationship between society and the natural world, see Ivanov-Omskii 1950, 147–242; Voskanian 1956; also see Matley 1966.

denounced as vulgar "geographical materialism." It was not merely antithetical to the spirit of genuine Marxist theory but indeed inherently reactionary, and in the present day appealed particularly to "bourgeois sociologists," "geopoliticians," and other assorted apologists for European imperialism and fascism.[16] Among other things, this new Stalinist credo brought about the fissure of the academic discipline of geography in the USSR, which up to that time had studied society-environment interactions as one of its leading themes. In the 1930s, the discipline was formally divided into the two separate branches of "economic" (study of society) and "physical" (study of the natural world) geography—a division that endures to the present day. Geography was not the only discipline to suffer this fate.[17]

The principled "dialectical" sectioning off of society from nature implied that the former could enjoy a radical freedom from the constraints of the natural world.[18] This perspective became the philosophical basis for a comprehensive program for the subjugation of nature by social forces in the USSR. Indeed, Soviet ideology from the 1930s not only emphatically embraced the Promethean vision but reified it as an all-subsuming and inflexible political imperative for the Soviet present. The immediate challenge and goal for Soviet society, in other words, was precisely to conquer the chaotic forces of nature and reconstruct them in accordance with society's needs and priorities. This imperative was expressed concisely in a single concept that became a defining keyword for the Stalinist ethos: *preobrazovanie*, or transformation, directed not only toward social organization but also toward a natural world that was seen as an obstacle to the fulfilment of human needs and a veritable "enemy" (*vrag*) of social progress. In line with the staggering ambition of this transformist project, the natural world was to be reconstructed in literally all of its various manifestations. "We cannot expect any favors from nature," the agronomist Ivan Vladimirovich Michurin (1885–1935) had famously declared, "our task is to take them from her."[19]

The external geographical environment would be comprehensively reshaped through massive projects of landscape engineering—canals, hydroelectric stations, railroads, dams, and so on. No objective was thought to be beyond the grasp of Soviet planning and science, as can be seen in the so-called "Great Stalin Plan for the Transformation of Nature" (*Velikii Stalinskii Plan Preobrazovaniia Prirody*) promulgated in 1948—a massive project of reforestation that aspired to

---

16. Konstantinov 1949; Matley 1966, 103.
17. Adams 1990a, 219.
18. Bassin 1996.
19. Cited in Konstantinov 1950, 628; Weiner 1984, 691. On Stalinist transformism, see the still-useful essay by Tucker 1956.

nothing less than redesigning climatic patterns over large parts of the country.[20] This Promethean exuberance infused literally all fields and activities in Stalinist Russia, and it was tirelessly propagandized in every public sphere, from official politics, cinema, and the popular press right through to children's literature.[21] One the eve of Stalin's death, the *Great Soviet Encyclopedia* proudly affirmed that the glorious successes of Soviet development have resulted in "the uninterrupted and ever-growing essential transformation of nature in the interests of socialist society."[22] In addition to transforming the external geographical environment, moreover, Soviet society would also extend its control over "inner" nature. Stalinism's support for Ivan Pavlov's psychological theory of "conditional reflexes" signaled its determination to develop a so-called Michurinism for man that would enable the deliberate conditioning and shaping of the individual human psyche.[23] Yet more famously (or infamously), the Ukrainian agronomist Trofim Lysenko seized the mantel of Michurin and gained immense power through his claim that the biological characteristics and genetic structures of food crops could be manipulated, reshaped, and "improved" at will through the rational intervention of socialist science.[24]

A transformist project of this magnitude called for its own dedicated agent and consummator, which Stalinist ideology provided with the notion of a *novyi sovetskii chelovek*, or "new Soviet person." Strictly speaking, this idea was not a creation of the Stalin era. The expectation that a new communist civilization would create a new sort of individual had been an article of faith for Russian Marxists since before the revolution, and the victorious Bolsheviks lost no time in specifying the qualities that would characterize the new socialist actor. Different periods, however, promoted different criteria for the sort of person this would be. In the 1920s, still under the strong influence of the postrevolutionary avant-garde, the image of the *vydvizhenets* or socialist hero as a sort of depersonalized man-machine dominated—effectively a virtuous superhuman robot, fully in tune with the rhythms of technology and liberated to the greatest possible extent from the encumbering weaknesses of natural bodily needs and inclinations.[25] By the end of the decade, however, the avant-garde had been crushed and a distinctively Stalinist prototype of the Soviet hero began to emerge. Stalin himself had issued

20. *Velikie stroiki stalinskoi epokhi* 1950; Kasimovskii 1951; Brain 2011, 140–67; Josephson 1995, 530–38.

21. Andreev 1927; Husband 2006.

22. "Geograficheskaia sreda" 1952, 543 (quote); Konstantinov 1950, 181.

23. Tucker 1956, 464.

24. On the history of Lysenkoism, see Joravsky 1970; Medvedev 1971; Pollock 2006, 41–71; Weiner 1985.

25. Rosenthal 2002, 189–95.

a call for heroes in the early 1930s, and *Pravda* duly demanded the "rehabilitation of the role of the individual in history"[26] The influence of Nietzschean categories and values was clearly apparent—irrespective of the fact that Nietzsche himself was officially denounced as a prophet of German fascism and his work proscribed.[27] Trotsky, for example, described how the new social system would produce an individual of a "higher social biologic [*sic*] type or, if you please, a superman (*sverkhchekovek*)."[28] And indeed, the Stalinist new Soviet person was projected as a kind of Nietzschean protagonist: a Dionysian activist fully personalized as a palpitating flesh-and-blood human being. This image drew on a novel Stalinist cult of the charismatic and heroic activist, which became a ubiquitous feature of socialist realist literature, exemplified by such memorable protagonists as Pavka Korchagin in Nikolai Ostrovskii's *Kak zakaialas' stal'* (1936) or Kirill Zhdarkin in Fedor Panferov's four-volume *Bruski* (1928–1937).[29]

This cultic mystique was also projected onto real-life characters, of course, and was disseminated through meticulously manufactured mythologies of such exemplary heroes of Soviet construction as the shock worker Aleksei Stakhanov, the pilot Valerii Chkalov, the agronomist Michurin, and many others.[30] In all cases, the essential elements of a standard prototype were recognizable. The Dionysian hero was a dynamic and intrepid actor, a Promethean agent in possession of inexhaustible stores of personal energy.[31] *Energiia*—the title of a 1933 novel by Fedor Gladkov, one of the highest-acclaimed authors of socialist realist prose—referred as much to the personal qualities of its Bolshevik superhero Baikalov as it did to the Dnieper hydroelectric station that was the object of his epic endeavor. Indeed, a "mystique of energy" was one of the essential components of this Stalinist image.[32] The Nietzschean inspiration was further apparent in the voluntarism of the hero, whose activist drive was spontaneous and personalized, quite beyond the control of external forces. It operated autonomously, the product of an irrepressible will-to-life and an unshakable resolution to build the communist future that resided deep inside the individual. Replacing the man-machine of the 1920s, the Stalinist hero was reemotionalized, and subjective personal sentiments such as rage, warmth, displeasure, courage, and enthusiasm were on prominent display as vital elements

---

26. Brandenberger and Dubrovsky 1998, 876, 886n.
27. Agursky 1994, 272. On the importance of the Nietzschean legacy for Stalinist ideology, also see Rosenthal 2002; Groys 1988; Groys 1994.
28. Trotsky 1971 [1924], 256.
29. Mikhail Agursky points to the Nietzschean overtones even in Ostrovskii's title, which resonates phonetically with *Tak govoril Zaratustra*—the Russian title of *Also Sprach Zarathustra*. Agursky 1994, 278.
30. Bergman 1998; McCannon 1997; Kaganovsky 2004.
31. Bergman 1998, 139–40; Agursky 1994, 261.
32. Rosenthal 2002, 267; Geller 2009, 22.

of the heroic personal psychology. The latter's dynamism was invariably described as *stikhiinyi* or elemental, which implied a commonality with the unbridled forces of the natural world, and it was precisely this elemental natural energy that drove the hero to perform *podvigi* or the magnificent feats of socialist construction.[33]

The superhero model was further marked by a tension between its "collectivist" and "vanguardist" tendencies.[34] On the one hand, the heroic individual was supposed to exemplify a sort of collective group identity, which subsumed and ultimately effaced its individual character. This point was ambivalent, however, for along with its commitment to the common good and to the virtue of self-sacrifice for the needs of the community, the Dionysian hero also clearly operated as an individual agent. Individualism was indeed an essential attribute, insofar as the hero was heroic precisely by virtue of qualities and achievements that were exceptional and served to distinguish him or her from the rank and file. Thus, although every member of Soviet society was exhorted to be like the socialist hero, the unspoken corollary was that not everyone would be able to do so. To this extent, the Stalinist protagonist was an *Übermensch* in a rather more literal Nietzschean sense, that is to say, a spectacularly exceptional and outstanding individual who, like Nietzsche's hero, stood not alongside the others but rather occupied a space above them, entirely on his or her own.[35] The first and greatest examples of this prototype were the deified figures of Lenin and Stalin themselves. The exceptionalism of the great leaders was then projected—in a carefully calibrated descending hierarchy—on the pantheon of Stalinist heroes mentioned above. In different ways, all of these figures were "leaders" who stood by definition apart from and above the laboring masses.

Passionarnost' and the New Soviet Person

Although Gumilev did not begin to publish his ideas on the subject until the 1960s, we have seen that he had "discovered" *passionarnost'* and begun developing the concept in the 1930s. His thinking in this early period was strongly influenced by the Stalinist model of the new Soviet person just described. On the one hand,

---

33. The emphasis on the *stikhiinost'* of the new Soviet person reveals a subtle but quite significant ambivalence in Stalinism. Although socialist society as a whole was deemed to operate separately from the natural world that it was supposed to conquer, as we have just seen, its leading figures were themselves represented as agents of powerful natural forces. The tensions that derived from this ambivalence can be clearly traced in the representation of landscape and nature in socialist realist art. See Bassin 2000; Bassin 2008.

34. Tirado 1994, 248.

35. Günther 1993; Scheibert 1961. For a more general consideration, see Thompson 2002.

passionarnost' was a physiological feature of the human organism that played a key role in the creation and the life history of all ethnic groups. At the same time, however, he used the concept for the purposes of developing his own version of a cult of the heroic. The combination of purposeful striving supported by a boundless capacity for physical exertion and struggle was for Gumilev a fundamental element of human existence, providing an impetus for great deeds and accomplishments that were witnessed throughout history. Gumilev's heroes were not Bolsheviks or shock workers, of course, and their goal was not the construction of socialism. But the special energy and dynamism that animated them was qualitatively identical to that of the Stalinist prototypes. Since his childhood, Gumilev had been fascinated by tales about the great historical figures, and he shared the idolization of them that inspired the Acmeist poetry of his father Nikolai Gumilev. Indeed, he would occasionally cite a verse from his father's poem *Captains* in his own work, as an illustration of his passionary heroes.

> All of you, noble knights of the green cathedral,
> Who follow the compass across stormy seas,
> Gonzalo, Captain Cook, La Perouse, and Da Gama,
> That visionary and king, Columbus of Genoa!
> Hanno of Carthage, the prince of Senegambia,
> Sinbad the Sailor, and mighty Ulysses,
> The grey waves that crash against the cape,
> Thunder their hymn to your glorious deeds.[36]

Used in this heroic sense, *passionarnost'* was disengaged from the complicated ebb and flow of the ethnogenetic process and identified more simply as an entirely personalized *élan vital* infecting only a few specific individuals. All of these great figures did what they did "not for the sake of wealth or revenge, but simply because they could not do otherwise. It was as if a propeller was turning inside of them, driving them into action."[37] These were passionary prototypes, whose personal qualities matched those of the new Soviet person in its Stalinist-Nietzschean casting: daring and courageous superindividuals rising above the level of the masses around them, capable of leading them and indeed "prepared to sacrifice their very lives for the sake of a common cause."[38]

Gumilev shared the admiration of Nietzsche that was common among Soviet intellectuals in the 1930s. At his arrest in 1935, a portrait of Nietzsche and a copy

---

36. Gumilev 1909, 137–41.
37. Gumilev 2003f, 63.
38. Gumilev and Balashov 1993, 139.

of *Also sprach Zarathustra* were found in his possession and added to his police file, as evidence of his anti-Soviet views.[39] Gumilev always discussed *passionarnost'* in Nietzschean terms, emphasizing its character as an elemental Dionysian force. "Like a fire, *passionarnost'* can provide warmth, but it can also burn you. When there is too little of it, things can be difficult, but it is awful (*strashno*) when there is too much."[40] Here as well, he would illustrate this awesome elementalism by citing a verse from his father, who himself had been influenced by Nietzsche:

Killing and bringing into life,
Swelling up with the soul of the universe—
This is the sacred will of the earth,
That she herself cannot understand.[41]

The very name he devised for this trait indicated its personalized and emotive quality, and he was always careful to explain to his readers that the Latin *passio* translated into Russian literally as *strast'*, or passion. His choice of this particular term was almost certainly influenced by the figure of the Basque communist Dolores Ibarruri (1895–1989), a hero of the Republican forces in the Spanish Civil War. Popularly known as "La Pasionaria," or the passion flower, Ibarruri fled into Soviet exile in 1939 and became a popular speaker there, thrilling her audiences with her dynamism and ardor.[42] *Passionarnost'* was a "feature of the psychological constitution of a given individual," located deep in the "sphere of the emotions" at the subconscious level of their personalities. Gumilev also invoked the authority of the Marxist classics on this point, maintaining that Engels had "determined that the stimulus for the development of civilization is not so much in the realm of ideas or political concepts but rather in *alchnost'* [lit: greed, avarice]—in other words, the emotions—which are located in the realm of the subconscious."[43] *Passionarnost'* was no less powerful for this, however, insofar as subconscious emotions "drive people to actions that integrate them into the processes of ethnogenesis and landscape formation to no less a degree than [rational] consciousness itself."[44] In a single individual, *passionarnost'* could be manifested across a wide variety of personality traits: selflessness, generosity, and loyalty, as well as greed, jealousy, and hubris.[45]

---

39. Beliakov 2012a, 147, 155. On Gumilev as a "young Nietzschean," see Demin 2008, 157–58; Kozyrev 2003, 279–80. For other discussions of Gumilev and Nietzsche, see Nifontov 2006; Frumkin 2001.

40. Gumilev 1970b, 48.

41. Gumilev 1921, 33. On Nikolai Gumilev and Nietzsche, see Rusinko 1994, 87–88.

42. Shnirel'man and Panarin 2000, 24; Klein 1992, 246; Beliakov 2012a, 144.

43. Gumilev 2004 [1967], 44; Efremov 1971, 79.

44. Gumilev 2001, 48–49; Gumilev 1970b, 50.

45. Gumilev 1970b, 46; Gumilev 1989c, 253, 292.

Gumilev's theory also reproduced the Stalinist ambivalence regarding the principle of collectivism. In our earlier discussion of *passionarnost'*, we saw that although he described it as a universal quality, at the same time he specified that certain individuals possessed it in a special way. Because Gumilev's heroic actor was the product of an energetic charge that far exceeded the norm, he or she necessarily stood apart from the masses, and all the personal characteristics and accomplishments associated with this heightened charge confirmed this individual's distinction as a sort of superperson. The priority of the collective was not displaced, however, and its group interests remained paramount. The passionary individual was not an egoist, but was rather motivated by an "antiegoistical ethics" in which "the interests of the collective—even if improperly understood—prevailed over the individual's survival instinct and concern with his own descendants." Spurred on by a shared inspiration, a small group of passionary individuals joined together in order to "smash the inertia of tradition and initiate [the formation of] new ethnies."[46] With this definitive act of passionary coalescence, a newborn ethnos drew its first breath. However, the particular "collective" that Gumilev had in mind still did not include the protoethnic masses in toto, but rather a "consortium," that is, a small assemblage of individuals set apart from these masses by the exceptionally high intensity of their passionary charge. Gumilev's lack of clarity on this point would seem to resonate with the ambivalences within the Stalinist prototype itself, as was unwittingly underscored in one discussion of Gumilev's ethnos theory, in which the dilemma of *passionarnost'* was framed in terms of the familiar Soviet juxtaposition of "the hero and the masses."[47]

As a final link to the Stalinist image of the new Soviet person, Gumilev made tentative efforts to frame his passionary individual as a sort of Promethean agent, driven to transform and reshape the world around him. This was both an immensely important and immensely problematic point for him. In his scientific formulation of his theory of ethnogenesis, Gumilev asserted unequivocally that ethnies were fully subject to the determining influence of the natural-geographical conditions in which they developed. It was, in other words, the ethnos that was shaped by the geographical environment and adapted to it, and not the other way around. This principle of dependency on external natural conditions was moreover essential for his more general argument that the ethnos was a natural part of a terrestrial biocenosis or ecological niche. But we have already seen that Gumilev was not entirely faithful to his own ecology of ethnicity. He subtly shifted his position by situating the ethnos—in addition to its local-ecological emplacement—within

---

46. Gumilev 1989c, 252; Gumilev 2004 [1970], 122.
47. Artamonov 1971, 75–77.

a grand biospheric network of cosmic energy circulation. Although such a dual arrangement was not contradictory and did not deny the principled determining influence of external natural conditions, it did serve to redefine the source of this influence by relocating it away from the earth's terrestrial environment and onto the cosmic bodies in outer space where the radiant energy in question originated.

Gumilev himself drew attention to this nuance. Insofar as *passionarnost'* was the product of variations in the radiation of cosmic energy, he explained, it was not really related to earth-bound "nature" (*priroda*) at all, but rather was linked to cosmic phenomena and hence was "of an entirely different order."[48] The clear implication was that the ethnogenetic process, which was most fundamentally driven by energetic *passionarnost'*, was liberated in significant ways from its dependency on "the external influences (*vozdeistviia*) or the conditions of the [earth's] landscape."[49] This liberation served to open up a certain space for autonomous activity on the part of the passionary agents of ethnogenesis. Their hyperactivism was driven by an internal dynamism that was no longer dependent, or at least not entirely dependent on its surrounding natural-geographical milieu. And this, in turn, meant that the relationship of the passionary individual to the earth's natural environment could be reformulated.

Gumilev signaled this reformulation in a not-so-subtle shift in terminology. Rather than "adapting" (*prisposobit'sia*) to the geographical environment, on occasion Gumilev spoke instead of the ethnic group "inscribing itself" (*vpisyvat'sia*) onto the surrounding natural landscape. While the process of inscription did not necessarily involve the alteration of natural conditions, it might under certain circumstances do so, as ethnic groups themselves now actively "reshape (*prisposobit'*)" the natural world around them.[50] "The landscape defines the possibilities of the ethnic collective at the moment of its creation, and the newborn ethnos changes (*izmeniaet*) the landscape in accordance with its needs."[51] Indeed, Gumilev implied that a passionary individual is an agent of transformation, in the sense that all passionary activity is distinguished by one universal feature, namely, "the ability and the determination to transform the natural world around them."[52] With this, Gumilev effectively abandoned his own description of ethnic groups as dependent subjects that adapt to the conditions of a natural landscape in favor of a position much more resonant with Stalinist transformism. Led by its dynamic passionary agents, the ethnos becomes an independent activist force, capable of creating and shaping the world around it. "Humankind

---

48. Gumilev 1971a, 81.
49. Gumilev 1978a, 98n.
50. Gumilev 1970a, 51 (quote), 54.
51. Gumilev 1989g.
52. Gumilev 1970b, 46 (quote); Gumilev 2004 [1970], 123.

not only adapts to the landscape but also uses its labor to adapt the landscape to its own needs and desires." *Passionarnost'* accordingly enables people to act not only as passive-adaptive agents but also to pursue creative (*tvorcheskie*) possibilities.[53] The capacity for hyperexertion that is part of the passionary condition is always directed toward the project of transforming the natural world. "The passionary individual [not only] carries out, but is unable not to carry out acts that lead to the alternation of its surrounding environment."[54] This process of landscape alternation through passionary intervention was pervasive throughout history and important enough for Gumilev—borrowing once again from ecological science—to give it a special name, calling it "anthropogenic succession."[55]

The fact that an ethnogenetic cycle was set in motion by a passionary surge meant that the emergence of each new ethnic group was marked by a new phase of landscape alternation. "The formation of a new ethnos always begins with a single peculiarity: an insuperable inner striving on the part of a small group of people toward an intensely active goal-oriented endeavor, which is always connected with the alteration of the external environment."[56] This correlation between ethnic formation and landscape alternation, Gumilev claimed, could be observed across five thousand years of human history.[57] Throughout this time, transformist activity was not merely a side product of the ethnogenetic process but a vital ethnogenetic rite of passage in and of itself. Moreover, each ethnos transformed the environment in unique manner.[58] Effectively, shared transformist activity represented a vital source of primordial ethnic solidarity. A collective (*kollektiv*) of passionary individuals, "cemented together by a goal they have chosen for themselves and by a common destiny," forms an initial protoethnic core that will eventually develop into an ethnos.[59] And the goal that animates them is nothing less than the reshaping of the natural world around them. "The collective undertakes a titanic project of the reconstruction (*perestroika*) of nature in order to secure what it needs from the environment. This task is more complicated than the conquest of neighboring groups, but having accomplished it, the collective—now welded together (*spaiannyi*) by a common cause—becomes an ethnos, lives off of the reshaped landscape, no longer transforming but only maintaining it."[60] Gumilev illustrated this process with examples from across the

53. Gumilev 1989c, 174.
54. Gumilev 1970b, 50 (quote); Gumilev 1970a, 55.
55. Gumilev 1989c, 179, 480.
56. Gumilev 1970b, 44 (quote); Gumilev 1989c, 91.
57. Gumilev 1970a, 51.
58. Gumilev 1970d.
59. Gumilev 2001, 44–45.
60. Gumilev 1970a, 54 (quote); Gumilev 1989c, 234.

historical record. His reference to a "common cause," however, came verbatim from the title of Nikolai Fedorov's *Filosofiia obshchego dela* and leaves no doubt as to the uncanny resonance between his theory of *passionarnost'*, the project of the new Soviet person, and the transformist *Zeitgeist* of Stalinist Russia.[61]

Despite these resonances, however, Gumilev's notion of *passionarnost'* cannot be reduced to a Stalinist essence. We have emphasized how the principle of heroic voluntarism contravened the environmental determinism that was an explicit condition of his natural-organic model of ethnicity, and we have also seen his own inconsistency as he tried to argue for both of these alternatives. In the final analysis, it was a contravention that Gumilev could not bring himself entirely to accept. He was obviously still struggling with it in an interview at the end of his life, in which he attempted to resolve the dilemma by drawing a simple but unconvincing equivalency. "An act of will"—in other words, an act of passionary voluntarism—"is also a natural phenomenon"—that is, compliant with natural determination.[62] In the final analysis, there really was no choice for him but to view *passionarnost'* as a natural phenomenon subject like everything else to universal natural laws. In any other case, his assertion that it obeyed the second law of thermodynamics would make no sense. This law set forth the principle of entropy, which for Gumilev meant that the initial charge of energy that drove his passionary actors necessarily dissipated over time and would eventually and inescapably be exhausted. The vitalistic dynamism of the Stalinist protagonist, by contrast, operated under no such constraints; to the contrary, it was the new Soviet person who would dictate the rules for the functioning of the natural world. Needless to say, Stalinism made no comparable provision for the decline and eventual exhaustion of the dynamic energy that powered *its* heroes.

Indeed, in a variety of ways Gumilev's *passionarnost'* operated entirely outside of the parameters that defined Stalinist Prometheanism and the new Soviet person. The Stalinist hero was invariably an ethical, morally just, and virtuous activist

---

61. Further evidence of this inclination can be seen in the following verse, which Gumilev composed during his Noril'sk exile in the early 1940s:

In the rain and frost I built this city,
And so that it would be higher than the hills around it
I turned my own soul in a stone,
And used the stone to decorate the road.

As Gumilev's biographer Sergei Beliakov observes, "these lines could have been published without censorship in any party or trade-union paper. Everything is there: optimism, the conquest of nature, and the great construction projects of socialism—that favorite theme of Soviet poets. If Gumilev were not an outcast prisoner in the Noril'sk labor camp but a member of the Union of Writers, this verse could even have been published in *Pravda*." Beliakov 2012a: 159.

62. Gumilev 1994c, 280; Demin 2008, 157.

whose grand deeds served the greatest historical endeavor to date—the construction of a socialist society.[63] It was true that Gumilev's passionary individuals, with their abundant energy and limitless personal determination, were as capable as these Stalinist heroes of great feats that carried a positive world-historical significance.[64] But this did not mean that the passionary individual was necessarily a moral actor, that *passionarnost'* was inherently a virtuous quality, or that in all cases it led to constructive and positive deeds. Very much to the contrary, Gumilev argued forcefully that the passionary impulse was strictly neutral in an ethical sense: neither inherently good nor bad, neither moral nor immoral. *Passionarnost'*, he explained, had no relation to ethical norms, and gave rise in equal measure to great accomplishments and heinous crimes, to creative genius and destructive will, to good and to evil.[65] The only thing it could not be is indifferent. In this regard, it might be noted, Gumilev was rather more careful than Stalinist ideologues in his adherence to the letter of the Nietzschean text, which described the *Übermensch*— rather like the passionary individual—as operating precisely *jenseits von Gut und Böse*: "beyond good and evil," entirely outside of and above all moral systems.

The goals that inspired passionary individuals, moreover, were unlike those of Soviet heroes. They were not conceived on the basis of rational deliberation and sober judgement, and they did not necessarily involve the ultimate betterment or perfection of society. Rather they were often, even usually, irrational, ephemeral, and, "as a rule, illusory."[66] In likening passionary eruptions of emerging ethnies to the migrations of lemmings, the swarming of locusts, or the irresistible assaults of ant armies, Gumilev was not only making a point about their naturalistic essence and the unity of the geobiochemical energy that drove them all. He was also emphasizing the irrational futility of these paroxysms of collective activity, which brought the lemmings, locusts, and ants no benefit but led them instead to certain death.[67] In this manner, Gumilev provided his own original twist on the Dionysian emotionalism of the day, suggesting that the passionary individual acted not in accordance with the impulses of unbridled human instinct but was rather motivated by precisely the opposite. *Passionarnost'*, that is to say, was counter- or anti-instinctual. It drove the individual who possessed it to override their natural inclinations and good sense, compelling them even to "destroy (*lomat'*) their instinct of self-preservation." This counterinstinctual passionary impulse could be so strong that those individuals affected by it "are unable to evaluate the consequences of their actions and—even if they sense that these actions will

63. McCannon 1997, 349–50.
64. Gumilev and Balashov 1993, 140.
65. Gumilev 2004 [1970], 122.
66. Gumilev 1978a, 98n; Gumilev 1990c, 4.
67. Gumilev 2003f.

lead to immanent death—still cannot refrain from carrying them out."[68] More often than not, *passionarnost'* stimulates behavior that diverges from the norms of the species and is thus clinically pathological rather than beneficial. Indeed, the passionary agent is often the very model of abnormality. "Of course, all passionary individuals are freaks (*urody*)," he observed matter-of-factly, adding that their lack of an instinct for self-preservation means they are relatively quickly eliminated in the course of "natural selection."[69]

This final point leads directly to Gumilev's most significant divergence with Soviet Prometheanism. The clearest evidence of passionary abnormality, he maintained, was to be seen in the effects of *passionarnost'* on the natural landscape. Like the new Soviet person, the passionary individual transforms the natural environment, but quite unlike the Stalinist agent does not necessarily do so in a rational, constructive, or beneficial manner. Indeed, the hyperenergized drive of *passionarnost'* to reshape the natural world, with the ostensible aim of better meeting the needs of the group, can easily result instead in environmental disruption and destruction. "No matter how viciously passionary individuals may fight with each other," the way they treat "the natural environment that provides their sustenance is far more deadly."[70] He listed numerous examples of the ill effects of passionary environmental alteration: the irrigation works of the ancient Sumerians led to the desiccation of Tigris-Euphrates delta, the clearing of primeval forests in North America by European settlers making way for cotton plantations resulted in erosion and soil degradation, and the ploughing of the grasslands in the American Midwest led directly to the dust storms of the 1930s.[71] Gumilev dismissed the official Soviet explanation that attributed the problem of environmental destruction to retrograde forms of socioeconomic organization, connected in the present day to the irrationalities of the capitalist system. "Humankind's rapacious treatment of the natural world can take place in all economic formations [and historical periods]," he insisted, "and for this reason cannot be seen as the result of social progress. Humankind deforms nature in all economic formations—it obviously possesses a special capacity for this."[72] Thus Gumilev saw environmental destruction as an inherent part of the human condition, inextricably interconnected with *passionarnost'* and the processes of ethnic formation and development.[73]

---

68. Gumilev 1970b, 50, 46 (quotes); Gumilev 2001, 66–67; Gumilev 1988b, 47; Gumilev 1978a, 99–100.

69. Gumilev 2003f, 64 (quote); Gumilev 1970b, 46; Gumilev 1989c, 308–9; Gumilev 2001, 49.

70. Gumilev 2001, 283.

71. Gumilev 2001, 284–86; Gumilev 1989c, 174–75.

72. Gumilev 1989c, 174 (quote); Gumilev 1989g.

73. Gumilev also identified environmental destruction as evidence of the negative effects of anti-systems and chimeras. Gumilev 1989h, 35, 448.

The great importance of this point for Gumilev can be seen in the critique he directed against one of the most important scientific formulations of the principles of Soviet transformism, namely, Vernadskii's concept of the "noosphere." As noted above, Vernadskii envisioned it as a realm of absolute human reason, developing in the modern world as an autonomous "geological force" ever more capable of shaping and directing the natural processes of the universe to better serve the needs of human society. Like Gumilev, Vernadskii assumed that the natural process of entropy described in the second law of thermodynamics played a significant role in the operations of the biosphere. Quite unlike Gumilev, however, Vernadskii believed that rational human intervention could eventually overcome the natural tendency to energy dissipation and overall decline and collapse.[74] This belief of course ran counter to the spirit of Gumilev's own naturalism, which did not question the natural inevitability of the effects of entropy in bringing about the demise of all ethnies. Despite Gumilev's veneration of Vernadskii and his repeated declarations that his own theories were based directly on the great scientist's ideas, he was outspoken in his skepticism regarding Vernadskii's theory about this "realm of rationality" or "technosphere."[75] "What has this noosphere—if it really exists—given us?" he queried incredulously. "From the Paleolithic age there are remains of flint chippings, discarded scrapers and blades, from the Neolithic there are trash mounds on the locations of former settlements. Antiquity had given us the ruins of cities, and the Middle Ages the ruins of castles. And even when ancient monuments survive to our day, such as the pyramids or the Acropolis, these are always inert structures that merely crumble at a slower rate than the rest." In our own day, he concluded, "you would hardly find someone who would prefer to see heaps of waste or concrete lots instead of forests and steppes."[76] In the fullness of time, he was suggesting, the products of human rationality would prove to be both transient and inconsequential in comparison with the truly enduring phenomena and processes of the natural world.[77]

Gumilev's final observation pointed to his most damning conclusion. Unbounded faith in the inevitable ascendance of human reason over the natural world was not merely misplaced but it was also destructive, for it led to the desecration and destruction of very natural environments that humankind needed in

---

74. Hagemeister 1989, 260n.

75. Gumilev 1989c, 23, 49; Mirzoian 1998; Beliakov 2012a, 713.

76. Gumilev 1989c, 316.

77. Much of the literature on Gumilev is anxious to situate him in the Cosmist tradition, and thus does not recognize this most important divergence with Vernadskii's teachings; e.g., Demin 2008, 193–99. In fact, Gumilev's association with Cosmism is highly tenuous: see Beliakov 2008; Ermekbaev 2003, 14; Petrov 2005, 258–60. On Gumilev and Cosmism in general, see Golovanov 1998; Kochanek 1998, 1186; Hagemeister 1997, 199; Lavreonova 2007, 116. In addition to the "noosphere," Gumilev also rejected the Fedorovian notion of the resurrection of the dead. Gumilev 2003f.

order to survive. It was, in other words, precisely the anthropocentric conceit of the noosphere that caused, or at least made possible, the "rapacious ravaging of natural resources or the disfiguration of the landscape" through various forms of human intervention.[78] In particular, this Promethean impulse had brought about the large-scale pollution and despoliation of the natural world across the Soviet Union. During the perestroika years, Gumilev was to speak out frequently about the "thoughtless distortions of nature"—for example the desiccation of the Aral Sea basin or the pollution of Lake Baikal—that were the consequence of the Soviet transformist project.[79] Two decades earlier, however, his readership was already picking up on this critical stance that was implicit in his work. As we will see, when a movement of environmental protection began to emerge in the 1960s, Gumilev would be regarded as one of its most important inspirers.

The Return of Ecology

In view of the central importance of the nature-society relationship for Stalinist ideology, it is not surprising that this issue should have reemerged prominently in the post-Stalinist debates of the 1960s and 1970s. On many fronts, the dogmatic assertion of an absolute separation between the social and the natural worlds was openly questioned. Nature and society were not in fact separate categories, it was now countered, but rather were existentially intertwined as part of a single integrated system, within which they operated synergically.[80] The Promethean premise that modern society, following inexorable laws of historical development, was destined to take ever-greater control over the natural world was challenged by a variety of more holistic perspectives. The notion that advanced human society remained dependent on the natural world, which had been triumphally banished from the Stalinist canon, found its way back in, along with a renewed appreciation of how the project of anthropogenic alteration can lead not to the betterment but rather to the destruction of the environment. The latter insight was abundantly supported by the material legacy of the despoliation of the Soviet landscape through decades of reckless pursuit of industrialization and *preobrazovanie*. The depth of the post-Stalinist concern for this problem can be seen in the emergence in the 1960s of popular movements for environmental protection—the first independent civic initiatives ever in the USSR.[81]

It is also not surprising that a critique of this particular dimension of Stalinist orthodoxy should have had a special resonance in those academic disciplines

---

78. Gumilev 1968b, 591.
79. Gumilev 1989a (quote); Gumilev 1988b.
80. Weiner 1999b, 312–75.
81. Komarov 1978; Ziegler 1985.

that had been particularly affected by it. Thus one of the earliest manifestations of the new holistic spirit came from the field of geography, which as noted had been divided in the 1930s into economic (society) and physical (nature) sections on the basis of the Stalinist position. In 1960, the Moscow geographer Vsevolod Aleksandrovich Anuchin (1913–1984) published *Theoretical Problems of Geography*, in which he called for the establishment of an *edinaia geografiia* or "unified geography" that would reassemble the sundered sections of the discipline and place the nature-society nexus at the very center of its attention.[82] Anuchin's thesis stimulated a nationwide debate that extended over many years and eventually culminated on the pages of the leading literary journal *Literaturnaia Gazeta*.

The liberalization of approaches to the nature-society juxtaposition was also reflected in the work of psychologists, who now began to study how the qualities of the "internal" nature of human psychology might influence different types of social behavior. The reemergence of the field of genetics after Lysenko's demise in the mid-1960s provided further stimulation for this line of inquiry, and within a few years Soviet scientists were openly and sympathetically discussing the tenets of sociobiology.[83] There was considerable public interest in these issues as well and they were debated in another popular forum, the journal *Novyi Mir*, in 1971.[84] The new focus on a nature-society synthesis was also evident in a wave of interest in the field of ecology. Vernadskii's teachings about the biosphere and noosphere were rediscovered at this time and became extremely popular. His scholarly works, now reissued (or in some cases published for the first time), offered an authoritative source of inspiration for what was effectively a post-Stalinist ecological *Weltanschauung*.[85] Indeed, the image of a richly bearded and contemplative Vernadskii achieved something of a cult status.[86] The legacy of other Cosmist thinkers such as Chizhevskii similarly attracted new interest, as their works as well were reissued and their ideas discussed afresh.[87]

Gumilev's thinking in the 1960s and 1970s was heavily influenced by these post-Stalinist developments. The new sociobiological tendencies in psychology, the revival of genetics, and the recovery of the works of Vernadskii all provided a critical foundation for him to develop further his own concepts and theories.

---

82. Anuchin 1960; Anuchin 1975; Anuchin 1972; Anuchin 1982; Gerasimov 1968; Khudushin 1966.
83. Graham 1987, 224, 226–44.
84. Graham 1987, 226–27, 244–47.
85. For example, Vernadskii 1965; Vernadskii 1978; Trusov 1969.
86. Graham 1993, 232.
87. Chizhevskii 1955; Chizhevskii 1963; Chizhevskii and Shishina 1969; Andrews 2009.

Gumilev's writings did not, however, merely reflect the ideas of the day. More than this, they played a highly significant role in their own right in the process of transcending the old Stalinist categories.[88] Gumilev's insistence on the organic interconnections between human ethnic communities and the natural world directly challenged the rigid Stalinist distinction between the realms of the social and the natural. In his historical-geographical studies of precipitation cycles in the Caspian basin, he developed a sort of early version of environmental history, arguing for the direct influence of changes in climatic and physical-geographical conditions on the historical fate of the Khazars and other peoples of the region.[89] His approach had something in common with the *Annales* school in France, and indeed he wrote a sympathetic review of Emmanuel Le Roy Ladurie's *Histoire du climat depuis l'an mil* (1967) when it appeared in Russian translation in 1971.[90] In a different regard, his ethnos theory asserted the ecological embeddedness of ethnic groups in the geographical landscapes in which they originated and developed. Although his magnum opus on the subject was not published until 1989, numerous copies of the dissertation on which it was based had been in circulation since the mid-1970s, and in any event he had set out the essentials of his perspective in a series of essays titled "Landscape and Ethnos," which appeared in fourteen installments from 1964 to 1973.[91]

Finally, Gumilev took a stand against the ongoing destruction of the natural world by grandiose Soviet construction projects—in other words, against the very transformist urge that elsewhere he had theorized as a ubiquitous and essential aspect of ethnic history. As he immodestly recalled in 1990, "I . . . was the first [in Russia] to take a stand as a 'green,' and I nearly lost my job because of it. I was saved by the fall of Khrushchev [in 1964]. I said that changing the course of Siberian rivers [to flow southward] into Kazakhstan would be ruinous. . . . How I was attacked for that!"[92] In the late 1980s he was a signatory to a letter to Mikhail Gorbachev protesting the planned construction of a chemical factory near Novgorod, and—despite his intense suspicion of all Western-sponsored international organizations—was a supporter of Greenpeace.[93] Inside the transformist project, he asserted, "lurks an evil will" that has deceived the "trusting peoples of Russia, and treats them cruelly and dishonorably."[94]

---

88. Iudel'son 2001, 157.
89. Bruno 2007, 642, 647. For a contemporary critique, see Andrianov 1968.
90. Le Rua Ladiuri 1971; Gumilev 1971d; Beliakov 2012a, 371–76.
91. For example, Gumilev 1964c; Gumilev 1967b.
92. Gumilev 1990b.
93. Beliakov 2012a, 690.
94. Gumilev 1989h, 34–35.

With his unconventional approach, fresh writing style, and disarmingly unorthodox conclusions, Gumilev was considered by many as a leading proponent for the new ecological perspective.[95] What he seemed to offer was quite simply one of the boldest, most imaginative, and most original attempts available to Soviet readers to bring nature and society together into a single conceptual framework, and with this to promote the new environmentalist sensibilities of the day. No less a luminary than Dmitrii Likhachev emphasized this fact retrospectively, in an evaluation of Gumilev's work prepared in the mid-1980s. Confirming his own belief in the importance of synthesizing the human and social sciences, Likhachev spoke of his pride in the fact that "the discovery of humankind's existence as part of the biosphere (*biosfernoe bytie cheloveka*) belongs to our compatriot" Lev Gumilev.[96] Indeed, interest in Gumilev as an advocate for a post-Stalinist perspective on the nature-society relationship extended beyond the Soviet Union. In France, the distinguished journal of the *Annales* school published an overview of his historical-geographical research on Khazaria,[97] and the first English-language translations of Gumilev appeared already in the 1960s in the American geographical journal *Soviet Geography: Review and Translation*, edited by Theodore Shabad (1922–1987). American geographers followed the Soviet nature-society debates in the 1960s and 1970s very closely, and were aware of Gumilev's position in them.[98] They did not, to be sure, understand the significance of his ethnos theory, and they certainly had no sense whatsoever of the deeper political content and implications of his ideas. They were, however, quite aware of the deleterious effect that the Stalinist canon had had on their discipline in the USSR and thus very much appreciated the challenge to this orthodoxy that they believed Gumilev was raising. Gumilev's Leningrad colleague Iurii Konstantinovich Efremov (1913–1999) testified to his friend's special popularity among the Americans. "American geographers visiting Soviet geographical

---

95. Podgorodnikov 1974; Koreniako 2005, 209–10.

96. Likhachev 2003a, 341. In the 1980s, Likhachev was asked on several occasions to write evaluations of Gumilev's work for the Central Committee. His tone was measured and he did not conceal his disagreements with Gumilev, but he consistently confirmed the importance of the latter's work for Soviet scholarship and urged that his doctoral dissertation be published. Likhachev 2003b, 338–40; Mirovich 1991, 158. Despite this, their respective political and intellectual orientations remained far apart, and recent attempts to harmonize them are not convincing; see Zapesotskii 2007; Zapesotskii and Zobnin 2007.

97. Szyszman 1970; also see Gumilev 1965.

98. Matley 1982; Hooson 1962; Chappell 1965; Chappell 1975. For Gumilev in *Soviet Geography*, see Gumilev 1964b; Gumilev 1968c. Gumilev's work was also published in the more prestigious American journal *Geographical Review*. Gumilev 1970c. On Shabad and Gumilev, see Lavrov 2000, 313.

congresses literally scrambled (*l'nut'*) to meet Gumilev and were proud of the opportunity" to have contact with him.[99]

Efremov, a distinguished physical geographer and ecologist in his own right who taught alongside Gumilev on the Faculty of Geography, was a leading specialist and spokesman for the new environmentalism and had helped draft some of the earliest Soviet legislation on environmental protection.[100] He enthusiastically described Gumilev's naturalistic perspective on ethnos as a "priceless contribution" to the project of overcoming the Stalinist legacy. "Stalin commanded us to think that the geographical environment was capable only of speeding up or slowing down social development, but could in no way [directly] influence it in any decisive manner whatsoever." Gumilev, however, demonstrated a direct link, in the sense that the behavioral stereotype of the ethnos represented "a higher form of adaptation to environmental conditions." Gumilev's arguments established "not only the possibility but indeed the necessity of studying precisely the connections between nature and society in any science."[101] Efremov recognized the internal/external bifurcation of the natural world and maintained that Gumilev's "great achievement" was his bold recognition of the influence of natural factors not only "in the natural environment and landscape" but also in the internal "psycho-physiological aspects of human communities" and human individuals.[102] When in the 1970s a new field of "social ecology" took shape in Soviet academics, devoted to the study of the interactions between society and the natural world, its founders acknowledged how they were inspired by Gumilev.[103]

A fuller indication of the contemporary appreciation of Gumilev as a proponent of ecological principles can be seen in a discussion of his work among a group of historians, geographers, and philosophers at Leningrad State University in the spring of 1975. Whereas some months earlier Soviet ethnographers had had subjected Gumilev's theories to withering criticism (examined in the next

---

99. Efremov 2003, 28. As a geography graduate student, the present writer shared this fascination, which led to the 1980 meeting with Gumilev described in the Introduction. For discussions of Gumilev's work by American geographers from this period see Chappell 1970, 369–71; Chappell 1975, 154; Matley 1982, 375, 378; Wagner 1991. Indeed, the very first of the now innumerable doctoral dissertations devoted to Gumilev was written in a Canadian department of geography. Brownson 1988. For the same reason, American geographers were also extremely interested in the work of Anuchin, whose book on *edinaia geografiia* was translated into English by Shabad's son. Anuchin 1977.

100. Efremov 2003, 31; Weiner 1999b, 260–62, 265–70.

101. Efremov 2003, 33; Efremov 1971, 79.

102. Efremov 1971, 79.

103. Komarov 1977; Girusov 1976; Komarov n.d.

chapter), most of the participants in the Leningrad symposium were sympathetic and positive, indeed very strongly so. Their favorable evaluations focused on Gumilev's success in bringing the realms of the social and national into a single conceptual framework. "At the present moment," one participant declared,

> the biological nature of human individuals and humankind is beginning to be of interest, not only to natural scientists but also to philosophers. At a time when there is talk of crisis in our interactions with the biosphere, the problem of the relationship between the biological and the social has assumed new relevance. . . . The whole phenomenon of man represents a unity of two systems, the organism as a biological system and the personality as a social system. . . . Nor can mankind be viewed simply as a social phenomenon, as society; the history of mankind at every stage also has to be considered on a biological level.

"It therefore seems to us," the speaker concluded, "that there is considerable value in Gumilev's attempt to look at history from a new point of view and to examine those aspects that derive from the biological nature of man and from the impact of biological environment."[104]

Gumilev's treatment of "geographical factors" attracted particular attention, for social organization and evolution should no longer be explained solely in terms of the standard Marxist criteria of economic base, superstructure, and means of production. On the one hand, Gumilev recognized that geographical conditions had in fact exerted an effect on social development throughout history that was, if not "determining," then at least direct and significant.[105] More urgently, however, Gumilev's environmentalism had an immediate relevance to the crisis of environmental destruction that was increasingly threatening not only Soviet but also world society. "If we want to prevent a negative impact," it was asserted at the symposium, "we must investigate the relationship between man and his natural habitat." Precisely this relationship had been discounted and even denied by Stalinism, but Gumilev's bold new ideas offered a chance to reconceptualize and reintroduce it back into contemporary understandings of the world.

The speakers at the 1975 meeting also largely endorsed Gumilev's argument for the positive resonance between his own conceptions and those of Marx. His theories of ethnogenesis were "not in conflict with Marxist philosophy" in regard to either dialectical or historical materialism.[106] But having established

---

104. "Critique of L. N. Gumilev's Work" 1977, 124.
105. Ibid., 125.
106. Ibid., 127.

Gumilev's conformity with this still-sacrosanct parameter of Soviet academic discourse, his commentators proceeded subtly to shift the juxtaposition by intimating that Gumilev offered a sort of valuable supplement to Marxism involving novel factors that were not in fact part of the classical Marxist legacy. At issue here was Gumilev's theory of *passionarnost'*, with its emphasis on the psychological and emotional dimension of human behavior. "History is made by people, and [thus] the subjective factor leaves its imprint on the course of world events." This subjective factor involved "socio-psychological dynamics," of which Gumilev's *passionarnost'*—inexplicable in terms of familiar Marxist categories—was an excellent example. "There are facts in history that we cannot explain in terms of productive forces." Another speaker went yet further, maintaining that the best way to achieve a new understanding of the society-nature relationship might be to disregard the Marxist principle of "modes of production" altogether. "Such an approach might make it easier to deal specifically with the mechanism of the man-nature relationship."[107]

Gumilev and The Neo-Stalinist Consensus

These challenges to the spirit of Stalinist Prometheanism encountered determined resistance from those still-considerable forces who remained faithful to the old status quo. The question about the relationship between nature and society, it turned out, had lost none of the ideological significance that Stalin and other Russian Marxist theoreticians had always accorded it. Indeed, Loren Graham has suggested that the disputations around this particular issue were emblematic of a more general "crisis of ideology" in the late Soviet period.[108] Thus a new, quasi-official position—a sort of tentative neo-Stalinist consensus on the nature-society question—took shape in opposition to the revisionist perspectives we have just considered. A significant concession was made to the revisionists with the acknowledgement that Stalin had pressed the absolute separation of nature and society too far, and there was now a preparedness to admit that the two did indeed "interact."[109] Nevertheless, the argument that the "two environments"—the realms of the natural and the social—operated according to different laws of the motion of matter was reasserted (albeit in somewhat softer terms), as was the original Stalinist distinction between them as distinct

107. Ibid., 123–24.
108. Graham 1987, 220.
109. Konstantinov 1964, 66–67; Ilyichev 1964, 32–33.

entities.[110] "The fact that the human individual is a living organism," admonished the leading Stalinist authority on Marxist philosophy and dialectical materialism Fedor Vasel'evich Konstantinov (1901–1991), "should not lead to the conclusion that society is a part of living nature."[111] Indeed, even as the popular new concerns with environmental destruction began to find some official support, the old transformist perspective that had created the problem in the first place was also firmly endorsed. A resolution of the Twenty-fourth Congress of the CPSU in 1971 called, surreally, for the "development of scientific principles for the protection *and* the transformation of nature, with the aim of improving man's natural environment and bettering his use of natural resources."[112]

Other advocates of a neo-Stalinist position on society and nature displayed no such ambivalence. Boris Nikolaevich Semevskii (1907–1976), the dean of the geography faculty at Leningrad State University, wrote a strongly worded denunciation of unified geography, castigating the "grossly erroneous" efforts on the part of Anuchin and his supporters to identify a seamless unity between society and nature.[113] In his article "The Geographical Environment" for the third, post-Stalinist, edition of the *Great Soviet Encyclopedia*, Stanislav Vikent'evich Kalesnik (1901–1977)—academician, director of the Oceanographic Institute, and influential president of the All-Union Russian Geographical Society—went yet further. In what was effectively a reassertion of the original Stalinist position, Kalesnik affirmed the qualitative separation of the social and the natural worlds and repeated that social development was determined above all by the means of production. Geographical conditions may have an influence in "accelerating" or "retarding" the pace of this development, precisely as Stalin had suggested, but otherwise they remain entirely detached from it.[114] Kalesnik argued that there can be no "qualitative hybrids" between nature and society, "no matter how closely they interpenetrate one another." Social organization represented the "aggregate of man's productive relationships," and as such it stood entirely apart from the natural world. By the same token, nature "cannot include social elements." The laws governing the operation of the social and natural worlds were entirely different. It was not possible directly to invoke the authority of Stalin on this point, and so Kalesnik referred instead to Lenin, who likened the contrast between nature and society (human labor) to the difference between *pudy* and *arshiny*—that is to

110. Khozin 1979, 30; Liamin 1967; Liamin 1978, 209; Konstantinov 1964, 62, 66–68; Matley 1982, 380–81.

111. Konstantinov 1964, 68.

112. *Materialy XXIV s"ezda KPSS* 1971, 244, cited in Efremov 1978, 14 (emphasis added).

113. Semevskii 1970, 506; Semevskii 1974.

114. Kalesnik 1971a.

say, between incommensurable units of weight and length.[115] The principled dis-association of society from the natural world, moreover, meant that the two were actively "opposed" to each other—a formulation which effectively brought the Promethean discourse of the 1930s over into the post-Stalin period.[116] The fundamental challenge for Soviet society, Kalesnik made clear, remained unchanged from the original Stalinist goal, namely, the "planned, rational transformation of nature."[117]

Gumilev's own perspective on these questions may have seemed clear enough to the audiences discussed in the previous section, but in fact his position in these post-Stalinist debates was profoundly ambiguous. Despite the iconoclastic ecological and holistic tone of his work, in important ways he sided with the neo-Stalinist establishment and against the revisionists. The basis for his position derived from his view of the nature of ethnicity. Gumilev's naturalization of ethnicity came at the expense of divorcing it ontologically from all aspects of social existence. As we have seen in an earlier chapter, Gumilev insisted on the radical and absolute differentiation between ethnic and social being, between the ethnosphere and the sociosphere. The ethnos stood completely outside of any social category and operated on an entirely different basis. This principled disas-sociation had two immediate implications. On the one hand, it made it possible to identity the ethnos explicitly as a biological-ecological entity and an organic part of the natural world. At the same time, however, the differentiation of *etnos* and *obshchestvo* meant that society itself remained in principle entirely separate from the natural world. The quirky upshot was that at the same time that Gumilev was flouting Stalinist orthodoxy in the most radical fashion with an elaborate naturalistic description of ethnic being, he was also simultaneously confirming and endorsing the essential Stalinist severance of the social from the natural.

This ambivalence was reflected precisely in Gumilev's schizophrenic attempts to correlate his theories to Soviet-Marxist doctrines. On the one hand, he appealed to the holistic aspiration of Marx's youthful works to combine the histories of the human and natural worlds into a single grand scheme. He took the title of his review of Le Roy Ladurie—"from the history of people to the history of nature"—from *The German Ideology*, and it was this aspiration that inspired his own argument that the ethnos was a part of the biosphere.[118] But the "history of people" that he had in mind included not all forms of human existence but only those parts of it that belonged to the realm of the natural—in

---

115. Kalesnik 1971b, 199, 200, 203; also see Kalesnik 1966, 50.
116. Konstantinov 1964, 61, 68 (quotes); Kalesnik 1971b, 204.
117. Kalesnik 1971b, 204.
118. Gumilev 1971c, 117.

other words, the ethnosphere. Social formations as such (the "sociosphere") he considered to be in fact *separate* from the natural world—a position comfortably in accord with Marxist teachings in their Stalinist redaction. Quite unlike his ideas about ethnies, Gumilev's conceptualization of social dynamics remained scrupulously faithful to Soviet-Marxist orthodoxy. Thus, he reaffirmed that the primary condition of social existence was "the means of production of material goods. People join together in the process of production, and the result of this union are social relations, which are framed in one of five famous formations: primitive communism, slave-owning, feudal, capitalist, and communist."[119] Societies were divided internally into classes on the basis of their relationship to the means of production.[120] Society was separated from the natural world by the unique human qualities of intelligence and reason, which enable social agents to shape their own destiny through the development of tools and technology—a process over which the natural world had no influence. "When we speak about the history of humankind, we usually have in mind the social form of the motion of matter—the progressive development of humanity. Neither geographical nor biological influences can significantly affect its internal regular operations (*zako-nomernosti*)."[121] The dependency on the natural world described in his theory of ethnogenesis "relates not to social, but to ethnic collectives."[122] Nature creates things "that humans cannot create: mountains and rivers, forests, steppes, and new forms of plants and animals. People [i.e. society] build houses, construct machines, erect statues, and write manifestos. Nature cannot do that. Is there a principled difference between the works of nature and the works of [social] man? Yes!"[123]

Gumilev accepted the Soviet-Marxist theory of historical materialism, with its notion of discrete laws of the motion of matter, as the most appropriate explanation for the historical development of society.[124] "Dialectical materialism distinguishes various forms of the movement of matter: mechanical, physical, chemical, and biological, all of which are categorized as natural (*prirodnye*). The *social* form of the movement of matter differs from all these by virtue of the fact that it is peculiar to humankind . . . ."[125] According to the theory of historical materialism, "society has its own special rhythm of autonomous [i.e., unaffected

119. Gumilev 1989c, 49.
120. Gumilev 1989c, 21.
121. Gumilev 1987a, Gumilev 1989c, 37.
122. Gumilev 1993a, 270.
123. Gumilev 1989c, 18 (quote), 23, 315.
124. Gumilev 1987a (quote); Gumilev 1989c, 22, 49; Gumilev 1970a, 50.
125. Gumilev 1989c, 50 (quote; emphasis added), 22–23, 132; Gumilev 1988d; Gumilev 1987a.

by natural influences] development (*samorazvitie*)."[126] All of this could have been taken from any standard Soviet text on Marxist theory. In his last interviews, Gumilev repeated that he "fully respected Marx" and had "no argument with Marxism"—no argument, in other words, with the specific *zakonomernosti* or laws of social development as set forth in the catechism of Soviet dialectical materialism.[127] The fact that he continued to emphasize his fidelity to Marxism at this late date, when there was no longer any censorial pressure for him to do so and his readers would indeed have been expecting something quite different, clearly indicates that it reflected his genuine conviction. He took pains to emphasize that his ethnos theory was not in any way intended "to replace [Marxist] teachings about the primacy of social development in history," but rather "to supplement it with the hard data of natural science."[128]

As is clear from the discussion earlier in the chapter, there was little appreciation among Gumilev's enthusiastic audiences of his fidelity to the Stalinist and neo-Stalinist disassociation of the social and the natural. To the contrary, they believed that what he offered was a complete departure from the official position. Efremov commented with fond bemusement on what seemed to him to be his friend's eccentric insistence on the distinction between the "sociosphere" and the "ethnosphere," while the deeper significance of Gumilev's position was completely lost on him.[129] Efremov failed to appreciate how this arcane but apparently innocuous rigidity in Gumilev's categories was in fact founded entirely logically and faithfully on the principles of Soviet dialectics. He mistakenly assumed that Gumilev recognized along with him the "absurdity" of the view that society did not conform to natural laws, and he tellingly mischaracterized Gumilev's concept of the ethnos as "biosocial." The latter, he maintained, represented "an invaluable contribution" to demonstrating "the connections between society and the natural world," and he suggested that in this regard there was a clear affinity between Gumilev's perspective and Anuchin's "unified geography."[130]

As far as Gumilev himself was concerned, there was nothing of the sort. The question of Anuchin's work was indeed a vital one, but not at all in the way that Efremov suggested. Not only was Gumilev's position not sympathetic to that of

---

126. Gumilev 1967b.

127. Gumilev 1994c, 271 (quote); Gumilev and Ivanov 1992, 51; Gumilev and Balashov 1993, 135.

128. Gumilev 1978a, 103. For confirmations of Gumilev's positive appreciation of Marx and Engels, see Luk"ianov 2003, 64; Loseff 1994, 3–4; Bogdanov 2002. For an alternative view (Gumilev "hated" Marx), see Borodai 1995, 112.

129. Gumilev 1989c, 315–16. Gumilev himself remarked on his colleague's incomplete understanding of this point.

130. Efremov 2003, 31, 33.

Anuchin, it was trenchantly opposed to it. Indeed, mindful perhaps of how the differences separating them might go unnoticed by undiscerning readers who understood them both in the same ecological spirit, Gumilev made considerable efforts to spell these out. He published an essay devoted solely to a critique of Anuchin, in which he maintained that the entire question of the relationship of humankind to nature rested on what he delicately referred to as a "small but very important terminological clarification": whether the humankind in question referred to communities that were ethnic or social. In regard to the former, it was correct to speak about a vital connection; in regard to the latter, it was not.[131] In *Ethnogenesis and the Earth's Biosphere* he castigated Anuchin's attempts to incorporate the social and the natural within the framework of a single "unified geography," claiming that by so doing he simplistically reduced "all human activity to natural laws."[132] Finally, to insure that his position on this issue could not be mistaken or misrepresented, he wrote a strongly worded letter to the editors of the journal of the All-Union Geographical Society, cataloguing once again his major disagreements with Anuchin. He reaffirmed the rationale for his own nature-society differentiation on the basis of differing "natural and social forms of motion of matter" and contrasted Anuchin's ideas with his own vision of ethnos.[133]

If Gumilev felt it important to emphasize his differences with Anuchin's notion of *edinaia geografiia*, he was equally determined to affirm his solidarity with another contemporary theoretician of the society-nature relationship with whom he happened to agree. This was none other than Stanislav Kalesnik, the same conservative president of the Geographical Society who in the 1960s and 1970s had reasserted the Stalinist position in such clear and unambiguous terms. Gumilev was active in the Society in Leningrad throughout this period and had a long-standing personal acquaintance with Kalesnik. The latter had extended a helping hand to him in the early postwar years when his background as a former convict was hindering the completion of his studies, and in the 1960s he helped Gumilev secure his research position on the geography faculty at Leningrad State University.[134] Beyond these personal connections, however, Gumilev genuinely

---

131. Gumilev 1967b.

132. Gumilev 1989c, 22. Ironically, this very accusation would be directed no less stridently against Gumilev himself; see below, 168–71.

133. Gumilev 1974b. For an insightful discussion of Gumilev and Anuchin, see Matley 1982, 375, 378.

134. Lavrov 2000, 59, 215–16. Like Gumilev, Kalesnik had had a youthful interest in ancient Asian history and languages. As a young professor of physical geography in Leningrad after the war, he summoned Gumilev—who had been accepted into the history faculty but as a former Gulag prisoner was not allowed to submit his thesis there—and offered to let him submit it in the geography faculty instead. "Sozdatel' global'noi ekologii" 2011. Gumilev's wife confirmed the friendly relationship that developed between the two in later years, noting that Kalesnik valued Gumilev's knowledge and opinion "very highly." Gumileva 2003b.

appreciated Kalesnik's position on the nature-society question and recognized its kinship with his own. Throughout his writings, he made numerous positive references to Kalesnik's work and consistently deferred to his authority on the issues we are considering. In particular, he endorsed Kalesnik's affirmation of the separation of society and the natural-geographical environment: "The point of departure" for the study of these issues, Gumilev clarified, "are the ideas formulated by S.V. Kalesnik . . . about the clear division of society and the geographical environment."[135] Kalesnik, he observed in the Introduction to *Ethnogenesis and the Earth's Biosphere*, "proposed the division of geography into two fields: (a) economic, which studies what has been created by people (*tvoreniia liudei*), and (b) physical, which studies the natural milieux of the earth and the biosphere. This is a very sensible division."[136] In stark contrast to the fatuous notion of a "unified geography," which misguidedly studied society as a part of nature, he maintained that his own perspective "fits totally with the conceptual framework of Kalesnik."[137] Kalesnik, for his part, returned the favor. In a highly laudatory review of Gumilev's *Drevnie Tiurki*, he noted approvingly how the latter "emphasizes that human society develops according to its own laws, which are different from the laws of development for the [natural-]geographical milieu."[138]

---

135. Gumilev 1967b (quote); Gumilev 1989c, 17, 38. For other references to Kalesnik's work, see Gumilev 1967c, 53; Gumilev 1968b, 560; Gumilev 2004 [1967], 52–53.

136. Gumilev 1989c, 17.

137. Gumilev 1974b; Ermolaev 1990, 31; Matley 1982, 375, 378.

138. Kalesnik 2012, 324–25. On Gumilev as a "follower" (*posledovatel'*) of Kalesnik's position, also see Petrov 2012, 287. Another spokesman for the neo-Stalinist position, Semevskii, also was supportive of Gumilev's work. Semevskii 1974, 75.

ETHNICITY AS IDEOLOGY AND POLITICS

The Equivocal Essentialism of Stalinism

Questions about the nature of ethnicity and the formulation of nationalities policy were central concerns in the ideological construction of Stalinism in the 1930s. The articulation of a coherent perspective was thwarted, however, by conflicting imperatives that pulled the issue in very different directions.[1] On the one hand, the classical Marxist scheme of social evolution postulated that over history societies advanced through a series of socioeconomic "formations" that were ever more highly developed. Nations and nationalism were associated with one particular stage—capitalism—and it was assumed that as society progressed beyond capitalism to socialism and eventually communism, the phenomenon of nationhood as such would eventually disappear and national populations would "merge" (*sliiat'*) together to form new social collectives. "The goal of socialism," declared Lenin in 1916, "is not only the destruction of the petty [national] states into which humankind is parcelized and isolated, not only the rapprochement (*sblizhenie*) of nations, but also their complete merger."[2] Stalinism accepted the principle of social evolution but readjusted its implications for the nationalities question in very significant ways. Nationhood, it was now suggested, was associated not with a single economic formation but rather itself evolved through a

---

1. Simon 1991, 135; Suny 2001, 876.
2. Lenin 1962, 256; Connor 1992, 31–32; Martin 2001a, 70.

succession of them. Thus, capitalist nations (*natsii*) evolved out of precapitalist "nationalities" (*natsional'nosti*) or "peoples" (*narody, narodnosti*), which in turn had evolved out of yet older "clans" (*rodovye obshchiny*) or "tribes" (*plemena*).[3] Earlier forms of nationhood differed from *natsii* in that, corresponding to their respective stage of economic development, they were more primitive.[4] This evolutionary process was ongoing at its various stages in the USSR. Stalinism believed that it could be controlled and directed through the social policies of the Soviet state—hence Francine Hirsch's term "state-sponsored evolutionism"—rather as the hack agronomist Lysenko maintained that the state could intervene into and control the evolutionary dynamics of the natural world.[5]

Another adjustment involved the classical Marxist—and early Bolshevik—teleology regarding the future direction and ultimate culmination of the evolution of these national formations. The inevitability of *sliianie*—that moment when these nations themselves would merge together and the national form as such would disappear—was not rejected, but it was now qualified with the proviso that it would occur only in the remote future, in "the epoch *after the victory of socialism* on a world scale." Only at this far-off point would national cultures finally dissolve into a common pool and reemerge as a single, genuinely postnational entity, which would possess a uniform set of cultural norms and "one common international language."[6] Until that time, precisely the opposite would take place: namely, the *rassvet* or blossoming and flourishing of national cultures with distinct separate identities.[7] This arrangement was related to another new condition that Stalinism wrote into the evolutionary scheme. Tribes might evolve into nationalities and then into nations—but at that point they would evolve no further. Socialism, it now transpired, would witness not the dissolution of nations but their transfiguration into a new form: *sotsialisticheskie natsii* or "socialist nations." To be sure, these were not the reactionary and oppressive nations associated with the capitalist past, but rather progressive national forms that were developing in the new socialist homeland. These, it was implied, effectively represented the culmination and end-form of social organization in the Soviet Union.[8] Stalin himself acknowledged the inconsistency of these positions on the national question, referring to the apparent "self-contradiction" of a doctrine that on the

---

3. Hirsch 2004, 10, 44–45, 266–67; Khazanov 1997, here 140n; Donahoe, Habeck, Halemba, and Santha 2008, 996–97.

4. Skalnik 1981, 185–86.

5. Hirsch 2004, 86, 103, 218, 250, 252, 262, 277, 312.

6. Stalin 1997, 135 (emphasis in original); Stalin 1951, 4–5, 7; Slezkine 1996b, 219; Martin 2001b, 246.

7. Simon 1991, 136–37; Suny 1998, 284, 289.

8. Hirsch 2004, 274, 310–11.

one hand stood "in favor of the fusion of national cultures in the future" while at the same time supported "the blossoming of [separate] national cultures at the present time." Although he dismissed this incongruity with a reference to the "dialectical character of the historical process," the contradiction was very real and the specter of *sliianie* would reassert itself with fresh vigor in later decades.[9]

The Stalinist recognition of a sort of permanence of socialist nations had its roots in the political realities that had confronted the Bolsheviks since before the revolution, when they were anxious to attract the support of the non-Russian nationalities of the empire for their cause. Insofar as these latter groups generally identified their goals in terms of "self-determination" in the form of national-political autonomy or independence, an accommodation had to be made.[10] Lenin endorsed the principle of national self-determination, referring to it as an "exclusive right to independence in the full sense," which included the option of formal political "separation from the oppressing nation."[11] As the political system of the Soviet Union took shape in the years after the revolution, moreover, this principled support for national self-determination and consolidation became one of the basic organizational principles of the new order. It was reflected most significantly in the strategic decision in the 1920s to federalize the country on the basis of ethno-territorial homelands rather than on regions defined in terms of economic functionality.[12] Eventually, the state developed an "affirmative action" policy of proactive enfranchisement and support for non-Russian nationalities that lasted into the late Soviet period.[13] Effectively, the principle of nationality became a *conditio sine qua non*, a veritable precondition for the Soviet order.

What had begun as a concern for the protection of national rights evolved into a proactive obsession with the creation and management of national entities themselves. The Soviet Union was not a unitary national state, but rather—as the titles of recent studies on this subject have alternatively phrased it—a "state" or "empire of nations."[14] The political-geographical realities of Soviet federalism needed the ideological support offered by the notion of "socialist nations." The Soviet federal structure always assumed, implicitly but necessarily, a certain permanence to the national form, in the face of which doctrinaire Marxist notions about the disappearance of nations as socialist society evolved to higher stages appeared increasingly awkward. Indeed, the Stalinist conceptualization of nationhood that developed in the 1930s reflected a highly essentialist and primordialist

9. Cited in Connor 1992, 31. Also see Suny 2001, 876; Fragner 2001, 13, 21.
10. Hirsch 2004, 24–25, 54–55.
11. Lenin 1962, 252, 255; Martin 2001a, 68, 71; Shanin 1989, 468; Slezkine 1996b, 206–7.
12. Hirsch 2004, 62–98.
13. Martin 2001b.
14. Suny and Martin 2001; Hirsch 2004.

perspective on the nature of these national communities. They were represented as objective, real-existing social entities. Membership in a national group was inherited as a birthright from one's parents, "passed on like genetic traits from one generation to another." It was assumed, moreover, that the qualities of the individual were determined to a significant extent by the qualities of the group.[15]

The new importance accorded to nationality or ethnicity was demonstrated early on in the Stalinist regime when in 1932 an internal passport was introduced that included a dedicated category—the *piataia grafa*—officially recording the nationality of the bearer.[16] Indeed, by the time of the Great Terror of 1937, the factor of ethnic or national identity had come to compete with and even displace the Marxist category of economic class.[17] This valorization of the factor of ethnicity made it possible, among other things, to identify entire nationalities as "enemies of the people"—an ominous categorization that would have fateful consequences for a number of national groups during the war years.[18] Eventually, Stalinist essentialism moved to disassociate ethnicity altogether from factors of class and from any dependence on an underlying economic "base"—a shift made easier by the proclamation in 1936 that the USSR had achieved socialism. As Stalin maintained in 1948, it was possible that ethno-cultural entities could persist in essentially the same form across a series of successive stages of social evolution.[19] The transition from feudalism to capitalism in France, it was pointed out, had not made the French any more or less French.

The principles of ethnic essentialism were, however, logically contravened by Stalinism's insistence on the plasticity of all individuals and forms of social organization, and also on their direct dependence on the material conditions in which they existed. In this sense, the ethnic essentialism of Stalinism was equivocal, for despite its affirmation of the fixity of ethnic being, it was unwilling to relinquish either the principle of "the malleability of its human subjects" or its pretense "to mould them at will."[20] The point was a subtle one, to be sure, but in the absolutist logic of totalitarian ideologies such subtleties could acquire great significance. This was certainly the case at hand, and the Stalinist position had at least one consequence that is of fundamental importance for our subject: its clear and consistent refusal to essentialize ethnic being in naturalist or biological

---

15. Suny 2001, 876 (quote); Suny 1998, 289; Martin 2000, 162–69.

16. Martin 2001b, 450–51; Slezkine 1996b, 206, 224.

17. Martin 1998, 852; Weiner 1999a, 1129.

18. Weiner 1999a, 1128–30, 1133; Martin 2001b, 449; Slezkine 1996b, 203, 221; Shanin 1989, 419.

19. Stalin 1997, 104–12; Slezkine 1996a, 852; Slezkine 1994, 310, 314–15; Ssorin-Chaikov 2003, 189.

20. Weiner 2002, 52.

terms.[21] The Soviets always explicitly opposed the reduction of ethnic characteristics to the biological qualities of an individual's genetic constitution, and they denounced the *Rassenkunde* in interwar Germany that was based on this perspective.[22] A fully naturalist view of nationality would have in principle removed it entirely from the sphere of social determination and rendered it impervious to all attempts at state intervention (aside from eugenics), which the Soviet state—keen to measure its achievements precisely in terms of the successes of its interventionist policies in shaping the social organization of its population—could not accept.[23] Although the Soviets actively studied race as a matter of physical anthropology, naturalistic or biological arguments about the nature of ethnicity were consistently denounced as reactionary and racist.[24] It was this background that was to make Gumilev's theories so unusual and controversial, but eventually also so influential.

The Emergence of Ethnogenesis

The principles of Stalinist ethnic essentialism were clearly reflected in the reorganization of the academic field of ethnography from the mid-1930s.[25] From what had been a social science stressing the interconnections with the broader socioeconomic structures in which it operated, ethnography was effectively redefined and recast as a subdiscipline of history, tasked with describing that which makes national groups different and tracing their ancient lineages. As the director of the Institute of Ethnography Sergei Pavlovich Tolstov (1907–1976) explained in 1946, "Ethnography is a branch of history, which researches the culture and customary distinctiveness of various peoples of the world in their historical

---

21. For a recent debate on this issue, see Weitz 2002; Weiner 2002; Hirsch 2002. Also see Weiner 1999a, 1115–16, 1123. The nineteenth-century background to this position is discussed in Laruelle 2006.

22. A striking indication of how foreign this sort of naturalism was not only to Soviet but more generally to Russian views of ethnicity and nationhood was the fact that even the self-declared "fascist" tendencies among Russian émigré circles in the 1930s explicitly rejected the racialist views of their German co-thinkers, with whom their solidarity was otherwise very strong. The "All-Russian Fascist Party" in Harbin, for example, "did not define the nation along genetic or racist lines, but as a historically constituted cultural and spiritual unit.... [M]embership in this culturally constructed nation did not come 'naturally', but had to be acquired.... Instead of the ethnically defined term *Russkaia natsiia* ['Ethnic' Russian Nation], they used the more open *Rossiiskaia natsiia*, which included all peoples living in the Russian empire regardless of their ethnicity." Hohler 2013, 135-36.

23. Hirsch 2004, 216–17, 231–72; Aksenova and Vasilev 1993, 88; Lariuel' 2009, 192; Slezkine 1996a, 847.

24. Laruelle 2008a, 176, 182.

25. Shnirelman 1995, 129–31; Laruelle 2008a, 173.

development, which studies the problems of origin and cultural-historical relations between these peoples, and which uncovers the history of their settlements and movements."[26] This strong historicist bias was apparent in the demarcation of a separate subfield within ethnographic science that focused specifically on the study of the origins of national groups and their development across the *longue durée* of their historical existence. In the 1920s, the archeologist Petr Petrovich Efimenko (1884–1969) suggested that this study of the life histories of ethnic groups could be called "ethnogeny" (*etnogoniia*) or "ethnogenics" (*etnogeniia*), and in the next decade the study of ethnogeny was taken up by the academic Nikolai Iakovlevich Marr (1865–1934) and others.[27] With the formation in 1939 of a special committee under the Presidium of the Academy of Sciences tasked with organizing the study of "ethnogenesis" (*etnogenez*), the approach was confirmed as a formal area of research within Soviet ethnography.[28] Significantly, three of Lev Gumilev's teachers and mentors from this period—Nikolai Kiuner, Vasilii Struve, and Mikhail Artamonov—served as members of the committee, and we can imagine that their engagement with this subject helped shape his own preoccupation with it.

The study of ethnogenesis focused on two related aspects of ethnic history. The first involved establishing the ancient historical origins of ethnic groups and tracing their development down to the present day. Insofar as these studies were driven by the belief that the antiquity of ethnic ancestors enhanced the legitimacy and importance of the group in the present day, Stalinist ethnogenesis often advanced primordialist reconstructions that were extravagant. The historian Vladimir Vasil'evich Mavrodin (1908–1987), for example, dated the origins of the early Slavs from the third century BC, while other specialists identified them with the Cherniakhovskii culture that flourished on the territories of present-day Ukraine, Moldavia, and Romania from the second to the fourth centuries.[29] A similar degree of deep antiquity was claimed for the Russians themselves as an ethno-national group, and leading historians including Nikolai Sevast'ianovich Derzhavin (1877–1953), Boris Dmitrievich Grekov (1882–1953), and Tolstov all argued for a direct ethnographic link between them and tribes such as the Cimmerians and Scythians that Herodotus had described in the fifth century BC.[30] Similar claims for ethnic superlongevity were advanced for other Soviet

---

26. Quoted in Sokolovskiy 2008, 5.

27. Hirsch 2004, 196–97; Uiama 2003, 23–31; Anderson and Arzyutov 2012.

28. Iusova 2008, 42–43; Aksenova and Vasilev 1993, 86–87; Slezkine 1991, 483; Slezkine 1994, 308–9.

29. Udal'tsov 1943; Tillett 1969, 87; Chernykh 1995, 142; Uiama 2003, 26–27, 42; Aksenova and Vasilev 1993, 93.

30. Tolstov 1947; Aksenova and Vasilev 1993, 100; Tillett 1969, 292–93.

nationalities; indeed Tolstov won a Stalin Prize for a work that maintained that the Uzbek, Tadzhik, Kazakh, and Kirgiz peoples all descended from a common Central Asian culture that flourished in the first century BC.[31]

In addition to this focus on primeval origins, Soviet ethnogenesis was preoccupied with the relationship between ethnic groups and the geographical habitat in which they emerged and developed. The notion of a vital bond connecting a nationality with its native homeland was a fundamental element of the Soviet epistemology of ethnicity in the 1920s, and ethno-territoriality became even more intense in the framework of Stalinism.[32] This bond was seen as crucial to the existence of the group, and the geographical features of the group's home region were assumed to help shape its ethnic character. The characteristically "joyful" and "sunny" disposition of the Georgians, for example, was linked to the fact that their homeland was itself a happy place drenched in the bright sun of the Caucasus, and this principle carried over to other nationalities.[33] In this regard Stalinist essentialism clearly echoed the romantic Herderian idealization of a peasant *Volk* rooted securely in its native soil, but it also resonated with the *Blut-und-Boden* doctrines of Walther Darré and others that were being developed as a key part of national socialist ideology in Germany in the 1930s.[34]

In order to describe the connections of a nationality to a geographical habitat, Stalinist ethnogenesis deployed a number of specialized scientific terms. These included concepts such as *prarodina* ("primeval" or "original" homeland), which represented the further primordialization of the already primeval *rodina*, and *avtokhtonnost'* (autochthony), which referred to the group's ancient habitation in this native region. *Avtokhtonnost'* conveyed a sense of what might be called a group's exclusive indigeneity, indicating that it had occupied its home region literally from the moment of its inception (and did not migrate into it at a later historical point) and that it had been this region's principal occupant.[35] In their

---

31. Tolstov 1948; Uiama 2003, 27–28; Tillett 1969, 104; Laruelle 2008a, 178.

32. Stalin himself had stressed this connection in his earliest discussions of nationhood. Stalin 1950 [1912–13], 22; Kushner 1951. Also see Hirsch 2004, 206, 208, 211, 238; Fragner 2001, 19–20; Suny 1998, 286; Martin 2001b, 73; Slezkine 1996a, 852; Blum and Filippova 2006, 321–22.

33. Martin 2001b, 443.

34. Darré 1930; Bramwell 1985; Bassin 2005. Darré was Reich Minister for Food and Agriculture from 1933 to 1942. To be sure, the Soviets denounced German *Blut und Boden* doctrines in the 1930s, maintaining that these theories treated nationality as a biological characteristic dependent on the natural conditions of its geographical environment, and thus represented a "slide into fascism." Dimitrov 1935, cited in Slezkine 1996a, 851; Soboleva 1936. Nonetheless, the resonances of the blood-and-soil topos within Stalinist and more broadly Soviet conceptions of nationality were obvious, as a number of recent studies point out. See Tishkov 1996, 27; Sokolovski n.d., 5, 7; Khazanov 1997, 126; Slezkine 1996a, 853; Shnirelman 2005, 105.

35. Laruelle 2008a, 174.

mutual deployment, these two concepts provided a sort of cross-legitimization: the *avtokhtonnost'* of a group in a genuine *prarodina* served at once to confirm the group's ethnic integrity as well as to legitimate its claim to the geographical region in question as its ethno-historical patrimony. This could be true even in regions where the group was not the majority population in the present day.[36]

The principles embodied in ethnogenesis—its exaggerated ethno-historical reconstructions on the one hand and its intense ethno-territoriality on the other—played a significant role in political discourse and practice in Stalinist Russia.[37] These political implications are of particular importance for the present study, and therefore need to be emphasized. From the standpoint of the central authorities, the emphasis on the primordial lineages of national groups, along with the historic association with defined geographical regions, served as an important buttress for the principles of ethnic federalism on which the territorial organization of the Soviet state was based. The new Soviet constitution of 1936 finally presented the definitive list of the nations and territories making up the political-geographical corpus of the Soviet Union, and after this point there was everything to be gained by "objectively" establishing the credentials of these national groups as genuinely "historical peoples" whose respective territorial allotments in the Soviet federal structure corresponded to ethnic homelands that they had occupied uninterruptedly since time immemorial.[38] In a different connection, numerous ethnogenetic studies detailing the extent of the Slavic *prarodina* across southeastern Europe were produced during the war. This mirrored the attempt of the Germans to extend the historical boundaries of their own nation through the historical-territorial concepts of *Kulturboden* and *Volksboden* developed by the geographer Albrecht Penck.[39] Soviet ethnogenetic research similarly supported the war effort and provided advance legitimation for the territorial claims that were anticipated after the war's end.[40]

At the same time, the Soviet nationalities themselves quickly embraced the Stalinist principles of ethnic primordialism and "authochthonism," and they turned their energies to the production of ethnogenetic myths of their own.[41] These were then put to use in the competition among the different groups for state resources and political authority, a struggle fundamentally exacerbated by the asymmetrical and hierarchical nature of Soviet federalism.[42] The differential

---

36. Ibid., 187.
37. Aksenova and Vasilev 1993, 91–92; Laruelle 2008a; Gullette 2006, 132; Shnirelman 2005.
38. Shnirelman 2005, 103; Blum and Filippova 2006, 322; Kohl 1998, 231–32.
39. Penck 1925; Herb 1997, 55–59.
40. Shnirelman 1995, 133–35; Shnirelman 2005.
41. Laruelle 2008a, 169; Shnirelman 2005, 95; Hirsch 2000, 212, 214–18, 224.
42. Khazanov 1997, 127.

access that different nationalities had to political power, social privileges, and control over resources produced an intense interethnic rivalry "which expressed itself in attempts by local intellectuals to emphasize the special role of their own ethnic groups in history." One common way to achieve this goal was through claims to "the great antiquity of one's own group and its particular historical and cultural traditions and achievements, connections and merits."[43]

Druzhba Narodov and the Stalinist Accommodation

The Stalinist doctrines that we have just considered defined the nature of ethnicity as manifested within the individual national groups that made up the Soviet population. But what of the Soviet Union as a collective whole? What was the glue that attached all the individual ethno-territorial entities into a single body, and what was the character of the multinational agglomeration that this bonding produced? In principle, the October revolution itself had provided the answer: it was the class solidarity of the liberated workers and peasants that underlay the fundamental alliance or *soiuz* (union) between the various parts and peoples of the former empire. With the accession of Stalin, however, this perspective began to be transformed in line with the new prioritization of ethno-national factors described above. In the late 1920s, a "brotherhood" (*bratstvo*) campaign was launched that promoted solidarity between Russia and Ukraine not only as a matter of class-economic affinities but also in terms of the inherent empathies between two neighboring peoples. By the mid-1930s the latter emphasis had become predominant. *Bratstvo* was replaced by the new designation *druzhba narodov*—"the friendship of the peoples"—and the vision of interethnic amity and what Stalin called a "feeling of mutual friendship" was extended beyond the Slavs to include all of the peoples of the USSR.[44]

The *druzhba narodov* concept represented the Soviet nationalities as a community (*obshchnost'*) of common destiny bound together by special affective ties. These ties—geographical proximity, shared historical experiences, and a range of shared social values—were deep and powerful enough to provide the

---

43. Shnirelman 2005, 95–96. For an insightful analysis of how this process played out in Stalinist Ukraine, see Yekelchyk 2002.

44. Cited in Vinogradov 1995, 456; Martin 2001b, 432–33, 441; Simon 1991, 150. For a comprehensive consideration of *druzhba narodov*, see Lowell Tillett's still-excellent study *The Great Friendship*.

unity for the mighty political formation that was the USSR.[45] Yet the doctrine of "indestructible" (*nerushimyi*) unity was formulated, paradoxically enough, entirely within the precepts of Stalinist ethnic essentialism. On the one hand, this meant that ethno-national affinity—as opposed to membership in a particular economic class—was the key index of social cohesion and solidarity. And this in turn meant that the primary unit of social organization was the national unit, or *narod*. What brought these national groups together was the principle of "friendship"—an emotive, voluntaristic, and ultimately subjective option that did not in any way challenge the essential distinctiveness of each constituent part. Indeed, precisely the opposite was the case. In a sort of dialectical juxtaposition, the greater unity implied by *druzhba narodov* presupposed—and served to enhance—the unique ethnic individuality of each of its members. The *druzhba narodov* doctrine "inescapably involved the constant affirmation of the peoples' ethnic differences."[46] And in the same way that friendship and unity were framed primarily in a matrix of interethnic relations, hostility and antagonism were similarly identified along the coordinates of ethnicity, with the result that entire peoples could now be stigmatized collectively—in practice if not in name—as "enemy nations" both inside the USSR and beyond its borders.[47] Ultimately, ethnic essentialism and interethnic fraternity combined to form what might called the Stalinist "accommodation" of the nationalities question: the affirmation of the essentialized integrity of national groups linked to a vision of the natural coherence of these groups to form a single harmonious and integrated political entity.

Dating the origins of this great friendship proved to be a critical question. In the 1930s, it was assumed that the revolution of 1917 was the major catalyst, which meant that *druzhba narodov* was a relatively recent product of socialist construction. This narrative began to be rearranged during the war years, however, and the notion of "fraternal cooperation" between Soviet nationalities and their collaborative resistance to external foes was increasingly historicized and pressed ever further back into the remote past. As this happened, a friendship that in the prewar decade had been merely "indestructible" was increasingly described as also being "age-old" (*vekovoi*).[48] This tendency intensified in the years after the war when the notion of *druzhba narodov* was primordialized along the same lines as nationality itself. Indeed, *druzhba narodov* itself came to represent a new dimension for the study of ethnogenesis. In addition to establishing the

45. Tillett 1969, 339.
46. Yekelchyk 2002, 40.
47. Martin 2001b, 442, 450, 461.
48. Tillett 1969, 66–67, 82, 86, 286; Szporluk 1979, 5.

ancient history of individual national groups, ethnogenetic research was now also charged with excavating the ancient roots of their fraternal association. As far as the Slavic peoples were concerned, wrote the historian Mavrodin in 1946, their great friendship formed deep in Russia's ancient past, when a "feeling of the unity" among them was already in clear evidence.[49] Similarly, Tolstov identified a "complex and powerful political system" among the ancient ancestors of the Soviet peoples in operation at the dawn of the first millennium. Significantly, Tolstov's scheme primordialized not only the internal friendship between the members of this "system" but also their collective external antagonisms toward the other great-power blocks of that day, namely, the Roman Empire in the west and the Han dynasty in China to the east.[50]

This primordialization of the Russian "system" involved a fundamental reevaluation of its imperial nature. A narrative of brutal colonial oppression within the tsarist "prison-house of peoples" had of course been fundamental to the revolutionary agitation of the Bolsheviks, and it continued to be developed extensively in the 1920s in the historiography of Mikhail Nikolaevich Pokrovskii (1868–1932) and others.[51] Such a narrative sat awkwardly with assertions of the age-old friendship and mutual support of all the Soviet nationalities, however, and in the 1930s it began to be rewritten. Tsarist imperialism may have been evil, but it was clearly a "lesser" evil than what its victim peoples would have experienced had they been conquered instead by other powers. And there was one great positive legacy of Russian imperialism, Stalin pointed out in 1937, namely, that it "put together an enormous Great Power, extending from the shores of the Baltic out to Kamchatka."[52] Hand in hand with this celebration of the empire went the prioritization of the national group most completely associated with it, namely, the Russians. References to the Russians as a "first among equals" appeared in 1936, and two years later Stalin himself described them as "the most Soviet and most revolutionary" of all the Soviet nations.[53] In his famous victory speech in 1945, Stalin toasted ethnic Russia as the teacher, cultural leader, and in general "elder brother" of all the Soviet peoples.[54] Like all other elements of the *druzhba narodov* doctrine, the notion of Russian preeminence was extended into

---

49. Mavrodin 1946, 307 (quote); Brandenberger 2002, 44; Tillett 1969, 87.

50. Tolstov 1947, 6–7. The clear implication, as Shnirel′man points out, was that the prerequisites for the formation of the USSR were already in place "by the beginning of the Christian period, if not earlier." Shnirelman 1995, 137 (quote); Shnirelman 2005, 104–5. Marlene Laruelle makes the same point: the Soviet Union projected itself onto the past "as a historical space unified since time immemorial." Laruelle 2008a, 172.

51. Tillett 1969, 26–34, 343–44.

52. Cited in Brandenberger 2002, 55; Tillett 1969, 45–46.

53. Martin 2001b, 452–53; Tillett 1969, 61.

54. Montefiore 2003, 555; Tillett 1969, 88.

the remote past and primordialized. Russians had traditionally led the defense against foreign invaders, and had consistently provided the dynamic impetus for cultural and social development.[55] Tolstov's conclusion that the incorporation of the peoples of Central Asia into the Russian empire was an "objectively progressive fact" because it enabled them to "come together with (*priobshchit'sia*) the leading culture of the Russian people" could be generalized across all of the non-Russian nationalities of the Soviet Union.[56]

The Return of *Sliianie*

In the years after Stalin's death, important aspects of Stalinist policies regarding nationality issues came under challenge. His successor Nikita Sergeevich Khrushchev (1894–1971) was unsympathetic to the principles of ethno-national essentialism and national consolidation among the Soviet population, believing them to be inherently reactionary and an obstacle to economic development and social integration across the country.[57] Beginning in the late 1950s, the notion of *sliianie* or "merging" of the different nationalities—an eventuality that Stalinism had acknowledged but relegated to the distant future—was increasingly described as an ongoing process in the present day.[58] At the Twenty-second Congress of the CPSU in 1961, this assimilationist perspective was given full expression. *Sliianie* was taking place in contemporary Soviet society, it was asserted, and had progressed to the point of creating a new sociopolitical entity, the *sovetskii narod*, or Soviet nation. This was described as a new historical community, the members of which shared a common homeland, civic identity, social values, and economic system. The continuing existence of individual nationalities was not denied, but they were now de facto subordinated to the homogenizing and integrationist dynamic of the larger entity. The implication was clear that with the continued progressive development of the USSR they would eventually be entirely absorbed and superseded by it.[59] The party program maintained that the internal boundaries of the Soviet federal structure, which were based on the principle of ethnonational territoriality, "were increasingly losing their former importance"—a point that Khrushchev had anticipated in dramatic fashion in 1954 by transferring the territory of the Crimean peninsula from the RSFSR to the Ukrainian SSR

---

55. Martin 2001b, 453.
56. Tolstov 1950, 10 (quote); Brandenberger 2002, 62.
57. Brudny 1998, 42.
58. Hodnett 1967, 2.
59. Thompson 1989, 71; Rutland 1984, 158–59; Simon 1991, 137, 254–55.

on the occasion of the three-hundred-year anniversary of their political union.[60] It was rumored at one point that the party was considering removing information about ethno-national origins from the internal Soviet passport, and there were suggestions that the national republics themselves should be abolished altogether and replaced by regions based on the more modern and "rational" principles of economic-territorial organization.[61]

Khrushchev's radical position on the nationality question was one of the factors that led to his downfall in 1964, and the Brezhnev regime that followed took a more moderate position. The provocative term *sliianie* was avoided in favor of the more measured *sblizhenie*, or rapprochement, and there was once again official acknowledgement of the integrity of ethno-national consolidation.[62] Yet Brezhnev himself shared many of Khrushchev's assimilationist inclinations, the clearest indication of which was the continued endorsement of the concept of *sovetskii narod*, with overtones not dissimilar to those emphasized by his predecessor.[63] From the late 1960s the concept proliferated to become a central element in Soviet nationalities discourse, with an abundant literature extolling its every aspect.[64] Brezhnev canonized the term on the occasion of the twenty-fourth CPSU conference in 1972, and it figured prominently in the preamble of the new Soviet constitution promulgated in 1977.[65] The powerful assimilationist impetus in the *sovetskii narod* concept can be seen in the third, so-called Brezhnev edition of the *Great Soviet Encyclopedia*, where it was described as "a new historical, social, and international collectivity of people, possessing a single territory and economy, a culture that is socialist in essence, . . . and a common goal: the construction of communism." Although its constituents were still distinguished by "national characteristics," the "members of any nation (*natsiia*) or nationality (*narodnost'*) within it consider themselves *first of all* to be Soviet people."[66]

The doctrines of *druzhba narodov* and *sovetskii narod* both characterized the Soviet population as a single cohesive entity. They differed fundamentally, however, in their premises and their implications, and it is critical to appreciate what these differences were. In the first place, the *sovetskii narod* concept did not endorse the primordialist and essentialist understanding of nationality that underpinned *druzhba narodov*. Nationality was rather viewed by the former

---

60. Cited in Gleason 1993, 89; Connor 1992, 42; Thompson 1989, 71.

61. Pimenov 2003, 15; Simon 1991, 254–56, 312–13; Semenov 1961; Semenov 1966.

62. Brezhnev 1970–1982, 1: 364, 2: 163–64, 409, 536; Hauner 1992, 29–30; Hodnett 1967, 3.

63. Thompson 1989, 73, 76–77.

64. For example, Veingol'd 1973; Kim 1975; Sherstobitov 1976; *Sovetskii narod—stroitel' kommunizma* 1977; Sherstobitov 1982; *Sovetskii narod: Novaia istoricheskaia obshchnost' liudei* 1987.

65. Gleason 1993, 308; Simon 1991, 307; Szporluk 1979, 17.

66. Kaltakhchian 1976, 25 (emphasis added); Simon 1991, 307.

as capable not only of evolving into something completely different but also of doing so under its very eyes. Second, as we have seen in the citation above, the *sovetskii narod* concept clearly prioritized the collectivity in toto over its individual constituent nationalities. There was no balance between the two levels, moreover, for as the *sovetskii narod* itself became more cohesive and better integrated, the national characteristics of its members were necessarily effaced and their nationality itself dissolved. Indeed, some ideologists, claiming that relations between the national groups in the Soviet Union had grown so close that the latter had lost their distinctiveness, explicitly rejected the very premise of *druzhba narodov* as outdated.[67]

Finally, and critically, the *sovetskii narod* concept did not follow *druzhba narodov* in primordializing the collectivity of Soviet peoples and locating its origins in the deep historical past. Very much to the contrary, the *sovetskii narod* was everywhere described as a *"new* collectivity of people," in other words, a product of the 1917 revolution, the victory of Marxism-Leninism and the "socialist transformation" that it brought about.[68] Still in the late Stalin period, Khrushchev himself demonstratively refused to backdate the great friendship to before the revolution, and this perspective was widely endorsed from the 1960s.[69] "In shared labor," declared Brezhnev at the Fourteenth Congress of the CPSU in 1971, "in the struggle for socialism and the struggle to defend it, new and harmonious relations were created between classes and social groups, nations and nationalities—relations of friendship and cooperation. Our people have been welded together by Marxist-Leninist ideology and the high goals of the construction of communism."[70] This was a clean break from the oppression and brutality of the old imperial regime, which had been characterized not by primordial harmonies and friendship but rather by mutual "national hatred." In tsarist Russia, "dozens of nations, nationalities and ethnic groups lived next to one another in a [single] territory but did not form a community."[71]

Theorizing Ethnicity after Stalin

We have noted how Stalinist primordialism accepted in principle that ethnic or national communities could survive intact across a series of social-economic formations. Indeed, the entire logic of the notion of ethnogenesis itself was founded

---

67. Simon 1991, 309.
68. Kaltakhchian 1976, 25 (quote, emphasis added); Hammer 1988, 21–22; Simon 1991, 307–8.
69. Khrushchev 1949, 80–81; Tillett 1969, 88n.
70. Brezhnev 1970–1982, 3: 279.
71. *Sovetskii narod—stroitel' kommunizma* 1977, 2: 7, 8; cited in Simon 1991, 311.

precisely on this assumption. In Soviet usage, however, terms such as *narod, narod-nost'*, *natsional'nost'*, or *natsiia* were still understood to be connected in some fashion to Marxist-Stalinist stages of historical development. How then was it possible to designate that ethnic essence or substratum that remained sufficiently detached from the process of social evolution to provide continuity throughout the historical transformation from *plemia* to *narodnost'* to *narod/national'nost'* and finally to *natsiia*? In the 1920s, the term "ethnos," first mooted in the work of prerevolutionary Russian ethnographers, began to attract attention.[72] It featured centrally in the work of the émigré ethnographer Sergei Shirokogorov (noted in chapter 1), while in the USSR, the archeologist and ethnographer Sergei Rudenko suggested that the term could be used to designate a community as an ethno-social entity that existed not merely at a single stage of economic development but across successive historical periods and socioeconomic formations, beginning in ancient times.[73] In later decades, Rudenko would be one of Gumilev's most important mentors, who strongly influenced the development of his thinking.[74]

As it happened, the term "ethnos" did not gain currency during the Stalinist period. Beginning in the 1960s, however, it came into broad usage as a central concept in post-Stalinist debates about the nature of ethnicity and nationality.[75] As Iulian Vladimirovich Bromlei (1921–1990), the head of the Institute of Ethnography of the Academy of Sciences and a principal architect of this innovation, explained, the new concept was intended to overcome the confusion by replacing a jumble of loosely defined but important concepts with a single term.[76] But Soviet "ethnos theory" represented not so much a new beginning or a clarification as a fresh reengagement with and in many ways a reproduction of the old, still-unresolved dilemmas and ambiguities in Stalinist theories of nationality of the 1930s and 1940s.[77] The emergence of the *sliianie* project as a political

---

72. For example, Mogilianskii 1908; Mogilianskii 1916; Hirsch 2004, 196n; Anderson and Arzyutov 2012.

73. Hirsch 2004, 196, 206, 313; Elfimov 2014, 73.

74. "To a large extent the complex historical-geographical and ethnographic approach in Gumilev's works was formed under Rudenko's influence." Burlaka 2012, 924. Rudenko wrote a review strongly supporting Gumilev's *Khunnu* against the criticism of the Sinologists (Rudenko 1965), and later contributed the preface for Gumilev's *Searches for an Imaginary Kingdom*. Also see Gumilev and Rudenko 1966; Gumilev 1970f; Gumilev 1971b.

75. On the history of Soviet ethnos theory, see Filippov 2010; *Akademik Iu. V. Bromlei i otechestvennaia etnologiia, 1960–1990e gody* 2003.

76. Bromley and Kozlov 1989, 425; Bromley 1974, 55–56; Poplinskii 1973; Klein 1992, 232; Sokolovskiy 2008. The scientific cachet of the term in the USSR was enhanced by the fact that questions of "ethnicity" and "ethnic groups" were similarly gaining new scholarly attention in the West at this time. Barth 1969; Shils 1975; Banks 1996, 17–24.

77. Ssorin-Chaikov 2003, 189; Skalnik 1986.

priority served to galvanize the debate, to be sure, but the result was to reaffirm the ambivalences underlying these questions rather than provide any resolution. Indeed, post-Stalinist ethnos theory was profoundly schizophrenic and contained within it two contradictory elements. On the one hand, it elaborated a theoretical model of ethnos that could accommodate the new political line of a burgeoning supranational *sovetskii narod*. This involved the clear acceptance of the evolutionist position and the Stalinist triad of *plemia*, *narodnost'*, and *natsiia*, which was adopted by Bromlei and others.[78] Like all other social formations, ethnies were malleable and in a state of constant change corresponding to the changes in the material conditions of their existence.[79] In the contemporary Soviet Union, the conditions of developed socialism had brought about the emergence of a new ethnic form: the "metaethnos." This was a scientific designation for the same sort of supraethnic integration of the peoples of the USSR expressed in political terms as the *sovetskii narod*.[80]

At the same time, however, ethnos theory resisted precisely this assimilationism and sought rather to develop what Victor Shnirelman calls a conceptual "language of resistance" to the cultural leveling inherent in the notion of a "new Soviet entity."[81] The effort involved the re-formulation of an explicitly primordialist perspective on ethnicity, which echoed the Stalinist essentialism described above.[82] Ethnic groups were reified as real-existing entities or "organisms" that had their own existence in history and developed according to their own dynamics and impulses, detached at least to some extent from the strict Marxist scheme of successive stages of socioeconomic evolution.[83] The study of ethnogenesis continued to play a vital role in supporting primordialist narratives, and the Stalinist tradition of gifting implausible life histories to Soviet nationalities that demonstrated that present-day ethnic structures were fully formed in ancient times was faithfully continued.[84] Implicitly at least, it was clear that *sliianie* could have no

---

78. Bromley and Kozlov 1989, 430–32; Bromlei 1983a, 6; Skalnik 1986, 164, 159; Drobizheva 1992, 112n.

79. Bromley and Kozlov 1989, 432; Gellner 1988, 132–33; Dragadze 1980, 163–64.

80. Bruk and Cheboksarov 1976; Tishkov 1997, 3–4.

81. Shnirelman 2005, 105.

82. Ssorin-Chaikov 2003, 189; Sokolovski n.d., 4, 11; Tishkov n.d.

83. Heikkinen 2000, 102–12; Sokolovski n.d., 11; Skalnik 1986, 158. Recent Western studies on how the concept of "ethnos" was understood in different countries have confirmed the strong essentialism characteristic of Soviet ethnography—which they were apparently surprised to find in a science that described itself as "Marxist." One survey concluded that Soviet ethnos theory was the "most strongly primordialist" of all those considered. Banks 1996, 18; also see Fenton 2003, 66–67; Shanin 1989, 415.

84. For example, Ermatov 1968, 8–9, 15–16; *Etnogenez mordovskogo naroda* 1965; Valiev 1966, 56–61; Gurvich 1980; Simon 1991, 281.

practical place in this scheme. Indeed, the primordialism of ethnos theory was in certain respects even more emphatic than its Stalinist precursor. Ethnic essentialism was now taken as a given, and considerable theoretical energies were devoted to defining what it consisted of and where it came from.

This "language of resistance" was not intended for internal academic purposes alone. The assimilationist challenge to the principles of ethnic essentialism and *druzhba narodov* was also viewed negatively by many of the Soviet nationalities themselves, who as we have seen had accepted the Stalinist accommodation and sought to secure their position within the Soviet state in terms of its values and priorities. From their point of view, the prospect of absorption into a homogeneous supranational *sovetskii narod* threatened not merely the loss of their national individuality but their political disenfranchisement as well. For these reasons, it was to be resisted at all costs. Thus, paradoxically, the period of the 1960s and 1970s witnessed not *sblizhenie* but an intensification of ethnic self-awareness, a heightened interest in ethnogenetic origins, and a sharp rise in ethno-national sentiment across the country.[85] Renewed attention was given to establishing ethnogenetic lineages and in some cases rearranging established historical narratives.[86] These sentiments affected ethnic Russians no less than the non-Russian nationalities, as we will consider in the next chapter. The professional formulators of Soviet ethnos theory were strongly influenced by these attitudes. The theories they devised, in turn, provided conceptual foundations for the more comprehensive development of ethno-nationalism in the USSR—the same ethno-nationalism that would eventually explode the unity of the country as a whole. And among the progenitors of ethnos theory, no one was more effective than Lev Gumilev.

Gumilev, Ethnos Theory, and the Stalinist Accommodation

Gumilev's theories occupied a special and extremely important position on the ideologically charged force field of ethnos discourse from the 1960s through the 1980s. This point needs to be emphasized, because at the time it was commonly assumed that he stood entirely outside the mainstream of post-Stalinist ethnography—a lone voice whose quirky ideas reflected not much more than his own ingenuity and encyclopedic historical knowledge. Indeed, the director of

---

85. Shnirelman 2005, 107, 112; Gellner 1988, 134; Pimenov 2003, 15.
86. Simon 1991, 279–81; Tolz 2001, 204.

the Institute of Ethnography in Leningrad, Rudol'f Ferdianandovich Its (1928–1990)—who as the author of the preface to the first edition of *Ethnogenesis and the Earth's Biosphere* was hardly unsympathetic—nevertheless reckoned that he knew of "no one among Soviet ethnographers who would accept" its author's ideas.[87] This impression of opposition was bolstered by the hostile attacks directed by some Soviet ethnographers against Gumilev's work, and no less by the latter's own persistent self-characterization as an unappreciated outcast whose audacious originality was too unsettling for his professional colleagues to be acceptable. The picture of Gumilev's absolute distinctiveness served the purposes of all parties involved—his own no less than the Soviet ethnographic establishment—and for this reason it was long the dominant view. It is, however, significantly misleading. Although Gumilev's theories about the nature of ethnicity and ethnogenesis were without any question distinctive and extremely controversial, they nonetheless formed an integral part of the discussions and debates among Soviet ethnographers of the day and were shaped by the same dilemmas regarding the Stalinist legacy and the doctrine of *sovetskii narod*.[88] Moreover, Gumilev's ideas had a direct influence on the development of mainstream ethnos theory itself, and more generally on thinking about ethnicity in the Soviet Union. This point is important not only for evaluating his significance in the Soviet period but also for understanding the enduring popularity of his ethnos theory in post-Soviet Russia.

Most immediately, Gumilev's ethnos theory represented a direct rebuttal to the assimilationist discourse of *sliianie* and the existence of a "Soviet people" as a supracthnic cntity. Wc have seen that the impossibility of artificially combining ethnic groups was a fundamental axiom for him, as was the categorical imperative to support ethnic individuality and autonomy. Although in his scholarly work Gumilev sought to avoid references to the present, and above all to contemporary politics, he made an exception for this particular point and indicated clearly that his theoretical position was aimed directly against an official state project of his day. "In bringing their political utopia to life, the authorities forcibly mixed the Ingush with the Baltic peoples in Siberia, and Koreans with Kalmyks in Kazakhstan."[89] He denounced the obliteration of ethnic difference inherent in the concept of "metaethnos," pointing out that every energetic process "requires a minimum of two poles. . . . Water flows from a higher vessel to a lower one. In electricity there are cations and anions, which move toward each other. If there

---

87. Its 1989, 4; also see Lavrov 2000, 304.
88. Gumilev's thinking "fit entirely into the tradition of Soviet ethnology." Lariuel' 2009, 190; Tishkov 1997, 2; Beliakov 2012a, 624n.
89. Gumilev and Ermolaev 1993, 186.

were only one or the other, there would be no electricity. For that reason, if everyone merges and becomes the same, then there will be no movement, no cultural development, and life will simply cease to exist."[90] There are no good reasons, he affirmed elsewhere, "for advocating the processes of *sblizhenie* and *sliianie*. Why should we try to squeeze the behavior of an Abkhazian and a Chukot, a Lithuanian and a Moldavian, all into a single frame?" Such an approach, he argued, "is pointless and harmful. How can we create a single ethnos for the entire planet [or our country]? For that, it would be necessary at the very least to destroy the differences between natural-climatic zones . . . , between the forest and the steppe, and of course between mountains and valleys. But this, happily, is impossible!"[91] The impossibility of *sliianie* did not, however, mean that the Soviet peoples could not live together in friendship and good faith. It was simply necessary to respect the single genuine principle capable of ensuring the coexistence of nations within a polyethnic state: "Live in peace, but separately (*v mire, no porozn'*)."[92]

Gumilev's strategy for resisting the assimilationist challenge, I would suggest, was to present a revised version of the original Stalinist accommodation described above, in which a primordial and essentialized view of individual Soviet nationalities was combined with a separate doctrine of organic corporate cohesion.[93] Numerous elements of Gumilev's complex theory of ethnos examined in the first part of this book resonated with the primordialism and essentialism of the Stalinist paradigm—a paradigm that some of his own teachers and mentors had been responsible for formulating. Thus for Gumilev, ethnic being was absolutized as an objective and real-existing quality, an indelible feature of every individual's persona. Beyond this, he repeated the primordialist insistence on the ancient lineages of all ethnic groups. Although his own scheme for the development of ethnies took the form of a universal template of life-cycle phases rather than an evolutionary succession through quasi-Marxist historical stages, the fact that he used the same term "ethnogenesis" to refer to it confirms its Stalinist origins. Relations within states, moreover, were determined on an ethnic basis, in the sense that the most important interface of interaction was between ethnic units (as opposed to economic classes) and was governed by the universal dynamics of ethnic behavior. As with Stalinism, so Gumilev as well reduced these interethnic relations to a simplistic binary of friend versus foe—"*druz'ia i nedrugi*," as he put it unsubtly in the subtitle to his collection *The Black Legend*—whose mutual

90. Gumilev 2003f; Gumilev and Ivanov 1992, 54.

91. Gumilev 1994c, 257, 293 (quotes); Gumilev 1989c, 305.

92. Gumilev and Ivanov 1992, 54 (quote), 55–56; Gumilev 2001, 35; Laruelle 2000, 181n.

93. Ivanov 2001, 216–17. Although Ivanov is correct in pointing out the Stalinist elements in Gumilev's own thinking, he does not appreciate the significant differences discussed below.

empathy or antipathy depended entirely on whether the ethnic feature of "complementarity" between the groups concerned was positive or negative. Indeed, he even developed his own version of internal "enemy nations" in the form of the chimera, which like the Stalinist equivalent was defined in ethnic terms and therefore applied indiscriminately to all members of the group across the entire duration of its historical existence.[94]

To balance this vision of essentialized ethnic individuality, Gumilev offered a theory of interethnic cohesion that resonated broadly, if not completely, with the doctrine of *druzhba narodov*.[95] Indeed, Gumilev made no secret of his admiration for the Stalinist precedent. Rejecting the *sovetskii narod* project as a dystopic attempt to "make everyone resemble yourself," he called for ethnic coexistence and the acceptance of difference, with the observation that "in general, *druzhba narodov* is the best [policy] on this question that has been devised over the millennia."[96] "Friendship and mutual aid is characteristic for the peoples of our country," he wrote, "and individual clashes in the course of the millennia were [mere] episodes against a general background of symbiosis."[97] In his view, *druzhba narodov* was quite simply the "holiest of holy" principles for Russian state policy.[98] Although Gumilev's own version of *druzhba narodov* was based on a Eurasianist reconstruction of Russian history, it corresponded with the Stalinist prototype in important ways. Like the latter, Gumilev's scheme was a two-tiered arrangement that preserved the individuality of each component ethno-national unit along with the unity of the greater corporate entity. Not only were these two principles not seen to be in any logical opposition, but they were treated as if they were mutually reinforcing.[99] As with *druzhba narodov*, so in Gumilev's scheme

---

94. While Stalinism had a term for an individual "enemy of the people," it did not provide a corresponding designation for those ethnies or nations which under the right circumstances it was capable of treating in the same manner. Perhaps formally acknowledging such an assumption by giving it a name would have seemed unacceptably fatalistic or reactionary. (I am grateful to Dr. Mikhail Suslov for his insights on this point.) Whatever the reason, Gumilev had no such scruples. From this standpoint, his notion of chimera represented what was effectively his own original, if post-dated contribution to Stalinist doctrine. It came too late to be of any use to Stalinism per se, but it appealed to his contemporaries in the Russian nationalist movement in the 1960s and 1970s, as we will see, and it has proved exceptionally popular and useful for post-Soviet public discourses.

95. Laruelle 2000, 188; Shlapentokh 2011, 107–8; Akaev 2011a, 23.

96. Gumilev 1994c, 261; Gumilev 1989a. Gumilev's support for Soviet internationalism and *druzhba narodov* was confirmed by Sergei Lavrov, his colleague for decades at the geographical faculty in Leningrad who knew him very well. Lavrov 2000, 354; Shlapentokh 2012. Gumilev dedicated his book *The Ancient Turks* (1967) "to our brothers—the Turkic peoples of the Soviet Union" and *Searches for an Imaginary Kingdom* (1970) "to the fraternal Mongol people."

97. Gumilev 2003h, 247 (quote), 234.

98. Gumilev 1988c, 3

99. Gumilev 1991e, 141.

interethnic amity was primordialized as the product of centuries of shared historical experience. Implicitly dismissing the notion that a "new historical entity" was created only under the conditions of Soviet socialism, he instead cited the works of Mavrodin and Tolstov to the effect that this reality had deep historical roots. "In the ancient past there were no boundaries. Polovtsy, Tatars, and Pechenegs all lived [peacefully] alongside the Slavs. . . . In the Great Steppe, an *old* historical totality, so to speak, was [already] in existence."[100] Finally, Gumilev's Eurasianist scenario similarly denied that there had ever been any oppression or domination of any nationality by Russia. Very much to the contrary, the Russian state developed as a joint project based not on conquest but on the principles of cooperation, voluntarism, and toleration.

And yet, for all of Gumilev's ingenuity, the Stalinist accommodation proved to be an ideological river into which he was unable to wade for a second time. In his attempt to reassert its guiding principles and priorities, he revised certain aspects of the original template, and these innovations served to alter the entire calculation and effect. In regard to his ethnos theory, his determination to resist the *sliianie* of the *sovetskii narod* project led him to embrace a model of ethnicity that was not "equivocally" essentialist like its Stalinist precedent but rather quite absolutely so. He achieved this very effectively, from a theoretical standpoint, by naturalizing ethnicity and describing it as a biological phenomenon that necessarily remained beyond the realms of social development and political policy. From this standpoint, *sliianie* indeed became a logical impossibility and lost its meaning as anything other than brutal policy of enforced and destructive assimilation.

But by naturalizing ethnicity, Gumilev was now asserting precisely what Soviet nationality theory had at all times strenuously resisted, namely, the biologization of ethnic being. Unquestionably, this was the most startling and sensational aspect of his ideas for his contemporaries, and it served more than anything else to attract broad attention to his work. The fact that Gumilev's biologization was not based primarily on factors of genetics or race, but rather on the principles of energy circulation and landscape science developed by great Russian scientists, did not mitigate its sensationalist effect in the slightest. Gumilev's naturalism was duly attacked by establishment ethnographers, but as we will see it also paradoxically began to influence the thinking even of his opponents among them. His influence would grow ever greater over time. No less significantly, Gumilev's audacity was inspirational for those who, like him, desired a model of ethnic

---

100. Gumilev 1988d (quote; emphasis added); Gumilev 2003e, 234.

essentialism—perhaps better called hyperessentialism—that could establish and legitimize the antiquity and absolute permanence of ethnic groups without any question or equivocation. Gumilev's improvement on Stalinist teachings in this respect was obvious. As ethno-nationalist sentiment grew stronger in the USSR from the 1970s, Gumilev's theories about the ethnos as a natural phenomenon correspondingly grew ever more popular. As we will see, his bold ethno-naturalism has proved to be one of the major sources of his continued popularity and influence in post-Soviet Russia.

Gumilev's picture of the primordial fraternity of the Soviet peoples similarly involved a number of departures from the model of *druzhba narodov*. The fact that he developed his perspective within a Eurasianist framework meant that the "old historical entity" he spoke about rested on a central axis of Turko-Slav affinity and unity—a prioritization that was absent from *druzhba narodov*. Indeed, as we have seen, Soviet historiography spoke largely with a single voice about the destructive effects of the Mongol invasion, effectively endorsing the very "Black Legend" that Gumilev took such pains to dispute.[101] No less important, Gumilev's account of Russia's historical relations with neighboring peoples said nothing about its role as a leader and first among Soviet equals. To the contrary, *his* Russia—born in the fourteenth-century crucible of Kulikovo—was in all respects a joint enterprise in which Slavic-Russian and Turkic-Mongol elements played essentially equal roles. We have seen that his account of relations between the Russians and the Golden Horde was actually quite critical of the Russian population, even suggesting that by not recognizing the good will of the Mongols it bore a certain culpability for the brutality it suffered. In his discussion of the post-Mongol period, Gumilev did not trumpet Russia's achievements in civilizing and enlightening other nationalities in the empire, but rather always emphasized the inherent virtues of the latter's traditional indigenous cultures. Finally, the correspondence between the Gumilevian superethnos and the single corporate entity created by *druzhba narodov* was highly problematic. Gumilev always maintained that Russia was not a single superethnos but instead represented seven distinct superethnies. It was his absolute determination to resist the specter of a homogenizing *sovetskii narod* that led him to this eccentric conclusion, which was quite fundamentally out of sync with the specifications of the Stalinist paradigm. He did relax this position at the very end of his life and recognize Russia as a single superethnic entity, as we will see, but even then he did so equivocally and inconsistently.

---

101. Tillett 1969, 322–23.

Mainstream Ethnography Critiques Gumilev

Gumilev began to present aspects of his thinking about ethnicity in the series of essays "Landscape and Ethnos" mentioned in the previous chapter. These were published in the reputable but obscure geological-geographical section of the *Vestnik Leningradskogo Gosudarstvennogo Universiteta*, and would have been seen by a small number of specialists at most.[102] His first full statement of his ethnos theory, however, was much more prominently featured in two installments that appeared in 1970 in the journal *Priroda* (Nature). Edited by the physicist and Nobel Laureate Nikolai Gennadievich Basov (1922–2001), *Priroda* was the premier general science journal in the USSR. It was read by professionals as well as lay audiences, and enjoyed a circulation of 41,000 copies, truly massive for the conditions of the day.[103] The fact that a little-known specialist in ancient steppe history with a highly problematic personal-political background, no particular professional standing, and no academic training in the natural sciences could publish his unorthodox research in such prestigious and influential pages was in itself remarkable and speaks to the extremely high interest in Gumilev's subject matter and his approach. Special attention was drawn to Gumilev's publication, moreover, by the fact that along with his short essays the editors included a collection of statements in which leading experts debated his ideas. A few of these expressed positive interest in different aspects of his work, notably the concept of *passionarnost'*, but for the most part their tone was highly critical and denunciatory.[104] The chorus of condemnation was led by Viktor Ivanovich Kozlov (1924–2013), a well-known and highly respected specialist in ethno-demography.

Kozlov identified three major errors in Gumilev's ideas. The first of these was the principled distinction between the social and the natural and the categorization of ethnies as part of the latter. Flatly contradicting Gumilev, Kozlov declared that an ethnos "relates not to biological but rather to social categories." It is, consequently, a "social organism," which operates in clear accordance with the laws of social development rather than those of the natural world.[105] In describing the nature of this organism, Kozlov referred to traditional Marxist teachings about nations and nationalism. Ethnic attachments were most powerful at the lower stages of social development and grew weaker as social organization progressed, increasingly replaced by affinities relating to economic class.[106] In the period of

---

102. As noted in chapter 5, most of these essays were translated into English. For a complete bibliographic listing, see Karimullin 1990.

103. Beliakov 2012a, 457.

104. Kurennoi 1974; Kuznetsov 1971; Drozdov 1974; Semevskii 1974, 74.

105. Kozlov 1971, 71, 74 (quotes); Kozlov and Pokshishevskii 1973, 9–10.

106. Kozlov 1971, 72.

capitalist development, ethnic identification was expressed in the form of a reactionary "nationalism" that objectively supported "the bourgeoisie and the intelligentsia who serve the bourgeoisie."[107] After the advent of socialist construction, however, the objective bases for ethnic consolidation were progressively eroded and ethnies were fated to grow ever weaker and more insignificant—a process that he believed to be taking place in his day in the Soviet Union. Kozlov spoke in support of the *sliianie* project, which he contrasted in stark terms to Gumilev's own insistence on the primordial immutability of ethnicity. "The existence of a state facilitates the creation within its boundaries of a single ethnos out of the different ethnic groups that make up its population." Socialism advances national equality, deprives nationalism of its ideological base, "and opens the way for the merging of nations, which was foreseen by the classics of Marxism-Leninism."[108]

Gumilev's naturalist perspective—his *biologizatsiia* of ethnos—provided a second object for attack.[109] He was accused on the one hand of a nihilistic social Darwinism, and on the other of endorsing the same brutal naturalist view of human culture as the proponents of *Rassenkunde* such as Autur de Gobineau or Ludwig Woltmann.[110] As Kozlov summarized, "it is readily apparent that Gumilev's conceptual structure leads to the justification of Nazi criminals, whose actions [he implies] were apparently conditioned by natural forces and genetic factors."[111] This led in turn to a third transgression. Gumilev's ethno-ecology amounted to nothing less than "geographical determinism"—a replacement term for what had earlier been called "geographical materialism." As we saw in the previous chapter, the topic had a palpable ideological purchase in post-Stalinist Russia: not strictly identical to racism but saturated with reactionary political significance in its own right. This particular issue was significant enough to merit a separate critique of Gumilev by Kozlov in the prominent journal *Voprosy Istorii*. Whereas in earlier centuries the exaggeration of environmental influences played an "objectively" progressive ideological role in helping to overcome antiquated feudal and clerical teachings, he maintained, by the nineteenth century it represented—still "objectively"—a fallback for the forces of bourgeois

---

108. Ibid., 73, 74. On Kozlov's embrace of *sliianie*, see Hirsch 2004, 321–22. It is interesting to note that some two decades later, in the rubble of the former Soviet Union, the old assimilationist Kozlov would finally discover the importance of ethnic individuality and gain a new voice as an ardent proponent of Russian ethno-nationalism. Kozlov 1996. Such a trajectory was not at all unusual, as we will see later in this book.

109. Kozlov 1971, 71.

110. Pershits and Pokshishevskii 1978, 107; "Critique of L. N. Gumilev's Work" 1977, 121; Shulyndin 1984, 11; Mashbits and Chistov 1986, 29–30. Also see Dunn 1975.

111. Kozlov 1990, 107.

reaction. It was eagerly embraced by an unsavory assortment of imperialists and racists and culminated in the notorious doctrines of German *Geopolitik* developed by Karl Haushofer, Carl Schmitt, and others who stood close to the Nazis. In all of these cases, geographical determinism filled the same function, namely, to demonstrate "scientifically" that differences and inequalities between peoples across the globe are natural, and thereby provide legitimation for the injustices of capitalism, imperialism, and fascism.[112] In his "biological-global" theories about ethnos, *landshaft*, and the biosphere, his critics maintained that Gumilev had de facto embraced this position. Referring to the interest in Gumilev on the part of American geographers, Kozlov pointed to the fact that his work "is eagerly published by the bourgeois press" as direct confirmation of its menacing potential for the Soviet state.[113]

In the 1970s Gumilev had his supporters as well as detractors, and despite the critique directed at him there was no consensus that his ideas had grievously transgressed accepted boundaries of scholarly debate. Indeed, in the years after the publication of his first controversial essays in *Priroda*, Gumilev was able to publish several more in the same journal, all without incident.[114] By the end of the decade, however, the situation began to change. His work on Russian history began to receive heavy criticism from leading Soviet historians, and the explosive potential of his radical conceptions of the nature of ethnicity and ethnic interaction became apparent as well. In 1981, *Priroda* once again published an essay dealing with Gumilev's ethnos theory, this time authored not by Gumilev himself but by Iurii Mefod'evich Borodai (1934–2006), a philosopher and one of his early disciples.[115] Presented as a sort of overview of Gumilev's unpublished three-volume dissertation, Borodai focused on the problem of environmental destruction. He explained the phenomenon in Gumilevian terms as the result of uncontrolled ethnic migration and mixing—processes that violated the integrity of individual ethnies, disrupted their "normal" interaction, and ultimately produced nature-hating chimeras and antisystems. Significantly, Gumilev's anti-Semitic undertones resonated in Borodai's essay as well.[116] On this occasion, Gumilev's

---

112. Kozlov 1974, 72–73; Pershits and Pokshishevskii 1978, 107, 110. For what it was worth, Gumilev himself categorically rejected the legacy of classical geographical determinism—he specifically noted Jean Bodin, Montesquieu, and Friedrich Ratzel—as "geographical nihilism." Gumilev 1989c, 89, 323; Gumilev 1967c, 53, 57; Gumilev 1970d; Rogachevskii 2001, 363; Bannykh 1997, 90–108; Beliakov 2012a, 256.

113. Kozlov 1974, 85.

114. Gumilev 1972a; Gumilev 1975; Gumilev 1976; Gumilev 1978a.

115. Iurii Borodai was the father of Aleksandr Borodai, whose evaluations of Gumilev have been cited at several points in this book.

116. Borodai 1981a. Borodai's essay is discussed in more detail in chapter 7.

assertions by proxy caused a real scandal. The deputy editor at the journal was fired and a special meeting of the Presidum of the Academy of Sciences was convened to denounce Borodai's essay. Responsibility for a rebuttal to the article was entrusted to a trio of senior Soviet academics.[117] It appeared the next year and Gumilev was clearly identified as the source of Borodai's ideas. Now with the full authority of the Soviet Union's highest academic establishment, his ideas were excoriated for their lack of Marxist content, their "antiscientific" and "antisocial" character, and their objective opposition to the basic values inspiring the Soviet people. Above all, however, the essay was castigated for its implicit critique of the assimilationist policy of *sovetskii narod*. The assertions of Borodai and Gumilev "are false, and they directly and immediately oppose the support of our party and our socialist government for the all-out (*vsemernoe*) rapprochement of nations and for the prospect (however far off) of their merging (*sliianie*) into a single socialist body of humanity."[118]

Gumilev and Bromlei

However much such trenchant critique may have worked to discredit Gumilev and further underscore his professional marginalization, the fact remained that his ideas exerted a highly significant influence on mainstream Soviet ethnos theory. This influence can be seen in the work of the most important official formulator of the ethnos concept, Iulian Bromlei, who sustained an active engagement with Gumilev and his ideas across several decades. Like Gumilev a historian by training, Bromlei was a specialist on the south Slavs. He was appointed director of the Academy of Science's Institute of Ethnography in 1966, and from this influential position acted as the principal inspiration behind the development of the ethnos concept.[119] From the outset, Bromlei paid extremely close attention to Gumilev's work. Although the two were separated by a wide gulf of academic status, scholarly orientation, and political legitimacy, there was nonetheless a

---

117. Andreev 2012; Beliakov 2012a, 562–65.

118. Kedrov, Grigulevich, and Kryvelev 1982. It is interesting to note that at least one of the authors of this critique—the academician Bonifatii Mikhailovich Kedrov (1903–1985)—recognized that the real basis of Gumilev's errant naturalism lay not in factors of genetics and race but in the ecological principles of landscape science, energy exchange, and Vernadskii's teaching about the biosphere. Kedrov made this point about Gumilev in private conversations at the time with Loren Graham. Graham 1987, 257. This insight did not, however, mollify Kedrov's condemnation of Gumilev's theories.

119. On Bromlei, see Mutschler 2011; *Akademik Iu. V. Bromlei i otechestvennaia etnologiia, 1960–1990e gody* 2003; Skalnik 1986.

resonance in their writings, which spoke not only to the fact that they were deal-ing with a common subject but also to more specific affinities in their approach and interpretation. They were themselves not unaware of a connection; indeed each viewed the other as a sort of personal nemesis and castigated their work correspondingly. This was especially true of Gumilev, who mockingly referred to Bromlei as "Barmalei"—the fearsome African pirate-cannibal character from Kornei Chukovskii's children's stories, who gobbled up little boys and girls as a hobby. For Gumilev's supporters, Bromlei was Gumilev's "principal opponent," and Gumilev himself regularly criticized him in his work.[120] Bromlei, for his part, did not fail to return the critique. In the late 1980s, the two engaged in a to-and-fro of bitter personal recrimination, in which they both spoke effectively in a single voice about the great conceptual differences that separated them.[121] Despite a certain "purely superficial agreement" in their perspectives, Bromlei insisted, "we have diametrically opposing views, not only in regard to individual questions but in our understanding of the essence of the theory of ethnogenesis, or ethnos."[122]

In fact, the agreement Bromlei spoke of here was rather more than superfi-cial. Although he always referred to Gumilev's theories critically, he nonetheless accepted them as a legitimate part of the debate around ethnos theory.[123] For his part, Gumilev was entirely aware of the deeper resonances between his thinking and Bromlei's, which he took as evidence that the latter was stealing his ideas.[124] Indeed, after the publication of Bromlei's monograph *Ethnos and Ethnography* in 1973, Gumilev was angry enough about this to challenge him to a public debate and set the record straight.[125] The affinities between the two were also noted by their respective camps of supporters. Kozlov, a close colleague and coauthor of Bromlei's, confirmed that a variety of the latter's positions "appeared to be analo-gous" to those of Gumilev.[126] Gumilev's acolytes were yet more vociferous on the point. One disciple published an entire essay asking if Gumilev and Bromlei had really advanced two distinct theories of ethnos in Soviet science, and concluded

---

120. Gumilev 1989c, 56, 74n, 164, 263; Gumilev 2001, 46; Mashbits and Chistov 1986. On Bromlei and Barmalei, see Lavrov 2000, 6, 304, 333.

121. Gumilev 1988a; Bromlei 1988b; Gumilev 1989f; Bromlei 1989; Bromlei 1988a. Also see Kozlov 1990.

122. Bromlei 1988b, 230. Also see Mashbits and Chistov 1986. The passions of this dispute between the two men were so strong that it was rumored to have hastened Bromlei's death in 1990. Beliakov 2012a, 624. For a discussion of Gumilev and Bromlei, also see Mutschler 2011, 221–33.

123. Bromley 1974, 56, 74; Bromley and Kozlov 1989, 425n, 428–29.

124. Gumilev 1989c, 90, 218, 234; Gumilev 2001, 21.

125. Gumilev 2008, 28; Lavrov 2000, 329.

126. Kozlov 1990, 95.

that they had not. To the contrary, there was "complete congruence" between them—the implication being that Bromlei had simply copied Gumilev.[127]

Both camps pointed to the obvious similarities in the concepts they deployed to analyze ethnies. Both Gumilev and Bromlei used the notion of a "behavioral stereotype," Bromlei referring to it as a "psychological stereotype" that, as in Gumilev's models, was not innate but needed to be learned.[128] Both described the ethnos as a "systemic totality" and an "organism" (in Bromlei's case an "ethno-social organism"), and both emphasized the importance of the us-them distinction as the basis of ethnic self-identification.[129] Finally, both deployed a tripartite scheme of ethnic hierarchy. Bromlei frequently used the term "subethnos," and his own notion of "metaethnos" corresponded at least structurally to Gumilev's "superethnos."[130] Along with these structural similarities went deeper affinities in their respective assumptions about the nature of ethnicity. Perhaps most striking in this regard was Bromlei's position regarding the ethnos as social or natural. On the one hand, he echoed the position set out by Kozlov above and insisted that ethnicity was a social category. "While in some theoretical propositions purely ethnic characteristics may be divorced from other social phenomena, in objective reality the ethnos cannot exist outside social institutions of all levels." An ethnos may be an "organism," but it was, as noted, an "ethno-social organism" in which ethnic being was integrated into and reflected through "macro-social formations."[131] He explicitly rejected Gumilev's naturalism and "biologization."[132]

Yet on this most important point Bromlei was ambivalent. In some of his descriptions, the ethnos was characterized as a social *and* biological entity, directly influenced by natural forces and processes. This influence was particularly strong in the early development of the ethnic group, but it did not necessarily dissipate entirely at higher levels.[133] Like Gumilev, Bromlei referred to the work of Marx in his attempts to elaborate this highly awkward position. While humankind is a "totality of all social relations," it is at the same time a "unity of the biological and

127. Ivanov 1985, 236, 238; Lavrov 2000, 25, 329. For a rebuttal, see Mashbits and Chistov 1986. Gumilev "drew attention to himself as a stern critic of Academician Bromlei" but the two "did not differ in any fundamental respect as regards the determination of what constitutes an ethnic group." Goudakov 2006, 83. Recent studies of Soviet ethnos theory have uniformly emphasized the affinities connecting Gumilev and Bromlei. Belkov 1993, 51–52, 56; Tishkov 1997, 2; Ssorin-Chaikov 2003, 189; Sokolovski n.d., 11.

128. Bromlei 1970, 53–54.

129. Bromlei 1970, 55; Bromley 1974, 61; Bromlei 1983a, 5; Porshnev 1973, 4ff.

130. Bromlei 1972; Bromley and Kozlov 1989, 432; Bromlei 1983b, 58; Bromlei 1983a, 6; Lavrov 2000, 25, 329; Mashbits and Chistov 1986, 32; Kozlov 1990, 95; Heikkinen 2000, 103–4. On the importance of hierarchy for ethnos theory, see Tishkov 1992; Drobizheva 1992, 112n.

131. Bromley 1974, 67, 69–72 (quotes); Bromlei 1983b, here 56; Bromley and Kozlov 1989, 433.

132. Bromlei 1988a, 17, 19; Bromlei and Doblaev 1988. Also see Gellner 1988, 135.

133. Bromlei 1971.

the social."[134] Bromlei spoke specifically about the "sociobiological aspects of ethnic life," in which connection he—again like Gumilev—emphasized the significance of the institution of endogamy. Indeed, he described the latter institution
in terms that were unmistakably Gumilevian. Endogamy acts as a "kind of genetic
barrier and ensures that ethnoses carry an attendant genetic pool."[135] And this, he
concluded, gives the ethnos the "function of a biological unit."[136] The resonances
between Bromlei's and Gumilev's positions on this question did not escape the
attention of the former's vigilant colleagues. In 1970, at the same moment that
Gumilev was being attacked for biologism and racism in *Priroda*, Bromlei himself
was subject to prominent public criticism in the journal *Sovetskaia Etnografiia* for
precisely the same errors. Despite Bromlei's strong protestations that he opposed
Gumilev's biological theories of ethnicity, his critics concluded to the contrary
that "in essence he himself acts as a supporter of this [Gumilevian] position."[137]
Even Gumilev was constrained to recognize the resonances of Bromlei's position
with his own, noting approvingly in *Ethnogenesis and the Earth's Biosphere* that
"Iu. V. Bromlei's comments about the stabilizing role of endogamy as a barrier
against assimilation (*inkorporatsiia*) are clearly correct."[138]

A second important affinity between Bromlei and Gumilev involved the relationship of the ethnos to the geographical environment. Once again, Bromlei
condemned what he described as Gumilev's exaggeration of the influence of
environmental factors on ethnic life and development, and echoed Kozlov that
Gumilev was reasoning in the spirit of the "anthropological school of Friedrich Ratzel"—in other words, the reactionary determinist tradition in German
geographical science that would lead to the doctrine of *Geopolitik*.[139] But at the
same time, Bromlei himself heavily stressed the importance of the environment
and landscape for ethnic being. His defined an ethnos in the first instance as an

---

134. Bromlei 1988a, 17–19.

135. Bromley and Kozlov 1989, 430; Bromlei 1970, 55.

136. Bromlei 1969, 89 (quote); Bromley 1974, 65; Pershits and Pokshishevskii 1978, 108–9; Dunn
1975, 69–70n. Like Gumilev, Bromlei had studied the naturalistic theories of Sergei Shirokogorov.
Bromley 1974, 55n; Skalnik 1986, 161–64; Tishkov 1997, 2–3; Sokolovski n.d., 6.

137. "Obsuzhdenie stat'i Iu. V. Bromleia" 1970, 89. Speaking after the collapse of the Soviet Union,
Lev Klein, a former colleague of both Bromlei and Gumilev, confirmed the importance of the biological dimension in the former's conceptualization of ethnos and specifically stressed its affinities to the
latter's ideas. Taylor 1993, 734. Also see Skalnik 1986, 160, 164; Sadokhin 2002, 26. Extraordinarily,
Bromlei in 1969 did not understand how his positive view of endogamy would "objectively" place
him—just like Gumilev a year later—in opposition to the official policy of *sovetskii narod*. When he
did eventually realize "the enormity of what he had done," he was terrified, convinced that such de
facto ideological heresy could lead to his dismissal and professional disgrace. Dragadze 2011, 29.

138. Gumilev 1989c, 90. On the similarities between the naturalism of Gumilev and Bromlei, see
Shnirel'man 2009, 209; Lariuel' 2001, 11; Filippov 2006, 92. Gumilev's biographer maintains that
Gumilev adopted his emphasis on endogamy from Bromlei. Beliakov 2012a, 621.

139. Bromlei 1983c, 213–14; Bromlei 1970, 55.

"intergenerational collection of people that is formed historically on a definite territory," and he confirmed Gumilev's point about the key role played by territory in the earlier stages of ethnogenesis. Indeed, at one point Bromlei even described the ethnos in Gumilevian terms as an "ethno-ecological system."[140] Nor was Bromlei alone in this conviction; indeed it has been argued that the "ideational linkage of ethnos to territory" was quite as important for the primordialism of post-Stalinist ethnos theory in general as it had been for Stalinist perspectives.[141] Writing in 1971, Mikhail Artamonov may have echoed Bromlei's criticism of his former student for exaggerating environmental influences, but he left no doubt about his own belief in the enduring importance of the geographical landscape for ethnic life: "the natural world (*priroda*) places its stamp on organisms, and people adapt to the particular landscape" that they occupy. The formation of ethnies is unquestionably influenced to a significant extent by their "interaction with the geographical environment."[142] Bromlei highlighted the importance of the territorial factor in the two fundamental categories of ethnic grouping that he described. The "ethno-social organism" was defined as a territorial community living compactly on its historical place of origin, whereas the so-called *etnikos* was a diaspora, dispersed away from its original homeland.[143]

Finally, and most remarkably, Bromlei shared at least some of Gumilev's principled reservations concerning the implications of ethnic merging and *sliianie*. On this subject as well, his position was fraught with ambivalences. On the one hand, he openly and enthusiastically endorsed the basic elements of the *sovetskii narod* project. We have noted his acceptance of the Stalinist scheme for the historical evolution of ethnies, and he used the terms "metaethnos" or "macroethnos" to describe new forms of "supranational" (*nadetnicheskii*) communities.[144] These took shape in a process of "ethno-transformation" (*etnotransformatsiia*), the most important example of which was "the formation of a new historical community: the Soviet nation."[145] The future development of Soviet society would lead inexorably to the "ever-greater unification (*edinenie*) of the peoples of our country [and] the onward movement of our society along the long path foreseen by Lenin, toward the *sliianie* of nations."[146] But he was clearly uncomfortable with this scenario. Regardless of its evolutionary character, he felt

---

140. Bromlei 1981, 246, 254, cited in Ivanov 1985, 237.

141. Sokolovski n.d., 18. It is worth noting that Sergei Shirokogorov also emphasized the importance of environmental adaptation in his own concept of ethnos. Shirokogoroff 1924, 5, 7–8, 10, 27, 32.

142. Artamonov 1971, 76.

143. Bromlei 1983a, 5; Bromley and Kozlov 1989, 428–29; Tishkov 1997, 3; Pimenov 2003, 16.

144. Bromlei 1983c, 82, 373, 375; Bromlei 1987, 37.

145. "Etnicheskie protsessy" 1978, 298.

146. Bromlei 1983b, 64 (quote), 59; Bromley and Kozlov 1989, 435–36; Bromlei 1983b, 57–58; Bromlei 1983c, 82, 375; Simon 1991, 312.

that ethnic being nonetheless possessed a certain autonomy from the material economic conditions of its respective society. Individual ethnies could be either advanced or backward in their level of socioeconomic development, and they can persist in the same form across a succession of historical formations.[147]

Although Bromlei used the term *sliianie*, he preferred to describe interethnic relations in terms of "integration" (*integratsiia*) or "consolidation" (*konsolidat-siia*)—the implication being that the latter processes amounted to rather less than the wholesale merger and mutual absorption of the groups concerned.[148] The existing ethnies of the USSR, he believed, could continue to survive long into the future. "In the conditions of mature socialism, nations will . . . retain much of their ethno-cultural character, [indeed] they will be not so much ethno-social as genuinely (*sobstvenno*) ethnic communities."[149] Qualitatively, the *sovetskii narod* was an entity of an entirely different type, a "polyethnic" and "supraethnic" (*nadetnicheskii*) assemblage based not on ethnic association but rather on shared cultural, social, and political values, a common language, and the "socialist way of life."[150] With this argument, he was suggesting that the development of the *sovetskii narod* would not necessarily involve the displacement or absorption of existing Soviet nationalities, but could rather coexist along with them far into the future. The two were eminently compatible. "In Soviet citizens feelings of love for one's people [i.e., ethnos] and for one's ethnic territory are combined with a growing sense of belonging to the Soviet people. . . . The identification of any individual with any definite ethnos usually combines with an awareness of being a Soviet citizen."[151] This position suggested a negative rather than positive nuance to the term "metaethnos," in the sense that the qualifier *meta* flagged the enduring differences from, rather than the growing similarities to, a "genuinely" ethnic community. Ironically, Bromlei criticized Gumilev's term "superethnos" because he mistakenly assumed that Gumilev intended it to refer to the entire country as a single ethnic or quasi-ethnic entity, something he—Bromlei—did not accept.[152] Had he read Gumilev more attentively and appreciated his careful delineation of the USSR into seven distinct and uncombinable superethnies, he would have seen that here as well their positions were very close.

---

147. Bromley 1974, 56–57; Bromley and Kozlov 1989, 425; Hirsch 2004, 314–15; Shanin 1989, 413.
148. Bromlei 1983a, 136, 139–40; Bromley and Kozlov 1989, 434.
149. Bromlei 1983b, 64; Bromlei 1983a, 141–43.
150. Bromlei 1983c, 82, 373; Bromlei 1983a, 163–64; Bromlei 1983b, 60.
151. Bromlei 1983a, 159, 165; Bromlei 1983b, 61.
152. Bromlei 1983c, 374.

1. Student portrait, 1934.

2. Returned from the camps, 1957.

3. After a lecture, Leningrad State University, mid-1970s.

4. Lecture at the Russian Geographical Society, late 1970s.

5. Gumilev at work, late 1970s.

6. With D. S. Likhachev, 1989.

7. Monument to Gumilev in central Kazan, erected in 2005.

Figures 1–6 are from the Gumilev Collection, St. Petersburg State University. Courtesy of the director of the collection, Dr. Marina Kozyreva. Figure 7 is provided by Dr. Ilya Vinkovetsky.

GUMILEV AND THE RUSSIAN NATIONALISTS

Gumilev remained a marginal figure up to the 1980s. As we have seen, only fragments and brief summaries of his historical accounts of Russian history were available, and it is safe to say that among the general reading public his neo-Eurasianist retelling of Russia's ancient encounters with the Golden Horde remained unknown. There was one exception, however—a group that was not only aware of his revisionist historiography but had strong views of its own about it and offered highly spirited reactions. This interest came from Russian ethno-nationalists, a tendency that first emerged in the 1960s.[1] The nationalists were highly critical of the Brezhnev regime but could support various elements of the Soviet system, including in some cases Stalinism, and their movement attracted some support from within the ranks of the Soviet political establishment. From the mid-1960s, nationalist sympathizers met in so-called Russian clubs to discuss issues that they felt related especially to Russian ethno-national interests, and at least two influential journals—*Nash Sovremennik* and *Molodaia Gvardiia*— were broadly supportive of their concerns.[2] The Russian nationalist reception of Gumilev is quite revealing, both for what it says about the ideological tensions of

---

1. On the development of post-Stalinist Russian nationalism, see Barghoorn 1956; Yanov 1978; Allworth 1980; Dunlop 1984; Dunlop 1993; Brudny 1998; Kochanek 1999; Mitrokhin 2003; Zubok 2011.

2. Semanov 1997; Baigushev 2006b, 257; Daniel' and Mitrokhin 1996, 24.

the day but also for the fact that these debates from the early 1980s anticipated issues that would continue to be relevant a decade and more later.

Russian Nationalism after Stalin

The nationalist reception of Gumilev's theories must be understood in the context of the movement's more general perspectives and concerns. Nationalism developed out of the ferment of the post-Stalinist period, largely as a reaction to aspects of Soviet society and official policy that were seen as threats to the welfare of ethnic Russia, its prospects for future development, and even its very survival. The nationality policies of the Soviet state were seen as a major source of these challenges. Many Russians felt that the "affirmative action" policies pursued since the 1930s to overcome the inequalities inherent in the legacy of tsarist imperialism had ended up benefitting non-Russians disproportionately in terms of economic prosperity and political power, at a direct cost to ethnic Russians.[3] This inequality was symbolized in the much-noted fact that the Russians were the only major Soviet nationality not to have been granted their own ethnically designated national republic with ethnically designated Communist parties and academies of sciences.[4] Within these Soviet republics, titular national groups occupied leadership positions, even in those cases where the groups did not represent the majority of the population. The burgeoning sense of Russian ethno-national disadvantage and discrimination was aggravated by demographic research in the 1970s that confirmed robust rates of population growth among non-Russian nationalities (in particular in the Central Asian republics), whereas those of the Russians were in decline. The prediction was that the proportion of Russians in the Soviet population would soon fall below 50 percent, meaning that ethnic Russians would for the first time in their history become a minority group within the Russian state.[5]

In contrast to the positive attempts to foster and develop other nationalities, Russian nationalists believed that for decades the Russians alone had been denied any ethnically based advantages and had been subjected instead to what was seen as an inexorable process of "de-nationalization." Under the holy motto of "socialist development," the Soviet state's reckless but relentless pursuit of industrialization and modernization had brought about the widespread destruction

---

3. Tolz 1996, 1003; Shnirelman 2005, 105; Martin 2001b.
4. "A Word" 1971, 40; Simonsen 1996, 97.
5. Shnirelman and Komarova 1997, 211–13; Dunlop 1997, 32; Tolz 2001, 148.

of ethnic Russia's most treasured cultural landmarks, the ravaging of the agricultural countryside, and the despoliation of its natural landscapes. The renewed determination shown by the post-Stalinist leadership to eradicate ethnic differentiation altogether through the promotion of a supranational "Soviet people" represented a sort of final insult.[6] From the nationalist standpoint, all of these factors combined to push their nation to the brink of ethno-national disaster, threatening not only the preeminence ethnic Russians had enjoyed historically as guardians of state power but indeed, as noted, their very survival as well.[7] This unprecedented perception of victimization and menace gave rise to a paranoia expressed in the concept of "Russophobia" coined by the dissident mathematician Igor' Rostislavovich Shafarevich, which implied that fear or indeed hatred of ethnic Russians had become a dominant social and political attitude.[8]

The Russian nationalism that emerged at this time was highly diversified ideologically.[9] Although nationalists were for the most part conservative, there was a liberal element that included the distinguished historian Dmitrii Likhachev. Moreover, the conservatives themselves were divided between those prioritizing ethno-cultural concerns—sometimes called *pochvenniki*—and those focused on enhancing the strength and cohesion of the Russian state, or the *gosudarstvenniki*. All of these different tendencies engaged in some way with Gumilev. The specific demands and goals of the nationalist movement reflected the ideological diversity just noted. One principal concern was the reassertion of the "organic unity" and "*monolitnost'*" of Russia's traditional forms of state life, which in practical terms meant the reassertion of a powerful and highly centralized state structure unobstructed by the pretensions of non-Russian nationalities ensconced in their federated seats of power.[10] Although this unity would be based on the voluntary association of all Soviet nationalities, the nationalists insisted that ethnic Russia must be accorded a special status within it, linked directly to Russia's preeminent historical role in the formation and development of the Russian state. "It is not by chance that the Russian nation became the unifier of our multi-national state," declared one nationalist manifesto: "The whole multi-national immensity of our state turns on an [ethnic] Russian pivot."[11] The legacy of Russian statehood had demonstrated the enduring "moral and political supremacy" of the Russians,

---

6. Brudny 1998, 43, 39–41, 45–46.
7. "A Word" 1971, 195; Shnirelman and Komarova 1997, 214; Drobizheva 1992, 101–2; Suny 1988, 40; Tolz 2001, 148, 205.
8. Shafarevich 1991.
9. Barghoorn 1980.
10. Semanov 1970, 317; Brudny 1998, 184–85.
11. "The Struggle against So-Called Russophilism" 1975, 328 (quote), 331.

who by all rights should now reclaim this preeminence as a national leader.[12] "In our state the Russian people must indeed become the ruling nation."[13] Moreover, the conservative nationalists reaffirmed the traditional sense of Russia's difference from and opposition to its most powerful neighbors, above all the capitalist West and the obstreperous Peoples Republic of China. It was hoped and believed that national unity could be reforged in the crucible of the current existential confrontation with these primordially hostile "principal enemies" of Russia.[14]

The nationalist concern with ethnic survival was articulated in various ways. Most generally, it was apparent in the widespread resistance to the official project promoting the *slianie* of the Soviet nations into a single "Soviet nation." The journal *Nash Sovremennik* flagged this resistance, subtly but unmistakably, by entitling one of its sections featuring writings from the national republics "Unified and Multinational," thereby opting for a vision of Soviet society as a collection of distinct nationalities rather than an integrated metaethnic amalgam. In the future, "Russians would remain Russian," asserted the Siberian writer Valentin Grigorevich Rasputin, "and Tatars would remain Tatars."[15] Influenced by the new thinking about ethnicity discussed in the previous chapter, some nationalists went further and concluded that "ethnic survival" was now a matter of "biological survival."[16] This particular concern may not have figured prominently in the nationalist discourse disseminated in popular periodical literature and books—all subject to official censorship—but it was a regular theme in the underground or samizdat literature of the nationalist movement. A samizdat declaration from the early 1970s spoke explicitly about the "biological degeneration" that Russia appeared fated to undergo. *Sliianie* was denounced not merely for its promotion of ethno-cultural integration, but much more specifically for the interbreeding between different races and ethnic groups that it encouraged. "When we talk of the [ethnic] Russian people we mean those people who are truly Russian, by blood and by spirit. We must put an end to random hybridization. Although periods of decadence are natural, there can be no fatal and inevitable degeneration as long as the healthy [biological] kernel of the nation is preserved."[17] "Hybridization" was a reference to intermarriage between different nationalities, which was common in the USSR; "degeneration" referred to declining Russian birth rates compared to the seemingly boundless fertility of many non-Russian nationalities. The brutal pessimism of this perspective was captured in the

---

12. Yanov 1978, 72; Shimanov 1974.
13. "A Word" 1971, 198 (quote), 195–96.
14. Semanov 1997, 180; Brudny 1998, 167, 171, 186, 189.
15. Cited in Agursky 1986, 97.
16. Tolz 1996, 1002; Graham 1987, 234.
17. "A Word" 1971, 198–99; Vanderheide 1980, 221; Shnirelman and Komarova 1997, 214, 217.

painting *Moscow in 50 Years' Time* by the nationalist artist and writer Aleksandr Aleksandrovich Zinov'ev (1922–2006). In it, the Orthodox cupolas adorning Moscow's skyline were replaced by the minarets of Islamic mosques, and the Soviet leaders solemnly assembled atop Lenin's mausoleum outside the Kremlin walls to oversee a parade were Central Asian in dress and appearance.[18]

For many of his contemporaries, Gumilev's origins in the cosmopolitan culture of prerevolutionary Russia, the suffering of his parents and his own grievous abuse by at the hands of the Bolshevik authorities, and his robust contravention of the holiest scholarly orthodoxies of the day all seemed to mark him as a natural sympathizer with the liberal and Western-oriented dissident intelligentsia of the post-Stalin period. Such an impression was widespread, and was in all probability part of the attraction in inviting him in the 1970s to speak in Akademgorodok in Western Siberia—one of the more freethinking academic centers in the country—to visit and deliver a special series of lectures.[19] In fact, the opposite was the case. As Aleksandr Borodai noted, Gumilev "believed that Soviet power was divided into two parts: a liberal-democratic part and a Black Hundreds-Cossack part. With the former, there was nothing to talk about. But with the Black Hundreds-Cossack part of Soviet power, [he felt] it was possible to have relations."[20] The Black Hundreds, of course, referred to an extreme Russian nationalist movement in the early twentieth century, notorious for its zealous support of autocracy, its violence toward the perceived enemies of Mother Russia, and its role in inciting anti-Jewish pogroms. Gumilev's sympathies clearly aligned with the conservative nationalists. Like them, he had nothing but scorn for the liberal Soviet intelligentsia, whom he contemptuously dismissed en bloc as Jews or Jewish-influenced traitors.[21] His feelings toward the regime that had condemned him for so many years to the gulag were highly complicated, as we have seen. But he steadfastly refrained from endorsing "the political resonance" of this awful legacy and never suggested that the legitimacy of the Soviet system itself was compromised by the terrible apparatus of repression that it maintained. If anything, indeed, he played down the significance of this particular aspect of the Soviet experience, pointing out that "Sof'ia Vlasovna had only perfected and given a broad Bolshevik scope (*razmakh*) to something that had long existed historically" in Russia and elsewhere.[22]

---

18. Tolz 2001, 148.

19. Author's interview with Andrei Rogachevskii, March 2015; Zubok 2011, 280–81.

20. "Passionarnost'" 2012. On the considerable confusion about Gumilev's political sympathies in this period, see Graham 1987, 252, 255–56. Gumilev himself commented on how his politics had been misunderstood. Gumilev 1989j.

21. Rogachevskii 2001, 360.

22. Mamaladze 1992, 7.

Ethnogenesis and the Environment

For the Russian nationalists, Gumilev represented a profound enigma, and their reception of him was highly mixed. There was great appreciation for many aspects of his work and he enjoyed the support of a number of influential figures within the nationalist ranks. Indeed, a recent study of the late-Soviet intelligentsia concluded that the nationalists as a whole "were particularly carried away" by his teachings.[23] His work obviously celebrated the greatness of Russia's national and state traditions and it was animated by a proud awareness of Russia's world-historical distinctiveness. His impressive historical research lent scholarly credibility to the argument about the elemental differences that separated Russia from the West and China; indeed, he considered the legacy of the latter's aggressive and antagonistic relations with the Great Steppe in much greater detail than that of the West.[24] By giving these civilizational entities the unusual new name of superethnies, moreover, he could include them in his theory of ethnicity, at once essentializing and eternalizing in natural-scientific terms the political and ideological hostility between them. Beyond this, his ethnos theory—as the only attempt to go beyond the long-standing Soviet taboo and treat ethnies unambiguously as natural and organic entities—attracted a good deal of positive attention in the nationalist literature.[25] His elaborate theories about ethnic groups as organic and biological entities were welcomed by many as an objective and apparently scientific basis for their own strongly essentialist ethnocentrism, and it clearly resonated with their apprehensions regarding the future survival of the Russian ethnic organism. With his trenchant condemnation of the official project of *sliianie* and the creation of a supranational *sovetskii narod*, Gumilev provided authoritative support for nationalist concerns. Lengthy extracts from his unpublished dissertation on ethnogenesis and the biosphere circulated in typescript and stimulated much discussion in nationalist circles.[26]

One important arena for this debate was the samizdat journal *Veche*, a leading forum for nationalist sentiments. Gumilev received this journal regularly and he was acquainted with its publishers Vladimir Nikolaevich Osipov and Svetlana Mel'nikova.[27] In the mid-1970s, the journal published an issue with a number of

---

23. Zubok 2011, 308 (quote); Beliakov 2012a, 565; Dunlop 1984, 83, 141, 145, 258–59; Malakhov 2006.

24. Gumilev 1960; Gumilev 1974a.

25. Shnirel'man and Panarin 2000, 26; Kochanek 1998, 1195; Tolz 1996, 1002–3.

26. For example, "Chast' shestaia: Passionarnost' v etnogeneze" 1972? On the samizdat circulation of Gumilev, also see "V samizdate, kak v Internete " 2005. Gumilev did not write expressly for samizdat publication, but he was aware that his work was being circulated in this format and was pleased with the praise it received there. Daniel' and Mitrokhin 1996, 26n.

27. Daniel' and Mitrokhin 1996, 25; Beliakov 2012a, 566.

essays devoted to a discussion of Gumilev's work. The authors were lavish in their praise, with one likening him to Pericles of Athens and another declaring that it was "difficult to doubt the correctness" of his conclusions.[28] Among other things, these essays demonstrated the specific appeal of Gumilev's biological-ecological perspective on the nature of ethnicity.[29] Ethnies were not malleable phantoms of group consciousness but real-existing human communities, it was affirmed, the "objective reality" (*ob"ektivnaia realiia*) and permanence of which were unquestionable. As Gumilev maintained, belonging to these groups was an inviolable and "inalienable" (*neottorzhim, neot"emlemost'*) aspect of an individual's personal being.[30] The belief in the natural fixity and immutability of ethnic character led the authors to echo Gumilev's stress on the importance of endogamy— what they referred to as "biological insulation" (*obosoblenie*)—for overcoming "random hybridization" and maintaining ethnic health.[31] They found Gumilev's notion of *passionarnost'* to be particularly compelling, and excerpts from his discussion of this subject were especially popular choices for samizdat circulation. Here the term was clearly deployed in the transformist sense we have discussed above. "The activity of a passionary person encompasses and sustains the most characteristic feature of life on earth: the miracle of the transformation of the chaos of stagnant, spiritless matter into the most highly organized structure of living nature, subjecting passive matter to [the passionary person's] own organizing principles."[32] The nature of ethnicity as a heritable genetic quality was emphasized, in the spirit of the nationalist belief that ethnic Russianness was defined "by blood"—inadvertently contravening Gumilev's own insistence that ethnic character is not inborn but rather acquired in childhood.[33] There was, however, a clear appreciation of Gumilev's insistence on the connections between an ethnos and the geographical landscape, and a corresponding recognition that some of the features characterizing a given ethnos could also form "as a result of adaptation to the conditions of the external natural environment."[34]

The nationalists identified the widespread destruction of Russia's natural environment through grand projects of industrial and urban development as a major threat to its ethnic integrity, providing incontrovertible evidence of the state's grossly misplaced priorities and, more specifically, of its indifference

---

28. Ruzhenkov 1975, 92; Vaniagin 1975, 102; Dunlop 1984, 141, 145.
29. Yanov 1978, 13; Vanderheide 1980, 221; Dunlop 1984, 42, 143–44, 263; Tolz 2001, 202, 205.
30. Vaniagin 1975, 98–99.
31. Vaniagin 1975, 118, Shnirelman and Komarova 1997, 214; Hammer 1988, 20.
32. Vaniagin 1975, 112–13 (quote), 100.
33. Vaniagin 1975, 118; Ruzhenkov 1975, 96.
34. Vaniagin 1975, 105, 107.

to protecting the national welfare of its own population.[35] Consequently, environmental protection became a central cause of the nationalist movement, which displayed increasingly determined opposition to the major industrial development projects of the day.[36] Massive hydroelectric projects such as those at Krasnoyarsk and Bratsk in the 1960s and 1970s were condemned for the inundation and destruction of local communities that their construction had involved, and a projected cellulose plant on the shores of Lake Baikal was denounced for the damage it would cause to the lake's pristine ecological conditions. Grandiose plans unveiled in the late 1970s for the so-called project of the century—the diversion of rivers in Siberia and the Russian North in order to deliver water to arid Central Asia—aroused particular consternation.[37] Environmental protection was a central theme for nationalist writers including Valentin Rasputin, Vladimir Alekseevich Chivilikhin (1928–1984), Viktor Petrovich Astaf'ef (1924–2001), Gleb Aleksandrovich Goryshin (1931–1998), and numerous others. In different ways, they all maintained that the natural environment represented Russia's invaluable national patrimony and that in the final analysis its despoliation amounted to nothing less than the desecration of the Russian nation itself.[38]

Nationalist concerns with the preservation of Russia's natural milieu and the yearning to reharmonize the Russian nation's interaction with it resonated quite powerfully with Gumilev's ethno-ecological teachings. He gained broad recognition as an authority on the subject, as we have seen, explaining the problem of environmental destruction as a result of ethnic dysfunction. Because he dealt primarily with examples drawn from foreign regions in the distant historical past, however, his detailed discussions of the subject remained somehow detached from the contemporary realities of Soviet conditions. It thus fell to his followers to bring out the more immediate significance of his perspective for nationalist concerns about Russia's environmental health and future. Two attempts in particular were important in this endeavor, by Iurii Borodai and Dmitrii Mikhailovich Balashov (1927–2000). Both were among Gumilev's closest associates and most devoted supporters who helped popularize his ideas in the late Soviet period and after the collapse of the USSR.

Balashov, a folklorist, ethnographer, and writer of historical fiction, had been active in nationalist circles since the 1960s. His work appeared in the journal *Molodaia Gvardiia* and he was a frequent speaker at the Russian Club.[39] His most

35. Dunlop 1984, 88–91.
36. Brudny 1998, 18, 45–46; Agursky 1986, 97.
37. Petro 1987; Darst 1988; Gustafson 1981.
38. Peterson 1994.
39. Krasnov 1991, 158–62; Brudny 1998, 70–71; Mitrokhin 2001.

important contribution to the dissemination of Gumilev's teachings came in a series of novels about ancient Russian history and Russia's relations with the Tatars and other steppe peoples. Balashov felt very strongly that environmental protection and the restoration of an ecological balance were imperative for the survival of ethnic Russia, and he framed his position using principles and categories taken directly from Gumilev.[40] Like all ethnies, he explained, the Russian ethnos was a part of the natural world and could operate in a normal fashion only when nature itself operated normally.[41] The so-called technical progress of Soviet development, however, had disrupted nature's normal functioning and poisoned its very essence, leading to the "destruction of [Russia's] primeval national foundations." It was not only the Russian ethnos, moreover, that was threatened in this manner. "Did it occur to a single one of the *povorotchiki*," he queried, referring to the advocates of diverting Siberian water to Central Asia, that building the necessary dam on the Ob' "would flood the territories of a number of nations: the Khanty, Mansy, Voguls, and others?" And this was only in Western Siberia. What about the threats to the natural environment in the Far East, Kamchatka, and Buriatia? "Land must be defended, and it must be defended on the basis of national principles (*berech' ee nado natsional'no*)." Balashov concluded on a Gumilevian note, linking the defense of the natural world to a return to the "established Russian principles of respect of national territory, national traditions, and the national way of life."[42]

A rather different attempt to refract the environmentalist concerns of Russian nationalists through a Gumilevian prism came from the philosopher Borodai. Borodai had been a student of the religious philosopher Aleksei Fedorovich Losev (1893–1988) and was also strongly influenced by the ideas of Igor' Shafarevich.[43] In the early 1980s, the two articles by him mentioned in the previous chapter appeared in *Priroda*, calling readers' attention to the existence of Gumilev's unpublished manuscript *Ethnogenesis and the Earth's Biosphere* and providing a general idea of its contents.[44] Both essays dealt almost exclusively with the issue of environmental destruction. What exactly was it, he asked, that brought about this sad and dangerous state of affairs? Was environmental destruction an inherent aspect of human activity, or was it rather a product of some sort of abnormal condition, an "illness, which is in no way necessary for human existence"? Gumilev, he reported, had carefully investigated the circumstances under which

---

40. On Balashov's environmentalism, see Krasnov 1991, 160–61; Paramonov 1992, 198.
41. Balashov 1989, 8.
42. Ibid., 9.
43. Rossman 2002b, 154–58; Mitrokhin 2001.
44. Borodai 1981a; Borodai 1981b.

"acts against nature" (*antiprirodnye*) were committed and came to the conclusion it was the latter.[45] Under normal conditions, most people were "preservers" (*okhraniteli*) of the natural world, for they understood that they depended on it for their existence. Under certain conditions, however, some groups became deformed and developed a warped psychological perspective that was categorically negative, "world denying" (*mirootritsaiushchii*), and life destroying. These were antisystems, entities that Gumilev called chimeras. With their rapacious practices, they acted not as preservers but rather "destroyers" (*gubiteli*) of nature.

Borodai explained this process in terms of Gumilev's scenario for the formation of ethnic aberrations. An invading chimera occupied the territory of a healthy ethnos and took control over it. This occupation initiated a far-reaching process of deformation, both of the subject ethnos and of the geographical landscape that was its ecological niche. The invader is afflicted by a massive psychological syndrome, expressed as an impulse to reshape (*peredelat'*) those aspects of the indigenous natural world and culture that do not suit it. "As a rule, . . . this 'reshaping' becomes an act of destruction."[46] Such a destructive imperative is overwhelming and irresistible, he maintained, and there is only one thing that can resist it: "*Passionarnost'*, with the help of which living nature is able to convey to newly formed ethnies the unique and harmonious rhythm [of coexistence with the natural world]. This is what can kill chimeras and the antisystems that are rooted in them. It is as if the passionary impulse generates an incandescence that bathes the chimeras and turns them into healthy ethnies, harmoniously ensconced in the landscape as a part of a biogeocenosis."[47] Borodai's description of *passionarnost'* conspicuously departs from Gumilev's own understanding of the phenomenon and provides an early demonstration of the great conceptual elasticity of this evocative term. Nonetheless, the identification of the deformed "life-destroying" ideologies of the antisystem as the most immediate cause of environmental destruction was thoroughly Gumilevian, as was Borodai's demonization of them as "diabolical" (*d'iavol'skie*) and "vampire conceptions" (*kontseptsii-vampiry*). These ideological aberrations were, however, themselves the product of "ethnic collisions" that came from intermingling and mixing of ethnic groups, and it was this latter phenomenon that must be seen as the real source of the problem. Although the Marxist-communist obsession with modernization and technological development were certainly the immediate causes for the degradation of the natural world in the Soviet Union, Borodai was indicating that this obsession itself was the product of dysfunctional patterns

---

45. Borodai 1981a, 82.
46. Ibid., 83.
47. Ibid., 85

of ethnic coexistence. The implication was clear that until the problem of "ethnic collisions" was resolved, environmental issues could not be effectively addressed.

The Jewish Question

In his essays, Borodai did not indicate what had caused such severe ethnic dysfunction in the USSR, preferring to dwell on Gumilev's own examples of chimeras and antisystems from antiquity and the Middle Ages.[48] The answer was obvious nonetheless, and it pointed to the final, and by far the most significant, contribution Gumilev made to nationalist discourse, namely, the elaboration and "scientific" justification of its strong anti-Semitic inclinations. The "Jewish question" had always been a major preoccupation for Russian nationalism, and it was certainly at the very center of concern in the period we are considering.[49] Beginning with the Stalinist campaign against "rootless cosmopolitanism" in the late 1940s and the Doctors' Plot on the eve of Stalin's death, anti-Semitism in the USSR received something resembling official endorsement, which survived Stalin himself and carried over into the period under discussion. This was apparent in the protracted campaign against so-called world Zionism, directed ostensibly against the policies of the state of Israel but implicitly indicating that the predatory behavior of this particular state was naturally related to the ethnic qualities of the nation that had created it. For the Russian nationalists, the Jews represented a particularly egregious example of ethnically based enfranchisement in the Soviet system that worked to their own detriment. The Jews "claim the role of a minority oppressed by the Russians, but meanwhile, by conducting a policy of national nepotism, they have all but gained the monopoly in the field of science and culture."[50] The debate around the position of the Jews in Russian society was further fired—and pressed ever more into the public domain—in the 1970s with the decision to allow a limited emigration of Soviet citizens of Jewish background to Israel and the West.[51]

A highly significant contribution to anti-Semitic discourses was the notion of *malye narody* or "small nations," made famous through the work of Igor' Shafarevich. A gifted mathematician of international renown, Shafarevich was also an active polemicist in the Russian nationalist movement. Along with his onetime colleague Aleksandr Solzhenitsyn he wrote several chapters for the landmark collection *From under the Rubble*, but his most important contribution

---

48. Ibid., 84.
49. Friedgut 1984; Woll 1989; Laqueur 1993.
50. "A Word" 1971, 197.
51. Mitrokhin 2001.

was the essay *Russophobia*, first circulated in samizdat form in the early 1980s.[52] Here Shafarevich developed the notion of a *malyi narod* or "little nation." The *malyi narod* Shafarevich had in mind was not one of the indigenous peoples of the Russian North or Siberia, but referred rather to a concept formulated in the early twentieth century by the conservative French historian Augustin Cochin (1876–1916). Cochin described *le petit peuple* as a small self-selected group of individuals drawn together by their hatred of the nation in which they originated. Operating as a hostile unit from within, they ceaselessly endeavored to bring about its destruction.[53] For Cochin, the little nation was the Freemasons, whereas for Shafarevich it was the Jews, whom he regarded as the principal destabilizing and destructive force throughout Russia's history.[54] Gumilev himself used the term *malyi narod* on several occasions in *Ancient Russia and the Great Steppe* as a synonym for an antisystem.[55] Although he referred directly to Cochin as his source and did not cite Shafarevich's writings, the two were acquainted and aware of each other's work. Indeed, it has been suggested that Shafarevich actually borrowed the term from Gumilev and not directly from Cochin.[56] However this may be, Gumilev's evaluation of Shafarevich was very positive. Speaking about the Jewish question in a radio broadcast at the end of his life, Gumilev confirmed that he had studied the samizdat publication of Shafarevich's *Russophobia*, concluding that it was an "excellent work" and that he "would have nothing to add to it."[57]

A major forum for the articulation of anti-Semitic sentiment was academic research on the ancient Jewish state of Khazaria by a young generation of nationalist historians in the 1960s to 1970s. This new Khazar historiography played an important role in the manipulation of negative stereotypes of the Jews as an ethnic group.[58] In the work of Svetlana Aleksandrovna Pletneva (1926–2008), Vadim Viktorovich Kargalov (1932–2009), Vladimir Nikolaevich Toporov (1928–2005), and others, Kharazia was depicted as a large and powerful aggressor empire

---

52. *Iz-pod glyb* 1974; Shafarevich 1991. On Shafarevich, see Horvath 2005, 153–59; Rossman 2002b, 168–72; Laqueur 1993, 99–101; Klier 1995; Ianov 1995a.
53. Devlin 2008.
54. Woll 1989, 6–7; Rossman 2002b, 77.
55. Gumilev 2004c, 227–28.
56. So in any event claimed the controversial Russian Jewish journalist Izrael′ Shamir. Shamir n.d. For an alternative view, see Mirovich 1991, 157–58.
57. Gumilev 1989i; Beliakov 2012a, 566. Gumilev made these comments in a lecture filmed for broadcast. The notoriety of Shafarevich's anti-Semitism in the early 1990s was such that Gumilev's supportive remarks were deleted from the recording and were not broadcast. They remained in the written transcript, however, and became available many years later when the point had come to seem less sensational. Gumilev and Shafarevich are also discussed below, 263–66.
58. Shnirelman 2002; Rossman 2002b.

under the ruthless control of a Judaic ruling elite.[59] Endemically hostile to ancient Russia, its overriding objective was the conquest of East Slav territories and the extraction of punitive tribute from their populations. It was, moreover, a state utterly without morals or humanity, which single-mindedly sought to gain material benefits by whatever means possible. Among other things, Kharazia sponsored a flourishing slave trade, in which endeavor they actively colluded with Western agents who shared the rabid Khazar hostility to the Russians. Ultimately, the Khazars were cast as a prototype of Russia's "internal enemy," and the "Khazar yoke" that they imposed on the shoulders of young Rus' wreaked devastation on a scale comparable to that of the Mongols.[60] This version of Khazar history became extremely popular among Russian nationalists, for whom it provided an ideal Aesopian foil for ruminating on the real nature of the Jews and their contemporary significance in Soviet society.[61]

Gumilev was a leading representative of this new generation of Khazar specialists; indeed, it was precisely in his work that their negative interpretative line found its culmination.[62] Gumilev was regarded by the nationalists as their most important spokesman for this most important of issues—indeed, many of those unfamiliar with the subject simply credited Gumilev as being the first and only one to have revealed the true history of young Russia's troubled relations with the Jewish Khazars.[63] Gumilev's historical reconstructions provided the nationalists with an apparently credible scientific-scholarly basis for a generalized critique of the role of the Jews in Russian history. The editors of the leading nationalist journals *Molodaia Gvardiia* and *Nash Sovremennik* commissioned articles about the Khazars from Gumilev—although ironically the anti-Semitic thrust of the essays he produced for them was so extreme that only the latter journal actually published them, and then only in the 1990s.[64] The recognition of Gumilev's Khazar expertise was all the more notable in that his major work on the subject, completed around 1980, was to remain unpublished for nearly another decade.[65]

---

59. Pletneva 1976; Kargalov 1985; Pletneva 1990; Sakharov 1982.

60. Tillett 1969, 313; Shnirelman 2002, 62–65.

61. Rossman 2002a, 34.

62. Shnirelman 2002, 28–29, 58.

63. Rossman 2002a, 34. For an early nationalist confirmation of the popularity of Gumilev's Khazar writings, see Semanov 1970, 318.

64. Gumilev 1991d; also see Kozhinov 1992b, 165–65; Shnirelman 2002, 47; Brudny 1998, 119.

65. Gumilev 1989b; Naarden 1996, 67. This work, Gumilev's *Ancient Rus' and the Great Steppe* (1989b), grew out of a project originally undertaken on a commission from the almanac *Prometei*. The latter was part of the book series *Zhizn' Zamechatel'nykh Liudei*, which was associated with the nationalist journal *Molodaia Gvardiia*. As noted, the manuscript he produced was deemed too radical in its anti-Semitism and was rejected. Beliakov 2012a, 567.

Gumilev's analyses were a critical milestone in the development of a Russian-nationalist narrative of Russia's Khazar experience, in a number of different
respects. Most significant was his insistence on the collusion of the Khazars with
pernicious Western agents, a link that other historians did not stress so heavily, if at all. This served to bring two of Russia's principal opponents together
into a united front of relentless and aggressive hostility, thereby simplifying and
intensifying the contours of the existential challenge faced by ancient Rus' (and,
by implication, by Russia in the present day). Gumilev also made a highly useful methodological contribution to Khazar discourse by framing the problem
in terms of his own naturalistic and ethno-ecological categories. This served
to transform the subject from a standard historical interpretation into a legitimate subject of natural-scientific analysis. These two approaches closely echoed
and reinforced each other, to be sure, but by refracting the history of Khazaria's
relations with Russia through the categories and processes of his ethnos theory,
Gumilev provided his arguments with a patina of scientific objectivity—and
hence credibility—that no standard historical study could reproduce. The highly
stylized vocabulary he used to describe his subject, notably the characterization
of Khazaria as an ecological chimera, quickly spread into common usage and was
repeated even by liberal nationalists such as Dmitrii Likhachev.[66]

Gumilev influenced the work of others writing about the relations of the
Khazars and ancient Russians. One example was Vadim Valerianovich Kozhinov
(1930–2001) a well-known literary scholar and critic and an important advocate of the nationalist cause.[67] For Kozhinov as for Gumilev, the Khazar theme
was an appealing basis for a comprehensive narrative of primordial Jewish hostility and malicious intent toward Russia.[68] Despite his extensive knowledge of
ancient Russian culture, however, Kozhinov had no particular expertise in the
field of Khazar-Russian relations, and thus his work on the subject relied almost
entirely on secondary sources. The most important was Gumilev. Kozhinov knew
Gumilev personally, had attended his lectures, and in the early 1990s facilitated
the publication of his work in *Nash Sovremennik*.[69] Although Kozhinov was
quite critical about certain aspects of his theories, in regard to Khazaria he fully

---

66. In a confidential review of Gumilev's work prepared for the authorities, Likhachev referred
approvingly to Gumilev's image of Khazaria as a "merchant octopus." Likhachev 2003b, 340. For a
revealing anecdotal account of Likhachev's enthusiasm for Gumilev's work on Khazaria, see Kozhinov
1992b, 164–65; Shnirelman 2002, 69.

67. Shafarevich 1993, 170–77.

68. Shnirel'man 2005b, 294–96; Rossman 2002b, 90–92.

69. Bondarenko 2002.

acknowledged Gumilev's authority.[70] In his own essays on the subject he cites Gumilev extensively—to the point, indeed, that he felt the need to make clear to his readers that he did not, in fact, agree entirely with everything Gumilev said.[71] Nonetheless, in his main points Kozhinov follows Gumilev very closely. The Khazar Khaganate, a large and powerful state, was the "most potent enemy" of Kievan Rus'.[72] In a sort of spiritual communion with the West, it waged aggressive wars against the Russians, occupied Slavic territories, enslaved their populations, and even ruled Kiev for some time. Kozhinov developed the image of a Khazar yoke, which "without question was much more dangerous for Rus' than that of the Mongols."[73] Compared with the brutal Khazars, he maintained, even the Varangians were benign occupiers.[74]

Yet whereas Gumilev remained consistently focused on the ancient Khazar past and painstakingly avoided any explicit reference to what this historical record might mean for the contemporary world, Kozhinov showed no such reserve. To the contrary, he was adamant that there was a direct link, "a deep, if not entirely obvious connection" between the "remote epoch" of the Khazars and the present day. It was precisely this connection, moreover, that provided the most compelling rationale for studying this historical past in the first place. "There is nothing artificial about the direct comparison (*sopostavlenie*) of the events of Russian history in the tenth century with those of the twentieth."[75] The pernicious influence of the Jews on the life of the Russian nation, he suggested, is as alive and real today as it had ever been in the past. His essays on Khazaria included extensive discussions of the early Soviet period, in which he repeated the conviction shared by Gumilev of the "immense role" played by nonethnic Russians—Jews above all—in the revolution itself and then in the bloody terror that followed. Effectively, Jews played the same role in postrevolutionary Russia that they had played in Khazaria, in both cases aiming at nothing less than the destruction of Russian culture.[76] Picking up directly on Gumilev's theories about

---

70. Kozhinov 2005, 310, 312, 331–32, 359–60, 500–502. In this particular work, Kozhinov hailed Gumilev as a "great representative" of Russian historical science. Elsewhere he took a narrower view, characterizing Gumilev as a poet rather than a historian, who all too often simply "thinks up, invents, and dreams up" his material. Gumilev's theory of *passionarnost'* he dismissed as "fantasy, of course." Kozhinov 1991; Beliakov 2012a, 647.

71. Kozhinov 1992b, 165; Kozhinov 1992a, 174; Kozhinov 1992c, 168; Kozhinov 1989.

72. Kozhinov 1989, 240.

73. Cited in "Eshche raz o morkovke" 1989; Shnirelman 2002, 66–67.

74. Kozhinov 1992b, 179.

75. Ibid., 168, 169.

76. Kozhinov 1992c, 173; Shnirelman 2002, 69.

the special role of Jewish women in gaining ethnic control of Khazar society, Kozhinov noted that if the Bolshevik leaders were not themselves Jewish then at least their wives were. "It is difficult to believe," he maintained, "that this 'unanimity' (*edinodushie*) [in their choice of marital partners] was accidental and inconsequential." Nor could it be a coincidence, he concluded, that the terror came to an end as soon as the political control of the state reverted back to the hands of ethnic Russians after the death of Stalin.[77]

Gumilev's powerful influence on the nationalist engagement with Khazaria can also be seen in the work of Aleksandr Innokent'evich Baigushev. A secret service agent attached to the Central Committee of the Communist Party, Baigushev was an early enthusiast for and heavily committed to the nationalist cause. He knew Gumilev well, referred to him as "my teacher," and claimed to have worked for many years under his "scientific direction."[78] Baigushev was interested in the story of ancient Khazaria and wrote a lengthy historical novel about it in the 1970s.[79] Gumilev was an important source of inspiration and information for him, and like Gumilev he was able to publish his work only with the onset of perestroika.[80] Baigushev repeated the Gumilevian scenario whereby Jewish invaders took control of Khazaria and turned it into a parasitic slave-trading state closely connected with corrupt Western networks and implacably hostile to the Russians. Baigushev used Gumilev's specialized terminology, characterizing the passionary Jews of Khazaria as the "clearest example" of an antisystem.[81] In regard to the twentieth century, Baigushev maintained not only that Jewish influence was behind the Russian revolution but also that the Soviet state had been thoroughly "judaized" (*iudaizirovannyi*), as was most recently apparent in Khrushchev's "Trotskyist-cosmopolitan thaw" that followed the death of Stalin.[82] The lessons he drew from the Khazar experience were thoroughly Gumilevian: if we want to avoid assimilation and preserve our ethnic integrity, "the heavens command us . . . to live separately!"[83]

A "Monstrous Distortion"

If Gumilev's positions on environmental protection and Russian-Khazar interaction resonated positively with Russian nationalist sentiments in the late Soviet period, there was another key aspect of the nationalist perspective that was notably

---

77. Kozhinov 1992c, 182n.
78. Baigushev 2006b, 79–81.
79. Shnirel'man 2005b, 299–301.
80. Baigushev 1990; Baigushev 1995.
81. Baigushev 2006b, 18, 21.
82. Ibid., 6, 11.
83. Cited in Shnirel'man 2005b, 301; Baigushev 1990, 252, 340–41; Shnirelman 2002, 122.

absent from his work. There was really nothing in his writings that reflected the exclusive preoccupation with ethnic Russia that was characteristic for the nationalists, and he did not seem to support—explicitly or even implicitly—the prioritization of ethnic Russia's interests over and above those of other Soviet nationalities. Gumilev's evenhandedness in this regard was reflected in his "science" of ethnology, in the sense that the universalism of the laws and processes he described meant that they functioned in the same way for all ethnies across all epochs of human history. This may have helped to provide his theories with an aura of scholarly objectivity useful for discourses of ethnic essentialism or anti-Semitism, but at the same time it mitigated against, indeed precluded, the sort of exceptionalist approach to ethnic Russia in particular that was the nationalist *conditio sine qua non*. But the uncomfortable fact was that—with the notable exception of the Jews—Gumilev simply did not share either the antipathy and defensiveness vis-à-vis non-Russian nationalities characteristic of many Russian nationalists or their belief in ethnic Russia's legitimate claim to preeminence.[84]

This problem came painfully into focus around Gumilev's revisionist account of the history of the relations between ancient Rus′ and the Golden Horde. On this important subject, the perspectives of the nationalists largely corresponded to official interpretations, which as we have seen were diametrically opposed to those expounded by Gumilev.[85] From the very inception of its historical life, nationalist historians argued, ancient Rus′ had been a beleaguered and isolated outpost, its very existence threatened by challengers on numerous fronts. From the West, it had had to contend with the relentless aggression of European powers, while from the southern and southeastern steppe came a constant stream of nomadic predators. The latter were not benign and friendly, as Gumilev would have it, but rather savagely hostile. As a result, Rus′ had been compelled to "maintain its defences on all fronts and survive under siege conditions that became the ordinary way of life."[86] Eventually it succumbed to the irresistible onslaught of the Golden Horde, which brought "countless misfortunes to the Russian people," interrupted the country's historical development for centuries, and left a deep scar on its national psychology.[87] For all of its hostility to the Soviet establishment, on this question

---

84. In my own extensive reading of Gumilev's work, I have come across only a single reference to the "leading Russian ethnos" (*vedushchii russkii etnos*), in an interview at the end of his life. But even here his point was to underscore not its greatness but rather its weakness. Because the travails of the revolution, civil war, and Stalinism had exhausted ethnic Russia's *passionarnost′*, he maintained, it "does not have the strength to realize its predominance" (*ne v silakh osushchestvliat′ svoe preobladanie*) in the present day. Gumilev 1992a.

85. Gammer 2004, 484, 486, 489; Shnirelman 1996, 22; Sheiko 2009, 149–50; Sorokin 2003, 21.

86. Liubomudrov 1981, 17; Nesterov 1980, 14.

87. Skrynnikov 1980, 9; Smirnov 1963, 81; Nechkina and Leibengrub 1970, 74–77; Tolstov 1950, 5.

the conclusion of the nationalist samizdat press was not very different: "The Tatar yoke dealt a heavy blow to Russia."[88] The eventual casting off of the Mongol yoke was of course the glorious achievement of the Battle of Kulikovo in 1380. The early victory of Russian forces over the Golden Horde assumed a great symbolic value and became one of the most important landmarks in Russia's national memory. It was cherished as a dramatic catharsis that at once brought liberation from foreign domination, moral renewal, the rediscovery of a common national ethos, and the foundations of a new political structure that would evolve into the mighty Russian state. As Likhachev observed, "the Kulikovo field is as holy to us as the field of Borodino or the land of Stalingrad."[89]

In regard to the related question about the origins of the Great Russian ethnos, the nationalists offered two scenarios, both of which differed significantly from Gumilev's account. According to one, ethnic Russia had been formed in Kievan Rus', prior to the Mongol invasion. It was at this time that "the ethnos, or nation (*narod*) took shape, with a unified territory, central political power, and a common language that could be understood by everyone from the Carpathians to the Volga and from Ladoga to the Sea of Azov." Along with this went an "all-Russian (*obshchrusskoe*) self-awareness and mentality."[90] The implication was that when centuries later the Russians were finally able to cast off the Tatar yoke and reclaim their national independence, they returned to the old traditions of Kievan Rus' and developed them in the novel geopolitical framework of the Muscovite state.[91] An alternative view maintained that it was the crucible of Kulikovo itself, where the armies of different proto-Russian principalities were assembled for the first time under unified leadership, that served to forged a self-conscious and unified Russian nation. The catalyst for unity was the common challenge that they confronted, in other words their "bitter struggle" against their nomadic Tatar adversaries from the steppe. "It was precisely on the Kulikovo field that those features that gave Russia its unique national character were first manifested."[92]

Whatever the precise ethnogenetic scenario, however, the nationalists drew the same historical conclusion. Ethnic Russia was forged *in struggle against* the forces of the Golden Horde, not in alliance or partnership with them. It logically followed that as a political formation, post-Tatar Muscovy was dominated exclusively by the Great Russian ethnos. The vast transcontinental Russian empire represented the achievement of ethnic Russia alone, the core nationality

88. "A Word" 1971, 195.
89. Cited in Kochanek 1999, 247; Likhachev 1980; Skrynnikov 1980.
90. Chivilikhin 1980, 105, 125 (quotes); Liubomudrov 1981, 17.
91. Likhachev 1980, 3, 6–8.
92. Kargalov 1981, 190.

that provided the creative impetus and initiative across the centuries and played the role of the "state-forming" (*gosudarstvennoobrazuiushchii*) element. And of course, this nationalist narrative about the early origins of Russia had everything to do with the present day. The historical remoteness of the events in question provided an ideal discursive field on which Russian nationalists could openly identify and denounce the challenges that that they believed non-Russian nationalities posed to ethnic Russia's survival in the present day, and on which they could defend the natural historical role of the latter as creator and leader of the modern Russian state. As one nationalist writer declared, "the multinational Soviet people were welded together forever by *velikaia Rus'*," which in the present day could only refer to ethnic Russia.[93]

Against this background, it can be readily appreciated that Gumilev's alternative narrative of early Russian history appeared scandalous and offended nationalist sensibilities to their very core. His suggestion of Russian-Tatar collusion at Kulikovo dismissed in the stroke of a pen the entire legacy of primordial struggle and heroic resistance that the nationalists cherished as the Russian nation's baptism in fire and one of its greatest historical accomplishments. At the same time, Gumilev's account offered no basis for prioritizing ethnic Russia as the preeminent nationality or first among equals—for the simple reason that Gumilev himself did not support this prioritization. For Gumilev, the historical collaboration of Russia's nationalities in a shared destiny was not the result of any one group's proactive leadership, but rather was a natural and organic development on the basis of mutual positive complementarity. From their earliest origins to the present, Russians had at all times coexisted peacefully with the steppe peoples, and indeed with all other nationalities of the empire, in a state of symbiosis, that is to say, mutual understanding, affection, and support. Although Gumilev made little attempt to spell out the implications of his historical scenarios for the present day, it is clear nonetheless that his ideal for Soviet society—or at least for its Slavic-Turkic axis—was a genuine fraternity of equally enfranchised ethnies between whom there could be no "first among equals." Gumilev's emphatic Turkophilism, along with his highly idealized "friendship of the peoples" scenario, were categorically unacceptable for many nationalists, and these alone sufficed to put him beyond the pale. Castigated as a "Tatar-lover" (*tataroliub*), Gumilev was never welcome to participate in the meetings of the Russian Club—precisely, as Baigushev explained, because "he was a Eurasianist."[94]

---

93. Liubomudrov 1981, 17.
94. Baigushev 2006b, 253; Koreniako 2000, 43; Laqueur 1993, 146–47. This question is also considered in Bassin 2015a.

The immense ideological stakes attending these differences in historical interpretation were confirmed by the harshness of the attacks that Gumilev's alternative
historical narrative attracted from the nationalist camp. The first of these came in
the form of an acerbic review by Boris Aleksandrovich Rybakov (1908–2001) of
Gumilev's book *Searches for an Imaginary Kingdom* (1970), which included fragments of his revisionist interpretation.[95] Rybakov was an eminent specialist on
ancient Russia, and as deputy dean of Moscow State University and director of the
Institute of Russian History of the Academy of Sciences he was extremely influential as well. He was an outspoken advocate of Russia's historical independence
from Western influence and an opponent of the "Norman" theory of the origins of
Russia, all of which made him particularly popular in nationalist circles.[96] Rybakov
was outraged by Gumilev's arguments. He rejected the assertions that from the
fall of the Khazars in the tenth century to the incursions of the Golden Horde in
the thirteenth, relations between Rus' and the steppe peoples were cooperative,
peaceful, and benign. All the historical evidence offered by the chronicles pointed
to precisely the opposite conclusion, he insisted, namely, that the nomads were
the scourge of ancient Russia and brought it nothing but misfortune and ruin.[97]
Rybakov was particularly scandalized by Gumilev's revisionist interpretation of
the chronicle *The Song of Igor's Campaign*—which claimed that the work was a
traitorous tract by a Russian turncoat in the service of the pro-Western camp—
and dismissed it as utterly ludicrous.[98] Rybakov's conclusions were unforgiving
in their ferocity. Gumilev's historical deductions were a "masquerade" confected
"without proof, analysis, or evidence." He could elaborate them only through the
"falsification of history": the "monstrous distortion" (*chudovishchnoe iskazhe-
nie*) of historical sources and their "dishonest manipulation" (*nedobrosovestnaia
podtasovka*).[99] Rybakov's denunciations were echoed a few years later by another
noted historian of ancient Russia, Nikolai Sergeevich Borisov, who denounced
Gumilev specifically for reviving the discredited theories of the Eurasianists.[100]

Gumilev as a Closet Zionist

Rybakov's sharp critique was, however, merely a foretaste of what was to come,
for it was only in the next decade that the nationalist movement would vent

---

95. Gumilev 1970e. On Rybakov and Gumilev, see Beliakov 2012a, 395–97, 503.
96. Semanov 1997, 181. Baigushev 2006b, 243–44.
97. "A bylo li igo?" 1997, 91.
98. See above, 97.
99. Rybakov 1971; Brudny 1998, 187. For Gumilev's rebuttal, see Gumilev 1972b.
100. Borisov 1976, 141–42; Halperin 1982b, 318n.

its full fury against Gumilev's historiographical heresies. The occasion was the six-hundred-year anniversary of the Kulikovo battle of 1380, which was memorialized in a national celebration that extended over several years and produced an abundance of historical studies, commentaries, and popular debates about Kulikovo and Russian history in general. This paroxysm of patriotic affirmation was very much encouraged by the party and state, not least in the hope that it would distract the attention of the Soviet public away from the unsettling invasion of Afghanistan (1979) and the emergence of the Solidarity movement in Poland (1980–1983). In view of the historical perspective of the nationalists just described, it can be readily appreciated that they were maximally mobilized by this memorialization project. Indeed, the victory at Kulikovo became one of Russian nationalism's "principal cultural symbols" in the late Soviet period, and the occasion of its six-hundred-year anniversary represented a major defining moment for them.[101] Among other things, it focused fresh attention on Gumilev's objectionable interpretations of Russia's experience with the Golden Horde. By this point, it should be noted, Gumilev had still not published a great deal on this particular topic. In addition to the original 1970 work that was the object of Rybakov's critique (of which only a small part dealt with the Mongols and Russia), he managed to publish all of two brief essays on the subject during the Kulikovo celebrations themselves.[102] This, however, was quite enough to excite what Brudny describes as "the most heated debate" of the entire period, as leading figures from the nationalist movement weighed in with extensive condemnations of his views.[103]

Among Gumilev's critics, the most significant were Vladimir Chivilikhin, an environmental activist and popular historian, and the academic historian Apollon Grigor'evich Kuz'min (1928–2004), an extreme anti-Semite and important contributor to nationalist publications.[104] Chivilikhin and Kuz'min were outraged by Gumilev's arguments, and both wrote spirited denunciations of his work.[105] Like Rybakov, the two historians objected most fundamentally to Gumilev's characterization of relations between the Russians and the Golden Horde as comradely and benign. To the contrary, they maintained, the tribulations of the Mongol conquest had been comparable to the fascist onslaught against Russia in

---

101. Brudny 1998, 117, 136, 181–91.

102. Gumilev 1980a; Gumilev 1980b. These two articles together totalled no more than four pages.

103. Brudny 1998, 186–87.

104. Kochanek 1999, 85, 251–54, 257, 255–58; Laqueur 1993, 114, 246; Brudny 1998, 55–56, 70, 105, 122, 131, 173, 184–85; Weiner 1999b, 334–37. This was the same Kuz'min who at the end of the 1980s denounced Gumilev's colleague, the geneticist Nikolai Timofeev-Resovskii. See above, 50n.

105. Lavrov 2000, 314–17, 364.

World War II, and the ensuing domination by the Golden Horde was a "harsh regime of plunder and genocide (*genotsid*)." How would the Soviet soldiers who fought and suffered at Stalingrad feel, they wondered, if they knew that, six hundred years from now, historians would write off *their* horrific experience in Gumilevian terms as "a couple of successful raids" by German fascists?[106]

They also questioned Gumilev's naturalist perspective on the nature of ethnicity. His theories were based on a flawed "vulgar-materialist" geographical determinism, and they denied outright that the phenomenon of *passionarnost'* even existed. Gumilev's ethnos theory, declared Chivilikhin, reduces to the proposition that all neighboring superethnies "should immediately go to war with each other."[107] "Human communities are not hordes of lemmings," they insisted, and maintained that ancient Russian history was to be explained not in reference to "climatic cycles or the *passionarnost'* of the region" but rather in the more reliable and familiar terms of "deep economic, social, and other objective historical processes."[108] They also rejected Gumilev's assertion of a primal ethnogenetic symbiosis between Slavs and Turks, and were particularly scandalized by Gumilev's "Russophobic" assertion that the "redemptive (*spasitel'nyi*) Tatar invasion" served to "breathe new life into Rus'" by infusing it with new sources of *passionarnost'*.[109] The murder of Russian princes, the enslavement of the people, and the wholesale destruction of their cultural heritage, they wrote scornfully—"that's what the symbiosis of Rus' and the Golden Horde actually amounted to!"[110]

Following Borisov, Kuz'min and Chivilikhin attacked the tradition of classical Eurasianism that inspired Gumilev's analysis. They identified the classical Eurasianists as renegade White Guards (perhaps partly for the sake of readers who might never have heard of them), and maintained that they, like Gumilev, exaggerated the role of geography and natural law in their historical explanations. Like Gumilev, moreover, the classical Eurasianists sought to justify the Tatar yoke by describing these Asiatic "oppressors and hangmen" of Russians as virtuous historical actors. By drawing on national historiographies hostile to Russia—for example, the work of the Ukrainian nationalist historian Mykhailo Serhiiovych Hrushevs'kyi (1866–1964)—the Eurasianist version of ancient Russian history betrayed ethnic Russia's genuine national interests. Simply put, like Gumilev himself the Eurasianists had expounded the "most vile form of Russophobia," which was "much more dangerous than the notorious Norman theory" about

---

106. Chivilikhin 1980, 102–25, 118–19, 111, 102, 107–8.
107. Ibid., 106.
108. Ibid., 103–4, 106 (quotes); Kuz'min 1982, 257.
109. Kuz'min 1982, 258–62; Kuz'min 1991, 262.
110. Chivilikhin 1980, 113–14, 118–19.

the origins of Russia.[111] Indeed, in their view Gumilev took this pernicious Russo-phobia one step further. Not content with spinning tendentious and flawed theo-ries about Russia's ancient past, they accused him of being a *Izhepatriot* or "false patriot" in the present day, actively siding with the very non-Russian nation-alities who struggle against ethnic Russians in the USSR. In the best traditions of Soviet conspiriology, Kuz'min darkly intimated that Gumilev developed his "anti-Russian tendency" through personal collusions not only with Tatar nation-alist historians but also—remarkably, in view of Gumilev's intense and well-publicized anti-Semitism—with "Zionist agents." There was no question that the Tatars were currently making full use of his incessant "juxtaposition of benevo-lent Mongols to Russian savages" in order to substantiate their own rejection of the "myth" of a Mongol yoke for their own nefarious ethno-national purposes.[112]

Kuz'min in particular nursed an antipathy toward Gumilev that was obsessive, and even delusional.[113] Not content with debunking his historical mythologies, he was determined to expose Gumilev personally for what he really believed him to be: a closet Judeophile. Gumilev's theory of ethnicity, he maintained, was very sim-ilar to that of Theodor Herzl, the founder of Zionism. Both Gumilev's and Herzl's theories made it possible for any group of people, no matter how cynically or indeed "mafia-like," to opportunistically claim the status of a legitimate ethnicity and on that basis demand protection against ethnic "discrimination" from other,

---

111. Chivilikhin 1980, 125; Kuz'min 1982, 256; Kuz'min 1991, 257–58; Kuz'min 1993b. It may be noted that Gumilev's was not the only Eurasianist exposition to attract nationalist ire. In 1975, the Kazakh poet Olzhas Omarovich Suleimenov published his own lengthy analysis of the epic poem *Song of Igor's Campaign*, in which he identified what he claimed to be a profusion of lexical and narrative elements that were of Turkic origin. This was evidence, he suggested, of the creative interaction and exchange between the cultures of the steppe peoples and the Russians (Suleimenov 1975). Suleimenov's book was denounced by the Russian nationalists—among them Apollon Kuz'min—and caused a mas-sive political uproar that went all the way to the Central Committee of the CPSU. Eventually, the book was banned and all copies were ordered destroyed. Kuz'min 1975; Brudny 1998, 172–75; Ram 2001; Frizman 2002. Gumilev himself was unsympathetic to Suleimenov's quasi-Eurasianist arguments and reviewed the book very critically (although Suleimenov later claimed that Gumilev really only resented the fact that his own work on the ancient Turks had not been mentioned). The two were acquainted personally, and Gumilev believed that he had known Suleimenov's father in a prison camp in Perm in the early 1950s. Gumilev's review remained unpublished in the Soviet period, but is now available online: Gumilev 1976?; Koreniako 2000, 43; "Olzhas Suleimenov" 2013.

112. Kuz'min 1991, 256, 263; Kuz'min 1993b, 276; Liubkin 2006. On accusations by Russian "patri-ots" that Gumilev sided with Tatars and Kazakhs against ethnic Russia, see Zholdasbekov and Kairzh-anov 2002, 8. An intelligence report prepared for the Central Committee of the CPSU in 1987 claimed that Gumilev's works were being used in Kazakhstan to encourage ethno-national and separatist sympathies. See below, 275–86.

113. Rossman 2002b, 92–93; Semanov n.d.; Shishkin 1995a; Liubkin 2006. According to a former student of Kuz'min, Gumilev was initially interested in getting to know the nationalist Kuz'min bet-ter, but Kuz'min proved to be even more dogmatic and intolerant than he, and rebuffed his overtures. Samovarov 2013.

larger groups. It was for this reason that the concept of *passionarnost'*—a critical ethnic marker—had become so popular, and there was no coincidence that it was particularly useful for the Jews. Gumilev's point that the Jews have demonstrated an inextinguishable *passionarnost'* for over two thousand years was "very flattering for the belief of the Zionist-Nazis (*siono-natsisty*) that they are the 'chosen people.'"[114] The vehemence of the anti-Semitic tone throughout all of Gumilev's work did not belie this appraisal, for Kuz'min claimed that there was not a bit of sincerity in the former's denunciations of the Jews. To the contrary, Kuz'min referred to the statements of Gumilev's old colleague Lev Klein that he was "in no way an anti-Semite," and he confirmed this assertion from his own personal contacts with Gumilev. "So what was it," he wondered, "that turned Gumilev from Judeophilia to Judeophobia?"[115] The sensational answer was that Lev Gumilev, son of Anna Akhmatova, "née Arens,"[116] was himself partly Jewish. This, for Kuz'min, explained everything.

> Where does [Gumilev's] unexpected and entirely uncharacteristic anti-Semitism come from? People of mixed background often experience sharp swings from "pro" to "contra." The extremes to which this can lead . . . were apparent in "Hitler's politbureau," where everyone was either of mixed background, a convert to Christianity, or married to a Jew. . . . In Gumilev's case, his anti-Semitism is obviously calculated [and false]. Its purpose is to act as bait (*nazhivka*) in order to hook *potential critics* from the anti-Zionist camp. So here anti-Semitism serves the purpose of Zionism, as the Zionist leaders have often noted.[117]

It was not only Gumilev's opponents who drew such a ludicrous conclusion. Sergei Semanov, who had a high regard for Gumilev, noted that when the latter complained to him about Kuz'min's unjust attacks, he responded in a similar spirit: "your boulevard (*bytovoi*) anti-Semitism fully suits the purposes of Zionism in destroying Russian history."[118]

---

114. Kuz'min 1993a, 251.

115. Ibid., 235–36.

116. Anna Evgen'evna Arens was Nikolai Punin's first wife, and in the early 1930s Gumilev lived for some time with her brother Lev. Kuz'min does not elaborate on his astonishing implication that the name somehow belonged to Akhmatova.

117. Kuz'min 1993a, 251–52, emphasis in original. Kuz'min was not the only one to maintain that Gumilev was partly Jewish; such claims were repeated even by his friends and admirers; see, for example, Burovskii 2004.

118. Semanov 2012. Gumilev wrote rebuttals to the criticism of Kuz'min and Chivilikhin, but was unable to find a journal willing to publish them. Gumilev 1976?; Gumilev 2003e; Lavrov 2000, 314–15. He returned to the subject frequently in interviews in the late 1980s: Suvorov 1988; Gumilev 1993b, 28; Gumilev 1989a; Gumilev 1991b.

Nationalist Eurasianism contra Gumilev

Although Chivilikhin's and Koz'min's critiques of Gumilev's historical scenario expressed the predominant view of Russian nationalism, the latter's peculiar interpretation of ancient Russia's relations with its steppe neighbors did have its adherents within the nationalist camp. One of these was Balashov, whose attempts to relate Gumilev's work to contemporary concerns about environmental protection we have considered. Balashov's real expertise was as a folklorist and prolific writer of historical fiction. He was a favorite in nationalist circles and a sought-after speaker at the Russian clubs.[119] From the 1970s to the early 1990s, he published a half-dozen novels that told the story of the formation of the Russian state and nation in the thirteenth and fourteenth centuries. Balashov's work was extremely popular—Brudny estimates that nearly eight hundred thousand copies of his novels were sold[120]—and their historical veracity was endorsed by Dmitrii Likhachev himself, who wrote an introduction to one of them.[121] It was from Gumilev, however, that Balashov took his vision of Russian history. He was a close associate and personal friend, and in his own words unquestioningly accepted the authority of his mentor's historical interpretation.[122] Thus, in Balashov's 1977 novel *Mladshii Syn* the Gumilevian scenario is readily recognizable: the passionary decline of pre-Mongol Kievan Rus', the natural empathy and complementarity between the Slavs and the steppe nomads, and the option for an alliance with the latter against the Catholics of the West, who were "yet more terrifying than the Mongol horde." As Gumilev taught, the Russian nation was born in the crucible of Kulikovo, an "eruption of spiritual energy of the people" that gave rise to the Muscovite state and shaped the rest of Russian history.[123] In an afterword, Balashov acknowledged Gumilev's extensive editorial input.[124]

The reaction to Gumilev's historical interpretation on the part of Vadim Kozhinov was rather more nuanced. Kozhinov's role in the reemergence of Eurasianism in the 1980s is of great importance, for it was really he—and not Gumilev—who first recognized and explored the potential of Eurasianism as an ideological framework specifically for Russian nationalism. His first discussions

---

119. "Prior to Balashov, we did not understand Holy Rus' so perfectly. He made a colossal contribution and was a rare zealot (*podvizhnik*) of the Russian Idea." Baigushev 2006b, 252–53; also see Semanov 1997, 181–82; Brudny 1998, 70–71.

120. Brudny 1998, 106, 313n; Beliakov 2012a, 547.

121. Balashov 2006 [1984].

122. Krasnov 1991, 158–62.

123. Balashov 1986, 14, 22–33, 37–38, 40, 449.

124. Balashov 1986, 591. For Gumilev's appreciation of Balashov, see his essay "The Burden of Talent." Gumilev 1991a.

of Eurasianist themes date from the early 1980s, the same time that Gumilev was publishing his own historical reinterpretation of the significance of Kulikovo.[125] Like Gumilev, Kozhinov was driven by an intense antipathy to the West, and he viewed Russian history as a dramatic struggle in defense of its national interests against Western influences. He as well drew on the work of classical Eurasianism in developing this perspective, notably the critique of Western cosmopolitanism presented by Nikolai Trubetskoi in *Europe and Humankind*.[126] Kozhinov's explanation of the existential significance of this struggle for the genesis of the Russian nation, however, came directly from Gumilev. On a basic level, he accepted Gumilev's argument for the close interaction between ancient Rus' and the nomadic peoples of the steppe. It was the latter—and "not the Normans, or the Varangians, or even Byzantium"—who exercised the "most powerful influence" on the young Russian nation from the ninth to the eleventh centuries.[127] Referring directly to Gumilev's work, he argued that this fateful association found its grand culmination three centuries later on the Kulikovo field. Far from representing a conflict between Russians and their supposed Asiatic Mongol-Tatar adversaries, Kulikovo actually witnessed an alliance of these two groups, united by their shared opposition to a common enemy from the west. "The struggle at Kulikovo, which [today] is understood by everyone exclusively as the repulsion of a specifically 'Asiatic' attack by Russians forces, was actually a struggle of the Russian people against the aggression of global cosmopolitanism."[128] The negative view of the Golden Horde as the oppressor of ancient Rus' emerged only in the eighteenth and nineteenth centuries, Kozhinov explained, inspired by "Western ideology."[129]

Yet although Kozhinov praised Gumilev for his clarification of the true nature of relations between the Russians and Golden Horde, he also criticized him for idealizing this relationship and overemphasizing the mutuality of their interests. Their shared natural opposition to Western aggression did not mean that their own relationship was entirely harmonious. In a substantial nod to the mainstream interpretation of these events, Kozhinov acknowledged that the Mongols could indeed be cruel conquerors and that their domination involved some measure of Russian suffering.[130] Kozhinov did not moreover accept Gumilev's

---

125. Kozhinov 1981. For discussions of this important essay, see Brudny 1998, 119–20, 189–90; Agursky 1986, 103–5; Kochanek 1999, 259–64. On Kozhinov's Eurasianism in general, see Beliakov 2012a, 647; Brazhnikov 2010; Malakhov 2006.

126. Kozhinov 2005, 285, 465; Kozhinov 1981, 162–63; Kozhinov 2000, 226–29; Samokhin 2004.

127. "Evraziistvo i sovremennost'" 1993.

128. Kozhinov 1981, 173–74 (quote); Kozhinov 2005, 294, 457, 459; Brudny 1998, 189.

129. Kozhinov 2005, 462.

130. Kozhinov 1981, 174, 172; Kozhinov 1991.

ascription of an ethnogenetic significance to Russia's early interaction with the nomadic steppe forces and their shared struggle against the West. Whatever sort of anti-Western alliance may have been realized at Kulikovo, it did not initiate a process of ethnic formation and did not result in an ethnic union between any of the different national groups involved. He rejected the suggestion of a symbiosis as "unacceptable" (*nepriemlemyi*). Rather than recognizing Kulikovo as a rupture with ancient Russian history and a new ethnogenetic Eurasian beginning, Kozhinov supported the more common nationalist view described above and insisted on the primeval (*iznachal'nyi*) continuity of the Russian ethnos extending back at least to the Nestorian Chronicles of Kievan Rus'.[131] This meant that Russia's special ethnic qualities were well formed by the fourteenth century when, according to Gumilev, Russian ethnogenesis was first initiated. To the extent that the "symbiosis" of Russians and nomads described by Gumilev had actually taken place, it involved nothing more than the assimilation by the latter of ethnic qualities that the Russians had long possessed.[132]

Thus although Kozhinov was prepared to embrace the notion of Russia's "Eurasian destiny," he did not see this as some sort of Gumilevian Slavo-Turkic symbiosis. He saw it rather exclusively in terms of Russia's own unique ethno-national qualities, above all Russia's *vsechelovechnost'*—the universalism or pan-humanism that enabled it to experience "genuine fraternity with any nation." Since the time of Petr Iakovlevich Chaadaev (1794–1856), he maintained, Russian thinkers had pointed to this quality as a defining feature of Russian culture on the world scene, which served at once to set it apart from all other cultures and provide it with an enduring world-historical mission, namely, the spiritual union of all humanity, in particular the reconciliation of East and West. Kozhinov scolded Gumilev for failing to appreciate the fundamental fact that Russia's national destiny was determined by the inherent "universalism of the [ethnic] Russian consciousness" rather than any constellation of mutual interethnic sympathies and affinities.[133] (Gumilev himself, as we have seen, flatly rejected the legacy of Chaadaev and *vsechelovechnost'* as a product of Russia's ethnogenetic degeneration in the nineteenth century.) Russia's national culture represented "a sort of spiritual bridge between Europe and Asia" that was endowed with the immense power of its "universalist elementalism."[134] But instead of the grand nineteenth-century projects of Chaadaev, Feodor Dostoevsky (1821–1881), and Vladimir Solov'ev—all of whom located Russia at the center of a panhuman

---

131. Kozhinov 1981, 158.
132. Kozhinov 2000, 224.
133. Kozhinov 1981, 174.
134. Ibid., 175.

reconciliation of genuinely universal dimensions—Kozhinov saw the ultimate consummation of Russia's *vsechelovechnost'* in the much more limited historical and geographical legacy of its engagement with the other nations occupying the spaces of Eurasia. This engagement began with the ancient interactions described by Gumilev and continued throughout Russia's subsequent empire-building to culminate in the Soviet Union of his day. The formation of Russia-Eurasia in its modern form was not the result of a spontaneous cosmically driven intermingling of the various national groups occupying these vast spaces, but rather testified to the dominating organizational capabilities and initiative of ethnic Russia alone.

With this analysis, Kozhinov effectively co-opted the most important aspect of the nationalist opposition to Gumilev into his own Eurasianist vision. The latter was permeated with an insistent ethno-national exclusivity, which spoke not about the shared attributes and commonality of the peoples involved but rather about their essential differences. The "Eurasian duality" (*dvoistvennost'*) that allowed the Russians to engage and interact with East and West was "precisely an ethnic Russian (*russkoe*) quality" that was simply foreign to all of Russia-Eurasia's other constituent nationalities.[135] Genuine "Eurasians" were not, as Gumilev and the classical Eurasians had taught, "ethnic Russians plus Turks, Finno-Ugric peoples, and so on." Very much to the contrary, it was really only ethnic Russia itself that could properly be called Eurasian. "It is *precisely and only* the ethnic Russian peoples (*russkii narod*) who are a Eurasian peoples." All of the other groups that make up the Russian state "are in their essence either European or Asiatic nations." They acquired whatever Eurasian features they may have "only in the 'magnetic field' (*magnitnoe pole*) of Russia," and once they left this field they quickly reverted back to their essential European or Asiatic type.[136] Indeed, Kozhinov maintained that in the final analysis ethnic Russia's Eurasian essence would not be affected even if its links with these groups were dissolved. "And for me personally, Eurasianism has nothing to do with the fact that Russia (*Rossiia*) unites in itself Slavs on the one hand together with Turks, Mongols, and Islamic peoples on the other. In the final analysis, this is not so important. If a part of Russia were to be broken off in order to create a national ethnic-Russian state (*russkoe gosudarstvo*) . . . then this state would in no way cease to be Eurasian."[137] The equality and fraternity among the Eurasian peoples is manifested above all in the universality of the Russian language. "All the nations of Russia are equal (*ravnopravnyi*) in their possession of Russian poetry, and of course

135. "Evraziistvo i sovremennost'" 1993.
136. Kozhinov 2000, 233 (emphasis added); Malashenko 1996, 101.
137. "Evraziistvo i sovremennost'" 1993.

Russian culture in general. . . . They all shared equally in the creation of Russian state life (*russkaia gosudarstvennost'*)."[138] It was only in these terms that Kozhinov understood the significance of *vsechelovechnost'*.

If Balashov's best-selling historical novels, inspired as they were by Gumilev's teachings, failed to excite much nationalist ire, the same cannot be said of Kozhinov's 1981 essay. Semanov recounts how the latter's Eurasianist ruminations stirred a storm of controversy among conservative nationalists and were denounced by Kuz'min and Chivilikhin in terms similar to those they had used against Gumilev.[139] Indeed, Kozhinov's essay was criticized in the mainstream press as well, including a dedicated article in *Pravda*.[140] But his argumentation, and in particular his differences with Gumilev, were significant; indeed, if looked at in hindsight, they were quite extraordinarily so. With his emphasis on the singular, dominating role of ethnic Russia in the development of Eurasian civilization, Kozhinov articulated a vital principle that Gumilev himself never mentioned and almost certainly never even recognized. A short decade later, however, this principle would prove to be vital in enabling Russian nationalism finally to come to terms with and embrace Eurasianism. As we will see, however, in the process Kozhinov's own formulation would be forgotten and everything would be ascribed to Lev Gumilev.

---

138. Kozhinov 1981, 158.
139. Semanov 2012.
140. Kuleshov 1982; Shubkin 1981; Suvortsev 1982.

Part 3

GUMILEV AFTER COMMUNISM

NEO-EURASIANISM AND THE RUSSIAN QUESTION

Gumilev and the Empire Savers

In the early 1980s, Gumilev's Eurasianist retelling of ancient Russian history was received for the most part with hostility and scorn. Within less than ten years, however, this critical stance was to undergo a striking transformation—not, to be sure, on the part of stalwarts such as Kuz'min or Chivilikhin, but from many others who carried forward the statist Russian nationalism of the early 1980s. The catalyst for this transformation was the change in Soviet politics and society associated with the perestroika of Mikhail Gorbachev. In a major policy revision, Gorbachev initiated a comprehensive program of national reform and concili-ation with the West that had no precedent in the country's history, either in its Soviet or imperial periods. Gorbachev's new "common European home" project envisioned not merely rapprochement with, but also a far-reaching integration into the West based on the assimilation of Western institutional structures and democratic norms. Such a policy was scandalous for the Russian nationalists, for whom the principle of difference from and opposition to the West remained an unquestionable article of faith. A further aspect of perestroika that facilitated the increasingly positive reception of Eurasianism was the accentuation of intereth-nic tensions and hostilities across the country. The new freedoms of expression offered by Gorbachev's *glasnost'* were intended to encourage the population to express their genuine views and aspirations. In the event, this policy had the spec-tacular if unanticipated result of facilitating the emergence of powerful national independence movements right across the country, movements that ultimately were to call into question the very legitimacy of the Soviet state. Secessionist tendencies were exacerbated by the discreditation of the traditional narratives of solidarity and fraternity among the Soviet nationalities that had legitimated the geopolitical cohesion of the state. As perestroika wore on, it seemed ever more possible that the mighty Soviet Union would fall victim to the increasingly irresistible strivings of its member nations for ethno-national autonomy and simply break apart.[1]

In response to these challenges, a loose formation of conservative-nationalist tendencies had begun to coalesce by the end of the 1980s. They were united in their determination to resist the secessionist challenge, defend the integrity and political-territorial unity of the Russian-Soviet state, and insure that Russia's national individuality and its distinction from the West would continue to be recognized and respected. This was no mere clustering of disaffected individuals, but a determined political movement that enjoyed significant support among the Soviet elite within the military, KGB, and party bureaucracies. Western observers writing at the time began to refer to this group as "empire savers," who indeed now began to use the term *imperiia* themselves in reference to the Soviet state.[2] Throughout the latter years of perestroika, these empire savers were increasingly open in their opposition to government policy. Their resistance would culminate in the desperate gambit of an attempted coup d'état in August 1991, the failure of which only accelerated the final collapse of the state entity that they struggled to maintain.[3]

Ideologically, the empire savers sought a new vision of Russia that could integrate two principal concerns: on the one hand the imperative to preserve the overall geopolitical integrity of the existing state, and on the other the determination—carried over from the priorities examined in the previous chapter—that the Russian nationality should reestablish its special role within the state as its leading or organizing element. Strictly speaking, such a vision was already available in the familiar policy of *druzhba narodov*. At this late date, however, it was no longer possible to redeploy the Stalinist doctrine as such, for any new ideological orientation now had to be formulated in terms of categories and values that at least appeared to be non-Marxist and non-Soviet. Beyond this, the heightened ethnic sensitivities on the part of all nationalities meant that any new collectivist vision would have to affirm the principle of ethno-national integrity more robustly and genuinely than such standard Soviet mantras as "national in form,

1. Dunlop 1993, 131.
2. Szporluk 1989, 17–20.
3. Dunlop 1993, 122; Dunlop 1997, 33–39; Verkhovskii 2007.

socialist in content." Against this background, the precepts of Eurasianism began to attract serious attention from the empire savers as an alternative ideological "glue" that might be able to hold the country together.[4] And indeed, in many respects, these precepts as elaborated by Gumilev spoke directly to their primary interests: the profound legitimacy of the traditional Russian state, its rightful domination of the continental spaces of Eurasia, and the unique greatness of Russian-Eurasian civilization. The natural polyethnic harmony described by Gumilev's Eurasianism was conditioned not by some contrived Marxist scheme of proletarian internationalism but by elemental ethnic and civilizational dynamics that were genuine and rooted deep in the primeval past. Similarly, the endemic hostility to the West was explained not in terms of socio-economic organization (capitalism versus communism) but through essentialized and unalterable dispositions that were anchored in ethnic character.[5] With certain adjustments, the concept of a Russian-Eurasian "superethnos" could provide a satisfactory terminological replacement for the USSR, not least because in a practical sense it was very similar, if not entirely identical. Gumilev's Eurasianist teachings had the further critical advantage of taking seriously and giving full attention to the complex problematic of ethnic individuality, and indeed precisely in a manner that did not challenge the more fundamental geopolitical imperative for multi-ethnic unity. Finally, all of this came appealingly gift-wrapped by Gumilev in a packaging of "objective" natural-scientific laws.

In principle, Gumilev's idiosyncratic Eurasianism should have been problematic for the empire savers for the same reason that the Russian nationalists had attacked him ten years earlier—namely, that he consistently failed to prioritize ethnic Russia as the leading nation among the Eurasian peoples. In his responses to the original criticism on this issue, he remained stubbornly faithful to his convictions and reaffirmed his commitment to the friendship of the peoples understood as a fraternal collection of nations that were genuinely equal and among whom there could be no "first." This was a fundamental principle for Gumilev, and down to his death he left no doubt whatsoever that he continued to support it. Recalling at the end of the decade his earlier struggles with nationalist historians—latter-day "Slavophiles," as he derisively called them—he restated his contempt for their Russoethnic exclusivity and ethnocentrism.

> The original Slavophiles were very highly educated people—[Aleksandr Semenovich] Shishkov, [Aleksei Stepanovich] Khomiakov, [Ivan Sergeevich] Aksakov. But our "Slavophiles" of today mistake crudeness for

---

4. Dunlop 1993, 292; Yasmann 1992, 23.
5. Hosking 2006, 371.

patriotism and grovelling for love of their homeland. For some reason, they believe it absolutely necessary to criticize other peoples and see them as a source of trouble and danger. [They do not] look at themselves and try to uproot and get rid of slavery in their own people. . . . I fear that today's "Slavophiles" are using a historical term to mask an ignorant, selfish, and unprincipled position.[6]

Elsewhere Gumilev condemned the legacy of ethnic discrimination in the USSR, noting with dismay that these attitudes "are still very apparent today."[7] On this question, for him clearly nothing had changed. But much had changed around him. By late perestroika, the appeal of Eurasianism and the determination to enlist Gumilev—who in the meantime had gained celebrity as a great national scholar and patriot—as its leading prophet was such that his manifest refusal to embrace Russian nationalism's ethnocentric bias was simply overlooked. Gumilev himself never spoke about ethnic Russians as the "organizers" of the Eurasian polity, and his detractors in the early 1980s understood this very clearly and correctly. It did not, however, prevent crowds of newfound acolytes at the end of perestroika from attributing such a perspective back to him.

It is difficult to overestimate Gumilev's importance for the late- and post-Soviet revival of Eurasianism. The Gorbachev regime had initiated the rehabilitation of generations of cultural and scholarly figures who had been repressed across the decades by the Soviet authorities. Out of this process, Gumilev emerged as a veritable living legend: a flesh-and-bones intermediary whose very existence directly connected the perestroika public both to the glorious heights of Silver Age culture as well as the darkest chapters of the Soviet passage through the twentieth century.[8] The fact that his parents were two of Russia's most brilliant and hard-suffering poetic talents would by itself have been enough to insure his celebrity, but in the case of Lev Nikolaevich it was just the beginning. As the circumstances of his own life became widely known, he gained general recognition in his own right as a unique witness to the arbitrary brutality of Stalinism and of the Soviet system more generally. In a very real sense, his had been a double victimhood: first through thirteen years of undeserved banishment in the Gulag, and second through a long career of academic marginalization, censorship, and lack of recognition. Throughout it all, he was seen to have acted with dignity, personal integrity, and professional honesty, and indeed at the end of his life he

---

6. Cited in Suvorov 1988. Gumilev also spoke about his detractors from the Russian nationalist camp as "black colonels"—a reference to the brutal Greek junta of the 1960s and 1970s. Lavrov 2000, 314–15; Mamaladze 1992, 7.
7. Gumilev 1989a.
8. Mamaladze 1992, 7.

could claim with justice that he never compromised with the system that had so mistreated him. But Gumilev's appeal did not rest solely on his parentage or the circumstances of his difficult life. Beyond this, and perhaps more important, was the immense scientific and scholarly authority that his work came to enjoy as it became increasingly known. An expert with an apparently encyclopedic knowledge of Eurasian and world history, a Soviet scholar with two doctoral degrees whose work was widely recognized internationally, a personal acquaintance of the émigré Eurasianists who fearlessly sought to advance their theories and had suffered the displeasure of the Soviet system for doing so—all this endowed Gumilev with a charisma and cachet of authority that was and still remains quite unique. It meant that his writings could play a vital legitimating function as a "respectable historical school," providing a rich patina of scientific credibility that the empire savers, among others, were most eager to claim.[9]

Gumilev himself was powerfully affected by the course of events during perestroika. In the beginning, he noted, he had "believed in perestroika" and shared the enthusiasm of many of his compatriots with the accession of someone as unconventional and apparently fresh-minded as Mikhail Gorbachev.[10] He even fancied that with Gorbachev, the ethnogenetic phase of *nadlom* that had been tearing the country apart since the early years of the century had finally come to an end, setting the stage for a transition to the more peaceful and productive phase of inertia. This confidence led him to dismiss the initial turbulences of perestroika as nothing more than a trifling ethnogenetic "growing pain."[11] Such benign optimism did not last very long, however, and he eventually joined the empire savers in their bitter denunciation of the entire Gorbachevian project. He could have no sympathy for the notion of a "common European home" that valorized democracy and other universal human values that Russia supposedly shared with the nations of the West. Reasserting a position staked out over decades, he insisted that by their very nature superethnies were mutually incompatible and could not be merged. So-called universal human values were nothing more than the dominant ethnic features (*dominanta*) of a foreign and hostile superethnos. "It would be a great error," he wrote,

> to think that the result of the construction of a "common European home" will be the mutual victory of common human values. The entry into a foreign superethnos always involves a rejection of one's own

---

9. Raskin 1996, 157.

10. Gumilev 1988b, 48 (quote); Gumilev 1988c, 3; Gumilev 1989a; Beliakov 2012a, 672; Laruelle 2000, 181.

11. Cited in Ianov 1995b, 206.

ethnic *dominanty* in exchange for the system of the new superethnos. It is highly unlike that this will be any different in our case. The price of joining civilization [i.e., the West] will be the domination of West European behavioral norms and psychology. And will it really be easier because this superethnic system of values is unjustifiably said to be "universal" (*obshchechelovecheskoi*)?

With the very same degree of justification, he insisted that "Orthodox Christian, Islamic, or Confucian perspectives and values could all be considered to be universal."[12] The cost of Russia's integration into a common European home would be the "total rejection of our national traditions" and the ascendance in Russia of the values and norms of Western Europe.[13] In the same way that in earlier times Gumilev had refused to identify with Soviet dissidents, so during perestroika he had no sympathy for those liberal forces who supported the democratization of Soviet society. Asked—perhaps playfully—by an interviewer in 1991 if he supported democracy ("*a Vy demokrat, Lev Nikolaevich?*"), he made no attempt to conceal his irritation: "No, by no means! . . . What sort of democrat am I supposed to be? I am an old soldier, my father was a soldier, and my grandfather as well."[14]

It was, however, the prospect of the territorial disintegration of the Soviet state that galvanized his indignation above all else. He was shocked and outraged by the "parade of sovereignties" and waves of separatist nationalism that were sweeping across the Soviet Union in the Baltic states, Central Asia, and the Caucasus.[15] "I support a united Russia," Gumilev declared, "in which there is one government, in one capital city—Moscow."[16] Indeed, if Aleksandr Prokhanov is to be believed, Gumilev was prepared even to support a post-Gorbachev Communist regime, if this could help avoid the impending territorial breakup of the country.[17] Like many Leningraders, Gumilev was particularly scandalized when the Baltic states of Estonia, Latvia, and Lithuania made their formal declarations of independence from the Soviet Union in 1990.[18] These sentiments led him,

---

12. Gumilev and Ermolaev 1993, 174.

13. Quoted in Luk"ianov 2003, 68–69; "Etnologicheskaia karta" 1988.

14. Gumilev 1991c; Beliakov 2012a, 683. In good Gumilevian fashion, he primordialized the traitorous dynamics of democracy, claiming that they were active already in ancient Russia as well. See above, 98n.

15. Gumilev and Ermolaev 1993, 186; Luk'ianov 2003, 67–68, 70; Lavrov 2001.

16. Gumilev 1991f, cited in Lavrov 2000, 350.

17. Author's interview with A. A. Prokhanov, Moscow, September 2007; also see Laruelle 2000, 182.

18. Iamshchikov 2006.

in the year before his death, to a liaison with the journalist Aleksandr Glebov-
ich Nevzorov, who presented the popular current-events television program *600
Sekund*. Nevzorov was a highly visible and committed empire saver, very much
out of favor with the perestroika leadership.[19] In 1991 he produced the film *Nashi*
(Ours), which heroicized the doomed attempts of Soviet special forces in Vilnius
to prevent the occupation of a television transmitting tower by supporters of
Lithuanian independence. The film detailed the failure of the authorities in the
Kremlin to support these troops, and implied that it represented a shameful surrender of the territorial integrity of the USSR. Gumilev regarded Nevzorov as a
genuinely passionary person and was moved by his engagement and efforts. He
welcomed him into his home, gave him lessons on Russian history, and eventually agreed to be interviewed on his television program.[20] At this time, Gumilev
was under consideration as a candidate for the title of "Corresponding Member"
(*Chlen-Korrespondent*) of the Russian Academy of Sciences, one of the most prestigious scholarly honors available in the Soviet system. Gumilev's friends, appre-
ciating the damage that a public display of solidarity with such a well-known
reactionary could do to his candidacy, pleaded with him not to appear on the
program, but he was not to be dissuaded.[21] He made his appearance, declared
his disdain for the Europhilism of perestroika, and confirmed his support for
Nevzorov and the struggle of the Soviet army in the Baltic states.[22]

The political polarization during perestroika led Gumilev to make one highly
significant theoretical modification in his concept of "superethnos." As we have
seen, he had always maintained that that the population of the Soviet Union
was divided among seven discrete superethnics. Confronted with the dramatic
growth of interethnic hostility and the increasing fragmentation of the country
along ethno-national lines, however, he began to reconceptualize the term. From
the late 1980s, he increasingly referred to the USSR in its entirety as a single
superethnos or a "collective superethnic concept" (*sobiratel'noe superetniches-
koe poniatie*).[23] "Our superethnos . . . was formerly called the Russian empire,

---

19. Dunlop 1993, 177–81, 183; Tishkov 1996, 32.

20. Nevzorov 2013; El'zon 2003, 207; Clark 1995, 31–32.

21. Ermolaev 2012, 214–15. In the event, Gumilev was not awarded the distinction. His student Ermolaev speculates that the eventual rejection of Gumilev's candidacy was related to his interview on Nevzorov's program. For a somewhat different version of Gumilev's rejection, however, see
Burovskii 2012.

22. Gumilev 1991c; Taylor 1993, 734; Beliakov 2012a, 682–85; Clark 1995, 31–32. When Gumilev
died in June 1992, Nevzorov was personally involved in the arrangements for his funeral, and his
youth group *Nashi*—which had links to the nationalist organization *Pamiat'*—oversaw security at
the ceremony. Beliakov 2012a, 696.

23. Gumilev 1994c, 297 (quote); Gumilev 1988b, 47.

and then the Soviet Union."[24] This shift was, however, obviously awkward for him, and his usage remained inconsistent. At one point, for example, he directly equated a single "Russian (*rossiiskii*) superethnos" with the entirety of the Soviet people (*sovetskii narod*), while noting in the same passage that the latter also contains "many different superethnies in the Far East."[25] In one essay, he referred specifically to the "two basic superethnies of our country: the *Rossiiskii* and the steppe superethnies."[26] However, in a televised lecture in 1988, he described a very different configuration.

> *Our* superethnos can be called the *Eurasian* superethnos because it includes, besides the Soviet Union, Mongolia and a significant part of Western Europe; the Baltic states, for example. Basically, the Baltic states are the boundary. They are borderlands of both Russia and Western Europe. [*Pointing to a wall map of the USSR.*] Here is our superethnos, look at how big and fine it is. It stretches to the Seas of Okhotsk and Japan. Not all of this territory is part of the Eurasian superethnos in a narrower sense of the term. Countries like Mongolia and Dzungaria are also part of the Eurasian superethnos, although they are not part of the USSR.[27]

Gumilev's new conception finally brought his thinking into line with the classical Eurasianist position, a point he drew himself by equating his "superethnos" concept with Nikolai Trubetskoi's description of Eurasian civilization in toto as a single *mnogonarodnaia lichnost'* (multinational individual). Its peoples were connected by "qualities of inner spiritual interrelatedness, an essential psychological similarity, and an often-demonstrated mutual sympathy or complementarity"[28] In short, Russia-Eurasia was a single, "ethnically unified" entity, a "multinational Eurasian superethnos."[29] Indeed, in order to stress this ethnic unity, Gumilev described it as a product of the *sliianie* process, and he now even maintained that the Eurasian superethnos possessed a political identity as well. "As a state structure as well as a spiritual culture, the Eurasian peoples long ago merged (*slity*) into a 'rainbow' of a single superethnic totality." Gumilev drew the obvious geopolitical conclusion that "any territorial question can be decided only on the basis of Eurasian unity."[30]

---

24. Gumilev and Ermolaev 1993, 183–84.
25. Gumilev 1989f, 159.
26. Gumilev and Ivanov 1992, 56.
27. "Etnologicheskaia karta" 1988, emphasis in original.
28. Gumilev 1995, 34.
29. Gumilev 1992b, 5; Gumilev 1995, 54.
30. Gumilev 1995, 53.

Gumilev may have always professed his disdain for politics and insisted that it had no relation to his scholarly work, but he had a network of significant connections within the Soviet political elite. Along with the ever-greater popularity of his written work, this personal network demonstrated the growing influence of his Eurasianist teachings. Probably the most prominent of these connections was his long-standing friendship with Anatolii Ivanovich Luk"ianov. A lawyer by training, Luk"ianov was appointed in 1972 to the Secretariat of the Presidium of the Supreme Soviet and by 1989 had risen to become head of Supreme Soviet of the USSR—constitutionally the most powerful political position in the country after that of Gorbachev himself.[31] The two had become acquainted in the late 1960s, when Luk"ianov—a great admirer of Akhmatova and himself an amateur poet—provided legal advice that helped Gumilev win a court case regarding the disposition of his mother's archive. They maintained a close personal connection until Gumilev's death.[32] It was only with Luk"ianov's support that Gumilev was finally permitted to publish his major works in the late 1980s.[33] Luk"ianov was a committed empire saver. In 1991, he ordered national television to broadcast Nevzorov's *Nashi* not once but three times, and under Gumilev's influence he embraced the view of Russia as a Eurasian superethnos.[34] He believed that Eurasianism offered a means by which the Soviet Union could maintain its territorial integrity and resist the Westernizing ambitions of perestroika.[35] Luk"ianov supported the coup against Gorbachev in August 1991 and was imprisoned for some time thereafter. Informed about Gumilev's death in June 1992, he wrote a poem to his friend's memory that neatly conveys the Gumilevian coloration of the empire savers' Eurasianism.

> We are both Europe and Asia. . . .
> We are not the enemies of [our national] differences,
> Rather commonality (*obshchnost'*) is our common destiny.
> Our formidable ethnos is Eurasia (*Evroaziia*). . . .
> Nations merged (*slivalis'*) into it like rivers. . . .
> And Western civilization
> Will not be able to get the better of us (*ne po zubam*).[36]

---

31. Kashin 2008.
32. Beliakov 2012a, 632–35.
33. For the documentation of this process, see "'Publikatsiia moikh rabot blokiruiutsia'" 1995; Brudny 1998, 313n; Iamshchikov 2006.
34. Clark 1995, 32, 226–27, 175.
35. Shlapentokh 1997, 148; Shnirelman 2001, 155.
36. Luk"ianov 2003, 70–71 (quote), 67.

If in the mid-1980s party censors still refused to allow publication of his work, and his "Eurasianist theories" and "biological-energetic approach to the past" were denounced on the pages of the official journal *Kommunist*,[37] by the end of the decade these same theories were attracting sympathizers from across the Soviet establishment. There was active interest from the Central Committee, two affiliates of which—the Sinologist Mikhail Leont'evich Titarenko and the journalist Leon Arshakovich Onikov (1924–2000)—knew Gumilev personally and supported him. Support also came from the International Department of the Communist Party, the KGB, the leadership of the Academy of Sciences, and the General Staff of the Armed Forces. Gorbachev's Minister of Defense Dmitrii Timofeevich Iazov in particular was an enthusiastic fan.[38] The deputy director of the Ideological Department of the Central Committee—one Gennadii Andreevich Ziuganov—was particularly drawn to Gumilev's teachings.[39] Indeed, even liberals such as the celebrated physicist and human rights activist Andrei Dmitrievich Sakharov (1921–1989) or the reformist politician Sergei Borisovich Stankevich were beguiled by the potential of Gumilev's Eurasianism as a replacement for Marxism-Leninism.[40] In the Ministry of Foreign Affairs, interest in Eurasianism was yet more pronounced. Gumilev had been invited there in 1986 to talk about his ideas, and although his lecture about the phases of ethnogenesis seems not to have been exactly what the diplomats expected to hear, enthusiasm for his teachings remained undiminished.[41] It was reflected in the ministry's official magazine *Mezhudnarodnaia Zhizn'*, which by the end of the decade had come to resemble what one observer described as a "podium for Eurasianists." Gumilev's particular contribution was appreciated: the senior diplomat Gennady Shevelev, for example, observed that his theories about the cosmic origins of ethnies provided a vital link between classical Eurasianism and the present day.[42]

After the collapse of the Soviet Union, the sentiments of the empire savers carried over into the political opposition to President Boris Yeltsin. The "red-brown" forces of this opposition—so-called because they comprised elements from the extreme Left as well as the Far Right—viewed Yeltsin as the principal perpetrator of the destruction of the Soviet state, and they were united in their hostility to

---

37. The author of this particular attack was the leading historian Iurii Nikolaevich Afanas'ev. Afanas'ev 1985, 110.
38. Voznesenskii 2003, 47; Sevast'ianov 2014; Shenfield 2001, 37; Yasmann 1992, 24.
39. Danks 2001, 68–69.
40. Stankevich 1993; Shatokhin 2010.
41. For Gumilev's account of this experience, see Gumilev 1990c, 7; Lavrov 2000, 347; Beliakov 2012a, 557, 629.
42. Yasmann 1992, 30.

his regime.[43] They rejected its pro-Western foreign policy and slavish idoliza-tion of Western values at home, in comparison to which Gorbachev's tentative Europhilism seemed tepid and halfhearted. They powerfully resented Russia's loss of its global status as a *derzhava* or great power, which was seen as an inevi-table consequence of its geopolitical dissolution. Finally, they could not abide the Yeltsin regime's advocacy of a novel civic *Rossiianin* identity for the citizens of the Russian Federation. They regarded this as nothing less than a return to the *sovetskii narod* project and were convinced that it was similarly intended to eradi-cate genuine ethnic identification altogether. The opposition carried forward the original quest of the empire savers for an "umbrella ideology" that could replace Marxism-Leninism—an ideology that as before needed to address their revan-chist yearning for a unified and mighty multinational Russia in a language and spirit that could resonate with the still-heightened ethno-national sensitivities of the entire population.[44] It needed to do all this, moreover, in a manner flexible enough to appeal both to the remnants of the Communist Party faithful as well as to adepts of post-Soviet Russia's new radical Right, who drew their inspiration more from the legacies of European fascism and German *Geopolitik* than from Marx or Lenin.

Although Eurasianism was not the only ideological orientation available to these revanchist forces, it seemed to offer the best potential as an umbrella ideol-ogy.[45] Indeed, the idiosyncratic mélange of scientistic determinism and volun-taristic emotionalism that characterized Gumilev's writings, pulsing as they did with undertones at once ethno-particularist and communitarian, could speak meaningfully to all of the various constituencies concerned. The fact that his work tended to deal with very obscure subjects, and for the most part had studi-ously avoided questions about political significances in the present day, provided a generous degree of interpretative elasticity, which further enhanced its useful-ness for the new ideological demands. By the same token, his death in 1992—however sincerely mourned—did conveniently insure that he would never be in a position to object either to subsequent interpretations of his ideas or to the uses to which they were put. For all of these reasons, after 1991 Gumilev's profile as an ideological *kumir* or idol for the conservative-nationalist tendencies in the Rus-sian opposition grew ever greater.[46] In 1993, the German newspaper *Frankfurter*

---

43. Higgins 1993. On the opposition to Yeltsin, see Laqueur 1993; Parland 2005; Allensworth 1998; Yanov 1995.

44. Ersen 2004, 141.

45. Tsygankov 1998. For a critique of Eurasianism from one such Russian nationalist, see Mialo 1992; Bassin 2010a; Laruelle 2004, 117–18, 134n.

46. Khazanov 2002, 476.

Allgemeine Zeitung published a lengthy article about him entitled "The Geneticist of History," reckoning that "no other scholar has influenced the politically fragmented [Russian] Right" as much as he.[47] In Russia itself, where the political and social instability of the early 1990s led to numerous comparisons with the volatile Weimar Republic, there was much speculation among liberal observers that Gumilev could provide an ideological foundation for the emergence of a fascist movement.[48] This view was supported by an eminent American authority on the history of European fascism, who maintained that Gumilev's ideas "share considerable similarities" with the doctrines of leading fascist theoreticians.[49]

On the right, Gumilev was embraced by two of the most important oppositionist ideologues, Aleksandr Gel'evich Dugin and Aleksandr Prokhanov. Dugin had been active in the dissident occultist underground during perestroika, but in the early 1990s he committed himself firmly to the Eurasianist project. By the end of the decade, he was to emerge as the most visible and influential proponent of neo-Eurasianism in post-Soviet Russia, a role that he has maintained down to the present day.[50] As we will consider in greater detail, Dugin's appreciation for Gumilev is unstinting in its grandiosity. With his historical accounts of the ancient Eurasian steppe, Dugin declared solemnly, Gumilev "has given two thousand years of our fate back to us" and thereby provided the vital stimulus for the contemporary renaissance of Eurasianist ideas.[51] Prokhanov, a well-established Soviet writer whose novels glorifying the exploits of the Soviet military earned him the touching sobriquet *solovei General'nogo Shtaba* or "the nightingale of the general staff," had been an admirer of Gumilev since the 1960s.[52] During perestroika Prokhanov emerged as a trenchant empire saver, and by the time of the collapse of the Soviet Union he had endorsed Eurasianism as the only ideological perspective that could insure the continued existence of the Russian state.[53] In 1990 Prokhanov founded the newspaper *Den'*, which quickly became the leading organ of the red-brown opposition. Gumilev himself supported this venture and

---

47. Holm 1994. Also see Loseff 1994, 12.

48. For discussions regarding the fascist potential of Gumilev's teachings, see Yanov 1995; Starovoitova 1993; Freidin 1996; Raskin 1996, Ianov 1992, 114, 112–13; Ianov 1995b, 212; Shnirel'man 2009; Diligenskii 1995, 37; Graev 1998; Novikov 1999, 11. Laqueur 1993, 146–47; Umland 2006, 620.

49. Gregor 2000, 151. For a dissenting view from another specialist on fascism, see Shenfield 2001, 44.

50. There is a large literature on Dugin. See especially Höllwerth 2007; Ivanov 2007; Kipp 2002; Laruelle n.d.; Laruelle 2001; Dunlop 2001.

51. Dugin 2002c.

52. On Prokhanov, see Rougle and Rich 1995; Livers 2010.

53. Prokhanov and Ianov 1992; Dunlop 1993, 176–77, 169–77; Allensworth 1998, 244–48; Simonsen 1996, 96.

his friend Dmitrii Balashov sat on the editorial board. The advocacy of Eurasianism was a principal goal of the journal, with entire pages in each issue dedicated to different aspects of it.[54] Shut down for its support of the parliamentary revolt again Yeltsin in 1993, the newspaper quickly reopened with the new name *Zavtra*, and its first edition displayed a large picture of Gumilev on the title page.[55]

On the left, Gumilev's Eurasianist banner was taken up by the leader of the reconstituted Communist Party, Gennadii Ziuganov, who as we have seen had been interested in his writings as a high-level Communist functionary in the 1980s. As part of his post-Soviet reinvention of Russian communism, Ziuganov made fundamental use of Eurasianist concepts.[56] He was aided in this process by Dugin, who for some time in the 1990s worked with him as a sort of ideological adviser. Ziuganov rated Gumilev particularly highly, reckoning him to be Eurasianism's "most brilliant representative." "With the boldness of his ideas, the breadth of his scientific discoveries, the strength of his spirit and moral greatness, there is no question that he belongs in the cohort of the greatest thinkers . . . of the twentieth century."[57] Gumilev's teachings influenced Ziuganov's formulation of a new doctrine of Russian communism that was anti-Western in principle and committed to the ideal of a grand multiethnic Eurasian amalgam.[58] Within this framework, Ziuganov cultivated Gumilev's notion of ethnos as a replacement for the Marxist category of class as the motor of history. He believed that the "voluntary reunion" of the former Soviet Union was inevitable, and that the resulting Eurasian entity would be "an imperial state (*imperskaia gosudarstvennost'*), the heart (*iadro*) of which would be the Russian ethnos."[59]

Gumilev's appeal was not, however, limited to these extremist tendencies of the political opposition. Very much to the contrary, there was also a significant measure of official appreciation and support, even from within the Yeltsin government itself.[60] One particularly significant example of the latter was Sergei Mikhailovich Shakhrai, a high government functionary who in the early 1990s headed the influential State Committee on Nationalities and was additionally charged with drafting a new constitution for the Russian Federation. In both these roles, Shakhrai sought to resist further ethno-national fragmentation

---

54. Kochanek 1999, 255; Tolz 2001, 150; Rossman 2002b, 2.

55. See Prokhanov's introduction to Avdeev 2005a.

56. Clover 1999, 12; Laruelle 2004, 126–27.

57. Ziuganov 1995, 18 (quote); Ziuganov 1993, 176.

58. Clark 1995, 1995. For Gumilev's influence on Ziuganov, also see Tsygankov 2003, 120–23; Parland 2005, 138.

59. Ziuganov 1997, 15–16; Ziuganov 2006; March 2002, 75.

60. On the influence of Eurasianism on foreign policy thinking within the government, see Kerr 1995; Morozova 2009, 669.

of the state by promoting a new supranational sense of community that was not reliant on Marxist-Soviet categories and values. Although he did not accept Gumilev's Eurasianist vision in its entirety, Shakhrai was drawn nonetheless by its compelling depictions of the harmony and mutual recognition of the Eurasian peoples throughout their history, and he recognized its potential for his own political purposes. He sponsored a project for the publication of Gumilev's collected works, and his enthusiasm was obvious enough to lead one foreign observer to the conclusion that Gumilev's "theories of the superethnos have arrived in the corridors of the Kremlin."[61] Although Shakhrai's publication project was not eventually realized, official acclaim of Gumilev's historical work was confirmed elsewhere. In 1995, the State Duma awarded Gumilev's historical survey *Ot Rusi do Rossii* (1992) the prestigious *Vekhi* prize, a distinction conferred in recognition of contributions to "the development and self-awareness (*samosoznanie*) of Russian civilization."[62] The book was also approved by the Ministry of Education of the Russian Federation as a text for the high school curriculum of the Russian Federation and reissued in a print run of one hundred thousand copies.[63]

Gumilev's Theoretical Contributions

Gumilev was by no means the only source of inspiration for the neo-Eurasianism that emerged at the end of perestroika and in the early years of the Russian Federation. The writings of the classical Eurasianists—fascinating and intellectually rich in their own right—were rediscovered and republished during this period, and in the search for new ideas certain aspects of Western conservative thought were drawn on as well. But Gumilev did make a number of original

---

61. Clark 1995, 328. Gumilev's widow also noted Shakhrai's interest in her husband's work. Gumileva 1993.

62. "O premii "Vekhi" Gosudarstvennoi Dumy Rossiiskoi Federatsii." n.d.

63. Shnirelman 2009b, 121–22; Beliakov 2012a, 586, 643; Lavrov 2003, 213. In general, the publication statistics for Gumilev's books are staggering. The first edition of *Ethnogenesis and the Earth's Biosphere*—published in 1989 in a print run of eleven thousand copies—sold out in a few months and was reissued in the same year. His subsequent publications were far more popular. *The Geography of the Ethnos in the Historical Period* (1990) had a print run of thirty thousand; *Rhythms of Eurasia* (1992) fifty thousand, and *The Black Legend* (1994) twenty thousand. Demand was so great that at one point in the early 1990s there were five separate projects to publish his collected works (not including Shakhrai's). Gumilev's widow complained about how these pirate editions wanted to "get rich in a hurry": publishing Gumilev's best-sellers was apparently a reliable way of doing so. Gumileva 1993, 10. In 1991, Gumilev's opponent Apollon Kuz'min confirmed that he had become the "most voluminously published historian" in Russia. Kuz'min 1991, 257.

contributions, without which it can be argued that the neo-Eurasianist renaissance would not have been possible. What he offered was a vividly imaginative mélange, in which elements of classical Eurasianism mixed freely with his own off-beat perspectives and with what were essentially Soviet doctrines, the latter, however, always described via Gumilev's special terminology so that their Soviet provenance was not immediately apparent. These qualities served not only to set Gumilev's contribution apart from that of his illustrious émigré predecessors, but also rendered it useful in a way that theirs could not be for the purposes of the neo-Eurasianist renaissance.[64]

This is most immediately apparent in the lexicon that Gumilev developed as part of his theoretical corpus and that was subsequently adapted for the purposes of neo-Eurasianism. Terms such as *passionarnost'* and chimera had a broad appeal and, as we will see, quickly became fundamental terms of reference in post-Soviet public discourse. Neither concept had a counterpart anywhere in the canon of classical Eurasianism, but both corresponded at least loosely to familiar Soviet concepts: the positive *élan vital* or *stikhiinost'* of the New Soviet Person on the one hand and the negative *vnutrennyi vrag* or *vrag naroda* on the other. Similarly, the special attribute of interethnic fraternity that Gumilev called *komplimentarnost'* was not extensively theorized in classical Eurasianism, but resonated directly with the key Soviet notion of *druzhba* or "friendship" that was supposed to exist between the country's assorted nationalities. In those cases where his concepts did correspond to those of the original Eurasianists, they were reformulated in ways that made them more relevant for contemporary purposes. Thus the most important of Gumilev's neologisms overall for the purposes of neo-Eurasianism—his notion of "superethnos"—corresponded directly, as we have seen, to what the classical Eurasianists had called a "multinational individual" (*mnogonarodnaia lichnost'*) or "multinational nation" and the Soviets had called a "historical community."[65] In all these variants, the term referred to a cohesive supranational entity formed out of an assemblage of discrete ethno-national units, which despite their higher unity retained their respective individuality. However, if Gumilev's new designation merely repeated the original Eurasian and Soviet belief in the authenticity of the polyethnic unity of the Russian-Eurasian peoples, it was formulated on an entirely novel basis, namely the objective natural laws of landscape science, ethology, and systems theory. Needless to say, the latter approach provided a dimension of discursive authority that was far greater than the classical Eurasianists' Spenglerian-historiosophical articulations of the same point.

---

64. Shlapentokh 2009, 12.
65. Bassin 2003, 257–67.

On a more subtle level, two basic elements of Gumilev's theories were fundamental to the elaboration of neo-Eurasianism in the early 1990s. One of these
was Gumilev's insistence on the absolute distinction between an ethnic community—ethnos—on the one hand and a sociopolitical community—*obshchestvo*
or *sotsiuum*—on the other.[66] Ethnies did not have a political structure, he had
maintained, and could not naturally serve as a basis for political formations.[67] For
post-Soviet Eurasianism, the place of *sotsiuum* in this juxtaposition was replaced
by *natsiia* or the nation. "L. N. Gumilev's great achievement was to distinguish
between the concepts of NATION and ETHNOS, which are often confused. . . .
The nation is the population of a country, the citizens of a state. An ethnos
(a people [*narod*]) originates as a geographical, culturological, and social-
psychological phenomenon. . . . The concept 'national belonging' has two [very
different] significations: ethnic belonging and citizenship."[68] By not making this
latter distinction, the modern European "nation-state" violated the natural order
of things.[69] In nation-states, political sovereignty is conflated with ethnic identification and a concept of national self-determination prevails that recognized
the unconditional right of all nationalities to aspire to sovereign political statehood or at least some form of political autonomy. These were positions that the
Russian neo-Eurasianists, with their strong opposition to the politics of ethno-
national separatism that had destroyed the unity of the Soviet state in the first
place, found completely unacceptable. They believed that Gumilev's principled
distinction between the ethnic and the political (or "national") offered an alternative to this conflation, which made it possible to support unequivocally the
ethnic individuality and integrity of all Eurasian peoples without acknowledging any concomitant right on their part to political self-determination in any
form, either as an independent state or an autonomous formation within a state.
Insofar as this latter aspiration still continued in various ways to challenge the
stability of the Russian state after 1991, the appeal of Gumilev's position was
extremely powerful.

The second point involved Gumilev's juxtaposition of ethnos to superethnos.
In the 1920s, classical Eurasianism acknowledged the legitimacy of what Nikolai Trubetskoi called "lower-level" ethno-national affinities, but it clearly subordinated these to the imperative for unity at the multiethnic "upper level" of

---

66. Gumilev 1989c, 85.
67. For an example of how this point can be misunderstood, see Turchin 2003, 43–44. "The main
kernel of Gumilev's theory is the explicit connection that he makes between ethnie and polity dynamics." The former Kirghiz president Askar Akaev, by contrast—an enthusiastic devotee of Gumilev—
appreciates the latter's real point very clearly. Akaev 2011a, 23–24.
68. Marochkin 1997, 226 (emphasis original).
69. For example, Malashenko 1991.

Eurasian civilization as a whole.[70] In this spirit, Trubetskoi had summoned all the peoples of Eurasia—ethnic Russians among them—to subordinate their local-ized ethnic loyalties to an all-embracing "pan-Eurasian nationalism."[71] In view of the overriding priority at that time—the geopolitical reassembly of territories that had broken away from the Russian empire in the wake of the revolution—this emphasis was entirely logical. The exigencies confronting Gumilev in the 1960s and 1970s, by contrast, were quite different: they were, namely, to resist the post-Stalinist *sliianie* project of merging ethnies into a supranational metaethnic Soviet people. He responded to this, again entirely logically, with his counter-emphasis on the natural integrity and inviolability of the lower-level ethnos, as distinct from and in a sense more fundamental than the superethnos. Indeed, as we have just seen, it was not until his final days that he even acknowledged the existence of a single Soviet (Eurasian) superethnos at all. Gumilev's bias toward the lower-level ethnos was an important element of the appeal of Eurasianism to various Russian conservative-nationalist tendencies after 1991. To be sure, the principle of a shared "pan-Eurasian" identity continued to be accepted. However, Eurasianism as refracted through a Gumilevian filter made it possible to retain a significant emphasis on the ethnos, which as we have seen for Russian neo-Eur-asianists meant first and foremost the Russian ethnos. Trubetskoi and the classi-cal Eurasianists had insisted that the ideal of a powerful multinational *derzhava* in the geopolitical tradition of the Russian empire could only be realized if eth-nic Russia abandoned or at least subordinated its own particular Russian ethno-national interests. With his relatively stronger emphasis on the importance of the ethnos, Gumilev was understood to be making no such demand. The effect was a vision of Eurasianism that both supported the principle of national diversity and at the same time defined Eurasia as an exclusive Russian identity.[72] Russian neo-Eurasianism could continue to insist not only on the essential "natural" dif-ferentiation of Eurasia's various nationalities but also—and in flagrant contra-vention of Gumilev's genuine inclinations—on the prioritization of the Russian (*russkii* or *velikorusskii*) ethnos above all the others. Russia was a Eurasian empire in which ethnic Russians represented the "pivotal" or "backbone" (*sterzhnevoi*) nationality, responsible more than any other group for its historical formation as well as its maintenance in the present day.[73]

A final point regarding Gumilev's contribution to neo-Eurasianism related to the question of the *Rossiianin* concept, much promoted in the 1990s as a nonethnic

---

70. Trubetskoi 1921b; Bassin 2011, 49–54; Bassin 2003.
71. Trubetskoi 1927.
72. Laruelle 2004, 133.
73. Marochkin 1997, 228; Makhnach 2001.

category encompassing all citizens of the Russian federation. The intention was to frame the latter as a multinational civic-political community or a "multiethnic nation" (*mnogonarodnaia natsiia*), as one of its principal advocates Valerii Aleksandrovich Tishkov put it.[74] Proponents of neo-Eurasianism roundly denounced this term, believing it to be a cover for the same leveling and assimilationist spirit as the *sovetskii narod* concept. In view of Gumilev's categorical opposition to the *sliianie* project of his own day, he was highly valued as an authoritative counterbalance on this issue, in particular to Tishkov's project.[75] This opposition to the term, however, revealed a nuanced but significant contradiction in the Eurasianist position itself. That a blatantly supraethnic concept such as *rossiianin* should be unacceptable to the latter was understandable. But what then exactly was the alternative designation *russkii* supposed to mean? Some Eurasianists intimated that the Russian (*russkii*) ethnos, as Eurasia's pivotal nationality, itself possessed a certain superethnic quality, in that it could subsume other ethnies. This was not the same as the *rossiianin* idea, which was an explicitly nonethnic category that by definition included all the nationalities of the state on an equal basis. But neither was *russkii* in this sense a strictly monoethnic entity like all the other nationalities of Eurasia. On the contrary, here the Russian ethnos appeared to possess a certain special ethnic capacity for including other ethnies inside it. Many Eurasianists, Gumilev's friend Balashov among them, extended the ethnic limits of the Russian (*russkii*) people to include Ukrainians and Belorussians.[76] In a public debate on Eurasianism in the early 1990s, another enthusiast pushed the point rather further. "The question has arisen: Who are the Russians (*russkie*)? . . . The Russian is not [only] a Slav. As Gumilev correctly maintained, a Russian is a Turk, an Alan, a Slav, and a Finno-Ugrian. The term '*rossiianin*' is inaccurate both politically and aesthetically because it emphasizes the differences between us. We are all Russian (*russkie*), and in the framework of a hyperethnos (*giperetnos*) a Russian can be

---

74. Tishkov 2007; Tishkov 1995. Tishkov was the director of the Institute of Ethnology and Ethnography of the Russian Academy of Sciences and briefly a Minister of Nationalities in the Yeltsin administration. Also see Tolz 1996: 1005–6; Simonsen 1996: 272, 277–78; Akturk 2010: 322–23.

75. Marochkin 1997, 230; Makhnach 2001. In 2005 a group of activists from a Eurasianist youth movement picketed Tishkov's office in Moscow, brandishing placards that read "Gumilev vs. Tishkov." Kanishchev n.d. The deployment of Gumilev against Tishkov on this issue is distinctly ironic, insofar as the latter's notion of a *mnogonarodnaia natsiia*, as Tishkov himself readily acknowledged, was actually very similar to the classical Eurasianist concept of a pan-Eurasian national entity formulated by Trubetskoi. "Druzhba s narodom" 2011. On Tishkov's "quasi-Eurasianism," also see Shlapentokh 2007a. Tishkov explicitly acknowledges a "Eurasian mission" on the part of the Russians, but it is not one the Eurasianists we are discussing would recognize. Tishkov 2005.

76. Balashov 2000b. The correct name for Ukrainians, in Balashov's view, was *Malorossy*. This was clearly not Gumilev's own view. He recognized Russians, Ukrainians, and Belorussians as separate ethnies which all belonged to the same superethnos. Luk"ianov 2003, 68.

a Jew, a German, or a Frenchman who lives here in Russia."[77] The paradox here is that the term "hyperethnos," obviously inspired by Gumilev, is intended to designate a phenomenon—a Jewish or French Russian—that Gumilev himself would never have accepted or even recognized. As we will see, this understanding of *russkii* persists into our own day, expounded among others by the Russian president Vladimir Putin.

Eurasianism and the Russian Ethnos

The different ways in which these aspects of Gumilev's theories are assimilated can be seen in a comparison of two articulations of post-Soviet Eurasianism. Aleksandr Dugin's Eurasianist perspective is a singularly complex and in many respects arcane amalgam of different political and philosophical theories, in which the Eurasianist legacy represents only one component part. He leaves no doubt, however, that Gumilev has played a critical role in the development of his own thinking. Gumilev's greatness is conveyed in his brilliant scholarly analyses, but is more fundamentally apparent in the powerful influence he has exerted on the process of rejuvenating Russia's self-image and self-understanding.[78] "Prior to Gumilev," Dugin asserts, "we typically looked at ourselves through the eyes of the West, seeing in our country . . . only oppressive centuries of barbarism, bloody conflicts, and senseless, stagnant, lifeless existence." Gumilev's teachings about ethnic history and ethnogenesis demonstrated dramatically how "our blood and our soil are saturated with the raw spirit of our ethnic and cultural roots, of our forebears—their passions, their strength, their special illumination and their energy."[79] This image was refracted through the prism of Russia's ancient Eurasian origins and its enduring Eurasian identity in the present. Through his life's work, Gumilev single-handedly succeeded in effecting the "*metaphysical rehabilitation of Eurasia*" that is inspiring the masses today. In doing so, he has "given us back two thousand years of our destiny."[80]

Dugin endorses Gumilev's teachings about the ethnos as the fundamental unit of human organization and the essential subject of historical development. "*The ethnos generalizes the laws of organic development, and completes the dialectical process of the evolution of matter.*" In it, universal laws of development "rise to the level of self-consciousness and self-comprehension (*samopostizheniia*). This takes

---

77. "Evraziistvo i sovremennost'" 1993.
78. See Dugin's lecture on Gumilev: http://www.youtube.com/watch?v=FgrWNmokmwk.
79. Dugin 2002c, 538.
80. Dugin 2002b; emphasis in original.

place precisely in an ethnos that is historically and empirically fixed, and not in some abstract conception of the human individual."[81] The unique significance of the ethnos rests above all on its function as medium for the "transformation of the natural into the social . . . and the historical and organic into the cultural," all effected through the dynamics of energy circulation. Dugin places particular emphasis on Gumilev's ecology of ethnicity and the dependency of ethnies as natural organisms on local environmental conditions. An ethnos is "organically and inseparably connected with its geographical environment, with the soil, the flora and fauna," and is "inscribed into the natural rhythms" of the landscape. "Climate, landscape, local geology, waterways, and mountains all play an active role in the formation of ethnic and civilizational types," whose characteristics are "strictly determined by geography" and necessarily obey special qualitative laws. For Dugin, as for Gumilev, all this points to the essential *biologichnost'* or biological quality of ethnies and their behavioral stereotypes.[82]

Along with these general principles, Dugin explains Russian national development essentially in terms of Gumilevian ethnogenesis. The Great Russian ethnos is not only Slavic but rather formed as a result of *sliianie* between Slavic and Turkic elements. Great Russian civilization took shape on the basis of a primeval Turkic-Slavic ethnogenesis, a "geopolitical synthesis" that was realized geographically through a "historic alliance" between forest and steppe.[83] The modern Russian nation is the product of this alliance. The sharing of cultural, administrative, geopolitical, and economic practices was accompanied by "ethnic mixing (*smeshenie*) on a broad scale, which gradually led to the creation of a *new ethnic unit*, bringing together the 'eastern Russians,' who after Kulikovo recognized themselves as 'Great Russians.'"[84] In all aspects of its civilization, ideology, and political destiny, Russia today is a product of this elemental geopolitical union, a "combination of sedentary and nomadic life, of West and East, rational and irrational, which is the source of the entire uniqueness and value of Russian culture."[85] *Passionarnost'* played a vital role in driving this process forward, and the characteristic aspects of Russia, or any nation at a given point in its historical development, can be explained in terms of the waxing and waning of its passionary energy as it progressed through successive ethnogenetic phases. "The ethnogenetic cycle is the principal instrument for the correct interpretation of . . . any historical culture."[86]

81. Dugin 2002b, emphasis in original.
82. Dugin 2000, 197 (quotes); Dugin 2002b.
83. Dugin 2000, 153, 155.
84. Dugin 2002a, 19, emphasis in original.
85. Dugin 2000, 539.
86. Dugin 2002b (quote); Dugin 2000, 155; Dugin 2002a, 24.

Dugin's discussion of the status of the Great Russian ethnos within the multi-national community of Eurasian peoples, however, brings out the tension in the neo-Eurasianist deployment of Gumilev's ideas. On the one hand, he prioritizes the Great Russian ethnos and accords it a special significance in the creation and development of Eurasian civilization. Simply put, the Great Russian nation represents Eurasia's basic "civilizational foundation" (*konstanta*), which provides the essential political, social, and cultural forms that dominated the life of the continent across the ages. The development of the Russian state in particular was a result of the special ethnic qualities of the Great Russian people. "It was not the state that formed the Russian nation (*russkaia natsiia*). On the contrary, the Russian nation, the Russian people (*narod*) experimented throughout history with different types of state systems, each one expressing in different ways the specific qualities of its unique mission." Alone of all the Eurasian nations, Russia "belongs to the group of messianic peoples" and has a "planetary-historical" significance that is "universal and panhuman." Ethnic Russians have every right, therefore, to see themselves as a "chosen peoples."[87]

The most important evidence of this, of course, was the Russians' special historical function as an "empire-forming" (*imperoobrazuiushchii*) and "empire-building" (*imperostroitel'nyi*) people in Eurasia, a function that not only created a magnificent and enduring geopolitical structure but maintained a constellation of civilizational values as well. The greatness of Eurasia in the past had always depended vitally on the preeminence of Great Russia, and it must continue to do so in the future. "It is precisely the Russian (*russkii*) people who should be seen as the principal political subject (*sub"ekt*), on the basis of which the scale of geopolitical, strategic, and social-economic interests of Russia is determined. Today, the Russian people are Russia (*russkii narod i est' segodnia Rossiia*)."[88] Dugin underscored the significance he attached to his point by including it in the first draft of his manifesto launching his political movement "Eurasia" in 2002. "We must resurrect the traditions of the Russian people . . . and reawaken in it the organic spirituality, the high ideals, the passionate patriotism that are characteristic for it. *Without prioritizing the resurrection of the Russian people (as an empire-forming nation) the Eurasian project cannot be realized.* The understanding of this point lays at the basis of our worldview."[89] To abandon its historical empire-building function, he argued elsewhere, would represent "national suicide" and signal nothing less than the end of the existence of the Russian people "as a historical reality."[90]

---

87. Dugin 2000, 188–89, 256.
88. Ibid., 189.
89. Dugin 2001 (emphasis added).
90. Dugin 2000, 197.

Yet despite this spirited prioritization of the Great Russian ethnos as an empire builder and Russia-Eurasia's "principal political subject," Dugin still fundamentally qualified the role of ethnicity—and the principle of ethnic Russian preeminence—in the political life of Eurasia in a manner as reminiscent of Trubetskoi as of Gumilev. Ethnic nationalism in all groups should be supported and fostered, but this nationalism must be based exclusively on cultural and religious criteria and cannot include any notion of ethno-national sovereignty or any potential for political mobilization. In the Eurasian order of the future, the Russian Federation's territorial-administrative system of *guberniia* would be replaced with a network of "ethno-religious regions (*oblasti*)" based on the distribution of ethnic groups. Although each of these entities would retain the maximal degree of cultural, linguistic, economic, and judicial autonomy, the more important point was that they would all be "strictly limited in terms of political, strategic, geopolitical, and ideological sovereignty."[91] Just like the classical Eurasians before him, Dugin clearly recognized that these principles would apply to ethnic Russia no less than anyone else. Nothing would be more harmful than succumbing to an isolationist "little Russian" (*mladorosskii*) desire for a mono-ethnic Russian "nation-state." The Russian ethnos is an imperial ethnos and can only prosper in an imperial state.[92] Thus, in his calls for a revival of Great Russian nationalism, he was careful to spell out exactly what he had in mind. Russian nationalism "should not use the [political] terminology of the state but rather an ethno-cultural terminology," with special emphasis on categories such as "the national ethos" (*narodnost'*) and "Russian Orthodoxy." It must be precisely a populist, ethnic, and ethno-religious nationalism, "without any trace of 'statism' (*gosudarstvennost'*)." It was precisely the recognition of the cultural-religious—and explicitly nonpolitical or imperial—basis of a Russian unity that would foster the "indivisibility, cohesiveness, totality, and unity of the Russian ethno-organism." This model of what Dugin called a "positive" nationalism applied not only to Russians but to all of Eurasia's ethnic groups as well.[93]

As an agglomeration of all of these groups, the Eurasian state itself was strictly multinational, and at the state level ethnicity per se was not an organizing principle. "Strategically, the neo-Eurasian worldview is supraethnic (*nadetnicheskoe*), and in a certain sense supranational (*nadnatsional'noe*). This is very important.

---

91. Ibid., 212. Indeed, Dugin would break up long-established national entities such as Yakutia or Tatarstan to thwart the possibility of ethno-political mobilization. Laruelle 2008b, 118.

92. Dugin 2000, 213.

93. Ibid., 255, 258. Tellingly, while Dugin referred to the Russian nation as "empire-forming" in a draft manifesto, as we saw in the previous paragraph, when this manifesto was published in its final form, the reference had been deleted. "Evraziia prezhde vsego" 2002, 15–16.

Neo-Eurasianism is the national idea for a supranational (*sverkhnatsional'nyi*) and metanational block."[94] The point was important, Dugin explained, because it served as a guarantee for Eurasia's non-Russian peoples against Great Russian domination within Eurasia, and insured that Eurasia as a political formation would not be subject to manipulation for the benefit of exclusively Russian ethno-national interests. Eurasia's non-Russian nationalities did not need to be concerned about possible Great Russian hegemony, for above all nationalities "there would always be a higher instance under which all ethno-religious communities [i.e., all ethnies] have equal status, and that is guided by the impartial principles of imperial harmony and justice."[95] This higher instance was the most important locus of identity and belonging in Eurasia, which subsumed ethnonational affinities and superseded the ethnos as the primary focus for popular allegiance. Dugin's uncompromisingly multinational and polyethnic vision of Eurasia was faithfully reflected in the leadership he assembled for his Eurasian movement, which included representatives of Muslim, Jewish, Buddhist, and other nationalities in the Russian Federation.[96]

In the final analysis, however, Dugin did not entirely dismiss the prospect that ethnic Russia might someday achieve its political consummation through the establishment of a sovereign "ethno-Russian state" (*russkoe gosudarstvo*) based exclusively on the Great Russian ethnos and devoted to advancing its interests.[97] When the united forces of Eurasia have secured their eventual global victory, he speculated, the logistical imperative that necessitated the continental or even multicontinental political union would lose its force. At this point individual ethnic units might finally emerge as sovereign states. "In this event, the Russian nation would need to be ready for the creation of its own state." The new entity would be shaped entirely by ethno-national criteria: shared territorial homeland, national traditions, culture, religion, and so on. But rather like Stalinism's conditional acceptance of the inevitability of *sliianie*, Dugin was careful to specify that this prospect could become a reality only in the very distant future. Although it was "entirely possible" that an ethnically Russian state may someday prove feasible, this could happen "only in a post-Eurasian period."[98]

A very different view of the relationship of the Great Russian ethnos to the rest of Eurasian society was elaborated by Igor' Shishkin, a journalist and deputy

94. "Kruglyi stol zhurnala *Filosofiia Prava*" 2000.
95. Dugin 2000, 258.
96. Laruelle 2008b, 118.
97. Dugin 2000, 262.
98. Ibid., 261.

director of Institute for the CIS Countries.[99] Shishkin had studied under Gumilev and therefore should have understood his thinking particularly well, but his formulations bear further witness to just how far the neo-Eurasianist perspective can diverge from the master's own intentions. Shishkin is very clear that post-Soviet Eurasianism must serve first and foremost as a Russian (*russkii*) ideology, which represents the specific interests of the Russian ethnos and offers a solution to the "Russian question." For these purposes, he argues, Gumilev represents a much more important locus of orientation than classical Eurasianism, for it is only on the basis of Gumilev's ethnogenetic perspective that a genuinely "national-state ideology" for Russia can be developed.[100] This involves above all the recognition of the primacy of ethnicity, in other words, that political and geopolitical structures are in the final analysis the direct product of specifically ethnic initiative and activity. Gumilev, he claims implausibly, demonstrated that ethnies "are natural phenomena that, in order to secure their existence, create the necessary social institutions, including states. Ethnies create states; states do not create ethnies." Russia stands as a prototypical example of this process. The Russian state emerged "not as the result of a 'voluntary union of peoples' but rather as the result of the deliberate historical creativity of the Russian ethnos." Whatever role other ethnies may have played in this process was only under the direction of the ethnic Russian element.[101] Unlike Dugin, Shishkin does not recognize a significant Turkic or Mongolian element either in the formation of the Russian state or the ethnogenesis of the Russian people.

Shishkin explained Russia's preeminence and its special state-building dynamism strictly in Gumilevian terms. On the one hand, it was related to the high passionary level of the Russians, which enabled them to "occupy and tame the necessary *Lebensraum* (*zhiznennoe prostranstvo*)" and in the process to "impose (*naviazat'*) their will" on the other Eurasian peoples. Along with this, the Russians possessed a unique behavioral stereotype in regard to interethnic relations. Despite their dominant position, they always treated other groups on an equal basis and with respect, never regarding them in any way as second class.[102] The historical legacy retains its full significance in the present day. Shishkin repeats Dugin's claim that ethnic Russia is Eurasia's sole empire-forming nation. "Not a single nation in Eurasia, aside from the Russians, possesses the level of

99. From 2000 to 2006 Shishkin published the Internet journal *Evraziiskii Vestnik*. http://gumilevica.kulichki.net/e-journal.html (accessed 13/1/2014). On Shishkin, see Tolz 1996, 1003–4; Beliakov 2012a, 704–5.

100. Shishkin 1998, 104.

101. Shishkin 1995b.

102. Shishkin n.d.

passionarnost' or the behavioral stereotype necessary to take on a state-forming function."[103] This means, again following Dugin, that "the resurrection (*vozrozh-denie*) of the Russian nation" becomes the central problem for the entire resurrection of Eurasia as a great power. "If the Russian ethnos is healthy and strong, then there will be a powerful Russian state (*velikaia Rossiia*), if not, then there will not be."[104]

Shishkin emphasizes the principle of ethnic differentiation, and for him the issue reveals the critical differences between classical Eurasianism and the teachings of his mentor. The classical Eurasianists, he suggests, believed that the peoples of Eurasia could somehow agglomerate at a macrolevel to form a sort of blended metaethnic entity, a vision clearly expressed in Trubetskoi's appeal for a "pan-Eurasian nationalism."[105] With his position that Russian-Eurasian civilization represented not one but seven distinct superethnies, however, Gumilev had implicitly rejected this vision, and for Shishkin the rejection was very important.[106] For Gumilev, the enduring strength of the Russian-Eurasian state was always based on intense ethnic diversity and the principle that these groups should all live "separately but in friendship" (*porozn' no druzhno*). Although the assimilation of one group by another is theoretically possible, it can only take place at an early point in the ethnogenetic cycle when the assimilating agent still possesses a high passionary charge. Insofar as the Russian ethnos today has long passed this point, it is no longer capable of absorbing other groups—indeed any attempt to do so could risk exhausting Russia's remaining passionary resources and thus prove fatal.[107] The powerful positive complementarity and "natural compatibility" (*sovmestimost'*) among its variegated ethnies has always been an essential element for the Russian-Eurasian *derzhava*, and it unites the interests of all into a seamless totality. "Founded on the teachings of Gumilev, Eurasianism for the first time joins the interests of the Russian (*russkii*) ethnos, the Russian (*rossiiskoe*) state, and all the peoples of Eurasia together into a single harmonious entity." Yet each ethnic group needed to recognize that the opportunity for free autonomous development could come only from its unconditional allegiance to a single overarching state structure that was controlled and directed by the Russian nationality. "To serve Russia (*Rossiia*) means to serve their own people (*narod*), and to serve their own people means to serve the Russian state.[108]

103. Shishkin 1998, 105.
104. Shishkin 1995b.
105. Shishkin n.d.
106. Shishkin 1994.
107. Shishkin 1995c.
108. Shishkin n.d.

Shishkin maintained that other versions of neo-Eurasianism ignore what he describes—again utterly implausibly—as Gumilev's message that Eurasianism is "a Russian (*russkaia*) ideology." They therefore fail to recognize the preeminence of the Russian ethnos and to acknowledge its claim as the exclusive state-forming nation in Eurasia.[109] "It is precisely Gumilev's teachings that demonstrate what a state-forming ethnos is. It is not a pretty label or privilege, but rather a reality. Without a state-forming ethnos a unified Eurasia cannot exist."[110] Most proponents of Russian neo-Eurasianism, he maintains, do not understand this. They believe "that to recognize the Russians as [the sole] state-forming ethnos is insulting to all the other nationalities," and so, "for the sake of the friendship of the peoples," they propose to consider *every* ethnos to be state-forming. "How very pleasant," he observed caustically, "how noble, how democratic." But because of this position, neo-Eurasianism has failed to become accepted as a valuable and strong national idea by most Russians, who are inclined to see it rather as an "anti-Russian ideology."[111]

The principal culprit, in Shishkin's view, is none other than Aleksandr Dugin. He argues—not incorrectly, as we have seen—that Dugin's state-centric focus ignores or at least deemphasizes the ethnic qualities of its population. The result is an instrumental conception of the Russian people as nothing more than an amorphous "means for the construction of a powerful Eurasian state."[112] Shishkin claims that Dugin treats ethnic diversity "as a threat to Russia's state life (*gosudarstennost'*)," and that his project for a Eurasian state would involve nothing less than the "obliteration" (*stiranie*) of ethnic differentiation among Russia's multinational population altogether. Dugin's guiding inspiration does not come from Gumilev or Eurasianism at all, Shishkin maintains, but rather—once again—from the vision of the "Soviet people" as a "new historical community" bequeathed by the Communists.[113] And this, in the final analysis, is why Dugin's false Eurasianism will never succeed in capturing the imagination of Russia's multinational population. "Taught by the bitter experience of the realization of a 'melting pot' in the form of the 'Soviet people,'" Russians recognize Dugin's position as "just one more attempt at the de-Russification of Russia," whereas other national groups see it just the opposite, namely, a veiled determination to Russify them. In the final analysis, however, Dugin's Eurasia is identical to the model of a "nation of *rossiianie*" much loved by the post-Soviet "democrats" of the Yeltsin era.[114]

---

109. Shishkin 2006.

110. "Passionarnost'" 2012.

111. Shishkin n.d. (quotes); Shishkin 1998, 103.

112. Ibid., 103–5.

113. Shishkin n.d.; Shishkin 2006.

114. Shishkin n.d. Shishkin is not the only one to denounce Dugin from an ostensibly Gumilevian position: see "Ne iavliaetsia li Aleksandr Gel'evich Dugin . . . predstavietlem antisistemy?" n.d.

Vladimir Putin's Eurasian Epiphany

The accession of Vladimir Putin to the Russian presidency in 2000 brought a sea change in the country's political life. He sought to reestablish stability in Russia after the chaos of the Yeltsin years, and his specific priorities in this regard—appropriately enough for someone who had enjoyed a long and successful career as a KGB officer—resonated clearly with the "patriotic" opposition to his chaotic predecessor. Putin was determined to restore Russia's lost status as a great-power *derzhava*, commanding the sort of political and military influence across the globe that the Soviet Union had once possessed. He expressed his conviction about the deleterious effects of the breakup of the Soviet state in the strongest terms, declaring in 2005 that this had been "the greatest geopolitical catastrophe of the century."[115] He also began to develop a much more nuanced position in regard to Russia's relationship with the West. He spoke consistently about Russia as a European country, to be sure, but he also stressed the need to appreciate its historical and civilizational individuality, and was not inclined to assume Russia's necessary commonality with the West. Already in 2000, Aleksandr Dugin was impressed enough by Putin's potential to engage positively with issues that were important to him that he left the opposition to declare his support for new Russian president. Since then, all of Dugin's considerable and on the whole highly successful efforts in promoting a Eurasianist platform have been aimed at securing the support of the mainstream political establishment and Vladimir Putin in particular.[116]

For many years, Putin did not openly endorse neo-Eurasianism; indeed, given its revanchist and extremist overtones from the 1990s, there was no way he could have done so. But from the beginning, some of his pronouncements had a clear Eurasianist resonance. Thus, in one of his first statements as Russian president he declared that Russia "has always perceived itself as a Euro-Asiatic (*evroasiatskaia*) country."[117] He was rather more explicit on this subject when speaking outside of the Russian capital, however, in particular during official visits to Kazakhstan, where a version of Eurasianism had been adopted in the mid-1990s as a sort of state ideology. Although Putin did not immediately endorse this initiative in its entirety, he did make some positive comments.[118] In October 2000 he traveled to the Kazakh capital Astana to sign an convention establishing a Eurasian Economic Community, and in a speech he related this project to the Commonwealth

---

115. Putin 2005a.
116. Laruelle 2004, 127.
117. Putin 2000a.
118. Humphrey 2002, 272; Kubicek 1997, 651.

of Independent States, maintaining that the latter "carried in itself the Eurasian idea."[119] Some years later, he declared that a Eurasian Union would make it possible to "resurrect that which was lost as a result of the collapse of the Soviet Union, but [would do so] on an entirely new basis."[120]

Speaking in both cases at the newly established Lev Gumilev Eurasian National University in the Kazakh capital Astana, the Russian president repeatedly called attention to the importance of Gumilev for this Eurasianism project. Gumilev had made a "brilliant contribution not only to the development of historical thinking but also to the affirmation of the ideas of commonality through the ages and the interrelatedness of the peoples who settled the massive spaces of Eurasia, from the Baltic to the Carpathians and the Pacific Ocean." There was no question, Putin maintained, that "Gumilev's ideas are today dominating (*ovladevaiut*) the masses." While in Astana, Putin laid a memorial wreath at a monument to Gumilev.[121] When Dugin established a Eurasian political party in 2002 in Moscow, the project apparently enjoyed the tacit support of the Russian leadership—indeed, the newspaper *Nezavisimaia Gazeta* reported that the political strategist Gleb Pavlovskii, who at the time had close connections with the Kremlin, had been installed as a sort of political "godfather" for Dugin.[122]

In the course of his second presidential term, the tone of Putin's Eurasianist pronouncements became more emphatic. At the 2005 celebration of the thousand-year anniversary of the city of Kazan in Tatarstan—where, as in Kazakhstan, Eurasianism enjoys a measure of official endorsement—Putin described the role of the Volga Tatars in Russian history in terms that distinctly echoed Gumilev's description of historical symbiosis between Russians and Tatars. "Features of Russia's imperial consciousness were predetermined precisely by relations with the Volga Khanate [of the Mongol empire]. Russia's centralized state assimilated many aspects of its financial, military, tax, and administrative structures from the Golden Horde."[123] In the same year, in an address to the Federal Assembly of the Russian Federation, Putin spoke about the need to continue "the civilizing mission of the Russian nation on the Eurasian continent."[124] Leading figures in Putin's own party, United Russia, openly acknowledged the inspiration of Dugin in some of their policies. All of this still fell short of an unequivocal endorsement

---

119. Putin 2000b; Alison 2000.

120. Putin 2004.

121. Putin 2000b; Putin 2004. Humphrey 2002, 263.

122. Veselov 2003; "Eurasia Party" 2003; Laruelle n.d., 3.

123. Putin 2005b. Putin repeated these points on the significance of Kulikovo more recently, in a televised question-and-answer session. https://www.youtube.com/watch?v=y2OJK8U1pt4 (accessed 3/2/2015).

124. Putin 2005a.

of Eurasianism on Putin's part, however, and indeed when in 2006 a group of foreign specialists meeting with Putin in the Kremlin queried him specifically about his views of Eurasianism and Nazarbaev's project, he was plainly uncomfortable with the question and avoided a direct response. Nonetheless, the Eurasianist undertones of his rhetoric and the political signals that he was giving were such that observers began to ask if Putin was, indeed, a Eurasianist.[125]

This question received a more definitive answer only in October 2011, in the course of Putin's electoral campaign for a third presidential term. As part of the campaign, Putin published a series of papers setting out his political position and his priorities for a third term. The first of these dealt with foreign policy. In it, Putin made the dramatic announcement that the top priority of his administration would be to carry out a "new integration project for Eurasia."[126] Although Putin's partiality to the project had long been apparent, as we have seen, this enthusiastic and very public endorsement of it as his principal policy objective was seen as sensational and immediately attracted international attention.[127] Putin had finally come out of the closet, so to speak, as an avowed supporter of the reintegration of Soviet space in the form of a Eurasian Union. But what exactly did this vision involve? The perspective he laid out in October 2011 was not new at all, but rather conformed more or less faithfully to the sort of Eurasianism that Nazarbaev in Kazakhstan had been advocating for fifteen years. In theory at least, the Eurasian Union would be an association of sovereign nations assembled strictly as equal partners in order to pool resources and create common economic and social advantages. Like Nazarbaev, Putin noted the positive comparisons with the European Union; indeed, the overall tone of his statement was highly positive in regard to relations between Eurasia and the West in general. The European Union did not represent merely an external model for how a Eurasian Union might develop, but it could also be a partner in a sort of collaborative macrocontinental effort toward integrated economic development, to create what Putin described as a "harmonious commonwealth of economies from Lisbon to Vladivostok."[128]

In the subsequent policy statement "The National Question in Russia," dealing with domestic policies for the Russian Federation, Putin struck a very

---

125. Shlapentokh 2005; Schmidt 2005; "Putin, Shaimiev Hail Eurasianism" 2005. Also see Pryce 2013, 31; Shlapentokh 2007a; Goble 2009. The question about Eurasianism was posed by the author in the course of a discussion between the Russian president and members of the Valdai Discussion Club, Moscow, September 2006.

126. Putin 2011.

127. Clover, Gorst, and Buckley 2011; Socor 2011; "Putin's Grandest Dream" 2012; Saari 2011; Markedonov 2012; Halbach 2012; Pryce 2013.

128. Putin 2011.

different tone, now making generous use of Russocentric concepts and the ter-minology of Russian Eurasianism that we have been considering.[129] Russia is a "polycultural community" and "polyethnic civilization" organized around the "backbone" of the ethnic Russian (*russkii*) people and Russian culture. In the past, Russians always played a special role as a "state-forming people" and they continue to do so. Putin attributed to them the same quasi-superethnic ability to subsume other nationalities described by the "hyperethnos" con-cept noted earlier in this chapter, with the effect of loosely Russianizing the country's non-Russian peoples. Russia's "civilizational identity," he explained somewhat confusingly, "is founded on the preservation of the Russian (*russkii*) cultural *dominanta*, the bearers of which are not only ethnic Russians but any bearers of this identity regardless of nationality." His point, however, was clear enough. "The great mission" of the Russians was to "use their language, culture, and universal empathy (*vsemirnaia otzychivost'*), about which Feodor Dosto-evsky spoke, in order to bond Russian Armenians (*russkie armiane*), Russian Germans (*russkie nemtsy*), Russian Azeris (*russkie azery*), and Russian Tatars (*russkie tatary*) together into a state-civilization." (Putin did not mention "Rus-sian Jews" as part of this mix, but he might well have.) This special quality of the Russians, he maintained, has nothing to do with separatist ethno-Russian "nationalism," that is to say, the false aspiration to "complete" the process begun in 1991 and achieve "racial purity" (*rasovaia chistota*) in a monoethnic state. In fine Duginesque spirit, Putin roundly denounced such aspirations as a mani-festation of "the notorious [principal of] self-determination"—something the Russian people do not need to struggle for insofar as they achieved it long ago. Russian self-determination comes in the form of a "polyethnic culture [that is] strengthened by the vital essence (*iadro*) of Russian culture." Putin's character-ization of Russian civilization as "unity in diversity" was classically Eurasian, and the balance he drew between ethnos and *obshchnost'* once again faithfully echoed that of Dugin. "Any person who lives in our country should not forget about their faith and ethnic belonging. But *above all* they should be a citizen of Russia and take pride in it. No one has the right to place national and religious affinities above the laws of the state."[130]

Although Gumilev was not mentioned in either of these statements, Putin's demonstrative embrace of the Eurasian vision—or visions—served to enhance the importance with which he and his legacy were viewed. This was true par-ticularly after Putin's electoral victory in March 2012, when the project of a

---

129. Putin 2012c. All of the citations in this paragraph are from this document.
130. Putin 2012c (emphasis added).

Eurasian Union moved as promised to the center of government attention and activity. The new "pro-Eurasia" orientation needed new explanatory rationales, for the purposes of which Gumilev's now well-known work and his legendary persona continued to offer a unique value and appeal. The new veneration with which the government treated his legacy was manifested on the occasion of the centenary of his birth in September 2012. A special conference in Gumilev's honor was convened at MGIMO, the elite diplomatic school in Moscow associated with the Ministry of Foreign Affairs. The conference opened with an unveiling of a bust of Gumilev, intended for permanent display on a central corridor of the institute. The event was presided over by the speaker of the State Duma Sergei Evgen'evich Naryshkin, and a number of other Duma deputies and government officials gave presentations. In his comments, Naryshkin underscored the enduring relevance of Gumilev's teachings for the present, noting "the sagacity and gift of foresight of this great scholar and thinker, whose ideas about Eurasianism are being realized today." The "thousand-year history of Eurasia about which Gumilev wrote," he asserted, "is being consistently developed in the twenty-first century."[131] Vladimir Putin himself was not in attendance, but he sent his greetings to the meeting: "With his extraordinary talents as an analyst and the courage of a true investigator and trailblazer," he declared, Gumilev "made a unique impact on the development of national and global science. His rich creative legacy has gained widespread international recognition. His original ideas are inspiring active studies and discussions of the most important historical events even today."[132] At a second official event in the same month, a roundtable in Gumilev's honor was held in the Civic Chamber (*Obshchestvennaia Palata*) of the State Duma. The organizer was Maksim Nikolaevich Mishchenko, a youthful Duma deputy from Putin's party United Russia who declared that Gumilev's works should "serve as the foundation for the construction of the Eurasian Union." With his brilliant discoveries of the laws of ethnic development and interaction, Mishchenko maintained that Gumilev could become the same sort of "founding father" for the contemporary Eurasianist project "that Marx had been for socialism."[133] In the wake of these events, there could no longer be any question about the official endorsement of Gumilev's ideas. "Eurasianism," announced a popular Russian news website, "is the state ideology of Putin's Russia."[134]

---

131. Naryshkin 2012. On the political significance of this high-level official homage for Gumilev, see Clover 2012.

132. Putin 2012a.

133. "Vnedrit'" 2012.

134. Chuprov 2012.

Eurasianism, Gumilev, and Popular Culture

A fascinating indication of the pervasiveness of Eurasianist sentiments and themes in post-Soviet Russia is the fact that they have proliferated beyond formal politics—official or oppositionist—and entered the realm of popular culture. This tendency was apparent even before the collapse of the Soviet Union. In 1991, one of Russia's leading directors, Nikita Sergeevich Mikhalkov, released the critically acclaimed film *Urga*, which drew heavily on Eurasianist themes. The film tells the story of a Russian truck driver in the steppes of Mongolia who seeks assistance from the local population and forms a close personal bond with them. *Urga* earned considerable critical acclaim in Russia and in the United States was nominated for an Academy Award. Mikhalkov, an outspoken conservative nationalist, is highly sympathetic to the Eurasianist perspective.[135] He knew Gumilev personally, and on the occasion of what would have been the latter's ninetieth birthday in 2002 organized a memorial celebration in his honor at the Russian Cultural Foundation. "I had the pleasure of meeting Lev Nikolaevich on several occasions, and I confess, after these meetings I was deeply struck because I had not been prepared to encounter such a powerful personality; I would say, the last poet of history. . . . It is thanks to Gumilev that we have the unique opportunity to understand that Russia is the only 'institution' on earth that is a genuine bridge between Europe and Asia."[136] In recent years Eurasianist themes have become commonplace in Russian cinema, although unlike *Urga* these are now generally developed via historical storylines. The epic film *Nomad* by Sergei Vladimirovich Bodrov (2005) tells the story of the Kazakh peoples in the eighteenth century. A second film of Bodrov's, *Mongol* (2007), and *The Secret of Chingis Khan* by the Yakut director Andrei Savvich Borisov (2009), both deal with the life of the great Mongolian empire-builder.[137] Bodrov stressed the debt that his project owed to Gumilev, not only for his historical reconstructions but also for the concept of *passionarnost'*, which inspired his representation of the great warrior.[138]

Eurasianism has also proven appealing for the world of Russian art. In the 1990s, the artist Timur Petrovich Novikov (1958–2002) was influenced by Gumilev's Eurasianist vision and for some time was associated with Aleksandr Dugin.[139] The work of Aleksei Iure'vich Beliaev-Gintovt and Andrei Molodkin, who style themselves as an "imperial avant-garde" with an unconcealed fascination for the

---

135. Mikhalkov 1991; Mikhalkov 1993.

136. Faustova 2002.

137. Borisov served as Minister for Culture and Spiritual Development in the Sakha-Yakut Republic from 1990 to 2014. His film is based on the best-selling novel by the Yakut writer Nikolai Alekseevich Luginov, whose connections to Gumilev are discussed below, 298–300.

138. "V chem sila, brat?" 2006; "Vtoroe nashestvie" 2007.

139. Stodolsky 2009.

grandeur of the Soviet past and even for Stalin's mystique, is similarly influenced by Gumilev. A recipient of the prestigious Kandinskii prize whose work has been exhibited in leading Russian art galleries and the state Duma, Beliaev-Gintovt is a particular admirer of Gumilev and produced a much-praised portrait of him in 2011.[140] The theme of Eurasianism has also been taken up in post-Soviet belles lettres. The cycle of novels *The Eurasian Symphony* by the fictional author Khol'm Van Zaichik—described as a "Euro-Chinese" humanist—are infused with Gumilevian ideas and images. They are set in a fantasyland created as a result of a union between the ancient Russians and the Mongol Golden Horde. This country is called *Ordus'*—a conflation of the words *orda* or "horde" and *Rus'*—and the storylines play heavily on themes of symbiosis and complementarity.[141] *The Eurasian Symphony* series was highly popular with readers and won numerous literary prizes. In 2009, the most ambitious Eurasianist literary project yet was launched, the name of which—*Etnogenez*—unmistakably points to a Gumilevian connection. Over fifty novels are projected, in some of which Gumilev himself figures as a heroic character, together with an invented son Andrei, a granddaughter Marusia, and numerous other descendants (the real Gumilev did not have any children). The series features such trademark Gumilevian tropes as *passionarnost'* and the protection of the Russian gene pool against foreign attempts to take advantage of its superior qualities. The *Etnogenez* project is the brainchild of the media specialist and former Duma deputy for Putin's United Russia Party Konstantin Igorevich Rykov, and through him has connections to the Kremlin. Rykov worked in the presidential administration of Aleksandr Medved'ev, and currently collaborates with, among others, the Minister of Culture Vladimir Rostislavovich Medinskii, who is himself a devotee of Gumilev.[142]

A particularly significant example of the influence of Gumilevian Eurasianism on popular culture can be seen in the genre of "alternative history" (also called "quasi-," "pseudo-," or "folk history"), which has flourished since the collapse of the Soviet Union. Conventional academic historians tend understandably to be quite critical of Gumilev's work, emphasizing the element of "unbridled fantasy" in it that undermines any pretensions to serious scholarship.[143] Gumilev's

---

140. "Portret L'va Gumileva rabota Alekseia Gintovta" 2011.

141. Van Zaichik 2003. Van Zaichik is the pseudonym of Viacheslav Mikhailovich Rybakov and Igor' Aleksandrovich Alimov, both of whom are senior scholars of Oriental studies in Moscow. For Gumilev's influence on the project, see Grmesov 2001.

142. Bassin and Kotkina Forthcoming; Klubkov 2013.

143. Khazanov 2002, 16–17. For criticism of Gumilev from professional historians, see Lur'e 1990, 129–31; Lur'e 1997, 125, 93–97; D'iakonov 1992; Eidel'man 1989, 31–32; Poluboiarinova 1997, 54–55, 57; Shnirel'man and Panarin 2000, 9, 20, 26, 32; Nikitin 2001, 412–13, 419; Khrustalev 2004, 69n, 227; Darkevich 1994, 50. For positive evaluations of Gumilev from Russian academic historians, however, see Krivosheev 2003, 89, 114–18, 130–31, 137–38; Trepavlov 2010.

reception by alternative history, by contrast, paints a very different picture. As its name suggests, alternative history challenges the canons of conventional history through the depiction of novel historical scenarios and interpretations that—so it is claimed—reveal a deeper reality about the past that has been neglected or even actively concealed by standard accounts, and that has direct implications for the present day. To be sure, alternative history is an international phenomenon, but it is particularly pervasive and popular in post-Soviet Russia.[144] In a sense, it developed directly out of Soviet historiography, where historical narratives were regularly rewritten in accordance with changes in the official political line.[145] Gumilev's work has been foundational for establishing the paradigm for this post-Soviet genre, in a number of different respects. His theories about the *Chernaia Legenda* or the chimera of Khazaria were themselves early examples of alternative history—if not nearly as grandiose or outrageous as those of later practitioners. Methodologically, moreover, Gumilev's work masterfully developed an important element of the alternative history paradigm, namely, the claim to a rigorous positivism on the basis of concepts and principles imported from the natural sciences into historical research. In his own day, as we have seen, Gumilev stimulated the historical imaginations of Balashov and Kozhinov. After 1992, his work served as a "ready-made bridge" enabling alternative historians "to cross the murky waters that separated conventional [historical] revisionism and pseudo-history."[146]

The most successful practitioner of alternative history is Anatolii Timofeevich Fomenko, with his so-called *Novaia Khronologiia* or "new chronology." A mathematician of international renown, Fomenko devised a new scheme of world history using statistical formulas to readjust the timescale of virtually all major historical events. Fomenko's books are extraordinarily popular and since the 1990s hundreds of thousands of copies have been sold—more even than Gumilev's own works.[147] Fomenko refers to Gumilev frequently throughout his analyses of Russian history. Although he disagrees with the latter on a number of significant issues (for example, he claims that the Khazars were ethnic Slavs), Gumilev's influence is readily apparent. Fomenko adopts Gumilev's notion of a fundamental Turko-Slavic symbiosis as the foundation of Russian history. This symbiosis produced a Russian-dominated superethnos that was ethnically and culturally diverse but galvanized by the ever-present threat of Western aggression. Like Gumilev, Fomenko denies there had ever been a Mongol conquest that

---

144. Sheiko 2009; Laruelle 2012; Volodikhin 1999.
145. Laruelle 2012, 566–67; Koreniako 2000, 44–45, 48–49.
146. Sheiko 2009, 87–88 (quote); Koreniako 2000, 39, 43.
147. Laruelle 2012, 575–79.

imposed a "yoke" on ancient Russia, claiming this to be a myth invented by the Romanov dynasty.[148] The importance of Gumilev for the alternative history project is advertised yet more prominently in the book series *The Secret of Lev Gumilev* (*Taina L'va Gumileva*), published by the Algoritm press in Moscow. Works in this series are focused on steppe history and Russian-nomad relations, and include reprints of Gumilev and Georgii Vernadskii, along with contemporary popular histories. The Gumilevian inspiration behind these latter works may be seen in an early volume, *Batyi: A Russian Tsar*, by Konstantin Aleksandrovich Penzev.[149] Like Fomenko, Penzev's contributions to the series all emphasize the themes of Slavic-Tatar cooperation and anti-Westernism, and at the end of one of them Penzev appended a brief exposition of Gumilev's theory of ethnogenetic cycles.[150]

---

148. Sheiko 2009, 70–71, 163, 155, 157, 173, 188.
149. Penzev 2007a.
150. Penzev 2006; also see Penzev 2007b.

BIOPOLITICS AND THE UBIQUITY OF ETHNICITY

Russia's Ethnic Renaissance

The so-called ethnic renaissance that developed during perestroika did not dissipate after 1991, but rather accelerated and intensified.[1] Although the essentialism of Soviet ethnos theory was sharply criticized in the 1990s by some professional ethnographers who sympathized with the constructivist approaches that had gained acceptance internationally, this was not the case among many of their colleagues or lay audiences. On the contrary, for many ethnicity seemed to be ever more objective and important—an all-subsuming ontological "category of existence" (*poriadok sushchestvovaniia*) that affected and even determined all other aspects of individual and collective being.[2] Today, the ethnos is valorized as the essential unit of social organization, more fundamental than the individual, family, or political state. This means, among other things, that the assumed "objective" realities of ethnic existence are no longer the exclusive concern of ethnographic or ethnological science, but serve instead as a sort of metaprism through which all aspects of collective life must be refracted: history becomes ethno-history, politics become ethno-politics, psychology is ethnopsychology, religious studies are ethno-religious studies, and so on.[3] Ethnos has

---

1. Schindler 1991, 68; Treisman 1997.
2. Sokolovski n.d., 5–6; Anderson and Arzyutov 2012; Zhade 2006, 117.
3. Makarikhina 2009, 147.

even become an object of formal philosophical inquiry.[4] The biologism that was so contentious in the Soviet period, moreover, is today entirely commonplace. Ethnies are widely and uncontroversially seen as "biosocial organisms" or "biological species"; indeed, no less an authority than a minister for nationalities in the Yeltsin government declared that ethnicity represents "biological belonging" (*biologicheskaia prenadlezhnost'*).[5] Rather than any identification with a state or nation, it is now the naturalness of the ethnic group that is understood as the factor insuring continuity across its life history.[6] Ethnies are animated by an inner "vital force" or "vital instinct" and can be diagnosed as healthy or ill in terms of the potency of this factor.[7] These new convictions about the biological status of ethnicity are expressed in evocative biopolitical narratives about Russia's "biological victimization" and the threats to its "biological vitality."[8]

In view of this heavily naturalist understanding of ethnos and ethnogenesis, the ascendance of Gumilev's theories to become a "dominant paradigm" in contemporary Russia can be readily appreciated.[9] Indeed, Gumilev's significance for post-Soviet discourses about ethnicity is greater even than his influence on neo-Eurasianism considered in the previous chapter. Gumilev may have made important contributions to the development of the Eurasianist canon, but he is by no means the only source of Eurasianist ideas and perspectives available to the post-Soviet public. In regard to a naturalistic view of ethnies as biological or sociobiological organisms, by contrast, Gumilev is much more on his own. Out of all the progenitors of Soviet ethnos theory (which incidentally began to enjoy a certain renaissance in its own right after 2000), it was he who developed this perspective most comprehensively.[10] To be sure, a variety of different naturalistic-organismic perspectives have been proposed in the years since the collapse of the Soviet Union, but none of them carry anything approaching the authority and legitimacy of Gumilev's theory. "If there is any new tendency in regard to the Soviet epoch," writes Elena Filippova, "it is above all the proliferation of the biological conceptions [about ethnies] inspired by Gumilev."[11] The specialized lexicon he developed

---

4. Rybakov 2001a; Anderson and Arzyutov 2012.

5. Tishkov 1997, 7–10; Sokolovski n.d., 6–7; Butenko and Kolesnichenko 1996, 96; Filippov 2010, 181–82.

6. Semilet 2004, 6, 54; cited in Oushakine 2007, 188–89; Humphrey 2002, 270.

7. Solovei 2006; Ushakin 2005. On "sick" and "healthy" ethnies, see Iskakov, Iskakov, and Gavrilov 2007.

8. These points are developed in Oushakine 2009.

9. Tishkov 1997, 2; Drobizheva 2001, 169; Zdravomyslov 1996, 7.

10. Zarinov 2002; Rybakov 2001b. Both single out Gumilev's naturalism for special comment. Also see Mutschler 2011, 16–17.

11. Filippova 2010, 53 (quote); Butenko and Kolesnichenko 1996, 96; Zhade 2006, 117; Savchenko and Smagin 2006.

to describe the spectrum of ethnic phenomena—*passionarnost'*, "complementarity," "symbiosis," "superethnos," "chimera," "antisystem," *nadlom*, "ecological niche," "nurturing landscape," and so on—has been widely adopted; indeed, it is not too much to say that in Russia there simply is no other vocabulary suitable for these purposes.[12] The fact that all of these evocative terms remain conceptually vague and malleable—despite Gumilev's own belief that he had described them with scientific rigor—only serves to enhance their usefulness and appeal.

The authority of Gumilev's teachings is apparent in the growth of the field devoted exclusively to the study of ethnies, namely, *etnologiia* or ethnology.[13] Although ethnology shares many of the same concerns and interests as ethnography, it differs in its inclination to essentialize ethnicity and view ethnic groupings as real-existing entities with immutable characteristics and a "unique individuality" or ethno-national character—precisely the spirit of Gumilev's own perspective. "In contrast to communities that are consciously created by people in the process of their cultural development, ethnies arise historically and are independent of the volition or consciousness of the people who form them. . . . All of the life processes connected with the existential needs of all of its members take place within the framework of each one of these."[14] Gumilev's leading role in discovering "the mechanism of the formation and development of ethnies" is widely acknowledged across much of the literature on the subject. Entire chapters of ethnological texts are devoted exclusively to a discussion of his theories, and the impact of his naturalist and biological vision of ethnicity is apparent throughout.[15] The ethnos is conceived as a "part of the bio-organic world of the planet" and ethnogenesis itself is described as a "natural process of the biosphere."[16] All of the important characteristics of ethnicity, moreover—identity, ethnic consciousness, and solidarity—can be understood "in terms of unconditional biological laws."[17] Gumilev's scheme of ethnogenetic phases, his model of super- and subethnic hierarchies, and concepts such as "positive and negative ethnic complementarity" are all discussed at great length.[18]

---

12. Ushakin 2005, 241–43; Mamaladze 1992, 7; Shnirel'man 2005a.

13. Filippova 2010.

14. Sadokhin 2004, 77.

15. Sadokhin 2004, 17 (quote), 80, 136–42; Bochkarev 2008, 13, 92–105, 161–67; Konstantinova 2005a, 36–38; Sadokhin 2002, 39ff., 199. The Russian Wikipedia entry on ethnology credits Gumilev for having made "the most significant contribution" to the field (http://ru.wikipedia.org/wiki/Этнология). For one example of an applied Gumilevian study of ethnogenesis and ethno-national character, see Dunichev 2001.

16. Sadokhin 2004, 136; Zarinov 2002, 8.

17. Sadokhin 2004, 303, 98; Sadokhin 2002, 198; Bochkarev 2008, 166; Konstantinova 2005a, 36–38; Abdulatipov 2004, 77–80.

18. Sadokhin 2002, 43, 64, 141, 154–56; Petrov 2002.

A clear indication of the proliferation of Gumilev's conceptual arsenal can be seen in the quite remarkable popularity of the term *passionarnost'*, which is now broadly accepted as a legitimate scientific concept describing a real-existing psychological and physiological feature.[19] In 2007, the Russian Academy of Natural Sciences sponsored a major interdisciplinary conference on "Passionary Energy and Ethnos in the Development of Civilization." The conference organizers emphasized the broad practical relevance of the *passionarnost'* concept, ambitiously claiming that it can be used "to predict the activity of large and small social groups, to reveal the tendencies of such social phenomena as political leadership, extremism, global and local conflicts, and to develop practical recommendations for the realization of geopolitical goals."[20] The *passionarnost'* concept has also been taken up in research across a range of different disciplines. In psychology, for example, it is treated as a key conceptual tool both for understanding the psychological dynamics of entire ethnies—so-called ethno-*passionarnost'*[21]—and for the analysis of the personalities and psychological complexes of individuals.[22] In the field of child psychology, one specialist has identified a special "passionary personality type" for a certain category of children.[23]

In the natural sciences, the relevance of *passionarnost'* for biology, genetics, cytology, energetics, and even chemistry has also been actively explored.[24] One astronomer studied the historical intervals of passionary eruptions as identified by Gumilev and concluded that their periodicity is related to the perihelion of the planet Pluto's orbit around the sun.[25] An entire subfield of research has developed devoted to the quantitative modeling of Gumilevian ethnogenesis and the mathematical description of passionary levels. At the Center for Mathematical Modeling at Omsk State University in western Siberia, a dedicated research team has devoted years to developing algorithmic models and differential equations to describe the "dynamics of ethnic systems," "distribution of ethnic fields," and fluctuations in "passionary tension," all based explicitly on Gumilev's theories.[26]

---

19. Frumkin 2008. Indeed, even Western scholars interested in the study of the history of emotions in Russia have picked up on the term. Plamper 2009, 232.

20. "Passionarnaia energiia i etnos v razvitoi tsivilitsii," 2007.

21. Iskakov, Iskakov, and Gavrilov 2007; Krylov and Kovalenko 1993, 78; Michurin 1992.

22. Bogdanov 2001; Kovalenko 1999. Also see the entries on *passionarnost'* in Krys'ko 1999; Zhmurov 2012.

23. Zimina 2007; Krylov and Kovalenko 1993, 79.

24. Vakhtin 2002; Gromov 2012; Maklakov 1996; Timashev n.d.

25. Butusov and Michurin 1995.

26. Guts, Korobitsyn, Pautova, and Frolova 2000, 108–24; Korobitsyn 2000; Korobitsyn and Frolova 2006; Krushel' and Surgutanov n.d. Interestingly and indicatively, the head of this team, the mathematician and computer scientist Aleksandr Konstantinovich Guts, has also written several works of alternative history. Guts 1999; Guts 2000; Sheiko 2009, 28–29; Laruelle 2012, 574.

The industrious researchers at Omsk have designed a software package, *ETNOS*, that simulates ethnic solidarity, interethnic interaction, and the territorial distribution of ethnic energy and claims to be able to predict points of ethnic conflict, declines in passionary levels, and so on.[27] One particularly imaginative attempt at the precise scientific quantification of *passionarnost'* proposed that levels of passionary tension be measured in standard energy units that could be called—in honor of their discoverer—*gumils* (plus *megagumils* and *gigagumils*).[28] The *passionarnost'* concept has also made its way into marketing and management studies.[29]

Passionarnost' has proven no less popular for the purposes of public political discourse. In his 2012 address to Russia's Federal Assembly, for example, Vladimir Putin spoke about the challenges of the burgeoning competition among the nations of the world. "Who leaps ahead, and who remains an outsider and inevitably loses their independence, will depend not only on economic potential but above all on the will of each nation, on its internal energy, as Lev Gumilev maintained, on its *passionarnost'*, its capability to move forward and to adapt."[30] Here Putin applies the term to an entire nation, although it is more commonly used in reference to the charismatic qualities of individual leaders and activists.[31] Gennadii Ziuganov, for example, greeted the late Venezuelan president Hugo Chavez as a "handsome, powerful and passionary leader."[32] The former president of Kyrgyzstan Askar Akaevich Akaev, who as a student in Leningrad heard Gumilev lecture and was captivated by his theories of ethnogenesis, wrote at length about *passionarnost'* and the "role of the Passionary Personality," whose chief characteristic is an "overwhelming Political Will."[33] Indeed, the term has become so colloquial that its original associations with other aspects of Gumilev's thinking can be lost. Thus Aleksandr Evseevich Khinshtein, a Duma deputy from Putin's United Russia Party who is Jewish, is described on a Jewish affairs website as a "passionary Jew"—an attribution that Gumilev intended to be menacing and odious but that Khinshtein today finds highly flattering. "I would like to think that I am also a passionary person," he explains. "All Jews are basically passionary people. If this were not the case, they could not have existed for so

---

27. Guts, Korobitsyn, Pautova, and Frolova 1998; Korobitsin and Frolova 2002.
28. Aizatullin 1999.
29. Nikishkin 2005; Nikishkin 2008; Zhuralev and Ladyzhets 2003.
30. Putin 2012b. For a mocking comment on Putin's use of the term *passionarnost'*, see Akopian 2012.
31. Shapkina 2007, 8.
32. "G. A. Ziuganov pozdravil Prezidenta Venesuely Ugo Chavesa . . ." 2009, http://kprf.ru/international/63793.html (accessed 21/2/2014).
33. Akaev 2011b: 24 (quote); Gullette 2008, 261, 267, 269–70.

long in a hostile environment."[34] And if Gumilev's terminology has been adopted by these representatives of Russia's political establishment, it is no less appealing for its sworn enemies. This can be seen vividly in the example of Aleksandr Aleksandrovich Tikhomirov (1982–2010), a Russian-Buriat convert to Islam who under the *nomme de guerre* Said abu Saad al'-Buriati became an ideologue for the so-called Caucasus Emirate in its struggle to establish an independent Sharia state. Said was inspired by Gumilev's notion of *passionarnost'*, which he incorporated into his own doctrine of *istishkhad*, or religious self-sacrifice. Gumilev's highly negative attitude toward Islam, of which he was fully aware, did nothing to diminish the appeal of the term for him. "*Istishkhad* is an eruption of *passionarnost'* ... which in our case will initiate the creation of the Caucasus Emirate."[35]

Ethno-Territoriality

A more specific indication of the influence of Gumilevian perspectives on the nature of ethnicity is the new interest in the existential dynamics between ethnos and territory and the emplacement of ethnies in particular geographical regions. The notion of a link between ethnicity and territory was not exclusive to Gumilev, of course, but the discussion of the topic in post-Soviet ethnological textbooks is often framed quite clearly in Gumilev's terms and concepts. Thus the homeland of a given ethnic group is described as its "containing" (*vmeshchaiushii*) or "nurturing landscape," its "ecological niche," or even its native *mestorazvitie*.[36] The functional significance of this relationship, moreover, is described in Gumilevian terms as a matter of ethnogenetic adaptation to the influence of external environmental conditions. The natural milieu is understood not only to influence the fate of ethnies across history but also to shape fundamental aspects of their ethno-national character. The behavioral stereotype of the ethnos "forms in the process of adaptation to the external natural environment," which defines its "unique character."[37] This involves not only customs and habits, but its psychological profile and *mentalité* as well.[38]

One line of research focuses exclusively on ethno-territoriality as *the* vital nexus for defining ethnic being. This perspective involves a highly complex

---

34. Bakulina 2011. For another example of Jewish *passionarnost'*, see Kramer n.d.

35. Saad 2009; Hahn 2009. Said was assassinated by Russian special forces in 2010.

36. Konstantinova 2005a, 30n. (quote), 38–39; Sadokhin 2002, 199–200; Oushakine 2007, 187–88.

37. Sadokhin 2002, 138 (quote); Konstantinova 2005b, 41.

38. Sadokhin 2004, 261–62.

description and analysis of the interconnections between ethnic unit and environment, with an emphasis on "the fundamental role played by the geographical factor in the origins of ethnies, in ethnic migrations, and in the history of ethnic development overall."[39] The degree to which the ethnos-environment nexus is prioritized and absolutized as the fundamental parameter of ethnicity is apparent in the concept of *etnicheskoe prostranstvo*, or ethnic space, developed into a veritable philosophical system in the work of Galina Petrovna Kibasova.[40] Building explicitly on Gumilevian foundations, Kibasova sets out to remove ethnic history from its "subordination" to social history, and consequently "to define its [autonomous] role and place in the macro-evolutionary process." The ethnos is an entirely "objective reality" of contemporary life, a natural organism and "biological subspecies of a single biological species [i.e., humankind], through which it secures its adaptation to concrete environmental conditions that provide the opportunity to support fertility, population size, and life spans." Each ethno-biological entity possesses its own specific ethnic space, which provides a dual character. On the one hand it is the same material "containing landscape" and "ecological niche" that Gumilev described. At the same time, however, it now represents rather more than this: a discrete ontological "order of existence" (*poriadok sushchestvovaniia*) that is the primary and necessary foundation of all ethnic life.[41]

A different line of research in ethno-territoriality is ethno-ecology, which developed in the 1980s as a sub-field within Soviet ethnography.[42] Generally speaking, ethno-ecology studies the ways in which ethnic groups are embedded in and interact with the natural landscapes and ecosystems in which they live, in terms of their material cultures but also in terms of their ethnic psychologies and perceptions of the environment.[43] The belief in the integration of ethnos and landscape into a single functional system is fundamental, and thus Gumilev—who better than anyone else "demonstrated the interdependence of the developmental processes of ethnies and their respective natural environments"—is recognized as an inspirational figure.[44] This sense of appreciation is enhanced by the fact that much ethno-ecological research is focused on the *malye narody* of the Russian north and east, about whom Gumilev himself wrote with special

---

39. Fedorova 2006.
40. Kibasova 2003. For different treatments of the term, see Sikevich 1999; Zhade 2006, 114–15.
41. Kibasova 2004, 7, 23, 49, 36, 22, 15.
42. One of ethno-ecology's early proponents, ironically enough, was Gumilev's bitter critic Viktor Kozlov. Kozlov 1983; Kozlov and Iamskov 1989; Kozlov 1994. For a strong appreciation of Gumilev's contribution to the field from one of Kozlov's coauthors, see Iamskov 2012.
43. Sadokhin 2002, 201.
44. Morokhin 1997, 6 (quote); Korotaev 1998; Gladkii 2006; Bruno 2007, 642.

interest and concern.[45] There are, however, significant departures from the letter of Gumilev's teachings. In accordance with his own model of the ethnogenetic cycle, Gumilev identified the *malye narody* as "vestiges," lingering in the final stage of their ethnic existence and destined inevitably to perish. "Not a single ethnos can escape this fate (*ot etogo ni odnomu etnosu ne uiti*)."[46] Ethno-ecology, by contrast, understands the integration of the ethnos into the natural environment in precisely the opposite way, as evidence of its objective "ethno-ecological balance (*ravnovesie*)," which provides for resilience, "stability," and long-term sustainability.[47]

A roughly similar ethno-ecological approach informs research in "ethnic geography," which has taken shape as subdiscipline of sorts within human geography.[48] This perspective, developed largely through the efforts of Gumilev's former students and disciples, takes his ethnogenetic paradigm as its point of departure and aims to refine the conceptual apparatus he developed through specific case studies of ethnogenetic development and ethnic interaction across the former Soviet Union.[49] Here again, interest focuses on the indigenous peoples of the Russian north and east who belonged to Gumilev's circumpolar superethnos. These were Gumilev's "vestiges"—"relict" ethnies in the final stages of their ethnogenetic cycle—that had largely exhausted their supply of *passionarnost'* and existed in a state of homeostatic adaptation within their native ecological niches. As with ethno-ecology, however, research in ethnic geography views homeostasis not as the precursor to inevitable ethnic collapse but rather as a sort of "sustainable" arrangement that—if respected and treated properly—is potentially open-ended.[50] Ethnic geography does, however, concur with Gumilev's emphasis on the passivity and fragility of these groups—characteristics which are linked directly to their position in the ethnogenetic cycle. "Homeostatic ethnies consist of people who are conservative and nonenterprising, although they are joyful and marvelously adapted in their natural native landscapes. Their inner energy or *passionarnost'* suffices only to preserve their traditional ways of life, which they inherited from older generations. The ethnos's resilience (*rezistentnost'*) is in constant decline, and it can very easily fall victim to its more passionary

---

45. A collection of highly sophisticated ethnographic studies by researchers from the Museum of Anthropology and Ethnography in St. Petersburg is dedicated to the "bright (*svetlaia*) memory" of Gumilev. Pavlinskaia 2001.

46. Gumilev and Okladnikov 1982.

47. Gladkii 2006.

48. Ivanov 1998; Ivanov 2005; Beliakov 2012a, 699, 702.

49. Khrushchev 2007, 5; Ivanov and Khrushchev 1998.

50. Ivanov, Gromova, and Khrushchev 1999, 60–61; Ivanov and Khrushchev 1998, 64; Khrushchev 2007, 8.

neighbors."[51] Ethnic geography is critical of the "state paternalism" of the USSR, which sought to align these groups forcibly with its own vision of modernity through intrusive policies of sedentarization and the establishment of *internaty* or boarding schools where indigenous children were separated from their parents and their traditional ways of life and routinized in the Soviet educational system. Ethnic geography describes the resulting alienation of the *malye narody* from their own native landscapes using its own Gumilevian neologism "disadaptation" (*desadptatsiia*), which involves the "lowering of the passionary level and the growth of subpassionaries in the ethnic population." In the present day, this condition causes social problems such as alcoholism and crime in these groups and threatens to bring about their "ethnic extinction."[52]

When asked in 1990 about how the situation of the *malye narody* could be improved, Gumilev replied: "I support the creation of reservations (*rezervatsii*). If the small nationalities of the north are left as they are, then scoundrels—of whom there quite a few in Siberia—will treat them badly. It is necessary that the government intervenes on their behalf. . . . Special protective zones should be created for them, where the nonindigenous population is permitted to enter only with passes."[53] This solution is not endorsed by his acolytes, who call instead for the authorities in the Russian Federation to respect the natural traditionalism of these groups and help them pursue their ancient practices without imposing upon them the technological paraphernalia of modern society. The difference between the traditionalist *malye narody* and the rest of modernized Russian society is natural and appropriate, they imply, and should not be represented as primitiveness or savagery contra development and progress.[54] In all events, the Gumilevian injunction not to "try to make them look like us" must be respected, and the northern environments that are their home should be protected.[55] But Gumilev's disciples also suggest that the passionary deficit among the *malye narody* could be ameliorated by the "naturally occurring interbreeding (*metisatsiia*)" that is now taking place among the northern peoples, making it possible for certain external groups to act as "donors (*donory*) of *passionarnost'*" that might help to revive the youthfulness (*omolozhenie*) of the relict ethnies.[56]

---

51. Ivanov, Gromova, and Khrushchev, 1999, 72 (quote), 62–64; Khrushchev 2007, 8.

52. Ivanov, Gromova, and Khrushchev, 1999, 87 (quote), 53, 63, 66, 72; Ivanov and Khrushchev 1998.

53. Gumilev 1990b. He was not consistent on the point, however, and elsewhere briskly dismissed the suggestion of reservations in the Soviet Union. Gumilev 1989a; Gumilev and Okladnikov 1982.

54. Ivanov and Khrushchev 1998.

55. Khrushchev 2007, 14–15; Ivanov, Gromova, and Khrushchev 1999, 63.

56. Ivanov and Khrushchev 1998. The authors of this essay include Yakuts as potential passionary donors. According to Gumilev, however, the latter were themselves a relict ethnos, characterized like all other *malye narody* not by a passionary surplus but rather a deficit. Ivanov, Gromova, and Khrushchev 1999, 63. Unsurprisingly, Gumilev's views on the imminent exhaustion of Yakut *passionarnost'* was an important issue in the reception of his theories in Yakutia (see below, 297–305).

Ethnos and International Relations

Naturalist views of ethnicity have also had a significant influence on post-Soviet thinking about politics and international relations.[57] In general, ethnic identification and attributes are appreciated as one of the important factors affecting how states are organized, how they behave, and how they interact.[58] The significance of ethnicity can, however, be amplified beyond this, to the extent that ethnos supersedes and replaces the state altogether as the essential subject of political analysis and the "primary basis (*nachalo*) of all systems of social relations, including international political relations."[59] Here again, Gumilev's teachings provide a special source of inspiration, as exemplified rather elaborately by the burgeoning field of *etnogeopolitika* or ethno-geopolitics.[60] Ethno-geopolitics views ethnicity in all of its various manifestations as the most fundamental force driving political life in the twenty-first century. Its analysis is based on the category of ethnic space, which represents the "most important invariable geopolitical condition (*invariant*)" for political relations at all geographical levels.[61] Gumilev's foundational influence on this new field is acknowledged and unquestioned, and his old disciple Iurii Borodai developed some of the early formulations of the ethno-geopolitical perspective.[62]

In its analysis of international politics, ethno-geopolitics regards the fundamental macrounits of global power as Gumilevian superethnies. As a generic category, "superethnos" is flexible: it can be projected on a Cold War model of a world bifurcated between two global superpowers, but it can also be applied to post–Cold War models of multiple power centers, variously designated as civilizations, global regions, or simply great powers. The notion of "civilization" is particularly conspicuous in this regard. In a sense, the deployment of Gumilev's "superethnos" concept represents the Russian ethno-geopolitical response to Samuel Huntington, and the affinities between Gumilev and Huntington are clearly recognized.[63] But it is important to note that "superethnos" is a much more elastic concept than Huntington's "civilization." While "the West," for example, may be treated as a single superethnic entity synonymous with Huntington's "Western civilization," it is alternatively possible to characterize the United States as a

57. Tsygankov and Tsygankov 2005, 280–300; Mukharyamov 2004.
58. Troitskii 2003; Abdulatipov 2004; Shabaev and Sadokhin 2005.
59. Tsygankov and Tsygankov 2005, 282.
60. For a fuller consideration, see Bassin 2009a.
61. Smirnov 1998 (quote); Mukharyamov 2004, 98.
62. Borodai 1994; Borodai 1995; Mukharyamov 2004, 98–99.
63. Smirnov 1998; Tsygankov and Tsygankov 1999. For a discussion of the geopolitics of Huntington's "clash of civilizations," see Bassin 2007.

self-contained superethnos in its own right, distinct from Europe and everyone else. In regard to Russia, the superethnos designation provides for a subtle but highly significant imprecision regarding its exact political-geographical contours. Ethno-geopoliticians can chose to describe the Russian (*rossiiskii*) superethnos either in its contemporary post-Soviet expression as the Russian Federation or alternatively as the more traditional—and decidedly grander—political space of the Russian empire and the USSR.

The identification of the principal power units of global politics as Gumilevian superethnies enables ethno-geopolitics to base its analyses on the same natural laws that control ethnogenesis and the patterns of interethnic relations. The first of these is the fact that superethnies, like ethnies, move through an ethnogenetic life cycle of development, maturity, decline, and ultimate collapse. As we have seen, different phases in this cycle are characterized by different levels of dynamism and vitality, and thus produce different sorts of activity. Insofar as an important expression of this activity is precisely the geopolitical ambitions of the superethnic entity and its behavior on the global arena, tracking its progression through the ethnogenetic cycle becomes a fundamental means for establishing the political dynamics of global relations. In this spirit, ethnogenesis can be treated "as a sort of matrix of the geopolitical aspirations (*ustremleniia*) of various states and political forces. Changes in these geopolitical aspirations correlate to phases of ethnogenesis, and can be observed in the historical record and projected as scenarios for future developments."[64] This dynamic immediately points to one significant insight in regard to the geopolitical potential of Russia's most important global competitor, namely, the West. Western civilization is currently going through a relatively advanced phase of ethnogenesis, meaning that it has ever less ethnogenetic energy and will necessarily become ever less dynamic. For this reason, in future the global "center of geopolitical ambitions (*pritiazaniia*) will inevitably shift to younger ethnies" and superethnies, prominent among them Russia.[65]

In the final analysis, however, relations among superethnies are governed by the degree and quality of their mutual complementarity.[66] The vital task of the ethno-geopolitician, therefore, is to determine whether the complementarity between two entities is negative or positive, in order to facilitate the choice of possible military-political allies.[67] Another important factor is the *passionarnost'* of the respective superethnos, the intensity of which varies as it moves through

---

64. Kefeli n.d.
65. Ibid.
66. Dergachev 2000, 84; Nartov 2003, 137.
67. Titenko 2005.

its ethnogenetic cycle. Early phases of ethnogenesis are always associated with high levels of passionary energy, for which reason the superethnies involved are more active and inclined to undertake territorial expansion (*nabukhanie*: literally, "swelling" or "bloating").[68] Through a comparative analysis of ethnogenetic progression and the associated dissipation of passionary energy, the ethnogeopolitician can provide political leaders with "timely warnings" about possible political and military "collisions" between superethnies.[69]

However preposterous these ethno-geopolitical postulates inspired by Gumilev may seem, their appeal at upper levels of policy analysis would appear to be very real. An indication of this can be seen in the work of Aleksandr Ivanovich Vladimirov, a retired army officer and president of the think tank Collegium of Military Experts who has advised the Putin administration on questions of military reform and national security. His treatise *The Conceptual Foundations of Russia's National Strategy* was formally sponsored by the Russian Academy of Sciences. Vladimirov explains his entire project as "the application of the teachings of our great compatriot L. N. Gumilev about ethnogenesis to an analysis of the leading [global] geopolitical players and to the search for the imperatives behind Russia's national strategy in the twenty-first century." Gumilevian superethnies are the "most fundamental subjects of geopolitical interaction" in global politics, and contemporary Russia finds itself confronted by four such superethnic formations: Europe, the United States, China, and Islam. Relations between these entities are conditioned by differences in their position in the ethnogenetic cycle, most significantly by the fact that the United States is the youngest of these superethnies and thus retains the highest level of passionary energy. At the same time, the nature of superethnic interaction is also determined by the quality of the complementarity between the entities, that is, whether it is positive or negative. Russia's relations with all four of its superethnic competitors fall into the latter category, although to different degrees. Negative complementarity, as Gumilev taught, necessarily involved a sort of absolute mutual hostility that denies the opponent any degree of legitimacy or even humanity. This could easily "lead to the mutual destruction" of the superethnies involved, for they all perceive their opponents to be "subhuman" (*neliud'*) and they deny the opposite camp "the right to life."[70] In this cheerless Gumilevian calculus, therefore, national survival becomes very much a zero-sum game in which the survival of one superethnos can be insured only through the destruction of its enemies.

---

68. Titenko 2005.
69. Dergachev 2000, 84 (quote); Kefeli n.d.
70. Vladimirov 2007, 168, 170, 173.

Russia as an *Etnosistema*

Gumilev's ideas are no less important for ethno-geopolitical analyses of the domestic affairs of individual states. The point is emphasized, among others, by the leader of the Liberal-Democratic Party of Russia, Vladimir Vol'fovich Zhirinovskii. A notorious extremist and Russian chauvinist, Zhirinovskii is also a student of geopolitics. In the late 1990s he published the bulky text *Geopolitics and the Russian Question*, and more recently has become an enthusiastic proponent of ethno-geopolitics as well.[71] He is attracted to the field partly out of his personal fascination for Gumilev, with whom he feels a special empathy. Like himself, Zhirinovskii points out grimly, Gumilev grew up without a father ("we both were bastards [*bastardy*]") and they both suffered for the social origins of their parents. "The sense of injustice, of being strangled by fate and the conditions of life, predetermined the unusual spiritual disposition of the future great scholar"—in the same way, he would like us to understand, as himself. "It seems," he observed self-importantly, "that I took the same path as Lev Gumilev."[72] Zhirinovskii claims to have conceived of a *passionarnost'*-like quality on his own, independently of Gumilev, and maintains that his manifesto *The Final Thrust to the South* (1993) anticipated and "in many respects confirms" Gumilev's theories.[73]

As formulated by Zhirinovskii and others, ethno-geopolitics strongly emphasizes the connection between an ethnos and its *rodina* or geographical homeland. "Like any biological species, an ethnos occupies a specific region that is necessary for its sustenance and reproduction."[74] This emplacement in a native "Lebensraum" (*zhiznennoe prostranstvo*) is a natural and necessary connection, as Gumilev taught, and the integrity of the ethnic group can only be maintained as long as it is respected and fostered.[75] At the same time, however, ethno-geopolitics echoes Russian neo-Eurasianism in the insistence that the natural right of all ethnies to their native homelands must not interfere with the greater imperative of preserving the coherence and unity of the superethnic entities that these ethnies cluster together to form. Such interference begins at that moment when the specifically ethnic character of a group's attachment to a particular region is recognized also to be a political prerogative.

---

71. Zhirinovskii 1998.

72. Zhirinovskii 2001b, 297, 294; *Nesgibaemyi Zhirinovskii* 2011, 86–87.

73. Zhirinovskii 1993; *Nesgibaemyi Zhirinovskii* 2011, 124. Recounting a story that Gumilev, in a prison camp in December 1953, had foretold the execution of Lavrentii Beria three days before it was officially announced, Zhirinovskii even claimed that the two shared the gift of prophecy. Zhirinovskii 2001b, 297.

74. Smirnov 1998.

75. Chernov 1999, 70, 77; Zhade 2006, 117; Zhirinovskii 2001a.

In this sense, ethno-geopolitics draws the familiar Gumilevian distinction between ethnic and political space. Boundaries of ethnic homelands only rarely coincide with those of political states, and ethnic groups have no inherent or automatic right to any national self-determination that involves sovereign political control of their ethnic space. "It is impossible to give power to all ethnies, nations, nationalities, and small ethnic groups, tribes and so on, and to allow them to form independent states." To do so would be to turn political relations across the entire globe "into an uninterrupted stream of wars small and large, national and ethnic conflicts, and religious clashes." Indeed, the "activation of the processes of political self-determination" that began in the twentieth century and carries over unabated into the twenty-first has destroyed the stability in the world order. "The absolute 'overlay' (*nalozhenie*) of political space onto ethnic space is not possible (*ne mozhet byt'*), by virtue of the concrete historical conditions of ethnic existence."[76] It is precisely the determination to force the two inherently unaligned categories of the "political" and the "ethnic" into an unnatural spatial-territorial alignment through the creation of "absurd monoethnic states" that calls forth the bitter "struggle for Lebensraum" that has once again become characteristic for our age.[77] This is a major problem for post-Soviet Russia. The recognition of national self-determination that came with the collapse of the USSR has not enhanced the rights and welfare of ethnic groups as a whole. Very much to the contrary, this "parade of sovereignties" served only to empower the self-selected and corrupt elites that lead them. The result is not "national liberation" at all but rather ethnocracy: oligarchic microregimes operating within the larger body politic under cover of a disingenuous appeal to national rights. By encouraging local self-sufficiency, a sense of opposition to the state's political center, and even separatist tendencies, ethnocracy represents the gravest internal threat to the cohesion of the Russian Federation.[78]

As an alternative, ethnogeopolitics offers its own model of an *etnosistema* or "ethnic system"—a collection of individual ethnies joined together to form a single entity. Effectively, this is a reworking of the "superethnos" concept, and the Gumilevian inspiration is readily apparent.[79] Like a superethnos, an ethnic system is a natural entity, a "living organism" that possesses its own unity and

76. Zhade 2006, 120 (quote); Smirnov 1998.

77. Borodai 1995, 114.

78. Chernov 1999, 6. On ethnocracy, see Toshchenko 2003.

79. Chernov 1999, 22. Gumilev himself occasionally used the term *etnosistema*, but always in reference to a single ethnos. Gumilev 1989c, 215; Gumilev 2003i, 117; Gumilev 2004c, 628. The terminological confusion in ethno-geopolitics is particularly apparent in Borodai's essay, where ethnos is juxtaposed to *natsiia*—which he treats as a sort of supraethnic entity akin to a superethnos. Borodai 1995, 112–15; Borodai 1994, 94. In all likelihood, Gumilev would not have understood this usage.

cohesiveness. As part of this, the principle of *korennost'* or "ethnic indigeneity" is vital, which means that different ethnic groups should live on "their specific historical territory of settlement (the place of their birth and development)."[80] And finally, as was the case with a superethnos, the unity and coherence of the groups that form the ethno-systemic organism is not an option but rather an existential necessity, for the "destruction of one element inevitably leads to the collapse of another." The groups that together make up an ethnic system "cannot separate peacefully," and any attempt to disassemble them can only result in "social cataclysms" across the entire system.[81]

The superethnos and *etnosistema* concepts differ, however, in one critical respect. For Gumilev, the superethnos was a balanced assemblage of freely associated ethnies that were all effectively equal. An ethnic system, by contrast, is based on the principle of "nonconflictual (*bezkonfliktnaia*) ethnic hierarchy." The ethno-geopoliticians call attention to this difference with Gumilev, describing the principle of a hierarchy of ethnies as "the most important feature" overall of an ethnic system and explicitly criticizing Gumilev—who himself had no notion whatsoever of any hierarchy within a superethnos—for his "rather narrow" appreciation of it.[82] They argue that the various constituent ethno-elements of the system are arrayed on different levels of what they call the "civilizational vertical" of the ethnic system. These different levels are associated with different degrees of "social maturity" (*sotsial'naia zrelost'*) and civilizational development within the respective ethno-systemic unit. Some are relatively less developed and others more advanced. The entire arrangement is described as a "clearly elaborated [pattern of] ethno-national subordination (*subordinatsiia*)."[83] The existence of the civilizational vertical is essential, for the system can only form "on the condition that the dominant ethnos is at a higher level of development [than the others] and is thus is able to insure the social integration and the regulation (*regulatsiia*) of the political community."[84]

At the top of this hierarchy sits the *etnodominanta*. As we have seen, Gumilev himself used the term to refer to the constellation of political, ideological, and religious values that form a basis for the consolidation of an ethnos in its earliest stages.[85] In post-Soviet usage, however, it is modified to refer more simply to

80. Chernov 1999, 77; Zhirinovskii 2001a, 305.
81. Zhirinovskii 2001a, 304.
82. Chernov 1999, 67.
83. Zhirinovskii 2001a, 300; Chernov 1999, 67–69.
84. Zhade 2006, 118 (quote); Chernov 1999, 71–72.
85. Gumilev 1989c, 251, 481; Gumilev 2004c, 73.

the most highly developed ethnos in any given grouping of ethnies. Historically, the *etnodominanta* acted as a "system-forming (*sistemoobrazuiushchii*) ethnos" that brought the entire system into being and continued to serve as a kind of overall guarantor of its integrity and stability.[86] The *etnodominanta* "groups other ethnies around itself, in which process elements of its culture become essential for the entire social system." Multinational societies that are not properly organized as ethnic systems generally lack these clear hierarchical structures, and this is always a source of weakness. In Canada, for example, "the primary ethnic elements (Anglo-Saxon and French) occupy approximately the same level of vertical-civilizational development," and the resulting friction works constantly to undermine national cohesion. In a structural sense, the same is true of many polyethnic African nations.[87] The situation is yet more critical in the United States, where multiculturalism prevents the emergence of an *etnodominanta* altogether and insures a more or less constant struggle between ethnic groups for dominance.[88]

Russia, by contrast, is organized—in principle at least—as a proper ethnic system, where the place of the *etnodominanta* is filled by ethnic Russia.[89] "Russia's polyethnic space has its own complex structure, the system-forming foundation of which is the ethnic space of the ethnically Russian (*russkii*) population. Historically, the Russian ethnos played the role of creating and consolidating the society (*sotsioobrazuiushchaia i sotsioskrepliaiushchaia rol'*), and in so doing provided for the cohesion of the country." Russia's polyethnicity is a necessary condition of its development, but this in turn depends on maintaining ethnic Russia's preeminent status of the system-forming ethnos.[90] To be sure, the natural domination of Russians within the system should not involve any sort of harmful subordination or oppression of the other constituent ethnies.[91] On the contrary, all ethnic groups that are a part of the Russian ethnic system are bonded together by mutual sympathy and "toleration"—a clear allusion to Gumilev's complementarity—and they all derive equal benefit from participation.[92] "The interconnection between the Russians and other peoples is indissoluble and mutual. The Russians need the large and small peoples who inhabit the vast spaces of the country just as much as the latter vitally need the Russians."[93]

---

86. Smirnov 1998.
87. Zhirinovskii 2001a, 303–4 (quote), 302; Chernov 1999, 71–72.
88. Vladimirov 2007, 174–75.
89. Zhirinovskii 2014, 8, 15, 44, 59ff.
90. Zhade 2006, 120.
91. Zhirinovskii 2001a, 304.
92. Zhade 2006, 119.
93. Chernov 1999, 70; Zhirinovskii 2001a, 301.

In view of the tribulations that Russia has undergone since 1991 and the challenges that face it in the immediate future, ethno-geopolitics calls for the decisive reaffirmation and enhancement of the country's ethno-systemic structure. Above all, this means that Russia must finally discard "ethnicity" altogether as a legal category for its federal subjects. Ethnicity was of course the basis of Soviet federalism, and the principal federal units—SSRs, ASSRs and so on—were all conceived as ethno-national entities. After 1991, the Russian Federation moved away from this principle, opting to designate most of its subjects as administrative units rather than ethnic homelands, but a significant number of the latter continue to be recognized as such. It is this harmful residual of Soviet practice that the ethno-geopoliticians want now to eliminate. "Within the framework of the Russian (*rossiiskii*) ethnic system," any division of territory on the basis of ethnicity "is not only illogical but positively dangerous. It will [necessarily] lead to interethnic clashes and wars, which will result in the dissolution of the country.... The Russian Federation should gradually eliminate any ethnic designation for its component territorial units and emphasize instead economic regionalization in the framework of national-cultural equality."[94] In this manner, ethnogeopolitics seeks to use Gumilev's concepts to undermine and eliminate one of his deepest principles, namely the right of all peoples to a free and autonomous national life on their own universally acknowledged ethno-territorial homelands.

Chimeras and the *Malyi Narod*

For Gumilev, chimeras and antisystems were closely related but not entirely identical phenomena. A chimera referred to the situation that resulted when a foreign ethnos was successful in invading and occupying the ecological niche of another ethnos. This created a profound aberration in which all of the organic relationships that had been developed within the ethnocenosis were disrupted, and which if uncorrected led inevitably to the demise of the indigenous ethnic group. An antisystem, on the other hand, was more specifically doctrinal or ideological in character: a negative and "life-denying" worldview propagated within an ethnic entity by alienated groupings that had become detached from their ethnic cohorts and struggled actively against them. One significant difference between the two is that while chimeras form in accordance with the laws of the ecology of ethnicity and are thus a product of natural determination, the development of antisystems involves a degree of voluntarism and free choice

---

94. Chernov 1999, 85, 173; also see Zhirinovskii 2014, 81.

inherent in what Gumilev referred to as the "bipolarity" of the ethnic field.[95] In the post-Soviet usage of these terms, however, such nuanced differences have become blurred. The terms are used much more loosely and interchangeably in order to characterize anything that induces "clever, good-hearted, and to all external appearances intelligent people to create nightmare images of monstrous philosophical systems . . . , compelling them to destroy their future and with this to destroy themselves."[96] Indeed, nurtured by the obsession in many corners of post-Soviet Russia with dark forces conspiring to destroy the Russian ethnic organism, Gumilevian chimeras and antisystems have become highly charged epithets for essentially any perceived opponent or enemy that happens to present itself at a given moment.[97]

Russia's political history in the nineteenth and twentieth centuries provides numerous examples of this tendency. The Decembrists, Nihilists, and Populists of the prerevolutionary period are all now described as examples of antisystems, as were all the revolutionary parties without exception. With the victory of the Bolsheviks, the antisystem of communism came to power—a catastrophe that insured the Soviet Union would necessarily develop as a chimera and would display the attendant deformations and dysfunctions.[98] The latter characteristics were apparent in all aspects of Soviet life, but nowhere more than in the official ambition to create a single metaethnos in the form of the "Soviet people." The refusal to acknowledge the inviolability of ethnic difference would always lead to what one of Gumilev's disciples refers to as the "chimerization" (*khimerizatsiia*) of the societies affected. This process was not limited to Russia—indeed, with its "melting pot," the United States (unlike Canada) had succumbed to this fate even earlier—but the USSR provided certainly the rawest and most tragic example.[99] "Did not great Russia begin to turn catastrophically into a chimera

95. Shishkin 1996.

96. Koriavtsev 1994.

97. An amusing example of the potency of these terms can be seen in the Russian take on the English word "Chimerica" coined by the Harvard historian Niall Ferguson to describe the defacto symbiosis between China and America in the twenty-first-century: the former as "the big saver" and the latter as "the big spender." Ferguson 2008. Russian commentators have cleverly transliterated the term not accurately as "*Kimerika*" (from the Russian word for China *Kitai*) but rather *Khimerika*, thereby evoking a Gumilevian chimera ("*khimera*") and indicating that such a symbiosis is intrinsically a threat to Russia. Ermachenkov 2009; Nurminen 2009. There is a web forum devoted entirely to *antisistemy*: http://antisys.b.qip.ru/ (accessed 4/2/2015).

98. Makhnach n.d. One of Gumilev's students attempted to sketch out a Gumilevian "ethnic history of Russian communism," arguing that the Bolsheviks were a consortium and the Communist Party a subethnos with its own behavioral stereotype. Ermolaev and Ermolaeva 1995.

99. Makhnach n.d.; Makhnach 2001. On *khimerizatsiia*, also see Efremov 2003, 32; Sevast'ianov 2003.

after 1917?" The contrived integration of the multinational population into a so-called Soviet nation had a clear "chimeric quality" (*khimerichnost'*). The project failed, of course, but only after it had ruined all aspects of Russia's national development for over a half century.[100]

In post-Soviet Russia, Gumilevian chimeras and antisystems have become key concepts in nationalist-conservative perspectives and are seen by many as virtually omnipresent.[101] Under the Yel'tsin administration, it is argued, their ideas achieved the status of state ideology, with devastating effects on Russia's genuine national interests. This was evident, for example, in the disastrous economic experiment with "shock therapy" inspired by the West, which culminated in the wholesale collapse of the economy.[102] The end of the Yeltsin era and Russia's reconsolidation under Vladimir Putin have reversed some of these negative tendencies, but there is a perceived "evergreen" quality to antisystems, which means that their danger cannot be entirely eliminated. Surviving parasitically within the corpus of ethnies, antisystemic elements lie today in waiting for the moment when there is "instability in social relations and a negative worldview becomes dominant." At this point they will reemerge and set about "destroying whatever they can."[103] The same Aleksandr Vladimirov whose perspectives on international relations we have just considered believes that in the case of either Chinese or Islamic incursion into Russia, a "superethnic geopolitical chimera" would take shape, with dire consequences. "The chimeric quality (*khimernost'*) of this possible formation can lead only to the annihilation of the great Russian (*rossiiskii*) superethnos and the disappearance of Russia as an independent civilization."[104] Indeed, this process has already begun on the territory of the former Soviet Union, in the form of an "Orange chimera" in Ukraine after 2006.[105] The following statement gives a taste of how such apprehensions can be expressed in a hysterical cascade of Gumilevian verbiage. "The situation in Ukraine is complicated by the presence of an ethnic chimera, which creates antisystemic communities of de-ethnicized people with negative worldviews, whose activities can only give rise to historical zigzags that deviate from the natural development of ethnogenesis."[106]

It is in anti-Semitic discourse, however, that the most elaborate post-Soviet deployment of the "antisystem" and "chimera" concepts is to be found.

---

100. Efremov 2003, 32.
101. Balashov 1992; Rossman 2002b, 48n.
102. Efanov 1998; Shishkin 1996.
103. Koriavtsev 1994.
104. Vladimirov 2007, 172.
105. "'Oranzhevaia khimera' na Ukraine" 2013.
106. Tanasov n.d.

This follows the lead of Gumilev himself, of course, who focused on the ancient Judaic khaganate of Khazaria as his leading example of chimeric deformation. He wrote at length and with great passion about the latter's pernicious character and its near-fatal hostility to Russia, and his Khazar historiography inspired an entire genre of anti-Semitic affirmation in the late Soviet Union. Interest in the Khazars carries over vigorously into the post-Soviet period, and as we will see in the following section there is an efflorescence of Gumilev-inspired writings about Russia's negative experience with the Khazarian antisystem. At the same time, however, Jews are directly implicated as part of those chimeric forces that have sought to harm Russia throughout the twentieth century. They are identified as a driving force among the revolutionaries in general and the Bolsheviks in particular. By their very nature, declared Dmitrii Balashov, Jews were sympathetic to the tenets of communism and cosmopolitanism, which demanded "the destruction of national differences, [and the establishment of] a single way of life, a single set of governmental principles, and even a single language." It is general knowledge, he insisted, that the Jews made up "nine-tenths" of Lenin's party, and that after the revolution they "seized the most powerful positions."[107] As a result of this political domination, the USSR formed as a "Judeo-khazar type of ethnic chimera."[108] It was true that Jewish influence receded from the late 1930s, but it reemerged in the 1970s in the form of special emigration privileges for Jews, and then in the next decade in the demands for democracy and the aspiration of a "common European home." Finally, with the collapse of the USSR, Balashov maintains that Russia once again came under the control of a Jewish antisystem in the form of the Yel'tsin administration.[109]

We have noted Gumilev's use of the term *malyi narod*, popularized by Igor' Shafarevich in his *Russophobia*. Shafarevich, for his part, wrote a warm memorial tribute after Gumilev's death for the newspaper *Den'*, in which he compared the latter's scholarly achievements to those of Herodotus.[110] The affinities between the two were strongly emphasized by Gumilev's student Igor' Shishkin, who maintained that Shafarevich's *malyi narod* was for all practical purposes identical with Gumilev's notion of "antisystem." Shishkin explained that the unity of their visions came from the fact that they studied the same problem from different perspectives: Gumilev sought natural causes of this development, whereas Shafarevich emphasized the social context. But they agreed that the success of the Jewish Bolshevik chimera represented "the political victory of a *malyi narod*,

107. Balashov 2000a.
108. Kosarenko 1993, cited in Graev 1998.
109. Balashov 1992, 150–51.
110. Shafarevich 1992, 5.

whose ascent to power unleashed powerful destructive forces and initiated the destruction of Russia and everything Russian, on a scale and level of brutality without historical precedent."[111] Shafarevich himself confirmed that although he had not read Gumilev's work when he first developed his ideas, he believed that the two had independently come to the same conclusions, and that his eventual discovery of Gumilev was a "great help" for him. He described the *malyi narod* in Gumilevian terms as a "systemic totality, with a negative worldview." Indeed, Gumilev's notion of "chimera" offered a significant "broadening" (*rasshirenie*) of the sense of *malyi narod*. Like many others, Shafarevich was attracted by the novelty of Gumilev's ethno-biological characterization, which helped establish the point that the *malyi narod* phenomenon was universal, limited neither to the Jews nor to Russia.[112]

Post-Soviet depictions of the Jews as an ethnic chimera pay special attention to the factor of *passionarnost'*. Gumilev had taught that the primordial rupture that separated the Jews from the natural environment had the vital effect of retarding the entropic process through which passionary energy was dissipated in the course of ethnogenetic development. They were thus uniquely able to conserve their *passionarnost'* on a fairly high level. This circumstance enabled the Jews not only to extend their existence well beyond the temporal limits of normal ethnogenesis but also to maintain a consistently high degree of ethnic vitality and activity throughout. And this in turn made it impossible for them "to establish [healthy] symbiotic contacts with indigenous peoples. . . . An ethnos with an elevated energetic profile (*energetika*) cannot live in isolation. It inevitably begins to act, . . . and having begun to act, it entirely naturally begins to refashion the ethnic system of its host nation in its own way. And this inevitably produces a chimera."[113] The dominant role of Jews in creating the Bolshevik antisystem was explained by another follower of Gumilev specifically in terms of this factor. Over many centuries, Jews had been able to preserve their passionary gene pool. "The revolutionary activity of the Jews was the work of passionary energy, torn out of the village and ghetto," with the result that "the Bolshevik empire was created with this passionary energy." The Stalinist repressions of the 1930s together with Hitler's predations significantly reduced Jewish *passionarnost'*, but it was not exhausted, and after a hiatus it reemerged to energize the Jewish dissidents in the 1960s and 1970s and then the *demokraty* of perestroika. "The history of the Jewish people," he concludes, "clearly illustrates Lev Nikolaevich Gumilev's

---

111. Shishkin 1996. On Gumilev and Shafarevich, also see Marochkin 1997, 228.
112. Shafarevich 2011; Shafarevich 2010.
113. Shishkin 1995c.

theories," which not only help us understand the past but also "aid the prognosis of the future."[114]

The principles of Gumilev's ecology of ethnicity serve a more general purpose for anti-Semitic discourse in post-Soviet Russia, one which cannot be provided by Shafarevich's *malyi narod*. The principles of natural law and environmental causation are used to frame Gumilev's theory as a dispassionate and objective scientific argument, uncolored by any sort of subjective bias in general or by anti-Semitism in particular. The inevitably calamitous consequences of contact with the Jewish ethnos thus has nothing to do with any "malign (*durnoi*) qualities" of the Jews but rather is the product of entirely natural processes, over which no one has any control. Neither ethnic bias nor any sort of "instinctive" anti-Semitic antipathy toward the Jews play any role.[115] The central postulate of Gumilev's theory of ethnic contact is that interaction between two or more ethnies is determined "by natural laws (*zakonomernosti*)," Shishkin insisted, "and not by our notions about political expediency or about what is good and what is bad."[116] In regard to the Jewish question in particular, "The greatest accomplishment of Gumilev's theory . . . is to remove it from the field of phantasmagoria and place it firmly on a scientific basis. Gumilev's theory explains the chimeric character of Jewish contacts with other ethnies neither in terms of [Jewish] underhand scheming (*proiskami*) nor by suggesting that some nations are good and others are bad, but rather exclusively in terms of natural laws."[117] We see here the efficacy of Gumilev's ecology of ethnicity as an explanatory framework for anti-Semitism, which explicitly and emphatically rejects any suggestion of racial valorization or genetic difference. In the final analysis, there is no Jewish "problem" at all, rather merely the objective scientific fact that all ethnies are fundamentally different, to the extent that "they must not be mixed."[118] As one commentator on the political valences of Gumilevian teachings observed, "In their search for a scientific apparatus that allows for an 'objective' evaluation of the role of the Jews . . . without attracting accusations of anti-Semitism," anti-Semitic Russian nationalists "turn to the theory of ethnogenesis developed by Gumilev."[119]

---

114. Zil'bert 1994, 1–3, 4, 7. For a more extensive consideration of how *passionarnost'* shaped the role of Jews in European civilization, see Zil'bert 2000.

115. Shishkin 1995c.

116. Shishkin 1994.

117. Shishkin 1995c; Tanasov n.d.

118. Shishkin 1995c.

119. Graev 1998.

"Project Khazaria"

A special dimension of Gumilev's influence on anti-Semitic discourse in Russia after 1991 relates to the perennial theme of Russia and Khazaria. The topic of Khazaria has flourished as a literary-historical genre, and Gumilev's influence over it is obvious and pervasive.[120] In one sense, post-Soviet interest merely carries forward the late- and post-Stalinist preoccupation with the historical saga of how a Jewish chimera state in the Middle Ages came to challenge the existence of ancient Rus'. Today, however, the Soviet censors are long gone and Gumilev's largely allegorical treatment of the issue has given way to open and explicit debate about the significance of that historical experience for the present day. Clearly inspired by Gumilev's work, Igor' Shafarevich has himself taken up the topic. He accepts Gumilev's characterization of the Khazar Khaganate as a unique "zigzag" in the historical development of this part of the world, and warns that this experience could easily repeat itself in the future, in which case "the 'zigzag' would become a regular pattern."[121] Others maintain that this has already happened, that Khazaria has returned to Russia not merely as a haunting saga of ancient ethnic injustice but also in the form of a menacing twenty-first-century Jewish chimera-in-formation. Contemporary Russia is portrayed as "Khazarstan"—an imaginative if logically implausible conflation of the Jewish and Islamic menaces—and paranoid apprehension is voiced about the establishment of a "New Khazaria," inspired by Jewish oligarchs and realized by émigré Jews who are allegedly repatriating and regrouping on Russia's defenseless southern shores.[122]

In the 1990s, the expression "Project Khazaria" was coined in specific reference to Boris Yel'tsin's regime. Today, the epithet has become popular as a way of emphasizing the planned and deliberate character of the Jewish threat to Russia. In this context, Gumilev's writings are invoked not only for their historical value but now explicitly for what they can reveal about Russia's current situation. An advertisement for a new edition of his *Discovery of Khazaria* promotes the book in the following terms:

> The history of the Khazars and Khazaria is closely interwoven with the history of the Russians and Russia. Khazar influence never really ceased to echo across Rus'. From the destruction of Belaia Vezha [a Khazar fortress on the Don River] to the Belovezha Accord and the collapse of the Soviet Union, the "Khazaria question" has been surrounded by turmoil.

---

120. Plotnikov 1994; Malikov 1996; Al'shevskii 1999. For a full discussion, see Shnirel'man 2005b.
121. Shafarevich 2002.
122. Beliakov 2012a, 573; Sevast'ianov 2003; "'Novaia Khazariia' na russkoi zemle" 2003; Lavrionov 2011.

What's more, today a *malyi narod* in Russia is raising the question of the resurrection of the Khazaria Khaganate in its historical boundaries. All of this makes Lev Gumilev's book exceptionally relevant.[123]

The neo-fascist National Front Party led by the white supremacist and Hitler enthusiast Il'ia Viktorovich Lazarenko invoked Gumilev in precisely this spirit. On the latter's authority, Lazarenko argued in the mid-1990s that Russia had always been an oppressed ethnic chimera, suffering under a "Jewish yoke" imposed through the "occupation of the country by the Judeans of the Khazar kaganat."[124]

The work of the political scientist Tat'iana Vasil'evna Gracheva provides a vivid example of how contemporary meaning can be read into the chronicles of Khazar history through a Gumilevian filter. Gracheva heads a department in the Military Academy of the General Staff of the Armed Forces of the Russian Federation and is also a senior research fellow at the latter's Center for Military and Strategic Studies. Although her academic specialization is national security, she has a strong interest in the Khazaria theme and has published two lengthy works on the subject: *Invisible Khazaria: The Algorithms of Geopolitics and the Strategies of Secret Wars behind the Scene Globally* and *Holy Russia against Khazaria*.[125] Although these books were published in limited editions by a provincial press, they have attracted a flurry of attention and comment, most of which is highly positive. The historical parts of her work are presented overwhelmingly in terms of Gumilev's categories and vocabulary, and they stand as compelling evidence of how the latter have become accepted as a standard framework for narrating and interpreting Khazar history. Thus, ancient Khazaria was a "classical chimera," more precisely an "ethnic chimera," which formed "as the result of the invasion of representatives of one superethnos into the zone of habitation of another incompatible superethnos." The chaotic nature of this chimera is conveyed in Gumilev's notion of an "ethnic field," on which "two incompatible rhythms are combined, creating cacophony" and degeneration within the system. This in turn gave rise to "the ideologies of antisystems," devised by people with "negative worldviews" and based on "nihilism" and the "principles of destruction." In characterizing these antisystems, Gracheva can do no better than to quote Gumilev himself: "'These negative formations exist at the expense of positive ethnic systems, which they eat away from within, like cancerous tumors.'"[126]

123. "Otkrytie Khazarii," http://www.ozon.ru/context/detail/id/3199685/ (accessed 4/2/2015).
124. Polivanov and Kosykh 1995: 11 (quote); Shenfield 2001, 249–50.
125. Gracheva 2008; Gracheva 2009; Beliakov 2012a, 574.
126. Gracheva 2008, 145, 147–49, 231–32.

If Gracheva's historical account of the Khazars is largely cribbed from Gumilev, however, her attempts to divine the significance of this historical legacy for the present are rather more original. This is not least because here she is able to put her analytical skills as a national security specialist—a subject about which Gumilev of course had no idea—to good use. Russia, she maintains, finds itself today involved in a "world war" that is constantly expanding to include new countries and regions. This is not the familiar war on terror or struggle against the forces of authoritarianism that the international media have drilled into the consciousness of ordinary citizens.[127] On the contrary, it is a secret war, the main protagonists of which are dark forces driven by the thirst for revenge. "The destructive passion for vengeance, to repeat the attempt to seize control, can have its roots in the past, even in the remote past. [This passion] suddenly animates and inflames the inner world of some group of people living in the present day and becomes the dominant factor of their personalities."[128] In order to understand the sources and dynamic forces of today's struggle,

> it is necessary to take a journey into the remote historical past, for the project that opposes our own "project" in all respects can be called "Project Khazaria." It is precisely here that the contemporary forces of anti-Russian revenge and opposition to the Russian state are united. Under its banner a global elite, which took over the baton from the war-mongering "unreasonable Khazars" [of old], is making its moves. Today's war is a war between the forces of historical revenge, united in "Project Khazaria," and the forces united in the "project" of defending the sacred historical state life of Russia.[129]

In contrast to ancient Khazaria, however, with its merchants, cities, and armies, the modern expression of the same struggle has no palpable form. Khazaria today is invisible (hence the book's title)—at once everywhere around the globe and nowhere at all. Gracheva insists on the universality of "Project Khazaria," which is not restricted to Russian soil but rather aims quite literally at world domination. It rests, accordingly, on the universalist ideologies of Zionism and cosmopolitan Marxism, which represent "the two component parts of a single antisystemic ideology of global Khazaria and the ideological foundations of the new world order."[130]

---

127. Ibid., 5.
128. Ibid., 141.
129. Ibid., 142–43.
130. Ibid., 232 (quote), 169, 229.

Gumilev's writings can, however, inspire very different sorts of conclusions about the implications of the Khazar threat to contemporary Russia, as can be seen in the example of Nikolai Lysenko, a prominent activist on the extreme radical right and leader in the 1990s of the National-Republican Party of Russia.[131] Through the agency of Jewish oligarchs such as Roman Abramovich, Lysenko maintained, Russia today is dominated by the world Jewish diaspora. "Under our very eyes, from the chrysalis of post-Bolshevism the disgusting insect of a Judeo-Christian chimera has emerged onto God's earth. In a series of works, L. N. Gumilev revealed the operational mechanism of this grotesque mutant, and we will not need to wait long to experience its deadly consequences." Relentless Westernization, the progressive "feminization" of Russian society, the decline of the family, alcoholism, narcotics, and sexual profligacy—"all of these negative processes are the necessary consequences of the rapid Khazarization (*khazarizatsiia*) of Russia, that is to say, the global process of transforming Russia into a new Khazaria." Ultimately, this would lead not merely to the total despoliation of Russian society but also to the further geopolitical fragmentation of the Russian state. The Russian Federation might "end its existence as a united Eurasian power" and break into three or four territorial enclaves. A new state would then be constructed "on the ruins of historical Russia," for which Judaism would be an "openly acknowledged foundation."[132]

In this process, ethnic Russians would not merely become thoroughly "Khazaricized" (*khazarizirovannyi*) but could even be ethnically cleansed altogether from their historical homeland. And insofar as the Russian people themselves are in a profound state of national collapse—which Lysenko characterizes as a Gumilevian *nadlom*—they will be unable to resist this omnipotent "Project Khazaria." There is only one source of effective opposition to the latter, which Lysenko locates—amazingly enough—in the global dynamism of resurgent Islam. Although in the 1990s Lysenko delivered virulent denunciations of Islamic elements in Russian society, the events of 9/11 seem to have changed his mind.[133] Lysenko praises the "courageous young Muslims" who gave their lives on that day in the struggle against the "inhuman Zionist-American regime," and he comes to the bizarre conclusion that the Russian people are now "objectively prepared for the Islamic alternative." At the very least, this is true for the most politically active and spiritually unbroken segments of the Russian population, who today are clear in their rejection of Western values. "The example of the Russian intelligentsia adopting Islam could serve as a spiritual beacon for thousands of Russian

---

131. Shnirelman 2002, 141; Shenfield 2001, 231–35; Laqueur 1993, 134, 268, 295.
132. Lysenko 2003.
133. Lysenko 1992; Shnirelman and Komarova 1997, 213; Verkhovskii 2007.

people" and thereby rescue the nation from the predations of New Khazaria.[134] What in the world, one wonders, would Gumilev have made of that?

The fact remains nonetheless that even Gumilev's most faithful adherents draw very different conclusions regarding the future of Russian-Jewish relations. One common perspective, stressing the principles of ethnic individuality and the natural-organic displacement of the Jews in an alien ecological niche, maintains that the latter will always be out of place in Russia and objectively represent an "internal enemy."[135] Yet even within this particular argument there are still discordant nuances in the deployment of Gumilevian principles. Some argue, for example, that the only abnormality about the Jews is their ecological displacement. This is an irregularity that has nothing to do with any inherent negative qualities of the Jews, much less with any "Jewish-Masonic conspiracy." Once the Jews resettle in their own natural homeland, this irregularity is removed and the ethnos is normalized. The conclusion is obvious: "from the standpoint of ethnogenesis, Israel represents a normal ethnos of this sort."[136] Aleksandr Dugin is one prominent adherent of this position, another is the very Nikolai Lysenko whom we have just discussed.[137] He rejected Jewish "*assimilianty*" in Russia who pretend to be Russian, but he was entirely prepared to accept Jews who did not deny their ethnic difference and acknowledged their formal allegiance to Israel rather than Russia.[138] The nontrivial corollary to this implicit acknowledgement of Israel's normalcy is the implication that the movement to gather the Jewish diaspora back into its original and natural ecological niche—that is, Zionism—is also normal and legitimate in terms of Gumilev's ecology of ethnicity.[139]

This implication would, however, logically undermine the identification of both Israel and Zionism as key operational elements in the diabolical project of the international Jewish diaspora to establish global domination. Determined to avoid such a conclusion, Tatiana Gracheva sought to delegitimize modern Israel as the rightful ecological homeland of the Jews by claiming—entirely contrary to Gumilev's own position—that the East European immigrants who made up most of the country's population after World War II were not actually genuine Jews at all. Rather, as Ashkenazi Jews they were not part of the original Judaic twelve tribes but descendants of the Khazars, that is, a Turkic Eurasian people who at certain historical moment had converted to Judaism. "Insofar as they were not genuine Semites, these Khazarian Jews occupied a territory [Israel] that they had

---

134. Lysenko 2003.
135. Shishkin 1996.
136. Kosarenko 1993, cited in Graev 1998; Rossman 2002a, 45.
137. On Dugin's complex and not entirely unambivalent position, see Laruelle n.d., 17–18.
138. Lysenko 1993, 151; also see Shnirelman 2002, 256.
139. For a discussion of this perspective in Western anti-Semitism, see Lariuel' 2009.

never owned and on which their forefathers had never lived."[140] Israel's current inhabitants thus have no genuine ethno-territorial connection to the lands in the Middle East they now inhabit, and the society they have created there is not a normal ethnic entity but rather an "Israeli Khazaria," with all that that implies.[141] Iurii Borodai concurred, describing Israel as a "brutal system based on apartheid, destined to end catastrophically . . . a chimera, according to L. N. Gumilev."[142]

A rather different perspective was advanced by Dmitrii Balashov. Balashov's underlying antipathy toward the Jews is not in question, and he faithfully repeated Gumilev's account of Khazaria as a dysfunctional ethnic chimera that nearly destroyed ancient Russian civilization. He also acknowledged the reemergence of this chimeric specter in the twentieth century, first in the form of the Judeo-Bolshevik antisystem of revolutionary Russia, and then in the Zionist conspiracy of the present day to gain global domination.[143] But it would be wrong, he pointed out, to project this clearly criminal activity of Jewish elites and international organizations onto the Jewish ethnic mass, for the same reason that one cannot "blame all ethnic Russians for the horrors of the Kolyma camps." The source of the problem was not only the ecological displacement of the Jews onto the homelands of other ethnies, but also the failure of the Jews to assimilate into the mass of the societies in which they lived. Because of this, "all of the normal laws of ethnogenesis were broken," according to which "migrants dissolved into the dominant nation by their fourth generation at the very latest."[144] Balashov clearly believed that such assimilation was not merely theoretically possible but could potentially be highly beneficial. "Who remembers today that [the great pianist Arthur] Rubinstein was a Jew? And is the pure-blooded Jew [Isaac] Levitan not a Russian national landscape artist? Even the Jews believe this, incidentally, because they praise [Marc] Chagall [i.e., consider him to be a Jew] but don't say anything about Levitan. I could also name our famous folklorist Pavel Shein, also a Jew, whose Jewishness did not prevent him from traveling around villages collecting Russian folksongs." Balashov was, however, careful to stipulate that in order for such assimilation to succeed, it would be necessary for Jews to adopt the religion, rituals, customs, and *genre de vie* of the Russian ethnos.[145]

The same sentiments were expressed in a more emphatic form by another of Gumilev's old associates, the secret service operative Aleksandr Baigushev. As we

---

140. Gracheva 2008, 160 (quote), 168.

141. Gracheva 2008, 164–66. This is a popular position in post-Soviet anti-Semitic discourse; see Shnirel'man 2005b, 306.

142. Borodai 1994.

143. Balashov 1992, 150–51; Balashov 2000a.

144. Balashov 2000a.

145. Ibid. On the issue of Levitan as a Russian, also see Malakhov 2006.

saw in chapter 7, Baigushev produced his own fictionalized accounts of the Khazar Khaganate in the 1970s and 1980s, which were prepared under Gumilev's supervision and reflected the latter's interpretation. In these early works, Baigushev had argued that Russia's ethnic survival depended on its strict separation from the Jews. More recently, Baigushev has examined the relationship between the two groups in rather different terms. He accepts the suggestion that the Jews of Russia and Eastern Europe are not part of the original twelve Judaic tribes but rather descendants of the Khazars, who converted to Judaism in the eighth and ninth centuries and subsequently experienced a "genetic passionary eruption" that led to their dispersal across Europe and into the New World. In contrast to Gracheva and others, however, he uses this circumstance not to ostracize but rather to nativize Russia's Jews, claiming that they naturally belong in Russia and are a natural ally for Russians in their struggle with the hostile forces of Westernization and globalization. It was worth noting that it was Gumilev's resistance to precisely this conclusion that led him to *reject* the notion of the Khazars as a thirteenth Judaic tribe.

Instead of emphasizing the inherent antipathy and hostility of the Jews toward the Russians, Baigushev now stresses the affinities of the two ethnies as "messianic nations" and maintains that salvation for either can come only through their unity. "Let us clasp hands, as two divine 'peoples of the idea'—Russians and Jews. Let us forget about both Russophobia and anti-Semitism and seek out our common ground instead. Perhaps we will be able to rescue the Judeo-Christian idea." The distasteful specter of the original Khazar chimera is highly diluted in Baigushev's most recent exhortation, where it is described in essentially neutral terms as the "historical source of the interactions between these two messianic peoples." Indeed, the very notion of a strict distinction between Jew and non-Jew now turns out to be "cultivated in the West" in order to divide Russia and conquer it. In the final analysis, however, Baigushev's vision of unity will only be achieved in the same spirit as Balashov's, that is to say, through the assimilation by Jews of the Russian language, Russian culture, Russian mentality, and "the mystical Russian messianic New Testament civilization." It is only the "ideal, unclouded, cleansing soul and transformative heart of Russian Orthodoxy" that can save the world from the "despiritualized globalism" that remains as part of the Jewish ethos. Baigushev urges Jews in Russia to "extend their hands" to Russians so that together "Russian (*russkaia*) civilization would flourish and Jewish civilization would preserve its best features."[146] Once again, one can only wonder what Gumilev himself—Baigushev's mentor and inspiration—could possibly have made of this.

---

146. Baigushev 2006a.

"THE PATRON OF THE TURKIC PEOPLES"

In a previous chapter we have seen how Russian nationalists in the 1980s accused Gumilev of providing material used by Tatar historians for "Russophobic" purposes. It was certainly true that from his earliest publications, Gumilev attracted special attention from the Soviet Union's non-Russian nationalities, especially those of Turkic origin.[1] His positive descriptions of the ancient nomadic civilizations of the Eurasian steppe understandably appealed to them, as did his rejection of the negative *igo* image and his counterarguments for the constructive role played by nomadic societies in Russia's historical development. Much of his analysis went against the grain of mainstream Soviet historiography, and the fact that it came from such an exceptional individual and learned historian—who happened to be ethnically Russian—made it all the more admirable and attractive. Their appreciation was enhanced by Gumilev's insistence on the inherent integrity of all ethnies and the equal value of their cultures. His opposition to the *sliianie* project, moreover, resonated with their own apprehensions about the threat it posed to their position in the Soviet social order; indeed his emphasis on the importance of ethnic life apparently inspired many to rediscover their own ethnic roots.[2] "I am happy" wrote the Kazakh journalist and folklorist Akselei

---

1. Lariuel' 2001, 17; Tishkov 1997, 3; Koreniako 2000, 44. In Central Asia, Gumilev's articles were reprinted in local publications as early as the 1970s. Lavrov 2000, 311.
2. Simon 1991, 283–90, 313; Hirsch 2004, 318; Brudny 1998, 43.

Slanovich Seidimbek (1942–2009) to Gumilev, "that thanks to you I came to understand myself (*poznal sebia*) as a member of an ethnos."[3] In a similar spirit, the Tatar writer Musagit Mudarisovich Khabibullin was inspired to write his historical novel about the ancient Bulgars, *Kubrat-Khan* through his acquaintance with Gumilev and the latter's primordialist vision of ethnogenetic antiquity. Khabibullin paid homage to Gumilev, referring to him as a "patron" of his people.[4] The surge of ethno-national sentiment across the Soviet Union during perestroika intensified this engagement with Gumilev. The lectures he gave in this period were eagerly attended by students and visitors to Leningrad, and scholarly delegations were dispatched from republic capitals to establish more formal contacts with him.[5] His growing popularity among non-Russians was even noted in an intelligence report prepared for the Central Committee of the CPSU in 1987, where it was claimed that Gumilev's works were being used in Kazakhstan "for all sorts of nationalist interpretations and justification of the superiority of the nomadic way of life."[6]

Since 1992, Gumilev's popularity among non-Russians has expanded exponentially.[7] The factors underlying his appeal relate directly to the political and social exigencies that confronted post-Soviet regimes at the moment of their formation and indeed continue to do so. One of these is the complex process of establishing and managing bilateral relations with the power center in Moscow, either on a federal level within the Russian Federation or internationally between now-independent states. For this purpose, non-Russian versions of Eurasianism, differing markedly from those considered in a previous chapter but similarly inspired by Gumilev, prove very useful.[8] No less important are the needs associated with "nation-building" within the numerous post-Soviet polities themselves: their self-representation (or invention) as coherent communities and their demand for external acknowledgement as legitimate national-political entities. The nation-building imperative is greatly complicated by the fact that standard ethno-national narratives of national consolidation—which in the 1980s provided the mobilizing energy that helped break apart the Soviet Union—often proved less suitable for the construction of new post-Soviet identities of inclusion among regional populations that were poly- rather than monoethnic.

---

3. For a reproduction of Seidimbek's dedication to Gumilev see https://www.flickr.com/photos/gumilyovenu/7364943556/in/photostream/ (accessed 18/7/2014).

4. Khabibullin 2009, 26, 31–32.

5. Zholdasbekov 2003, 6, 8.

6. "'Publikatsiia moikh rabot blokiruiutsia'" 1995, 88. On how Gumilev's theories indeed "strengthened the desire to secede from the Soviet Union," see Gullette 2006, 146.

7. Humphrey 2002, 263; Edgar 2012, 435.

8. For an insightful consideration of non-Russian Eurasianism, see Humphrey 2002.

In these cases, new visions of community and coherence had to be elaborated. Ideologically, these various exigencies pull in different and even opposing directions. The unintended but entirely extraordinary genius of Gumilev's teachings is that they can be deployed on one way or another to serve virtually all of them.[9] For this reason, he has emerged as a familiar and influential figure in a variety of non-Russian political and national discourses right across the former Soviet Union. In this chapter, we will consider how his influence developed in three Turkic regions.

Kazakhstan

In 1994, President Nursultan Nazarbaev of Kazakhstan became the first post-Soviet leader to call for the creation of a "Eurasian Union" that would include the states of the former Soviet Union and in effect replace the Commonwealth of Independent States. His regime has advocated this project ever since, and Eurasianism has de facto become the ideology of state in Kazakhstan.[10] Yet despite the "similarities in mentality and worldview" supposedly bonding Kazakhstan with other Eurasian nations—in particular Russia—Kazakh Eurasianism is driven very much by its own imperatives and priorities.[11] What it envisages is a qualified reintegration of post-Soviet states that would create a common economic space but retain the structures of political independence and state sovereignty established in 1991.[12] The primary impetus for reintegration comes not from cultural or historical factors but from the economic imperatives of a globalizing world, in which individual states are compelled to join together into powerful regional blocks capable of protecting their members from international competition and enabling them to compete successfully in global networks.[13] In contrast to Dugin's and Shishkin's conservative-nationalist visions, Nazarbaev's is a rather more liberal Eurasianism. He sees the Eurasian Union as a confederation: a body of sovereign nations joined together strictly as equal partners in order to pool resources and create common economic and social advantages. The best model for Kazakh Eurasianism is therefore neither the Mongol empire nor some sort of neo-Soviet geopolitical conglomerate assembled around a Russian "leading ethnos," but rather a free association of modernized states organized along the lines

9. On the "flexibility" in his theories, see Gullette 2006, 133, 134, 136.
10. Spivakovskii 1995, 170–71; Laruelle 2008b, 171–87.
11. Nazarbaev 1995, 7.
12. Nazarbaev 1996, 7; *Evraziistvo* 2004, 23; Shnirelman 2009a, 70–72.
13. Nazarbaev 1995, 6–8; Nazarbaev 1996, 4, 7.

of the European Union. Indeed, in a sense Nazarbaev conceives of the Eurasian Union as a sort of eastern counterpart to the European Union.[14] In 2012 Vladimir Putin gave his public endorsement to Nazarbaev's project, and in January 2015 the Eurasian Economic Union came into existence.

Eurasianism in Kazakhstan has, however, been deployed not only for the purposes of rapprochement and cooperation between the post-Soviet states. Along with these aims, and no less important, Eurasianism is projected internally onto the domestic arena.[15] Official narratives about the country's unique geographical positioning "at the center of Eurasia" subtly but clearly imply that Kazakhstan by itself represents a self-contained Eurasia—a "Eurasia in miniature" independent of or even instead of Russia.[16] From this perspective, Eurasianist doctrines about interethnic commonality and harmony are intended to provide an aspirational vision directed specifically at the Kazakh polity, demonstrating how the different national groups inhabiting its "polycultural space"—Kazakhs, Russians, Ukrainians, Tatars, Uzbeks, Uyghurs, Germans, Koreans, and dozens of others—can cohere to form a single national body.[17] The implication is that, in addition to their particular ethnic identities, all the inhabitants of Kazakhstan also belong to a single multinational nation of "Kazakhstanis" (*kazakhstantsy*). This latter notion has roots in Soviet discourse of *sovetskii narod*, and indeed the first attempts to localize it within Kazakhstan date from the 1970s when the term *kazakhstanets* was first mooted.[18] Today, however, it is not proletarian internationalism but rather the premises of Eurasianism that provide the ideological basis for the model of a "monolithic Kazakhstani ethnos."[19] And in elaborating and legitimizing this vision, Gumilev's teachings play a vital role.

From the outset, Gumilev has been venerated as an iconic figure at the very center of the discourse around Kazakh Eurasianism. He had been "discovered" by Kazakhs in the Soviet period, as noted, when his work on the history of the steppe peoples and his emphasis on their role in the origins and development of the Russian state stirred considerable interest and sympathy in the republic. With the official ideological embrace of Eurasianism, his authority and influence were much enhanced. Gumilev is credited with having resurrected the forgotten teachings of the classical Eurasianists and reformulated them in a manner that brought out their full meaning for the contemporary world. "Only a person of

---

14. *Evraziistvo* 2004, 17, 24–25; Zholdasbekov 2003, 7; Anceschi 2014, 738.
15. Schatz 2000, 492; Anceschi 2014, 740.
16. *Evraziistvo* 2004, 28; Doronin 2002; Zholdasbekov 2001, 19–20; Zholdasbekov 2003, 6; Schatz 2000, 491–92; Surucu 2005.
17. Nazarbaev 1995, 10; Jones 2010.
18. Olcott 2002, 55; Ermekbaev 2003, 60.
19. Schatz 2000, 491; Frolovskaia 2005.

titanic breadth was able to carry out a genuine renaissance of Eurasianism and rescue it from its condition of intellectual lethargy. The 'last Eurasian,' as Lev Nikolaevich called himself, was precisely this sort of person."[20] That such accolade should be showered upon the Russian Gumilev is all the more significant in view of the fact that the Kazakhs have their own native prophet of Eurasianism, namely the writer and poet Olzhas Suleimenov.[21] Suleimenov remains a highly visible public figure in his own right—since 2002 he has served as Kazakhstan's ambassador to UNESCO—but he does not challenge Gumilev's preeminence as the key inspiration of the Eurasianist project.

A grandiose indication of Gumilev's intimate connection to Kazakh Eurasianism was the establishment in 1996 of the "Lev Gumilev Eurasian National University" in the new Kazakh capital of Astana.[22] The Eurasianist character of the institution is apparent in its profile as an "international" university with formal institutional links to Moscow State University and other universities in Siberia, Central Asia, and the Caucasus.[23] The university's first rector described the importance of Gumilev and Eurasianism in the following terms. "In our difficult times, with the threats of terrorism, destructive wars, and ecological catastrophes, people seek out those teachings that can provide answers to the eternal questions 'who are we?' and 'where are we headed?' Our youth can find answers to many of the questions in the work of Lev Nikolaevich Gumilev. Eurasianism is like an inoculation (*privivka*) against racism, nationalism, and Eurocentrism. Eurasianism is our future."[24] On the centenary of Gumilev's birth in 2012, the Kazakh government reaffirmed its continuing veneration for his legacy. A republic-wide "Gumilev Olympics" was organized for high school students; a new book series, *Gumilev's World*, was launched; a jubilee postage stamp bearing his image was issued; and in the Altai mountain range a peak was named in his honor, thereby inscribing his name quite literally on the country's map.[25]

Gumilev's role in Kazakh Eurasianism is not merely symbolic or ceremonial, however, and his historical research and ethnographic theories are actively deployed in support of its basic principles. Most important are his arguments

20. Frolovskaia 2005 (quote); Abdymanapov 2004, 16.

21. See below, 199n.

22. "Ukaz Prezidenta Respubliki Kazakhstana, Nr. 2996" 1996; Nazarbaev 2001, 78; Zholdasbekov 2003, 6.

23. Zholdasbekov 2003, 8; Olcott 2002, 66–67; Doronin 2002. Aleksandr Dugin, who briefly held a professorial chair in the Faculty of Sociology at Moscow State University, is an adjunct professor at this university. He is a strong advocate of Nazarbaev's Eurasianism and produced an entire book extolling the Kazakh president's "Eurasian mission." Dugin 2004.

24. Abdymanapov 2004, 3.

25. "Bezymiannaia gornaia" 2012. *Pik Gumileva* along with its near neighbor *Pik Voroshilova*, is located in eastern Kazakhstan on the border with China.

about the special interconnection and synergy between the peoples historically inhabiting the various regions and landscapes of Eurasia. Gumilev was the first "to recognize the world significance of the history of the Eurasian ethnies—the Turkic, Mongolian, East Slavic, and Finno-Ugric peoples"—and to recognize the entire region as a "common hearth (*kolybel'*) and shared fatherland" for all of the native Eurasian groups.[26] Relations between forest and steppe were historically not antagonistic but synergetic, characterized by a mutual understanding and empathy best described using Gumilev's trademark terminology. "Gumilev called this phenomenon complementarity—a 'feeling of positive resonance between the behavioral stereotypes [of the respective groups].' Each of the ethnies of [imperial] Russia contributed to the general culture while at the same time maintaining their individuality."[27] Unlike the West European empires, which oppressed the societies they incorporated, Russia was a benevolent patron, acting always with lenience (*miagkost'*) and tolerance to support and protect the peoples under its aegis.[28] The complementarity between Russians, Kazakhs, and other Eurasian peoples makes possible the "resurrection of Eurasian culture" in the present day—a renaissance that supports interethnic coexistence and fraternity while at the same time protecting ethnic and national differences.[29] Drawing on another Gumilevian concept, the historical assemblage of ethnies collected together within the corpus of the Russian state is described as a single "gigantic Eurasian superethnos" that "provided for stability in the region and the opportunity for each [constituent] ethnos to conduct its accustomed way of life."[30] All of this points the way to the future. "From the history of the Great Steppe," concluded another rector of Gumilev University, Gumilev "demonstrated the preconditions for Eurasian integration" in the twenty-first century.[31]

Along with this celebration of pan-Eurasian commonality, Gumilev's positive judgements in specific regard to Kazakh civilization and history are of great importance. Simply put, he is recognized as the first and still one of the very few Russians to defend the *samobytnost'* or originality of its Turkic culture.[32] "Gumilev affirmed the full and equal value (*polnotsennost'*) of nomadic history and culture—a point that naturally could not fail to please the descendants of these very nomads."[33] He not only discounted the claim of endemic hostility between forest

26. Zholdasbekov and Kairzhanov 2002, 20 (quote), 14.
27. Akhmetov 2002, 19 (quote); Zholdasbekov and Kairzhanov 2002, 14.
28. Ermekbaev 2003, 56; also see Gumilev 2003g, 18.
29. Akhmetov 2002, 19; Temirgaliev 2007a.
30. Abdymanapov 2004, 17.
31. Zholdasbekov 2003, 9.
32. Zholdasbekov and Kairzhanov 2002, 16.
33. Temirgaliev 2007b.

and steppe, but went further by rejecting categorically the "Eurocentric" Black Legend about the *igo* with which the Golden Horde was supposed to have subdued ancient Rus'. Gumilev rejected the assumption of "higher" and "lower" levels of cultural development, with Eurasian cultures traditionally relegated to the latter category. Whereas a "Eurocentrist" (who in Kazakh discourse could well be a Russian) might scoff at the primitiveness of the Kazakh yurt as an aboriginal dwelling structure, for example, Gumilev always spoke respectfully, indeed "rapturously" (*s vostorgom*), about the yurt as a magnificent invention of a nomadic peoples.[34]

The discourse of polyethnic Kazakstani nationhood also makes active use of Gumilev's scientific theories about ethnogenesis and the ecology of ethnicity. The concepts of "ecological niches" and "nurturing landscapes" are used to help explain how the country's separate ethnic groups maintained their autonomy and individuality across the centuries, at the same time that they were developing a superethnic commonality.[35] More specifically, attempts have been made to locate the position of the novel Kazakstani nationality on Gumilev's ethnogenetic timeline. One analysis maintained that the breakup of the USSR delivered a "passionary jolt," thereby initiating a new process of Kazakhstani ethnogenesis. Faithfully following Gumilev's model, the emergent Kazakhstani ethnos is described as currently moving through the initial ethnogenetic phase of "incubation." This process affects the entirety of Kazakhstan's multinational population—all of whom, conveniently, share a common "perception of the world" and "behavioral stereotype"—and it will succeed to the extent that it can overcome the "differences between clans and nationalities." Indeed, multinational Kazakhstan will succeed in realizing its "historical chance" to consolidate itself as a political state only to the extent that its entire population is able "to perceive itself consciously to be a single [Kazakhstani] ethnos."[36]

At the center of this Gumilevian conceptualization of an emerging Kazakhstani ethnos is the belief that the latter is animated by naturalistic "vital energies" (*zhizennaia energiia*) and *passionarnost'*.[37] As is the case in post-Soviet Russia, for Kazakhstan as well the latter term is powerfully evocative and appealing. It is similarly deployed in a dual sense, referring on the one hand to the enthusiasm of the national masses and their engagement in the nation-building project, but on the other more exclusively to the charismatic leaders of the national renaissance

---

34. Frolovskaia 2005; Abdymanapov 2004, 19; Ermekbaev 2003, 41, 63.

35. Abdymanapov 2004, 17; Akhmetov 2002, 17; Ermekbaev 2003, 16; Zholdasbekov and Kairzhanov 2002, 14.

36. Kulataev 2002; Medeu-Uly and Kulataev 2002. For an alternative Gumilevian reading of the Kazakh (rather than Kazakhstani) ethnos by itself as a "completely new ethnic system," see Temirgaliev 2007b.

37. Akhmetov 2002, 19; Dzhilkibaev 2001.

in politics, economic development, and culture.[38] *Passionarnost'* is, for example, a central theme in a heavily promoted book about Kazakhstan's national development by two prominent politicians, who define it as a "creative passion" that stimulates selfless activity and sacrifice for the sake of a designated goal.[39] "Gumilev . . . emphasized that *passionarnost'* does not . . . create 'heroes' who lead the 'masses,' for most passionary individuals are within the latter group, where they define the internal potential of the ethnos."[40] Despite this populist spin, however, the authors used Gumilev's terminolgy specifically in order to flatter the national leader. The "founder of cities"—a reference to Nazarbaev and his construction of a new Kazakh capital—was a special type of passionary individual: a "passionary builder" (*stroitel'*). "For the passionary builder, yearly and five-year plans are constraining. For him, the growth and prosperity of the economy are only part of a much greater goal, of a planetary and even cosmic scale. He senses the breath of a new epoch and strives to bring it closer. His thoughts and actions are devoted to the future of his state, and he develops its economy, its social sphere, culture, and relationships between its citizens all according to new plans, on the principles of the future." To recognize these plans and bring them into life "to the extent possible for human effort"—this is the passionary Nazarbaev's "principal spiritual vector."[41]

If Gumilev stands as a figurehead for internationalist Eurasianism, however, his ideas are no less appealing for Kazakh ethno-nationalism, which has been growing relatively more pronounced since the turn of the century.[42] Most generally, the ethno-nationalist perspective views Kazakhstan as national and not a multinational state, in which ethnic Kazakhs should be accorded the same leading role that titular groups enjoy in other such national states.[43] Having been denied this status across all of its modern history, the most pressing political task in the country today is to translate this imperative into political reality. In contrast to the Eurasian narrative of civilizational commonality and historical solidarity between Russians and Kazakhs, Kazakh ethno-nationalism maintains that the two groups do not share a basic common civilizational background. For the present day, therefore, there is a pressing need to replace Russian "domination" (*dominirovanie*) of Kazakhstan with the "domination by the priorities of the

---

38. On the cult of charismatic leadership in Kazakhstan, see Isaacs 2010.

39. Shalakhmetov and Iskakov 2005.

40. Ibid.

41. Ibid. Other writers describe these *stroiteli* as a special Gumilevian "subethnos" of the Kazak people which brings innovation and modernity in the form of technological capabilities and urban infrastructure. Gali 2002.

42. On the juxtaposition of "civic" to "ethnic" nationalism in Kazakhstan, see Ó Beacháin and Kevlihan 2011.

43. Kolstø 1998, 54; "National Problems in the State Policy of Kazakhstan" 1998; Surucu 2005.

indigenous nation," that is to say, the "nation that forms the state."[44] This will be accomplished through a process of *kazakhizatsiia* or "Kazakhification" of the state. Kazakhification would involve a broad affirmative-action program of ethnic promotion, including the establishment of Kazakh as the language of state and official lingua franca for interethnic interaction, the recognition of Kazakh culture as the country's essential and guiding (*strezhnevaia*) culture, and the preferential advancement of ethnic Kazakhs in the country's leading political, economic, and cultural institutions.[45] The eventual goal is the formation of a so-called greater Kazakh—as opposed to Kazakstani—nation (*bol'shaia kazakhskaia natsiia*). The creation of such an entity would involve the active assimilation of the country's diverse multinational population into a Kazakh mainstream and the acknowledgement of the preeminence of the Kazakh ethnos.[46]

Ethno-national sentiment shares Eurasianism's fascination with Gumilev's narratives of steppe history, but it interprets the significance of his research in a very different way. Rather than describing the origins of the commonality uniting all the Eurasian peoples—and in particular Kazakhs and Russians—it sees his work as an affirmation of the primordial roots of the Kazakh nation and its unbroken lineage down to the present day. The rather anxious concern of post-Soviet Kazakh historiography to establish such a lineage can be seen, for example, in the extravagant argument advanced by some historians that the origin of the Kazak nation can be traced all the way back to the Saka peoples, a nomadic tribe associated with the Scythians around the first century BC.[47] Although Gumilev himself did not specifically confirm this, he did begin his own account of Kazakh ethnogenesis at the satisfyingly early date of the fifth century AD.[48] Gumilev's work on the Xiongnu and ancient Turks, which "were also the times of the beginning of Kazak ethnogenesis," is seen as another aspect of his contribution to Kazak ethnic history.[49] A more specific concern is to establish the antiquity of Kazakhstan's *gosudarstvennost'*, or state tradition. Relying on the authority of Gumilev, the historian Kinaiat Zardykhan argued that the emergence of a Kazak state dates back to the thirteenth and fourteenth centuries, in the form of the *Ak Orda* or White Horde.[50] In Zardykhan's account, Gumilevian ethno-energetics figured centrally in this process: "As a state, ancient Kazakhstan . . . acted as a sort of transmission state (*gosudarstvo-retransliator*)," he explained imaginatively, "which was able to

44. Gali 2007.
45. Smagulova 2006, 309; Hale 2009, 20–23; Gali 2004a.
46. Gali 2007.
47. Schatz 2000, 496–97; Shnirelman 2005, 105; Suny 2001, 882.
48. Gumilev 2003g, 12ff.
49. Temirgaliev 2011.
50. Zardykhan n.d.

accumulate the energy of the Turko-Mongolian Chingisid horde and redirect it toward the expansion of the boundaries of the Golden Horde."[51]

Kazakh ethno-nationalists are reserved and even sceptical about the Eurasianist project in Kazakhstan. In particular, there are deep suspicions of Aleksandr's Dugin's neo-Eurasianist appeals to the Kazakhstan leadership, which are seen as a cover for deeper hegemonic intentions. As one academic notes, Russian Eurasianists reckon that "Kazakhstan is like a big fat pie: it has gas, oil, and other natural resources . . . and its political elite is weak, with no supporters of a strong state."[52] Indeed, in the final analysis it is not merely Eurasianism that is the problem but the very fabric of Russian-Kazakh relations. Rather than a chronicle of tolerance and brotherhood, Kazakh nationalists see relations with tsarist Russia and then the USSR as a legacy of conquest, colonial disenfranchisement, and national oppression. Although the dissolution of the Soviet Union provided an opportunity to break this syndrome, Eurasianism in Kazakhstan would simply return the country back into its former status as a Russian "satellite" and "colony."[53] In view of Gumilev's official association with the cause of Eurasianism and alliance with Russia, this anti-Eurasianist stance leads some ethno-nationalists to question and reject him as well. Paradoxically, this is the position of the historian Zardykhan, who, as we have just seen, was prepared to invoke his authority in other connections.[54] It is by no means a universal position, however, and there is considerable support for him among nationalists, as can be seen in the work of another historian Makash Baigalievich Tatimov. Although Tatimov takes a highly negative view of Russia's historical role in Kazakhstan and calls for his compatriots to "break away from their dependency" on ethnocentric Russian historiography, he singles Gumilev out as a great exception who is worthy of the highest praise. "In my opinion, Gumilev is the very best historian, and I bow (*priklonit'sia*) before him." He summoned all other scholars "to remain faithful to the traditions of the great scholar Gumilev. . . . We should think in precisely the manner he did."[55]

---

51. Zardykhan 2007.
52. Gali 2003; Gali 2002.
53. Gali 2003; Surucu 2005; "National Problems in the State Policy of Kazakhstan" 1998.
54. Zardykhan n.d.; Asadullaev 2004; Serikbai 2002.
55. Cited in Masanov and Savin 2004. There was a certain schizophrenia in Gumilev's position on the question of Russia's imperial legacy that illustrates the tensions that pulled him toward Russian ethno-nationalism on the one hand and non-Russian ethno-nationalism on the other. We have seen his vigorous defense of Russia's imperial expansion and his denials that it involved hegemonic conquest. At the same time, however—in a demonstration of his sympathies with the non-Russian nationalities—he was also on occasion prepared to concede that the Russian empire had indeed "conquered" indigenous peoples and lands. He attempted to mollify the effect of the latter point, however, by asserting that this was universal practice and that not a single ethnos in the world "lives on land that is not conquered" from someone else. Gumilev 1990b; Lavrov 2000, 355.

The influence of Gumilev is also apparent in discussions about the nature of ethnicity and ethnos. Ethno-national discourse in Kazakhstan commonly describes an ethnos in Gumilevian terms as a natural entity distinct from social communities. Membership in a given ethnic unit is not a matter of preference or choice but is rather a natural condition, an inborn quality more closely associated with the spontaneous inclination of the subconscious than with rational deliberation. The debt that this perspective owes to Gumilev, moreover, is clearly acknowledged: "Ethnic belonging is based on a feeling (*oshchushchenie*), on which Gumilev's entire theory is based. Gumilev's notion of 'behavioral stereotype' corresponds to the specific rules and standards of behavior that one generation teaches to the next. The 'difference from others' marks the most profound aspect of the ethnos that provides us with a definition of who we are. The sense of 'who we are' remains in our subconscious. It emerged out of the depths of the millennia . . . it is that which we imbibe along with our mother's milk."[56] Gumilev's insistence on the vital function of endogamy in preserving the process of intergenerational transfer is also endorsed, which leads to questions about the ethnic status of children of mixed marriages.[57] This biologization of Kazakh ethnicity affirms that ethnic identity is reflected in genetic makeup and that each individual ethnos possesses its own respective genofond, which must be protected if the group is to survive.[58]

Of all the elements of Gumilev's natural-organic understanding of ethnicity, however, his teachings about the vital link connecting an ethnos to the natural-geographical environment have a special significance. The literature on Gumilev pays particular attention to this subject, emphasizing his argument that different groups are naturally attached to different geographical regions—the Russians to river valleys, for example, the Finno-Ugric peoples to the spaces between water basins, and the Turkic-Mongol peoples to the steppe. "The life activity (*zhiznedeiatel'nost'*) of the ethnos . . . cannot be separated from its accommodating and nurturing landscape."[59] The specific implications of the latter point for the Kazakhs are elaborated in Gumilev's ecology of nomadism, which explains aspects of Kazakh national culture in terms of the geographical conditions of the steppes in which it developed.[60] Finally, Gumilev's point that ethnies were characterized by their own distinctive genetic makeup was carried over into the ecological relationship with a native landscape. For the Kazakhs, this means that

---

56. Serazhieva 2002.
57. Kolstø 1998, 55.
58. Segizbaev 2007; Atabek 2004a.
59. Abdymanapov 2004, 21 (quote), 13, 16.
60. Ermekbaev 2003, 16, 30; Amanov and Mukhambetova 2002, cited in Adams 2011, 108.

the "steppe is not only a manifestation of their historical memory but also a bio-logically active condition of their [ethnic] gene pool."[61]

For some ethno-nationalists, Gumilev's ethno-territoriality has a rather more practical significance. Questions of homeland rights for indigenous peoples and claims for jurisdiction over putatively national territories are important and highly sensitive issues all across the former Soviet Union. They are especially so in multinational Kazakhstan, where for historical reasons and as a result of Soviet policy the settlement of ethnic Russian population is disproportionately dense in its northern regions. This geographical imbalance is exacerbated by the argu-ment made by some Russian nationalists that these territories are not legitimately Kazakh at all but rather historically Russian lands, alienated as a consequence of the arbitrary Soviet redesignation of national republic boundaries in the 1920s.[62] There are indications that these sentiments have some resonance with at least sec-tions of the Russian population in these areas, raising the prospect of irredentism and a full-fledged separatist movement against the Kazakh state.[63] These possi-bilities are taken very seriously by Kazakh nationalists, who maintain to the con-trary that although these territories may have been a constant object of Russian colonization, in fact they "always remained primordially Kazakh lands."[64] Indeed, there seems to be little doubt that Nazarbaev's radical decision to heighten the Kazakh presence in the north by relocating the capital city was influenced by these considerations. The desire to alienate the Kazakhs' traditional homeland is assumed to a hidden agenda of Russian Eurasianism, and the call for Kazakhstan to join a common Eurasian state is believed to conceal a deeper intention "to legally divorce the [Kazakh] ethnos from its concrete territory."[65]

Some Kazakh nationalists have mobilized Gumilev's ecology of ethnicity into a firm position on the question of homeland rights and entitlements. This position might be described as "exclusive territoriality," and it forms a critical element in the process of *kazakhizatsiia*.[66] The argument is that the entirety of the state territory of Kazakhstan is the natural historical homeland for only one ethnic group, the Kazakhs, who have occupied it effectively from time immemo-rial. All other groups, taken together, form a great collection of ethnic diasporas, each of which migrated into Kazakhstan at some later point.[67] "In every [ethnic]

61. Abdymanapov 2004, 17–18; also see Shalakhmetov and Iskakov 2005.
62. Kubicek 1997, 645; Olcott 2002, 56.
63. Laruelle and Peyrouse 2004, 221–29.
64. Toleshovich 1998.
65. Gali 2002; Gali 2003.
66. Smagulova 2006, 306, 309.
67. Nysanbaev and Kadyrzhanov 2006.

Kazakh flows the blood of an aborigine (*avtokhton*, i.e., original inhabitant)."[68] This means that the Kazakhs alone are entitled to exercise patrimonial rights across all Kazakh lands, and consequently that the Kazakh ethnos—its language, culture, and so on—should by rights be able to play a dominating role. Although other ethnic groups are also entitled to such ethno-territorial prerogatives, their entitlement is valid only in regard to their own aboriginal homelands, which in all cases are located somewhere beyond the geographical space of the Kazakh state. Traces of this perspective can be seen even in official pronouncements on nationalities policy, with Nazarbaev himself emphasizing the special rights of ethnic Kazakhs to their "historic homeland, age-old Kazakh land" and suggesting that other ethnic groups "who do not have deep roots on Kazakh soil" might find it easier to leave the republic than those who do.[69] The suggestion is that Kazaks are somehow more native that the other nontitular groups, all of whom naturally retain an attachment of some sort to an external homeland in addition to their commitment to Kazakhstan itself.

This point was put bluntly in a declaration by Aron Kabyshevich Atabek, a poet and leader of the "Alash National Freedom Party," an extremist Kazakh ethno-national political movement. "Historical truth and reality consist in the following," he asserted:

> Kazakhstan is inhabited by a TITULAR, STATE-FORMING NATION, that is, the KAZAKHS. Together with them—on their KAZAKH LANDS—live representatives of more than 120 national foreign dia-sporas (communities). The latter live in Kazakhstan with the rights of good guests (*na pravakh dobrykh gostei*), no matter whether they came here voluntarily or involuntarily, or whether their presence is desirable or not. Each one of these diasporas has its own historical Motherland and its own primordial ethnos: for the Russians this is Russia, for the Germans Germany, for the Koreans Korea (both of them), and so on.[70]

For Atabek, the implications of this situation are unambiguous and compelling. Simply put, the very presence on Kazakh soil of these "foreign" guest nationalities is inherently disruptive. He spelled this out clearly, using Gumilev's naturalist

---

68. Gali 2004b.

69. Cited in Hale 2009, 22 (quote), 24–25. On Nazarbaev's oscillations between multinationalism and ethno-nationalism, see Suny 1999, 4–5; Schatz 2000, 492–93; Kolstø 1998, 56–57; Olcott 2002, 65; Bremmer and Welt 1995.

70. Atabek 2004b (emphasis in original).

teachings about the organic links between ethnicity and environment, and about intruder groups whose very presence disrupts them:

> As Gumilev wrote, there is a "sacred (*sakral'naia*) connection between ethnos and landscape." Practically speaking, this connection is genetic. Only the local ethnos understands the "intimate" needs of the given landscape. The unity of the aboriginal group (*avtokhton*) and the land is cosmic and mystical. Those who migrate into the region at a later point destroy this deep connection (if only inadvertently). In this manner, Mesopotamia was undermined by the Egyptians, North Africa by the Romans, and Kazakhstan [by the Russians] during the Virgin Lands program.[71]

The implied alternatives for Kazakhstan's non-Kazakh population are unalluring: they must either accept the preeminence of the Kazakh ethnos in Kazakhstan or repatriate back to their group's original native homeland. It may be noted that by placing an absolute priority on the natural-organic emplacement of an ethnos in its exclusive ecological niche, Atabek's shrill homily is able to claim a special preeminence for Kazakhs in Kazakhstan without in any way stigmatizing other nationalities as less worthy or inferior. The problem, as he would have it, has nothing whatsoever to do with ethno-national inequalities, much less those of race. To the contrary, he can genuinely argue that all nationalities are strictly equal. They are so, however, only insofar as they respect the natural order of things as described by Gumilev, which dictates that they must remain ensconced within their own respective primordial homelands and not seek to occupy others. In this way, Gumilev provides the basis and justification for a narrative of social exclusion that avoids the familiar and immediately objectionable language of bigotry and racism.[72]

Tatarstan

In certain respects, the ethno-political dynamics in post-Soviet Tatarstan resemble those of Kazakhstan. The massive political mobilization and momentum for change in the republic during perestroika was largely ethno-national in character. No sooner had the ancien régime collapsed, however, than the local political elite began to promote an alternative view of "civic" nationhood, which represented Tatarstan as a civic political community based not on national criteria but rather on the principle that all citizens were equal members, regardless of ethnic

---

71. Ibid.
72. Kolstø 1999, 614–15.

affiliation.[73] The principal architect of this new vision was Mintimer Sharipo-vich Shaimiev—like Nazarbaev a former Communist leader who became the republic's first president.[74] The polyethnic character of post-Soviet Tatarstan was emphasized by the same juxtaposition we have seen in Kazakhstan between the Tatar ethnos on the one hand and the "Tatarstani nation" (*tatarstanskii narod*) on the other hand, the latter being an amalgam of ethnic Tatars, Russians, and other groups.[75] Tatarstan's multinational and multicultural identity was officially confirmed in its 1992 constitution and further explicated in a plethora of mani-festos and statements put out by key ideologues of the regime—notably Rafael Sibgatovich Khakimov, a key political adviser for Shaimiev, vice president of the Tatar Academy of Sciences, and director of the Academy's Institute of History.[76] In 1994—the same year in which Tatarstan finally signed a bilateral treaty with Russia—Shaimiev presented this perspective in an address at Harvard University, where he offered his program as a "Tatarstan model" for the development of local and federal politics in the Russian Federation. This model emphasized the same two priorities that we have seen in Kazakhstan, namely, the peaceful cohabita-tion of ethnic groups within the Tatar republic together with the development of harmonious interaction and cooperation between it and the federal center.[77]

In its efforts to legitimize this perspective, the political leadership in Tatarstan has formally embraced Lev Gumilev's legacy, and Gumilev's per-sona has become an object of official veneration similar to that in Kazakhstan. President Shaimiev frequently invoked the memory of this "great scholar and civic actor," whose brilliant and profound scientific theories "we are today only beginning to appreciate."[78] After Gumilev's death in 1992, the Tatarstan govern-ment quickly established itself as a guardian of his memory in St. Petersburg by erecting a memorial at his gravesite in the Aleksandr Nevskii Monastery, and in 1997 it commissioned a memorial plaque commemorating Gumilev, which was mounted on the apartment block where he last lived.[79] The images on the plaque evoke Gumilev's engagement with the steppe nomads, a connection emphasized in its simple inscription: "To the outstanding historian and Turkologist Gumilev, from the Republic of Tatarstan."[80] A large international conference on "The Ideas

73. Khakimov 1993, 12, 14, 17; Khakimov 2002; Mukhametshin 2004, 290–91; Walker 1998, 233; Giuliano 2000, 295.

74. Unlike Nazarbaev, however, Shaimiev stepped down from office in 2010.

75. Khakimov 1993, 15; Khakimov 2002; Sharapov 1998, 62; Gorenburg 1999, 252.

76. Mukhametshin 2004, 291; Gorenburg 1999, 252; Shnirelman 2009a, 74–75.

77. Iskhakov 1995. For discussions, see Veinguer and Davis 2007, 188; Giuliano 2000, 309–10; Raviot 1992.

78. Shaimiev 1997 (quotes); Shaimiev 2005; Tol'ts 2005.

79. This plaque is reproduced on the cover of this book.

80. Mansurova 2005; Lavrov 2000, 354n.

of Eurasianism in the Scientific Legacy of Lev Nikolaevich Gumilev" was held in Kazan in 2004, with presidents Shaimiev and Nazarbaev in attendance, and the official embrace was confirmed the following year with the erection of a statue to his memory as part of the thousand-year anniversary of the city of Kazan. The choice of Gumilev for this distinction was all the more significant in view of the fact that the statue was originally intended to be of the Russian tsar Peter the Great. Shaimiev and Vladimir Putin both attended the unveiling of the monument in August 2005, and the Tatar president cited Gumilev's memorable declaration of solidarity with the Tatar peoples that is inscribed at the base of the monument: "I am a Russian who has spent his entire life defending Tatars against insults."[81] Shaimiev's successor as Tatar president, Rustam Nurgalievich Minnikhanov, has made his own expression of the "enormous respect and deep gratitude" of the Tatar people to Gumilev's memory.[82]

The most important element of Gumilev's legacy in Tatarstan is his Eurasian-ist historiography, which has enjoyed an official endorsement similar to, if some-what less intense than, that in Kazakhstan.[83] He is celebrated above all for his debunking of the "Black Legend" about the Tatar yoke as a pernicious historical invention—an "ideological aggression" inspired by anti-Russian agents in the West and East—and his insistence that relations between the Russians and the Golden Horde were fraternal and mutually supportive.[84] "I think that Gumilev is a very important figure," observed the historian Damir Mavliaveevich Iskhakov, who maintained that his work is "critical for the future reconceptualization of Russian [rossiiskii] history." Gumilev not only "demonstrated the positive role of nomadic peoples in Russian history" but also established more generally that the ancestors of many non-Russian nations made vital contributions over the centuries to the development of Russian society and state life.[85]

The influence of Gumilev's historical interpretations can be readily seen in the writings of a variety of leading historians in Tatarstan.[86] Khakimov himself summarized the significance of the Golden Horde for Russia using Gumilev's own characterization.

---

81. "Gumilev Monument Opened on St. Petersburg Street" 2005; "Lev Gumilev primirit stolitsu Tatarstana s Rossiiskoi imperii" 2005. For Gumilev's original statement, see Gumilev 1994c. For a photo of this monument see figure 7.

82. See Minnikhanov's introduction to Akhmetshin 2011.

83. Shaimiev 2005. On Tatar Eurasianism, see Laruelle 2008b, 162–67.

84. Shaimiev 1997, 6; Iskhakov 1999, 278; Enikeev 2007b; Khakim n.d.

85. "Who Is Who" 2006.

86. Fakhrutdinov 2000; Fakhrutdinov 1993; Iskhakov 1993; Teliashov 2001. On post-Soviet Tatar historiography, see Shnirelman 1996, 36–40.

The spirit of Ghingiz Khan always lived in Russia . . . Moscow was born of the Golden Horde because it was revived and became powerful thanks to [its role in collecting] the "Tatar tribute." Later, it used this privilege to unite the other Russian principalities around itself. It never occurred to Dmitrii Donskoi to fight with the Tatars, [rather] he acted together with loyal Tatars on the side of the legitimate power against the *uzurpator* Mamai, who was supported by the Lithuanians. And if Khan Tokhtamysh marched on Moscow, then it was only in order to compel Dmitrii to pay the tribute.[87]

The Gumilevian inspiration motivating the work of the popular historian Gali Rashitovich Enikeev is even clearer. In *The Imperial Crown of the Golden Horde*, which appeared in the popular history series *The Secret of Lev Gumilev* mentioned above, Enikeev explained that his perspective was based entirely "on the Eurasian views and methodology of Lev Nikolaevich Gumilev."[88] Enikeev's book is essentially a colorful account of how the experience of the Golden Horde brought Russians and Tatars together to establish the foundations for a "great Eurasian empire," and how this sacred collaborative legacy was subsequently concealed and denied. Enikeev took up this latter issue in a sequel volume that he graced with an explicitly Gumilevian title: *Following the Traces of the "Black Legend."*[89] Enikeev's work has attracted high praise in Tatarstan, not only from official historians but from religious and cultural figures as well. Such indeed is the appreciation for Gumilev's historiography that even Tatar historians unsympathetic to Eurasianism as a political project in the present day concede that Gumilev is the only Russian to have delivered a balanced account of ancient Russian history "capable of reconciling (*primirit'*) the history" of the Russians and Tatars.[90]

For Tatar Eurasianism, Gumilev's historical research established conclusively that the Russian state is the product of two distinct historical and cultural traditions. "On the basis of Gumilev's legacy," noted Shaimiev, "a very important conclusion can be drawn: that Russia has two sources, Slavic and Turkic, Orthodoxy and Islam." Indeed, were it not for "the khan [of the Golden Horde], with his harsh laws, systems of communication, and population censuses," the warring Russian princedoms would never have united around Moscow and "there would

87. Khakim 2002.

88. Enikeev 2007a; Enikeev 2007b.

89. Enikeev 2009.

90. See the comments of Iskander Lerunovich Izmailov and Damir Mavliaveevich Iskhakov in "A bylo li igo?" 1997, 86, 90.

have been no Great Russia."[91] His adviser Khakimov was yet more emphatic. "Moscow is the creation of the Golden Horde," he asserted. "The sources of Russia are Orthodoxy as well as Islam—Slavic as well as Turkic. This is Russia's genetic code, which it is not possible to get away from. It will determine the country's future. In other words, Russia has two foundations, two legs—Kievan Rus' and the Golden Horde. All of its problems, all of the lack of clarity surrounding Russia's national idea and the country's politics are caused by ignoring this fact, [which is] a shameful denial of the Tatar legacy [developed] under the influence of the tradition of Peter and Catherine."[92] The basis for this relationship was the existence of positive complementarity between the two ethnies, which as Gumilev taught led early on to their symbiosis and subsequent co-development as a single entity. "Lev Gumilev was not far from the truth when he spoke about the Russians and Tatars as a single people (*narod*), separated only by language and religion."[93] To emphasize the point, Napoleon's notorious observation, "scratch a Russian and you will find a Tatar"—originally intended as an insult—is now invoked by Tatars in a positive spirit.[94] The grand culmination of this symbiosis is a supranational amalgam best described once again in Gumilevian terms as a superethnos.

Again as in Kazakhstan, Gumilevian Eurasianism in Tatarstan plays a significant ideological role in domestic politics. The "superethnos" concept is highly valuable for developing a vision of "Tatarstani" society as a multinational or community (*obshchnost'*) based on interethnic harmony, cohesion, and mutual good will. Khakimov was pressing this point in 1993 when the precise form and composition of the Tatar republic was still not entirely clear.[95] In regard to Tatarstan's dealings with the federal center, Eurasianism acts as a singularly useful discourse that can articulate and accommodate different aspects of what is a profoundly ambivalent relationship. On the one hand, it conveys a message of fraternity and natural unity with Russia on the basis of ethno-cultural affinities, a shared historical experience, and—most critically—a full accounting for the contribution that non-Russian peoples have made to the creation and development of the Russian state. In order that all of Russia's nationalities have their proper place, maintained Iskhakov, "it is necessary to understand history from a Gumilevian perspective (*s gumilevskikh pozitsii*)—broadly and without prejudice."[96] This was the message of Tatarstan's official representative in St. Petersburg in 1997, who explained

---

91. "Prezident Tatarstana vystupaet za rasprostranenie 'liberal'nogo islama'" 2004; Shaimiev 1997, 6; Shaimiev 2005; Khazanov 2002, 477; Tagirov 2001.

92. Khakim 2002 (quote); Khakimov 2005.

93. Tagirov 2001 (quote).

94. Khakim 1998, 42.

95. Khakimov 1993, 10.

96. "Who Is Who" 2006.

that the memorial plaque offered by his government was intended to "continue the tradition established by Gumilev and become a symbol of cooperation and friendship between the two peoples."[97] The historian Enikeev insists that all of Gumilev's historical work points precisely to the need for statesmen of today to maintain the closest unity between the two peoples, and he even reproaches the Tatar "elite" for failing fully to appreciate this point.[98] The Institute of History of the Tatar Academy of Sciences echoed this assertion by praising Enikeev's work precisely for illuminating "the age-old tolerant relations of the Tatar peoples with other nations of Eurasia."[99]

Along with harmony and cooperation, however, Gumilev's legacy can also be invoked to legitimize the principle of diversity and ethnic heterogeneity—a principle that can in turn be deployed to enhance claims for greater political autonomy within the federal arrangement. Tatarstan declared itself a sovereign entity in 1990, even before the collapse of the USSR, and it was only after several years of difficult negotiation that a treaty stipulating Tatarstan nebulously as an "associated state" was signed with Moscow. The subsequent debate about precisely what this means has served to unsettle relations with Moscow down to the present day. The "diversity" that Gumilev had in mind, of course, related to the freedom of ethnies to live undisturbed in their own ecological niche in accordance with their own particular behavioral stereotypes and had nothing to do with politics. For the Tatarstan government, the argument is transformed into a claim for enhancement of federal prerogatives and thus takes on very clear political resonances. Despite Tatarstan's de facto status as a federal subject, Tatarstan has used the doctrines of Eurasianism in order to claim equality with Russia itself, even to the point of participating with other CIS states on the same legal footing as the Russian Federation.[100] It is in regard to these latter points that in one interview Khakimov delicately characterized the Tatar leadership's embrace of Gumilev as "politically advantageous."[101]

Gumilev's naturalistic perspective on ethnicity figures prominently in Tatar discourses about nationhood and identity, official as well as popular.[102] It can be seen in calls to foster the Tatar behavioral stereotype and maintain endogamy in order to preserve the cultural cohesiveness of the national group.[103] The

---

97. See the comments of Sh. K. Akhmetshin at http://gumilevica.kulichki.net/fund/fund02.htm, accessed 2/5/2015.

98. Enikeev 2005.

99. Mamleev n.d.

100. Likhachev 1996, 7, 8, 10; Laruelle 2008b, 62–63.

101. Interview with the author, Kazan, July 2004.

102. Shnirel'man 2009, 214; "Who Is Who" 2006.

103. Veinguer and Davis 2007, 201.

same Khakimov whose strong support of interethnic Eurasianist concord we have just noted was also an outspoken early proponent of ethnic essentialism. Acknowledging his debt to Gumilev, he described the character of the ethnos in the following terms.

> An ethnos is a biosocial phenomenon, which connects the natural world with society. The ethnos contains biological energy, and it obeys laws that are different from those controlling social processes. We sometimes hear appeals that we should forget about our ethnic origins and not divide people according to this criterion. Such appeals are based on a misunderstanding of the nature of the phenomenon. Ethnicity does not come from wishful thinking, or much less from some evil plot on the part of "separatists," but rather it is given by birth. . . . The biological nature of ethnicity becomes clearly apparent in situations of interethnic conflicts.[104]

The concept of *passionarnost'* has become a popular keyword in discussions of the dynamics of ethnic development, and as we have seen with Nazarbaev in Kazakhstan, it is frequently associated specifically with the person of the president. "The passionary energy of the Tatar people has not been exhausted," maintained one syncophant, "but rather, thanks to the president, is gaining new strength and cogency."[105] As is the case in Russia itself, extravagant conclusions are attributed to Gumilev's ethno-naturalism—conclusions that he himself would not have recognized. The editor of the newspaper *Zvezda Povol'zhia*, for example, claimed that Gumilev defined each nationality as a "special frequency of the human biological field" tuned to its own unique "electro-paramagnetic frequency." He suggested that audio tests could therefore be effective in measuring the precise amount of "Tatarness" (*tatarskost'*) present in ethnic Russians or "Russianness" in Tatars.[106]

One aspect of Gumilev's ethnos theory that does not figure very prominently in Tatar ethno-national discourse is his ecology of ethnicity. The reasons for this relate to the highly fragmented demographics of the Tatar peoples, who are widely dispersed across Russia and other states of the former Soviet Union. Only about one-third of ethnic Tatars actually live in the Tatar Republic. The Tatar diaspora is, moreover, of very long standing historically, and the different branches of it have put down deep roots in very different regions: Kazan,

---

104. Khakimov 1993, 11 (quote), 12; Drobizheva 2001, 169.
105. Mingazov 2007 (quote); Aisin 2006; also see Shagbanova 1998.
106. Akhmetov 2008a; Akhmetov 2007.

Astrakhan, Siberia, Crimea, Uzbekistan, Kazakhstan, Turkmenia, and else-where.[107] For this reason, the attempt to describe a sort of greater ethnic Tatar nation that would include all of these groups cannot easily fit with the notion of a clearly delimited and shared homeland—something that is rather more straightforward in Kazakhstan, as we have seen. To be sure, Khakimov's discussion of the nature of ethnicity is careful to include the Gumilevian principle that ethnies "are formations with deep roots in a specific territory, to which only one ethnos may lay claim," and he refers to the Tatars in particular as living on "their primordial lands."[108] But in his more practical thinking about ethnic nation-building, this principle is not actively deployed. Indeed, by rejecting the "Stalinist" definition of ethnos, Khakimov implied among other things that a common shared territorial base was *not* a necessary condition for the existence of an ethnic group.[109]

Khakimov rejected the idea that Tatar ethnic essentialism amounted to separatism, as we have seen, and this position is repeated more emphatically by others. "Wherever, in whatever region of the Russian Federation Tatars may live, they always support the unity and cohesiveness of Russia. The Tatar national renaissance is not separatist, but rather unifying and stabilizing."[110] Nonetheless, the very logic of ethno-national affirmation necessarily involves a certain critical juxtaposition of Tatars to Russians, which emphasizes not unity and shared destiny but rather difference and contrast. And as this juxtaposition is developed, it leads to a certain qualification of, and even a retreat from, the unambiguous Gumilevian declarations of solidarity and commonality cited above. Thus, Khakimov maintains that although Russians and Tatars may be joined in a single superethnos, the two groups remain "divided by many things: their relation to the state, society, the family, and their work." Indeed, their superethnic unity "must not be absolutized (*absoliutizirovat'*), for the Russians formed as Russians, after all, and the Tatars as Tatars."[111] And throughout the historical process of symbiosis, the Tatars still managed to preserve their distinct identity and culture as "an island of Islamic and Turkic civilization in the middle of a Russian Orthodox ocean." Contradicting his own argument for a Russian-Tatar superethnos, Khakimov maintained that the alliance of what he describes as two "counterposing civilizations" is to be explained "not by some sort of special sympathies"—by which he means Gumilevian complementarity—but rather by the common strategic

---

107. Khakim 1998, 56; Khakim 2002.
108. Cited in Tishkov 1997, 8; Khakim 2002.
109. Khakimov 1993, 11.
110. Tagirov 2001 (quote); Enikeev 2005.
111. Khakim n.d.; Tagirov 2001.

imperative of confronting an external threat from the West.[112] This logic led him at one point to add his voice to that of other skeptics in Tatarstan and dismiss the very existence of a common Eurasian civilization as a historical fiction that only "very naïve people" can find convincing.[113]

The juxtaposition between the Tatar and Russian ethnies is emphasized in the rejection by Tatar ethno-nationalists of the Soviet account of Tatar ethnogenesis.[114] According to the latter, the Tatars originated out of local Turkic-Bulgar tribes who inhabited the Volga region prior to the Mongol onslaught and suffered like the Russians themselves under the oppressive domination of the foreign Golden Horde.[115] Today, by contrast, nationalist Tatar historiography celebrates the great antiquity and geographical range of the Tatar ethnos—a perspective for which Gumilev provides due inspiration. Relations between the Bulgar state and Golden Horde are no longer depicted in negative but rather in strongly positive terms, as a sort of vital formative phase in the ethnogenesis of the Tatar nation of today.[116] This stress on positive connections with the Golden Horde allows Tatar historians to lay claim to an imperial heritage of their own, to the extent indeed that they now describe themselves as an "empire-forming" peoples in their own right. Once again, this perspective leads to a break with Gumilevian doctrine, in this case his rejection of the legend about the Tatar yoke. It turns out that his categorical dismissal of it—a dismissal faithfully embraced in the official discourse of the Tatarstan model—is not so self-evident, and that the entire matter is rather more complicated than Gumilev himself would have us think. As Khakimov explained, "Lev Gumilev claimed that there had been no Tatar-Mongol yoke, but rather a union of Tatars and Russians, [who together] faced an onslaught of Teutons and Lithuanians. Perhaps he idealized the situation somewhat. [In fact,] the Tatar-Mongols were not humanitarians, and in their brutality they were no different from the Europe of their time."[117] His point

---

112. Khakim 1998, 44, 58, 38.

113. Khakim 1998, 49. The historian Iskander Izmailov rejects the Eurasian assumption of mutual Tatar-Russian influences altogether. He explains that although he can appreciate the effects of the Golden Horde on ethnic Russian history, he cannot see a reciprocal Russian influence on the Tatars, and dismisses the notion that any Gumilevian "symbiosis" ever took place. Interview with the author, Kazan, July 2004; also see "A bylo li igo?" 1997, 87, 89; "Who Is Who" 2006. For other skeptical evaluations of Eurasianism, see Iskhakov 2002; Buravleva 1998.

114. For an excellent overview of the contorted ideological history of this question, see Uiama 2003.

115. Tillett 1969, 314–15.

116. Zverev 2002, 79, 81; Shnirel'man 2003; Shnirelman 1996, 36–37; Khakim 1998, 34–35; Fakhrutdinov 1993; Usmanov 1997., Even those Tatar historians who continue to describe Bulgar-Mongol relations as antagonistic can however find great inspiration in Gumilev's accounts. Bariev 2005.

117. Khakim 2002.

was not of course to celebrate the brutality of the Golden Horde, but rather to make it very clear that, as an imperial nation, the forebears of today's Tatars could act indeed like one and leave a corresponding mark on Russia. Gumilevian harmony, symbiosis, and *komplimentarnost'* would not really allow for this. Another historian made this point yet more clearly, asserting—contra Gumilev—that the Golden Horde did engage in the conquest of Rus' after all, and did actually "colonize" (*kolonizatsiia*) its lands. The experience might not have been as abject and destructive as the *igo* image suggests, but there was no question that these were "quite difficult times" for Rus'. "I think that it is not very convincing to assume that just because there was no *igo* [in the traditional Russian understanding], there is nothing to talk about. History cannot be entirely rewritten. By all means, the Golden Horde forms a period of Russian history."[118]

The standard Eurasianist scenario depicting the development of the Russian state out of foundations established by Genghis Khan generates an entirely novel ideological dynamic when it is detached from the context of Russian debates about ancient Russian history and inserted instead into the center of contemporary Tatar ethno-political discourses.[119] Gumilev's historiographical authority is co-opted for these purposes, moreover, and he is redeployed on the front line of a revisionist argumentation—where we may assume he would not really have wanted to be. Now Gumilev is praised for having "convincingly demonstrated what Russia grew out of and to whom the Russians owe the fact that they became a great nation."[120] It was the Mongol-Tatar imperial legacy—presented as vitally relevant for the present day—that explains why Stalin and other Russian rulers always feared Tatar culture, for the latter "is potentially powerful in its *passionarnost'* (*passionarno*), possibly more powerful than Russian culture." And all this "is precisely what Lev Gumilev was writing about."[121]

No less significant than these claims to a robust ethno-imperial legacy are resentments about the subsequent historical fate of the Tatar peoples within the Russian imperial state. Here again Khakimov contradicts himself, asserting that the latter was built not on the basis of voluntaristic cooperation at all but rather by means of coercion, annexation, and forced assimilation.[122] The degree of public sensitivity in post-Soviet Tatarstan that attaches to this historical legacy can be seen in the widespread indignation against a plan to commemorate the

118. See the comments of Aleksandr Salagaev in "Who Is Who" 2006.
119. Aleksandr Dugin has picked up on this and denounces Khakimov's (as opposed to Nazarbaev's) Eurasianism for its blatant "Tatar nationalism" and "Russophobic artificiality." Dugin n.d.
120. Mulladzhanov 2007.
121. Akhmetov 2008b.
122. Khakimov 1993, 19, 31.

city of Kazan's millennium in 2005 by erecting a statue to Peter the Great—a veritable hate figure, as it turned out, who Tatar protestors denounced as having "deliberately pursued a policy of the destruction of the Tatar nation."[123] In this dispute as well Gumilev was implicated, and indeed in the most public of ways, for it was none other than he himself who was selected as an alternative Russian figure preferable to the great tsar. In contrast to Peter, Gumilev was someone that the Tatar people could accept, and a statue in *his* memory "would not have to be protected against a dissatisfied local population."[124] These sensitivities about the historical legacy of Russian imperialism are exacerbated by what is widely interpreted as its reappearance in the contemporary policies of the Russian Federation, specifically in the centralizing inclinations of the Putin administration. The effects of centralization are seen as the strengthening of the "imperial principles" and the "imperial tradition" of the Russian center, with the obvious goal of further restricting Tatarstan's autonomy and obstructing the consolidation of the greater Tatar ethnos.[125]

One example of the perceived challenges to the latter project came in the form of "Federal Law 309" adopted by the Russian Duma in 2007. This highly controversial law stipulated that decisions about the language of instruction in the country's autonomous republics would no longer be made by the republic in question but rather by individual schools, which had the effect of handing the prerogative over to the federal Ministry of Education.[126] This was seen in Tatarstan as a naked attempt to undermine indigenous Tatar culture and further Russify the population, and it was bitterly denounced. Among its critics was the historian Enikeev, whose enthusiastic popularizations of Gumilev's account of the historical friendship and unity of the two peoples we have noted above. Enikeev used Gumilevian arguments to respond to this challenge as well, in this case drawing on his theory of ethnic essentialism. Moscow's latest attempt to Russify and assimilate Tatars cannot possibly work, Enikeev explained, for the latter "have not inherited, in line with the objective laws of nature, the corresponding behavioral stereotype, culture, and traditions of the Great Russian ethnos." The Russian center was violating clear legal norms and even its own constitution, to be sure, but more grievous was their violation of the fundamental ethno-natural principles of the biosphere. "As the great Russian scholar, humanist, historian, and ethnologist Lev Nikolaevich Gumilev repeatedly emphasized, ethnies or

---

123. Tol'ts 2005.

124. "Gumilev Monument Opened on St. Petersburg Street" 2005; "Lev Gumilev primirit stolitsu Tatarstana s rossiiskoi imperii" 2005.

125. Khakim 2002; Mukhametshin 2004, 287.

126. Lobjakas 2009.

nations (*narody*)—including those occupying the territory of our own country—do not rise and fall 'on the orders of a king or sultan.' Nations cannot be 'created' and 'abolished' by politicians. Rather, they are objects with natural origins,
and develop and survive precisely according to natural laws." Ignorant bureau-
crats do not understand this, of course, and thus cannot heed Gumilev's warning
that their "reckless violence against nature"—that is, against ethnic individuality and autonomy—is committed in vain. "As objects of natural origin, ethnies
will struggle—to some extent unconsciously and in different ways—against all
attempts to change them."[127] In a sense, Enikeev is deploying Gumilev in the same
manner as we have noted in Tatar Eurasianism, in order to legitimate a claim for
Tatar autonomy from the federal center. At question here, however, is not the
autonomy of a multinational "Tatarstani" civil community, but rather respect for
ethno-national diversity and the right for all ethnies to live—as Gumilev himself
put it—"peacefully but separately."

Sakha-Yakutia

The final example in our consideration of Gumilev beyond ethnic Russia is the
Republic of Sakha. Sakha shares certain sociopolitical characteristics with Kazakh-
stan and Tatarstan in regard to the multiethnic composition of its population, the
Turkic identity of the titular Yakut nationality, and the republic's early and sustained attempts to maximize its autonomous status vis-à-vis the federal center.
Sakha differs, however, in that a narrative about the republic's population as a sort
of multiethnic "Yakuti" civil community—along the lines of "Kazakhstani" and
"Tatarstani" nationhood—has not been developed in the same manner. Moreover,
Eurasianism does not enjoy the same status as an ideology of state as in Kazakhstan—although in its own way it does remain highly significant.[128] Nevertheless,
the level of public esteem for Gumilev in Sakha is comparable to that in Kazakhstan and Tatarstan, and his concepts and theories play a special role in ethno-
political discourses for many of the same reasons. As was the case with the other
national groups considered in this chapter, Yakut interest in his work was apparent
in the 1980s, and at that time Gumilev expressed his own special appreciation for
it. "Through difficult years," he explained in an interview for a Yakutsk newspaper
at the end of the decade, "I was very grateful for the fact that the Yakuts were the
only ones who were interested in me, my books, and my ideas."[129]

---

127. Enikeev 2008.
128. Shnirelman 2009a, 73.
129. "Prarodina Iakutov" 1989.

From the moment the republic was established in the early 1990s, the Sakha leadership has taken care to affirm its allegiance to the Russian state and the importance of its inclusion in the latter's federal structure. In a 2002 speech commemorating Yakutia's "becoming a part" (*vkhozhdenie v sostav*) of the Russian state in the seventeenth century, the republic's new president Viacheslav Anatolevich Shtyrov stressed this point and immediately referred to the authority of Gumilev. "The mentality and psychology of the two peoples served as important factors" for insuring their successful integration over the centuries. "This is what the great Russian scholar Nikolai [*sic*] Gumilev called *komplimentarnost'*: a sympathy between nations for each other, a striving for collaboration, and a preparedness to live together." It was important to preserve the elemental "friendship between our peoples" and "to strengthen the unified Russian state," which was the principal guarantor of "our [Sakha] state life." Shtyrov gave this Gumilevian perspective a distinctly post-Yeltsinist or "Putinist" spin, asserting—contra the Tatar position we have just considered—not only that tsarist Russia was not really a notorious "prison-house of peoples" but that even the Soviet Union itself did not suppress the free development of its nationalities. a conclusion that would have Gumilev most certainly spinning in his grave. To the contrary, Shtyrov explained, the USSR actually saved the "small peoples" of the North from extinction and made it possible "to realize the ideas and dreams of the Yakut people about their consolidation (*splochenie*) into a nation with its own state life."[130] Shtyrov's confusion as to which Gumilev he had in mind exposes an apparatchik's comical ignorance about his own country's most important cultural landmarks. At the same time, however, it underscores the pervasiveness of popular associations of the name Gumilev with this particular post-Soviet version of interethnic solidarity, even on the part of those with only the shallowest sense of who he was and what he actually said.

Some of the same points are articulated by the celebrated Yakut writer and dramatist Nikolai Alekseevich Luginov. Luginov does not dispute the historical image of Russia as an empire, however, but rather confirmed and even celebrated it—not as an evil "prison house of peoples," to be sure, but rather as a supportive and protective guardian. In this, Luginov echoes the spirit of the post-Soviet Russian "imperial" nationalism promoted by such journals as Aleksandr Prokhanov's *Zavtra* (in which Luginov has published). It was, however, Gumilev's work that has had a particular influence on his thinking in this regard.[131] There can be

---

130. Shtyrov 2002.
131. "Nikolai Luginov ob Olonkho" 2009. For Gumilev's influence, also see "Nikolai Luginov pokazal panoramnuiu kartinu" 2008.

no question of a Russian "conquest" of Sakha, or for that matter of Siberia, he explained, for all these territories were "primordially imperial lands" In his view, this is the most important insight of the Eurasian perspective. The "principal unifying factor" of Eurasian space is its imperial character.[132] "I am convinced that only [Russia's] imperial will—at once merciless toward its enemies and righteous toward its own people—is the sole guarantor of the preservation of all of the nations of Russia." The Yakuts and other peoples of the north were able to survive "thanks exclusively to healthy and strong Russian blood." Both Shtyrov's and Luginov's deferential acknowledgements of Russia's preeminence are clearly at odds with Eurasianist doctrines in Kazakhstan and Tatarstan, which insist on strict parity with, or even primacy over, Russia. Where Luginov maintains that Yakut culture developed "in the bosom (*lono*) of Russian culture," Mintimer Shaimiev precisely reversed these roles.[133]

Indeed, Luginov offers himself as a sort of personal prototype of Gumilevian symbiosis between the Russian and Yakut ethnies. Asked by an interviewer to describe his sense of national identity, he responded: "As strange as it may sound, I do not feel in any way different from [ethnic] Russian writers. Perhaps this is because the Russian and Yakut languages are both native for me.... Like an ancient Asiatic (*slovno drevnii aziat*) I have been nurtured by two mothers—an elder and a younger, and raised in common by two cultures." And this commonality is not merely cultural, but has a foundation in Gumilevian naturalism as well, and he points out that contemporary scientific research confirms the "genetic unity" of the two peoples.[134] Along with this intense avowal of symbiotic oneness with the Great Russian ethnos, however, Luginov's self-reference as an "ancient Asiatic" indicated a more exclusively ethno-national dimension of his identity. He sought the sources for it in a distinctively Yakut "primeval memory" (*prapamiat'*), which he traced—with the assistance of Gumilev's historical research—back into the "deep antiquity" of the Xiongnu period in the fifth century BC. "It is here that I discovered the roots of our ethnos with its clans."[135] This ethnic prehistory was embellished by the rich folkloric tradition associated with the Yakut epic poem *Olonkho*, and it culminated in the awesome catharsis of the encounter between Rus' and the Mongol empire.

Luginov has focused considerable creative energy on this latter period, most significantly in his historical novel *On the Orders of Genghis Khan*. First published in Yakut in 1996, it was quickly translated into Russian and in 2009 was made into

132. "Nikolai Luginov ob Olonkho" 2009; Fedorov 1999, 130; Shnirelman 2009a, 74.
133. "Nikolai Luginov ob Olonkho" 2009.
134. Luginov 2008; Antonov 1999.
135. Luginov 2008.

a blockbuster film by the Yakut director Andrei Borisov.[136] Luginov's conclusions about the formative influence of the Mongol experience in shaping the emergence of the Russian ethnos and the development of the Russian state reflected the same sort of overenthusiastic reading of the Eurasianist narratives of Gumilev, Trubetskoi, and Vernadskii that we have seen in Kazakhstan and Tatarstan. "At first glance," he maintained, it might be difficult to believe that

> a Russian (*russkii chelovek*) is [in fact] the blood descendant of a Xiongnu, or more precisely a Turkic milieu, a person who—in terms of upbringing, worldview, and traditions—developed out of the Mongol epoch, [in other words] out of a milieu of an entirely different people with an entirely different racial composition (*prinadlezhnost'*) and a different form of state life. The point may be difficult to digest, but that's the way it is. The Russian empire grew and strengthened, developing out of the world of the Mongol empire and under its influence. The Russian (*russkoe*) state was a part, an autonomous element of the Mongol empire.

The Russian empire adopted in full the state ideology, administrative structure, and methods of governance that had been developed by the Golden Horde. "This much," he concludes, "is obvious."[137]

In addition to these reconstructions of Russia's experience with the Golden Horde, Yakut ethno-nationalism draws directly from Gumilev's theories of ethnicity. In a discussion with Gumilev in the final days of perestroika, a Yakut interviewer declared that the "global scope" and "explosive power" of *Ethnogenesis and the Earth's Biosphere* was matched only by that of Albert Einstein's theory of relativity.[138] In more measured tones, the Yakut academic Anatolii Georgievich Novikov confirmed Gumilev's importance for an understanding of ethnic being. "Whoever is interested in the historical fate of their ethnos must consult Gumilev's ethnography, for without it there cannot be a full scientific historical picture."[139] The principle of ancient historical lineage that is the foundation of Gumilev's ethnogenetic theories is extremely significant—one historian refers to how the "search for noble ancestors" is critical for ethno-political consolidation in the republic today.[140] In this quest, Gumilev's ethno-environmental history has particular salience by virtue of the widespread belief that Yakut ethnogenesis was

136. Luginov 1997.
137. "Nikolai Luginov ob Olonkho" 2009.
138. "Prarodina Iakutov" 1989.
139. Novikov 2002.
140. Borisov 2002, 35.

shaped by the sort of interactions between ethnos and geographical environment that Gumilev described in his ecology of ethnicity.[141] These were understood to have conditioned one of the great formative events in Yakut ethnic history, namely, the group's migration in the thirteenth and fourteenth centuries from its original home around Lake Baikal northeast to its present position on the middle reaches of the Lena River and the lower Vilyuy and Aldan Rivers.[142] Although folk legends recount how the Yakuts were driven out of their primeval homeland by the hostility of the neighboring Buriats, Gumilev suggested that the same climatic fluctuations in temperature and precipitation that influenced population movements in the Caspian Basin were at work in southeastern Siberia as well. His account figured importantly in post-Soviet attempts to provide a "scientific" basis for Yakut ethnic history.[143]

Such attempts also use Gumilev's notion of an "ecological niche," that is to say, the assumption of an inviolable organic connection between an ethnos and the specific "nurturing landscape" in which it develops.[144] "These landscapes dictate (*diktovat'*) definite behavioral rules to people, unite them, make them ethnically original and unique."[145] In the case of Yakut ethnogenesis, this theory resonates in a number of powerfully suggestive ways. The "primeval homeland" or *prarodina* of the Yakuts was set in the open steppes around Lake Baikal, where they had practiced cattle and horse breeding. Gumilev himself argued that, when forced to migrate, they sought out areas in their new regions that physically resembled those they had abandoned. They settled in grassy and relatively well-watered lowland pastures or *alaas*, where they could "imitate their earlier life" around Baikal.[146] This behavior in turn implied an unbroken continuity in Yakut ethnic life extending back into ancient times, and lent support to contemporary arguments about its primordial antiquity. This point was illustrated by the example of the *serge* (Yakut *сэргэ*), a traditional wooden post erected for the purpose of tying up cattle and horses. The Yakuts brought the *serge* with them from the treeless steppe and continued to use it in their new homeland as a "memory of their life in the steppes"—although in the abundant woodlands of the Lena Valley it had quite lost its purpose.[147] Finally, the "ecological niche" notion is deployed in a way that closely mimics Gumilev's own use of the concept, namely, to establish

141. Novikov 1999, 26; Gavrilova 1999, 38–39.

142. Vitebsky 1990, 304; Balzar and Vinokurova 1996, 103–4.

143. Borisov 2002; 35, 37; Borisov 1996.

144. For example, Jordan 2002, 18, 21, 22, 101, and passim. Jordan's study of Yakut ethnogenesis was inspired by Gumilev's geographical approach but takes a critical perspective on it.

145. Novikov 1999, 23; Krivoshapkin 1999, 115.

146. Gumilev 1972a; Borisov 2012.

147. Novikov 1999, 31; "Prarodina Iakutov" 1989; Mészáros 2008.

and rationalize the principles of harmonious ethnic interaction and coexistence. Yakuts settled in the open plains of the *alaas*, where they could continue their traditional pursuit of horse and cattle husbandry. The aboriginal groups that already inhabited the region, however, were either hunters and gathers or practiced reindeer herding, and required very different geographical conditions. The Yukagiry settled in the tundra, whereas the Even and Evenk peoples occupied the forested upland zones. The Russians who began to penetrate into the region in the seventeenth century brought with them agriculture and orchardry, for which they needed the well-watered meadowlands along the river banks. By virtue of this entirely natural ecological segregation of ethnic life, Yakutia was able to preserve ethnic peace and avoid "serious ethnic collisions" across the centuries, and this noble pattern continued to characterize interethnic relations in the republic to the present day.[148]

Another aspect of Gumilev's ethnos theory that has entered public discourses about national development is his concept of *passionarnost'*. Although we have noted the resonance of the term in Kazakhstan and Tatarstan, it would appear to be particularly evocative in post-Soviet Sakha, where it is likened in an exclusively positive sense to such New Age trends as dianetics, scientology, socionics (*sotsionika*), and "transpersonal psychology."[149] Mikhail Efimovich Nikolaev, the first president of Sakha, used *passionarnost'* to describe the special *élan vital* of the Yakut nation as a whole, which was instrumental in helping to mobilize national self-confidence. The "transformation of social consciousness" that had come with the acquisition of sovereign republic status "began to unfreeze age-old doubts that a small people, who apparently had begun to lose their roots and their belief in their own special destiny, could once again acquire their passionary energetics and new stimuli for advancing into world civilization." Indeed, because the presence of *passionarnost'* was—so he maintained—particularly stimulated by "extreme geographical conditions," the Yakuts had every right to view themselves as a sort of natural "advanced model for Russian (*rossiiskii*) and indeed for world culture as a whole" in this respect.[150] In a speech at the opening of a new research center for science and technology in Yakutsk in 2006, he asserted that a "surge (*vsplesk*) of a new wave of *passionarnost'*" was imminent in Yakutia, an efflorescence that would "transform the culture of the people, its spiritual condition, way of life, and interpersonal relationships." Nikolaev concluded his panegyric with a truly spectacular mixing of Gumilevian metaphors. The construction of a new scientific facility, he affirmed triumphantly, heralded

---

148. Gavrilova 1999, 37; Novikov 1999, 23, 31; Borisov 2002, 35.
149. Innokent'ev 1999, 145.
150. Nikolaev 2002.

the "transition from a 'nurturing landscape' to a 'nurturing technology' (*kormiashchaia tekhnologiia*)"![151]

If Nikolaev represented *passionarnost'* as a national trait, others stress its function as a marker of social elites and specially endowed individuals. One notable example of such usage is provided by Mikhail Il'ich Everstov. Everstov is an important political figure in Yakutia, a former Duma deputy with a doctoral degree in economics who served as secretary of Putin's *Edinaia Rossiia* Party in the republic. Everstov defined *passionarnost'* as the "ability of individuals or a small part of the nation to mobilize the rest of the people for grandiose social-political and economic reconstruction." In the first instance, the principal passionary individuals are the national leaders Vladimir Putin and president of the Sakha republic Viacheslav Shtyrov. These were visionaries who "with their *passionarnost'* are leading the multinational Russian people" on its historic transition to a globalized world. In addition to them, Everstov continued, it had been scientifically established that approximately 2 percent of the republic's youth were born "with the genetic qualities of genius" and a further 15 percent with the "genetic qualities of talented people."[152] Everstov then processed this data through a Gumilevian calculus and came to the following precise conclusion:

> According to Lev Gumilev, among Yakutia's young generation today there should be approximately 11,500–23,000 potential passionary individuals. Together with the potential passionaries among older generations, the republic should possess a potential passionary reserve of 30,000 to 60,000 people. I assume that this number of passionary individuals is entirely sufficient in order to lead the rest of Yakutia's population on the basic path of social-economic reconstruction of the republic. For this reason, we should use all of our means to foster *passionarnost'* among our young generation.

The young passionary individuals of today, he concluded, "should form new generations of political, technocratic, scientific, financial, economic, IT, cultural, and ecological elites" that would lead the republic over the next two decades and beyond.[153]

---

151. Nikolaev 2006. For a satirical sketch about the "muscular and fearless passionaries" among the political leadership in Yakutia, see Porfir'ev n.d.

152. Everstov 2008.

153. Everstov 2008. Everstov might have based these calculations on a comment by Gumilev that in an "actively functioning [i.e., normal] country," 5–7 percent of the population should be made up of passionary individuals. "If there is less than this, then it is bad for the country (*to dlia strany eto plokho*)." Gumilev 1988d.

In adapting Gumilev's ethnogenetic scheme for Yakut purposes, however, there is a rather large elephant in the room, a problematic detail that challenges even his most devoted adherents. The issue relates to Yakutia's exact position on the ethnogenetic cycle. Although he was not entirely consistent on the point, Gumilev generally dated the inception of Yakut ethnogenesis in the fourth and fifth centuries, which would mean that by the time the ethnos first encountered the Russians in the seventeenth century it had exhausted most of its reserves of passionary energy.[154] According to Gumilev, this circumstance explains Yakut lassitude in the face of the initial Russian incursion and of all subsequent state-sponsored projects for ethno-cultural domination and assimilation. His conclusion—entirely consistent with the scheme for the progression of ethnogenetic phases described on "Gumilev's graph"—is that Yakuts today find themselves in the final phase, and thus constitute a "relict" ethnos on the very brink of collapse. This was an extremely awkward and even counterfactual position for Gumilev to take, insofar as the new Yakut engagement with his theories that he witnessed would appear to be evidence of a renaissance of ethnic energetics and dynamism. His discomforting inability to reconcile these conflicting conclusions was clearly apparent in his 1989 interview cited above. In it, he affirmed that "contemporary Yakuts comprise, to a significant extent, a relict ethnos." "But," he hastened to add—obviously mindful of the sensitivities of his young Yakut interviewer and the eventual audience for his comments—it is nonetheless "the sturdiest and most powerful relict in Siberia! . . . The Yakuts are a very poetic, cultured, and civilized people, which still has its word to say to the world!" Their impending and inevitable decline may lead to the dissipation of the ethnos, but even "if in the future they become mixed with other groups, then no matter what language they may speak they will remain catalyzers of historical processes."[155] Gumilev was doing the best he could, but still could not offer much encouragement for the hopeful advocates of Yakutia's ethnic renaissance. After all, the scientific credibility of his theory rested entirely on its *zakonnomernost'* and deterministic inviolability, which meant that ethnic decline could not be resisted, circumvented or undone.

Unsubtle enthusiasts such as the politicians Nikolaev and Everstov—who opportunistically invoke Gumilevian principles in order to attach scientific credibility to their bombastic claims about Yakutia's national dynamism and the passionary genius of its leadership—are hardly aware of the problematic

---

154. Gumilev 1972a; "Prarodina Iakutov" 1989. For discussions of Gumilev's inconsistent dating of Yakut ethnogenesis, see Krivoshapkin 1999, 117; Novikov 1999, 27–28; Borisov 1999; Gogolev 1989.

155. "Prarodina Iakutov" 1989.

implications inherent in Gumilev's actual theories, much less troubled by them. Some of the latter's more learned admirers, however, have not failed to pick up on the unsettling inconsistency in Gumilev's pronouncements about the age of their ethnos, and for them the matter is not so simple.[156] One such scholar, for example, accepts the proposition that the Yakut ethnos is a relict at the end of its ethnogenetic cycle, but then goes on to make the very un-Gumilevian proposal that a new ethnogenetic cycle (*vitok*) could be jump-started deliberately in order to initiate an "ethno-cultural renaissance" leading to the formation of a "neo-Yakut culture."[157] The reactions of Ul'iana Alekseevna Vinokurova, a Yakut ethnographer concerned precisely with establishing her people's ethnogenetic scenario, are somewhat more reasoned. Vinokurova had considerable sympathy for Gumilev's essentialist arguments about ethnies as real-existing natural communities. However, she categorically rejected his ascription of great antiquity to the Yakuts, for two reasons. One was the associated conclusion about their "relict" status and the current exhaustion of their ethnic energies. "It is sad," she mused with ironic scepticism, "to belong to an ethnos that is disappearing, even hypothetically."[158] The second reason is her insistence that the territory of Yakutia today is not the second homeland of the Yakuts, as Gumilev suggested, but rather the original homeland of a much younger ethnos "that formed on the territory where it is currently settled." This latter point is significant for both ethnographic and ethno-political reasons, since it is intended to establish the Yakuts today as the true and exclusive *avtokhton* or "indigenous people of Yakutia," with all the attendant implications for their status and role in the political life of the region.[159]

---

156. Novikov 1999, 29.
157. Borisov 1999, 42–43.
158. Vinokurova 1994, 27.
159. Vinokurova 1994, 31; also see the discussion in Tishkov 1997, 8; Shnirelman 2003, 34.

THE POLITICAL SIGNIFICANCE OF GUMILEV

Writing on the centenary of Gumilev's birth in 2012, the journalist Mikhail Leontiev observed that "all of the concepts presented [in Gumilev's writings] are political instruments (*politicheskoe instrumentarie*). They are a political evaluation . . . they are in fact ideology, but it is the ideology of Gumilev. It doesn't fit into any other ideology because it is deeply individual."[1] Although Leontiev's identification of the political instrumentalism pervasive throughout all of Gumilev's work is accurate, his conclusion about Gumilev not fitting into "any other ideology" is not. Very much to the contrary, rather than having created any separate ideology of his own, different elements of Gumilev's theories correlate with and precisely "fit into" a broad range of different and even opposing ideological perspectives that were pervasive in the USSR and have continued to develop after 1991. Indeed, if Gumilev's real distinctiveness can be reduced to a single element, it would arguably be this great ideological malleability and "pick-and-chose" adaptability. It is these latter qualities, and not any genuine exceptionalism, that explain the universality of Gumilev's popularity and the ubiquity of his ideas.

In this book, I have argued that Gumilev's work straddled one of the deepest and most important fault lines of Soviet politics and society: the fissure formed by the collision of ethno-national individualism and polyethnic collectivism. From its inception, the Soviet state struggled to reconcile these two alternative

---

1. "Gumilev: Poet, politik, passionarii" 2012.

principles of social organization. Thus the Soviets emphasized the distinctive-ness of the country's non-Russian nationalities, whose "liberation" from Russo-centric imperial oppression had been secured through guarantees of political and cultural autonomy, while at the same time actively promoting the notion that all of these groups combined naturally with the Russians to form an inte-grated polyethnic *obshchnost'*. The latter was projected as a multinational com-munity sufficiently cohesive and homogeneous to possess its own quasi-ethnic characteristics. In different ways, and despite their potential incompatibility, both principles played essential roles in the organization of the Soviet Union. An ideological balance of sorts between them had been struck in the form of what I called the Stalinist "accommodation" of the 1930s and 1940s. This was, however, upset by Stalin's successors, who advocated an assimilationist model of an international *sovetskii narod*, in which the factor of ethnic individuality was downplayed and even dismissed as increasingly irrelevant. Gumilev's immediate project developed as a reaction against this latter policy and had two objectives: to revalorize the principle of ethnic individuality and to reestablish the earlier positive synergy between it and polyethnic integration. In a sense, Gumilev's the-ories were a new iteration of the Stalinist accommodation, but with his natural-scientific rationalizations and arguments he produced something that was in fact entirely new. For many in his day, Gumilev's unorthodox ideas were appealing and even compelling, such that despite the inauspicious circumstances of his professional marginalization they enjoyed a broad circulation and influence.

By the 1970s, however, ethno-exclusivism and polyethnic collectivism in the Soviet Union were beginning to harden into mutually exclusive options that would not be reconciled. This process intensified after the accession of Gor-bachev, and it was a major factor in the breakup of the Soviet Union. Yet rather than abating after the catharsis of 1992, the confrontation between these two principles was further aggravated, and powerful metadiscourses of identity and politics have developed around each one, right across the former Soviet Union. The fact that the confrontation between them is utterly at odds with Gumi-lev's own deeper purpose of reconciliation has done nothing to undermine the appeal of his ideas. To the contrary, it has actually worked to enhance it. Gumilev believed that he had developed a holistic and tightly integrated "systems theory" of ethnicity, in which each element—as in the biosphere itself—was necessarily interlinked with everything else and could not be detached. As it turned out, however, his post-Soviet audiences have had no difficulty whatsoever in disas-sembling his holistic *Denkgebäude*, selecting out of it those conceptual elements that suited their own purposes, while leaving—indeed even rejecting—the rest. Effectively, Gumilev's work has an à la carte quality, which makes it possible for some concepts and theories to be isolated and discarded while others remain intact without losing any of their apparent credibility. His complex ecological theories about the biological nature of ethnies can be endorsed while his associated arguments for the natural cohesion of these ethnic units into greater superethnic entities are ignored or shunned.[2] Alternatively, his historically based arguments for the necessary *obshchnost'* of different ethnic groups across Eurasia may be embraced by admirers who are entirely unreceptive to his naturalistic understanding of the ethnogenetic process as driven by variations in the levels of *passionarnost'*.[3] Indeed, the reality of *passionarnost'* can even be accepted while at the same time his explanations of it as the product of cosmic energy are lightly dismissed.[4] Gumilev's authority can be invoked by supporters of interethnic mixing and no less stridently by those calling for ethnic segregation and racial purity. This à la carte quality combines with the inherent malleability and ambivalence of many of Gumilev's arguments to render them appealing and useful for a wide variety of differing and even contending constituencies. It also means that his concepts and terminology can be developed in ways and to extremes that he himself could not have imagined.

The collectivist inclination is apparent most popularly in the vision of Eurasianism, which owes its fin de siècle reemergence in no small measure to Gumilev's efforts. Eurasianism is in itself remarkable in its ideological flexibility. It is popular in a variety of different post-Soviet regions, where it means different things and is deployed for different political purposes. In Russia, it was taken up first of all by revanchist nationalists such as Dugin and Prokhanov, who during perestroika saw it as an alternative ideological vision that could replace a failing Soviet Marxism and help preserve the geopolitical unity of the Soviet state. After 1991, it helped provide an ideological rationale for their determination to resurrect some sort of neo-Soviet entity. At the end of the Yeltsin era, Russia's new president Vladimir Putin himself began subtly to signal his interest in aspects of the Eurasianist program, an interest that finally culminated in 2012 with an official declaration of support for the creation of a Eurasian union. Dugin and Prokhanov, who in the 1990s formed part of the radical opposition to the status quo, became integrated into the political establishment after 2000, along with

---

2. Lariuel' 2001, 17. Even Gumilev's most devoted students and colleagues could not always accept his arguments for Eurasianism. Viacheslav Ermolaev, for example, saw it as nothing more than a pretext for the Kazakhs and other ethnies suffering from a "profound passionary impotence" to siphon off surplus Russian *passionarnost'* for their own purposes. Ermolaev 2000, 13. Also see Makhnach 1995, 126; Makhnach 2008. Similarly, Gumilev's biographer Beliakov wholeheartedly accepted his theory of ethnos while writing off his Eurasianist-inspired historiography as a fanciful mixture of "[Theodore] Mommsen and Maine Reid" that cannot be taken seriously. Beliakov 2012a, 402.

3. Ivanov 1992, 11; Mamonov 1995, 60–61.

4. Akaev 2011a, 23; Saifullin 2012, 178–79.

their Eurasianist ideas. It is critical to appreciate, however, that although the Russian Eurasianists all emphasize Gumilev's inspirational importance and invoke his "scientific" demonstration of an insuperable opposition between Russia-Eurasia and the West, they do not for the most part share his utopic vision of a genuinely egalitarian Eurasian superethnos or collection of superethnies in which all nations are equally balanced and equally enfranchised. Rather, they insist on the natural preeminence of Russia over all other Eurasian nations as Eurasia's "backbone" and "system-forming" ethnos, and ascribe this view back to him. Gumilev "did not for a minute doubt the right of the Russian people to create their own empire (*pravo russkogo naroda na sozdanie svoei Imperii*)," declared a former associate. "He was an imperial individual (*imperskii chelovek*), literally a native son of the immense Russian empire."[5]

The growing nostalgia in recent years for the idealized interethnic harmony, economic security, and ideological unity of the Soviet period serves increasingly to position Russian Eurasianism as what Laruelle terms "a substitute ideology for Sovietism."[6] Insofar as Gumilev's ideas themselves in important respects mirrored Soviet doctrines and institutions, they appear in this context ever more relevant and appealing. The use of Gumilev for the purpose of a positive reaffirmation of the Soviet experience may seem logically awkward, in view of his own and his parents' suffering at the hands of the Bolsheviks, but in fact this background proves to be not very problematic. When a journalist asked the Duma deputy and Gumilev enthusiast Maksim Mishchenko to clarify the "nuance" of how Gumilev could be used in connection with positive evocations of the USSR, the parliamentarian remained unperturbed. "It's true, it wasn't very easy in those days," he conceded blandly. "But on the whole, the people developed and moved forward. Gumilev understood this, and did not for one second become a dissident or a traitor—someone prepared to go against the interests of his homeland."[7] However people may or may not have "developed and moved forward" in the USSR, the implication that by not opposing the interests of the Soviet state Gumilev supported it was, in important respects, accurate enough.

Eurasianism has however also been embraced by non-Russian elites across the former Soviet Union. Here it is deployed for the very different purpose of legitimizing a claim for greater parity or indeed equality with the Russian center. The Lev Gumilev Center, based in Moscow and with a growing number of branches across the country, was established largely by representatives of

---

5. Burovskii 2012.
6. Laruelle 2004, 119; Shlapentokh 2011, 113. On the phenomenon of Soviet nostalgia, see White 2010.
7. "Vnedrit'" 2012 (quote); Shishkin 1996.

non-Russian nationalities of the Russian Federation, who promote Gumilevian Eurasianism as a means for guaranteeing recognition of their identities and their rights. "Eurasianism provides comfort and consolation (*prikhodit kak Uteshitel'*) for the small indigenous peoples," declared their 2010 manifesto, "Eurasianism is an advocate for the oppressed (*pritesniaemykh*)." The potential of Gumilev's teachings for conflict resolution is stressed: "Eurasianists are able to prevent ethnic conflicts, foster [native] cultures and traditions, and defend the humiliated and scorned. . . . Yes, Eurasianism is Love."[8] In Tatarstan, officially sponsored Eurasianism focuses in particular on Gumilev's historiography, which is used to argue that the modern Russian state is as much a product of the Eurasian steppe as of the Slavic Rus' territories. Beyond the Russian Federation, the leadership of newly independent Kazakhstan was the first to embrace Eurasianism in the early 1990s. Here as well, the intention was to provide an ideological foundation for a relationship with the Russian center, but Eurasianism was additionally used for domestic purposes for constructing a "Kazakhstani" national identity, of which the Russian state as such is not a part. In all these different cases, Eurasianism is always firmly associated with the person of Gumilev, and the same Gumilevian conceptual building blocks are in place: a radically revisionist historical narrative locating the primordial unity of the Eurasian peoples in the remote past and a "scientific" explanation of the dynamics of interethnic unity in Eurasia, based on the concepts of "superethnos," "complementarity," and "symbiosis."

Like neo-Eurasianist collectivism, contemporary ethno-exclusivism or ethno-nationalism also has roots in Soviet nationality policies. In the USSR, however, it was ideologically modulated and counterbalanced by the assimilationist elements of official policy, as well as the awkward fact that Soviet Marxism never managed convincingly to theorize the role of ethnicity in social development. These constraints fell away after 1992, with the result that ethnicity has acquired the unprecedented potency described in this book. For many, the ethnos has become the major locus for social mobilization and the negotiation of power and control, superseding even the political state as the essential social collective possessing its own inherent rights and entitlements. Narratives of primeval ethnogenetic origins continue as before to support and legitimate processes of state-building, and today the simple fact of ethnic identification itself can represent a claim to power. These principles are invoked by virtually all national groups, such that when in 1997 the Yeltsin government proposed removing the famous *piataia grafa* (indicating ethnic background) from the internal passport of the Russian Federation, there was fierce opposition across the board, from the

---

8. "Manifest Tsentra L'va Gumileva" 2011.

smallest nationalities to ethnic Russians themselves. All of these groups believed that the removal of this public marker of ethnic belonging portended a reduction in the political and social significance of ethnicity, which would in turn lead inevitably to the loss of ethnically based rights and privileges.[9]

Gumilev's theories of "ethnos" and "ethnogenesis" have a played an influential role in this biopolitical valorization of ethnic being. His essentialized biological model fits ideally into the paradigm of ethno-national exclusivity and offers a compelling conceptual framework for the "scientific" reification of ethnicity as an ontological reality. Gumilev provides complex but comprehensible explanations for what the ethnos is, how it develops, what it needs to prosper, and how it can tell its friends from its enemies. His emphasis on the organic territoriality of ethnicity and the special connection of each ethnos to its own native landscape is particularly important. The Soviet principle of *korennost'* or autochthony has survived the demise of the Soviet Union, and contemporary claims for territorial control and political status are routinely buttressed as before with exaggerated accounts of ethnogenetic lineage.[10] In the post-Soviet context, moreover, the Gumilevian valorization of indigeneity opens up the possibility for very new sorts of ethno-political discourses. For example, whereas in the Soviet Union the *korennost'* and legitimacy of the *malye narody* of the Russian north and east were acknowledged, the Soviet-Marxist teleology of social development and modernization still implicitly stigmatized these groups as backward and primitive. The Gumilevian perspective, by contrast, categorically rejects the notion of "historical progress" and the associated characterizations of societies as "advanced" or "backward," and thus liberates the *malye narody* in principle from any such stigmatization. Instead, the very traditionalism of these groups—the primordial originality of their cultures, their deep empathy for the natural world, and the ecological sustainability of their traditional *genres de vie*—is now valorized positively. In this new framework of Gumilevian values, qualities that earlier seemed retrograde become robust evidence of ethnic integrity and can be deployed to enhance political demands for recognition of ethnic distinctiveness.[11]

In an earlier chapter it was noted how, directly after the collapse of the USSR, some observers in Russia and the West believed that Gumilev's teachings could provide an ideological platform for the emergence of Russian fascism. We can see

---

9. Akturk 2010, 324–26; Donahoe, Habeck, Halemba, and Santha 2008, 998.

10. Laruelle 2008a, 185–86; Sokolovski n.d., 19; Shnirelman 2005.

11. Heikkinen 2000, 99; Sokolovskiy 2000; Donahoe, Habeck, Halemba, and Santha 2008, 1014. This particular valorization of indigeneity resonates in many respects with the so-called First Nations movement that has developed globally since the 1990s. Here as well, ethnic status can serve as the basis for political claims. Kuper 2003; Merlan 2009; "The Concept of Indigeneity" 2006.

in our own day that this has not come to pass: not for any lack of fascistic tendencies in Russia but rather because these perspectives do not draw primarily on Gumilev. More prevalent and pernicious than neofascism, however, are the simple racist antagonisms expressed by ethnic Russians against "foreigners" from Central Asia, the Caucasus, and elsewhere, and Gumilev's theories have been described as providing an important source of legitimation for this racial discrimination and bias.[12] The question of race and racism in Gumilev's work goes to the heart of one of the main themes of this book. There is obviously no question that Gumilev was a zealous anti-Semite, and his teachings certainly continue today to feed these particular flames. Beyond this, his biological model of ethnicity can be appealing to advocates of social exclusion, who support discrimination against other groups based on putative racial differences. But Gumilev's theories themselves are not racialist in a strict sense, and comparisons that have been drawn between them and German *Rassenkunde* are not accurate. This point is well appreciated, among others, by those genuinely attempting to resurrect the teachings of *Rassenkunde* in Russia today, in the form of *rasologiia*. The ambivalence toward Gumilev on the part of these latter-day adepts of "racial scientists" such as Ludwig Woltmann (1871–1907) and Hans F. K. Günther (1891–1968) is revealing. On the one hand, they have no choice but to acknowledge Gumilev's positive contribution in establishing the natural-biological essence of the ethnos, and they regularly invoke his authority on this fundamental point. At the same time, they are loud in their denunciations of his "failure" to appreciate that this essence is rooted not in the relationship to the natural environment but in the genetics of race.[13] We have seen that Gumilev himself vigorously denied that race played any role in his conceptualization of ethnos, and in this case he may be taken at his word. He categorically refused to identify ethnies as races; indeed, he argued that the development of ethnies always involved the mixing of different races.

Instead of race, Gumilev based his biologization of ethnicity on ecological principles, which he drew from natural-scientific theory that had nothing to do with racial science. From his own standpoint, a great strength of his theory was that it naturalized and biologized ethnicity precisely on a nonracial basis. Indeed, it can be argued that the real ideological value of Gumilev's teachings for the purposes of radical ethno-nationalism today is not their racialist potential but rather the precise opposite: the fact that they can justify social discrimination and the exclusion of "foreign" groups on the basis of scientific-ecological principles

---

12. Shnirel'man 2005a; Shnirel'man 2009, 207n, 208n, 210n, 211n, 216–17; Shlapentokh 2011, 103; Rossman 2002b, 24.

13. One work on the subject devotes an entire chapter to "Gumilev: pro et contra." Sevast'ianov 2008: 42–50; Savel'ev 2010: 41, 48–49, 53–55, 149; Avdeev 2005b.

that apparently have nothing to do with racialist bias or motivation. In this sense, the function of Gumilev's ecology of ethnicity is very similar to that of so-called ethno-pluralism as it has been conceptualized and promoted by the West European New Right since the 1970s.[14] Ethno-pluralism is an avowedly nonracial strategy for social exclusion, which recognizes the principle of equality of all nations but maintains that they can function normally only if they are kept separate on their "natural" historical homelands.[15] Contemporary theoreticians of the European New Right such as Alain de Benoist and Robert Steuckers are well aware of Gumilev's ethnos theory and clearly appreciate its resonances with their own views; indeed, a recently published German Far Right text even includes a full-page portrait of Gumilev as one of the most important proponents of ethnos theory.[16] The all-critical difference is that whereas in Western Europe this rationale is intended to be used by majority national groups for the purpose of excluding ethnic minorities, in Russia it can be deployed by the latter as well, to defend themselves against encroachment and disenfranchisement by the central authorities. The example of the *malye narody* noted above would be a case in point.

A no less significant problem with characterizing Gumilev's theories as racialist is the outspoken internationalism of his Eurasianism. This again was something Gumilev strongly insisted on, and once again there is no reason to question his sincerity. He may not have liked the Jews or the Chinese or the "foreign" superethnies in the USSR such as the Baltic peoples, but the solidarity he felt for the other Soviet nationalities was entirely genuine and practically unlimited. As we have seen, he was a determined advocate of the friendship of the peoples, which he understood in a strictly literal, even utopic sense as a genuine fraternity of equally enfranchised nations. His theory about positive complementarity and symbiosis provided a conceptual basis for this friendship and it inspired his reconstructions of Russian history. Gumilev's internationalism was well-known in his own day and it strongly influenced his reception across the USSR, winning him enduring appreciation from non-Russian nationalities and bitter resentment from some of his more genuinely racist Russian-nationalist colleagues. In the present day, Eurasianism in all of its many variants is inspired by his idealized vision of a polyethnic community that is consensual, cohesive, and united.

---

14. In general, the resonances between Gumilev's theories and those of the contemporaneous European New Right—parties who were unaware of the other's existence—were remarkably precise and powerful. Bassin 2015b; Lariuel' 2009, 195–96; Laruelle 2008b, 141; Kochanek 1998, 1193–94.

15. Spektorowski 2003; Karklins 2000.

16. Steuckers n.d.; Verslius and de Benoist 2014, 83–84; de Benoist 2012, 244; Andersen 2010; Bar-On 2013, 204–5. The picture of Gumilev is in Böttger 2014, 216.

But if Gumilev's theories are not racist in the strict sense we have considered here, they have nonetheless made a substantial contribution to the climate of ethnic intolerance and social exclusion that has become increasingly pronounced in Russian society since the 1990s.[17] His potency in this regard rests on the specific "scientific" allegations he makes about the nature of ethnicity: that individual members of an ethnic group all necessarily share the same character and act the same way, that ethnies are not merely different from each other but in principle incompatible (*nesovmestimyi*) and cannot be harmoniously integrated, that ethnies have moral characteristics that render them either collectively good or bad, and that some degree of hostility between them is natural and insuperable.[18] This final point refers to his notion of "positive and negative complementarity." Although some of his contemporary followers may understand Gumilevian Eurasianism as a program of conflict resolution and the ideological enactment of "love" between peoples, as we have just seen, Gumilev himself was very clear that conflict between ethnies was an intrinsic reality of ethnic life itself. "Blood does flow, but not very much, and life goes on," was how he described relations between fraternal ethnies sharing positive complementarity. The immanence of interethnic hostility was apparent "already in Paleolithic times," he explained: it was as natural as "the sparks produced by a voltaic arc as it passes from cathode to anode."[19] "Clashes" (*stolknoveniia*) between superethnies were similarly natural and inexorable.[20] It is entirely indicative that Aleksandr Borodai—the son of Gumilev's old friend and cothinker and himself strongly influenced by Gumilev from childhood—should have played an active role as one of the leaders of the Russian forces in Russia's "confrontation with the West" in Eastern Ukraine in 2014.[21] A commentator recently reflected on Gumilev's belief in the inevitability of ethnic discord:

> I only want one simple fact to be recognized: that animosities between nations do not need to be "aroused" or "excited," for they simply exist as a given. To close one's eyes to this is foolish and grievously wrong....

---

17. Shnirel'man 2005a; Shnirel'man 2009; Sokolovski n.d., 5; Temirgaliev 2007b,

18. Loseff 1994, 6, 10.

19. Gumilev 1990b (quote); Gumilev 1990c, 8; Beliakov 2012a, 722, 729.

20. Gumilev 2004c, 6; Yasmann 1992, 29. There is a striking resonance on this point between Gumilev and the American Samuel Huntington, who essentialized the "clash of civilizations" in precisely the same spirit. "It is human to hate," Huntington wrote. "For self-definition and motivation people need enemies.... The resolution of one conflict and the disappearance of one enemy generate personal, social and political forces that give rise to new ones." Huntington 1996, 129.

21. From May to August 2014 Borodai served as self-styled prime minister of the "Donetsk People's Republic." Balmforth 2014. Borodai's connection to Gumilev is frequently noted, e.g., Prokhanov 2014.

> Above all, it is necessary to appreciate Lev Gumilev's theory about complementary and noncomplementary nations. [His conclusions] have been all too conclusively confirmed over the past quarter century, when across the territory of the former Soviet Union—with its supposedly unified *sovetskii narod*—no fewer than 150 bloody conflicts have broken out.[22]

Indeed, Gumilev's entire vision of history, as we have seen, was cast as an existential struggle between the forces of good and evil. Shortly after his death, his wife reaffirmed this perspective, maintaining that the future could be saved only if new generations charged with positive passionary energy can continue to resist Russia's ethnic and superethnic foes and "rescue our land from complete chimerical-diabolical destruction."[23]

This extremist potential in Gumilev's teachings is taken up enthusiastically by radical Russian ethno-nationalists, for whom notions of ethnic *nesovmestimost'* and "chimera-ethnies" provide vital rationalizations for their resentments against Jews and other "foreign" nationalities. They are not, however, alone in this usage, and non-Russians themselves can deploy the same aspects of Gumilev's teachings for their own assertions of ethno-exclusivist hostility. We saw in the previous chapter how his ethno-ecological principles are used in Kazakhstan to claim the exclusive patrimony of the Kazakh ethno-nation over the entire territory of the Kazakh state. A more hysterical example can be seen in a book by the Chechen writer Khasan Bakaev.[24] Bakaev's work is a deliriously anti-Semitic and hyperbiologized diatribe about ethnicity, nationhood, and the Chechen wars. The author is obsessed with the imperative to prevent ethnic mixing and maintain purity within ethnic groups, and cites Gumilev copiously in support of this position. He describes how Gumilev "categorically warned that the 'mixing of blood' will lead any nation or state quickly and directly to its demise."[25] Before Gumilev, the author maintains, the same convictions had inspired the German Nazis with their *Rassenkunde*, on which basis he calls for a positive reevaluation of the latter. Indeed, Bakaev cannot understand why the Nazis should be universally condemned when they did nothing more than to place "the notion of 'pure blood' at the basis of their state policies." After all, he points out, "the Russian scholar L. N. Gumilev's concept of the 'ethnic field'" is not subjected to the same critique, despite the fact that "using a different terminology, he made

---

22. Sevast'ianov 2014.
23. Gumileva 1994, 618.
24. Bakaev published his work under the pseudonym Deni Baksan. Baksan 1998.
25. Baksan 1998, 199–200.

the same point as Hitler."[26] Gumilev's identification of the Jews as a universal ethnic chimera ("established on the basis of facts") also resonated with the Nazi position, he maintains: "Hitler came to precisely the same conclusion. . . . Hitler, like Gumilev, opposed the Jews to the rest of humanity."[27] All of this was positive and laudable. In the final analysis, the Chechen crisis was to be explained in Gumilevian terms as a simple, if tragic example of ethnic incompatibility. In affairs between nations, "ethnic incompatibility (or 'negative complementarity' in Gumilev's terminology) can only result in mutual disdain, conflicts, and wars." This is all the more true if the ethno-nations in question "are contained within a single state, with no possibility of separating their border."[28]

Yet although it is important to appreciate the ways in which Gumilev's ideas and images help to feed post-Soviet discourses of ethnic intolerance and discrimination, they are perhaps not the most important point to take away from a broader consideration of his work and influence. Paradoxically, at least parts of his audience understood and still understand his message as one of mutual understanding and tolerance between peoples. But Gumilev was not a progressive or leftist, although for some time in the 1960s and 1970s many assumed that he was. He was rather an "old soldier," a self-acknowledged conservative and a committed Russian nationalist. As nationalism and conservatism have grown stronger across Russia since the end of the Cold War—as they have across much of the world—Gumilev's star has naturally shone ever brighter. The source of Gumilev's special genius and the "mystique" noted in title of this book was not any particular idea or theory or line of influence but rather the remarkable assemblage of arguments and viewpoints that he gathered together into the corpus of his work. Gumilev spoke and speaks today to a diverse variety of constituencies—from the Russian president to fundamentalist insurgents—and offers a diverse (and contradictory) array of explanations for the most important social and national issues. The fact that these explanations do not for the most part withstand scholarly and scientific scrutiny would seem to be entirely beside the point, for it does not in any way undermine the authority that his work continues to enjoy. It is not too much to say that Lev Gumilev has become a universal point of reference and metadiscourse in his own right: a venerable and apparently inexhaustible wellspring of ideas and inspiration for pretty much anyone seeking to make sense of the Russian past, present, and future.

---

26. Ibid., 248.
27. Ibid., 205.
28. Ibid., 319–20.

Bibliography

"25-letie vykhoda v svet 'Etnogenez i biosfera zemli.'" 2004. http://gumilevica.ku lichki.net/fund/fund33.htm, accessed 21/7/2014.

Abdulatipov, R. G. 2004. *Etnopolitologiia*. St. Petersburg: Piter.

Abdymanapov, S. A. 2004. *Zhizn' i deiatel'nost' L. N. Gumileva*. Astana: Iz-vo ENU.

Adams, Margarethe Ann. 2011. "Music and Entertainment in Post-Soviet Kazakhstan: Ideology and Legacy." PhD diss., University of Illinois at Urbana-Champaign.

Adams, Mark B. 1979. "From 'Gene Fund' to 'Gene Pool': On the Evolution of Evolutionary Language." In *Studies in the History of Biology*, edited by William Coleman and Camille Limoges, 241–85. Baltimore, MD: Johns Hopkins University Press.

———. 1990a. "Eugenics as Social Medicine in Revolutionary Russia." In *Health and Society in Revolutionary Russia*, edited by S. G. Solomon and J. F. Hutchinson, 200–223. Bloomington: Indiana University Press.

———. 1990b. "Eugenics in Russia, 1900–1940." In *The Wellborn Science: Eugenics in Germany, France, Brazil, and Russia*, edited by M. B. Adams, 153–216. New York: Oxford University Press.

———. 1990c. "The Soviet Nature-Nurture Debate." In *Science and the Soviet Social Order*, edited by Loren R. Graham, 94–138. Cambridge MA: Harvard University Press.

Afanas'ev, Iu. N. 1985. "Proshloe i my." *Kommunist* 14: 105–16.

Agursky, Mikhail. 1986. "The Prospects of National Bolshevism." In *The Last Empire: Nationality and the Soviet Future*, edited by Robert Conquest, 87–108. Palo Alto, CA: Hoover Institution Press.

———. 1994. "Nietzschean Roots of Stalinist Culture." In Rosenthal, *Nietzsche and Soviet Culture*, 256–86.

Aisin, Ruslan. 2006. "Tatary i globalizm." http://tatpolit.ru/category/context/2006-05-13/51, accessed 3/6/2014.

Aizatullin, T. A. 1999. "Teoriia Rossii." http://aizatulin.chat.ru/aizatul1.html, accessed 10/2/2014.

Akademik Iu. V. Bromlei i otechestvennaia etnologiia, 1960–1990e gody. 2003. Moscow: Nauka.

Akaev, Askar. 2011a. "Dmitrii Likhachev i Lev Gumilev: Sopriazhenie sudeb." In *Dialog kul'tur v usloviiakh globalizatsii: IX Mezhdunarodnoe Likhachevskie nauchnye chteniia*, edited by A. C. Zapesotskii, 21–24. St. Petersburg: SPbGUP.

———. 2011b. "Passionarnost' glazami fizika." *Geopolitika i Bezopasnost'* 4/16: 16–27.

Akhmetov, K. A. 2002. *Lev Nikolaevich Gumilev: Zhizn' i tvorchestvo*. Astana: n.p.

Akhmetov, Rashit. 2007. "Avangardist." *Zvezda Povolzh'ia* 20 (24–30 May), http://tat polit.ru/category/discussion/2007-06-02/321, accessed 3/6/2014.

———. 2008a. "Kev Salikhov." *Zvezda Povolzh'ia* 46 (4–10 December), http://tatpolit.ru/category/zvezda/2009-02-26/1407, accessed 3/6/2014.

———. 2008b. "Tatarskii teatr." *Zvezda Povolzh'ia* 12 (27 March–2 April), http://tatpolit.ru/category/tema/brend-tatar/2008-05-21/770, accessed 3/6/2014.

Akhmetshin, Sh. K. 2011. *Lev Nikolaevich Gumilev*. St. Petersburg: Slaviia.

Akopian, Al'bert. 2012. "Putin: Budushchee za passionarizatsiei i deoffshorizatsiei." *Russian Reality* (12 December), http://www.russianrealty.ru/analytic/articles/rr/262102/, accessed 21/2/2014.

Aksenov, G. P. 1988. "Poniatie zhivogo veshchestva: Ot Biuffona do Vernadskogo." *Voprosy Istorii Estestvoznaniia i Tekhniki* 1: 57–66.

———. 1994. *Vernadskii.* Moscow: Soratnik.

Aksenova, E. P., and M. A. Vasilev. 1993. "Problemy etnogonii slavianstva i ego vetvei v akademicheskikh diskusiiakh rubezha 1930–1940-kh godov." *Slavianovedenie* 2: 86–104.

Akturk, Sener. 2010. "Passport Identification and Nation-Building in Post-Soviet Russia." *Post-Soviet Affairs* 26, no. 4: 314–41.

Al'shevskii, M. 1999. *Khazary.* Moscow: Terra.

Aleksin, A. A., and L. N. Gumilev. 1962. "Khazarskaia Atlantida." *Aziia i Afrika segodnia* 2: 52–53.

Alison, Sebastian. 2000. "Putin Pushes for 'Eurasian Union.'" *Moscow Times* (10 October), http://www.themoscowtimes.com/stories/2000/10/10/011.html, accessed 8/11/06.

Allensworth, Wayne. 1998. *The Russian Question: Nationalism, Modernization, and Post-Communist Russia.* Lanham, MD: Rowman & Littlefield.

Allworth, Edward, ed. 1980. *Ethnic Russia in the USSR: The Dilemma of Dominance.* New York: Pergamon.

Amanov, Bagdaulet, and Asiya Mukhambetova. 2002. *Kazakhskaia traditsionnaia muzyka i XX vek.* Almaty: Daik-Press.

Anceschi, Luca. 2014. "Regime-Building, Identity Making and Foreign Policy: Neo-Eurasianist Rhetoric in Post-Soviet Kazakhstan." *Nationalities Papers* 42, no. 5: 733–49.

Andersen, Joakim. 2010. "Lev Gumilev och etnogenesis." *Motpol.* http://www.motpol.nu/oskorei/2010/09/11/lev-gumilev-och-etnogenesis/, accessed 4/11/2014.

Anderson, D. G., and D. V. Arzyutov. 2012. "Etnos in the Life-History of Soviet and Russian Anthropology." Unpublished manuscript presented at the Wenner Gren International Seminar "Etnos, Etnogenez and the Peoples of Siberia," Dom Uchenykh, St. Petersburg, December.

Andreev, A. F. 2012. "Zhurnal 'Priroda'—100 let." *Uspekhi fizizicheskikh nauk* 182: 105–10.

Andreev, B. 1927. *Zavoevanie prirody.* Moscow: Gosizdat.

Andrews, James T. 2009. *Red Cosmos: K. E. Tsiolkovskii, Grandfather of Soviet Rocketry.* College Station: Texas A&M University Press.

Andrianov, B. A. 1968. "Nekotorye zamechaniia po povodu stat'i L. N. Gumileva. . . ." *Istoriia SSSR* 1: 233–34.

Annenskii, L. 2005. "Chto znachit urusnichat'?" *Rodina* 8: 141.

Antonov, E. P. 1999. "'Sliianie' ('simbioz') kak osnovnoi faktor etnogeneza russkogo naroda." In Borisov, *Materialy Gumilevskikh chtenii 1995–96 gg.*, 151–55.

Anuchin, V. A. 1960. *Teoreticheskie problemy geografii.* Moscow: Gos. Iz-vo Geog. Lit.

———. 1972. *Teoreticheskie osnovy geografii.* Moscow: Mysl'.

———. 1975. "Sootnoshenie obshchestva i prirody v geograficheskoi srede i filosofskie problemy geografii." *Voprosy Filosofii* 4: 80–91.

———. 1977. *Theoretical Problems of Geography.* Translated by Steven Shabad. Columbus: The Ohio State University Press.

———. 1982. *Geograficheskii faktor v razvitii obshchestva.* Moscow: Mysl'.

Artamonov, M. I. 1937. *Ocherki drevneishei istorii khazar.* Leningrad: Sotsekgiz.

———. 1962. *Istoriia khazar.* Leningrad: Iz-vo Gos. Ermitazha.

———. 1971. "Snova 'geroi' i 'tolpa'?" *Priroda* 2: 75–77.

Asadullaev, I. 2004. "V zashchitu evraziistva." *Zavtra* 35, no. 562 (30 August), http://www.zavtra.ru/content/view/2004-08-2542/, accessed 3/6/2014.

Atabek, Aron. 2004a. "Kazakhstanskaia natsiia, ili put' v reservatsiiu." *Internet-Gazeta "Zona KZ"* 150/2675 (6 October), http://zonakz.net/articles/?artid=7183, accessed 3/6/2014.

———. 2004b. "V Kazakhstane est' tol'ko odin narod i odna natsiia—kazakhi, vse ostal'nye—diaspory." *Internet-Gazeta "Zona KZ"* 122/4924 (18 November), http://zonakz.net/articles/?artid=7484, accessed 3/6/2014.

Avdeev, V. B. 2005a. "Nado uchit'sia prikladnoi biologii." *Zavtra* 32 (10 August), http://www.zavtra.ru/content/view/2005-08-1081/, accessed 8/4/2014.

———. 2005b. *Rasologiia*. Moscow: Belye al'vy.

Avins, Carol. 1983. *Border Crossings: The West and Russian Identity in Soviet Literature, 1917–1934*. Berkeley: University of California Press.

Baigushev, A. I. 1990. *Plach po narzumnym Khazaram*. Moscow: Stolitsa.

———. 1995. *Khazary*. Moscow: Lirus.

———. 2006a. "Khazarskie strasti: K russko-evreiskomu dialogu." *Zavtra* 34 (23 August), http://zavtra.ru/content/view/2006-09-0631/, accessed 11/7/2014.

———. 2006b. *Russkii orden vnutri KPSS : Pomoshchnik M. A. Suslova vspominaet. . . .* Moscow: Algoritm.

Bailes, Kendall E. 1990. *Science and Russian Culture in an Age of Revolutions: V. I. Vernadsky and His Scientific School, 1863–1945*. Bloomington: Indiana University Press.

Bairamova, L. K., ed. 1998. *Sistema tsennostei rossiiskoi national'noi politiki*. Kazan: Apparat Prez. Res. Tatarstana.

Baksan, Deni. 1998. *Sled Satany na tainykh tropakh istorii*. 2nd ed. Groznyi: n.p.

Bakulina, Sonia. 2011. "Passionarnyi evrei." *jewish.ru* (20 May), http://www.jewish.ru/theme/cis/2011/05/news994296611.php, accessed 10/2/2014.

Balashov, D. M. 1986. *Mladshii Syn*. Moscow: Sovremennik.

———. 1989. "I nuzhna liubov': Formirovanie russkoi natsii i sovremennye problemy nashego natsional'nogo bytiia." *Literaturnaia Rossiia* 8, no. 1360 (24 February): 8–9.

———. 1992. "Anatomiia antisistemy." *Nash Sovremennik* 4: 150–54.

———. 2000a. "Cherez bezdnu." *Zavtra* 6 (28 March 2000), http://www.kulichki.com/~gumilev/BDM/bdm03.htm, accessed 11/7/2014.

———. 2000b. "Nashikh b'iut." *Sovetskaia Rossiia* 124 (26 October), http://gumilevica.kulichki.net/BDM/bdm04.htm, accessed 10/7/2014.

———. 2006 [1984]. *Simeon Gordyi*. Moscow: AST.

Balmforth, Tom. 2014. "Russia's Nationalist Fringe Takes Center Stage in Eastern Ukraine." *Radio Free Europe/Radio Liberty* (17 June), http://www.rferl.org/content/russias-nationalist-fringe-take-center-stage-in-eastern-ukraine/25425155.html, accessed 2/10/2014.

Balzar, Marjorie, and A. V. Vinokurova. 1996. "Nationalism, Interethnic Relations, and Federalism: The Case of the Sakha Republic." *Europe-Asia Studies* 48, no. 1: 101–20.

Banks, Marcus. 1996. *Ethnicity: Anthropological Constructions*. London: Routledge.

Bannykh, S. G. 1997. *Geograficheskii determinizm ot L'va Mechnikova do L'va Gumileva*. Ekaterinburg: n.p.

Bar-On, Tamir. 2013. *Rethinking the French New Right: Alternatives to Modernity*. London: Routledge.

Barghoorn, Frederick C. 1956. *Soviet Russian Nationalism*. New York: Oxford University Press.

———. 1980. "Four Faces of Soviet Russian Ethnocentrism." In *Ethnic Russia in the USSR: The Dilemma of Dominance*, edited by Edward Allworth, 55–66. New York: Pergamon.

Bariev, R. Kh. 2005. *Volzhskie Bulgary: Istoriia i kul'tura*. St. Petersburg: Agat.

Barnakov, N. V. 2004. *O vospitanii talanta i drugikh kachestv cheloveka*. . . . Ulan-Ude: Iz-vo Buriat. gos. s-kh. akademii. http://rus.triz-guide.com/2126.html, accessed 22/4/2014.

Barth, Frederik. 1969. *Ethnic Groups and Boundaries. The Social Organization of Cultural Difference*. Oslo: Universitetsforlaget.

Bassin, Mark. 1992. "Geographical Determinism in Fin de Siècle Marxism: Georgii Plekhanov and the Environmental Basis of Russian History." *Annals of the Association of American Geographers* 82, no. 1: 3–22.

———. 1996. "Nature, Geopolitics, and Marxism: Ecological Contestations in the Weimar Republic." *Transactions of the Institute of British Geographers* 21, no. 2: 315–41.

———. 2000. "'I Object to Rain That Is Cheerless': Landscape Art and the Stalinist Aesthetic Imagination." *Ecumene* 7, no. 3: 313–36.

———. 2003. "Classical Eurasianism and the Geopolitics of Russian Identity." *Ab Imperio* 2: 257–67.

———. 2005. "Blood or Soil? The Volkisch Movement, the Nazis, and the Legacy of Geopolitik." In *How Green Were the Nazis?: Nature, Environment, and Nation in the Third Reich*, edited by F-J Brüggemeier, Marc Cioc, and Thomas Zeller, 204–42. Athens, OH: Ohio University Press.

———. 2007. "Civilizations and Their Discontents: Geography and Geopolitics in the Huntington Thesis." *Geopolitics* 12: 351–74.

———. 2008. "The Morning of Our Motherland: Fedor Shurpin's Portrait of Stalin (1949)." In *Picturing Russia: Explorations in Visual Culture*, edited by Valerie Kievelson and Joan Newberger, 214–17. New Haven, CT: Yale University Press.

———. 2009a. "The Emergence of Ethno-Geopolitics in Post-Soviet Russia." *Eurasian Geography and Economics* 50, no. 2: 131–49.

———. 2009b. "Nurture *Is* Nature: Lev Gumilev and the Ecology of Ethnicity." *Slavic Review* 68, no. 4: 872–97.

———. 2009c. "Rodina kak ekologicheskoe nishe: Lev Gumilev ob etnose i landshafte." In *Rossiia: Voobrazhenie prostranstva/prostranstvo voobrazheniia*, edited by D. N. Zamiatin and I. I. Mitin, 109–19. Moscow: Agaf.

———. 2010a. "Is There Room for Russia in Eurasia?': Neo-Eurasianism and the Problem of Russian Nationalism." In *Ofiary imperium—Imperia jako ofiary*, edited by Andrzej Nowak, 169–80. Warsaw: IH/PAN.

———. 2010b. "Nationhood, Natural Region, *Mestorazvitie*: Environmentalist Discourses in Classical Eurasianism." In *Space, Place and Power in Modern Russia: Essays in the New Spatial History*, edited by Mark Bassin, Chris Ely, and Melissa Stockdale, 49–80. De Kalb: Northern Illinois University Press.

———. 2011. "*Etnos vs Obshchnost'*: Eurasianist Visions of Russian Nationhood in Space." In *Mastering Russian Spaces: Raum und Raumbewältigung als Probleme der russischen Geschichte*, edited by Karl Schlögel, 47–72. Munich: R. Oldenbourg.

———. 2015a. "Narrating Kulikovo: Lev Gumilev, Russian Nationalists, and the Troubled Emergence of Neo-Eurasianism." In *Between Europe and Asia: The Origins, Theories and Legacies of Russian Eurasianism*, edited by Mark Bassin, Marlene Laruelle, and Sergey Glebov, 165–86. Pittsburgh: University of Pittsburgh Press.

———. 2015b. "Lev Gumilev and the European New Right." *Nationalities Papers*, 43, no. 6.

Bassin, Mark, and Irina Kotkina. Forthcoming. "The *Etnogenez* Project: Ideology And Science Fiction in Putin's Russia." *Utopian Studies*.

Bassin, Mark, Marlene Laruelle, and Sergei Glebov, eds. 2015. *Between Europe and Asia: The Origins, Theories and Legacies of Russian Eurasianism*. Pittsburgh, PA: University of Pittsburgh Press.

Beisswenger, Martin. 2013. "Was Lev Gumilev a 'Eurasianist'?: A New Look at his Post-War Contacts with Petr Savitskii." *Ab Imperio* 1: 85–108.

Beliakov, S. S. 2008. "V. N. Demin: Lev Gumilev." *Voprosy Literatury* 6, http://maga zines.russ.ru/voplit/2008/6/be26-pr.html, accessed 10/5/2012.

———. 2012a. *Gumilev syn Gumileva*. Moscow: Astrel'.

———. 2012b. "Lev Gumilev: Glavy iz knigi." *Novyi Mir* 4: 78–123, http://magazines. russ.ru/novyi_mi/2012/4/b8.html, accessed 19/5/2012.

Belkov, P. L. 1993. "O metode postroeniia teorii etnosa." In *Etnosy i etnicheskie protsessy: Pamiati R. F. Itsa*. Moscow: Vostochnaia Literatura.

Berg, L. S. 1947. *Geograficheskie zony Sovetskogo Soiuza*. 3rd ed. vol. 1. Moscow: OGIZ.

———. 1969 [1922]. *Nomogenesis, or Evolution Determined by Law*. Translated by J. N. Rostovtsov. Cambridge, MA: MIT Press.

Berg, R. L. 1979. "The Life and Research of Boris L. Astaurov." *Quarterly Review of Biology* 54: 397–416.

———. 1990. "In Defense of Timofeeff-Ressovsky." *Quarterly Review of Biology* 65, no. 4: 457–79.

———. 2003. *Sukhovei: Vospominaniia genetika*. Moscow: Pamiatniki istoricheskoi mysli.

Bergman, Jay. 1998. "Valerii Chkalov: Soviet Pilot as New Soviet Man." *Journal of Contemporary History* 33, no. 1: 135–52.

Bernshtam, A. N. 1946. *Sotsial'no-ekonomicheskii stroi orkhono-eniseiskikh tiurok VI–VIII vv*. Moscow-Leningrad: Institut Vostokovedeniia.

———. 1951. *Ocherk istorii gunnov*. Leningrad: LGU.

Bertalanfi, L. 1969. *Obshchaia teoriia sistem—kriticheskii obzor*. Moscow: Progress.

"Bezymiannaia gornaia vershina v okrestnostiakh Riddera poluchila nazvanie pik Gumileva." 2012. *YK-news.kz* (21 July), http://www.yk-news.kz/novost/bezymyanna ya-gornaya-vershina-v-okrestnostyakh-riddera-poluchila-nazvanie-pik-gumileva, accessed 5/6/2014.

Birstein, Vadim J. 2001. *The Perversion of Knowledge: The True Story of Soviet Science*. Boulder, CO: Westview Press.

Blum, Alain, and Elena Filippova. 2006. "Territorialisation de l'ethnicité, ethnicisa-tion du territoire: La cas du systèm politique soviétique et russe." *L'Espace géographique* 35, no. 4: 317–27.

Bochkarev, A. I. 2008. *Fundamental'nye osnovy etnogeneza*. Moscow: Flinta.

Bogdanov, A. A. 1989 [1913]. *Tektologiia: Vseobshchaia organizatsionnaia nauka*. 2 vols. Moscow: Ekonomika.

Bogdanov, Ia. V. 2001. "Tipologiia lichnostei L. N. Gumileva s pozitsii ucheniia ob aktsentuatsiiakh." http://gumilevica.kulichki.net/debate/Article33.htm, accessed 11/7/2014.

———. 2002. "Ot idei L'va Gumileva k natsional'noi ideologii Rossii." http://www.left. ru/2003/7/bogdanov83.html, accessed 3/3/2014.

Bondarenko, Grigorii, Viacheslav Ermolaev, and Konstantin Ivanov. 1992. "V gostiakh u L'va Gumileva." *Den'* 12, no. 40 (22–28 March): 6

Bondarenko, Vladimir. 2002. "Rytsar' russkoi mysli." *Zavtra* 6, no. 429 (5 February), http://www.zavtra.ru/content/view/2002-02-0561/, accessed 24/3/2014.

Borisov, A. A. 1996. "Lev Gumilev o proiskhozhdenii naroda sakhaa." *Ilin* 1–2 (7–8), http://ilin.sakhaopenworld.org/1996-12/68.htm, accessed 4/6/2014.

——. ¨1999. "Iakutskii etnos v svete gumilevskoi teorii passionarnosti." In Borisov, *Materialy Gumilevskikh chtenii 1995–96 gg.*, 41–44.

——, ed. 1999. *Materialy Gumilevskikh chtenii 1995–96 gg.* Iakutsk: Iz-vo IaGU., 151–55.

——. 2002. "L. N. Gumilev i Iakutiia." In Shevchenko, *Lev Nikolaevich Gumilev*, 1: 34–37.

——. 2012. "Velikii evraziets i Iakutiia." *Ilin* 4, http://ilin-yakutsk.narod.ru/2012-4/32. htm, accessed 17/7/2014.

Borisov, N. S. 1976. "Otechestvennaia istoriografiia o vliianii tataro-mongol'skogo nashestviia na russkuiu kul'turu." *Problemy Istorii SSSR* 5: 129–48.

Borodai, Iu. M. 1981a. "Etnicheskie kontakty i okruzhaiushchaia sreda." *Priroda* 9: 82–85.

——. 1981b. "V poiskakh etnogennogo faktora." *Priroda* 4: 124–26.

——. 1994. "Ot imperii k natsional'nomu edinstvu." *Novaia Rossiia*, nos. 3–4, http://gumilevica.kulichki.net/BUM/bum02.htm, accessed 11/7/2014.

——. 1995. "Puti stanovleniia natsional'nogo edinstva." *Nash Sovremennik* 1: 112–32.

Böss, Otto. 1961. *Die Lehre der Eurasier: Ein Beitrag zur russischen Ideengeschichte des 20. Jahrhunderts*. Wiesbaden: Otto Harassowitz.

Böttger, Christian. 2014. *Ethnos: Der Nebel um den Volksbegriff*. Schnellbach: Lindenbaum Verlag.

Boym, Svetlana. 1995. "From the Russian Soul to Post-Communist Nostalgia." *Representations* 49 (Winter): 133–66.

Brain, Stephen. 2011. *Song of the Forest: Russian Forestry and Stalinist Environmentalism, 1905–1953*. Pittsburgh, PA: University of Pittsburgh Press.

Bramwell, Anna. 1985. *Blood and Soil: Richard Walther Darré and Hitler's Green Party*. Bourne End, England: Kensal.

Brandenberger, David. 2002. *National Bolshevism: Stalinist Mass Culture and the Formation of Modern Russian Identity, 1931–1956*. Cambridge, MA: Harvard University Press.

Brandenberger, David, and A. M. Dubrovsky. 1998. "'The People Need a Tsar': The Emergence of National Bolshevism as Stalinist Ideology, 1931–1941." *Europe-Asia Studies* 50, no. 5: 873–92.

Bratel', B. I. 1993. "Uchenie V. I. Vernadskogo o noosfere i solnechnaia energiia." In *Uchenie V. I. Vernadskogo i sovremennaia ekologicheskaia situatsiia: Tezisy vystuplenii na mezhdunarodnoi nauchnoi konferentsii*, 98–99. Akmola-Borovoe: AIPP "Zhanna Arka."

Brazhnikov, I. L. 2010. "Vospominaniia o Vadime Kozhinove: Nesostoiavshaiasia istoriia." http://pravaya.ru/names/19790?print=1, accessed 4/1/2014.

——. 2011. "'Skifskii siuzhet' v russkoi kul'ture." *Vestnik Nizhegorodskogo Universiteta* 4, no. 1: 332–37.

Bremmer, Ian, and Cory Welt. 1995. "Kazakhstan's Quandray." *Journal of Democracy* 6, no. 3: 139–54.

Brezhnev, Leonid Il'ich. 1970–1982. *Leninskim Kursom: Rechi i Stat'i*. 9 vols. Moscow: Iz-vo Politicheskoi Literatury.

Bromlei, Iu. V. 1969. "Etnos i endogamiia." *Sovetskaia Etnografiia* 6: 84–91.

——. 1970. "K voprosu o sushchnosti etnosa." *Priroda* 2: 51–55.

——. 1971. "Neskol'ko zamechanii o sotsial'nykh i prirodnykh faktorakh etnogeneza." *Priroda* 2: 83–84.

——. 1972. "Opyt tipologizatsii etnicheskikh obshchnostei." *Sovetskaia Etnografiia* 5: 61–81.

——. 1981. *Sovremennye problemy etnografii: Ocherki teorii i istorii.* Moscow: Nauka.

——. 1983a. *Ethnic Processes.* Translated by V. Epstein. Moscow: USSR Academy of Sciences.

——. 1983b. "Etnicheskie protsessy v SSSR." *Kommunist* 5: 56–64.

——. 1983c. *Ocherki teorii etnosa.* Moscow: Nauka.

——. 1987. *Etnosotsial'nye protsessy: Teoriia, istoriia, sovremennost'.* Moscow: Nauka.

——. 1988a. "Chelovek v etnicheskoi (natsional'noi) sisteme." *Voprosy Filosofii* 7: 16–28.

——. 1988b. "Po povodu odnogo 'avtonekrologa.'" *Znamia* 12: 229–32.

——. 1989. "Pis'mo v radaktsiiu." *Voprosy Filosofii* 12: 158–61.

Bromlei, Iu. V., and V. L. Doblaev. 1988. "O stat'e L. N. Gumileva 'Biografia nauchnoi teorii, ili Avtonekrolog.'" *Znamia* 12: 229–33.

Bromley, Yulian. 1974. "The Term *Ethnos* and Its Definition." In *Soviet Ethnology and Anthropology Today,* edited by Yulian Bromley, 55–72. The Hague: Mouton.

Bromley, Yulian, and V. I. Kozlov. 1989. "The Theory of Ethnos and Ethnic Processes in Soviet Social Science." *Comparative Studies in Society and History* 31, no. 3: 425–38.

Brownson, John Austin Jamil. 1988. "Landscape and Ethnos: An Assessment of L. N. Gumilev's Theories on Historical Ethnology and Implications on Russian Geopolitical Policies." PhD thesis, Simon Fraser University, Vancouver, BC.

Brudny, Yitzhak M. 1998. *Reinventing Russia: Russian Nationalism and the Soviet State, 1953–1991.* Cambridge, MA: Harvard University Press.

Bruk, S. I., and N. N. Cheboksarov. 1976. "Metaetnicheskie obshchnosti." *Rasy i Narody: Ezhegodnik* 6: 15–41.

Bruno, Andy. 2007. "Russian Environmental History: Directions and Potentials." *Kritika* 8, no. 3: 635–50.

Burlaka. D. K., ed. 2012. *Lev Gumilev: Pro et Contra: Lichnost' i tvorchestvo L. N. Gumileva v otsenkakh rossiiskikh myslitelei i issledovatelei: Antologiia.* St. Peterburg: Nauchno-Obraz. Kul't. Obshchestvo.

Buravleva, V. V. 1998. "Rossiia—Zapad—Vostok v kontseptsii evraziistva." In Bairamova, *Sistema tsennostei rossiiskoi natsional'noi politiki,* 30–31.

Burovskii, A. M. 2004. *Evrei, kotorykh ne bylo.* vol. 2. Moscow: Iz-vo AST.

——. 2012. "Lev Nikolaevich Gumilev, kakim ia ego zapomnil." http://www.s-pe.ru/notes/russia/93-lev-nikolaevich-gumiljov-kakim-ja-ego-zapomnil, accessed 20/9/2014.

Butenko, L. P., and Iu. V. Kolesnichenko. 1996. "Mentalitet rossian i evraziistvo: Ikh sushchnost' i obshchestvenno-politicheskii smysl." *Sotsis* 5: 92–102.

Butusov, K. P., and V. A. Michurin. 1995. "Lev Gumilev: Kosmos i chelevechestvo." *Terminator* 4, no. 5: 8–9.

"A bylo li igo?" 1997. *Rodina,* nos. 3–4: 85–92.

Carlson, Elof Axel. 1981. *Genes, Radiation, and Society: The Life and Work of H. J. Muller.* Ithaca, NY: Cornell University Press.

Chappell, John E. 1965. "Marxism and Geography." *Problems of Communism* 14, no. 6: 12–22.

——. 1970. "Climatic Change Reconsidered." *Goegraphical Review* 60, no. 3: 347–73.

——. 1975. "The Ecological Dimension: Russian and American Views." *Annals of the Association of American Geographers* 65, no. 2: 144–62.

Chase, Jonathan M., and Matthew A. Leibold. 2003. *Ecological Niches: Linking Classical and Contemporary Approaches.* Chicago: University of Chicago Press.

"Chast' shestaia: Passionarnost' v etnogeneze." 1972? *Antologiia samizdata,* http://antology.igrunov.ru/authors/lev_gumilev/passoinarn.html, accessed 22/3/2014.

Chebanov, S. B. 1998. "Istoriia odnogo seminara." *Pchela* 12, http://www.pchela.ru/podshiv/12/honesem.htm—top, accessed 10/6/2014.

Chernov, P. V. 1999. *Rossiia: Etnogeopoliticheskie osnovy gosudarstvennosti*. Moscow: "Vostochnaia Literatura."

Chernykh, E. N. 1995. "Postscript: Russian Archaeology after the Collapse of the USSR." In Kohl and Fawcett, *Nationalism, Politics, and the Practice of Archeology*, 139–48.

Chesnokov, V. S. 2010. "S. A. Podolinskii: Kontseptsiia sotsial'noi energetiki." *Vek Globalizatsiia* 2, no. 6: 181–87.

Chivilikhin, V. A. 1980. "Pamiat'." *Nash Sovremennik* 12: 102–25.

Chizhevskii, A. L. 1955. *Kosmicheskii pul's zhizni: Zemli v ob"iatiiakh solntsa. Geliotaraksiia*. Moscow.

———. 1963. *Solntse i my*. Moscow: Znanie.

———. 1973. *Zemnoe ekho solnechnykh bor'*. Moscow: Mysl'.

Chizhevskii, A. L., and Iu. G. Shishina. 1969. *V ritme solntsa*. Moscow: Nauka.

Chuprov, Aleksei. 2012. "Evraziistvo: Gosudarstvennaia ideologiia putinskoi Rossii." *newsland* (9 December), http://newsland.com/news/detail/id/1093886/, accessed 19/1/2014.

Clark, Bruce. 1995. *An Empire's New Clothes: The End of Russia's Liberal Dream*. London: Vintage.

Clover, Charles. 1999. "Dreams of the Eurasian Heartland." *Foreign Affairs* 78, no. 2: 9–13.

———. 2012. "Kremlin Gets Inspiration from Famous Dissident." *Financial Times* (1 October), http://blogs.ft.com/the-world/2012/10/135601/, accessed 10/7/2014.

Clover, Charles, Isabel Gorst, and Neil Buckley. 2011. "Putin Calls for New 'Eurasian Union.'" *Financial Times* (4 October), http://www.ft.com/intl/cms/s/0/3901988c-eea2-11e0-9a9a-00144feab49a.html—axzz2mcmTI99T, accessed 19/1/2014.

"The Concept of Indigeneity." 2006. *Social Anthropology* 14, no. 1: 17–32.

Connor, Walker. 1992. "Soviet Policies toward the Non-Russian Peoples in Theoretic and Historic Perspective: What Gorbachev Inherited." In *The Post-Soviet Nations: Perspectives on the Demise of the USSR*, edited by Alexander J. Motyl, 30–50. New York: Columbia University Press.

"A Critique of L. N. Gumilev's Work on Ethnography at a Meeting at Leningrad University." 1977. *Soviet Geography: Review and Translation* 18, no. 2: 119–28.

D'iakonov, I. M. 1992. "Ognennyi d'iavol: Po povodu rabot L. N. Gumileva." *Neva* 4: 225–28, http://passiorush.h1.ru/Path-Kritika/Diakonov-2.htm, accessed 11/3/2014.

Dalos, Gyorgy. 1998. *The Guest from the Future: Anna Akhmatova and Isaiah Berlin*. Translated by Anthony Wood. London: John Murray.

Danchenko, E. M. 1997. "O skhodstve vzgliadov S. M. Shirokogorova i L. N. Gumileva na prirodu etnosa." *Gumanitarnoe znanie*. vyp. 1: 72–74.

Daniel', Aleksandr, and Nikolai Mitrokhin. 1996. "Dissidentskie korni 'novykh kraine pravykh' v Rossii." In Iliushenko, *Nuzhen li Gitler Rossii?*, 20–29.

Danilevskii, N. Ia. 1895 [1871]. *Rossiia i Evropa: Vzgliad na kul'turnye i politicheskie otnosheniia slavianskogo mira k Germano-Romanskomu*. 5th ed. St. Petersburg: Panteleev.

Danks, Catherine. 2001. *Russian Politics and Society*. Harlow: Longman.

Darkevich, V. P. 1994. "Proiskhodezhdenie i razvitie gorodov dreveni Rusi (X–XIII vv.)." *Voprosy Istorii* 10: 43–60.

Darré, R. Walther. 1930. *Neuadel aus Blut und Boden*. Munich: Lehmann.

Darst, Robert G. 1988. "Environmentalism in the USSR: The Opposition of the River Diversion Projects." *Soviet Economy* 4, no. 3: 223–52.

De Benoist, Alain. 2012. *Mémoire vive*. Paris: Éditions de Fallois.

Demin, V. M. 2008. *Lev Gumilev*. 2nd ed. Moscow: Molodaia Gvardiia.

Dergachev, V. A. 2000. *Geopolitika*. Kiev: VIRA-R.

Devlin, F. Roger. 2008. "From Salon to Guillotine." *The Occidental Quarterly* 8, no. 2: 63–90.

Diagileva, T. D. 2012. *Lev Nikolaevich Gumilev: K 100-letiiu so dnia rozhdeniia; bibliograficheskii ukazatel'*. St. Petersburg: TsRB im. V. G. Belinskogo.

Diligenskii, G. G. 1995. "Staryi i novyi oblik fashizma." *Polis* 2: 34–37.

Dimitrov, D. 1935. "Slavianskaia filologiia na putiakh fashizatsii." *Iazyk i myshlenie* 5: 125–33.

Djordjević, R. 1999. "Russian Cosmism[. . . .]" *Serbian Journal of Astronomy* 159: 105–9.

Dokuchaev, V. V. 1899. *K ucheniiu o zonakh prirody*. St. Petersburg: Tip. SPb. Gradonachal'stva.

Donahoe, Brian, Joachim Otto Habeck, Agnieszka Halemba, and Istvan Santha. 2008. "Size and Place in the Construction of Indigeneity in the Russian Federation." *Current Anthropolgy* 49, no. 6: 993–1020.

Doronin, Gennadii. 2002. "Teoriia, stavshaia mirovozzreniem." *Kazakhstanskaia Pravda* (5 October), http://newsite.kazpravda.kz/rus/nauka/teorija_stavshaja_miro vozzreniem.html, accessed 3/6/2014.

Dragadze, Tamara. 1980. "The Place of Ethnos Theory in Soviet Anthropology." In *Soviet and Western Anthropology*, edited by Ernst Gellner, 161–70. London: Duckworth.

———. 2011. "Soviet Ethnography: Structure and Sentiment." In *Exploring the Edge of Empire: Soviet Era Anthropology in the Caucasus and Central Asia*, edited by Florian Mühlfried and Sergey Sokolovskiy, 21–34. Berlin: LIT Verlag.

Drobizheva, L. M. 1992. "*Perestroika* and the Ethnic Consciousness of Russians." In *From Union to Commonwealth: Nationalism and Separatism in the Soviet Republics*, edited by Gail W. Lapidus and Victor Zaslavsky, 98–113. Cambridge: Cambridge University Press.

———. 2001. "Etnichnost' v sovremennom obshchestve." *Mir Rossii* 2: 167–80.

Drozdov, O. A. 1974. "Etnos i prirodnaia sreda." *Priroda* 8: 75–76.

"Druzhba s narodom." 2011. *Izvestiia* (9 February), http://izvestia.ru/news/371091, accessed 17/4/2014.

Dugin, A. G. 2000. *Osnovy geopolitiki: Geopoliticheskoe budushchee Rossii: Myslit' prostranstvom*. 2nd ed. Moscow: Arktogeia-tsentr.

———. 2001. "Evraziia prevyshe vsego." http://www.arctogaia.com/public/vtor9.htm, accessed 13/1/2014.

———. 2002a. "Evoliutsiia natsional'noi idei rusi (Rossii) na raznykh istoricheskikh etapakh." In Shevchenko, *Lev Nikolaevich Gumilev*, 2: 9–36.

———. 2002b. "Lev Gumilev: Nauka 'zhivoi zhizni.'" http://evrazia.org/modules.php?name+News&file=article&sid=634, accessed 8/2/2014.

———. 2002c. "On vernul nam dve tysiachi let nashei sud'by!" In *Osnovy Evrazistva*, edited by N. Agamalian et al, 534–40. Moscow: Arktogeia.

———. 2004. *Evraziiskaia missiia Nursultana Nazarbaeva*. Moscow: ROF "Evraziia."

———. n.d. "Vekhi Evraziistva." *Evraziia*, http://eurasia.com.ru/vehi1.html, accessed 3/6/2014.

Dunichev, V. M. 2001. *Anglichane, Russkie, Iapontsy (poiavlenie i razvitie etnosov)*. Iuzhno-Sakhalinsk: Sakhalinskoe knizhnoe iz-vo.

Dunlop, John. 1984. *The Faces of Contemporary Russian Nationalism*. Princeton, NJ: Princeton University Press.

——. 1993. *The Rise of Russia and the Fall of the Soviet Empire*. Princeton, NJ: Princeton University Press.

——. 1997. "Russia: In Search of an Identity?" In *New States, New Politics: Building the Post-Soviet Nations*, edited by Ian Bremmer and Ray Taras, 29–95. Cambridge: Cambridge University Press.

——. 2001. "Alexandr Dugin's 'Neo-Eurasian' Textbook. . . ." *Harvard Ukrainian Studies* 25, nos. 1–2: 91–127.

Dunn, Stephen P. 1975. "New Departures in Soviet Theory and Practice of Ethnicity." *Dialectical Anthropology* 1: 61–70.

Dylis, N. V. 1969. "Biogeosfera, ee svoistva i osobennosti." *Izvestiia AN SSSR: Seriia biologicheskiaia* 4: 497–504.

Dzhilkibaev, Berik. 2001. "Passionarnost' podlinnaia i mnimaia." *Internet-Gazeta "Zona KZ"* 0–135 (14 September), http://www.zonakz.net/articles/11449, accessed 3/6/2014.

Edgar, Adrienne. 2012. "*Rulers and Victims* Reconsidered." *Kritika* 13, no. 2: 429–40.

Efanov, L. E. 1998. "Eshche raz ob itogakh 'shokovoi terapii' ili antisistemy v ekonomike." In Ganzha,*Uchenie L. N. Gumileva*, 94–98.

Efremov, Iu. K. 1971. "Vazhnoe zveno v tsepi sviazei cheloveka s prirodoi." *Priroda* 2: 77–80.

——. 1978. "Preobrazovanie prirody kak sostavnaia chast' prirodopol'zovaniia." *Voprosy Geografii* 108: 14–26.

——. 2003. "Slovo o L've Nikolaeviche Gumileve (1912–1992)." In Voronovich and Kozyreva, *Vspominaia L. N. Gumileva*, 22–40.

Eidel'man, N. Ia. 1989. "*Revoliutsiia sverkhu*" *v Rossii*. Moscow: Kniga.

El'zon, M. D. 2003. "Chto pomniu." In Voronovich and Kozyreva, *Vspominaia L. N. Gumileva*, 206–8.

Elez, A. I. 2001. *Kritika etnologii*. Moscow: MAIK "Nauka/Interperiodika."

Elfimov, Alexei. 2014. "Russian Ethnography as a Science: Truths Claimed, Trails Followed." In *An Empire of Others: Creating Ethographic Knowledge in Imperial Russia and the USSR*, edited by Roland Cvetkovski and Alexis Hofmeister, 51–80. Budapest: CEU Press.

Engel'gart, L.T. 2000. "Kak upoitel'no prostranstvo." In *A. L. Chizhevskii: Vremena goda: Zhivopis'. Poeziia*, edited by L. T. Engel'gart, 7–34. Moscow.

Engels, Friedrich. 1974. *Dialectics of Nature*. Translated by Clemens Duttt. Moscow: Progress.

Enikeev, G. R. 2005. "Lideram i elite tatarskoi natsii." http://tatarlar.3bb.ru/viewtopic.php?id=23, accessed 3/6/2014.

——. 2007a. *Korona ordynskoi imperii*. Moscow: Algoritm.

——. 2007b. "Vspomnim imia svoe. . . ." *Zvezda Povolzh'ia* 10 (15–21 March), http://tatpolit.ru/category/zvezda/2007-03-19/215, accessed 3/6/2014.

——. 2008. *Moskovskoe Tatarskoe Studencheskoe Sobranie*, http://www.mtss.ru/pages/conf250209er.htm, accessed 3/6/2014.

——. 2009. *Po sledam chernoi legendy: Pravda i lozh' o tatarakh Rossii: Istoki, prichiny, avtory*. Moscow: Medina.

Ermachenkov, Igor'. 2009. "Chimerica: Soiuz titanov ili khimera?" *Finam.ru* (20 July), http://www.finam.ru/analysis/forecasts00E76/default.asp, accessed 16/3/2014.

Ermatov, M. 1968. *Etnogenez i formirovanie predkov uzbekskogo naroda*. Tashkent: "Uzbekistan."

Ermekbaev, Zh. A. 2003. *Teoriia etnogenez i evraziiskie idei L. N. Gumileva v prepodavanii istoricheskikh distsiplin.* Astana: ENU.

Ermolaev, V. Iu. 1990. "Samoorganizatsiia v prirode i etnogenez." *Izvestiia Vsesoiuznogo Geograficheskogo Obshchestva* 122, no. 1: 26–32.

———. 2000. "Sumerki na golubom nebe: Kazakhstan i 'evraziiskie' legendy'." *Deti Fel'dmarshala* 10: 12–13.

———. 2012. "Lev Nikolaevich Gumilev: Shtrikhi k portretu." In Burlaka, *Lev Gumilev: Pro et Contra*, 198–217.

Ermolaev, V. Iu., and M. A. Ermolaeva. 1995. "Russkii kommunizm i Evraziia: Al'ternativa ili edinstvo?" In *Geopoliticheskie i geoekonomicheskie problemy Rossii*, edited by S.B. Lavrov, 70–75. St. Petersburg: Russkoe Geograficheskoe Obshchestvo.

Ersen, Emre. 2004. "Neo-Eurasianism and Putin's 'Multipolarism' in Russian Foreign Policy." *Turkish Review of Eurasian Studies* 4: 135–72.

"Eshche raz o morkovke." 1989. *Ogonek* 41: 29.

"Etnicheskie protsessy." 1978. In *Bol'shaia Sovetskaia Entsiklopediia.* 3rd ed., vol. 30, 298. Moscow: Sovetskaia Entsliklopediia.

Etnogenez mordovskogo naroda. 1965. Saransk: Mordovskoe kn. izd-vo.

"Etnologicheskaia karta sovremennogo sostoianiia mira." 1988. http://www.kulichki.com/~gumilev/fund/fund21.htm, accessed 7/4/2014.

"Eurasia Party-Union of Patriots Sets Ambitious Goal." 2003. *RFE/RL Newsline* (23 May), http://www.rferl.org/content/article/1142922.html, accessed 16/1/2014.

Everstov, M. I. 2008. "Globalizatsiia i molodezh' Iakutii." *Molodezh' Iakutiia* (18 January), http://uhhan.ru/publ/50-1-0-218, accessed 18/4/2014.

"Evraziia prezhde vsego." 2002. In *Evraziiskii Vzgliad: Mirovozzrencheskaia platforma OPOD "Evraziia,"* 3–17. Moscow: Arktogeia-tsentr.

"Evraziistvo i sovremennost': kruglyi stol." 1993. *Liki Rossii: Al'manakh* 2, http://www.patriotica.ru/actual/stol_eurasia.html, accessed 16/6/2014.

Evraziistvo: Ot idei k praktike. 2004. Astana: ENU.

Fakhrutdinov, R. G. 1993. *Zolotaia orda i tatary: Chto v dushe u naroda.* Naberezhnye Chelnye: KAMAZ.

———. 2000. *Istoriia tatarskogo naroda i Tatarstana (Drevnost; i srednevekov'e).* Kazan: Magarif.

Faustova, Milena. 2002. "Lev Gumilev: Poet istorii." http://gumilevica.kulichki.net/fund/fund31.htm, accessed 14/7/2014.

Fedorov, M. M. 1999. "K voprosu o vkhozhdenii Vostochnoi Sibiri v sostav Rossii." In Borisov, *Materialy Gumilevskikh chtenii 1995–96 gg.*, 130–42.

Fedorov, N. F. 1906–1913. *Filosofiia obshchego dela.* 2 vols. Moscow-Vernyi: n.p.

Fedorova, N. V. 2006. "Analiticheskii obzor osnovnykh sovremennykh etnolandshaftnykh kontseptsii." *Uchenye zapiski Tavricheskogo Natsional'nogo Universiteta; Seriia "Geografiia"* 14, no. 53: 1, http://www3.crimea.edu/tnu/magazine/scientist/edition14/tom1geography/article30.htm, accessed 19/06/2008.

Feinstein, Elaine. 2005. *Anna of All the Russias: The Life of Anna Akhmatova.* London: Phoenix.

Fenton, Steve. 2003. *Ethnicity.* Cambridge: Polity.

Ferguson, Niall. 2008. "Team 'Chimerica.'" *Washington Post* (17 November): A19.

Filippov, V. R. 2006. "S. Shirokogorov: U istokov biosotsial'noi intepretatsii etnosa." *Etnograficheskoe Obozrenie* 3: 86–93.

———. 2010. *"Sovetskaia teoriia etnosa": Istoricheskii ocherk.* Moscow: Inst. Afriki RAN.

Filippova, Elena. 2010. "De l'ethnographie à l'ethnologie: Changer de nom ou changer de paradigme?" *L'Homme* 194: 41–56.

Fragner, Bert G. 2001. "'Soviet Nationalism': An Ideological Legacy to the Independent Republics of Central Asia." In *Identity Politics in Central Asia and the Muslim World: Nationalism, Ethnicity and Labour in the Twentieth Century*, edited by Willem Van Schendel and Erik Jan Zürcher, 13–33. London: I. B. Tauris.

Freidin, Gregory. 1996. "Weimar Russia?" *Los Angeles Times* (7 January), http://www.stanford.edu/~gfreidin/Publications/columns/weimar.htm, accessed 9/1/2012.

Friedgut, Theodore H. 1984. *Soviet Anti-Zionism and Anti-Semitism*. Jerusalem: Soviet and East European Research Center.

Frizman, L. 2002. "Vozmutitel' spokoistviia: Kniga O. Suleimenova *Az i Iai* pod ognem ideologicheskoi kritiki." *NLO* 55, http://magazines.russ.ru/nlo/2002/55/friz.html, accessed 6/17/2014.

Frolovskaia, Tat'iana. 2005. "Kul'tura Kazakhstana—evraziiskii vektor." *Kazakhstan* 4 (1/2/2008), http://www.investkz.com/openkz/9.html, accessed 3/6/2014.

Frumkin, K. G. 2001. "Passionarnost': K istorii idei." *Rossiia XXI* 3, http://www.ecc.ru/XXI/RUS_21/ARXIV/2001/frumkin_2001_3.htm, accessed 6/7/2014.

———. 2008. *Passionarnost': Prikliucheniia odnoi idei*. Moscow: LKI.

"G. A. Ziuganov pozdravil Prezidenta Venesuely Ugo Chavesa . . ." 2009. *KPRF*, 16 February, http://kprf.ru/international/63793.html; accessed 23/6/2015.

Gaissinovitch, A. E. 1980. "The Origins of Soviet Genetics and the Struggle with Lamarckism, 1922–1929." *Journal of the History of Biology* 13, no. 1: 1–51.

Gali, Azimbai. 2002. "Russkoe vizantiistvo i paradigmy dlia russkopodannogo nerusskogo." *Internet-Gazeta "Zona KZ"* 0/702 (10 April), http://www.zonakz.net/articles/155, accessed 3/6/2014.

———. 2003. "Azimbai Gali protiv Aleksandra Dugina." *Internet-Gazeta "Zona KZ"* 17/768 (14 October), http://zonakz.net/articles/4642, accessed 3/6/2014.

———. 2004a. "Kazakhizatsiia, kak etnosotsial'naia mobilizatsiia dlia sozdaniia postetnicheskogo kazakhstana." http://www.centrasia.ru/newsA.php?st=1074842940, accessed 3/6/2014.

———. 2004b. "Ratsional'noe soznanie i irratsional'noe videnie." *Kazkhskaia Pravda* 123 (9 May), http://kazpravda.by.ru/archive2/2004-may-09(123)_article02.htm, accessed 26/2/2008.

———. 2007. "Kontseptsiia 'bol'shoi kazakhskoi natsii.'" *Nachnem s ponedel'nika* 12/674 (30 March–35 April), http://www.centrasia.ru/newsA.php?st=1182676440, accessed 3/6/2014.

Galkovskii, D. E. 1995. "Russkaia politika i russkaia filosofiia." http://old.russ.ru/antolog/inoe/galkov.htm, accessed 31/7/2014.

Gammer, Moshe. 2004. "Russian and the Eurasian Steppe Nomads: An Overview." In *Mongols, Turks and Others: Eurasian Nomads and the Sedentary World*, edited by Reuven Amitai, 483–502. Leiden: Brill.

Ganzha, A. G., and I. S. Shishkin, eds. 1998. *Uchenie L. N. Gumileva: opyt osmysleniia. Vtorye gumilevskie chteniia*. Moscow: RAN.

Gare, Arran. 2000. "Aleksandr Bogdanov's History, Sociology and Philosophy of Science." *Studies in the History and Philosphy of Science* 31, no. 2: 231–48.

Gavrilova, M. K. 1999. "Chelovek i priroda." In Borisov *Materialy Gumilevskikh chtenii 1995–96 gg.*, 35–40.

Geller, Leonid. 2009. "Ostval'd, Bogdanov, Malevich i mnogie drugie: Zametki o russkikh sud'bakh energetizma." In *Literaturovedenie na sovremennom etape . . . Materialy mezhdunarodnogo kongressa literaturovedov: K 125-letiiu E. I. Zamiatina*, edited by L. V. Poliakova. Tambov: Izd. dom TGU.

Gellner, Ernst. 1988. "Modern Ethnicity." In *State and Society in Soviet Social Thought*, edited by Ernst Gellner, 115–36. Oxford: Blackwell.

"Geograficheskaia sreda." 1952. In *Bol'shaia Sovetskaia Entsiklopediia*. 2nd ed. 10: 452–53. Moscow: "Bol'shaia Sovetskaia Entsiklopediia."

Gerasimov, I. P., ed. 1968. *Priroda i obshchestvo*. Moscow: Nauka.

Gershtein, E. G. 1993. "Lishniaia liubov': Stseny iz moskovskoi zhizni." *Novyi Mir* 11, 12: 151–85, 139–74.

———. 1998. *Memuary*. St. Petersburg: Inapress.

Gerstein, Emma. 2004. *Moscow Memoirs*. Translated by J. Crowfoot. London: Harvill Press.

Girusov, E. V. 1976. *Sistema "obshchestvo-priroda" (problema sotsial'noi ekologii)*. Moscow: Iz-vo MGU.

Giuliano, Elise. 2000. "Who Determines the Self in the Politics of Self-Determination?: Identity and Preference Formation in Tatarstan's Nationalist Mobilization." *Comparative Politics* 32, no. 3: 295–316.

Gladkii, I. O. 2006. "Geograficheskie osnovy etnicheskoi ekologii." Avtoreferat, Doctoral diss., St. Petersburg University, http://www.dissercat.com/content/geogra ficheskie-osnovy-etnicheskoi-ekologii, accessed 15/6/2011.

Gleason, Gregory. 1993. "Nationalism and Its Discontents." *Russian Review* 52, no. 1: 79–90.

Goble, Paul. 2009. "Putin's 'Vulgar Eurasianism' Has Chekist Roots." *Window on Eurasia* (8 June), http://windowoneurasia.blogspot.co.uk/2009/06/window-on-eurasia-putins-vulgar.html, accessed 10/7/2014.

Gogolev, A. I. 1989. "Resonans: Tiurkskaia kul'tura: Proshloe i busushchee." *Molodezh' Iakutii*, 20 April, http://gumilevica.kulichki.net/debate/Article38.htm, accessed 4/6/2014.

Gołąbek, Bartosz. 2008. "Lew Gumilow i Aleksander Dugin: O dwóch obliczach euroazjatyzmu w Rosji po 1991 roku." PhD thesis, Jagiellonian University, Krakow.

Golovanov, L. V. 1995. "Chizhevskii, Aleksandr Leonidovich." In *Russkaia filosofiia: Slovar'*, edited by M. A. Maslina, 608–9. Moscow: Respublika.

———. 1998. "'Kosmizm' L'va Gumileva." In Ganzha and Shishkin, *Uchenie L. N. Gumileva*, 7–11.

Golovnikova, O. V., and N. S. Tarkhova. 2001. "'Iosif Vissarionovich!: Spasite sovetskogo istorika' (o neizvestnoi pis'me Anny Akhmatovoi Stalinu)." *Otechestvennaia Istoriia* 3: 149–57.

Goncharova, E. M., ed. 1995. *Dni L. N. Gumileva v Bezhetske*. Bezhetsk: "Ekopros."

———, ed. 2003. *Lev Gumilev: Sud'ba i idei*. Moscow: Airis.

Gorenburg, Dmitry. 1999. "Regional Separatism in Russia: Ethnic Russia or Power Grab?" *Europe-Asia Studies* 51, no. 2: 245–74.

Gorham, Eville. 1991. "Biogeochemistry: Its Origins and Development." *Biogeochemistry* 13, no. 3: 199–239.

Goudakov, Vladimir. 2006. "Gumilev and Huntington: Approaches and Terminologies." *Diogenes* 210: 82–90.

Gracheva, Tat'iana V. 2008. *Nevidimaia Khazariia: Algoritmy geopolitiki i strategii tainykh voin mirovoi zakulisy*. Riazan': Zerna.

———. 2009. *Sviataia Rus' protiv Khazarii*. Riazan': Zerna.

Graev, Viktor. 1998. "'Produkt prirody' i revolutsiia." *TUM Balalaika* 7 (January–February): 6–7, http://feedbackgroup.info/proetcon/produkt.html, accessed 30/6/2014.

Graham, Loren R. 1987. *Science, Philosophy, and Human Behavior in the Soviet Union*. New York: Columbia University Press.

———. 1993. *Science in Russia and the Soviet Union: A Short History*. Cambridge: Cambridge University Press.

Granin, Daniil. 1987. *Zubr*. Leningrad: Sovetskii Pisatel'.

———. 1989. *The Bison: A Novel about a Scientist Who Defined Stalin*. Translated by A. W. Bouis. New York: Doubleday.

Gregor, A. James. 2000. *The Faces of Janus: Marxism and Fascism in the Twentieth Century*. New Haven, CT: Yale University Press.

Grinnell, Joseph. 1917. "The Niche-Relationships of the California Thrasher." *The Auk* 34, no. 4: 427–33.

Grmesov, Peresvet Chelubeevich. 2001. "Rassuzhdeniia o pervom romane tsikla *Plokhikh liudei net*." http://orduss.pvost.org/old/pages/peresvet.html, accessed 14/7/2014.

Gromov, A. I. 2012. "Energeticheskaia osnova global'noi sistemy 'priroda-obshchestvo-chelovek.'" *Partnerstvo Tsivilizatsii* 3: 30–36.

Groys, Boris. 1988. *Gesamtkunstwerk Stalin: Die gespaltene Kultur in der Sowjetunion*. Munich: Hanser.

———. 1994. "Nietzsche's Influence on the Non-Official Culture of the 1930s." In Rosenthal, *Nietzsche and Soviet Culture*, 367–90.

Gullette, David. 2006. "Kinship, State, and 'Tribalism': The Genealogical Construction of the Kyrgyz Republic." PhD diss., University of Cambridge.

———. 2008. "A State of Passion: The Use of Ethnogenesis in Kyrgyzstan." *Inner Asia* 10: 261–79.

Gumilev, L. N. 1956. Letter to P. N. Savitskii, 19 December, personal archive of author.

———. 1960. *Khunnu : Sredinnaia Aziia v drevnie vremena*. Moscow: Inst. Vostoch. Litry AN SSSR.

———. 1963. "Pul's klimata." *Komsomol'skaia Pravda* (27 July).

———. 1964a. "Gde ona, strana Khazariia?" *Nedelia* 24 (7–13 June).

———. 1964b. "Khazaria and the Caspian Sea (Landscape and Etnos I)." *Soviet Geography: Review and Translation* 5, no. 6: 54–69.

———. 1964c. "Khazariia i Kaspii." *Vestnik Leningradskogo Universiteta: Seriia Geograficheskaia* 6, no. 1: 83–95.

———. 1965. "Les fluctuations du niveau de la mer Caspienne (Variations climatiques et histoire des peuples nomades au sud de la plaine russe)." *Cahiers du monde russe et soviétique* 6, no. 3: 331–66.

———. 1966. *Otkrytie Khazarii: Istoriko-geograficheskii etiud*. Moscow: Nauka.

———. 1967a. *Drevnie Tiurki*. Moscow: Nauka.

———. 1967b. "Po povodu 'edinoi' geografii (Landshaft i etnos, III)." *Vestnik Leningradskogo Universiteta: Seriia Geograficheskaia* 6, no. 1: 120–29, http://gumilevica.kulichki.net/articles/Article86.htm, accessed 6/6/2011.

———. 1967c. "Rol' klimaticheskikh kolebanii v istorii narodov stepnoi zony Evrazii." *Istoriia SSSR* 1: 53–66.

———. 1968a. "Etnos i landshaft." *Izvestiia Vsesoiuznogo Geograficheskogo Obshchestva* 3: 97–106.

———. 1968b. "On the Anthropogenic Factor in Landscape Formation." *Soviet Geography* 9: 590–602.

———. 1968c. "On the Subject of the 'Unified Geography' (Landscape and Etnos, VI)." *Soviet Geography: Review and Translation* 9, no. 1: 36–47.

———. 1970a. "Etnogenez i etnosfera." *Priroda* 2: 43–50.

———. 1970b. "Etnogenez i etnosfera." *Priroda* 1: 46–55.

———. 1970c. "Khazaria and the Caspian Sea." *Geographical Review* 60, no. 3: 363–77.

———. 1970d. "Mesto istoricheskoi geografii v vostokovednykh issledovaniiakh." *Narody Azii i Afriki* 1: 85–94, http://gumilevica.kulichki.net/articles/Article13.htm—Article13note2, accessed 10/3/2014.

——. 1970e. *Poiski vymyshlennogo tsarstva: Legenda o "Gosudarstve 'presvitera Ioanna.'"* Moscow: Nauka.

——. 1970f. "Sergei Ivanovich Rudenko: Nekrolog." *Izvestiia Vsesoiuz. Geogr. O-va* 102, no. 1: 91–93.

——. 1971a. "Etnogenez: Prirodnyi protsess." *Priroda* 2: 80–82.

——. 1971b. "Kollektsii S. I. Rudenko v Gosudarstvennom muzee narodov SSSR." In *Etnografiia narodov SSSR*, A.N. Arkhangel'skii, 6–15. Leningrad: Geog. Obshchestvo SSSR.

——. 1971c. "Ot istorii liudei k istorii prirody." *Priroda* 11: 117–18.

——. 1971d. "Ot istorii liudei k istorii prirody: Rets. na knigu E. Le Rua Ladiuri *Istoriia klimata s 1000 goda.*" *Priroda* 11: 116–17.

——. 1972a. "Izmeneniia klimata i migratsii kochevnikov." *Priroda* 4: 44–52, http://gumilevica.kulichki.net/articles/Article15.htm, accessed 7/3/2014.

——. 1972b. "Mozhet li proizvedenie iziashchnoi slovesnosti byt' istoricheskim istochnikom?" *Russkaia Literatura* 1: 73–82.

——. 1974a. *Khunny v Kitae: Tri veka voiny Kitaia so stepnymi narodami.* Moscow: Nauka.

——. 1974b. "Letter to the Editors of *Izvestiya Vsesoyuznogo Geograficheskogo Obshchestva.*" *Soviet Geography: Review and Translation* 15, no. 6: 376.

——. 1975. "Vikingi ne solgali." *Priroda* 5: 95–99.

——. 1976. "G. E. Grumm-Grzhimailo i rozhdenie nauki ob etnogeneze." *Priroda* 5: 112–21.

——. 1976? "Spor s poetom." http://gumilevica.kulichki.net/articles/Article02.htm, accessed 5/4/2014.

——. 1977. "Mongoly i merkity v XII veke." *Studia orientalla et Antiqua* 416 (23/4/2007), http://gumilevica.kulichki.com/articles/Article78.htm, accessed 8/6/2015.

——. 1978a. "Biosfera i impul'sy soznaniia." *Priroda* 12: 97–105.

——. 1980a. "Epokha kulikovskoi bitvy." *Ogonek* 36: 16–17.

——. 1980b. "God rozhdeniia 1380." *Dekorativnoe Iskusstvo* 12: 34–37.

——. 1987a. "Liudi i priroda velikoi stepi." *Voprosy Istorii* 11: 64–77, http://gumilevica.kulichki.net/articles/Article16.htm, accessed 10/3/2014.

——. 1987b. *Searches for an Imaginary Kingdom: The Legend of the Kingdom of Prester John* Translated by R. E. F. Smith. Cambridge: Cambridge University Press.

——. 1988a. "Biografiia nauchnoi teorii, ili avtonekrolog." *Znamia* 4: 202–16.

——. 1988b. "Imia sobstvennoe." *Priroda i chelovek* 9: 46–48.

——. 1988c. "Korni nashego rodstva." *Izvestiia* (13 April): 3.

——. 1988d. "Negasimye kostry." *Leningradskii rabochii* (14 March), http://gumilevi ca.kulichki.net/articles/Article57.htm, accessed 3/3/2014.

——. 1989a. "Chelovechnost' prevyshe vsego." *Izvestiia* (24 June), http://gumilevica.kulichki.net/articles/Article45.htm, accessed 19/3/2014.

——. 1989b. *Drevniaia Rus' i velikaia step'.* Moscow: Mysl'.

——. 1989c. *Etnogenez i biosfera Zemli.* 2nd ed. Leningrad: Iz-vo Len. Universiteta.

——. 1989d. "Etnos, istoriia, kul'tura." *Dekorativnoe Iskusstvo SSSR* 5: 30–33.

——. 1989e. "Etnos, istoriia, kul'tura." *Dekorativnoe Iskusstvo SSSR* 10: 30.

——. 1989f. "Pis'mo v radaktsiiu 'Voprosov filosofii.'" *Voprosy Filosofii* 5: 157–60.

——. 1989g. "Pomni o Vavilone." *Istoki* 20: 359–72, http://gumilevica.kulichki.net/articles/Article62.htm, accessed 2/3/2014.

——. 1989h. "Sila epokhi." *Dekorativnoe Iskusstvo SSSR* 7: 34–35.

——. 1989i. "Sinkhronnyi tekst iz peredachi 'Grani Rossiiskogo etnogeneza.'" http://gumilevica.kulichki.net/articles/Article27.htm, accessed 4/4/2014.

———. 1989j. "Vsem nam zaveshchana Rossiia." *Krasnaia Zvezda* (21 September), http://www.patriotica.ru/religion/gumilev_int2.html, accessed 19/3/2014.

———. 1990a. *Geografiia etnosa v istoricheskii period*. Leningrad: Nauka.

———. 1990b. "Iskat' to, chto verno." *Sovetskaia Literatura* 1: 72–76, http://gumilevica.kulichki.net/articles/Article06.htm, accessed 25/2/2014.

———. 1990c. "Zakony vremeni." *Literaturnoe Obozrenie* 3: 3–9.

———. 1991a. "Bremia talanta." In D. M. Balashov, *Sobranie sochinenii*. Moscow: Khudozhestvennaia Literatura. http://gumilevica.kulichki.net/articles/Article55.htm, accessed 5/4/2014.

———. 1991b. "Chto-to s pamiat'iu. . . ." *Den'* 1, no. 29 (29 December 1991): 5.

———. 1991c. "Kakoi ia demokrat?: Ia staryi soldat!" http://nevzorov.tv/2012/03/lev-gumilyov-kakoj-ya-demokrat-ya-starij-soldat/, accessed 17/4/2014.

———. 1991d. "Kniaz' Sviatoslav Igorevich." *Nash Sovremennik* 7: 43–149.

———. 1991e. "'Menia nazyvaiut evraziitsem.'" *Nash Sovremennik* 1: 132–41.

———. 1991f. "My zhivem v bol'shoi kommunal'noi kvartire." *Nedelia* 6: 10–11.

———. 1992a. "My absoliutno samobytny." *Nevskoe Vremia* (12 August), http://gumilevica.kulichki.net/articles/Article52.htm, accessed 21/3/2014.

———. 1992b. "Ritmy Evrazii." *Nash Sovremennik* 10: 3–7.

———. 1993. *Ritmy Evrazii: Epokhi i tsivilizatsii*. Moscow: Ekopros.

———. 1993a. "Etno-landshaftnye regiony evrazii za istoricheskii period." In Gumilev, *Ritmy Evrazii*, 252–70.

———. 1993b. "Skazhu Vam po sekretu, chto esli Rossiia budet spasena, to tol'ko kak evraziiskaia derzhava. . . ." In Gumilev, *Ritmy Evrazii*, 25–32.

———. 1994a. "Chernaia Legenda." In Gumilev, *Chernaia Legenda*, 42–147.

———. 1994b. *Chernaia Legenda: Druz'ia i nedrugi Velikoi stepi*. Moscow: Ekopros.

———. 1994c. "'Ia, russkii chelovek, vsiu zhizn' zashchishchaiu tatar ot klevety.'" In Gumilev, *Chernaia Legenda*, 247–323.

———. 1994d. "Poisk neprotivorechivoi versii'." In Gumilev, *Chernaia Legenda*, 209–26.

———. 1994e. *Poiski vymyshlennogo tsarstva*. St. Petersburg: Arbis.

———. 1995. "Istoriko-filosofskie trudy kniazia N. S. Trubetskogo (zametki poslednego evraziitsa)." In N. S. Trubetskoi, *Istoriia. Kul'tura. Iazyk*, edited by V. M. Zhivov, 31–54. Moscow: Progress-Univers.

———. 2000. *Ot rusi do rossii: Ocherki etnicheskoi istorii*. Moscow: Airis-Press.

———. 2001. *Konets i vnov' nachalo: Populiarnye lektsii po narodovedeniiu*. Moscow: Rol'f.

———. 2003. *Chtoby svecha ne pogasla. Sbornik esse, interv'iu, stikhotvorenii, perevodov*. Moscow: Airis Press.

———. 2003a. "Avtobiografiia." In Goncharova, *Lev Gumilev: Sud'ba i idei*, 7–16.

———. 2003b. "Avtonekrolog." In Goncharova, *Lev Gumilev: Sud'ba i idei*, 17–36.

———. 2003c. "'Chtoby svecha ne pogasla.'" In Gumilev, *Chtoby svecha ne pogasla*, 7–15.

———. 2003d. "Dovoennyi Noril'sk." In Voronovich and Kozyreva, *Vspominaia L. N. Gumileva*, 221–30.

———. 2003e. "Glavnomu redaktoru zhurnala *Kommunist* R. I. Kosolapovu [1982]." In Voronovich and Kozyreva, *Vspominaia L. N. Gumileva*, 230–36.

———. 2003f. "Nikakoi mistiki." In Gumilev, *Chtoby svecha ne pogasla*, 51–68.

———. 2003g. "Proiskhozhdenie kazakhskogo etnosa." In Zholdasbekov, *Evraziistvo i Kazakhstan*, 1: 11–18.

———. 2003h. "'Publikatsiia moikh rabot blokiruiutsia': Kto i pochemu otvergal L. N. Gumilevu." In Voronovich and Kozyreva, *Vspominaia L. N. Gumileva*, 246–56.

———. 2003i. *Tysiacheletie vokrug Kaspiia*. Moscow: Airis-Press.

———. 2004a. "Apokrif." In *Etnosfera. Istoriia liudei i istoriia prirody*, 499–500. Moscow: AST.

———. 2004b. "Bipoliarnost' etnosfery." In *Etnosfera. Istoriia liudei i istoriia prirody*, 354–75. Moscow: AST.

———. 2004c. *Drevniaia Rus' i velikaia step'*. Moscow: Airis.

———. 2004d. "Otritsatel'nye znacheniia v etnogeneze." In *Etnosfera. Istoriia liudei i istoriia prirody*, 335–3\53. Moscow: AST.

———. 2004e. "Zigzag istorii." In *Etnosfera. Istoriia liudei i istoriia prirody*, 376–498. Moscow: AST.

———. 2004 [1967]. "O termine etnos." In *Etnosfera. Istoriia liudei i istoriia prirody*, 38–55. Moscow: AST.

———. 2004 [1970]. "Etnogenez i etnosfera." In *Etnosfera. Istoriia liudei i istoriia prirody*, 97–132. Moscow: Ast.

———. 2008. *Struna istorii: Lektsii po etnologii*. Moscow: Airis-Press.

Gumilev, L. N., and D. M. Balashov. 1993. "V kakoe vremia my zhivem?" In Gumilev, *Ritmy Evrazii*, 133–60.

Gumilev, L. N., and V. Iu. Ermolaev. 1993. "Gore ot illiuzii." In Gumilev, *Ritmy Evrazii*, 174–87.

———. 1997. "Problemy predskazuemosti v izuchenii protsessov etnogeneza." In *Predely predskazuemosti*, edited by Iu. A. Kravtsov, 236–47. Moscow: TsentrKom.

Gumilev, L. N., and K. P. Ivanov. 1984. "Etnosfera i kosmos." In *Materialy vtorogo vsesiuznogo soveshchaniia po kosmicheskoi antropoekologii*, edited by E. I. Slepiana, 211–20. Moscow: Nauka http://gumilevica.kulichki.net/articles/Article08.htm, accessed 30/4/2014.

———. 1992. "Etnicheskie protsessy: Dva podkhoda k izucheniiu." *Sotsiologicheskie Issledovaniia* 1: 50–57.

Gumilev, L. N., and A. P. Okladnikov. 1982. "Fenomen kul'tury malykh narodov Severa." *Dekorativnoe Iskusstvo* 8: 23–28, http://gumilevica.kulichki.net/articles/Ar ticle102.htm, accessed 17/5/2014.

Gumilev, L. N., and A. M. Panchenko. 1990. *Chtoby svecha ne pogasla: Dialog*. Leningrad: Sovetskii Pisatel'.

Gumilev, L. N., and S. I. Rudenko. 1966. "Arkheologicheskie issledovaniia P. K. Kozlova v aspekte istoricheskoi geografii." *Izvestiia Vsesoiuz. Geogr. O-va* 98, no. 3: 240–46.

"Gumilev Monument Opened on St. Petersburg Street." 2005. *Radio Free Europe/ Radio Liberty* (25 August), http://www.rferl.org/content/article/1345169.html, accessed 3/6/2014.

Gumilev, N. S. 1909. "Kapitany." *Apollon* 1: 137–41.

———. 1921. "Poema nachala." In *Drakon: Almanakh stikhov*. Petrograd: "Izdanie Tsekha Poetov."

Gumileva, N. V. 1993. "Passionarii ne obiaztel'no byvaiut vozhdam (Interv'iu s N. V. Gumilevoi)." *Moskovskii Zhurnal* 12: 2–10.

———. 1994. "Dokumenty." In Gumilev, *Etnogenez i biosfera Zemli*, 615–31, Moscow: Tanais.

———. 2003a. "15 Iiunia." In Voronovich and Kozyreva, *Vspominaia L. N. Gumileva*, 13–21.

———. 2003b. "Vospominaniia." In Goncharova, *Lev Gumilev: Sud'ba i idei*, 457–85, http://gumilevica.kulichki.net/fund/fund32.htm, accessed 10/5/2014.

"Gumilev: Poet, politik, passionarii." 2012. *Den' TV* (1 October), http://www.dentv.ru/ content/view/gumilyov-poet-politik-passionarij/, accessed 2/10/2014.

Günther, Hans. 1993. *Der sozialistische Übermensch: M. Gorkij und der sowjetische Heldenmythos*. Stuttgart: Metzler.

Gurvich, I. S., ed. 1980. *Etnogenez narodov Severa*. Moscow.

Gustafson, Thane. 1981. *Reform in Soviet Politics: Lessons of Recent Policies on Land and Water*. New York: Cambridge University Press.

Guts, A. K. 1999. *Podlinnaia istoriia Rossii*. Omsk: OmGU.

———. 2000. *Mnogovariantnaia istoriia Rossii*. Moscow: AST.

Guts, A. K., V. V. Korobitsyn, A. A. Laptev, L. A. Pautova, and Iu.V. Frolova. 2000. *Sotsial'nye sistemy: Formalizatsiia i komp'iuternoe modelirovanie*. Omsk: Omsk. Gos. Un-ta.

Guts, A. K., D. A. Lanin, and S. V. Nikitin. 1998. "Uchebnyi paket programm ETNOS dlia modelirovaniia evoliutsii etnicheskikh sistem." *Matematicheskie struktury i modelirovanie* 2: 128–31.

Hagemeister, Michael. 1989. *Nikolaj Fedorov: Studien zu Leben, Werk und Wirkung*. Munich: Otto Sagner.

———. 1997. "Russian Cosmism in the 1920s and Today." In *The Occult in Russian and Soviet Culture*, edited by Bernice Glatzer Rosenthal, 185–202. Ithaca, NY: Cornell University Press.

———. 2003. "Die Eroberung des Raums und die Beherrschung der Zeit: Utopische, apokalyptische und magisch-okkulte Elemente in den Zukunftsentwürfen der Sowjetzeit." In *Die Musen der Macht*, edited by Jurij Murasov and Georg Witte, 257–84. Munich: Fink.

Hahn, Gordon M. 2009. "Buryatskii, Istishkhad, and the Riyadus-Salikhin Suicide Martyrs' Battalion." *Islam, Islamism, and Politcs in Eurasia Report*. no. 5, http://www.miis.edu/academics/faculty/ghahn/report, accessed 19/2/2014.

Halbach, Uwe. 2012. "Vladimir Putin's Eurasian Union." *SWP Comments* 1: http://www.swp-berlin.org/fileadmin/contents/products/comments/2012C01_hlb.pdf; accessed 9/6/2015.

Hale, Henry E. 2009. "Cause without a Rebel: Kazakhstan's Unionist Nationalism in the USSR and CIS." *Nationalities Papers* 37, no. 1: 1–32.

Halperin, Charles J. 1982a. "George Vernadsky, Eurasianism, the Mongols and Russia." *Slavic Review* 41, no. 1: 477–93.

———. 1982b. "Soviet Historiography on Russia and the Mongols." *Russian Review* 41, no. 3: 306–22.

———. 1983. "Russia in the Mongol Empire in Comparative Perspective." *Harvard Jounal of Asiatic Studies* 43, no. 1: 239–61.

Hammer, Darrell P. 1988. "*Glasnost'* and the 'Russian Idea.'" *Russian Nationalism Today. Radio Liberty Research Bulletin, Special Edition* (19 December): 11–25.

Hauner, Milan. 1992. *What Is Asia to Us?: Russia's Asian Heartland Yesterday and Today*. London: Routledge.

Heikkinen, Kaija. 2000. "Ethnicity and Nationalism in Contemporary Russian Ethnography." In *The Fall of an Empire, the Birth of a Nation: National Identities in Russia*, edited by Chris J. Chulos and Timo Piirainen, 98–115. Aldershot: Ashgate.

Herb, Guntram. 1997. *Under the Map of Germany: Nationalism and Propaganda, 1918–1945*. London: Routledge.

Higgins, Andrew. 1993. "Russian Crisis: Fears of Fascism Grow as 'Red-Brown' Allies Emerge." *The Independent* (4 October), http://www.independent.co.uk/news/world/europe/russian-crisis-fears-of-fascism-grow-as-redbrown-allies-emerge-1508578.html, accessed 15/1/2014.

Hirsch, Francine. 2000. "Towards an Empire of Nations: Border-Making and the Formation of Soviet National Identities." *Russian Review* 59: 201–26.

———. 2002. "Race without the Practice of Racial Politics." *Slavic Review* 61, no. 1: 30–43.

——. 2004. *Empire of Nations: Ethnographic Knowledge and the Making of the Soviet Union.* Ithaca, NY: Cornell University Press.

Hodgson, Katharine. 1998. "The Poetry of Rudyard Kipling in Soviet Russia." *Modern Language Review* 93, no. 4: 1058–71.

Hodnett, Grey. 1967. "What's in a Nation?" *Problems of Communism* 16, no. 5: 2–15.

Hoffman, Stefani. 1979. "Scythian Theory and Literature 1917–1924." In *Art, Society, Revolution: Russia 1917–1921,* edited by Nils Åke Nilsson, 138–64. Stockholm: Almqvist & Wiksell International.

Hohler, Susanne. 2013. "Russian Fascism in Exile: A Historical and Phenomenological Perspective on Transnational Fascism." *Fascism. Journal of Comparative Fascist Studies* 2: 121–40.

Höllwerth, Alexander. 2007. *Das sakrale Eurasische Imperium des Aleksandr Dugin: Eine Diskursanalyse zum postsowjetischen russischen Rechtsextremismus.* Stuttgart: ibidem-Verlag.

Holm, Kerstin. 1994. "Genetiker der Geschichte: Russische Parawissenschaft, Der Ethnologe Lew Gumiljow." *Frankfurter Allgemeine Zeitung* (28 December): 0N5.

Hooson, David. 1962. "Methodological Clashes in Moscow." *Annals of the Association of American Geographers* 52: 469–75.

Hornborg, Alf, John McNeill, and Juan Martínez Alier. 2007. *Rethinking Environmental History: World-System History and Global Environmental Change.* Lanham MD: Altamira, 2007.

Horvath, Robert. 2005. *The Legacy of Soviet Dissent: Dissidents, Democratisation and Radical Nationalism in Russia.* Abingdon: RoutledgeCurzon.

Hosking, Geoffrey. 2006. *Rulers and Victims: The Russians in the Soviet Union.* Cambridge, MA: Harvard University Press.

Hughes, H. Stuart. 1992. *Oswald Spengler.* New Brunswick, NJ: Transaction.

Humphrey, Caroline. 2002. "'Eurasia,' Ideology, and the Political Imagination in Provincial Russia." In *Postsocialism: Ideals, Ideologies, and Practices in Eurasia,* edited by C. M. Hann, 258–76. London: Routledge.

Huntington, Samuel P. 1993. "The Clash of Civiliations?" *Foreign Affairs* 72: 21–49.

——. 1996. *The Clash of Civilizations and the Remaking of World Order.* London: Simon and Schuster.

Husband, William B. 2006. "'Correcting Nature's Mistakes: The Environment and Soviet Children's Literature, 1928–1941." *Environmental History* 11: 300–318.

Iagodinskii, V. N. 1987. *Aleksandr Leonidovich Chizhevskii.* Moscow: Nauka.

Iamshchikov, S. V. 2006. "On ostavil nam nazhdedu." *Zavtra* 8, no. 640 (22 February), http://www.zavtra.ru/cgi/veil/data/zavtra/06/640/71.html, accessed 31/7/2011.

Iamskov, A. N. 2006. "'Novye klassiki': L. N. Gumilev i S. Khantington v obrazovatel'nykh programmakh." In *Etnologiia obshchestvu: Prikladnye issledovaniia v etnologii,* edited by S. V. Cheshko, 176–99. Moscow: Orgservis-2000.

——. 2012. "Idei L. N. Gumileva o vzaimootnosheniiakh etnosov i landshaftov i razvitie poniatiino-terminologicheskogo apparata otechestvennoi etnoekologii." In *Nauchnoe nasledie L. N. Gumileva: Istoki, evoliutsiia, problemy, vospriiatiia,* 16–20. St. Petersburg: Iz-vo SPb Un-ta.

Ianov, Aleksandr. 1992. "Uchenie L'va Gumileva." *Svobodnaia Mysl'* 17: 104–16.

——. 1995a. "Personal'naia voina Professora Shafarevicha." In Ivanov, *Posle El'tsyna,* 191–200.

——. 1995b. *Posle El'tsyna: "Veimarskaia Rossiia."* Moscow: Kruk.

Ianshina, F. T. 1996. *Evoliutsiia vzgliadov V. I.Vernadskogo na biosferu i razvitie ucheniia o noosfere.* Moscow: Nauka.

Iarilin, A. A. n.d. "Vecherami u Timofeeva-Resovskogo." http://wwwinfo.jinr.ru/drrr/Timofeeff/auto/yarilin.html, accessed 10/5/2014.

Ignatieff, Michael. 1998. *Isaiah Berlin*. London: Chatto & Windus.

Ignatova, E. A. 2008. "N. A. Kozyrev i L. N. Gumilev." In *Vremia i zvezdy: K 100-letiiu N. A. Kozyreva*, 777–78. St. Petersburg: Nestor-Istoriia.

Iliushenko, V., ed. 1996. *Nuzhen li Gitler Rossii?* Moscow: Nezavisimoe Iz-vo PIK.

Ilyichev, L. F. 1964. "I. F. Ilyichev's Remarks about a Unified Geography." *Soviet Geography* 5, no. 4: 32–34.

Innokent'ev, A. I. 1999. "Gumilevskoe nasledie kak odin iz sposobov vospitaniia tolerantnosti—put' k evraziiskomu edinstvu." In Borisov, *Materialy Gumilevskikh chtenii 1995–96 gg.*, 144–47.

Isaacs, Rico. 2010. "'Papa'—Nursultan Nazarbayev and the Discourse of Charismatic Leadership and Nation-Building in Post-Soviet Kazakhstan." *Studies in Ethnicities and Nationalism* 10. no. 3: 435–52.

Iskakov, B. I., A. B. Iskakov, and A. A. Gavrilov. 2007. "Ethnopassionarnost' i upravliaemye tsepnye reaktsii v reshenii demograficheskikh i sotsial'no-ekonomicheskikh problem." Paper presented at the conference *Passionarnaia energiia i etnos v razvitoi tsivilizatsii*, Moscow, 2007.

Iskhakov, D. M. 1993. *Tatary (populiarnyi ocherk etnicheskoi istorii i demografii)*. Naberezhnye Chelny: KAMAZ.

——. 1995. "Tatarstanskii model': Za i protiv." *Panorama-Forum* 1: 46–58.

——. 2002. "Kritika novoi evraziiskoi ideologii v sovremennom Tatarstane." In *Evraziistvo: Problemy osmysleniia*, 24–29. Ufa: Vostochnyi Universitet.

Iskhakov, Salavat. 1999. "Istoriia narodov Povolzh'ia i Urala: Problemy i perspektivy 'natsionalizatsii.'" In *Natsional'nye istorii v sovetskom i postsovetskikh gosudarstvakh*, edited by Karl Aimermakher and Gennadii Bordiugov, 275–98. Moscow: AIRO-XX.

Its, R. F. 1989. "Neskol'ko slov o knige L. N. Gumileva *Etnogenez i biosfera Zemli*." In Gumilev, *Etnogenez i biosfera Zemli*, 3–13.

Iudel'son, A. V. 2001. "Metodologicheskii poisk sovetskikh istorikov v 1960-e gg.: K voprosu ob 'ottaiavshem' vo vremia istoriograficheskoi 'ottepeli.'" In *Obrazy istoriografii: Sbornik statei*, edited by A. P. Logunov, 147–72. Moscow: RGGU.

Iusova, N. N. 2008. "Pervoe akademicheskoe soveshchanie po voprosam etnogeneza (konets 1930-kh gg.)." In *Slavianskie forumy i problemy slavianovedeniia: Sbornik statei*, edited by M. Iu. Dostal', 40–56. Moscow: Iz-vo SGU.

Ivakhiv, Adrian. 2005. "Nature and Ethnicity in East European Paganism: An Environmental Ethic of the Religious Right." *The Pomegranate* 7, no. 2: 194–225.

Ivanov, Anatolii. 1992. "Passionarnaia polemika." *Russkii Vestnik* 15 (8–15 April): 11.

Ivanov, K. P. 1985. "Vzgliady na etnografiiu ili est' li v sovetskoi nauke dva ucheniia ob etnose." *Izvestiia Vsesoiuznogo Geograficheskogo Obshchestva* 117, no. 3: 232–38.

——. 1998. *Problemy Etnicheskaia Geografiia*. St. Petersburg: SPbGU.

Ivanov, K. P., Iu. V. Gromova, and S. A. Khrushchev. 1999. "Oskol'ki ukhodiashchikh tsivilizatsii: Malye narody Severa Rossii na grani ischeznoveniia." In Borisov, *Materialy Gumilevskikh chtenii 1995–96 gg.*, 51–88.

Ivanov, K. P., and S. A. Khrushchev. 1998. "Znachenie teorii L. N. Gumileva dlia izucheniia malochislennykh narodov severa Rossii." In Ganzha and Shishkin, *Uchenie L. N. Gumileva*.

Ivanov, P. 1951. "Ob odnoi oshibochnoi kontseptsii." *Pravda* (25 December).

Ivanov, S. A. 2001. "Vzaimootnosheniia Rusi i Stepi v kontseptsiiakh evraziitsev i L'va Gumileva." *Slaviane i ikh sosedi: Slaviane i kochevoi mir* 10: 213–18.

Ivanov, V. P. 2005. *Etnicheskaia geografiia chuvashskogo naroda: Istoricheskaia dinamika chislennosti i regional'nye osobennosti rasseleniia*. Cheboksary: Chuv. kn. iz-vo.

Ivanov, Vladimir. 2007. *Alexander Dugin und die rechtsextremen Netzwerke*. Stuttgart: ibidem-Verlag.

Ivanov-Omskii, I. I. 1950. *Istoricheskii materializm o roli geograficheskoi sredy v razvitii obshchestva*. Moscow: Gosudarstvennoe Iz-vo Politicheskoi Literatury.

Iz-pod glyb. 1974. Paris: YMCA.

Jammer, M. 1967. "Energy." In *Encyclopedia of Philosophy*, 2nd ed., 2: 511–17. New York: Macmillan.

Jones, Nathan Paul. 2010. "'Assembling' a Civic Nation in Kazakhstan: The Nation-Building Role of the Assembly of the Peoples of Kazakhstan." *Caucasian Review of International Affairs* 4, no. 2: 159–68.

Joravsky, David. 1970. *The Lysenko Affair*. Chicago: University of Chicago Press.

———. 1977. "The Mechanical Spirit: The Stalinist Marriage of Pavlov to Marx." *Theory and Society* 4, no. 4: 457–77.

Jordan, Bella Bychkova. 2002. "A Geographical Perspective on Ethnogenesis: The Case of the Sakha Republic (Yakutia)." PhD diss., Austin: University of Texas Press.

Josephson, Paul R. 1995. "'Projects of the Century' in Soviet History: Large-Scale Technologies from Lenin to Gorbachev." *Technology and Culture* 36, no. 3: 519–59.

Juderías, Julián. 1914. *La leyenda negra y la verdad histórica*. Madrid: Tip. de la Rev. de Arch.

Kaganovsky, Lilya. 2004. "How the Soviet Man Was (Un)Made." *Slavic Review* 63, no. 3: 577–96.

Kalesnik, S. V. 1966. "A Few More Words about the Geographical Environment." *Soviet Geography: Review and Translation* 7, no. 10: 46–52.

———. 1971a. "Geograficheskaia sreda." In *Bol'shaia Sovetskaia Entsiklopediia*, 3rd ed., 6: 254–55. Moscow: Sovetskaia Entsiklopediia.

———. 1971b. "On the Significance of Lenin's Ideas for Soviet Geography." *Soviet Geography: Review and Translation* 12, no. 4: 196–205.

———. 2012 [1964]. "O rukopisi L. N. Gumileva *Drevnie Tiurki*." In Burlaka, *Lev Gumilev: Pro et Contra*, 324–26.

Kaltakhchian, S. T. 1976. "Sovetskii narod." In *Bol'shaia Sovetskaia Entsiklopediia*, 3rd ed., vol. 24. Moscow: Sovetskaia Entsliklopediia.

Kanishchev, Pavel. n.d. "Tishkov, za vami zaedut!" http://rossia3.ru/mer/ti_shock, accessed 13/1/2014.

Karel'skaia, L. P. 2005. *L. N. Gumilev*. Moscow: MarT.

Kargalov, V. V. 1981. "*Preemstvennost'*" (Review of F. Nesterov, *Sviaz' Vremen*). *Nash Sovremennik* 1: 187–91.

———. 1985. "Sviatolsav'." In *Polkovodtsy Drevnei Rusi*, edited by V. V. Kargalov and A. N. Sakharov. Moscow: Molodaia Gvardiia.

Karimullin, A. G. 1990. *Lev Nikolaevich Gumilev: Bibliograficheskii ukazatel'*. Kazan: Resp. Nauch. B-ka Tat. SSR. http://gumilevica.kulichki.net/matter/Article15.htm, accessed 30/5/2014.

Karklins, Rasma. 2000. "Ethno-pluralism: Panacea for East Central Europe?" *Nationalities Papers* 28, no. 2: 219–41.

Karpenko, M. P. 2011. "O vzaimodeistvii idei V. I. Vernadskogo i L. N. Gumileva pri izuchenii evoliutsii sotsiosfery." *Vestnik Rossiiskoi Akademii Estestvennykh Nauk* 2: 16–19.

Kashin, Oleg. 2008. "Anatolii Ivanovich: Chto rasskazal poet Osenev." *Russkaia Zhizn'* (24 September), http://www.rulife.ru/mode/article/939/, accessed 17/4/2014.

Kasimovskii, E. 1951. *Velikie stroiki kommunizma.* Moscow: Gosizdatpolitlit.

Kedrov, B. M., I. R. Grigulevich, and I. A. Kryvelev. 1982. "Po povodu stat'i Iu. M. Borodaia 'Etnicheskie kontakty i okruzhaiushchaia sreda.'" *Priroda* 3: 88–91, http://scepsis.net/library/id_1110.html, accessed 30/5/2014.

Keen, Benjamin. 1969. "The Black Legend Revisited: Assumptions and Realities." *Hispanic American Historical Review* 49, no. 4: 703–19.

Kefeli, I. F. n.d. "Istoriia razvitiia geopoliticheskikh vozzrenii v otechestvennoi nauke i uchenie L. N. Gumileva." http://levgumilev.spbu.ru/node/156, accessed 11/7/2014.

Kerr, David. 1995. "The New Eurasianism: The Rise of Geopolitics in Russia's Foreign Policy." *Europe-Asia Studies* 47, no. 6: 977–88.

Khabibullin, Musagit. 2009. "Zaputnik." *Agramak* 1: 24–39.

Khakim, Rafael'. 1998. "Russia and Tatarstan: At the Crossroads of History." *Anthropology and Archaeology of Eurasia* 37, no. 1: 30–71.

——. 2002. "Kto ty, tatarin?" *Vostochnyi Ekspress* nos. 17–18 (26 April), http://kitap.net.ru/hakim/1.php, accessed 3/6/2014.

——. n.d. "Metamorfozy dukha." *Tatarskie Novosti,* http://1997-2011.tatarstan.ru/?DNSID=b3cd09cc7e23286c19e7d764c7fd44c7&node_id=2903, accessed 3/6/2014.

Khakimov, Rafael. 1993. *Sumerki imperii: K voprosu o natsii i gosudarstve.* Kazan: Tatarskoe kn. iz-vo.

——. 2002. "Ia—samyi tatarstanskii natsionalist!" *Komsomol'skaia Pravda* (21 March), http://1997-2011.tatarstan.ru/?DNSID=14f6db3c59a3612d20b26c0c6c4bee5d&node_id=416, accessed 3/6/2014.

——. 2005. "Dva istoka rossiiskoi gosudarstvennosti." *Rodina* 8: 45–47.

Khazanov, Anatoly M. 1997. "Ethnic Nationalism in the Russian Federation." *Daedalus* 126, no. 3: 121–42.

——. 2002. *Kochevniki i vneshnyi mir.* 3rd ed. Almaty: Daik-Press.

Khozin, G. 1979. *The Biosphere and Politics.* Moscow: Progress.

Khrushchev, N. S. 1949. "Stalinskaia druzhba narodov—zalog nepobedimosti nashei Rodiny." *Bol'shevik* 24: 80–85.

Khrushchev, S. A. 2007. "Geograficheskoe issledovanie ustoichivosti etnotsenozov korennykh narodov Severa." Avtoreferat kandidatskoi dissertatsii, St-Pet. Gos. Univ.

Khrustalev, D. G. 2004. *Rus': Ot nashestviia do 'iga' (30–40 gg. XIII veka).* St. Petersburg: Evraziia.

Khudushin, F. S. 1966. *Chelovek i priroda.* Moscow: Iz-vo politicheskoi literatury.

Kibasova, G. P. 2003. *Etnicheskoe prostranstvo.* Volgograd: Volgogradskii gos. meditsinskii uni-tet.

——. 2004. "Etnicheskoe prostranstvo Rossii: Sotsial'no-filosofskii analiz." Avtoreferat, doctoral diss., Volgogradskii Gos. Med. Universitet.

Kim, M. P. 1975. *Sovetskii narod: Novaia istoricheskaia obshchnost' liudei.* Moscow: Nauka.

Kipp, Jacob W. 2002. "Aleksandr Dugin and the Ideology of National Revival: Geopolitics, Eurasianism and the Conservative Revolution." *European Security* 11, no. 3: 91–125.

Klein, Lev. 1992. "Gor'kie mysli 'priveredlivogo retsenzenta' ob uchenii L. N. Gumileva." *Neva* 4: 228–46.

Klenskaia, I. V. 1985. *V solnechnom ritme: A. Chizhevskii.* Moscow: Znanie.

Klier, John. 1995. "Russian Jewry as the 'Little Nation' of the Russian Revolution." In *Jews and Jewish Life in Russia and the Soviet Union,* edited by Yaacov Ro'i, 146–56. Ilford, UK: Frank Cass.

Kline, George L. 1968. *Religious and Anti-Religious Thought in Russia.* Chicago: University of Chicago Press.

Klubkov, Anton. 2013. "Vladimir Medinskii o evraziistve." http://a-klubkov.livejournal.com/7220.html, accessed 14/7/2014.

Kneen, Peter. 1998. "Physics, Genetics and the Zhdanovshchina." *Europe-Asia Studies* 50, no. 7: 1183–1202.

Kochanek, Hildegard. 1998. "Die Ethnienlehre Lev N. Gumilevs: Zu den Anfängen neu-rechter Ideologie-Entwicklung im spätkommunistischen Russland." *Osteuropa* 48, nos. 11–12: 1184–97.

———. 1999. *Die russisch-nationale Rechte von 1968 bis zum Ende der Sowjetunion: Eine Diskursanalyse.* Stuttgart: Franz Steiner.

Koestler, Arthur. 1976. *The Thirteenth Tribe: Khazar Empire and Its Heritage.* London: Hutchinson.

Kohl, Philip L. 1998. "Nationalism and Archeology: On the Constructions of Nations and the Reconstructions of the Remote Past." *Annual Review of Archeology* 27: 233–46.

Kohl, Philip, and Clare Fawcett, eds. 1995. *Nationalism, Politics, and the Practice of Archeology.* Cambridge: Cambridge University Press.

Kołakowski, Leszek. 1978. *Main Currents of Marxism.* 3 vols. Oxford: Oxford University Press.

Kolstø, Pål. 1998. "Anticipating Demographic Superiority: Kazakh Thinking on Integration and Nation Building." *Europe-Asia Studies* 50, no. 1: 51–69.

———. 1999. "Territorialising Diasporas: The Case of the Russians in the Former Soviet Republics." *Millennium* 28, no. 3: 607–31.

Komarov, Boris. 1978. *Unichtozhenie prirody.* Frankfurt: Posev.

Komarov, V. D. 1977. *Nauchno-tekhnicheskaia revoliutsiia i sotsial'naia ekologiia.* Leningrad: Iz-vo LGU.

———. n.d. "Vklad L. N. Gumileva v sotsial'nuiu ekologiiu." http://levgumilev.spbu.ru/node/181, accessed 2/3/2014.

Kon'shina, L. F. 1993. "Idei V. I. Vernadskogo, K. E. Tsiolkovskogo, A. L. Chizhevskogo o kosmichnosti iavlenii zhizni i cheloveka." In *Uchenie V. I. Vernadskogo i sovremennaia ekologicheskaia situatsiia: Tezisy vystuplenii na mezhdunarodnoi nauchnoi konferentsii,* 33–35. Akmola-Borovoe: AIPP "Zhanna Arka."

Konstantinov, F. V. 1949. *Razvitie istoricheskogo materializma Leninym i Stalinym.* Moscow: Pravda. http://www.biografia.ru/arhiv/razvmat01.html, accessed 28/2/2014.

———. 1950. *Istoricheskii materializm.* Moscow: Gos. iz-vo pol. lit.

———. 1964. "Interaction between Nature and Society and Modern Geography." *Soviet Geography: Review and Translation* 5, no. 10: 61–73.

Konstantinova, S. S. 2005a. *Etnologiia: Konspekt lektsii.* Rostov-na-Donu: Feniks.

———. 2005b. *Etnologiia: Uchebnoe posobie.* Moscow: RIOR.

Koreniako, Vladimir. 2000. "Etnonatsionalizm, kvaziistoriografiia i akademicheskaia nauka." In *Real'nost etnicheskikh mifov,* edited by Marta Brill Olkott and Aleksei Malashenko, 34–52. Moscow: Gendal'f.

———. 2005. "Mezhdunarodnaia konferentsiia "Mezhdu etnosom i Evrazii." *Vestnik Evrazii* 3, no. 29: 206–13.

Koriavtsev, P. M. 1994. *Filosofiia antisistem: Opyt prilozheniia teorii etnogeneza,* http://gumilevica.kulichki.net/debate/Article05.htm, accessed 11/7/2014.

Korobitsyn, V. V. 2000. "Model' territorial'nogo raspredeleniia passionarnoi energii etnosa." *Matematicheskie struktury i modelirovanie* 5: 44–53.

Korobitsyn, V. V., and Iu. V. Frolova. 2006. "Mathematicheskoe modelirovanie dinamiki etnicheskikh sistem." *Sotsial'naia Politika i Sotsiologii* 3: 205–21.

Korobitsin, Victor V., and Julia V. Frolova. 2002. "Simulation of Evolution Dynamics of Social System: Ethnic Solidarity Level." http://www.systemdynamics.org/conferences/2002/proceed/papers/Korobit1.pdf, accessed 18/2/2014.

Korogodin, V. I., G. G. Polikarpov, and V. V. Velkov. 2000. "The Blazing Life of N. V. Timofeev-Resovskii." *Journal of Bioscience* 25, no. 2: 125–31.

Korotaev, V. I. 1998. *Russkii sever v kontse XIX-pervoi treti XX veka: Problemy modernizatsii i sotsial'noi ekologi*. Arkhangel'sk: IPGU.

Kosarenko, S. 1993. "Antisistema: Rossiia v tochke bifurkatsii." *Den'* 8 (28 February–6 March), 10 (14 March–20 March): 3.

Kovach, Joseph K. 1971. "Ethology in the Soviet Union." *Behaviour* 39, nos. 2–4: 237–65.

Kovalenko, M. I. 1999. "Passionarnost' kak psikhologicheskii fenomen." In *Psikhologicheskie problemy samorealizatsii lichnosti*. St. Petersburg: Iz-vo SPb Un-ta. http://gumilevica.kulichki.net/debate/Article13.htm, accessed 25/06/2009.

Kozhinov, V. V. 1981. "'I nazovet menia vsiak sushchii v nei iazyk.'" *Nash Sovremennik* 11: 153–76.

——. 1989. "Nesostoiatel'nye ssylki." *Voprosy literatury* 9: 236–42.

——. 1991. "Poiski Budushchego." *Nash Sovremennik* 3: 127–28.

——. 1992a. "Istoriia Rusi i russkogo slova (a)." *Nash Sovremennik* 10: 173–87.

——. 1992b. "Istoriia Rusi i russkogo slova (b)." *Nash Sovremennik* 11: 161–81.

——. 1992c. "Istoriia Rusi i russkogo slova (c)." *Nash Sovremennik* 12: 167–82.

——. 2000. "O evraziiskoi kontseptsii russkogo puti." In *O russkom natsional'nom soznanii*, edited by A. Ul'ianov, 223–39. Moscow: Algoritm.

——. 2005. *Velikaia Voina Rossii*. Moscow: Iazua-Eksmo.

Kozlov, V. I. 1971. "Chto zhe takoe etnos?" *Priroda* 2: 71–74.

——. 1974. "O biologo-istoricheskoi kontseptsii etnicheskoi istorii." *Voprosy Istorii* 12: 72–85.

——. 1983. "Osnovnye problemy etnicheskoi ekologii." *Sovetskaia Etnografiia* 1: 3–16.

——. 1990. "Puti okoloetnicheskoi passionarnosti." *Sovetskaia Ethnografiia* 4: 94–110.

——. 1994. *Etnicheskaia ekologiia: Stanovlenie ditsipliny i istoriia problem*. Moscow: RAN.

——. 1996. *Istoriia tragedii velikogo naroda: Russkii vopros*. Moscow: n.p.

Kozlov, V. I., and A. N. Iamskov. 1989. "Etnicheskaia ekologiia." In *Etnologiia v SShA i Kanade*, edited by V. A. Tishkov, 86–107. Moscow: Nauka.

Kozlov, V. I., and V. V. Pokshishevskii. 1973. "Etnografiia i geografiia." *Sovetskaia Etnografiia* 1: 3–13.

Kozyrev, A. N. 2003. "Kak eto bylo: Materialy sledstevennogo dela L. N. Gumileva i N. N. Punina 1935 goda." In Voronovich and Kozyreva, *Vspominaia L. N. Gumileva*, 257–331.

Kramer, Asia. n.d. "Passionarii my ili kto, v nature?" http://berkovich-zametki.com/Nomer42/Kramer1.htm, accessed 1/23/2014.

Krasnov, Vladislav. 1991. *Russia beyond Communism: A Chronicle of National Rebirth*. Boulder: Westview.

Krivoshapkin, A. I. 1999. "K voprosu o rasselenii iakutov do prikhoda russkikh." In Borisov, *Materialy Gumilevskikh chtenii 1995–96 gg.*, 115–20.

Krivosheev, Iu. V. 2003. *Rusy i mongoly: Issledovanie po istorii severo-vostochnoi rusi XII–XIV vv.* St. Petersburg: Iz-vo St. Petersburgskogo Universiteta.

"Kruglyi stol zhurnala *Filosofiia Prava*." 2000. http://evraz-info.narod.ru/157.htm, accessed 8/2/2014.

Krushel', E. G., and G. G. Surgutanov. n.d. "Model evoliutsii etnosov i ee realizat-sii na baze geneticheskikh algoritmov." http://www.library.biophys.msu.ru/mce/20021505.htm, accessed 18/2/2014.

Krylov, A. A., and M. I. Kovalenko. 1993. "Problemy etnicheskoi psikhologii v svete teorii etnogeneza L. N. Gumileva." *Vestnik Sankt-Peterburgskogo Universiteta* Seriia 6, no. 4 (27): 73–80.

Krys'ko, V. G. 1999. *Etnopsikhologicheskii slovar'*. Moscow: MPSI. http://onlineslovari. com/etnopsihologicheskiy_slovar/page/passionarnost.274/, accessed 12/2/2014.

Kubicek, Paul. 1997. "Regionalism, Nationalism and Realpolitik in Central Asia." *Europe-Asia Studies* 49, no. 4: 637–55.

Kulataev, Saken. 2002. "Etnogenez i sovremennaia politika." *Internet-Gazeta "Zona KZ"* 0/1376 (4 September), http://www.zonakz.net/articles/641, accessed 24/2/2014.

Kuleshov, V. 1982. "Tochnost' kriteriev." *Pravda* 1 February.

Kuper, Adam. 2003. "The Return of the Native." *Current Anthropolgy* 44, no. 3: 389–402.

Kupriianov, D. V. 1995. "Lev Gumilev i bezhetskii krai." In Goncharova, *Dni L. N. Gumileva v Bezhetske*, 14–21.

Kurennoi, V. N. 1974. "Passionarnost' i landshaft." *Priroda* 8: 76–77.

Kurkchi, Aider. 1994. "L. N. Gumilev i ego vremia." In *Poiski vymyshlennogo tsarstva*, 24–78. Moscow: Tanais. http://gumilevica.tripod.com/Matter/Article041.htm, accessed 18/3/2014.

Kushner, P. I. 1951. *Etnicheskie territorii i etnicheskie granitsy*. Moscow: AN SSSR.

Kuz'min, A. G. 1975. "Tochka v kruge, iz kotoroi vyrastaet repei." *Molodaia Gvardiia* 12: 270–80.

——. 1982. "Sviashchennye kamni pamiati." *Molodaia Gvardiia* 1: 252–66.

——. 1988. "K kakomu khramu ischem my dorogu?" *Nash Sovremennik* 3: 154–64.

——. 1991. "Propeller passionarnosti. . . ." *Molodaia Gvardiia* 9: 256–76.

——. 1993a. "Khazarskie stradaniia." *Molodaia Gvardiia*, nos. 5–6: 231–52.

——. 1993b. "Otvety ili navety." *Molodaia Gvardiia*, nos. 11–12: 276–80.

Kuz'min, Mikhail. 1998. "Social Genetics and Organizational Science." In *Alexander Bogdanov and the Origins of Systems Thinking in Russia*, edited by John Biggart, Peter Dudley, and Francis King, 278–303. Aldershot, England: Ashgate.

Kuznetsov, B. I. 1971. "Proverka gipotezy Gumileva." *Priroda* 2: 74–75.

"L. N. Gumilev—A. A. Akhmatovoi: Pis'ma, ne doshedshie do adresata." 2011. *Znamia* 6: 141–51.

Lamanskii, V. I. 1916 [1892]. *Tri mira aziiskogo-evropeiskogo materika*. 2nd ed. Petrograd: Novoe Vremia.

Laqueur, Walter. 1993. *Black Hundred: The Rise of the Extreme Right in Russia*. New York: HarperCollins.

Lariuel', Marlen. 2001. "Kogda prisvaivaetsia intellektual'naia sobstvennost', ili O protivopolozhnosti L. N. Gumileva i P. N. Savitskogo." *Vestnik Evrazii* 4, no. 15: 5–19.

——. 2009. "Opyt sravnitel'nogo analiza teorii etnosa L'va Gumileva i zapadnykh novykh pravykh." *Forum Noveishei Vostochnoevropeiskoi Istorii i Kul'tury* 1: 189–200, http://www1.ku-eichstaett.de/ZIMOS/forum/docs/forumruss11/a10LaruellGumilev.pdf, accessed 11/7/2014.

Laruelle, Marlène. 2000. "Lev Nikolaevic Gumilev (1912–1992): Biologisme et eurasisme dans la penseé russe." *Revue des Études Slaves*, nos. 1–2: 163–89.

——. 2001. "Alexandre Dugin: Esquisse d'un eurasisme d'extrême-droite en Russie post-soviétique." *Revue d'études comparatives Est-Ouest* 32, no. 3: 85–103.

——. 2004. "The Two Faces of Contemporary Eurasianism: An Imperial Version of Russian Nationalism." *Nationalities Papers* 32. no. 1: 115–36.

——. 2006. "Regards sur la réception du racialisme allemand chez les panslavistes et les eurasistes russes." In *L'Allemagne des linguistes russes*, edited by Celine Trautmann-Waller, 145–56. Paris: CNRS.

——. 2008a. "The Concept of Ethnogenesis in Central Asia: Political Context and Institutional Mediators (1940–1950)." *Kritika* 9, no. 1: 169–88.

——. 2008b. *Russian Eurasianism. An Ideology of Empire.* Washington, DC: Woodrow Wilson Center Press.

——. 2012. "Conspiracy and Alternative History: A Nationalist Equation for Success." *Russian Review* 71: 565–80.

——. 2015. "Conceiving the Territory: Eurasianism as a Geographical Ideology." In Bassin, Laruelle and Glebov, *Between Europe and Asia*, 68–83.

——. n.d. "Aleksandr Dugin: A Russian Version of the European Radical Right?" *Kennan Institute Occasional Papers*, no. 272, http://www.wilsoncenter.org/sites/default/files/op272_structures_russian_discourse_Sokolovski_1999.pdf, accessed 24/2/2014.

Laruelle, Marlène, and Sébastian Peyrouse. 2004. *Les Russes du Kazakhstan: Identités nationales et nouveaux etats dans l'espace post-soviétique.* Paris: Maisonneuve et Larose.

Lattimore, Owen. 1940. *Inner Asian Frontiers of China.* New York: American Geographical Society.

Lavreonova, O. A. 2007. "Ot Zemli k kosmosu: Noosfernaia kontseptsiia V. I. Vernadskogo i kosmicheskii determinizm A. L. Chizhevskogo." *Gumanitarnaia Geografiia* 4: 100–120.

Lavrionov, Pavel. 2011. "Novyi Khazarstan." http://www.ruskolan.info/article/69/, accessed 25/2/2014.

Lavrov, S. B. 1993. "L. N. Gumilev i evraziistvo." In Gumilev, *Ritmy Evrazii*, 7–22.

——. 2000. *Lev Gumilev: Sud'ba i idei.* Moscow: Svarog i K.

——. 2001. "Uroki L'va Gumileva." *Zavtra* 31, no. 400 (31 July), http://zavtra.ru/content/view/2001-07-3172/, accessed 24/1/2014.

——. 2003. "Paradoksy L'va Gumileva." In Voronovich and Kozyreva, *Vspominaia L. N. Gumileva*, 209–16.

Le Rua Ladiuri, E. 1971. *Istoriia klimata c 1000 goda.* Leningrad: Gidrometeorologicheskoe Iz-vo.

Lenin, V. I. 1962. "Sotsialisticheskaia revoliutsiia i pravo natsii na samoopredelenie (1916)." In *Polnoe Sobranie Sochinenii*, 5th ed., 27: 252–66. Moscow: Politizdat.

Leont'ev, K. N. 2007 [1875]. *Vizantizm i slavianstvo.* Moscow: AST.

"Lev Gumilev primirit stolitsu Tatarstana s rossiiskoi imperii." 2005. *Vremia Novostei* (18 August), http://www.vremya.ru/2005/150/4/132261.html, accessed 3/6/2014.

Levit, George S. 2000. "The Biosphere and the Noosphere Theories of V. I. Vernadsky and P. Teilhard de Chardin." *International Archives on the History of Science* 50 (144): 160–76.

——. 2001. *Biogeochemistry—Biosphere—Noosphere: The Growth of the Theoretical System of Vladimir Ivanovich Vernadsky.* Berlin: Verlag für Wissenschaft und Bildung.

Liamin, V. S. 1967. "O dvukh urovniakh vzaimodeistviia prirody i obshchestva." *Vestnik Moskovskogo Universiteta: Seriia Filosofia* 22: 48–58.

——. 1978. *Priroda i obshchestvo.* Moscow: Mysl'.

Likhachev, D. S. 1980. "Russkaia kul'tura i srazhenie na Kulikovom Pole za Donom." *Zvezda* 9: 3–8.

———. 2003a. "Otzyv na knigu doktora istoricheskikh nauk L. N. Gumileva *Etnogenez i biosfera Zemli* [23 November 1987]." In Voronovich and Kozyreva, *Vspominaia L. N. Gumileva*, 341–43.

———. 2003b. "Otzyv o rukopisi d.i.n. L. N. Gumileva *Etnogenez i biosfera Zemli* [6–1– 1984]." In Voronovich and Kozyreva, *Vspominaia L. N. Gumileva*, 338–40.

Likhachev, V. N. 1996. "Evraziiskii proekt: Balans interesov gosudarstv i regionov." In *Klub "Realisty": Informatsionno-analiticheskii biulleten'. no. 16*, edited by N. N. Beliakov and V. A. Perov, 5–15. Moscow: Klub "Realisty."

Liubkin, S. G. 2006. "A. Kuz'min i L. Gumilev." *Duel'* 24, no. 472 (13 June), http://www.duel.ru/200624/?24_6_2, accessed 3/4/2014.

Liubomudrov, Mark. 1981. "Sila edinstva." *Ogonek* 4: 17.

Livers, Keith. 2010. "The Tower or the Labyrinth: Conspiracy, Occult, and Empire-Nostalgia in the Work of Viktor Pelevin and Aleksandr Prokhanov." *Russian Review* 69, 3: 477–503.

Lobashev, M. E. 1947. "Fiziologicheskaia (paranekroticheskaia) gipoteza mutatsion-nogo protsessa." *Vestnik Leningradskogo Universiteta* 8: 10–29.

———. 1961. "Signal'naia nasledstvennost'." In *Issledovaniia po genetike*, edited by M. E. Lobashev, 1: 7–11. Leningrad: Iz-vo LGU.

———. 1967. *Genetika*. Leningrad: Leningrad. Gos. Un-t.

Lobjakas, Ahto. 2009. "Apparently, Russia Needs Just One 'National Component.'" *Radio Free Europe/Radio Liberty* (April 23), http://www.rferl.org/content/Apparently_Russia_Needs_Just_One_National_Component/1614655.html, accessed 3/6/2014.

Loseff, Lev. 1994. "The Not-So-Gay Science: The Scientific and the Poetic in L. N. Gumilev's Neo-Eurasianism." Unpublished paper.

Luginov, N. A. 1997. *Po veleniiu Chingis Khana*. Moscow: Sovremennyi Pisatel'.

———. 2008. "Sozidaiushchii real'nost'." *Den' Literatury* 11, no. 147 (22 November), http://mreadz.net/new/index.php?id=122486&pages=13, accessed 4/6/2014.

Luk'ianov, A. I. 2003. "Passionarii otechestvennoi nauki i kul'tury." In Voronovich and Kozyreva, *Vspominaia L. N. Gumileva*, 62–72.

Lur'e, Ia. S. 1990. "K istorii odnoi diskussii." *Istoriia SSSR* 4: 128–33.

———. 1997. *Rossiia drevniaia i Rossiia novaia*. St. Petersburg: Dmitrii Bulanin.

Lysenko, N. N. 1992. "Nasha tsel'—sozdanie velikoi imperii." *Nash Sovremennik* 9: 122–30.

———. 1993. "Otkrovennyi razgovor o 'druziakh.'" *Nash Sovremennik* 7: 150–58.

———. 2003. "Stanet li Rossiia novoi Khazariei?: Razmyshleniia russkogo traditsion-alista." *Vse ob Islame* 11 (March), http://malikit.livejournal.com/394355.html, accessed 11/7/2014.

M. E. Lobashev i problemy sovremennoi genetiki. 1978. Leningrad: Lenin. Gos. Universitet.

Makarikhina, O. A. 2009. "Istoriia terminov v istorii gumanitarnykh nauk (na primere termina 'etnos')." *Vestnik Nizhegorodskogo Universiteta* 1: 46–51.

Makhnach, V. L. 1995. "Imperii v mirovoi istorii." In *Inoe: Khrestomatiia novogo rossi-iskogo samosoznaniia*, edited by S. B. Chernyshev, 109–26. Moscow: Argus.

———. 2001. "Chto takoe Rossiia." In *Rossiia—posledniaia krepost'*. Moscow: Slovo. http://www.hrono.info/statii/2001/mahnach02.html, accessed 17/4/2014.

———. 2008. "Avtobiograficheskii ocherk." http://www.pravaya.ru/ludi/2487/15900, accessed 25/6/2014.

———. n.d. "Khimera i antisistema." http://mahnach.ru/articles/ikvp/3.html, accessed 16/3/2014.

Maklakov, Kirill. 1996. "Teoriia etnogeneza s tochki zreniia biologa." *Ural* 10: 164–78.

Malakhov, V. 2006. "Sovremennyi russkii natsional'izm." http://iph.ras.ru/
page50523858.htm, accessed 2/4/2014.

Malashenko, Aleksei. 1996. "Russkii natsionalizm i islam." *Vestnik Evrazii* 2, no. 3: 98–112.

Malashenko, Igor'. 1991. "Na polputi k Evrope: Sostoitsia li evraziiskoe soob-
shchestvo?" *Nezavisimaia Gazeta*, 21 November, 5.

Malikov, V. 1996. "Skazaniia o Khazarakh." In *Mify drevnei Volgi*, edited by V. I. Vardu-
gin, 118–44. Saratov: Nadezhda.

Malinovskii, A. A. 1970. "Obshchee voprosy stroeniia sistemy i ikh znacheniia dlia
biologii." In *Problemy metodologii sistemnogo issledovaniia*, edited by I. V. Blau-
berg, 145–50. Moscow.

Maltby, William S. 1971. *The Black Legend in England: the Development of Anti-Spanish
Sentiment, 1558–1660*. Durham: Duke University Press.

Mamaladze, Irma. 1992. "Beznadezhno, esli. . . ." *Literaturnaia Gazeta* 42, no. 5419 (14
October): 7.

Mamleev, Maksat. n.d. "Otkroi svoiu istoriiu. . . .," http://kitap.net.ru/mamleev/1.php,
accessed 3/6/2014.

Mamonov, V. F. 1995. "Zapad, Vostok, Evraziia (Tvorchestvo L. N. Gumileva i sovremennost')." *Urzhumka (Chelyabinsk)* 1: 49–63.

"Manifest Tsentra L'va Gumileva." 2011. http://www.gumilev-center.ru/manifest-
centra-lva-gumiljova-2/, accessed 11/10/2014.

Mansurova, Diliara. 2005. "Tatarstan i Sankt-Peterburg: mezhregional'noe sotrudnichestvo." *Tatarskie Novosti* 2, no. 139, http://1997-2011.tatarstan.ru/?DNSID=
82425ade98ce0760f332cd0bbda80bbd&node_id=1185&full=1636, accessed
3/6/2014.

March, Luke. 2002. *The Communist Party in Post-Soviet Russia*. Manchester: Manchester University Press.

Markedonov, Sergey. 2012. "Putin's Eurasian Aspirations." *The National Interest*
(29 May), http://nationalinterest.org/commentary/putins-eurasian-aspira-
tions-6973, accessed 10/7/2014.

Marochkin, Sergei N. 1997. "Russkie i imperiia." In *Russkii stroi*, edited by A. N.
Savel'ev, 222–42. Moscow: Intellekt.

Martin, Terry. 1998. "The Origins of Soviet Ethnic Cleansing." *Journal of Modern History* 70, no. 4: 813–61.

——. 2000. "Modernization or Neo-Traditionalism?: Ascribed Nationality and Soviet
Primordialism." In *Russian Modernity: Politics, Practices, Knowledge*, edited by
David Hoffmann and Yanni Kotsonis, 161–82. New York: St. Martin's Press.

——. 2001a. "An Affirmative Action Empire: The Soviet Union as the Highest Form
of Imperialism." In *A State of Nations: Empire and Nation-Making in the Age
of Lenin and Stalin*, edited by Ronald Grigor Suny and Terry Martin, 67–90.
Oxford: Oxford University Press.

——. 2001b. *The Affirmative Action Empire: Nations and Nationalism in the Soviet
Union, 1923–1939*. Ithaca, NY: Cornell University Press.

Martinez-Alier, Juan. 1987. *Ecological Economics: Energy, Environment and Society*.
Oxford: Blackwell.

Martynov, I. F. 1987. "Kipling i Gumilev: Poety dvukh imperii: K voprosu o sud'be
poeticheskogo naslediia R. Kiplinga v Rossii." *Vestnik Russkogo Studencheskogo
Khristianskogo Dvizheniia* 3: 166–89.

Masanov, N., and I. Savin. 2004. "Rossiia v Kazakhskikh uchebnikakh istorii." *Mir Istorii* 1, http://history.krsu.edu.kg/index.php?option=com_content&id=211&Item
id=40&limit=9&limitstart=275, accessed 3/6/2014.

Mashbits, Ia. G., and K. V. Chistov. 1986. "Eshche raz k voprosu o dvukh kontseptsiiakh 'etnosa' (po povodu stat'i K. P. Ivanova)." *Izvestiia Vsesoiuznogo Geograficheskogo Obshchestva* 118, no. 1: 29–37.

Materialy XXIV s"ezda KPSS. 1971. Moscow: "Politizdat."

Matern, Frederick. 2007. "The Discourse of Civilization in the Works of Russia's New Eurasianists: Lev Gumilev and Alexander Panarin." MA thesis, York University, Toronto.

Matley, I. M. 1966. "The Marxist Approach to the Geographical Environment." *Annals of the Association of American Geographers* 56: 97–111.

——. 1982. "Nature and Society: The Continuing Soviet Debate." *Progress in Human Geography* 6: 367–96.

"Matvei Grubian slushaet Vladimira Vysotskogo." 2009. http://dorobok.com/vysotsky_ls/blog/matvej-grubiyan-slushaet-vyisoczkogo.html, accessed 11/3/2014.

Mavrodin, V. V. 1946. *Drevniaia Rus': Proiskhozhdenie russkogo naroda i obrazovanie kievskogo gosudarstva*. Moscow: Gospolizdat.

Mccannon, John. 1997. "Positive Heroes at the Pole: Celebrity Status, Socialist-Realist Ideals and the Soviet Myth of the Arctic, 1932–39." *Russian Review* 56, no. 3: 346–65.

Medeu-Uly, Tel'man, and Saken Kulataev. 2002. "I vse-taki nashe godusarstvo dolzhno byt' treugol'nym!" *Internet-Gazeta "Zona KZ"* 14/1490 (18 September), http://www.zonakz.net/articles/1466, accessed 3/6/2014.

Medved', A. N. 1994. "Idei V. I. Vernadskogo i nauchnoe tvorchestvo L. N. Gumileva." *Voprosy Istorii Estestvoznaniia i Tekhniki* 3: 119–21.

Medvedev, Zhores A. 1971. *The Rise and Fall of T. D. Lysenko*. Garden City, NY: Anchor.

Menzel, Birgit. 2007. "The Occult Revival in Russia Today and Its Impact on Literature." *Harriman Review* 16, no. 1: 1–14.

Merlan, Francesca. 2009. "Indigeneity: Global and Local." *Current Anthropolgy* 50, no. 3: 303–33.

Mészáros, Csaba. 2008. "The Alaas, a Symbolic Landscape in Yakutia: Tradition and Public Representation in a Siberian Community." *Tabula* 11: 1–2, http://www.neprajz.hu/tabula/szam19/reza.shtml, accessed 4/6/2014.

Mialo, Kseniia. 1992. "Est' li v Evrazii mesto dlia russkikh?" *Literaturnaia Rossiia* 32 (7 August): 4–5.

Michurin, V. A. 1992. "O podkhodakh k izucheniiu passionarnosti." *Izvestiia Russkogo Geograficheskogo Obshchestva* 124, no. 6: 525–30.

——. 2004. "Slovar' poniatii i terminov teorii etnogeneza L. N. Gumileva." In *Etnosfera. Istoriia liudei i istoriia prirody*, 517–72. Moscow: AST.

Mikhalkov, Nikita. 1991. "Most mezhdu Evropoi i Aziei." *Pravda*, 7 November, 2.

——. 1993. "'O dukhovnosti ne govoriat—dukhovno zhivut.'" *Evraziia* 2: 68–72.

Mingazov, R. Kh. 2007. "Vremena Shaimieva." *Zvezda Povolzh'ia* 17 (4–10 May), http://tatpolit.ru/category/zvezda/2007-05-09/295, accessed 3/6/2014.

Mirovich, I. 1991. "Lev Gumilev i drugie." *Strana i mir* 2, no. 62: 155–58.

Mirzoian, E. N. 1998. "Teoriia etnogeneza i noosfery." In Ganzha and Shishkin, *Uchenie L. N. Gumileva*, 23–25.

Mitrokhin, Nikolai. 2001. "'Russkaia partiia': Fragmenty issledovaniia." *NLO* 48, http://magazines.russ.ru/nlo/2001/48/mitr.html, accessed 2/4/2014.

——. 2003. *Russkaia partiia*. Moscow: NLO.

Mogilianskii, N. M. 1908. "Etnografiia i ee zadachi (po povodu odnoi knigi)." *Ezhegodnik Russkogo Antropologicheskogo Obshchestva* 3: 1–14.

——. 1916. "Predmet i zadachi etnografii." *Zhivaia Starina* 25, no. 1: 1–22.

Montefiore, Serge Sebag. 2003. *Stalin: The Court of the Red Tsar*. London: Weidenfeld and Nicholson.

Morgan, David O. 1989. "Review of L. N.Gumilev, *Searches for an Imaginary Kingdom*." *Journal of the Royal Asiatic Society* 1: 161–62.

Morokhin, N. V. 1997. *Fol'klor v traditsionnoi regional'noi ekologicheskoi kul'ture Nizhegorodskogo Povolzh'ia.* Kiev: Kievskii ekologo-kul'turnyi tsentr.

Morozova, Natalia. 2009. "Geopolitics, Eurasianism and Russian Foreign Policy Under Putin." *Geopolitics* 14, no. 4: 667–86.

Mukhametshin, Rafik. 2004. "Post-Soviet Tatarstan: Democratic Strains in the Ideological Evolution of the Tatar National Movement." In *Democracy and Pluralism in Muslim Eurasia*, edited by Yaacov Ro'i, 287–305. London: Frank Cass.

Mukharyamov, Nayil' M. 2004. "Ethnicity and the Study of International Relations in the Post-Soviet Russia." *Communist and Post-Communist Studies* 37, no. 1: 97–109.

Mulladzhanov, Narkas. 2007. "Pochemu v Kazani net pamiatnika Chingiskhanu?" *Zvezda Povolzh'ia* 15 (19–25 April), http://tatpolit.ru/category/zvezda/ 2007-05-01/267, accessed 3/6/2014.

Mutschler, Helene. 2011. "Julian V. Bromlejs 'Theorie des Ethnos' und die sowjetische Ethnographie 1966–1989: Traditionslinien und Transformationen, Grundbegriffe und politische Implikationen eines sowjetischen Ethnizitätskonzepts." PhD thesis, University of Bonn, Germany.

"Mutter-Sohn-Konflikt in Künstlerinnen- und Historienoper: Bruno Mantovanis 'Akhmatova' an der Opéra Bastille Paris." 2011. *neue musikzeitung*, http://www. nmz.de/online/mutter-sohn-konflikt-in-kuenstlerinnen-und-historienoper-bruno-mantovanis-akhmatova-an-der-op, accessed 4/8/2014.

Myers, Greg. 1985. "Nineteenth-Century Popularizations of Thermodynamics and the Rhetoric of Social Prophecy." *Victorian Studies* 29, no. 1: 35–66.

Naarden, Bruno. 1996. "'I Am a Genius, but No More Than That': Lev Gumilev (1912–1992), Ethnogenesis, the Russian Past, and World History." *Jahrbücher für Geschichte Osteuropas* 44: 54–82.

Nartov, Nikolai Aleksandrovich. 2003. *Geopolitika*. 2nd ed. Moscow: Edinstvo.

Naryshkin, S. E. 2012. "Evraziiskaia integratsiia—istoricheskaia, ekonomicheskaia i parlamentskaia izmereniia." http://yeurasia.org/2012/10/02/сергей-нарышкин-евразийская-интегра/, accessed 10/7/2014.

"National Problems in the State Policy of Kazakhstan." 1998. *International Eurasian Institute for Economic and Political Research*, http://www.iicas.org/ publeng/?id=989, accessed 3/3/2008.

Nazarbaev, N. A. 1995. "Ideia, kotoroi prinadlezhit budushchee." *Evraziia* 1: 5–11.

——. 1996. "Evraziiskii soiuz: Strategiia integratsii." *Evraziia* 1: 3–8.

——. 2001. "Vystuplenie Prezidenta Respubliki Kazakhstana (10 October 2000)." In *Evraziiskii universitet i mir: Vzglaid v budushchee*, 78–80. Astana: Izd-vo EGU.

"Ne iavliaetsia li Aleksandr Gel'evich Dugin . . . predstavietlem antisistemy?" n.d., http://www.kulichki.com/~gumilev/matter/Article31.htm, accessed 8/4/2014.

Nechkina, M. V., and P. S. Leibengrub, eds. 1970. *Istoriia SSSR: Uchebnoe posobie dlia 7 klassa*. 5th ed. Moscow: Iz-vo "Prosveshchenie."

Negrobov, B. V., and K. V. Khmelev. 2000. "Sovremennye kontseptsii konsortsiologii." *Vestnik Voronezhskii Gos. Un-ta.: Seriia khimii, biologii*: 118–21.

Nesgibaemyi Zhirinovskii. 2011. Moscow: LDPR.

Nesterov, Fedor. 1980. *Sviaz' vremen*. Moscow: Molodaia Gvardiia.

Nevzorov, A. 2013. "Zhivi mnogie tainy, ne poteriavshie etogo statusa." *Svobodnaia pressa*, 2 October, http://www.svpressa.ru/online/article/74968/, accessed 2/4/2014.

Nifontov, Vadim. 2006. "Nitsshe kak vospitatel'." (09/08/2007), http://www.intelros. org/nicsshe/nifontov.htm, accessed 6/7/2014.

Nikishkin, V. V. 2005. "K voprosu o proiavleniiakh passionarnosti sovremennogo marketinga." *Prakticheskii Marketing* 1, http://www.marketologi.ru/publikatsii/stati/k-voprosu-o-projavlenijakh-passionarnosti-sovremennogo-marketinga/, accessed 20/2/2014.

———. 2008. "Marketing i passionarnost'." *Display Russia* 19, http://www.marketologi.ru/publikatsii/stati/marketing-i-passionarnost/, accessed 20/2/2014.

Nikitin, A. L. 2001. *Osnovaniia Russkoi istorii: Mifologemy i fakty.* Moscow: Agraf.

Nikolaev, M. E. 2002. "Ia veriu v mudrost' naroda." (18 April), http://www.sakhagov.ykt.ru/main.asp?c=5306, accessed 4/6/2014.

———. 2006. "'Tri doliny': Territoriia respubliki." *Respublika Sakha-Iakutiia* (14 March), http://sakhagov.ykt.ru/main.asp?c=10468, accessed 4/6/2014.

"Nikolai Luginov ob Olonkho, Chingiskhane i literaturnom slove." 2009. *SakhaLife* (3 March), http://museum.sakha.ru/show.php?i=509, accessed 3/6/2014.

"Nikolai Luginov pokazal panoramnuiu kartinu imperskikh sostoianii natsii i narodov." 2008. *SakhaLife* (29 November), http://sakhalife.ru/node/8253, accessed 4/6/2014.

"'Novaia Khazariia' na russkoi zemle." 2003. *Novaia Sistema* 29, http://www.slavrus.net/digest/article.php?n=0310&a=11, accessed 25/2/2014.

Novikov, A. G. 1999. "L. N. Gumilev ob istorii etnosov." In Borisov, *Materialy Gumilevskikh chtenii 1995–96 gg.,* 23–35.

———. 2002. "'I vymyshlennaia legenda o presvitere Ioanne': Metodologiia L'va Gumileva." *Ilin* 4, no. 31, http://www.sakhaopenworld.org/ilin/2002-4/novikov.htm, accessed 4/6/2014.

Novikova, Ol'ga. 2007. "Lev Gumilev: 'Ia, russkii soldat.'" *Nevskoe Vremia*, 12 December, http://gumilevica.kulichki.net/NOG/nog01.htm, accessed 11/10/2014.

Nurminen, Pavel. 2009. "Khimery khimeriki." *Globalist* (15 June), http://globalist.org.ua/?p=17851, accessed 16/3/2014.

Nysanbaev, Abdumalik, and Rustem Kadyrzhanov. 2006. "National'naia ideia: Grazhdanskaia ili etnicheskaia." *Kazakhstanskaia Pravda* (23 December), http://www.centrasia.ru/newsA.php?st=1166999820, accessed 3/6/2014.

Ó BeacháIn, Donnacha, and Don Kevlihan. 2011. "State-Building, Identity and Nationalism in Kazakhstan: Some Preliminary Thoughts." Working Papers in International Studies, Centre for International Studies, Dublin City University, No. 1.

"O premii "Vekhi" Gosudarstvennoi Dumy Rossiiskoi Federatsii." n.d. http://gumilevica.kulichki.net/fund/fund07.htm, accessed 18/6/2015.

"Obsuzhdenie stat'i Iu. V. Bromleia 'Etnos i endogamiia.'" 1970. *Sovetskaia Etnografiia* 3: 86–103.

Olcott, Martha Brill. 2002. *Kazakhstan: Unfulfilled Promise.* Washington, DC: Carnegie Endowment for International Peace.

"Olzhas Suleimenov: Budet vtoraia *Az i Ia.*" 2013. *Radio Azattyk* (27 February), http://rus.azattyk.org/content/kyrgyzstan_culture_suleymenov/24914057.html, accessed 9/7/2014.

"'Oranzhevaia khimera' na Ukraine." 2013. *Regnum* (25 November), http://www.regnum.ru/news/1737311.html, accessed 22/4/2014.

Ostwald, Wilhelm. 1912. *Der energetische Imperativ.* Leipzig: Akademie Verlag.

"'Osvobodit' iz-pod aresta i Punina i Gumileva i soobshchit' ob ispolnenii.'" 1999. *Istochnik* 1: 77–82.

Oushakine, Serguei. 2007. "Vitality Rediscovered: Theorizing Post-Soviet Ethnicity in Russian Social Sciences." *Studies in East European Thought* 59: 171–93.

———. 2009. *The Patriotism of Despair: Nation, War, and Loss in Russia.* Ithaca, NY: Cornell University Press.

Panchenko, A. 1997. "Ia poterial sobesednika." *Nevskoe Vremia* 188, no. 1591, http://www.kulichki.com/~gumilev/matter/Article07.htm, accessed 11/10/2014.

Paramonov, Boris. 1992. "Sovetskoe Evraziistvo." *Zvezda* 4: 195–99.

Parland, Thomas. 2005. *The Extreme Nationalist Threat in Russia: The Growing Influence of Western Rightist Ideas.* London: Routledge.

"Passionarnaia energiia i etnos v razvitoi tsivilizatsii." 2007. http://www.conf.muh.ru/archive/7%E2%80%932007/40%E2%80%93191207, accessed 23/6/2015.

"Passionarnost'." 2012. *Zavtra* 41, no. 985 (3 October), http://zavtra.ru/content/view/passionarnost/, accessed 7/9/2014.

Pavlinskaia, L. P., ed. 2001. *Evraziia: Etnos, landshaft, kul'tura.* St. Petersburg: Evropeiskii Dom.

Pavochka, S. G. 2011. *L. N. Gumilev: Istoki i sushchnost'.* Grodno: IGAU.

Penck, Albrecht. 1925. "Deutscher Volks- und Kulturboden." In *Volk unter Völkern,* edited by K. C. von Loesch, 62–73. Breslau: F. Hirt.

Penzev, K. A. 2006. *Velikaia Tatariia: Istoriia zemli russkoi.* Moscow: Algoritm.

———. 2007a. *Russkii tsar' Batyi.* Moscow: Algoritm.

———. 2007b. *Zemli Chingiskhana.* Moscow: Algoritm.

"Perepiska A. A. Akhmatovoi i L. N. Gumileva." 1994. *Zvezda* 4: 170–88.

Pershits, A. I., and V. V. Pokshishevskii. 1978. "Ipostasi etnosa." *Priroda* 12: 106–13.

Peterson, Dale E. 1994. "'Samovar Life': Russian Nurture and Russian Nature in the Rural Prose of Valentin Rasputin." *Russian Review* 53, no. 1: 81–96.

Petro, Nikolai N. 1987. "The Project of the Century: A Case Study of Russian Nationalist Dissent." *Studies in Comparative Communism* 20, nos. 3–4: 235–52.

Petrov, A. N. 2002. "O vliianii etnogeneza na dinamiku narodonaseleniia." *Izvestiia Russkogo Geograficheskogo Obshchestva* 134, no. 2: 85–92.

Petrov, K. M. 2005. *Filosofskie problemy geografii.* St. Petersburg: Iz-vo SPb. Un-ta.

Petrov, M.P. 2012 [1974]. "Priroda i istoriia v knige L.N. Gumileva. S tochki zrenia geografa." In Burlaka, *Lev Gumilev: Pro et Contra*: 287–90.

Pimenov, V. V. 2003. "Poniatie 'etnos' v teoreticheskoi kontseptsii Iu. V. Bromleia." In *Akademik Iu. V. Bromlei i otechestvennaia etnologiia, 1960–1990e gody,* 12–17. Moscow: Nauka.

Plamper, Jan. 2009. "Emotional Turn?: Feelings in Russian History and Culture." *Slavic Review* 68, no. 2: 229–37.

Pletneva, S. A. 1976. *Khazary.* Moscow: Nauka.

———. 1990. "Khazarskie problemy v arkheologii." *Sovetskaia Arkheologiia* 2: 77–91.

Plotnikov, V. 1994. "Peshchery kamenny. . . ." *Sever* 11.

Podgorodnikov, M. I. 1974. "Trudnye voprosy biosfery." *Literaturnaia Gazeta* 21 (22 May): 22.

Podolinskii, S. A. 1880. "Trud cheloveka i ego otnoshenie k raspredeleniiu energii." *Slovo,* nos. 4–5: 135–211.

Polienovich, Ia. V. 2005. *V. I. Vernadskii.* Moscow: MarT.

Polivanov, S., and I. Kosykh. 1995. "Svoikh' u korichnevoi partii net." *Moskovskie Novosti* 11 (12–19 February): 11.

Pollock, Ethan. 2006. *Stalin and the Soviet Science Wars.* Princeton, NJ: Princeton University Press.

Polonsky, Rachel. 2012. "Russia: The Citizen Poet." *New York Review of Books* 59, no. 17 (8 November).

Poluboiarinova, Marina. 1997. "Russkie v Zolotoi Orde." *Rodina,* nos. 3–4: 53–57.

Poplinskii, Iu. K. 1973. "K istorii vozniknoveniia termina 'etnosa.'" *Sovetskaia Etnografiia* 1: 128–34.

Porfir'ev, Maksim. n.d. "Tri tolstiaka i toshchie chleny profsoiuza." http://www.compromat.ru/page_23295.htm, accessed 4/6/2014.

Porshnev, B. F. 1973. *Protivopostavlenie kak komponent etnicheskogo samosoznaniia.* Moscow: Gl. Red. Vost. Lit.

"Portret L'va Gumileva rabota Alekseia Gintovta." 2011. http://www.gumilev-center. ru/portret-lva-gumiljova-raboty-alekseya-gintovta/, accessed 14/7/2014.

Pozdniakova, Tat'iana, and Marina Kozyreva. 2005. "'Sladko l' uzhinal, padishakh?'" In *"I zachem nuzhno bylo stol'ko lgat'?": Pis'ma L'va Gumileva k Natal'e Barbanets iz lageria 1950–1956*, 5–54. St. Petersburg: AGAT.

"Prarodina Iakutov: Gde Ona?" 1989. *Molodezh' Iakutiia* (20 March), http://gumilevica. kulichki.net/articles/Article73.htm, accessed 3/6/2014.

"Prezident Tatarstana vystupaet za rasprostranenie 'liberal'nogo islama.'" 2004. *NEWSru.com* (7 July), http://www.newsru.com/religy/07jul2004/shaimiev_ print.html, accessed 3/6/2014.

Prokhanov, Aleksandr, and Aleksandr Ianov. 1992. "Dva vzgliada na russkuiu ideiu." *Literaturnaia Gazeta*, no. 36 (2 September): 13

Prokhanov, A. A. 2014. "Borodai: Syn druga Gumileva, intellektual i polevoi komandir." *Navigator* (19 May), http://www.politnavigator.net/prokhanov-borodajj-syn-druga-gumileva-intellektual-i-polevojj-komandir.html, accessed 3/10/2014.

Pryce, Paul. 2013. "Putin's Third Term: The Triumph of Eurasianism." *Romanian Journal of European Affairs* 13, no. 1: 25–43.

"'Publikatsiia moikh rabot blokiruiutsia': Kto i pochemu otvergal L. N. Gumilevu." 1995. *Istochnik* 5: 84–89.

Pursiainen, Christer. 1998. *Eurasianism and Neo-Eurasianism: The Past, Present, and Postmodernity of a Russian Integration Ideology.* UPI Working Papers 5. Helsinki: Finnish Institute of International Affairs.

Putin, V. V. 2000a. "Rossiia: Novye vostochnye perspektivy." 9 November, http://ar chive.kremlin.ru/text/appears/2000/11/28426.shtml, accessed 10/12/2013.

———. 2000b. "Vystuplenie Prezidenta . . . Putina v Universitete imeni L. Gumileva." 10 October, http://gumilevica.kulichki.com/matter/Article26.htm, accessed 11/01/2010.

———. 2004. "Vystuplenie na mezhdunarodnom forume 'Evraziiskiaia integrat-siia'. . . .'"(Astana). 18 July, http://archive.kremlin.ru/appears/2004/06/18/1149_ type63377_72959.shtml, accessed 8/2/2014.

———. 2005a. "Poslanie Federal'nomu Sobraniiu Rossiiskoi Federatsii." 25 April, http:// archive.kremlin.ru/text/appears/2005/04/87049.shtml, accessed 11/12/2013.

———. 2005b. "Rechi i obrashcheniia po sluchaiu pamiatnykh sobytii. . . ." 26 August, http:// archive.kremlin.ru/appears/2005/08/26/2353_type122346_92947.shtml, accessed 8/4/2014.

———. 2011. "Novyi integratsionnyi proekt dlia Evrazii." *Izvestiia*, 3 October, http:// izvestia.ru/news/502761, accessed 21/5/2013.

———. 2012a. "Greetings to International Academic Congress Honouring the Legacy of Lev Gumilev." 1 October, http://eng.kremlin.ru/news/4460, accessed 10/7/2014.

———. 2012b. "Poslanie Federal'nomu Sobraniiu Rossiiskoi Federatsii." 12 December, http://www.kremlin.ru/transcripts/1711el=, accessed 21/2/2014.

———. 2012c. "Rossiia: Natsional'nyi vopros." *Nezavisimaia Gazeta*, 23 January, http:// www.ng.ru/politics/2012-01-23/1_national.html, accessed 10/7/2014.

"Putin, Shaimiev hail Eurasianism." 2005. *RFE/RL Newsline* 9, no. 163 (29 August), http://www.hri.org/news/balkans/rferl/2005/05-08-30.rferl.html—04, accessed 10/7/2014.

"Putin's Grandest Dream: Could His 'Eurasian Union' Work?" 2012. *The Atlantic*, 18 March, http://www.theatlantic.com/international/archive/2012/03/putins-grandest-dream-could-his-eurasian-union-work/254651/, accessed 19/1/2014.

Ram, Harsha. 2001. "Imagining Eurasia: The Poetics and Ideology of Olzhas Suleimenov's *AZ i IA*." *Slavic Review* 60, no. 2: 289–311.

Raney, Franklin C. 1966. "Geobiocenology." *Ecology* 47, no. 1: 170–71.

Raskin, David. 1996. "Ob odnoi istoricheskoi teorii, unasledovannoi russkim fashizmom." In Iliushenko, *Nuzhen li Gitler Rossii?*, 157–58.

Ratner, Vadim A. 2001. "Nikolay Vladimirovich Timofeeff-Ressovsky (1900–1981): Twin of the Century of Genetics." *Genetics* 158: 933–39.

Raviot, Jean-Robert. 1992. "Tipy natsionalizma, obshchestvo i politika v Tatarstane." *Polis*, nos. 5–6: 42–58, http://www.tatar-history.narod.ru/ravio.htm, accessed 3/6/2014.

Reif, Wolf-Ernst, Thomas Junker, and Uwe Hossfeld. 2000. "The Synthetic Theory of Evolution: General Problems and the German Contribution to the Synthesis." *Theory in Biosciences* 119: 41–91.

Revunenkova, E. V., and A. M. Reshetov. 2003. "Sergei Mikhailovich Shirokogorov." *Etnograficheskoe Obozrenie* 3: 100–119.

Rindzeviciute, Egle. 2010. "Purification and Hybridisation of Soviet Cybernetics." *Archiv für Sozialgeschichte* 50: 289–309.

Rogachevskii, Andrei. 2001. "Lev Gumilev i evreiskii vopros (po lichnym vospominaniiam)." *Solnechnoe Spletenie*, nos. 18–19: 358–68.

Rooney, Victoria. 1986. "Nietzschean Elements in Zamyatin's Ideology: A Study of His Essays." *The Modern Language Review* 81, no. 3: 675–86.

Rosenthal, Bernice Glatzer, ed. 1994. *Nietzsche and Soviet Culture. Ally and Adversary*. Cambridge: Cambridge University Press.

——. 1997. "Political Implications of the Early Twentieth-Century Occult Revival." In *The Occult in Russian and Soviet Culture*, edited by Bernice Glatzer Rosenthal, 379–418. Ithaca, NY: Cornell University Press.

——. 2002. *New Myth, New World: From Nietzsche to Stalin*. University Park: The Pennsylvania State University Press.

Rossman, Vadim. 2002a. "Lev Gumilev, Eurasianism and Khazaria." *East European Jewish Affairs* 32, no. 1: 30–51.

——. 2002b. *Russian Intellectual Antisemitism in the Post-Communist Era*. Lincoln: University of Nebraska Press.

Rudenko, S.I. 1965. "K voprosu ob istoricheskom sinteze (po povodu odnoi diskussii)" *Geograficheskoe obshchestvo SSSR. Doklady po etnografii* 1, no. 4: 59–65.

Rougle, Charles, and Elisabeth Rich. 1995. "Aleksandr Prokhanov." *South Central Review* 12, nos. 3–4: 18–27.

Rumiantseva, T. G. 2008. *Osval'd Shpengler*. Minsk: Knizhniy Dom.

Rusinko, Elaine. 1994. "Apollonianism and Christian Art: Nietzsche's Influence on Acmeism." In Rosenthal, *Nietzsche and Soviet Culture*, 84–106.

Russell, Robert. 1992. "The Drama of Evgenii Zamiatin." *Slavonic and East European Review* 70, no. 2: 228–48.

Rutland, Peter. 1984. "The Nationality Problem and the Soviet State." In *The State in Socialist Society*, edited by Neil Harding, 150–78. Albany: SUNY Press.

Ruzhenkov, Mikhail. 1975. "Passionarnaia teoriia L. N. Gumileva." *Vol'noe Slovo*, nos. 17–18: 93–96.

Rybakov, B. A. 1953. "K voprosu o roli Khazarskogo kaganata v istorii Rusi." *Sovetskaia Arkheologiia* 18: 128–50.

——. 1971. "O preodolenii samoobmana." *Voprosy Istorii* 3: 153–59, http://gumilevica.kulichki.net/debate/Article34.htm, accessed 24/3/2014.

Rybakov, S. E. 2001a. *Filosofiia etnosa*. Moscow: IPK Gossluzhby.

——. 2001b. "Sud'by teorii etnosa." *Etnograficheskoe Obozrenie* 1: 3–22.

Ryzhkov, Vladimir. 2003. "Lev Gumilev: Vremia Karlaga." *Kazakhstanskaia Pravda*, 13 August, http://www.kazpravda.kz/rus/nauka/lev_gumilev_vremja_karlaga.html, accessed 22/7/2011.

Saad, Said Abu. 2009. "Istishkhad: Mezhdu pravoi i lozh'iu." *Kavkazcenter.com* (11 December), http://www.kavkazcenter.com/russ/content/2009/12/11/69600.shtml, accessed 21/1/2014.

Saari, Sinikukka. 2011. "Putin's Eurasian Union Initiative." *UI brief* 9 (1 November), http://www.ui.se/upl/files/65793.pdf, accessed 9/6/2015.

Sadokhin, A. P. 2002. *Etnologiia: Uchenyi slovar'*. Moscow: Gardariki.

——. 2004. *Etnologiia : Uchebnoe posobie*. 3rd ed. Moscow: Al'fa-M.

Saifullin, R. G. 2012. "Passionarnost' kak odin iz vedushchikh faktorov politicheskoi dinamiki." In *Istoricheskie, filosofskie, politicheskie i iuridicheskie nauki, kul'turologiia i iskusstvovedenie: Voprosy teorii i praktiki*, 177–80. Tambov: Gramota.

Sakharov, A. N. 1982. *Diplomatiia Sviatoslava*. Moscow: Mezhdunarodnoe Otnosheniia.

Samokhin, A. V. 2004. "Istoricheskii put' evraziistva kak ideino-politicheskogo techeniia (ch. 2)." *Al'manakh "Vostok"* 3, no. 15, http://www.situation.ru/app/j_art_317.htm, accessed 16/6/2014.

Samovarov, Aleksandr. 2013. "Lev Gumilev: Pokhod protiv bol'shevizma." *APN* (4 December), http://www.apn.ru/publications/print30678.htm, accessed 3/4/2014.

Sapronov, P. A. n.d. "Ot Rusi do Rossii vmeste s L. N. Gumilevym." http://nationalism.org/aziopa/sapronov.htm, accessed 18/6/2014.

Savchenko, A. 1996. "Sem' let riadom so L'vom Gumilevym." *Novyi Mir* 2: 240–50.

Savchenko, V. N., and V. P. Smagin. 2006. *Nachala sovremennogo estestvoznaniia: Kontseptsii i printsipi*. Rostov-na-Donu: Feniks.

Savitskii, P. N. 1994. "Iz pisem P. N. Savitskogo L. N. Gumilevu." In Gumilev, *Chernaia Legenda*, 164–66.

Schatz, Edward. 2000. "The Politics of Multiple Identities: Lineage and Ethnicity in Kazakhstan." *Europe-Asia Studies* 52, no. 3: 489–506.

Scheibert, Peter. 1961. "Der Übermensch in der russischen Revolution." In *Der Übermensch: Eine Disskusion*, edited by Ernst Benz, 179–96. Stuttgart: "Rhein."

Schenk, Frithjof Benjamin. 2004. *Aleksandr Nevskij: Heiliger—Fürst—Nationalheld: Eine Erinnerungsfigur im russischen kulturellen Gedächtnis (1263–2000)*. Cologne: Böhlau Verlag.

Schindler, Debra A. 1991. "Theory, Policy and the *Narody Severa*." *Anthropological Quarterly* 64, no. 2: 68–79.

Schmidt, Matthew. 2005. "Is Putin Pursuing a Policy of Eurasianism?" *Demokratizatsiya* 13, no. 1: 87–100.

Schoener, T. 1989. "The Ecological Niche." In *Ecological Concepts*, edited by J. Cherrett, 79–113. Oxford: Blackwell Scientific Publications.

Segizbaev, Kanat. 2007. "S chego nachinaetsia Rodina?" *Internet-Gazeta "Zona KZ"* 70/2496 (17 July), http://zonakz.net/articles/18542, accessed 3/6/2014.

Semanov, S. N. 1970. "O tsennostiakh otnositel'nykh i vechnykh." *Molodaia Gvardiia* 8: 308–20.

——. 1997. "Russkii klub." *Moskva* 3: 177–82.

——. 2012. *Russkii klub : Pochemu ne pobediat evrei*. Moscow: Algoritm. http://coollib.com/b/250689/read, accessed 5/4/2014.

——. n.d. "Chem bol'she rodinu my liubim." http://www.moskvam.ru/1999/11_99/semanov.htm, accessed 16/11/2008.

Semenov, P. G. 1961. "Programma KPSS o razvitii sovetskikh natsional'no-gosudarstvennykh otnoshenii." *Sovetskoe Gosudarstvo i Pravo* 12: 15–25.

———. 1966. "Natsiia i natsional'naia gosudarstvennost' v SSSR." *Voprosy Istorii* 7: 73–81.

Semenova, S. G., and A. G. Gacheva, eds. 1993. *Russkii Kosmizm: Antologiia filosofii mysli*. Moscow: Pedagogika-Press.

Semevskii, B. N. 1970. "Propaganda for a 'Unified Geography.'" *Soviet Geography* 11, no. 6: 501–9.

———. 1974. "Vzaimodeistvie sistemy 'chelovek-priroda.'" *Priroda* 8: 74–75.

Semilet, T. 2004. *Kulturvitalizm: Kontseptsiia zhiznennykh sil kul'tury*. Barnaul: n.p.

Serazhieva, S. Kh. 2002. "K voprosu o poniatiiakh 'etnopolitika' i 'natsional'naia politika.'" Kazakhstanskii Institut Strategicheskikh Issledovanii pri Prezidente Res. Kaz., http://kisi.kz/site.html?id=3836, accessed 3/6/2014.

Serikbai, S. 2002. "Evraziistvo i Kazakhstan." *Internet-Gazeta "Zona KZ"* 0/712 (5 August), http://analytics-iss.ru/articles/library/09_08_02_libr_rusev.htm, accessed 3/6/2014.

Sevast'ianov, A. N. 2003. *Chego ot nas khotiat evrei*, http://www.sevastianov.ru/vre mya-bytj-russkim/vremya-bytj-russkim-chego-ot-nas-hotyat-evrei-chastj-1. html, accessed 7/11/2014.

———. 2008. *Etnos i natsiia*. Moscow: Knizhnyi Mir.

———. 2014. "Lev Gumilev i Ministerstvo oborony SSSR." *APN* (19 February), http:// www.apn.ru/publications/article31094.htm, accessed 17/3/2014.

Shabaev, Iu. P., and A. P. Sadokhin. 2005. *Etnopolitologiia*. Moscow: IUnity.

Shafarevich, I. R. 1991. *Rusofobiia: Dve dorogi k odnomu obryvu*. Moscow: Tovarishchestvo russkikh khudozhnikov.

———. 1992. "Iz roda gerodotov: Pamiati L'va Gumileva." *Den'* 25, no. 53 (21–27 June): 5.

———. 1993. "Shtrikhi k tvorcheskomu portretu Vadima Valerianovicha Kozhinova." *Nash Sovremennik* 9: 170–77.

———. 2002. "Khazariia." In *Trekhtysiacheletniaia zagadka: Istoriia evreistva iz perespektivy sovremennoi Rossii*, 33–36. St. Petersburg: Bibliopolis.

———. 2010. "Sovremennaia Rossiia i vlast' 'malogo naroda.'" *Zolotoi Lev*, 261–62, http://www.zlev.ru/index.php?p=article&nomer=50&article=3016, accessed 28/11/2012.

———. 2011. "Akhillesova piata Malogo naroda." traditio-ru.org/wiki/Игорь_Шафаревич: Ахиллесова_пята_Малого_народа, accessed 11/7/2014.

Shagbanova, Iu. B. 1998. "Etnodiaspora i izmeneniia v etnosrede." In Bairamova, *Sistema tsennostei rossiiskoi natsional'noi politiki*, 85.

Shaimiev, M. Sh. 1997. "V istorii naroda—ego nastoiashchee i budushchee!" *Rodina*, nos. 3–4: 6.

———. 2005. "My s russkim narodom srodnilis' davno." *Mezhdunarodnaia Zhizn* 10: 11–13, http://shaimiev.tatar.ru/pub/view/977, accessed 3/6/2014.

Shalakhmetov, G. M., and N. A. Iskakov. 2005. *Printsip piramidy*. Moscow: Evraziia. http://www.pobisk-memory.narod.ru/book/piramida/prefrase.htm, accessed 3/6/2014.

Shamir, Israel'. n.d. "Pis'ma iz Moskvy—bez tsenzury: Ego posledovateli." http://www. israelshamir.net/ru/letters40.htm, accessed 4/4/2014.

Shanin, Teodor. 1989. "Ethnicity in the Soviet Union: Analytical Perceptions and Political Strategies." *Comparative Studies in Society and History* 31, no. 3: 409–24.

Shapkina, E. V. 2007. "Kharizmaticheskoe liderstvo v politicheskom protsesse: Regional'nyi aspekt." Avtoreferat kand. diss., Sibirskii gos. industral'ny un-t, Ulan-Ude.

Sharapov, Ia. Sh. 1998. "Etnopolitika respubliki Tatarstana." In Bairamova, *Sistema tsennostei rossiiskoi natsional'noi politiki*, 61–63.

Shatokhin, Sergei. 2010. "Sovremennoe evraziistvo: Politicheskaia demagogiia." *Stoletie* (10 June), http://www.stoletie.ru/geopolitika/sergej_shatohin_sovremennoje_jevrazijstvo__politicheskaja_demagogija_2010-06-10.htm, accessed 18/6/2014.

Shaw, Denis J. B., and Jonathan D. Oldfield. 2006. "V. I. Vernadsky and the Noosphere Concept." *Geoforum* 37: 145–54.

———. 2007. "Landscape Science: A Russian Geographical Tradition." *Annals of the Association of American Geographers* 97, no. 1: 111–26.

Sheiko, Konstantin. 2009. *Nationalist Imaginings of the Russian Past: Anatolii Fomenko and the Rise of Alternative History in Post-Communist Russia*. Stuttgart: *ibidem*-Verlag.

Shenfield, Stephen D. 2001. *Russian Fascism: Traditions, Tendencies, Movements*. Armonk, NY: M. E. Sharpe.

Sherstobitov, V. P., ed. 1976. *Sovetskii narod: Monolitnaia obshchnost' stroitelei kommunizma*. Moscow: Mysl'.

———, ed. 1982. *Internatsionalizm sovetskogo naroda*. Moscow: Nauka.

Shevchenko, Iu. Iu., ed. 2002. *Lev Nikolaevich Gumilev: Teoriia etnogeneza i istoricheskie sud'by Evrazii*. St. Petersburg: Evropeiskii Dom.

Shils, Edward. 1975. *Center and Periphery: Essays in Macrosociology*. Chicago: University of Chicago Press.

Shimanov, G. M. 1974. "Kak ponimat' nashu istoriiu i k chemu v nei stremit'sia." http://chri-soc.narod.ru/sh_kak_ponimat_nashu_istoriu.htm, accessed 16/6/2014.

Shirokogoroff, S. M. 1924. *Ethnical Unit and Milieu*. Shanghai: Edward Evans and Sons.

Shirokogorov, S. M. 1923. *Etnos: Issledovanie osnovnykh printsipov izmeneniia etnicheskikh i etnograficheskikh iavlenii*. Shanghai: Izd. Vostochnogo Fakul'teta Gos. Dal<pre-Vostochnogo Un-ta.

Shishkin, I. S. 1994. "'Obshchevropeiskii dom'; Vot bog, a vot porog." *Zavtra* 45, no. 50 (20/6/2008), http://www.kulichki.com/~gumilev/debate/Article16.htm, accessed 8/4/2014.

———. 1995a. "Chitaite L. N. Gumileva." In Goncharova, *Dni L. N. Gumileva v Bezhetske*, 75–84.

———. 1995b. "Rossiia bez russkikh." *Zavtra* 35, no. 91, http://www.kulichki.com/~gumilev/debate/Article16.htm, accessed 8/4/2014.

———. 1995c. "Simbioz, kseniia, i khimera." *Zavtra* 4, no. 60: 4.

———. 1996. "Vnutrennii vrag." *Derzhava* 6 and 7, http://gumilevica.kulichki.net/debate/Article03.htm, accessed 11/6/2015.

———. 1998. "Uchenie L. N. Gumileva, evraziistvo i russkii vopros." In Ganzha and Shishkin, *Uchenie L. N. Gumileva*, 103–5.

———. 2006. "Piatyi punkt v neoevraziistve." *Nezavisimaia Gazeta*, 5 June, http://www.ng.ru/ideas/2002-06-05/11_punkt.html, accessed 8/4/2014.

———. n.d. "Russkii vopros i evraziistvo." http://levgumilev.spbu.ru/node/157, accessed 13/1/2014.

Shitikhin, P. 2012. "Sravnitel'nyi analiz istoriosofskikh vzgliadov N. Ia. Danilevskogo i L. N. Gumileva." Avtoreferat kand. diss., Moskovskaia Dukhovnaia Akademiia, Moscow.

Shlapentokh, Dmitry. 1996a. "Bolshevism as a Fedorovian Regime." *Cahiers du Monde Russe* 37, no. 4: 429–66.

———. 1996b. "The Fedorovian Roots of Stalinism." *Philosophy Today* 40: 388–404.

——. 1997. "Eurasianism: Past and Present." *Communist and Post-Communist Studies* 30, no. 2: 129–51.

——. 2001. "Cosmism in European Thought: Humanity without Future in Cosmos." *Journal of Philosophical Research* 26: 497–546.

——. 2005. "Is Putin Really a Eurasianist?" *Transitions Online* (5 September), http://www.tol.org/client/article/14429-the-allure-of-eurasianism.html, accessed 10/7/2014.

——. 2007a. "Putin's Neo-Eurasianism." *Prague Watchdog* (16 January), http://www.watchdog.cz/?show=000000-000004-000002-000028&lang=1, accessed 10/7/2014.

——, ed. 2007b. *Russia Between East and West: Scholarly Debates on Eurasianism.* Leiden: Brill.

——. 2009. "Russian Elite Image of Iran: From the Late Soviet Era to the Present." http://www.strategicstudiesinstitute.army.mil/pdffiles/pub936.pdf, accessed 17/4/2014.

——. 2011. "Huns in Eurasianist Thought: The Case of Lev Gumilev." *International Journal of Turkish Studies* 17, nos. 1–2: 95–114.

——. 2012. "Lev Gumilev: The Ideologist of the Soviet Empire." *History of European Ideas* 38, no. 3: 483–92.

Shnirel'man, V. A. 2003. "Ot konfessional'nogo k etnicheskomu: Bulgarskaia ideia v natsional'nom samosoznanii kazanskikh tatar v XX veke." In *Evraziia: Liudi i Mify*, edited by Sergei Panarin, 450–73. Moscow: Natalis.

——. 2005a. "Novyi rasizm v Rossii." *Ezhednevyi Zhurnal* (12 October), http://www.ej.ru/?a=note&id=2073, accessed 18/9/2014.

——. 2005b. "'Svirepye khazary' i rossiiskie pisateli: Istoriia vzaimootnoshenii." In *Khazary: Evrei i slaviane*, edited by I. Ablina and M. Iaglom, 287–309. Jerusalem: Mosty kul'tury.

——. 2009. "Lev Gumilev: Ot 'passionarnogo napriazheniia' do 'nesovmestimosti kul'tur.'" *Politicheskaia Kontseptologiia* 3: 205–22.

Shnirel'man, V. A., and S. A. Panarin. 2000. "Lev Nikolaevich Gumilev: Osnovatel' etnologii?" *Vestnik Evrazii* 3, no. 10: 5–37.

Shnirelman, Victor A. 1995. "The Grand Result, Taking Shape under His Eyes, Was the "Formation of a New People—the Soviet People. . . ." In Kohl and Fawcett, *Nationalism, Politics, and the Practice of Archeology*, 120–38.

——. 1996. *Who Gets the Past?: Competition for Ancestors among Non-Russian Intellectuals in Russia.* Washington, DC: Woodrow Wilson Center Press.

——. 2001. "The Fate of Empires and Eurasian Federalism: A Discussion between the Eurasianists and Their Opponents in the 1920s." *Inner Asia* 3: 153–73.

——. 2002. *The Myth of the Khazars and Intellectual Antisemitism in Russia, 1970s–1990s.* Jerusalem: Vidal Sassoon International Center for the Study of Antisemitism, Hebrew University.

——. 2003. "Myths of Descent: Views of the Remote Past, as Reflected in School Textbooks in Contemporary Russia." *Public Archaeology* 3, no. 1: 33–51.

——. 2005. "Politics of Ethnogenesis in the USSR and After." *Bulletin of the National Museum of Ethnology* 30, no. 1: 93–119.

——. 2009a. "To Make a Bridge: Eurasian Discourse in the Post-Soviet World " *Anthropology of East Europe Review* 23, no. 2: 68–85.

——. 2009b. "Stigmatized by History or Historians? The Peoples of Russia in School History Textbooks." *History and Memory* 21, no. 2: 110–49.

Shnirelman, Victor A., and Galina Komarova. 1997. "Majority as a Minority: The Russian Ethno-Nationalism and Its Ideology in the 1970s–1990s." In *Rethinking*

Nationalism and Ethnicity: The Struggle for Meaning and Order in Europe, edited by Hans-Rudolf Wicker, 211–24. Oxford: Berg.

Shtyrov, V. A. 2002. "V ednioi sem'e narodov Rossii." *Respublika Sakha-Iakutiia* (1 October), http://sakha.gov.ru/node/1486, accessed 3/6/2014.

Shubkin, Vladimir. 1981. "Neopalimaia kupina: Zametki o traditsiiakh russkoi klassiki v sovremennoi proze." *Nash Sovremennik* 12: 175–88.

Shulyndin, P. P. 1984. "Etnos i etnopsikhologiia (o 'geografo-psikholgicheskoi' kontseptsii L. N.Gumileva)." Unpublished ms, dep. at INION (Moscow), no. 19238.

Shumovskii, T. A. 2003. "Besedy s pamiat'iu." In Voronovich and Kozyreva, *Vspominaia L. N. Gumileva*, 87–115.

Sikevich, Z. V. 1999. "O sootnoshenii etnicheskogo i sotsial'nogo." *Zhurnal sotsiologii i sotsial'noi antropologii* 2, no. 2: 71–81.

Simon, Gerhard. 1991. *Nationalism and Policy toward the Nationalities in the Soviet Union: From Totalitarian Dictatorship to Post-Stalinist Society*. Translated by Karen Forster and Oswald Forster. Boulder, CO: Westview.

Simonsen, Sven Gunnar. 1996. "Raising 'The Russian Question': Ethnicity and Statehood—*Russkie* and *Rossiya*." *Nationalism and Ethnic Politics* 2, no. 1: 91–110.

Simmons, Ian. 1993. *Environmental History: A Concise Introduction*. Oxford: Blackwell.

Skalnik, Peter. 1981. "Community: Struggle for a Key Concept in Soviet Ethnography." *Dialectical Anthropology* 6: 171–82.

———. 1986. "Towards an Understanding of Soviet *Etnos* theory." *South African Journal of Ethnology* 9, no. 4: 157–66.

Skrynnikov, Ruslan. 1980. "Kulikovskaia bitva." *Zvezda* 9: 9–20.

Slezkine, Yuri. 1991. "The Fall of Soviet Ethnography, 1928–38." *Current Anthropology* 32, no. 4: 476–84.

———. 1994. *Arctic Mirrors: Russia and the Small Peoples of the North*. Ithaca, NY: Cornell University Press.

———. 1996a. "N. Ia. Marr and the National Origins of Soviet Ethnogenetics." *Slavic Review* 55, no. 4: 826–62.

———. 1996b. "The USSR as a Communal Apartment, or How a Socialist State Promoted Ethnic Particurlarism." In *Becoming National: A Reader*, edited by Geoff Eley and Ronald Grigor Suny, 203–38. New York: Oxford University Press.

Smagulova, Juldyz. 2006. "Kazakhstan: Language, Identity, and Conflict." *Innovation* 19, nos. 3–4: 303–20.

Smirnov, I. I., ed. 1963. *Kratkaia Istoriia SSSR: Chast' Pervaia*. Moscow-Leningrad: Iz-vo AN SSSR.

Smirnov, Sergei. 1998. "Est' li u Rossii svoia geopolitika?" *Rossiiskoe Analiticheskoe Obozrenie*, no. 8–9, http://metuniv.chat.ru/rao/98-8-9/09smirn.htm, accessed 12/2/2014.

Sobolev, D. 1997. "V storonu Khazarii." *Dvadtsat' dva* [Tel Aviv] 103: 114–29, http://www.sunround.com/club/22/vstoronu.htm, accessed 27/1/2015.

Soboleva, G. 1936. "'Volk und Rasse': Kriticheskii obzor." *Antropologicheskii Zhurnal* 1: 110–16.

Socor, Vladimir. 2011. "Putin's Eurasian Manifesto Charts Russia's Return to Great Power Status." *Eurasia Daily Monitor* 8: 185 (7 October), http://www.jamestown.org/programs/edm/single/?tx_ttnews%5Btt_news%5D=38501&tx_ttnews%5BbackPid%5D=512&no_cache=1—.UtvKMmQ1hcw, accessed 19/1/2014.

Sokolovski, Sergei V. n.d. "Structures of Russian Political Discourse on Nationality Problems: Anthropological Perspectives." *Kennan Institute Occasional Papers*,

no. 272, http://www.wilsoncenter.org/sites/default/files/op272_structures_
russian_discourse_Sokolovski_1999.pdf, accessed 24/2/2014.

Sokolovskiy, S.V. 2000. "The Construction of 'Indigenousness' in Russian Science, Politics, and Law." *Journal of Legal Pluralism* 45, no. 91–113.

——. 2008. "Anthropology and Ethnology in Russia." Unpublished paper. http://pen
dientedemigracion.ucm.es/info/antrosim/docs/Sokolovskiy_Anthropology_
Ethnology_in_Russia.pdf, accessed 9/6/2015.

Solovei, Valerii. 2006. "Osnovnoi Faktor." *APN*, http://www.apn.ru/publications/
print1790.htm, accessed 24/1/2014.

Solzhenitsyn, Aleksandr I. 1973. *The Gulag Archipelago*. Translated by Thomas P. Whitney. New York: Harper & Row.

Sorokin, Iu. A. 2003. "L. N. Gumilev o vzaimootnosheniiakh velikoi stepi i russkogo
gosudarstva v IX–XVIII vv." In Zholdasbekov, *Evraziistvo i Kazakhstan*, 1: 19–25.

Sovetskii narod—stroitel' kommunizma. 1977. 2 vols. Frunze: Iv-vo "Kyrgyzstan."

Sovetskii narod: Novaia istoricheskaia obshchnost' liudei. 1987. Kishinev: Shtiintsa.

"Sozdatel' global'noi ekologii." 2011. http://old.rgo.ru/2011/01/sozdatel-globalnoj-
ekologii/, accessed 28/7/2014.

Spektorowski, Alberto. 2003. "The New Right: Ethno-regionalism, Ethno-pluralism
and the Emergence of a Neo-fascist 'Third Way.'" *Journal of Political Ideologies* 8,
1: 111–30.

Spengler, Oswald. 1918–1923. *Der Untergang des Abendlandes: Umrisse einer Morphologie der Weltgeschichte*. 2 vols. Vienna: Braumüller; Munich: C. H. Beck.

Spivakovskii, P. E. 1995. "Evroaziatskoe sotrudnichestvo ili 'evraziiskii tupik'?" In
Novoe zarubezh'e: Poiski putei obnovleniia, edited by V. A. Vinogradov, 170–73.
Moscow: INION RAN.

Ssorin-Chaikov, Nikolai V. 2003. *The Social Life of the State in Subarctic Siberia*. Stanford, CA: Stanford University Press.

Stalin, I. V. 1946 [1906]. "Anarkhizm ili sotsializm?" In *Sochineniia*, 1: 294–392.
Moscow: Gos. Iz-vo. Pol. Lit.

——. 1950 [1912–1913]. *Marksizm i natsional'nyi vopros*. Moscow: Glavpoligrafizdat.

——. 1951 [1930]. "Zakliuchitel'noe slovo po politicheskomu otchetu TsK XVI S'ezdu
BKP(b)." In *Sochineniia*, 13: 1–16. Moscow: Gos. Iz-vo Pol Lit.

——. 1997 [1950]. "Marksizm i voprosy iazykoznaniia." In *Sochinenii*, 16: 104–38.
Moscow: Pisatel'.

Stankevich, Sergei. 1993. "Russia's New Model: East Asia Plus West Europe." *New Perspectives Quarterly* (Spring): 41–43.

Starovoitova, G. V. 1993. "Weimar Russia?" *Journal of Democracy* 4, no. 3: 106–9.

Stekliannokova, L. D. 2003. "Vechnaia pamiat'." In Goncharova, *Lev Gumilev: Sud'ba
i idei*, 528–57, http://gumilevica.kulichki.net/matter/Article40.htm, accessed
6/7/2014.

Steuckers, Robert. n.d. "Foundations of Russian Nationalism." http://www.counter-
currents.com/2014/04/foundations-of-russian-nationalism-2/, accessed
26/11/2014.

Stigall, Alycia L. 2012. "Using Ecological Niche Modelling to Evaluate Niche Stability
in Deep Time." *Journal of Biogeography* 39: 772–81.

Stodolsky, Ivor. 2009. "Cultural Geopolitics in the New Russian Intelligentsia: A Case
Study of Timur Novikov, Artist and Cultural Ideologue." In *Eurasie: Espace
mythique ou réalite en construction?*, edited by Wanda Dressler, 287–320. Brussels: Établissements Émile Bruylant.

Stokes, Kenneth Michael. 1995. *Paradigm Lost: A Cultural and Systems Theoretical Critique of Political Economy*. Armonk, NY: M. E. Sharpe.

"The Struggle against So-Called Russophilism, or the Path to National Suicide." 1975. *Vol'noe Slovo*, nos. 17–18.

Sukachev, V. N. 1947. "Osnovy biogeotsenologii." In *Iubeleinyi sbornik, posviashchennyi 30-letiiu Velikoi Oktiabr'skoi sotsialisticheskoi revoliutsii*. Moscow-Leningrad: Akademiia Nauk SSSR.

———. 1949. "O sootnoshenii poniatii geograficheskii landshaft i biogeotsenos." *Voprosy Geografii* 16: 45–60.

———. 1961. "Obshchie printsipy i programma izucheniia tipov lesa." In *Metodicheskie ukazaniia k izucheniiu tipov lesa*, edited by V. N. Sukachev and S. B. Zonn, 9–75. Moscow: AN SSSR.

"Sukachev Vladimir Nikolaevich (1880–1967)." 2007. http://biogeographers.dvo.ru/pages/0238.htm, accessed 10/5/2014.

Suleimenov, Olzhas. 1975. *AZ i Ia: Kniga blagonamerennogo chitatelia*. Alma-Ata: Zhazushy.

Suny, Ronald Grigor. 1988. "Russian Nationalism in the Era of *Glasnost'* and *Perestroika*." *Russian Nationalism Today: Radio Liberty Research Bulletin, Special Edition* (19 December): 37–42.

———. 1998. *The Soviet Experiment: Russia, the USSR, and the Successor States*. Oxford: Oxford University Press.

———. 1999. "Provisional Stabilities: The Politics of Identities in Post-Soviet Eurasia." *International Security* 24, no. 3: 139–78.

———. 2001. "Constructing Primordialism: Old Histories for New Nations." *Journal of Modern History* 73: 862–96.

Suny, Ronald Grigor, and Terry Martin, eds. 2001. *A State of Nations: Empire and Nation-Making in the Age of Lenin and Stalin*. Oxford: Oxford University Press.

Surucu, Cengiz. 2005. "'Western in Form, Eastern in Content': Negotiating Time and Space in Post-Soviet Kazakhstan." Unpublished paper, http://www.toscca.co.uk/publications.htm, accessed 18/5/2014.

Susiluoto, I. 1982. *The Origins and Development of Systems Thinking in the Soviet Union: Political and Philosophical Controversies from Bogdanov and Bukharin to Present-Day Reevaluations*. Helsinki: Suomalainen Tiedeakatemia.

Suvorov, Vladimir. 1988. "Istoriia—nauka estestvennaia, ili vizit k professory Gumilevu." *Sel'skaia Molodezh'* 2: 44–49, http://gumilevica.kulichki.net/articles/Article66.htm, accessed 5/4/2014.

Suvortsev, Iurii. 1982. "V stile ekstaza." *Znamia* 3: 202–24.

Szporluk, Roman. 1979. "History and Russian Nationalism." *Survey* 24, no. 3 (108): 1–17.

———. 1989. "Dilemmas of Russian Nationalism." *Problems of Communism* 38, no. 4: 15–35.

Szyszman, Simon. 1970. "Découverte de la Khazarie." *Annales: Économies, Sociétés, Civilisations* 25, no. 3: 818–24.

Tagirov, Indus. 2001. "Bez tatarskogo naroda Rossiiskoe Gosdarstvo—nepolnoe." *Nezavisimaia Gazeta* (27 February), http://www.ng.ru/specfile/2001-02-27/9_people.html, accessed 3/6/2014.

Tanasov, Valentin. n.d. "Opyt superetnicheskikh kontaktov na Ukraine: Period passionarnoi depressiia fazy nadloma." http://melot.h16.ru/H-Ximera/Opit-2.htm, accessed 17/3/2014.

Taylor, Timothy. 1993. "Conversations with Leo Klejn." *Current Anthropology* 34, no. 5: 723–35.

Tchijevsky, A. L. 1971. "Physical Factors of the Historical Process." *Cycles* (January): 11–27.

Teliashov, Rakhim. 2001. *Ot indeitsev i gunnov do Zolotoi Ordy*. St. Petersburg: Sankt-Peterburgskaia Panorama.

Temirgaliev, Radik. 2007a. "Eshche raz k voprosu o mezhnatsional'nykh otnosheniiakh v Kazakhstane." *Internet-Gazeta "Zona KZ"* (9 January), http://www.zakon.kz/80676-eshhe-raz-k-voprosu-o-mezhnacionalnykh.html, accessed 3/6/2014.

——. 2007b. "Kazakhi i Gumilev." *Internet-Gazeta "Zona KZ"* 142–2939, zonakz.net/articles/20205, accessed 3/6/2014.

——. 2011. "O Gumileve." yvi.kz/community/История%20Казахстана/149128.html, accessed 8/7/2011.

Thompson, Peter. 2002. "'The Ubermensch is the Proletariat': Marx + Neitzsche = ?" *Debatte* 10, no. 2: 201–19.

Thompson, Terry L. 1989. *Ideology and Policy: The Political Uses of Doctrine in the Soviet Union*. Boulder, CO: Westview.

Tillett, Lowell. 1969. *The Great Friendship: Soviet Historians on the Non-Russian Nationalities*. Chapel Hill: University of North Carolina Press.

Timashev, S. F. n.d. "O fiziko-khimicheskoi sushchnosti passionarnykh tolchkov." http://gumilevica.kulichki.net/debate/Article08.htm, accessed 29/4/2014.

Timofeev-Resovskii, N. V. 1962. *Nekotorye problemy radiatsionnoi biogeotsenologii*. Sverdlovsk: UF AN SSSR.

Tirado, Isabel A. 1994. "Nietzschean Motifs in the Komsomol's Vanguardism." In Rosenthal, *Nietzsche and Soviet Culture*, 235–55.

Tishkov, V. A. 1992. "The Crisis in Soviet Ethnography." *Current Anthropology* 33, no. 4: 371–94.

——. 1995. "What Is Russia?: Prospects for Nation-Building." *Security Dialog* 26, no. 1: 41–54.

——. 1996. "Post-Soviet Nationalism." In *Europe's New Nationalism: States and Minorities in Conflict*, edited by Richard Caplan and John Feffer, 23–41. Oxford: Oxford University Press.

——. 1997. *Ethnicity, Nationalism, and Conflict in and after the Soviet Union: The Mind Aflame*. London: Sage.

——. 2005. "Rossiiskii narod kak evropeiskaia natsiia i ego evraziiskaia missiia." *Politicheskii Klass* 5: 73–78.

——. 2007. "Rossiiskaia natsiia i ego kritiki." In *Nationalizm v mirovoi istorii*, edited by V. A. Tishkov and V. A. Shnirel'man, 558–601. Moscow: Nauka.

——. n.d. "Etnos ili etnichnost'?" http://valerytishkov.ru/cntnt/publikacii3/publikacii/etnos_ili_.html, accessed 2/5/2014.

Titenko, Igor'. 2005. "Strategicheskaia nestabil'nost' i etno-geopolitika." *Moskva* 2: 129–55.

Titov, Alexander Sergeevich. 2005. "Lev Gumilev, Ethnogenesis and Eurasianism." PhD diss., School of Slavonic and Eastern European Studies, London University.

Tiurin, Aleksandr. 1992. "Pis'mo v redaktsiiu." *Neva* 4: 223–25.

Tol'ts, Vladimir. 2005. "Tysiacheletie Kazanii: Politicheskaia arifmetika istoricheskogo vremeni." *Radio Svoboda* (27 August), http://www.svobodanews.ru/content/article/127644.html, accessed 3/6/2014.

Toleshovich, Umirserik. 1998. "Natsional'naia bezopasnost' Respubliki Kazakhstana: 'Okna uiazvimosti.'" *Delovaia Nedelia* (11 September), http://globalteka.ru/books/doc_download/3845——.html, accessed 3/6/2014.

Tolstov, S. P. 1947. "Iz predystorii Rusi." *Sovetskaia Etnografiia*, nos. 6–7: 39–59.

——. 1948. *Drevnii Khorezm: Opyt istoriko-arkheologicheskogo issledovaniia*. Moscow: Izdanie MGU.

———. 1950. "Velikaia pobeda leninsko-stalinskoi natsional'noi politiki (k dvadtsatipi-atiletiiu natsional'nogo razmezhevaniia Srednei Azii)." *Sovetskaia Ethnografiia* 1: 3–24.

Tolz, Vera. 1996. "Forging the Nation: National Identity and Nation Building in Post-Communist Russia." *Europe-Asia Studies* 50, no. 6: 993–1022.

———. 2001. *Russia: Inventing the Nation.* London: Arnold.

Toshchenko, Zh. T. 2003. *Etnokratiia: Istoriia i sovremennost' (sotsiologicheskie ocherki).* Moscow: ROSSPEN.

Toynbee, Arnold. 1934–1961. *A Study in History.* 12 vols. Oxford: Oxford University Press.

Treisman, Daniel S. 1997. "Russia's 'Ethnic Revival': The Separatist Activism of Regional Leaders in a Postcommunist Order." *World Politics* 49, no. 2: 212–49.

Trepavlov, V. V. 2010. *Zolotaia Orda v XIV stoletii.* Moscow: Kvadriga.

Troitskii, E. S. 2003. *Russkaia etnopolitologiia.* 3 vols. Moscow: Granitsa.

Trotsky, Leon. 1971 [1924]. *Literature and Revolution.* Translated by Rose Strunsky. Ann Arbor: University of Michigan Press.

Trubetskoi, N. S. 1921a. *Evropa i chelovechestvo.* Sofia: Rossiisko-Bolgarskoe knigoizdatel'stvo.

———. 1921b. "Verkhi i nizy russkoi kul'tury." In *Iskhod v vostoku,* 86–103. Sofia: Rossiisko-Bolgarskoe knigoizdatel'stvo.

———. 1925. *Nasledie Chingiskhana: Vzgliad na russkuiu istoriiu ne s Zapada, a s Vostoka.* Berlin: Evraziiskoe Knigoizdatel'stvo.

———. 1927. "Obshcheevraziiskii natsionalizm." *Evraziiskaia khronika* 9: 24–31.

Trusov, Iu. P. 1969. "The Concept of the Noosphere." *Soviet Geography* 10: 220–37.

Tsvetaeva, Marina. 2009. *Molitva: Stikhotvoreniia.* Khar'kov: Folio.

Tsygankov, A. P. 1998. "Hard-Line Eurasianism and Russia's Contending Geopolitical Perspectives." *East European Quarterly* 32, no. 3: 315–34.

———. 2003. "Mastering Space in Eurasia: Russia's Geopolitical Thinking after the Soviet Break-up." *Communist and Post-Communist Studies* 36, no. 1 (March): 101–27.

Tsygankov, A. P., and P. A. Tsygankov. 1999. "Pluralism or Isolation of Civilizations?: Russia's Foreign Policy Discourse and the Reception of Huntington's Paradigm of the Post-Cold War World." *Geopolitics* 4, no. 3: 47–72.

———. 2005. *Rossiiskaia nauka mezhdunarodnykh otnoshenii: Novye napravleniia.* Moscow: ПЕР СЭ.

Tucker, Robert C. 1956. "Stalin and the Uses of Psychology." *World Politics* 8, no. 4: 455–83.

Turchin, Peter. 2003. *Historical Dynamics: Why States Rise and Fall.* Princeton, NJ: Princeton University Press.

Udal'tsov, A. D. 1943. "Nachal'nyi period vostochnoslavianskogo etnogeneza." *Istoricheskii Zhurnal,* nos. 11–12: 67–72.

von Uexküll, Jakob. 1920. *Staatsbiologie: Anatomie, Physiologie, Pathologie des Staates.* Berlin: Paetel.

Uiama, Tomokhiko. 2003. "Ot 'Bulgarizma' cherez 'Marrizm' k natsionalisticheskim mifam: Diskursy o Tatarskom, Chuvashskom i Bashkirskom etnogeneze." In *Novaia volna v izuchenii etnopoliticheskoi istorii Volgo-Ural'skogo regiona,* edited by Matsuzato Kimitaka, 16–51. Sapporo: Slavic Research Center.

"Ukaz Prezidenta Respubliki Kazakhstana, Nr. 2996." 1996. 23 May, http://www.ku lichki.com/~gumilev/matter/Article13.htm, accessed 3/6/2014.

Umland, Andreas. 2006. "The Soviet Union." In *World Fascism: A Historical Encyclope-dia,* edited by Cyprian P. Blamires and Paul Jackson. Santa Barbara, CA: ABC-Clio.

Ushakin, Sergei. 2005. "Zhiznennye sily russkoi tragedii: O postsovetskikh teoriiakh etnosa." *Ab Imperio* 4: 233–77.

Usmanov, M. A. 1997. "Sosedy nazyvali ikh 'tatarami.'" *Rodina*, nos. 3–4: 40–44.

"V chem sila, brat?" 2006. *Rossiiskaia Gazeta-Nedelia*, 15 December, http://www.rg.ru/2006/12/15/bodrov.html, accessed 14/7/2014.

"V prokuraturu SSSR: Otzyvy uchenykh o L. N. Gumileve." 2003. In Voronovich and Kozyreva, *Vspominaia L. N. Gumileva*, 332–36.

"V samizdate, kak v Internete, mnogo khoroshego i plokhogo." 2005. *Pravda*, 3 June, http://www.pravda.ru/culture/2005/4/9/21/19994_samizdat.html, accessed 4/5/2014.

Vakhtin, Iu. B. 2002. "Mutatsii passionarnosti L. N. Gumileva: Vozniknovenie i fenotipicheskoe proiavlenie." In *Uchenie L. N. Gumileva i sovremennost'*, edited by L. A. Verbitskaia, 213–33. St. Petersburg: SPbGU.

Valiev, A. K. 1966. *Formirovanie i razvitie sovetskoi natsional'noi intelligentsii v Srednei Azii.* Tashkent: FAN.

Van Zaichik, Khol'm. 2003. *Delo zhadnogo varvara.* Moscow: Azbuka-Klassika.

Vanderheide, Daniel. 1980. "Ethnic Significance of the Non-Black Earth Renovation Project." In *Ethnic Russia in the USSR: The Dilemma of Dominance*, edited by Edward Allworth, 218–28. New York: Pergamon.

Vaniagin, A. 1975. "Rozhdenie Nauki." *Vol'noe Slovo*, nos. 17–18: 96–119.

Varustin, L. E. 1990. "Lev Gumilev: 'Povoda dlia aresta ne daval.'" *Avrora* 11: 3–30.

Vasilii (Butylo) (Sviashch.). 2012. "Moi vstrechi s L. N. Gumilevym." In Burlaka, *Lev Gumilev: Pro et Contra*, 163–65.

Veingol'd, Iu. Iu. 1973. *Sovetskii narod: Novaia istoricheskaia obshchnost' liudei: Sotsiologicheskii ocherk.* Frunze: "Kyrgyzstan."

Veinguer, Aurora Alvarez, and Howard H. Davis. 2007. "Building a Tatar Elite: Langague and National Schooling in Kazan." *Ethnicities* 7, no. 2: 186–207.

Velikie stroiki stalinskoi epokhi: Kratkii rekomendatel'nyi ukazatel' literatury. 1950. Moscow: Biblioteka im. Lenina.

Verkhovskii, Aleksandr. 2007. "Ideinaia evolutsiia russkogo natsionalizma: 1990-e i 2000-e gody." In *Verkhi i nizy russkogo natsionalizma*, edited by A. Verkhovskii, 6–32. Moscow: Sova. http://www.polit.ru/research/2007/12/28/verhovsky.html, accessed 1/7/2014.

Vernadskii, V. I. 1926. *Biosfera.* Leningrad: NKhTI.

——. 1965. *Khimicheskoe stroenie biosfery Zemli i ee okruzheniia.* Moscow: Nauka.

——. 1978. *Zhivoe veshchestvo.* Moscow: Nauka.

——. 1994. *Zhivoe veshchestvo i biosfera.* Moscow: Nauka.

Vernadsky, George. 1961. Review of L. N. Gumilev, *Khunnu: Sredniaia Aziia v drevnie vremena* (1960). *The American Historical Review* 66, no. 3: 711–12.

Vernadsky, Vladimir I. 1998. *The Biosphere.* Translated by David B. Langmuir. New York: Copernicus/Springer Verlag.

Vernadsky, W. I. 1945. "The Biosphere and the Noösphere." *American Scientist* 33, no. 1: 1–12.

Verslius, Arthur, and Alain De Benoist. 2014. "A Conversation with Alain de Benoist." *Journal for the Study of Radicalism* 8, no. 2: 79–106.

Veselov, Arkadii. 2003. "Vesennee obostrenie evraziistvom." *Nezavisimaia Gazeta*, 21 May, http://www.ng.ru/ideas/2003-05-21/7_obostreniye.html, accessed 17/1/2014.

Vidershpan, A. V. 2004. "Istorifsofiskie idei L. N. Gumileva v kontekste razvitiia evraziistva." Aftoreferat kandidatskoi dissertatsii, Kostanaiskii Iuridicheskii Institut, Almaty.

Vinogradov, Igor'. 1995. "Zhizh' i smert' sovetskogo poniatiia 'Druzhba Narodov.'" *Cahiers du monde russe* 36, no. 4: 455–62.

Vinokurova, Ul'iana Alekseevna. 1994. *Skaz o narode Sakha*. Yatkutsk: Bichhik.

Vitebsky, P. 1990. "Yakuts." In *The Nationalities Question in the Soviet Union*, edited by Graham Smith. London: Longman.

Vladimirov, A. I. 2007. *Kontseptual'nye osnovy Natsional'noi strategii Rossii: Politicheskii aspekt*. Moscow: Nauka.

"Vnedrit' v obrazovatel'nyi protsess." 2012. *Vzgliad* (29 October), http://vz.ru/cul ture/2012/10/29/604838.html, accessed 10/7/2014.

Volodikhin, Dmitrii. 1999. "Fenomen Fol'k-Khistori." *Mezhdunarodnyi Istoricheskii Zhurnal* 5, http://scepsis.net/library/print/id_148.html, accessed 15/7/2014.

Voronovich, V. N., and M. G. Kozyreva, eds. *Vspominaia L. N. Gumileva: Vospomina-niia. Publikatsii. Issledovaniia*. St. Petersburg: Iz-vo "Rostok."

Voskanian, A. M. 1956. *O roli geograficheskoi sredy v razvitii obshchestva*. Erevan: AN Arm.SSR.

Voznesenskii, L. A. 2003. "'Mozhno, ia budu otvechat' stikhami?'" In Voronovich and Kozyreva, *Vspominaia L. N. Gumileva:*, 41–61.

"Vse svobodny: Razgovor na svobodnye temy: V studii Dmitrii Oreshkin." 2005. *Radio Svoboda* (16 October), http://archive.svoboda.org/programs/shen/2005/ shen.101605.asp, accessed 11/6/2014.

"Vtoroe nashestvie." 2007. *Isskustvo Kino*, no. 9, http://kinoart.ru/archive/2007/09/n9-article3, accessed 14/7/2014.

Vucinich, Alexander. 1988. *Darwin in Russian Thought*. Berkeley: University of California Press.

Wagner, Philip L. 1991. Review of L. N. Gumilev, *Ethnogenez i biosferea Zemli* (1989). *Geographical Review* 81, no. 2: 232–34.

Walker, Edward W. 1998. "Negotiating Autonomy: Tatarstan, Asymmetrical Federalism, and State Consolidation in Russia." In *Separatism: Democracy and Disintegration*, edited by Metta Spencer, 227–52. Lanham, MD: Rowman & Littlefield.

Weatherford, Jack. 2004. *Ghengis Khan and the Making of the Modern World*. New York: Three Rivers Press.

Weikart, Richard. 1998. *Socialist Darwinism: Evolution in German Socialist Thought from Marx to Bernstein*. San Francisco: International Scholars Publications.

Weiner, Amir. 1999a. "Nature, Nurture, and Memory in a Socialist Utopia: Delineating the Soviet Socio-Ethnic Body in the Age of Socialism." *American Historical Review* 104, no. 4: 1114–55.

———. 2002. "Nothing but Certainty." *Slavic Review* 61, no. 1: 44–53.

Weiner, Douglas R. 1982. "The Historical Origins of Soviet Environmentalism." *Environmental Review* 6, no. 2: 42–62.

———. 1984. "Community Ecology in Stalin's Russia: 'Socialist' and 'Bourgeois' Science." *Isis* 75, no. 4: 684–96.

———. 1985. "The Roots of 'Michurinism': Transformist Biology and Acclimatization as Currents in the Russian Life Sciences." *Annals of Science* 42: 243–60.

———. 1987. *Models of Nature: Conservation and Ecology in the Soviet Union*. Bloomington: Indiana University Press.

———. 1999b. *A Little Corner of Freedom: Russian Nature Protection from Stalin to Gorbachev*. Berkeley: University of California Press.

Weitz, Eric D. 2002. "Racial Politics without the Concept of Race: Reevaluating Soviet Ethnic and National Purges." *Slavic Review* 61, no. 1: 1–29.

White, Stephen. 2010. "Soviet Nostalgia and Russian Politics." *Journal of Eurasian Studies* 1: 1–9.

"Who Is Who: Mister Gumilev." 2006. *Elita Tatarstana* (January–February): 82–87, http://www.elitat.ru/index.php?link=2&st=513&type=3&lang=1, accessed 3/6/2014.

Wiederkehr, Stefan. 2007. *Die eurasische Bewegung: Wissenschaft und Politik in der russischen Emigration der Zwischenkriegszeit und im Postsowjetischen Russland.* Cologne: Boehlau.

Woll, Josephine. 1989. "Russians and Russophobes: Antisemitism on the Russian Literary Scene." *Soviet Jewish Affairs* 19, no. 3: 3–21.

"A Word to the Nation." 1971. *Survey* 17, no. 3: 191–99.

Worster, Donald. 1988. *The Ends of the Earth: Perspectives on Modern Environmental History.* Cambridge: Cambridge University Press.

Yanov, Alexander. 1978. *The Russian New Right: Right-Wing Ideologies in the Contemporary USSR.* Berkeley: Institute of International Studies, University of California.

———. 1995. *Weimar Russia and What We Can Do about It.* New York: Slovo-Word.

Yasmann, Victor. 1992. "Red Religion: An Ideology of Neo-Messianic Russian Fundamentalism." *Demokratizatsiya: The Journal of Post-Soviet Democratization* 1, no. 2: 20–39.

Yekelchyk, Serhy. 2002. "Stalinist Patriotism as Imperial Discourse: Reconciling the Ukrainian and Russsian 'Heroic Pasts,' 1939–1945." *Kritika* 3, no. 1: 51–80.

Young, George M. 2012. *The Russian Cosmists: The Esoteric Futurism of Nikolai Fedorov and His Followers.* Oxford: Oxford University Press.

Zakharov, I. A. 1999. *Kratkie ocherki po istorii genetiki.* Moscow: Bioinformservis.

Zapesotskii, A. C. 2007. "Likhachev i Gumilev: Spor o Evraziistve." In *Dmitrii Likhachev: Velikii russkii kul'turolog,* 72–90. St. Petersburg: SPbGUP.

Zapesotskii, A. C., and Iu. V. Zobnin. 2007. "Nam iasen dolgii put'?: Dmitrii Likhachev i Lev Gumilev: Diskussiia prodolzhaetsia. . . ." *Nevskoe Vremia,* 2 February.

Zardykhan, Kinaiat. 2007. "Chingiskhan byl Mongolom." *Megapolis* 39, no. 354 (8 October), http://www.megapolis.kz/show_article.php?art_id=6942, accessed 3/6/2014.

———. n.d. "Vzgliady L. N. Gumileva na voprosy obrazovaniia gosudarstvennosti u kochevykh narodov." http://bibliofond.ru/view.aspx?id=72215, accessed 3/6/2014.

Zarinov, I. Iu. 2002. "Sotsiuum—etnos—etnichnost'—natsiia—natsionalizm." *Etnograficheskoe Obozrenie* 1: 3–30.

Zdravomyslov, A. G. 1996. *Mezhnatsional'nye konflikty v postsovetskom prostranstve.* Moscow: Aspekt Press.

Zelinskii, A. N. 2012. "Pamiati uchitelia." In Burlaka, *Lev Gumilev: Pro et Contra,* 96–107.

Zhade, Z. A. 2006. "Etnicheskoe prostranstvo kak faktor geopolitiki." *Vestnik Adygeiskogo Gosudarstvennogo Universiteta* 3: 114–21.

Zhirinovskii, V. V. 1993. *Poslednyi brosok na iug.* Moscow: Pisatel'.

———. 1998. *Geopolitika i russkii vopros.* Moscow: Geleriia.

———. 2001a. "Etnogeopolitika." In *Utomlennaia planeta,* 288–305. Moscow: LDPR.

———. 2001b. *Utomlennaia planeta.* Moscow: LDPR.

———. 2014. *Vostochno-khristianskaia pravoslavnaia tsivilizatsiia: Uchebnoe posobie.* Moscow: LDPR.

Zhmurov, V. A. 2012. *Bol'shaia entsiklopediia po psikhiatrii.* 2nd ed. http://vocabulary.ru/dictionary/978/word/pasionarnost, accessed 12/2/2014.

Zholdasbekov, M. Zh. 2001. "Mezhdunarodno-predstavitel'skaia missiia Evraziiskogo Gosudarstvennogo Universiteta." In *Evraziiskii Universitet i mir: Vzglaid v budushchee*, 4–31. Astana: Izd-vo EGU.

———. 2003. "Evraziistvo i Kazakhstan." In Zholdasbekov, *Evraziistvo i Kazakhstan*, 1: 5–10.

Zholdasbekov, M. Zh., and Abai Kairzhanov. 2002. *Evraziiskaia teoriia L. N. Gumileva*. Astana: n.p.

Zhuralev, V. A., and N. S. Ladyzhets. 2003. "Passionarnyi universitetskii menedzhment." *Universitetskoe Upravlenie: Praktika i Analiz* 1, no. 24: 4–8.

Ziegler, Charles E. 1985. "Soviet Images of the Environment." *British Journal of Political Science* 15, no. 3: 365–80.

Zil'bert, Maks M. 1994. *Evrei i proletarskaia revoliutsiia: Po prochtenii L. N. Gumileva*. Moscow: n.p.

———. 2000. "Fenomen ashkenazskikh evreev." http://zhurnal.lib.ru/z/zilxbert_m_m/ ashktextdoc.shtml, accessed 11/7/2014.

Zimina, I. S. 2007. "Razvitie passionarnykh kachestv u detei kak sredstvo preodoleniia leni, apatii, boleznennosti." *Psikhologiia: Perm'* 11: 14–17.

Ziuganov, G. A. 1993. *Drama Vlasti: Stranitsy politicheskoi avtobiografii*. Moscow: Paleia.

———. 1995. *Rossiia i sovremennyi mir*. Moscow: Obozrevatel'.

———. 1997. *Uroki Zhizni*. Moscow: Sankt-Peterburgskaia Tipografiia.

———. 2006. "Russian Socialism: An Answer to the Russian Question." *Pravda*, 6 April, http://cprf.info/news/articles/we/40891.html, accessed 9/1/2014.

Zubok, Vladislav. 2011. *Zhivago's Children: The Last Russian Intelligentsia*. Cambridge, MA: Belknap Press.

Zverev, Alexei. 2002. "'The Patience of a Nation Is Measured in Centuries': National Revival in Tatarstan and Historiography." In *Secession, History and the Social Sciences*, edited by Bruno Coppieters and Michel Huysseune, 69–87. Brussels: VUB Brussels University Press.

Index

Abramovich, Roman, 269
Abrosov, V. N., 84
Acmatic phase (*peregrev*), in ethnogenesis
  life cycle, 57, 93–94, 107
Adaptation
  environment and, 58
  ethnies and, 34–42
Affirmative action policies, of Soviet
  Union, 148, 178, 281
Afghanistan, Soviet invasion of, 114n141
Akaev, Askar Akaevich, 81n2, 224n67, 248
Akhmatova, Anna Andreevna, 103, 200,
  200n116, 217
  death of, 12
  Gumilev and, 7, 9, 10, 11–13, 12n33, 14
  poetry of, 9, 12, 16
  Zhdanov's denunciation of, 10
Alash National Freedom Party
  (Kazakhstan), 285
Albigensianism (Catharism), in medieval
  France, 75
Aleksandrov, Aleksandr Danilovich,
  15, 16
Alekseev, Nikolai Nikolaevich, 51n43
Aleksin, A. A., 84
Alimov, Igor' Aleksandrovich, 241n141
Also sprach Zarathustra (Nietzsche),
  124–25
Alternative history, 82
  in post-Soviet popular culture, 241–43
"Americanoid" superethnos, 71
Ancient Russia and the Great Steppe
  (Gumilev), 188
Annales school, 135, 136
Annihilation (*annigiliatsiia*), chimera
  and, 79–80
Anthropogenic succession, 128
Anti-Semitism. *See* Jews
Antisystem (*antisistema*)
  chimera as, 73–75
  ethical and moral dimensions of,
  78–80
Jews and, 75–77, 188, 192

post-Soviet comparison with chimeras,
  260–61
post-Soviet usage of, 261–65
Project Khazaria and, 267
Russian ethno-nationalism and,
  186–87
Anuchin, Vsevolod Aleksandrovich, 134,
  137n99, 140, 143–44
Arens, Anna Evgen'evna, 200, 200n116
Artamonov, Mikhail Illarionovich, 8, 15,
  85, 86n24, 104, 151, 175
Ascendancy phase (*pod"em*), in
  ethnogenesis life cycle, 57, 107
Ashkenazi Jews, 89n37, 270
Assimilation (*assimiliatsiia*), as category
  of ethnic interaction, 60
Astaf'ef, Viktor Petrovich, 184
Astaurov, Boris L'vovich, 51
Atabek, Aron Kabyshevich, 285–86
Auguste de Thou, Jacques, 96n70
Avtokhtonnost' (autochthony), 152–54,
  258, 278, 285, 286, 305, 311

Babylon, 76
Baigushev, Aleksandr Innokent'evich,
  192, 195, 271–72
Baikal, Lake, 30, 133, 184
Bakaev, Khasan, 315–16
Balashov, Dmitrii Mikhailovich, 184–85,
  201, 201n119, 205, 221, 226, 226n76,
  271–72
Basov, Nikolai Gennadievich, 168
Batu (Mongol khan), 94–96, 98
Batyi: A Russian Tsar (Penzev), 243
Begich, Murza, 100
Behavioral stereotype (*stereotip
  povedeniia*)
  Bromlei and, 173
  cosmic radiation and mutations,
  53–54
  ecological niche and, 40
  as embodiment of ethnicity, 24–26
  environment and, 137

Behavioral stereotype *(continued)*
  ethnogenesis and, 39, 55
  ethnos and natural environment
    and, 249
  ethnos and superethnos and, 66–67
  heredity and, 32
  Kazakhstan and, 283
  Russian ethnos and, 232
  superethnos and, 65
  Tatars and, 291–92
Behavioral syndrome, annihilation and,
    79–80
Beliaev-Gintovt, Aleksei Iure'vich, 240–41
Berg, Lev Semenovich, 31n42, 36, 37, 38,
    38n78, 45, 54n61, 58
Berg, Raisa L'vovna, 30, 31n42, 50n42,
    54n61
Beria, Lavrentii, 256n73
Berlin, Isaiah, 10, 10n25
Bernshtam, Aleksandr Natanovich,
    14n44, 104, 105
Bertalanfi, Ludwig von, 25n12
Biocenosis, 35, 37, 126. *See also*
    Ecological niche
Biogeocenosis, 35–37, 45–46, 186
Biogeochemical energy, ethnogenesis and,
    47–49, 55–56
Biogeosphere, 46n16
Biologism *(biologizm)*, 33, 35, 174, 245
Biopolitics
  ethnos theory and, 5–6
  Gumilev's post-Soviet legacy and,
    244–46
  origin of conception of, 5
Biosphere concept, 46–48
  principles of, 48–49
Black Hundreds, 181
Black Legend *(Chernaia Legenda)*, 96–97,
    96n70, 164–65, 167, 222n63, 242,
    279, 288. *See also Leyenda Negra*
Blok, Alexandr Aleksandrovich, 103–4
Blue Horde (Mongol Empire), 99, 100
Blut-und-Boden doctrines (Nazi
    Germany), 152, 152n34
Bodrov, Sergei Vladimirovich, 240
Bogdanov, Aleksandr, 25n12, 45
Bogomilstvo (Gnostic Balkan sect), 76
Bolshevism, 85, 121, 124, 147–48, 156
  Gumilev's family and, 181, 309
  Jews and, 111–12, 192, 263–64, 271
  revolution and ethnogenesis life cycle,
    108, 261

Borisov, Andrei Savvich, 240,
    240n137, 300
Borisov, Nikolai Sergeevich, 196
Borodai, Aleksandr Iur'evich, 13–14,
    13n37, 111–13, 181, 253, 314
Borodai, Iurii Mefod'evich, 170–71, 184,
    185–87, 253, 257n79, 271
Bratstvo (Soviet nationalities
    campaign), 154
Breakdown *(nadlom)* phase. *See Nadlom*
    (breakdown) phase
Brezhnev, Leonid, 158, 159, 177
Brodsky, Joseph, 12, 14n42
Bromlei, Iulian Vladimirovich, 160,
    161, 171–76, 172n122, 173n127,
    174n137
Brudny, Yitzhak M., 197, 201
Bruski (Panferov), 122
Buddhism, 69, 75
Bukharin, Nikolai Ivanovich, 45
Byzantine superetnos, 70–71
Byzantium, 63, 69, 86, 87, 92, 99, 109, 202

Canada, 259, 261
Capitalism, association with nationalism,
    146–47
Catherine the Great, 290
Center for Mathematical Modeling, at
    Omsk State University, 247–48
Chaadaev, Petr Iakovlevich, 203
Chagall, Marc, 271
Chavez, Hugo, 248
Chechen crisis, 315–16
*Chemical Structure of the Earth's
    Atmosphere* (Vernadskii), 48
Chernaia Legenda. See Black Legend
Chimera. *See* Ethnic chimeras
"Chimerica"/*Khimerika*, 261n97
China, 55, 82, 261n97
  as superetnos or civilization, 69, 255
  viewed as hostile, 70, 90, 113, 113n140,
    156, 180, 182
Chivilikhin, Vladimir Alekseevich, 184,
    197–98, 201, 205
Chizhevskii, Aleksandr Leonidovich,
    47–48, 48n26, 134
Chkalov, Valerii, 122
Christianity, Christians, 63, 69, 77, 87, 91,
    200, 214
  Olga's conversion to, 92
  Russian history and, 94, 98, 99, 103,
    107, 109, 201

Circumpolar superethnos, 65, 70, 71, 251
Civilizations, superethnies and, 68–71
Clash of Civilizations (Huntington), 68–69
Climate. *See* Ecological history
Cochin, Augustin, 188
Collectivism
  new Soviet person and, 126–28
  Soviet superhero and tension with vanguardism, 123
Collisions (*kollizii*), between superethnies, 67, 69
Common cause (*obshchee delo*), of humanity, 118, 124, 128–29
Communism, 159, 221
  as antisystem, 231, 231n98
  hostility toward West, 211, 213–14
  Jews and, 263
  nationhood and, 146, 158
Complementarity (*komplimentarnost'*), 2, 223, 295, 298
  ethnic interaction and, 61–62, 71
  ethno-geopolitics and, 254, 259
  Kazakhstan and, 278
  Sakha-Yakutia and, 298
  Tatars and, 293–95
Conceptual Foundations of Russia's National Strategy, The (Vladimirov), 253
Consortium (*konsortiia*), ethnic hierarchy and, 62–63, 66
Conviction (*konviksiia*), ethnic hierarchy and, 62–63
Cosmic radiation, ethnogenesis and, 44–49, 46n16, 52–56, 58, 75, 127
Cosmism, 118, 132n77
Cossacks, 63, 181
Council of Lyons, 94
Crimea, 100, 157–58

Danilevskii, Nikolai Iakovlevich, 68, 70
Darré, Walther, 152, 152n34
Davidenkov, Nikolai, 49
de Benoist, Alain, 313
Decembrists, 108, 261
Degeneration (*vyrozhdenie*), in ethnogenesis life cycle, 57, 99, 100, 108, 180–81, 203, 267
Deianie (domain of deliberate activity), 78–80
Den', 220, 263
Derzhavin, Nikolai Sevast'ianovich, 151

Dialectical materialism, 138–39, 140, 142
Dialectics of Nature (Engels), 56n66, 119
Discovery of Khazaria (Gumilev), 266–67
Dmitrii Ivanovich ("Donskoi"), 100–101
Doctors' Plot (1953), 85, 113, 187
Dokuchaev, Vasilii Vasil'vich, 35–37, 46
Dominanty, ethno-cultural, 66–67, 69, 213, 238
Dostoevsky, Feodor, 203, 238
Drevnie Tiurki (Gumilev), 145
Druzhba narodov (friendship of the peoples)
  contemporary significance of, 307
  differs from *sovetskii narod*, 158–59
  empire savers and, 210–12
  Gumilev and, 165, 165–66, 165n96, 167, 195, 223
  neo-Eurasianism and, 211, 223
  Sakha-Yakutia and, 298
  Stalinist doctrine of, 154–56, 158–59, 162–64, 166, 307
Dugin, Aleksandr Gel'evich, 240, 270, 277n23, 308
  Gumilevian denunciation of, 234, 234n114
  Gumilev and, 220, 221
  Kazakhstan and, 282
  on Khakimov, 295n119
  Putin and, 235, 236–39
  Russian ethnos and, 227–31
  Shishkin on, 234
Dzerzhinskii, Feliks, 111

Ecological history, Khazaria and, 84–90
Ecological niche, 35, 40, 49, 58, 64–65, 79, 186, 249–50
  ethnic settlement in Siberia and, 61, 302
  Jews and chimeras, 42, 72–73, 76, 88, 270–71
  Kazakhstan and, 279, 286
  Tatars and, 291, 301–2
  see also Biocenosis
Ecology, science of, 35–37, 133–34
Ecology of ethnicity
  antisystems and, 74–75
  as non-racialist legitimation for social exclusion, 265, 284–86
  chimeras and, 260–61, 265, 270
  contemporary significance of, 312–13
  Dugin and, 228
  Gumilev's theory of, 29, 34–42, 126–27

Ecology of ethnicity *(continued)*
Kazakhstan and, 279, 284
Tatars and, 292–93
Yakuts and, 301–2, 313
Economic geography, 120, 134
Edinaia geografiia (unified geography)
concept, of Anuchin, 134, 144–45
Efimenko, Petr Petrovich, 151
Efremov, Iurii Konstantinovich,
136–37, 143
Ehrenburg, Ilya Grigor'evich, 11
Einstein, Albert, 2, 4, 300
Élan vital, 124, 223, 302
El'zon, Mikhail Davidovich, 14
Empire savers
Gumilev's fame and, 211–13
perestroika and, 209–10, 212–18
principle concerns of, 210–11
Yeltsin and, 218–22
Endogamy
Bromlei and, 174, 174n137
Islam and undermining of ethnos, 99
Kazakhstan and, 283
protection of ethnos and, 29–30,
34, 183
Russian ethno-nationals and, 109–10,
181–83
Tatars and, 291–92
see also Metisatsiia (intermarriage/
mixing)
Enemies of the people, 149, 165n94
Energetics/energeticism
(*energetika/energetizm*), 45–46
Energiia (Gladkov), 122
Engels, Friedrich, 56n66, 119, 125
Enikeev, Gali Rashitovich, 289, 291,
296–97
Entropy, ethnogenesis life cycle and, 56,
57–58, 68n43, 129, 132
Environmental destruction
Gumilev condemns Soviet, 135
linked to high levels of *passionarnost'*,
131–33
Russian nationalists condemn Soviet,
170, 182–87
Environmental history, 84–85
Environmentalism
adaptation and ethnicity, 34–42
annihilation and, 79–80
Borodia and, 170
history adapted to, 135
neo-Stalinism and, 139–40

Sakha-Yakutia and
ethno-environmental history,
300–304
transcending of Stalinist categories
and, 133–39
Ermolaev, Viacheslav, 215n21, 308n2
Ethnic chimeras, 42, 71–72
annihilation and, 79–80
antisystems compared, 260–61
contemporary significance of, 315
enemy nations as, 165, 165n94
ethical and moral dimensions of,
78–80
ethnogenetic dysfunctionality of,
73–75
Jews as, 75–77, 83, 85–90, 242
parasitic comparisons, 72–73
post-Soviet usage of, 260–65
Russian ethno-nationalism and
Borodai, 186
used in neo-Eurasianism era, 223
Ethnic divergence, 41–42, 131–32
Ethnic essentialism, 149–50, 152, 155,
157, 161–62, 161n83, 164, 244
hyperessentialism, 166–67
Tatarstan and, 291–97, 295n119
Ethnic field concept (*etnicheskoe pole*), 34,
57, 247, 267, 315–16
contemporary significance of, 315–16
Ethnic geography, 251–52
Ethnic interaction
categories of, 60–62, 71
chimera and, 71–75
ethnic hierarchy and, 62–67, 173, 246,
258–59
ethnosphere as moral domain, 78–80
Jews as chimera, 75–77
superethnos and civilizations, 68–71
Ethnicity, nature of
ethnos as natural formation, 23–29
genetics and, 29–33
geography and adaptation and, 34–42
neo-Stalinism and, 141
race dismissed from, 33–34, 149–50
Ethnic space (*etnicheskoe
prostranstvo*), 250
political space and, 70, 254–57
Ethnocenosis, 37, 58, 260. *See also*
Biocenosis
Ethno-ecology, 72–73, 76, 169, 178,
184, 250–51, 250n42, 315. *See also*
Environmentalism

Ethnogenesis (*etnogenez*), 11n29, 15, 17,
    23, 31, 38–39
  contemporary significance of, 311
  cosmic energy sources of, 44–49,
    46n16, 52–56, 58, 75, 127
  ethno-geopolitics and, 253–55
  Gumilev's uses of term, 54
  Kazakhstan and, 278–80
  as life cycle, 24, 54–59, 254–55
  as natural law, 55
  origin of use of term, 151
  origins of theory of, 43–44
  radiation mutogenesis and mechanics
    of, 49–54
  Stalinism and, 15o–54
  Tatars on timeline of, 294–96
  Yakuts and, 301, 304–5
Ethnogenesis and the Earth's Biosphere
    (Gumilev), 38n78, 144, 145, 163,
    174, 185–86, 222n63, 300
Ethnogenics, 151
Ethnogeny, 151
Ethno-geopolitics, post–Soviet Union,
    253–55
  Russians as *etnosistema*, 256–60
Ethnography
  ethnology differs from, 246
  redefined in 1930, 150–51
Ethnology (*etnologiia*), post-Soviet, 246
Ethno-nationalism, 4–5, 151–52,
    158, 162
  contemporary significance of, 310–11
  Kazakhstan and, 280–83, 282n55
  Stalin and, 154–57
  see also Russian nationalism
Ethno-naturalism, 116–17, 162–67
  Tatarstan and, 291–97, 295n119
Ethno-pluralism, 313
Ethnos
  as closed system, 56
  contemporary significance of, 311
  distinguished from *natsiia*, 224,
    257n79
  Dugin and Russian, 227–31
  early use of term, 160
  ethnic hierarchy and, 63–64
  nationality debates after Stalin and,
    161–62
  as natural, not social, formation,
    23–29
  shaped by natural-geographical
    world, 126

  as social organism, 168
  superethnos differences, 66–67
  superethnos similarities, 63–64, 65–66
  21st century social organization and,
    244–45
Ethnos and Ethnography (Bromlei), 172
Ethno-social organism, of Bromlei, 173,
    175, 176
Ethnosphere, 24, 48, 64n23, 72
  as moral domain, 78–80
  sociosphere and, 141–43
"Ethnos theory"
  post-Soviet revival of interest in, 245
  Soviet, 159–63
Ethno-territoriality
  Israel and, 271
  Kazakhstan and, 282–86
  post–Soviet Union, 249–52, 260
  Stalin and federalization of homelands,
    148, 152, 153
Etnodominanta, in ethnic hierarchy,
    258–60
Etnogenez science-fiction series, 241
Etnos
  gosudarstvo and, 6
  obshchestvo and, 141
Etnosistema, 257n79
  post-Soviet ethno-politics and,
    257–60
ETNOS software package, 248
Eugenics in the USSR, 31n44, 150
Eurasianism, 51, 51n43
  contemporary significance of,
    308–10
  Gumilev and Russian history, 82–85,
    103–7
  Gumilev's ethno-naturalism and,
    166–67
  Russian nationalism and, 195–96,
    198–99, 199n11, 201–5
  see also Neo-Eurasianism
Eurasian Symphony, The (Van Zaichik),
    241, 241n141
Eurasian Union
  Nazarbaev's vision of, 275–76
  Putin and, 237, 238–39
Europe and Humankind (Trubetskoi),
    68, 202
European New Right, 313, 313n14
Everstov, Mikhail Il'ich, 303, 303n153,
    304–5
Exogamy. *See Metisatsiia*

Fascism, 122, 219
  Gershtein and prediction about, 30n40
  Gumilev's theories and, 170, 197–98,
    219–20, 311–12
  Russian émigrés and, 150n22
Federal Law 309, in Russia, 296–97
Fedorov, Nikolai Fedorovich, 118, 129,
    132n77
Ferguson, Niall, 261n97
Filippova, Elena, 245–46
Filosofiia obshchego dela (Fedorov), 129
Final Thrust to the South, The
    (Zhirinovskii), 256
First Nations movement, 311n11
Following the Traces of the "Black Legend"
    (Enikeev), 289
Fomenko, Anatolii Timofeevich, 242–43
Foucault, Michel, 5
France, 63, 135, 136, 149
Frankfurter Allgemeine Zeitung, 219–20
Freemasons, 108, 188
Friendship of the peoples. *See Druzhba
    narodov*
Fusion. *See Sliianie*

Gemeinwesen (Marx), 27
Genafond. See Gene pool
Gene pool, 30, 33, 52, 174, 241, 264, 284
Genetics
  ethnos and, 29–33
  race and, 312
  Soviet ecology movement and, 134
Genghis Khan, 53, 63, 94, 100, 103, 104,
    106, 295, 299
Geographical determinism, 169–70,
    170n112, 198
Geographical materialism, 119–20, 169
Geography, 15n46
  adaptation and ethnicity, 34–42
  ethnic geography, 251–52
  ethnogenesis and, 152–54
  Stalinist division of, 120, 134
  superethnos and, 65–66
  in U.S., 136–37, 170
*Geography of the Ethnos in the Historical
    Period, The* (Gumilev), 222n63
Geopolitik (inter-war German
    geopolitics), 170, 174, 219,
Geopolitics and the Russian Question
    (Zhirinoskii), 256, 256n73
German Ideology, The (Marx), 141

Gershtein, Emma Grigor'evna, 9, 9n18,
    11, 12, 12n33, 30n40
Gladkov, Fedor, 122
Gnosticism, as example of antisystem,
    75, 108
Gobineau, Autur de, 169
God-building (*bogostroitel'stvo*)
    movement, 117–18
Göktürk Khaganates, 15, 16, 17, 82, 87–88
Golden Horde, 83, 94–95, 167, 236
  Russian nationalists and Gumilev's
    account of, 192–98, 202
  Russian alliance with, 94–103, 202,
    204, 236, 242–43
  Kazakh lineage and, 279, 282
  Sakha-Yakutia and, 299–300
  Tatars and, 288–90, 294–95, 294n113
Gorbachev, Mikhail, 18, 135, 209–10,
    213, 217
Gorkii, Maksim, 45
Goryshin, Gleb Aleksandrovich, 184
Gracheva, Tat'iana Vasil'evna,
    267–68, 270
Graham, Loren, 4, 18n52, 139, 171n18
Great Soviet Encyclopedia, 121, 140, 158
"Great Stalin Plan for the Transformation
    of Nature," 120–21
Gregory IX, pope, 94
Grekov, Boris Dmitrievich, 8, 151
Grinnell, Joseph, 40n91
Grubiian, Matvei Mikhailovich, 14n39
Grumm-Grzhimailo, Gregorii Efimovich,
    84n15
Gumilev, Lev Nikolaevich
  accused of Zionism, 196–200
  arrests and sentencing to gulag, 9–10,
    11–13, 13n36
  centenary of birth of, 3, 239, 277, 306
  childhood of, 6–7
  contemporary significance of, 2–6,
    238–39, 306–16
  death of, 18–19, 215n22, 219
  education and dissertations, 7–9, 10,
    15–16, 17
  post-gulag professional life and
    reputation, 15–18
  Putin on, 236, 239
  theories of, generally, 3–4
  in post-Soviet popular culture, 240–43
Gumilev, Nikolai Stepanovich, 6–7, 8, 124
Gumileva, Natal'ia Viktorovna, 7, 113

Günther, Hans F. K., 312
Guts, Aleksandr Konstantinovich, 247n26

Haushofer, Karl, 170
Hermitage Museum, 8, 15
Herodotus, 2, 151, 263
Herzl, Theodor, 199
Hierarchy, of ethnic systems, 62–67, 173,
    246, 258–59
"Highlander in the Kremlin, The"
    (Mandel'sham), 9
Hirsch, Francine, 147
Histoire du climat depuis l'an mil (Le Roy
    Ladurie), 135
Historical materialism, 138–39, 142–43
Hitler, Adolf, 200, 264, 267, 316
Holy Russia against Khazaria
    (Gracheva), 267
Hrushevs'kyi, Mykhailo Serhiiovych,
    198
Huntington, Samuel, 68–69, 253–54,
    314n20
Hyperethnos (giperetnos), 67,
    226–27, 238

Iakubovskii, Aleksandr Iur'evich, 8
Iavlenie (worldly natural phenomena),
    78–80
Iazov, Dmitrii Timofeevich, 218
Ibarruri, Dolores (La Pasionaria), 125
Ierarcheskaia sopodchinennost', ethnic
    hierarchy and, 62, 64
Igor', Varangian prince, 92
Igor Svyatoslavich, prince, 97
Imperial Crown of the Golden Horde, The
    (Enikeev), 289
Incubation phase, in ethnogenesis life
    cycle, 57, 101, 279
Inertia phase, in ethnogenesis life cycle,
    56–57, 91, 93, 126, 213
Innocent IV, pope, 94
Intermarriage. See Metisatsiia
Internal passport, in Soviet Union, 149,
    158, 310–11
Internationalism, 5, 165n, 211, 276,
    313–14. See also Ethno-geopolitics,
    post–Soviet Union
International relations. See Ethno-
    geopolitics, post–Soviet Union
Invisible Khazaria: The Algorithms of
    Geopolitics and the Strategies of

Secret Wars behind the Scene Globally
    (Gracheva), 267
Iskhakov, Damir Mavliaveevich, 288, 290
Islam, 87, 204, 262, 289–90
    Gumilev's negative attitude
        toward, 249
    Khazars and, 89, 266
    Lysenko sees as positive choice for
        Russia's future, 269–70
    recognized as civilization, 55, 69–70
    Russian history and, 97, 99, 102
    Tatars and, 293
Islamic superethnos, 71, 109, 255
Ismailism (branch of Shi'a Islam), 75
Israel. See Jews; Zionism
Istishkhad (Islamic doctrine of
    martyrdom) and passionarnost', 249
Itil (capital of Khazaria), 84, 86, 88, 93
Its, Rudol'f Ferdinandovich, 163
Ivan I, prince, 102
Ivan the Terrible, 107
Izmailov, Iskander Lerunovich, 294n113

Jahweh, 77
Jaspers, Karl, 75
Jews
    Borodai dismisses as traitors, 181
    as ethnic chimera in Russian history,
        75–77, 83, 85–90, 242
    ethnic interaction and, 71
    Eurasian history and, 83
    Gumilev's anti-Semitism and, 13–15,
        14nn39, 42
    Gumilev's contemporary significance
        and, 312, 315–16
    as passionary people, 248–49
    as post-Soviet chimera and antisystem,
        262–65
    post-Soviet era and assimilation, 271–72
    Russian nationalism and "scientific"
        justification of anti-Semitism,
        187–92
    Soviet Union and, 110–14
    Stalin's campaign against rootless
        cosmopolitanism, 76, 85,
        113n144, 187
    as superethnos, 71, 76
Juderías y Loyot, Julián, 96n70

Kabbalah, 77
Kak zakaialas' stal' (Ostrovskii), 122

Kalesnik, Stanislav Vikent'evich, 140–41,
  144–45, 144n134
Karaite Judaism (Karaism), 87–88
Kargalov, Vadim Viktorovich, 188
Kazakhstan, 274, 275–86
  contemporary Eurasianism in,
    275–76, 310
  ethnogenesis and, 278–80
  ethno-nationalism and, 280–83,
    282n55, 315
  ethno-territoriality and homeland
    rights in, 282–86
  Eurasianism and, 275–78
  Gumilev honored in, 3, 276–78
  Gumilev's works stimulating Kazakh
    nationalism in, 274
  Putin and, 235–36, 237, 276
Kazakhizatsiia, 276, 281, 284
Kedrov, Bonifatii Mikhailovich, 171n118
KGB, 16, 210, 218, 235
Khabibullin, Musagit Mudarisovich, 274
Khakimov, Rafael Sibgatovich, 287,
  290–95, 295n119
Khazaria, 15, 82, 242,
  as classical chimera, 86–90, 267, 271
  environmental history of, 83–85, 135,
    136,
  Gumilev's narrative of ancient Russia's
    relations with, 90–93
  "Khazar/Jewish yoke", 189, 191, 267
  post-Soviet views of, 263, 266–72
  Russian nationalists in USSR and,
    188–92, 196
  Soviet historiography on, 85–86
  USSR as "Sovetskaia Khazaria,"
    110–11, 113n144
Khinshtein, Aleksandr Evseevich, 248–49
Khrushchev, Nikita Sergeevich, 135,
  157–59, 192
Kibasova, Galina Petrovna, 250
Kievan Rus', 85, 91–95, 97, 101–2, 107,
  191, 194, 201, 203, 290
Kingsblood Royal (Lewis), 30
Kipling, Rudyard, 7
Kiuner, Nikolai Vasil'evich, 8, 151
Kjellén, Rudolf, 5
Klein, Lev Samuelovich, 14, 174n137, 200
Kliuev, Nikolai Alekseevich, 9
Klychkov, Sergei Antonovich, 8, 9n17
Koestler, Arthur, 89n37
Kommunist (journal), 218

Komplimentarnost'. See Complementarity
Konstantinov, Fedor Vasel'evich, 140
Korennost'. See Avtokhtonnost'
Kozhinov, Vadim Valerianovich, 190–92,
  191n70, 201–5
Kozlov, Viktor Ivanovich, 168–73,
  169n108, 250n42
Kozyrev, Nikolai Aleksandrovich, 10,
  44, 44n3
"Krivaia Gumileva" ("Gumilev's Graph"),
  57n69, 304
Kulikovo, Battle of, 100, 101–2, 106,
  167, 194, 194–95, 197, 201–3, 228,
  236n123
Kulturboden concept, of Penck, 153
Kuz'min, Apollon Grigor'evich,
  50n42, 197–200, 199nn111, 113,
  200nn116,117, 201, 205, 222n63

Lamanskii, Vladimir Ivanovich, 68
Lamarckian environmentalism, 54n61
"Landscape and Ethnos" (Gumilev),
  135, 168
Landscape zone, 36, 39–41, 58
  superethnies and, 65–66
Laruelle, Marlene, 156n50, 309
Lattimore, Owen, 84n15
Lavrov, Sergei Borisovich, 11, 108n121,
  165n96
Lazarenko, Il'ia Viktorovich, 267
Lebensraum (zhiznennoe prostranstvo),
  232, 256–57
Lenin, Vladimir, 111, 123, 140–41, 146, 148
Leningrad State University, 10, 15, 17,
  30–31, 137–38
Leont'ev, Konstantin Nikolaevich, 68
Leont'ev, Mikhail, 306
Le Roy Ladurie, Emmanuel, 135, 141
Lev Gumilev Center, 3, 309–10
Lev Gumilev Eurasian National
  University, 236, 277, 278
Levitan, Isaak, 271
Lewis, Sinclair, 30
Leyenda Negra, 96n70. See also Black
  Legend
Likhachev, Dmitrii Sergeevich, 97, 136,
  136n96, 179, 190, 190n66, 194, 201
"Living matter" of the universe. See
  Zhivoe veshchestv
Lobashev, Mikhail Efimovich, 31–32,
  31n43, 32n48, 34, 49–50

Losev, Aleksei Fedorovich, 185
Luginov, Nikolai Alekseevich, 240n137, 298–300
Luk"ianov, Anatolii Ivanovich, 217
Lunacharskii, Anatolii Vasil'evich, 45
Lysenko, Nikolai, 269, 270
Lysenko, Trofim Denisovich, 30, 31, 121, 134, 147

Malinovskii, Aleksandr Aleksandrovich, 25, 25n12, 30, 54n61
Malye narody (indigenous peoples of the Russian North and Siberia), 71, 250–52, 311, 313
   Reservations proposed for, 252, 252n53
Malyi narod (pejorative designation for "foreign" ethnies)
   anti-Semitism and, 187–88
   antisystems and, 260, 263–65, 267
Mamai, 99–102
Mandels'tam, Osip Emilevich, 8–9, 16
Manicheism, 75, 82, 113
Mantovani, Bruno, 3
Marr, Nikolai Iakovlevich, 151
Marx, Karl, 3, 4, 26–27, 219
Marxism, 17, 18, 268, 308–10, 187, 269
   Gumilev's Eurasianism as a replacement for, 16, 18, 44, 210, 211, 218, 219, 221, 222, 239, 308
   Gumilev's theories and, 26–27, 112, 125, 138–39, 141–43, 164, 171
   Soviet concepts of ethnicity and, 26, 146, 147, 148, 149, 159–61, 168–69, 173, 310, 311,
   Soviet views of nature and, 117–20, 140
Marxism-Leninism, 159, 169, 218–19
Mavrodin, Vladimir Vasil'evich, 8, 151, 156, 166
Mazdaism (Zoroastrian sect), 75
Medinskii, Vladimir Rostislavovich, 241
Melkii Bes (Sologub), 13
Mel'nikova, Svetlana, 182–83
Memorial (*homeostasis*) phase, in ethnogenesis life cycle, 57, 59, 93, 251
Mendeleev, Dmitrii Ivanovich, 45
Mestorazvitie (topogenesis), 106, 249
Metaethnos, 161, 163–64, 173, 175, 176, 261

Metisatsiia (intermarriage/mixing), 30, 33–34, 228
   Borodai and, 170, 186
   as category of ethnic interaction, 60
   Golden Horde and, 102
   Jews and, 77, 88, 110
   in Soviet Union, 180–81, 252
   superethnies and, 64–65, 67
   see also Endogamy
Mezhudnarodnaia Zhizn', 218
MGIMO, 239
Michurin, Ivan Vladimirovich, 120–22
Migration/emigration, consequences to ethnos, 41–42, 72
Mikhalkov, Nikita Sergeevich, 240
Minnikhanov, Rustam Nurgalievich, 288
Mishchenko, Maksim Nikolaevich, 239, 309
Mishnah, 87
Ministry of Foreign Affairs, interest in Gumilev, 218, 239
Mladshii Syn (Balashov), 201
Molodaia Gvardiia, 177, 184, 189
Molodkin, Andrei, 240–41
Mongolia, 40, 82, 165n96, 216, 240
Mongol empire, 15, 63, 104, 241, 275, 282, 299–300
   mongolskoe igo, 106, 167, 189, 191, 194, 199
   Russians themselves to blame for Mongol brutality, 96, 101
   see also Golden Horde
Mongol (film), 240
Monomakh, Vladimir, 110
Morozov, Georgii Fedorovich, 35
Moscow in 50 Years' Time (Zinov'ev), 181
Mstislav of Chernigov, 110
Muller, Herman J., 49–50
Multiethnic nation (*mnogonarodnaia natsiia*)
   of Kazakhstanis, 276
   neo-Eurasianism and, 223, 226, 226n7
Multinational individual (*mnogonarodnaia lichnost'*), neo-Eurasianism and, 69, 216, 223
Muslims, 69, 91, 269
Mutagenesis, 31, 49–52, 53, 55
Mutual dependency (*obratnaia zavisimost'*), 35, 58
Mutual interaction (*vzaimodeistvie*), 24, 58

Nadlom (breakdown) phase, of
    ethnogenesis
    as Russia's current condition, 246, 269
    in ethnogenetic life cycle, 57–59, 108
    in Russian history, 108, 110–11, 213
Napoleon Bonaparte, 54, 108, 290
Naryshkin, Sergei Evgen'evich, 239
Nashi (Ours) (film), 215, 217
Nash Sovremennik, 150, 177, 189, 190
Nationalities policies, ethnicity and,
    146–76
    ethnic essentialism and, 146–50, 152,
        155, 157, 161–62, 164, 166–67
    ethnogenesis and, 150–54
    ethnos theory after Stalin, 159–62
    ethnos theory and Gumilev's
        ethno-naturalism, 162–67
    Gumilev's disagreements and affinities
        with Bromlei, 171–76
    mainstream criticisms of Gumilev,
        168–71
    sovetskii narod and assimilation,
        157–59
    see also *Druzhba narodov*
"National Question in Russia, The"
    (Putin), 237–38
Natsiia (nation), 158, 160, 161
    Gumilev distinguishes ethnos from,
        224, 257n79
    neo-Eurasianism and, 224, 226,
        226n75, 229
Natural-geographical world, 247–48
    environmental protection and, 133–39
    man's relationship to, 117–21
    neo-Stalinism and, 139–45
    new Soviet person and, 121–23
    new Soviet person and *passionarnost'*
        123–33, 223
Natural zone concept, of Dokuchaev, 35
Nazarbaev, Nursultan, 237, 275–76, 280,
    284, 285, 287, 288
Nazis, 50n42, 169, 170, 200, 315, 316,
Negative complementarity
    ethnic hierarchy and, 67
    ethnic interaction and, 61–62
    ethno-geopolitics and, 255
Neo-Eurasianism
    Gumilev and empire savers, 209–22
    Gumilev and popular culture, 240–43
    Gumilev's theoretical contributions,
        222–27

Putin and, 235–39
    Russian ethnos and, 227–34
Neo-Stalinism, Gumilev's theories and,
    139–45
Nestorian Chronicles, 203
Nestorians (Christian sect), 82–83,
    97–99, 102–3, 106, 203
Nevskii, Aleksandr Iaroslavich, 94, 98,
    98n77, 101
Nevzorov, Aleksandr Glebovich, 215,
    215n22, 217
New Soviet person (*novyi sovetskii
    chelovek*), 44
    history of concept, 121–22
    passionarnost' and, 123–33, 223
    Stalin and, 121, 122–23
    see also *Übermensch*
Nezavisimaia Gazeta, 236
Nietzsche, Friedrich, 122, 123,
    124–25, 130
Nikolaev, Mikhail Efimovich, 302–5
Nikon, Patriarch, 107
Nomad (film), 240
Nonantagonistic competition
    (*neantagonisticheskaia
    sopernichestva*), ethnic hierarchy
    and, 62, 63, 64–65, 67
Noosphere concept, of V. Vernadskii, 118,
    131–34, 132n77
Novaia Khronologiia (New Chronology),
    242–43
Novikov, Anatolii Georgievich, 300
Novikov, Timur Petrovich, 240
Novyi Mir, 134

Obadiah, Jewish-Khazar prince, 88–89
Obscurity phase, in ethnogenesis life
    cycle, 56–57
Obshchestvennyi (social category), 26
Obshchnost' (community of peoples)
    contemporary significance of, 317, 318
    druzhba narodov and, 154–55
    Eurasia and, 83, 238
    Russia as, 307–8
    superethnos and, 71, 290
"Occidentalization"
    (*oksidentalizatsiia*), 108
Okladnikov, Aleksei Pavlovich, 8
Old Believers, 64, 64n21
Oleg, Varangian prince, 91–92
Olga, Varangian princess, 92–93

Olonkho (Yakut epic poem), 299
Onikov, Leon Arshakovich, 218
On the Orders of Genghis Khan (Luginov),
    299–300
Orange chimera, in Ukraine, 262
Orbeli, Leon Abgarovich, 32
Oreshkin, Dmitrii Borisovich, 16
Osipov, Vladimir Nikolaevich, 182–83
Ostrovskii, Nikolai, 122
Ostwald, Wilhelm, 45, 49
Ot Rusi do Rossii (Gumilev), 222

Panferov, Fedor, 122
Passionarnost', 2, 168
    categories of ethnic interaction and, 60
    contemporary significance of, 308
    cosmic origins of, 44–49
    energy and, 48
    energy units of, 248
    ethnic geography and, 251–52
    ethnogenesis and, 49–54
    ethnogenesis life cycle and, 55–59
    ethno-geopolitics and, 254–55
    ethno-nationalists and, 198, 200
    as genetic and universal feature, 54
    Gumilev and popular culture, 240, 241
    Jews and, 248–49, 264
    Kazakhstan and, 279–80
    origins of, 44, 125
    post-Mongol Russian imperialism and,
        107–10
    post-Soviet use of concept, 247–49
    Russian ethno-nationalism and, 183, 186
    Russian ethnos and, 228, 232–33
    Saka-Yakutia and, 302–3
    superethnos and, 65
    Tatars and, 292, 295
    used in neo-Eurasianism, 223
    Yakuts and, 252n56, 302–4, 303n153
    Zhirinovskii and, 256
Passionarnost', and new Soviet person,
    123–24
    collectivism and, 126–29
    counterinstinctual impulse and,
        130–32
    destructiveness of human reason and,
        132–33
    ethical neutrality and, 129–30
    individuals' *élan vital* and, 124–26
Pasternak, Boris, 9, 16
Pavlov, Ivan Petrovich, 31–32, 121

Pavlovskii, Gleb, 236
Penck, Albrecht, 153
Penzev, Konstantin Aleksandrovich, 243
Perestroika, 2, 14n40, 18, 98n77
    Jews and, 264–65
    neo-Eurasianism during, 209–10,
        213–18
Pesakh (Khazar general), 92
Peter the Great, 108, 288, 290, 296
Physical geography, 120, 134
Piataia grafa (designation of nationality
    in Soviet passport), 149, 310
Plekhanov, Georgii Valentinovich, 117
Pletneva, Svetlana Aleksandrovna, 188
Podolinskii, Sergei Andreevich, 45, 46
Political space, ethnic space and, 70,
    254–57
Politics, post–Soviet Union, 244–72
    chimeras and *malye narod*, 260–65
    ethno-geopolitics, 253–55
    ethno-geopolitics, Russian superethnos
        and, 256–60
    ethno-territoriality and, 249–52
    Gumilev's influence on, generally,
        244–49
    Project Khazaria and anti-Semitism,
        266–72
Popular culture, post-Soviet, 240–43
Positive complementarity
    contemporary significance of, 313–14
    ethnic hierarchy and, 62, 65, 67
    ethnic interaction and, 61
    Eurasian history and, 83
    Russian ethnos and, 233
    Tatars and Russians and, 290
Prarodina ("primeval" or "original"
    homeland), 152–54
Pravda, 85, 86n24, 122, 205
Preobrazovanie (transformism), 120–21
    as element of ethnogenesis, 58–59,
        73, 79
    passionarnost' and, 126–29, 131–33
Prester John, 82–83
Priroda (Nature) journal, 168, 170, 174
Project Khazaria, 266–72
Prokhanov, Aleksandr Andreevich, 113,
    214, 220–21, 298–300, 308
Prokhorov, Gelian Mikhailovich, 14n39
Prometheanism, 117–23, 126–29,
    131, 139
Psychological stereotype, of Bromlei, 173

Psychology
    passionarnost', 247
    Soviet ecology movement and, 134
Punin, Nikolai Nikolaevich, 7–8, 45, 105,
    200n116
Purposeful unanimity (*tseleustremlennoe
    edinoobrazie*), 66
Pushkin, Alexander, 34, 108
Putin, Vladimir
    antisystems and, 262
    Kazakhstan and, 235–36, 237, 276
    neo-Eurasianism and, 227, 235–39,
        298, 308
    as passionary individual, 303
    praises Gumilev, 3, 236, 239
    uses *passionarnost'* concept, 248
    Tatarstan and, 288, 296

Race
    contemporary significance of, 312–15
    Gumilev's dismissal of significance of,
        33–34
    Putin's dismissal of significance of, 238
Radhanite (Radaniya) Jews, 87–89, 91
Radiation (*izlucheniia*). *See* Cosmic
    radiation; Mutagenesis
Radioecology, 50
Rakovor, battle of, 98
Rasologiia, 312
Rasputin, Valentin Grigorevich, 180, 184
Rassenkunde (racial science), 33, 150, 169,
    312, 315
Rassvet of Soviet nations, 147
Ratzel, Friedrich, 170n112, 174
Razin, Stenka, 107
"Reflections on the Decline of Europe"
    (Gumilev), 68
Relict ethnos, 59, 93, 251–52
    Khazars as, 86–87
    Sakha-Yakutia as, 252n56, 304–5
Requiem (Akhmatova), 9, 12, 16
Rhythms of Eurasia (Gumilev), 222n63
Roman Empire, 55, 156
Romano-Germanic superethnos, 69,
    93–94, 98, 102
Rossiianin, post-Soviet concept, 219,
    225–27
Rossiiskaia natsiia, 150n22
Rossiiskii superethnos, 71, 107, 216, 254,
    262

Rubinstein, Artur, 271
Rudenko, Sergei Ivanovich, 10, 160,
    160n74
Rus' Khaganate, 90–91
Russia
    Federal Law 309 in, 296–97
    nationalist discourse and civilizations,
        68–70
    subethnos in, 63–64
Russian empire, 45, 72, 157, 194, 215, 225,
    254, 300, 309
    Gumilev on, 108–10, 282n55
Russian ethnos, formation of
    first ethnogenetic cycle, 90–91
    second ethnogenetic cycle (Battle of
        Kulikovo), 99–103
Russian Federation
    ethno-geopolitics and, 231, 236–38,
        252, 254, 257, 260, 269
    neo-Eurasianism and, 219, 221–22
Russian history, ethnogenesis in
    Eurasianism and, 82–85, 103–7
    Golden Horde and, 94–102
    Gumilev as historian and, 81–82,
        81n2
    Khazars and Jews, 85–93, 89n37
    post-Mongol upheavals and Russian
        imperialism, 107–10
    Romano-German superethnos and,
        93–94, 98
Russian nationalists (Soviet period),
    177–205
    attack on Gumilev's revisionist
        accounts of Golden Horde, 192–96
    biological view of ethnicity, 180–81
    ethnic Russians disadvantaged after
        Stalin, 178–81
    Eurasianism and, 195, 196, 198–99,
        199n11, 201–5
    Gumilev accused of Zionism, 196–200
    Gumilev's ethnogenesis and Soviet
        environmental destruction, 182–87
    prioritized in *druzhba narodov*
        doctrine, 156–57
    "scientific" justification of
        anti-Semitism, 187–92
Russophobia (Shafarevich), 188, 263
Russophobia, Gumilev accused of, 179,
    198–99, 272–73
Rybakov, Boris Aleksandrovich, 196, 197

Rybakov, Viacheslav Mikhailovich, 241n141
Rykov, Konstantin Igor'evich, 241

Saka peoples, 281
Sakharov, Andrei Dmitrievich, 218
Sakha-Yakutia, 297–305
  allegiance to Russian imperial tradition, 298–99
  ethno-environmental history and, 300–304
  pre-history of, 61, 110, 299
  relict ethnos status of, 252n56, 304–5
Sartaq (son of Batu), 98
Savitskii, Petr Nikolaevich, 51n43, 89n36, 104, 105, 106–7
Sblizhenie (rapprochement) of nations, 146, 158, 162, 164
Schmitt, Carl, 170
Scythianism, 103–4
Scythians, 103, 151, 281
"Scythians, The" (Blok), 103–4
Searches for an Imaginary Kingdom (Gumilev), 97, 196
Secret of Chingis Khan, The (film), 240
Secret of Lev Gumilev, The (book series), 243, 289
Seidimbek, Akselei Slanovich, 273–74
Self-determination
  ethnic identity and, 224
  Putin and, 238
  Soviet Union and, 148, 257
Semanov, Sergei Nikolaevich, 13, 200, 205
Semevskii, Boris Nikolaevich, 140
Seminar on Theoretical Biology, at Leningrad University, 30–31
Separatist nationalism, during perestroika, 210, 214–15
Serge, of Yakuts, 301
Shabad, Theodore, 136
Shein, Pavel, 271
Shafarevich, Igor' Rostislavovich, 179, 185, 187–88, 188n57, 189n57, 263–65, 266
Shaimiev, Mintimer Sharipovich, 287, 289–90, 299
Shakhrai, Sergei Mikhailovich, 221–22
Shevelev, Gennady, 218
Shirokogorov, Sergei Mikhailovich, 29n33, 160, 174n36, 175n141

Shishkin, Igor', 231–34, 263, 265
Shnirel'man, Viktor, 86n24, 156n50, 161
Sholokhov, Mikhail Aleksandrovich, 11
Shtyrov, Viacheslav Anatolevich, 298, 299, 303
Siberia, 10, 42, 63, 71, 101, 109, 163, 181, 184, 185, 188, 247, 252, 293, 299, 301, 305
  ecological niches in, 61
  symbiosis and, 61
Signal inheritance (signal'naia nasledstvennost') theory, of Lobashev), 32, 34
Skobelev, Mikhail Dmitrievich, 109
Sliianie (merging of ethnic groups), 67, 163–67, 175
  after Stalin, 157–61, 169, 171
  Bromlei ambivalent about, 175–76
  as category of ethnic interaction, 60–61, 64, 67
  emergence of new ethnies and, 55–56
  Gumilev's views of, 163–64, 166, 216, 225, 226, 273
  neo-Eurasianism and, 228, 232
  Russian ethnos and Eurasian superethnos and, 103, 216
  Russian nationalists and, 180–82
  Stalinist nationality policy and, 147–48
Snegov, Sergei Aleksandrovich, 10, 44n3
Social class (soslovie), subethnos and, 64
Social Darwinism, 33
Social ecology, 137
Social energetics, 45
Socialism, 117–18, 239
  in evolution of societies, 27, 146–47, 169
  Lenin on goal of, 146
  in Soviet Union, 121–24, 123n33, 129, 146–49, 158–61, 166
"Socialist nations," Stalinist concept of, 148–49
Social organism, ethnos and, 168
Society (sotsiuum), ethnos and, 26–28
Sociobiology, 6, 134, 174
Sociosphere, 141–43
Solar energy, ethnogenesis and, 45, 47, 52
Sologub, Fedor Kuz'mich, 13
Solov'ev, Vladimir Sergeevich, 108, 203
Solzhenitsyn, Aleksandr, 187

Song of Igor's Campaign, The (epic poem), 97, 196, 199n111
Sovetskaia Etnografiia journal, 174
Sovetskii narod (Soviet nation), 157–59, 171, 174n137, 175
  differs from *druzhba narodov*, 158–59
  Gumilev and, 165, 165n96
  Kazakhstan and, 276
  resistance to, 162, 163–67
  Russian nationalists and, 182
  compared to *rossiianin* identity, 219
Soviet Geography: Review and Translation (journal), 136
Soviet Union
  chimeric quality of, 261–62
  Gumilev ambivalent about, 110–14
  post-Soviet nostalgia for, 309–10
  seen as social phenomenon, 26
  superethnies and, 70–71
Spengler, Oswald, 2, 68–69, 223
Staatsbiologie ("state biology"), 5
Stakhanov, Aleksei, 122
Stalin, Joseph, 111, 118, 147, 295
  Akhmatova defends Gumilev to, 9
  anti-Semitic campaign against rootless cosmopolitanism, 76, 85, 113n144, 187, 318
  death of, 11, 113, 192
  Gumilev approves "Doctors' Affair," 114
  Gumilev critical of, 1–2, 111–13, 137
  Mandel'stam's satirical caricature of, 9
  social evolution and, 146–47
  transformation of inner nature of man, 121–23
  transformation of external natural environment, 117–21, 137–39, 178–79, 183–84
  see also Ethnic essentialism; Neo-Stalinism
"Stalinist accommodation," 154–57, 162, 164–67, 307
Stankevich, Sergei Borisovich, 218
"State-sponsored evolutionism," 147
Steppe superethnos, 70, 71, 216
Steuckers, Robert, 313
Struve, Vasilii Vasil'vich, 8, 151
Study in History, A (Toynbee), 68
Subethnos, ethnic hierarchy and, 63–64
Suess, Eduard, 46

Sukachev, Vladimir Nikolaevich, 35, 37, 45–46, 50
Suleimenov, Olzhas Omarovich, 199n111, 277
Superethnos
  empire savers and hostility toward West, 211, 213–14
  ethnic hierarchy and, 63–65, 64n23
  ethno-geopolitics and, 253–55
  ethnos differences, 66–67
  ethnos similarities, 63–64, 65–66
  Gumilev's theoretical modification of, during perestroika, 215–16
  Jews as, 76
  neo-Eurasianism and, 223–25
  Russia as single, 278
  Russia as comprised of seven, 70–71
  Tatars and, 290–91
Superman, of Nietzsche. *See Übermensch*
Surplus energy (*energeticheskie perepady*), chimeras and, 75
Sviatoslav, Varangian prince, 93, 110
Symbiosis (*simbios*), 35, 58
  as category of ethnic interaction, 60, 61–62
  contemporary significance of, 313–14
  ethnicity and ideology and, 165
  ethnic Russians and, 198
  Golden Horde and Khazars, 98, 103, 198, 203, 236, 242
  Jews and Khazars, 87
  Kozhinov and, 203
  Tatars and, 293–95, 294n113
Systems theory, ethnos and, 25–26, 307

Talmud, 77, 87
Tarle, Evgenii Viktorovich, 8
Tatarstan, 286–97
  contemporary Eurasianism in, 288–91, 310
  ethno-naturalism and ethnic essentialism, 291–97, 295n119
  Eurasianism and two historical and cultural traditions, 288–91
  Gumilev honored in, 287–88
  multicultural identity and, 286–87
Tatimov, Makash Baigalievich, 282
Technosphere, 118, 132
Teutonic knights, 94, 98
Theoretical Problems of Geography (Anuchin), 134

"Thirteenth tribe," Jewish Khazars as, 89n37, 272
Tikhomirov, Aleksandr Aleksandrovich, 249
Timofeev-Resovskii, Nikolai Vladimirovich, 31, 50–52, 50n, 51nn43, 45
Tishkov, Valerii Aleksandrovich, 74, 226, 226n75
Titarenko, Mikhail Leont'evich, 218
Tokhtamysh, 100–101
Tolstov, Sergei Pavlovich, 150–52, 156, 157, 166
Toporov, Vladimir Nikolaevich, 188
Torah, 87
Toynbee, Arnold, 68, 108
Trotsky, Leon, 118, 122
Trubetskoi, Nikolai Sergeevich, 68–69, 70, 103, 104, 105, 202, 216, 224–25, 233, 300
Tselostnost', 37, 62, 64, 69, 83
Tsvetaeva, Marina Ivanovna, 6, 16
Turkic peoples, Gumilev's popularity with, 273–75. See also Kazakhstan; Sakha-Yakutia; Tatarstan

Übermensch (superman), Soviet person as, 122, 123, 130
Ukraine, 157–58, 262
United States, 30, 51, 63, 105, 108, 109, 240, 262n97, 269
American geographers interested in Gumilev, 1–2, 136–37, 137n99, 170
as superethnos, 71, 253–55, 259, 262
environmental destruction in, 70, 79, 131
Untergang des Abendlandes, Der (Spengler), 68
Urga (film), 240
Uzbek (Mongol khan), 99, 102

Van Zaichik, Khol'm, 241, 241n141
Varangians, 90, 91–93, 191, 202
Veche (samizdat Russian nationalist journal), 182–83
Vernadskii, Georgii Vladimirovich, 51n43, 104, 105, 107, 134, 243, 300
Vernadskii, Vladimir Ivanovich, 46–48, 46n16, 48n26, 50, 118, 131–32, 134, 171n118. See also Noosphere
Vestnik Leningradskogo Gosudarstvennogo Universiteta, 168

VINITI (Moscow center for scientific information), 17–18
Vinokurova, Ul'iana Alekseevna, 305
Vladimirov, Aleksandr Ivanovich, 255, 262
Volksboden concept (Penck), 153
Voluntarism, of new Soviet person, 122, 129, 166, 260
Von Herberstein, Sigismund, 96n70
Voprosy Istorii journal, 169
Voznesenskii, Aleksandr Alekseevich, 10, 16
Vrag (enemy), 120, 223
Vyshii Atestatsionnyi Komitet (VAK), 17
Vysotskii, Georgii Nikolaevich, 35

Western civilization
in advanced phase of ethnogenesis, 253–55
hostility toward, 211, 213–14
West-European superethnos, 70, 71,
White Guards, 198
White Horde (Mongol Empire), 99, 100, 281
Woltmann, Ludwig, 169, 312
Written tests, chimeras and, 74–75, 77

Xiongnu people, 15, 82, 83, 113n140, 299–300
Kazakh lineage and, 281
Yakut prehistory and, 299–300

Yakuts. See Sakha-Yakutia
Yeltsin, Boris/Yeltsin era, 218–19, 221, 234–35, 245, 262, 266, 298, 308, 310–11
Yoke (igo), of Tatars
Classical Eurasianism on, 106, 198
denial of existence of, 96–97, 242–43, 273, 288, 294
place in Russian history, 95–96, 194, 198–99
see also Black Legend; Golden Horde; Mongol empire, Khazaria
Yurt, Kazakh culture and, 279

Zamiatin, Evgenii Ivanovich, 104
Zardykhan, Kinaiat, 281–82
Zavtra, 221, 298
Zhdanov, Andrei Aleksandrovich, 9, 10

Zhirinovskii, Vladimir Vol'fovich, 256, 256n73
Zhivoe veshchestvo (living matter of the biosphere), 46, 52
Zhiznennoe prostranstvo. *See Lebensraum*
Zigzags, in history, 55
   chimeras and, 73, 75, 262
   Jews and Khazaria, 93, 110, 266

Zinov'ev, Aleksandr Aleksandrovich, 181
Zionism, 268–71
   Gumilev accused of, 196–200
   Russian nationalism and "scientific" justification of anti-Semitism, 187–92
Ziuganov, Gennadii Andreevich, 218, 221, 248
Zvezda Povol'zhia, 292